SCIENCE DISCOVERYWORKS
CONCORDIA EDITION

Concordia Publishing House

St. Louis, MO

SCIENCE DiscoveryWorks
CONCORDIA EDITION

Scripture quotations taken from the HOLY BIBLE: NEW INTERNATIONAL VERSION® NIV®. Copyright ©1973, 1978, 1984 by International Bible Society. Used by permission of Zondervan Publishing House. All rights reserved.

Copyright 1999 by Concordia Publishing House
3558 S. Jefferson Avenue, St. Louis, MO 63118-3968
Manufactured in the United States of America

Original edition published by
Silver Burdett Ginn Inc.
Parsippany, NJ USA
Copyright ©1999
by Silver Burdett Ginn Inc.

Silver Burdett Ginn Inc. does not express any view or opinion as to the religious content and views included in this edition. The religious views and beliefs presented are those authored and authorized by Concordia Publishing House.

All rights reserved. No part of this publication may be reproduced, stored in a retrieval system, or transmitted, in any form or by any means, electronic, mechanical, photocopying, recording, or otherwise, without the prior written permission of Concordia Publishing House.

ISBN 0-570-02510-9

1 2 3 4 5 6 7 8 9 10 RRD 08 07 06 05 04 03 02 01 00 99

CONTENTS

UNIT A: Cells and Microbes

THEME: MODELS
GET READY TO INVESTIGATE! A2

1 Cells A4

INVESTIGATION 1

What Are Cells? A6

Activity: Observing Plant Cells A6
Activity: Observing Animal Cells A8
Resource: Animal and Plant Cells A9
Resource: Closer Look at Cells A12

INVESTIGATION 2

What Are Some Life Processes of Cells? A14

Activity: Moving In and Out of Cells A14
Resource: Coming and Going With Cells A16
Resource: Cells and Energy A18

INVESTIGATION 3

How Do Cells Make More Cells? A20

Activity: Multiplying by Dividing A20
Resource: Cell Division A22
Resource: Artificial Blood A24
Resource: Tissues, Organs, and Systems A25
Reflect and Evaluate A27

2 Protists and Fungi A28

INVESTIGATION 1

What Are Protists? A30

Activity: Microorganisms A30
Activity: Observing an Animal-like Protist A31
Activity: Observing a Plantlike Protist A32
Resource: The World of Protists A33
Resource: Protozoan Diseases A38

INVESTIGATION 2
What Are Fungi? — **A40**

Activity: Lifestyles of Fungi.................A40
Resource: Yeasts, Bread, and Fuels A42
Resource: Fungi—Good and Bad...............A43
Reflect and Evaluate A45

3 Bacteria and Viruses — **A46**

INVESTIGATION 1
What Are Bacteria and Viruses? — **A48**

Activity: Classifying Bacteria................A48
Resource: Bacteria and Viruses A50
Resource: Microbe Discoverers A54

INVESTIGATION 2
How Do Bacteria and Viruses Affect Other Living Things? **A56**

Activity: Warm Milk..........................A56
Resource: Bacterial and Viral Diseases A58
Resource: AIDS: Searching for a Cure A60
Resource: Helpful Bacteria A61
Reflect and Evaluate A63
Investigate Further! A64

UNIT B The Changing Earth

THEME: MODELS
GET READY TO INVESTIGATE! **B2**

1 Cracked Crust — **B4**

INVESTIGATION 1
Do Continents Really Drift About? — **B6**

Activity: The Great Puzzle B6
Resource: Alfred Wegener and the Drifting Continents B8
Resource: Evidence for Continental Drift B10
Resource: Continents on the Move B12

INVESTIGATION 2
What Do the Locations of Volcanoes and Earthquakes Tell Us? **B16**

Activity: Earth—Always Rockin' and Rollin'! B16
Activity: Volcanoes and Earth's Plates B18
Resource: The Cracked Crust: Tectonic Plates B19

INVESTIGATION 3
What Does the Sea Floor Tell Us About Plate Tectonics? **B22**

Activity: Sea-Floor Spreading B22
Activity: Building a Model of the Ocean Floor B23
Activity: Mapping the Ocean Floor B24
Resource: Sonar: Mapping the Sea Floor B26
Resource: Magnetism Tells a Story B28
Resource: Heating Up Iceland B31
Reflect and Evaluate **B33**

2 Tectonic Plates and Mountains B34

INVESTIGATION 1
Why Do Tectonic Plates Move? **B36**

Activity: The Conveyor B36
Resource: Moving Plates B38

INVESTIGATION 2
How Does the Motion of Tectonic Plates Build Mountains? **B42**

Activity: Colliding Plates B42
Activity: A Big Fender Bender B44
Resource: Mountain-Building B45
Resource: Life at the Top B49
Reflect and Evaluate **B51**

3 Shake, Rattle, and Roll B52

INVESTIGATION 1
What Causes Earthquakes, and How Can They Be Compared? **B54**

Activity: A Model of Sliding Plates B54
Resource: Sliding Plates B56
Resource: Our Active Earth B58

v

Investigation 2
What Happens to Earth's Crust During an Earthquake? — B62
Activity: Shake It! B62
Resource: Bend Till It Breaks B64

Investigation 3
How Are Earthquakes Located and Measured? — B68
Activity: Shake It Harder! B68
Activity: Locating Earthquakes B70
Activity: Be an Architect B72
Resource: The Seismograph B74
Resource: Earthquakes on the Sea Floor B76
Resource: Designing for Survival B79
Reflect and Evaluate B81

4 Volcanoes — B82

Investigation 1
Where Do Volcanoes Occur, and How Are They Classified? — B84
Activity: Worldwide Eruptions B84
Resource: Volcanoes and Plate Tectonics B86
Resource: Surtsey B90
Resource: Mount Vesuvius B92

Investigation 2
How Do Volcanic Eruptions Affect Earth? — B94
Activity: Volcanoes You Can Eat! B94
Resource: Mount Pinatubo B96

Investigation 3
In What Other Places Can Volcanoes Occur? — B100
Activity: How Hawaii Formed B100
Resource: An Island in the Making B102
Resource: Using Robots to Investigate Volcanoes B106
Resource: Great Rift Valley of Africa B108
Reflect and Evaluate B111
Investigate Further! B112

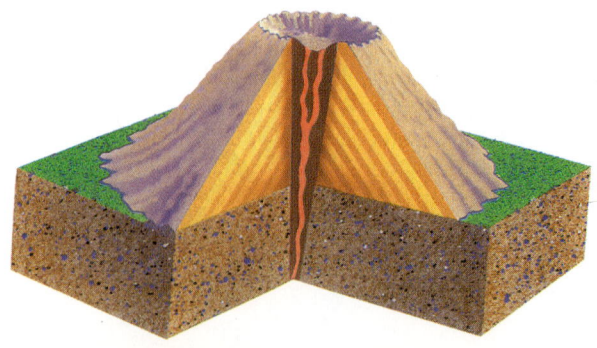

UNIT C — The Nature of Matter

THEME: SCALE
GET READY TO INVESTIGATE C2

1 Characteristics of Matter — C4

Investigation 1

How Can You Describe Matter? — C6

- **Activity:** A Matter of Mass C6
- **Activity:** A Matter of Space C8
- **Activity:** Checking for Purity C9
- **Resource:** Measuring Mass and Volume C10
- **Resource:** Density C13

Investigation 2

What Makes Up Matter? — C16

- **Activity:** Always Room for More C16
- **Activity:** Racing Liquids C18
- **Resource:** Structure of Matter C19

Investigation 3

How Does Energy Affect Matter? — C22

- **Activity:** Cooling Race C22
- **Activity:** Speeding Up Change C24
- **Resource:** Particle Energy C25
- **Reflect and Evaluate** C29

2 Kinds of Matter — C30

Investigation 1

How Can Matter Be Classified? — C32

- **Activity:** Testing Your Metal C32
- **Activity:** A Change for the Wetter C33
- **Resource:** Elements C34
- **Resource:** Compounds C39
- **Resource:** Ancient Elements C42

Investigation 2

What Is a Mixture? — C44

- **Activity:** Working with Mixtures C44
- **Activity:** Racing Colors C46
- **Activity:** A Mixed-Up State C47
- **Resource:** Mixtures C48

INVESTIGATION 3
What Are Liquid Mixtures Like? **C52**

Activity: Mixing Solids into Liquids C52
Activity: To Mix or Not to Mix C54
Activity: Making Water Wetter C55
Resource: What's the Solution? C56
Resource: Bubbles C58
Resource: Alloys C59
Reflect and Evaluate **C61**

3 How Matter Changes **C62**

INVESTIGATION 1
How Can Matter Change? **C64**

Activity: Balloon Blower C64
Activity: Making a Fire Extinguisher C66
Activity: Solids From Liquids C67
Resource: Physical and Chemical Change C68
Resource: Atomic Structure and Chemical Change C71
Resource: Conservation of Mass C75
Resource: Radioactive Elements C76

INVESTIGATION 2
What Are Acids and Bases? **C78**

Activity: Cabbage-Juice Science C78
Activity: The Litmus Test C80
Resource: Acids, Bases, and Salts C81
Resource: Acid Rain C84

INVESTIGATION 3
What Do Chemists Do? **C86**

Activity: Testing a Tablet C86
Activity: Mystery Powders C88
Activity: "Slime" Time C90
Resource: Polymers and Plastics C91
Resource: What Chemists Do C93
Reflect and Evaluate **C95**
Investigate Further! **C96**

UNIT D: Continuity of Life

THEME: CONSTANCY AND CHANGE
GET READY TO INVESTIGATE! D2

1 Reproduction — D4

INVESTIGATION 1: What Is Asexual Reproduction? — D6

Activity: Divide and Conquer! D6
Activity: The "Budding" System D8
Resource: Fission: Splitting Heirs D10
Resource: Reproduction by Budding D13
Resource: New Plants From Old D15

INVESTIGATION 2: What Is Sexual Reproduction? — D18

Activity: Splitting Pairs D18
Activity: Combining Cells D20
Resource: Meiosis and Fertilization D22
Resource: Saving Species D25
Reflect and Evaluate D27

2 Heredity — D28

INVESTIGATION 1: What Are Inherited Traits? — D30

Activity: What Can You Do? D30
Activity: Environmental Influence D32
Resource: Genes, Traits, and Environment D34

INVESTIGATION 2: How Are Traits Inherited? — D38

Activity: Scrambled Genes D38
Activity: Inheriting Traits D40
Activity: All in the Family D42
Resource: Laws of Heredity D44
Resource: Designer Genes D47
Reflect and Evaluate D49

3 Change Through Time — D50

Investigation 1: What Do Fossils Tell Us About Life—Past and Present? — D52

- **Activity:** Examine a Fossil D52
- **Activity:** Make a Model Fossil D54
- **Resource:** How Fossils Form D56
- **Resource:** The Geologic Time Scale D59
- **Resource:** What Happened to the Dinosaurs? D62

Investigation 2: What Evidence Do Scientists Have That Species Change Over Time — D64

- **Activity:** Out on a Limb D64
- **Resource:** Comparing Limbs D66
- **Resource:** Darwin's Voyage D68
- **Resource:** Selective Breeding D70

Investigation 3: How Do Changes in Species Occur? — D72

- **Activity:** A Variety of Peanuts D72
- **Resource:** Natural Selection, Variation, and Mutation D74
- **Resource:** Competition and Isolation D77
- Reflect and Evaluate D79
- Investigate Further! D80

UNIT E — Oceanography

THEME: SYSTEMS
GET READY TO INVESTIGATE! — E2

1 Ocean Water — E4

Investigation 1: What Makes Up Ocean Water? — E6

- **Activity:** A Closer Look at Ocean Water E6
- **Resource:** What's in the Water? E8

Investigation 2: What Are the Properties of Ocean Water? — E12

- **Activity:** Lighting the Water E12
- **Activity:** Dense Water E14
- **Activity:** Under Pressure E16

Resource: The Bends E17
Resource: Ocean Temperatures and Pressure E18
Resource: That's Dense! E20

INVESTIGATION 3

What Living Things Are in Ocean Water? — E22

Activity: Let the Sun Shine E22
Resource: All Creatures Great and Small E24
Reflect and Evaluate E27

2 The Ocean Floor — E28

INVESTIGATION 1

What Features and Sediments Occur on the Ocean Floor? — E30

Activity: Graphing the Ocean Floor E30
Activity: Modeling Ocean Sediments E31
Resource: Features of the Ocean Floor E32
Resource: Sediments on the Ocean Floor E36

INVESTIGATION 2

How Do Scientists Study the Ocean Floor? — E40

Activity: Hear the Distance E40
Activity: Modeling Sonar E42
Resource: Sonar E43
Resource: Underwater Exploration E44
Resource: Exploring the Oceans E46
Reflect and Evaluate E49

3 Moving Ocean Water — E50

INVESTIGATION 1

What Causes Ocean Currents? — E52

Activity: Current Trends E52
Activity: Modeling Density Currents E54
Resource: World Currents E55
Resource: How Deep Water Moves E58

INVESTIGATION 2

What Causes Ocean Waves? — E62

Activity: Making Waves E62
Activity: Wave Motion E64
Resource: What Are Waves? E65

INVESTIGATION 3
What Causes Tides? **E68**

Activity: Making a Tide Model E68
Resource: The Moon, Sun, and Tides E70
Reflect and Evaluate **E73**

4 Ocean Resources **E74**

INVESTIGATION 1
What Resources Can the Oceans Provide? **E76**

Activity: What You See From the Sea E76
Activity: Desalination E77
Activity: Obtaining Energy E78
Resource: Treasures From the Sea E79
Resource: Treasures Through Time E82
Resource: Energy and the Sea E84

INVESTIGATION 2
How Does Pollution Affect the Oceans and Their Resources? **E88**

Activity: Investigating Oil Spills E88
Activity: Cleaning Up the Mess E90
Resource: Pollution of the Oceans E91
Reflect and Evaluate **E95**
Investigate Further! E96

UNIT F — Forces and Motion

THEME: SCALE
GET READY TO INVESTIGATE! **F2**

1 Moving On **F4**

INVESTIGATION 1
How Do You Describe Motion? **F6**

Activity: The Ant Maze F6
Resource: From Feet to Fathoms F8

INVESTIGATION 2: How Do You Measure Speed? — **F12**

- **Activity:** Speeding Marbles F12
- **Resource:** Bicycle Cyclometers F14
- **Resource:** What Is Speed? F15

INVESTIGATION 3: How Do You Describe Changes in Motion? — **F18**

- **Activity:** Swinging Speeds F18
- **Activity:** Twin Pendulums F20
- **Resource:** Acceleration F21
- **Resource:** Stopping Power F24
- **Reflect and Evaluate** **F27**

2 Getting a Grip on Gravity — **F28**

INVESTIGATION 1: How Can The Force of Gravity Be Measured? — **F30**

- **Activity:** Measuring Gravity's Pull F30
- **Resource:** Weighing In F32

INVESTIGATION 2: Do All Objects Fall at the Same Rate? — **F36**

- **Activity:** The Great Gravity Race F36
- **Activity:** Falling Together F37
- **Resource:** Galileos's Great Gravity Discovery F38
- **Resource:** How High? F39

INVESTIGATION 3: How Does Air Change the Rate at Which an Object Falls? — **F42**

- **Activity:** Paper Race F42
- **Activity:** Parachuting F44
- **Resource:** Feather Falling on The Moon F46
- **Resource:** Sky Divers and Their Parachutes F48
- **Reflect and Evaluate** **F51**

3 Making and Measuring Motion — **F52**

INVESTIGATION 1: How Are Objects at Rest and Objects in Motion Alike? — **F54**

- **Activity:** Rider Moves F54
- **Activity:** Crash-test Dummies F56
- **Resource:** Sir Isaac Newton's First Law F58
- **Resource:** Seat Belts and Air Bags F60

INVESTIGATION 2 — How Do Forces Affect Motion? — **F62**

Activity: Starting and Stopping F62
Activity: The Problem With Big Trucks F64
Resource: Sir Isaac Newton's Second Law F65

INVESTIGATION 3 — How Does Friction Affect the Motion of Objects? — **F70**

Activity: Friction Floors F70
Activity: Wheel Power F72
Resource: Friction F73
Reflect and Evaluate F77

4 Forces in Pairs — **F78**

INVESTIGATION 1 — What Property Do All Moving Objects Share? — **F80**

Activity: Marble Collisions F80
Activity: Football Momentum F82
Resource: Playing Pool F84
Resource: Momentum Sharing F85

INVESTIGATION 2 — How Do Actions Cause Reactions? — **F88**

Activity: Bouncing Balls F88
Activity: Double-Ball Bounce F90
Resource: Actions Cause Reactions F91
Resource: Trampoline Fun F94

INVESTIGATION 3 — How Are Action-Reaction Forces Used? — **F96**

Activity: Action-Reaction Wheels F96
Resource: Civilization and The Wheel F98
Resource: Faster Fins F101
Reflect and Evaluate F103

5 Real-World Forces — **F104**

INVESTIGATION 1 — How Do Heavy Things Fly? — **F106**

Activity: Making a Paper Glider F106
Activity: Propeller Power! F108
Resource: Designing Fliers F109
Resource: Flying Forces F110

INVESTIGATION 2
How Do Rockets Use Action-Reaction Forces? **F114**
- **Activity:** Balloon Rocket Race F114
- **Activity:** Straw Rockets F116
- **Resource:** Rocket Launch F118

INVESTIGATION 3
How Do Things Float? **F120**
- **Activity:** Clay Boats F120
- **Activity:** Floating Egg F122
- **Resource:** Forces In Fluids F123
- **Reflect and Evaluate** **F127**
- **Investigate Further!** **F128**

SCIENCE Handbook

- Think Like a Scientist H2
- Safety H8
- Science Tools H10
- Measurements H16
- Glossary H18
- Index H38
- Credits H46

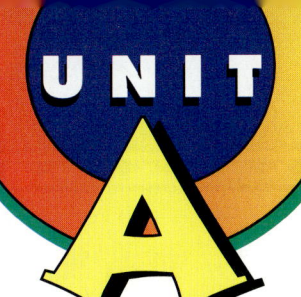

CELLS AND MICROBES
Theme: Models

Get Ready to Investigate! A2

1 Cells A4
Investigation 1   What Are Cells? A6
Investigation 2   What Are Some Life Processes of Cells? A14
Investigation 3   How Do Cells Make More Cells? A20

2 Protists and Fungi A28
Investigation 1   What Are Protists? A30
Investigation 2   What Are Fungi? A40

3 Bacteria and Viruses A46
Investigation 1   What Are Bacteria and Viruses? A48
Investigation 2   How Do Bacteria and Viruses Affect
                                  Other Living Things? A56

Investigate Further! A64

GET READY TO

OBSERVE & QUESTION

How do bacteria and viruses affect other living things?

When plants and animals die, what do you think happens to the remains? Did you know that without bacteria, Earth would be covered with dead leaves, plants, and other organisms? In addition, did you know that your survival depends on bacteria living in your large intestine? These bacteria produce vitamins you need to survive. Look around you. What else can you observe about bacteria?

EXPERIMENT & HYPOTHESIZE

What are some life processes of cells?

How is a cell like a plastic bag? If you pour water into a plastic bag and seal the bag, can the water get out? If you place an empty, sealed plastic bag in a bucket of water, can the water get in? When you do the activities in this chapter, you may be surprised to find out how a plastic bag is like a cell in your body.

INVESTIGATE!

RESEARCH & ANALYZE

As you investigate, find out more from these books.

- **Microscope: How to Use and Enjoy It** by Eve and Albert Stwertka (Julian Messner, 1988). This book will help you get up close to an invisible world you may have never seen before and may not have even known existed. Yet it is a world that is all around you—populated by organisms too tiny to see without the aid of a microscope.

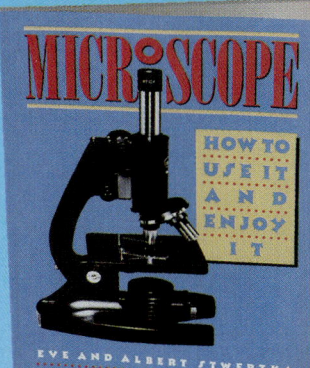

- **Black Pioneers of Science and Invention** (Harcourt Brace, 1970). When you think of surgery, do you think of sterile instruments and sterile conditions? In the 1880s, doctors used scalpels over and over without cleaning them, and the operating room might have been someone's kitchen. Read how Dr. Daniel Hale Williams changed those conditions, and then read about other African American pioneers and their contributions to medicine and science.

WORK TOGETHER & SHARE IDEAS

How would you model the world of microscopic organisms you will study in this unit?

Working together, you'll have a chance to apply what you have learned about protists, fungi, bacteria, and viruses. Plan and develop models for a "micromenagerie" of these organisms. Put your models on display and see if your classmates can identify fungi, bacteria, and viruses.

CHAPTER 1

CELLS

The brain and liver are very important organs. But then, so are the body's muscles. God created these body parts to do very different and vital jobs. Yet they all are similar in one way—they are all made up of cells. Cells are the basic units of life.

A Blood Cell Tester

Carlton Donovan is a phlebotomist (flē bät'ə mist). His job involves obtaining and testing the blood of patients such as Meghan Delaney. To get a sample of Meghan's blood, Mr. Donovan inserts a needle into a blood vessel in her arm. He draws blood up the needle into a test tube.

To see whether Meghan's blood is healthy, Mr. Donovan must place the blood in a machine that will count the red and white blood cells in the sample. Too few red blood cells could mean that Meghan has been exposed to a poison, such as lead. Too many white blood cells could mean that her body is fighting off an infection.

There are many types of cells besides red blood cells and white blood cells. In this chapter you'll learn what cells are, what they do, and how cells make more cells.

Coming Up

INVESTIGATION 1

WHAT ARE CELLS?
.... A6

INVESTIGATION 2

WHAT ARE SOME LIFE PROCESSES OF CELLS?
.... A14

INVESTIGATION 3

HOW DO CELLS MAKE MORE CELLS?
.... A20

◀ Phlebotomist Carlton Donovan prepares to take blood from patient Meghan Delaney.

INVESTIGATION 1

WHAT ARE CELLS?

Look at the skin on the back of one of your hands. What do you think you would see if you could look at a layer of your skin under a microscope? You would see cells—the tiny basic units that make up all living organisms. But what are cells made of? Are all cells alike? These are some of the questions you'll find answers to in Investigation 1.

Activity
Observing Plant Cells

In this activity you'll use a microscope to examine some plant cells. You might be surprised at what you see.

MATERIALS
- goggles
- 2 microscope slides
- 2 droppers
- aquarium water
- *Elodea* leaves
- 3 cover slips
- microscope
- 2 percent salt solution
- iodine solution
- onion section
- tweezers
- *Science Notebook*

SAFETY
Wear goggles. Clean up spills immediately. Iodine will stain clothing and is poisonous if swallowed.

Procedure

1. Place a drop of aquarium water on a clean microscope slide. Add a small piece of *Elodea* leaf to the drop.

2. Hold a cover slip by two corners and gently lower it onto the microscope slide as shown.

3. Remove your goggles. Use a microscope to **observe** the slide you made under low power. In your *Science Notebook*, **draw** what you see.

4. Focus the microscope to **observe** the slide under high power. **Make a drawing** of one cell, including any structures you see.

5. Locate the outer border, or **cell wall**, of one *Elodea* cell. Next look for small round green structures in the cell. These are **chloroplasts**. **Label** these structures.

Step 2

6. Now locate the light-colored material, called **cytoplasm**, that fills much of the cell. In the cytoplasm, look for spaces that appear empty. These are fluid-filled spaces called **vacuoles**. In your drawing show and **label** a vacuole. Also **label** the cytoplasm.

7. Put on your goggles. Repeat step 1 using the salt solution instead of aquarium water. Then repeat steps 2 through 4. **Describe** any differences you observe between the *Elodea* in salt water and the *Elodea* in aquarium water.

Step 8

8. Put on your goggles. Place one drop of iodine solution on a microscope slide. Bend an onion section backward (against its curve) until it breaks. Use tweezers to pull off a layer of onion skin and place it in the drop of iodine solution. Add a cover slip to the slide.

9. Use the microscope to **observe** the onion cell under low power and then under high power. Locate the **nucleus**—the large dark structure. **Make a drawing** of the onion cell and label the nucleus and any other structures you can identify.

Analyze and Conclude

1. Each cell you observed was surrounded by a cell wall. **Infer** the function of this structure.

2. The cell theory states that all organisms are made of cells. How did your observations support or not support this theory?

INVESTIGATE FURTHER!

EXPERIMENT

Make a slide of tomato skin in a drop of water. Observe the skin under a microscope, using low power and high power. Draw what you see. What cell parts are similar to those in the onion skin? What cell parts are different from the onion cells? How can you account for these differences?

Step 1

◀ *Elodea* in fresh water

A7

Activity
Observing Animal Cells

MATERIALS
- prepared slide of human cheek cells
- prepared slide of frog blood
- microscope
- *Science Notebook*

You've seen that plants are made up of cells. Animals are also made up of cells. How do animal and plant cells compare? Find out in this activity.

Procedure

1. Observe a slide of cheek cells under the low power of the microscope. Describe what you see and **record** your observations in your *Science Notebook*.

2. Observe the cheek cells under high power. **Make a drawing** of one cell. Label any structures you can identify.

3. Repeat steps 1 and 2, using a slide of frog blood.

4. The outer border of animal cells is the **cell membrane**. Label the cell membrane in each of your drawings.

Step 1

Analyze and Conclude

1. Infer the function of the cell membrane. All cells have a cell membrane. Where do you think the cell membrane of a plant cell is located?

2. Compare the drawings you made in this activity with those you made of the plant cells in the activity on pages A6 and A7. In what ways are animal cells similar to plant cells? In what ways are animal cells different from plant cells?

3. Do your observations in this activity support the theory that all organisms are made up of cells? Explain your answer.

INVESTIGATE FURTHER!

RESEARCH

You observed the red blood cells of a frog. Observe prepared slides of human red blood cells. What difference do you observe between the two types of red blood cells? Use a reference book to find out why this difference exists.

Animal and Plant Cells

From a distance the surface of a brick wall looks smooth. However, as you get closer, you can see the individual bricks. If you get close enough to examine one of the bricks, you can see the texture and maybe even some large particles of the brick.

What if you get close to a plant or an animal? Can you see any of the "building blocks" that make up each organism? How close do you have to get to an organism to see its building blocks?

The Cell Theory

In the activities on pages A6 through A8, you used a microscope to observe material from plants and animals closely enough to see their building blocks. In a sense, you got close enough to see the details of the building blocks. The building blocks you were able to observe with the microscope are called cells. Just as bricks are the basic units of a wall, **cells** are the basic units of all God's living creations.

The cells of an organism are, in some ways, like the bricks in this building. From a distance all you see is the solid wall (*above*). But up close you can see the characteristics of each brick (*inset*).

The idea that all living things are made of cells led to the development of the cell theory. This theory resulted from the work of many scientists. The main points of the **cell theory** are listed here.
- Cells are the basic units of structure and function of all living things.
- All life processes are carried out by cells.
- New cells are produced from existing cells.

Cells Are Alike

From your observations of plant cells and animal cells, you know that all cells are not identical. For example, you observed structures called chloroplasts in the *Elodea* cells, but not in the onion cells nor in the cheek cells. In fact, cells from different parts of the same organism can differ. However, as the drawings on these two pages show, cells are remarkably similar. All cells are bounded

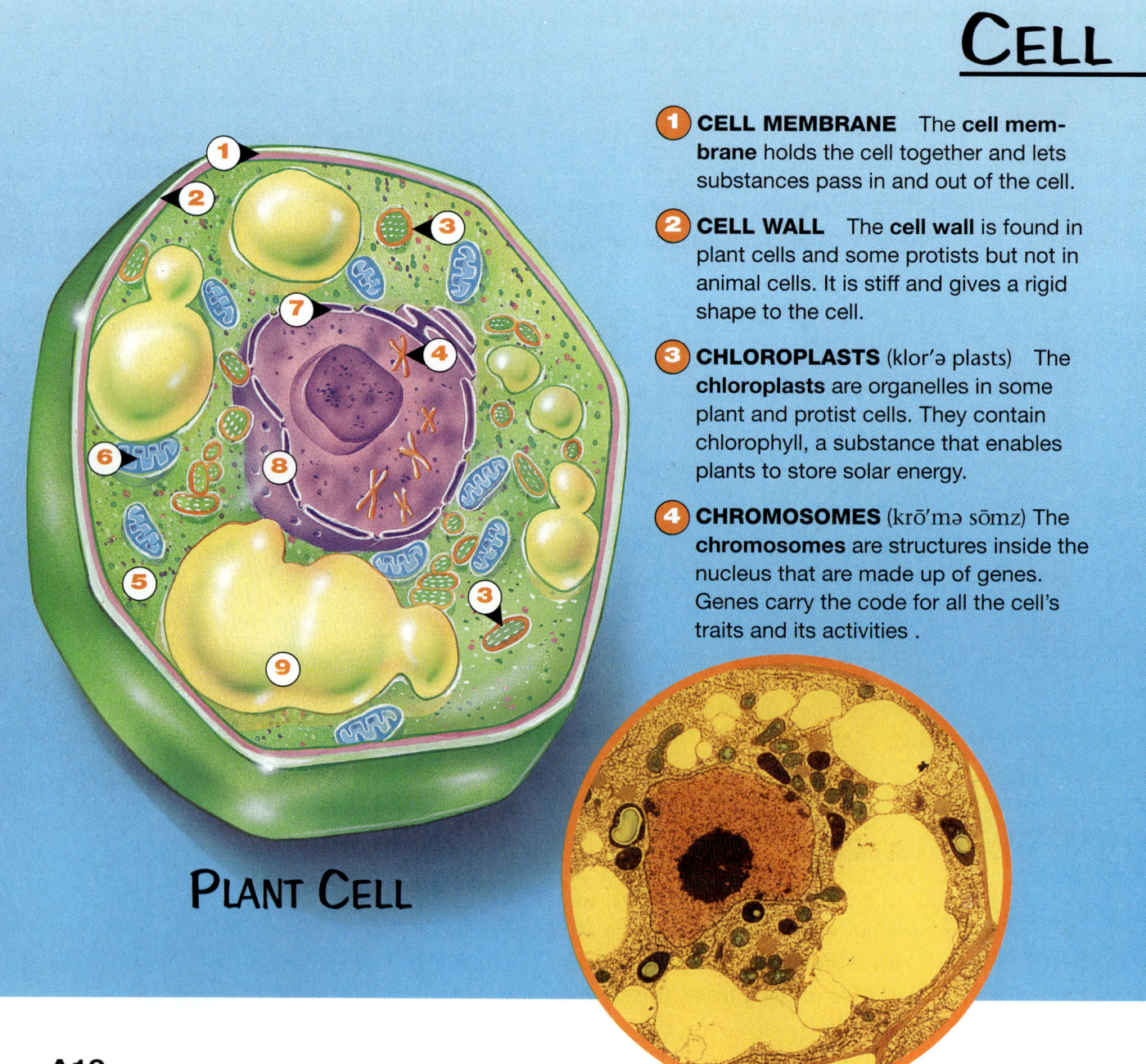

CELL

1. **CELL MEMBRANE** The **cell membrane** holds the cell together and lets substances pass in and out of the cell.

2. **CELL WALL** The **cell wall** is found in plant cells and some protists but not in animal cells. It is stiff and gives a rigid shape to the cell.

3. **CHLOROPLASTS** (klor′ə plasts) The **chloroplasts** are organelles in some plant and protist cells. They contain chlorophyll, a substance that enables plants to store solar energy.

4. **CHROMOSOMES** (krō′mə sōmz) The **chromosomes** are structures inside the nucleus that are made up of genes. Genes carry the code for all the cell's traits and its activities.

PLANT CELL

A10

by a cell membrane and contain cytoplasm. Within the cytoplasm of most cells can be found mitochondria, vacuoles, and a nucleus that contains chromosomes and that is surrounded by a nuclear membrane. Although there are some differences between their cells, all living things must carry out similar life processes. Therefore, it should not be surprising that their cells are so similar. ■

> # UNIT PROJECT LINK
>
> With your group, choose a specific kind of plant or animal cell. Build a model of your cell to display in a Micromenagerie. Work with your group to select the materials you will need to make a true representation of the cell that will catch the interest of others.

PARTS

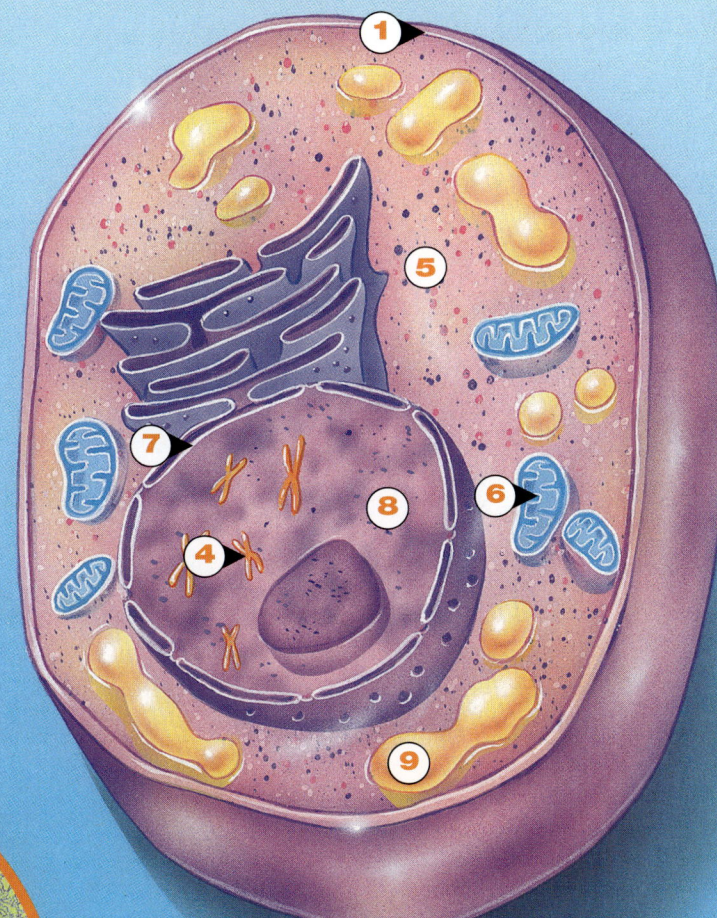

5 **CYTOPLASM** (sīt'ō plaz əm) The **cytoplasm** is the watery gel inside the cell. Many materials are dissolved or suspended in the cytoplasm. Various structures called organelles are found in the cytoplasm.

6 **MITOCHONDRIA** (mīt ō kän'drē ə) The **mitochondria** are organelles in which energy is released from food.

7 **NUCLEAR** (nōō'klē ər) **MEMBRANE** The **nuclear membrane** allows substances to pass in and out of the nucleus.

8 **NUCLEUS** (nōō'klē əs) The **nucleus** controls cell activities.

9 **VACUOLES** (vak'yōō'ōlz) The **vacuoles** are spaces in the cytoplasm where food and chemicals are stored.

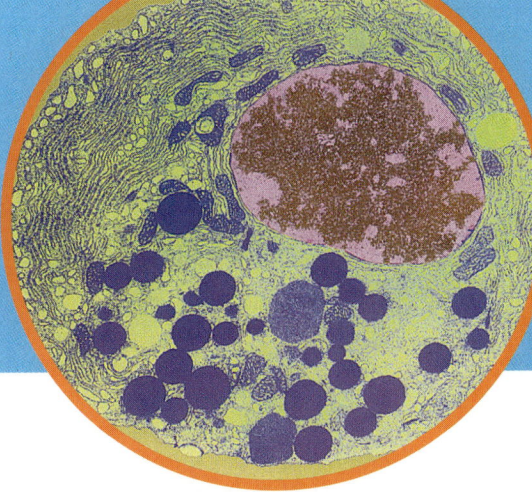

ANIMAL CELL

Closer Look at Cells

When the first microscopes were made, a new world opened up for scientists. For the first time, scientists could see single cells and single-celled organisms—things invisible to the eye alone. How does a microscope make these tiny cells visible? The magnifying power of a microscope comes from its lenses. A lens is a thin piece of glass with at least one curved surface. In a microscope, lenses create an enlarged image of a tiny specimen.

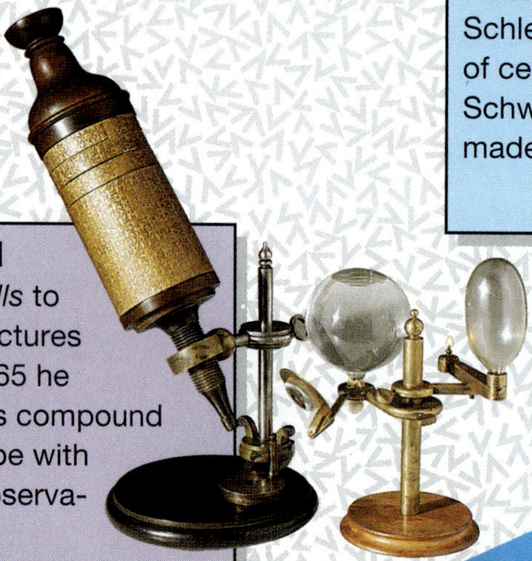

Matthias Schleiden, Germany
Schleiden states that all plants are made up of cells. In 1839, German biologist Theodor Schwann concludes that all animals are made up of cells.

1838

Robert Hooke, England
Hooke coins the term *cells* to describe the boxlike structures that make up cork. In 1665 he publishes drawings of his compound microscope (a microscope with two lenses) and of his observations in *Micrographica*.

1665

1674
Anton van Leeuwenhoek, Netherlands
Leeuwenhoek builds a simple microscope (a microscope with only one lens). The microscope magnifies objects 270 times. Van Leeuwenhoek is the first to see one-celled organisms, which he calls "wee beasties."

Rudolph Virchow, Germany
Virchow states that cells can come only from other living cells. This idea, along with the hypotheses of Schleiden and Schwann, becomes part of the cell theory.
1855

The scanning electron microscope (SEM) is developed. The SEM allows scientists to create three-dimensional (3-D) images of the surfaces of specimens.
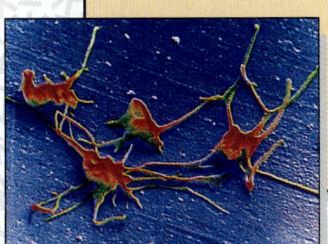
1969

1931
Ernst Ruska, Germany
Ruska builds the first transmission electron microscope (TEM). The TEM uses a beam of electrons and magnets to create an image. In 1933, Ruska builds a second TEM with magnification so great that scientists can use it to study the insides of cells.

1980
Heinrich Roher, Germany
Roher and Gerd Binning develop the scanning tunneling microscope (STM). Using the STM, scientists can see the smallest units of matter—individual atoms!

INVESTIGATION 1

1. You are observing two unlabeled cells. What can you look for to determine which is a plant cell and which is an animal cell?

2. Why do scientists infer from the cell theory that all living things are related?

A13

INVESTIGATION 2

WHAT ARE SOME LIFE PROCESSES OF CELLS?

In order to survive, your body must use oxygen from the air you breathe to get energy from the food you eat. Processes that occur within your cells make these activities possible. In this investigation you'll discover what these cell processes are and how they occur.

Activity

Moving In and Out of Cells

When you breathe, air moves in and out of your body. Inside your body, materials move in and out of cells. These materials move from areas where they are concentrated (present in great amounts) to areas where they are less concentrated. This movement of materials is called diffusion. Make a model of a cell membrane to see how diffusion works.

MATERIALS
- goggles
- spoon
- starch
- 2 beakers
- water
- sealable plastic bag
- container of iodine solution
- *Science Notebook*

SAFETY
Wear goggles. Iodine will stain clothing and is poisonous if swallowed. Clean up spills immediately.

Procedure

1. Put a spoonful of starch into a beaker of water. Stir until well mixed.

2. Pour the starch mixture into a plastic bag. Seal the bag.

Step 1

Step 2

3. When iodine mixes with starch, the mixture changes in color to a dark blue-black. **Talk with your group** and together **predict** what will happen if you place the bag containing the starch mixture in contact with the iodine solution. **Record** your prediction in your *Science Notebook*.

4. Place the bag into a beaker containing iodine solution.

5. Observe the setup every 15 minutes for the next 2 hours. **Record** your observations.

Analyze and Conclude

1. You have made a model that shows how substances move into or out of a cell. What cell part does the plastic bag represent?

2. Infer which substance moved through the plastic bag—the iodine or the starch. How can you tell? How did your prediction compare with your observations?

3. Having **observed** this model, what conclusions can you make about how materials enter and leave cells?

4. Hypothesize as to why only one substance seemed to move through the bag. Explain your hypothesis.

INVESTIGATE FURTHER!

EXPERIMENT

Repeat the above procedure, using food coloring in the beaker instead of iodine. How would you be able to tell that diffusion has taken place?

Coming and Going With Cells

How It Works

In the activity on pages A14 and A15, you saw that a substance, iodine, could pass through a thin layer of plastic. The iodine moved from the fluid in the beaker to the starch-water mixture in the bag. You could tell that the iodine had moved from one side of the plastic to the other because the starch solution turned blue-black in color.

Like the plastic, a cell membrane is also a thin layer. However, a cell membrane is living material. Water, oxygen, salts, and some waste products can pass through the cell membrane by diffusion. **Diffusion** is the tendency of a substance to move from an area of greater concentration to an area of lesser concentration. It continues until the two areas have equal concentrations of a substance.

Cells are mostly water. Water moves freely from regions with lesser concentrations of dissolved substances (high concentrations of water) to regions with greater concentrations of dissolved substances (lesser concentrations of water). The diffusion of water through a membrane, called **osmosis**, maintains the balance of water inside and outside a cell.

The ability of substances to move through the cell membrane is called cell transport. This life process ensures that needed materials, such as food and oxy-

▲ *Elodea* cells in fresh water (*top*); when placed in salt water (*bottom*), water leaves the cells and the cell membrane shrinks.

gen, are able to pass into the cell. These materials are normally in greater concentration outside the cell and so move through the cell membrane by diffusion.

Within a cell, the release of energy from food, in addition to other processes taking place, results in the buildup of waste materials. These waste materials move out of the cell by diffusion.

The movement of materials through the cell membrane by diffusion does not require any "action" by the cell. In other words, the cell uses no energy to move these materials through the cell membrane. However, needed materials (such as chemicals used to make proteins) that are in low concentration outside the cell can also be moved through the cell membrane. In this type of cell transport, the cell uses energy to move the material through the cell membrane. ■

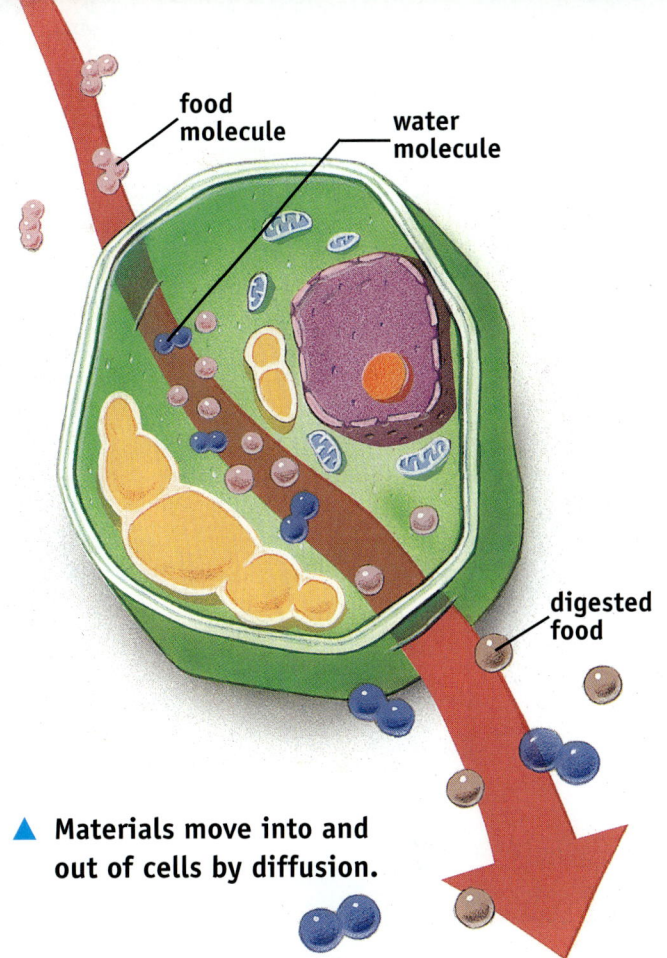

▲ Materials move into and out of cells by diffusion.

SCIENCE IN LITERATURE

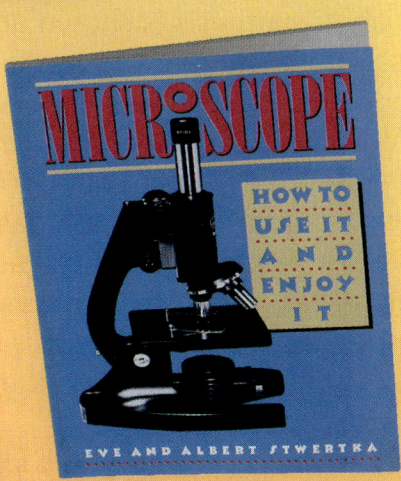

MICROSCOPE: HOW TO USE IT AND ENJOY IT
by Eve and Albert Stwertka
Julian Messner, 1988

By now you are aware of the importance of the microscope in learning about cells and tiny living things. Using a microscope is a skill that takes a little practice. The book *Microscope: How to Use It and Enjoy It* by Eve and Albert Stwertka can be your guide to developing that skill.

Do you want to see what Robert Hooke saw under the microscope he invented in 1665? Look on pages 1 through 8. Are you wondering how using lenses to bend light makes things look bigger? You'll find answers on pages 9 through 13. This book has everything you want to know about microscopes—and probably a few things you hadn't considered!

▲ God designed a way for green plants to make their own nourishment and to supply the needs of other living things. Through photosynthesis, the rain forests of the world provide much of the oxygen needed by other organisms.

Cells grow, reproduce, and carry out other life processes. All of these life processes require energy. Cells obtain energy from food. But plant cells and animal cells differ in the ways that they obtain food.

Photosynthesis

In the *Elodea* leaf that you observed in the activity on pages A6 and A7, you saw structures called chloroplasts. These structures do not occur in animal cells. Chloroplasts contain a green chemical called chlorophyll that is able to capture, or absorb, the energy in sunlight. Plant cells are able to use this energy to build sugar from carbon dioxide and water. So, plant cells make their own food. Animal cells must absorb food from their environment.

The process by which light energy is used to make food is called **photosynthesis** (fōt ō sin'thə sis). The equation for photosynthesis is shown at the top of this page. Note that oxygen is a waste product of this process.

Where do plants get the carbon dioxide and water to carry out photosynthesis? Carbon dioxide is a gas found in air. Most plants absorb this gas through their leaves, and in most plants, photosynthesis takes place in the leaves. Water, found in the soil, is absorbed by the roots and carried to the leaves.

In the next chapter you'll learn about some other organisms that also contain chlorophyll and carry out photosynthesis. All organisms that can carry out photosynthesis are called producers.

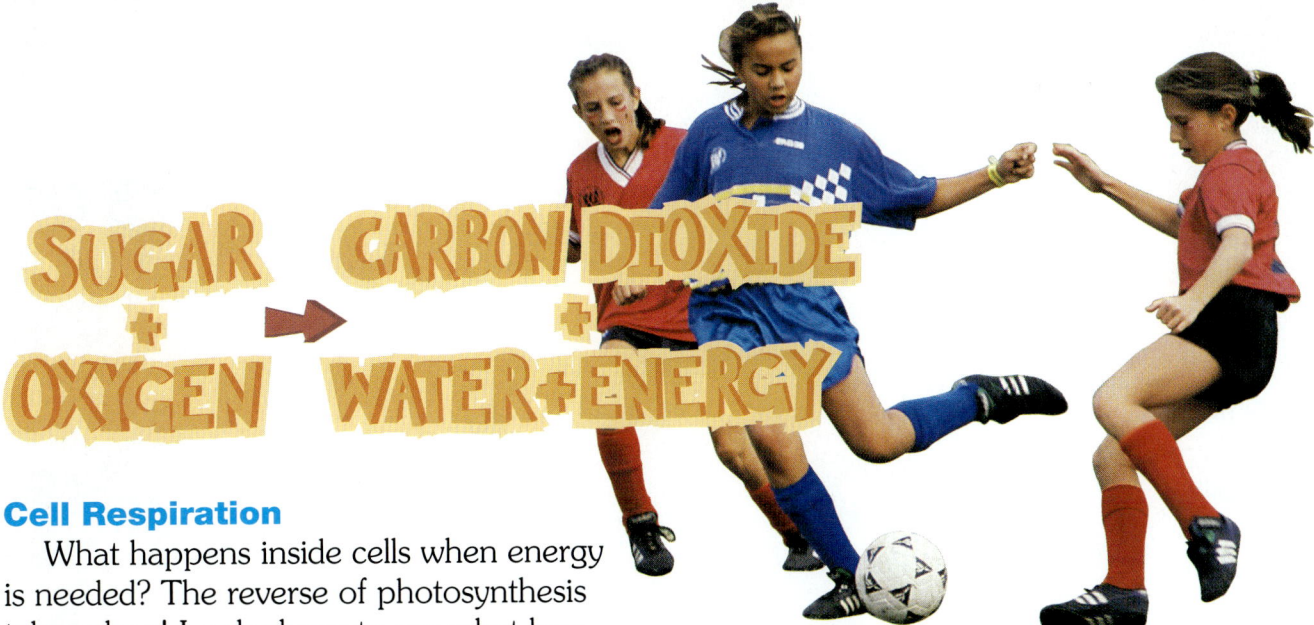

SUGAR + OXYGEN → CARBON DIOXIDE + WATER + ENERGY

Cell Respiration

What happens inside cells when energy is needed? The reverse of photosynthesis takes place! Look above to see what happens when the photosynthesis equation is turned around.

The process of using oxygen to release stored energy by breaking down sugar molecules is called **cell respiration** (res pə rā′shən). This process occurs in the mitochondria of both plant and animal cells. Plants use the energy they have stored as a result of photosynthesis. Animals use energy they receive when they eat plants or eat animals that have eaten plants.

The equation at the top of this page summarizes cell respiration. Notice that cell respiration produces the same materials that are used for photosynthesis.

When oxygen isn't available in sufficient amounts, some cells obtain energy

▲ Physical activity requires respiration—the reverse process of photosynthesis—to provide energy.

from sugar in a different way. In the process, called **fermentation** (fʉr mən tā′shən), the sugar is only partly broken down. This occurs, for example, when you exercise very hard. Your heart cannot pump blood fast enough to keep your muscle cells supplied with oxygen, so the sugar cannot be broken down into carbon dioxide and water. Fermentation causes your cells to produce a waste product called lactic acid. Fermentation and cell respiration are both life processes that release the energy stored in food. ■

INVESTIGATION 2

1. How is diffusion important to cell processes such as photosynthesis?

2. How might your life be affected if your cells contained chloroplasts?

INVESTIGATION 3

How Do Cells Make More Cells?

You've grown a lot since you were very young. Your cells have been busy making new cells to add to your body. Investigation 3 will give you some clues as to how cells reproduce and specialize to do specific jobs.

Activity

Multiplying by Dividing

MATERIALS
- microscope
- prepared slide of onion root tip
- *Science Notebook*

When an organism grows, it adds new cells. Cells also wear out and are continually replaced by new cells, even after the organism is fully grown. In this activity you will learn how cells multiply by dividing.

Procedure

1. Observe a root tip under low and high power of the microscope. Try to locate cells that look like the photographs on page A21. Study each cell and each photograph and **record** your observations in your *Science Notebook*.

Step 1

Can you put these stages in order? ▼

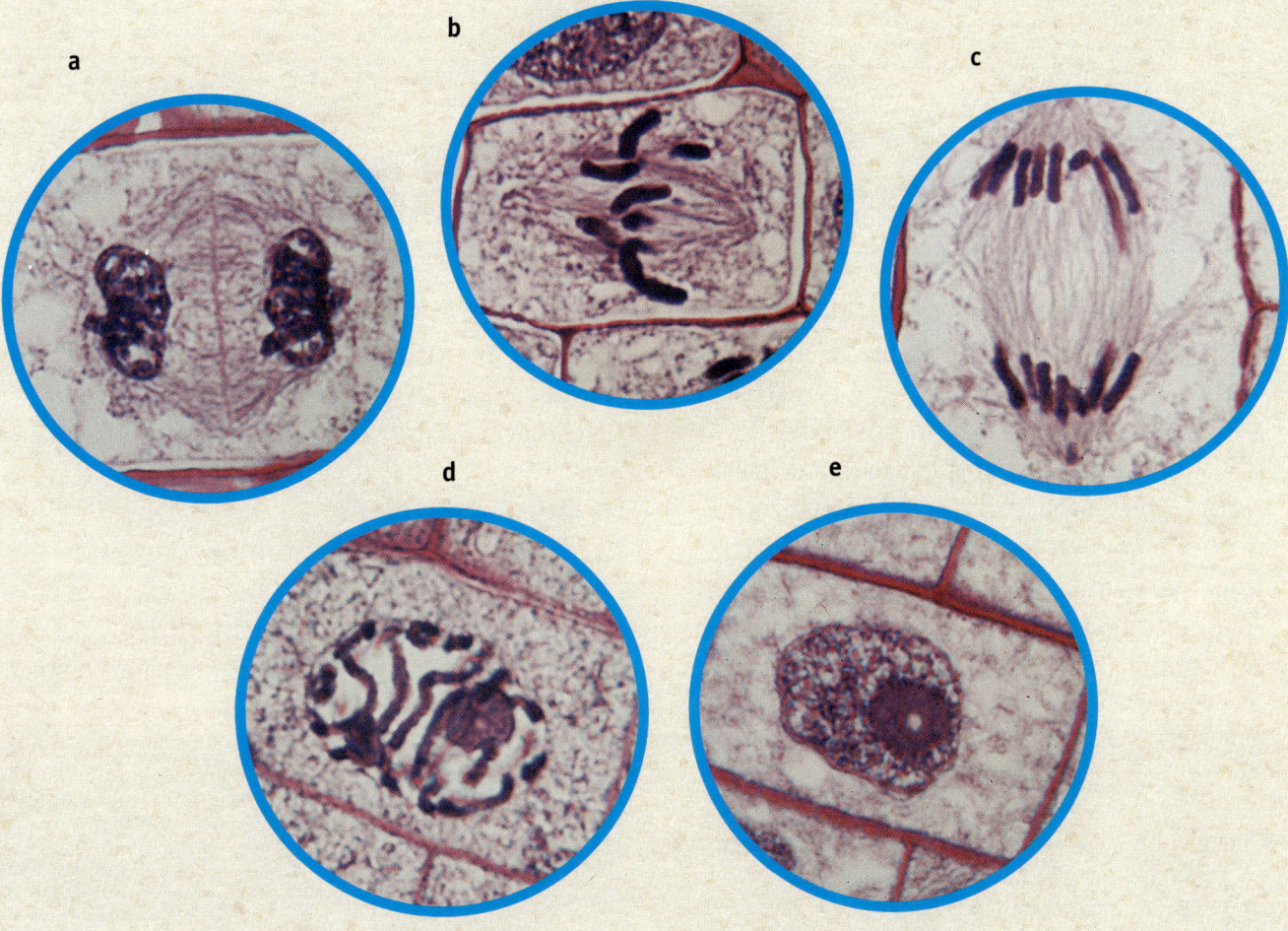

2. The photographs shown above are not in the proper order to show the process of cell division. Look for evidence that one cell is dividing into two and **hypothesize** about the correct sequence of the photos. **Compare** your sequence with that of another student. Work together to order the pictures. Then **draw a diagram** to **record** your suggested sequence.

Analyze and Conclude

1. What evidence did you **observe** that suggests that one cell is dividing into two?

2. Infer why the tip of an onion root is a good place to look for dividing cells.

3. Infer where you might find dividing cells in a human being.

INVESTIGATE FURTHER!

RESEARCH

What is cloning? Consult library sources to find out about the cloning of plant and animal cells.

Cell Division

A meteorite flashes out of the night sky and into a small lake. Deep in the water, a single-celled amoeba absorbs radiation given off by the space rock. The amoeba begins to grow rapidly. Within hours, it's the size of a car. Slowly, the amoeba begins to ooze its way toward a nearby town.

Feeding on everything in its path, the amoeba continues to grow and move. As it approaches the first house, the residents peer out at the blob. Are they in danger? Can anything stop the blob? Could something like this really happen?

Is Bigger Better?

Recall how cells get the oxygen and food they need. These substances must move into the cell by diffusing through the cell membrane. Cell wastes must also

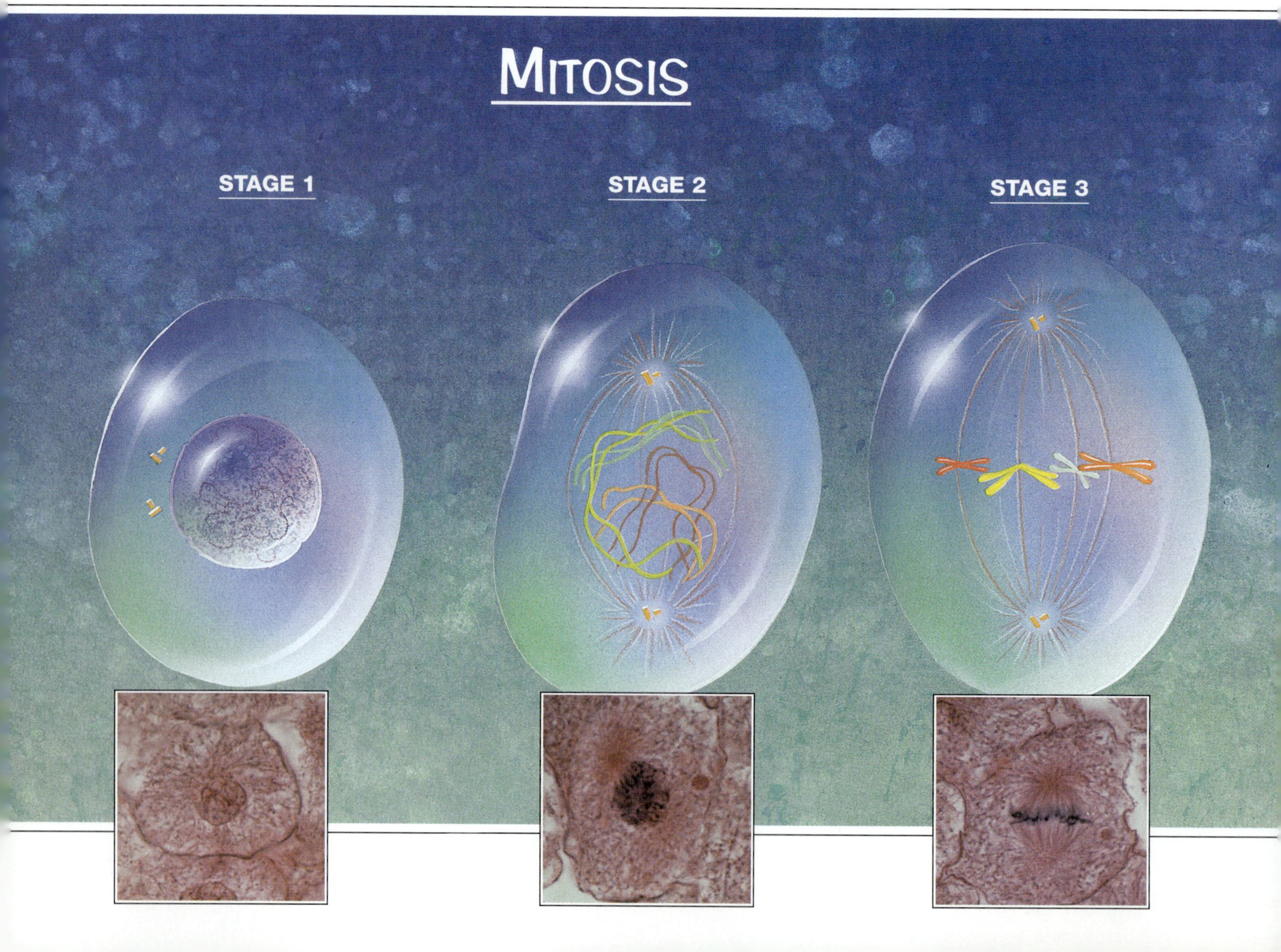

MITOSIS

STAGE 1   STAGE 2   STAGE 3

move out through the cell membrane by diffusion.

As a cell grows larger, it requires more and more energy and thus needs increasing amounts of sugar. More and more oxygen is needed to react with the sugar and release the energy. The growing cell also produces greater amounts of carbon dioxide and other waste products.

As a cell gets bigger, both its cell membrane and its volume get bigger. But the volume actually increases faster than the cell membrane. At some point, the cell membrane wouldn't be large enough to let enough materials in (or out) quickly enough to keep the cell's life processes going. God in His wisdom starts another life process before cells reach this point.

Splitting in Two

Instead of continuing to grow, cells divide once they reach a certain size. (For this reason, giant amoeba could never exist.)

When a cell divides, two new cells are formed. Most of the cells in living organisms divide by a process called mitosis (mī tō′sis). In **mitosis**, a cell divides into two exact copies of itself.

Before mitosis begins, the cell's chromosomes make copies of themselves. During mitosis the copies are pulled to opposite ends of the cell, and the cell splits in half. The two daughter cells, each with a complete set of chromosomes, now begin to grow. Follow the stages of mitosis in the diagram and compare the drawings to those you made in the activity.

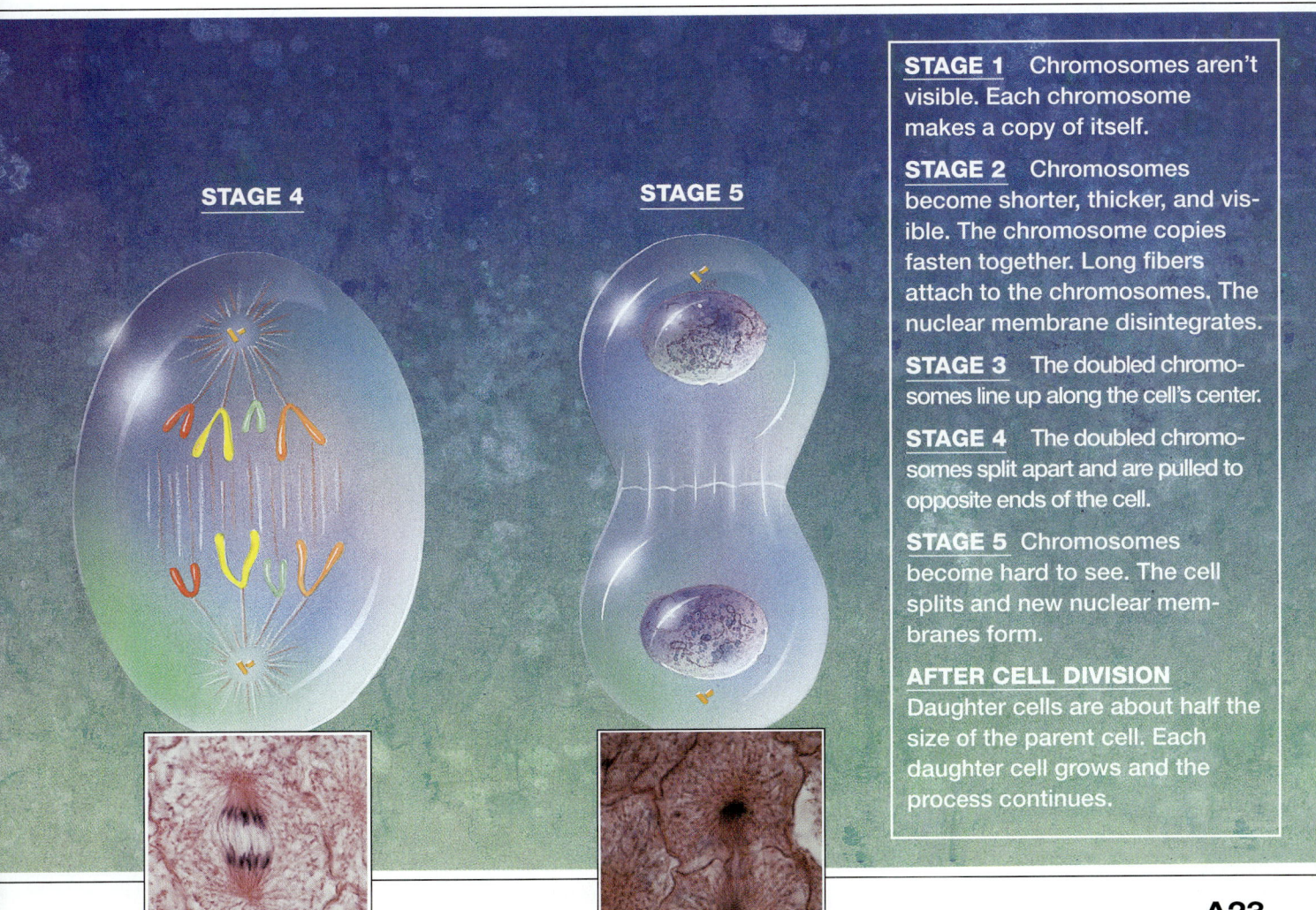

STAGE 1 Chromosomes aren't visible. Each chromosome makes a copy of itself.

STAGE 2 Chromosomes become shorter, thicker, and visible. The chromosome copies fasten together. Long fibers attach to the chromosomes. The nuclear membrane disintegrates.

STAGE 3 The doubled chromosomes line up along the cell's center.

STAGE 4 The doubled chromosomes split apart and are pulled to opposite ends of the cell.

STAGE 5 Chromosomes become hard to see. The cell splits and new nuclear membranes form.

AFTER CELL DIVISION Daughter cells are about half the size of the parent cell. Each daughter cell grows and the process continues.

Artificial Blood

Have you ever heard a radio or television announcement asking people to donate blood? People need blood for a variety of reasons. Some have been in in major accidents and have suffered a loss of blood. Others require blood during surgery. Still others have blood diseases that cause them to need blood on a regular basis.

The transfer of blood from one person to another is called a transfusion. The person donating the blood is the donor. The person receiving the blood is the recipient. Although many recipients receive whole blood, blood banks routinely separate blood into its parts because some patients need only certain types of blood cells.

Unfortunately the need for blood is so great that the demand often exceeds the supply. What can be done when there are not enough blood donors?

A Possible Answer

One answer is to use artificial blood. Whereas real blood is a complex tissue that performs many functions, artificial blood is much simpler. It's designed and used for only one of the jobs that blood does—carrying oxygen, for example. Oxygen is carried by a protein in red blood cells. The protein captures oxygen when blood passes through the lungs and releases the oxygen as blood flows through the body.

In one process for making artificial blood, blood is obtained from a blood bank. To isolate the oxygen-carrying protein, red blood cells are separated out and broken down. The oxygen-carrying protein is processed to kill any viruses. Then the protein is enveloped in an artificial membrane, bottled, and packaged in transfusion bags for shipment. Since only the oxygen-carrying protein is being used, there is no need to worry about matching blood types. ■

The creation of artificial blood depends upon blood donations. It is the artificial membrane that gives it its name. ▼

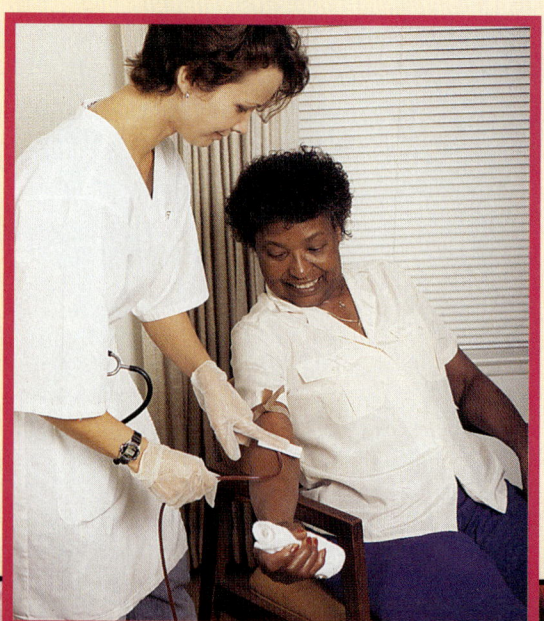

Tissues, Organs, and Systems

As organisms grow, their cells continue to divide. The cells develop into different and specialized cell types. Each type of cell has certain structures and characteristics that make the specialized cell better at its job than a cell that must carry out many tasks.

The specialization of cells is called **cell differentiation** (dif ər en shē ā'shən). It begins early in development, when organisms still consist of only a few cells. In humans, once a cell differentiates, it never becomes anything different.

But in some other organisms, cells can change their specialties throughout the organism's life. Salamanders can grow a new leg or tail if they lose one. One piece of a planarian, a type of flatworm, can grow into a whole new planarian.

God's insurance policy--
Because their cells can differentiate throughout their lives, salamanders can replace body parts that are lost. ▼

Some plants can even grow a whole new plant from just a leaf or stem.

Groups of specialized cells that work together to do a specific job form **tissues**. Take, for example, muscle tissue. Muscles contain cells that contract. These contracting cells make it possible for you to move. Another example is the nerve tissue that carries information between different parts of your body. Messages from your muscle tissue are carried to your spinal cord and brain by nerve tissue. Other nerve tissue carries messages back to tell your muscle tissue when to contract.

Tissues Make Up Organs

The heart and liver are examples of organs. An **organ** is a group of tissues that function together to do a specific job. Organs are usually made of several different kinds of tissues.

The heart, for example, has muscle tissue, which contracts, squeezing the blood out of the heart's chambers and into your arteries. The heart also has tissue that forms membranes that cover and protect the muscle tissue of the heart. Nerve tissue is also present in the heart. This tissue carries signals to the heart from the brain.

Organ Systems

Specialized cells combine to form tissues. Tissues connect to form organs, each with its own task. But in many living things, groups of organs work together. An **organ system** is a group of organs that work together to do a job.

An example of an organ system is your digestive system. This system includes the group of organs that work to digest food. These include the esophagus, the stomach, and the intestines. Each has its specific job in the process of digestion.

Plants also have organs and organ systems. Leaves, stems, and roots are all organs. They work together to transport water throughout the plant. ■

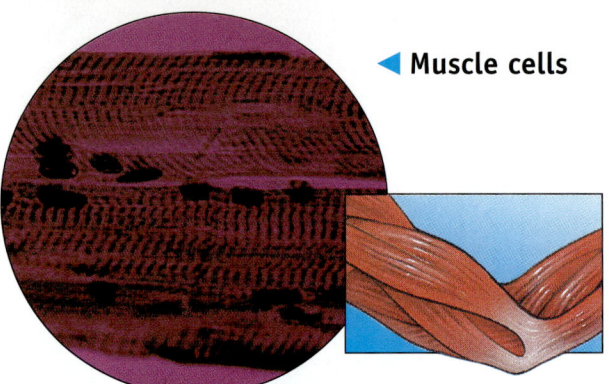

◄ Muscle cells

▲ Individual muscle cells work together to form this striated muscle tissue.

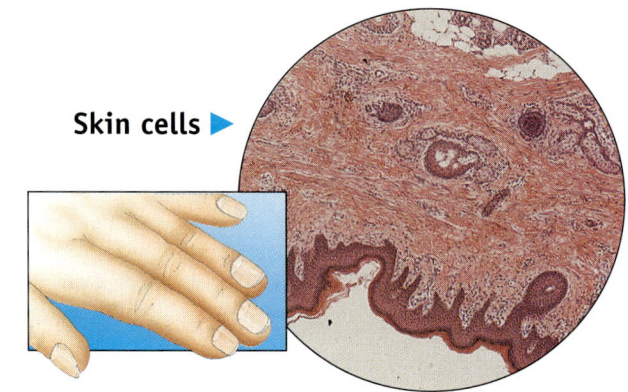

Skin cells ▶

▲ Many tissues combine to form an organ, such as the skin.

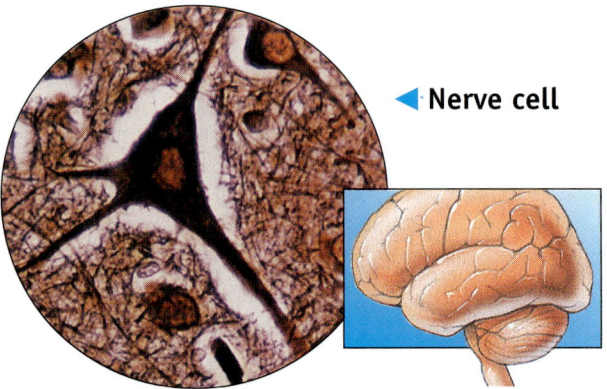

◄ Nerve cell

▲ The brain, which is an organ made of nerve cells and other tissues, is part of the nervous system.

INVESTIGATION 3

1. When a cell divides, how do the two new cells end up with the correct number of chromosomes?

2. Why do the cells in multi-celled organisms specialize?

REFLECT & EVALUATE

WORD POWER

cell membrane
cell
cell theory
cell wall
cell respiration
diffusion
chloroplast
mitosis
chromosome
nucleus
cytoplasm
organ
fermentation
osmosis
mitochondria
vacuole
cell differentiation
nuclear membrane
organ system
photosynthesis
tissues

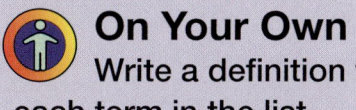

On Your Own
Write a definition for each term in the list.

With a Partner
Write a clue for each term in the list. Then design a crossword puzzle using the terms. Trade puzzles with your partner.

Create drawings or models of plant and animal cells to include in your portfolio.

Analyze Information

Study the micrograph of the cell. Then identify as many cell structures as you can. Do you think this is a plant cell or an animal cell? Why?

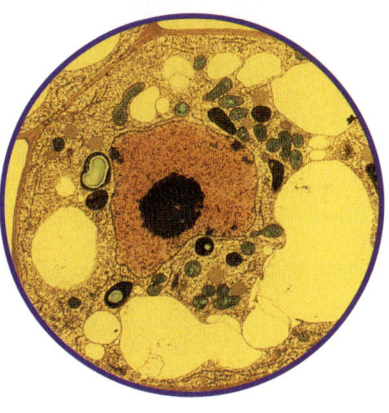

Assess Performance

Using water and food coloring, design an experiment to demonstrate diffusion. After your teacher has approved it, conduct the experiment and report your results to the class.

Problem Solving

1. Why do you think plant cells have both a cell membrane and a cell wall?

2. What are some life processes of cells? How do cells carry out these processes? Do animal cells carry out any of these processes in different ways than plant cells? Explain.

3. Based on your knowledge of cells, why do you think it is possible for a one-celled organism to survive? What advantages or disadvantages do you think a multi-celled organism possesses?

4. What compliment would you pay God now that you know more about how organized and well-made humans are?

CHAPTER 2

PROTISTS AND FUNGI

It might look like green scum, but it's part of God's creation. Amoeba grow and move like an animal in a bowl of pond water. Yet scum isn't a plant, and an amoeba isn't an animal. In real life, as in fairy tales, things are not always what they seem.

A Strange Encounter

Have you read *Alice's Adventures in Wonderland*? It tells of a curious girl named Alice, who follows a rabbit into an underground world. In the passage below, Alice has shrunk to a fraction of her normal size, and she finds herself under a mushroom.

[Alice] stretched herself up on tiptoe, and peeped over the edge of the mushroom, and her eyes immediately met those of a large caterpillar that was sitting on the top . . . taking not the smallest notice of her or of anything else. The Caterpillar and Alice looked at each other for some time in silence; at last the Caterpillar . . . addressed her in a languid, sleepy voice.

"Who are you?" said the Caterpillar.

— Lewis Carroll

In real life, as in Wonderland, a mushroom looks like a plant. Yet in this chapter you'll find out the true identity of mushrooms and other organisms sometimes mistaken for plants.

Coming Up

WHAT ARE PROTISTS? A30

WHAT ARE FUNGI? A40

◀ Alice encounters a caterpillar sitting atop a fungus in Lewis Carroll's *Alice's Adventures in Wonderland*.

INVESTIGATION 1

WHAT ARE PROTISTS?

You've just entered a world of tiny, unusual organisms. Some act like plants, while others act like animals. A few of these organisms seem to be both plants and animals! Welcome to the kingdom of protists. Find out about the characteristics of these organisms in this investigation.

Activity

Microorganisms

The kingdom of living things known as protists includes mostly single-celled, microscopic organisms. In this activity you'll examine some of these fascinating creatures.

MATERIALS
- dropper
- pond water
- microscope slide
- cover slip
- microscope
- *Science Notebook*

Paramecium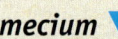

Procedure

Place a drop of pond water on a clean microscope slide. Then place a cover slip on the drop. Look at the slide under the low power and then the high power of the microscope. **Observe** any tiny organisms you see and **sketch** them in your *Science Notebook*.

Analyze and Conclude

1. **Identify** the shapes of some of the organisms you observed.
2. **Describe** how the organisms move.
3. **Infer** how the organisms obtain food.

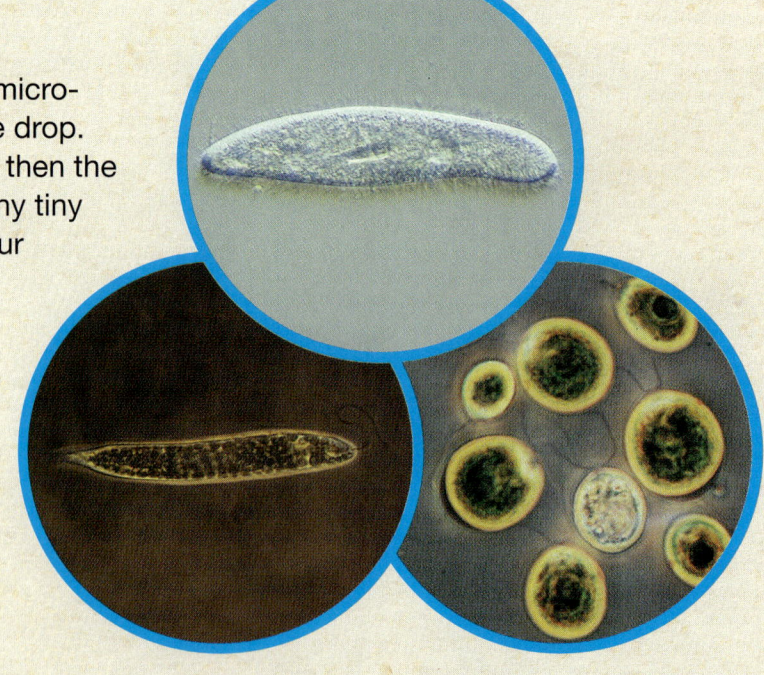

▲ Euglena   ▲ Chlamydomonas

Activity
Observing an Animal-like Protist

MATERIALS
- dropper
- culture of amoebas
- microscope slide
- cover slip
- microscope
- timer
- *Science Notebook*

Most of the animals you know move around—running, flying, swimming. How does a one-celled, animal-like protist move? How does it perform other life processes? In this activity you'll explore the life of a one-celled animal-like protist.

Procedure

1. Place a drop of the amoeba culture on a clean microscope slide. Then place a cover slip on top of the drop. Look at the slide under the low power of the microscope.

2. Observe an amoeba and **make a drawing** of it in your *Science Notebook*.

3. Make two or more sketches showing the outline of the amoeba at 1-minute intervals. **Talk with your group** about how the amoeba seems to be changing.

4. Compare the amoeba on your slide with the one in the photograph. How is the amoeba on your slide similar to or different from the one in the photograph?

Analyze and Conclude

1. How does an amoeba move? Based on your observations, **hypothesize** how an amoeba may obtain its food.

2. Amoebas were once classified as one-celled animals. In what ways are these tiny protists like animals?

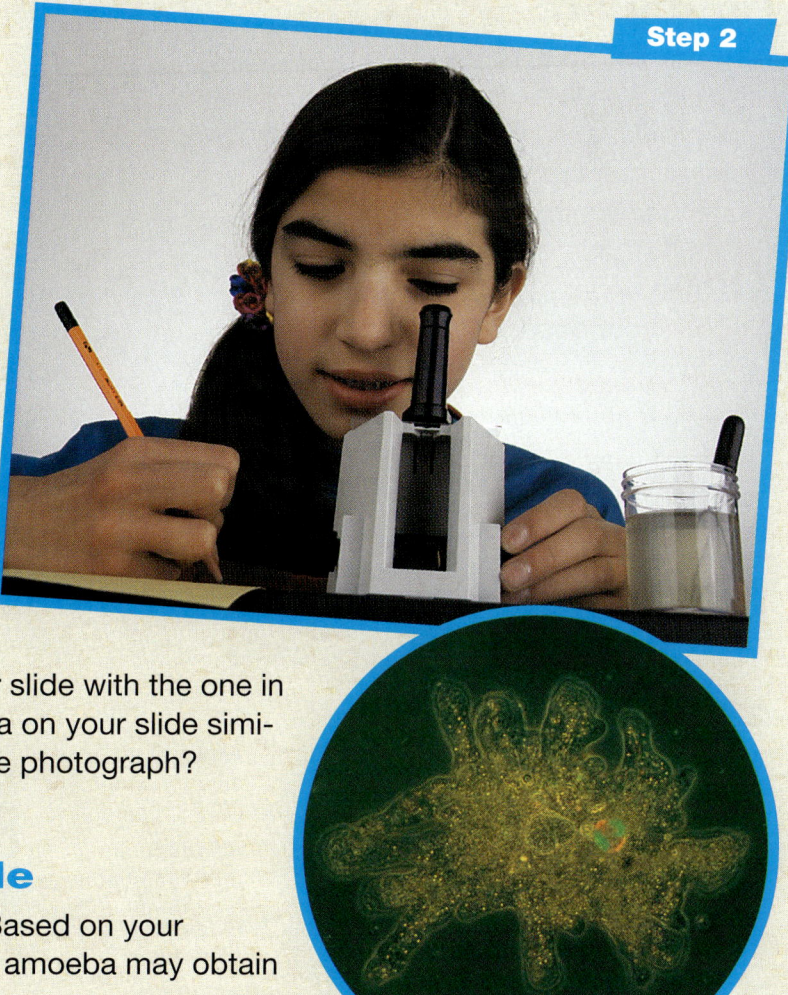

▲ Amoeba

Activity
Observing a Plantlike Protist

MATERIALS
- prepared slides of *Spirogyra*
- microscope
- *Science Notebook*

Have you seen green scum growing on a pond? If so, you've seen plantlike protists. Some plantlike protists are multicellular; they have more than one cell. You'll observe a multicellular plantlike protist in this activity.

Procedure

1. Predict how a plantlike protist may be different from an animal-like protist. **Record** your prediction in your *Science Notebook*. Obtain a prepared slide of *Spirogyra*. Place the slide on the microscope. Focus the slide under low power and then under high power. **Record** your observations.

2. Make a drawing of several *Spirogyra* cells that show the shape of the cells and how they are arranged.

▲ *Spirogyra*

Analyze and Conclude

1. Describe the structure of *Spirogyra*.

2. Based on your observations, how are plantlike protists similar to animal-like protists? How are they different?

3. A *Spirogyra* cell usually has one chloroplast. Can you **identify** the chloroplast in a cell on your slide? What is the shape and size of the chloroplast?

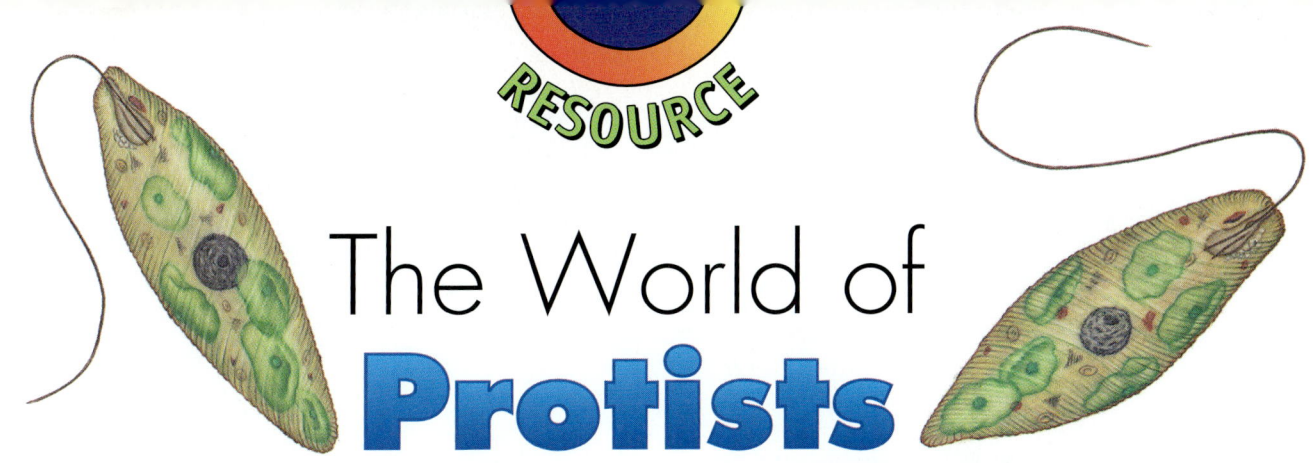

The World of Protists

Swarming in the murky water of a lake, strange-looking creatures dart here and there in search of prey or the bright rays of sunlight. If you could shrink yourself down even smaller than Alice was in Wonderland, you'd be surrounded by millions of these creatures. This is the world of **protists**, a kingdom of mostly single-celled, microscopic organisms that have traits of animals, plants, or both.

As you saw when you did the activity on page A30, pond water teems with a variety of protists. However, protists also live in lakes, rivers, oceans, and damp soil. Some protists even live inside other organisms. Scientists have found many thousands of protist species in all parts of the environment.

A single drop of pond water may contain a world of life—much of it protist. ▼

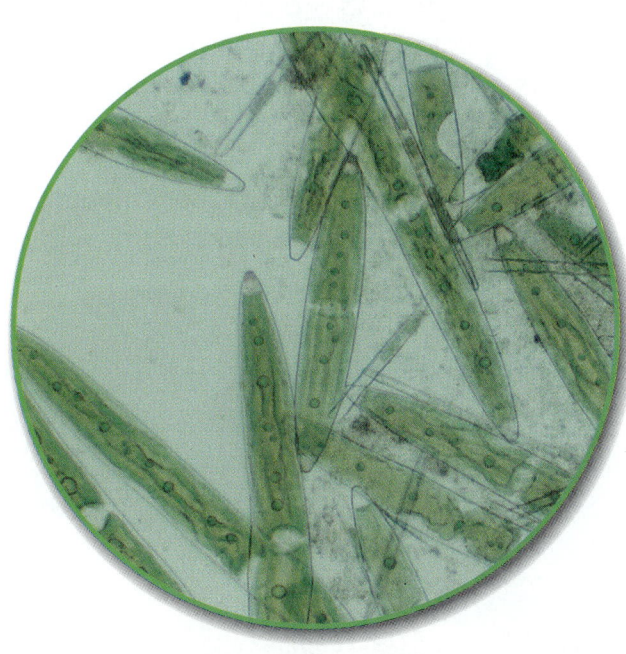

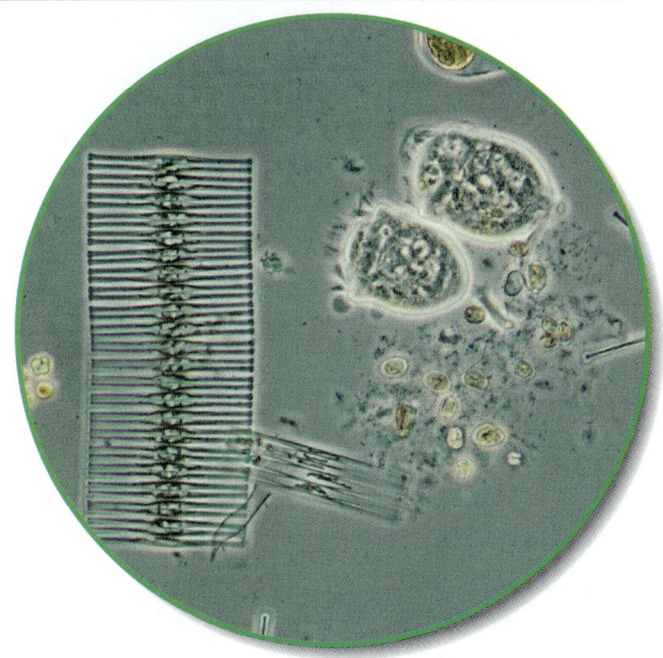

▲ **What is animal, what is plant, and what is protist? You've seen some of these organisms in the activities.**

Most protists are single-celled and contain a nucleus and the other cell structures needed to carry out all basic life functions. Some protists are **multicellular** (mul ti sel′yoo lər), which means they are made up of more than one cell. Multicellular protists may not be microscopic. In fact, some grow to be many meters in length. But all the cells of multicellular protists are very similar, and each carries out its own life functions.

Most protists reproduce by fission, the dividing of a cell to produce two new cells. In this form of reproduction, there is only one parent, and the new cells are

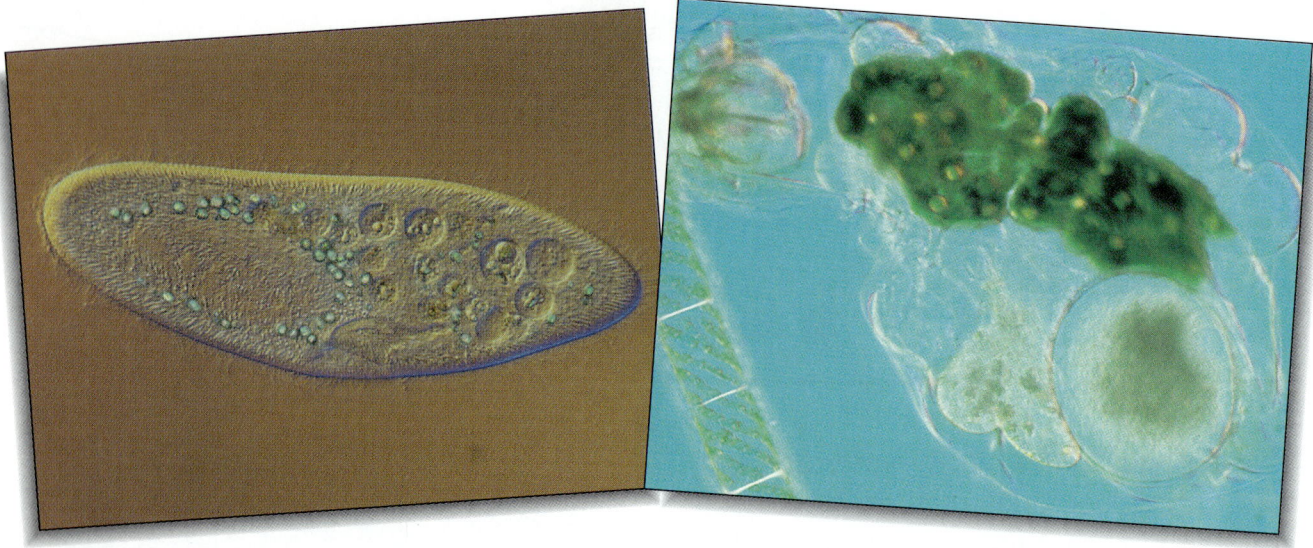

▲ The tiny cilia on a paramecium enable it to move and gather food.

▲ These organisms may be green like plants, but they are protists.

identical to the parent. In some protists, cells from two parents join and produce new cells that are not identical to either parent.

Animal-like Protists

Many protists have traits that are like those of animals. Such protists are called **protozoans**. Like animals, these protists get their energy by feeding on other organisms. Most protozoans have some method of locomotion to help them obtain food.

In the activity on page A31, you observed an amoeba that was moving by pushing out its cytoplasm and forming pseudopods (sōō′ dō pädz). Amoebas also use their pseudopods to capture food. An amoeba completely surrounds the food and ingests it. Once inside the amoeba, the food is digested and used for energy.

Other kinds of protozoans have different methods of locomotion. Parameciums (par ə mē′sē əmz) have hairlike structures called cilia (sil′ē ə). The beating of the cilia propels a paramecium. Cilia also draw water and food into the paramecium's mouthlike opening. Some protozoans have threadlike tails, called flagella (flə jel′ə), that whip around to cause movement.

There are also protozoans that do not move on their own. Most of these protozoans are parasites, meaning they live in or on other organisms. While some parasitic (par ə sit′ik) protozoans are harmless to their hosts, others are extremely harmful and may even be deadly.

Plantlike Protists

Plantlike protists are capable of producing their own food. Like plants, these protists contain chlorophyll, a green pigment. Chlorophyll is held in structures

A diatom, a single-celled alga, has chlorophyll and a rigid cell wall like a plant. ▼

Spirogyra is a common freshwater alga.

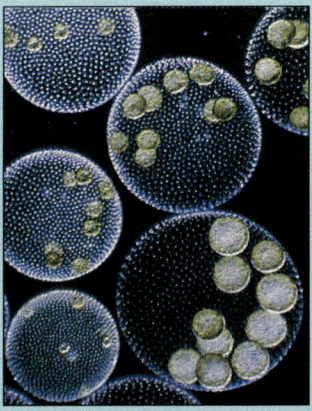
Volvox is a freshwater alga that lives in colonies.

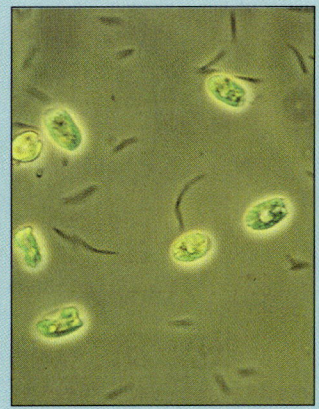
Chlorella is a freshwater alga with one large chloroplast.

Sargassum is an algal seaweed. It can cover miles of ocean surface.

called chloroplasts, which you observed in the activity on page A32. As in plants, chlorophyll helps plantlike protists make food, using the Sun's energy.

Some plantlike protists are able to move on their own. The *Euglena*, for example, has a flagellum. It also has a light-sensitive eyespot that helps it locate the brightest areas in its surroundings. The *Euglena* is also animal-like because it can feed on other organisms when there is not enough light for it to make food.

Many plantlike protists are called **algae** (al′jē). If you've ever been to the beach, you've probably seen seaweed. But those plantlike strips aren't weeds at all, they're algae.

Most kinds of algae, such as the **diatoms** (dī′ ə tämz) on these two pages, are single-celled. The most plentiful of all algae, diatoms are found in both fresh water and seawater. Like other algae, diatoms contain chlorophyll. But the green color is hidden by yellow and brown pigments. The cell walls of diatoms are tiny glasslike shells, resembling little boxes with lids. The jewel-like organisms come in a variety of shapes and colors.

In addition to their beauty, diatoms are important to other organisms. A large part of ocean plankton is made of diatoms. **Plankton** includes all the tiny organisms that float freely near the surface of the ocean. It is plantlike plankton that forms the base of the ocean food chain. Tiny animals that live in the plankton feed on diatoms. Small fish also feed on them. In turn, larger fish feed on the small fish. Even some very large marine animals, such as the baleen whale, have a diet that consists mainly of plankton!

▼ A diatom

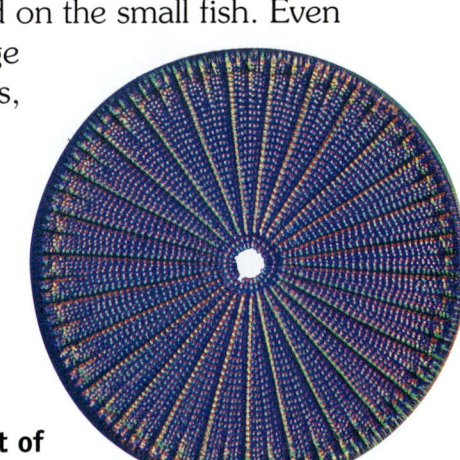

Why is the first hundred feet of the ocean so thick with diatoms? ▶

How an Amoeba Captures Food

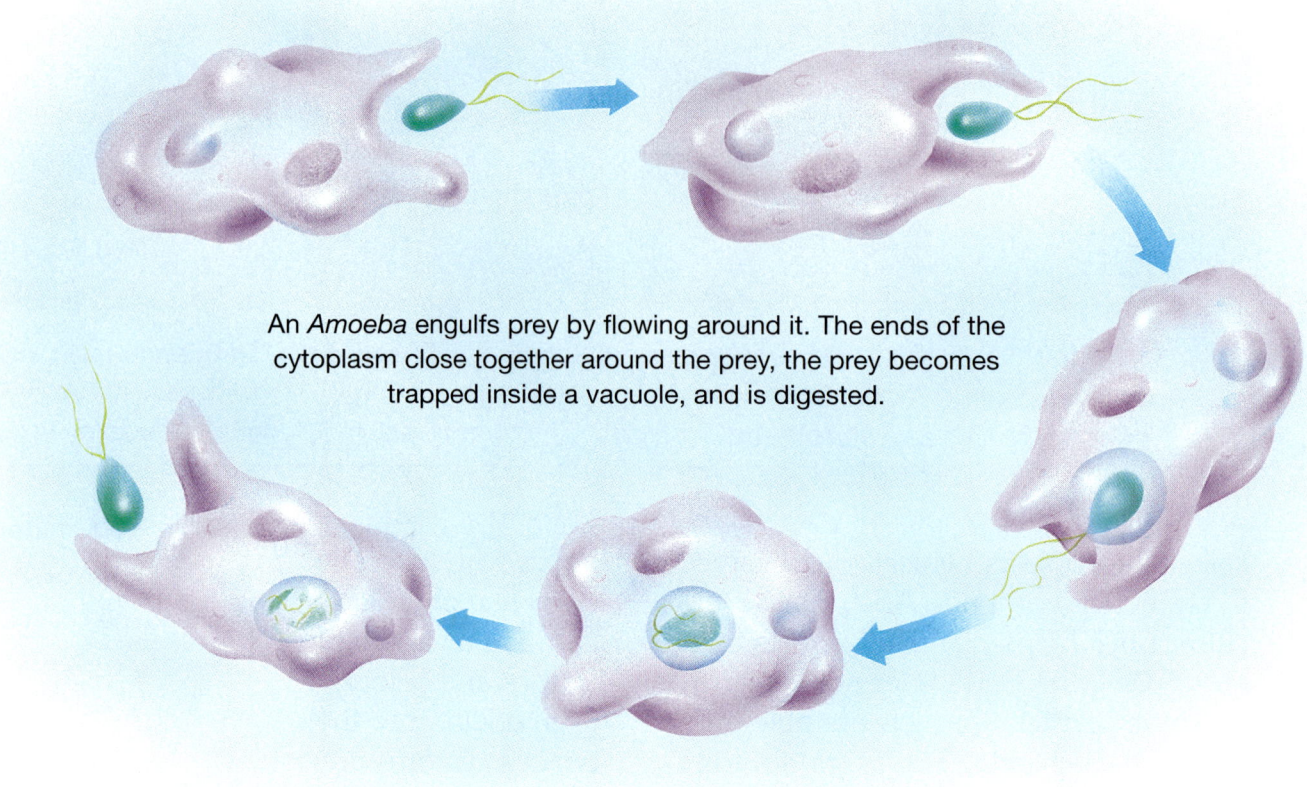

An *Amoeba* engulfs prey by flowing around it. The ends of the cytoplasm close together around the prey, the prey becomes trapped inside a vacuole, and is digested.

How Protists Reproduce

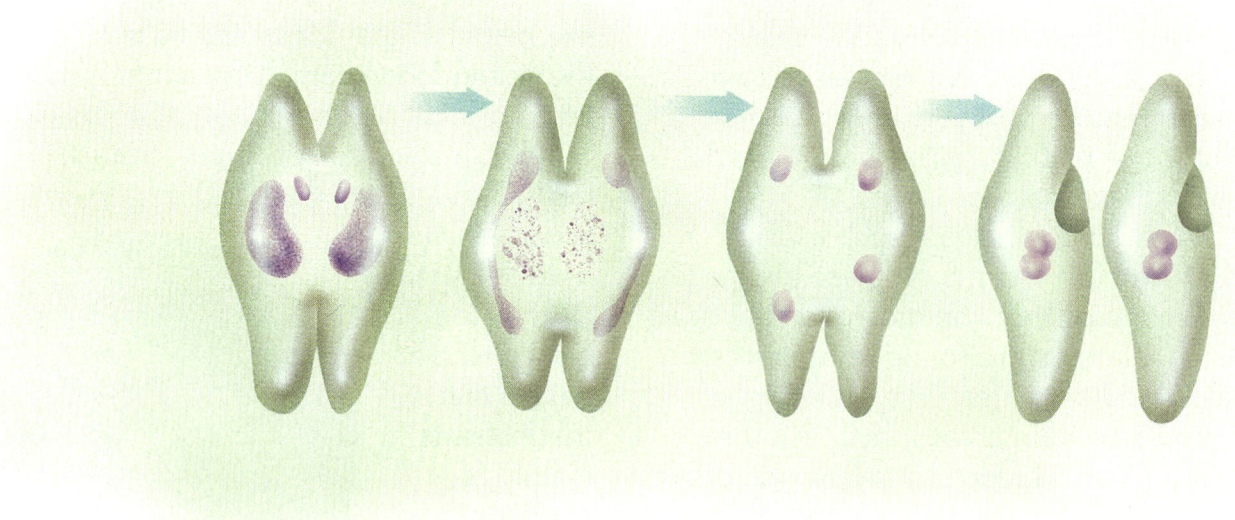

Most protists reproduce by fission, or cell division. This process results in two identical cells.

Multicellular Protists

The most familiar kinds of multicellular protists are the algae commonly called seaweed. The *Spirogyra* that you observed in the activity on page A32 is a microscopic multicellular alga found in fresh water. Kelp, a multicellular saltwater alga, grows to be many meters long and is made up of millions of cells. If you've ever eaten Japanese food, you may have tasted kelp. Algae is also used to make products such as cosmetics, dog food, and ice cream.

Like plants, all algae contain chlorophyll. Some algae contain other pigments in addition to chlorophyll. These pigments may cause the algae to be a color other than green, such as brown, gold, or red. Algae are also like plants in another way—they have cell walls.

Multicellular algae play an important role in the life cycles of Earth. Many animals depend on them for food and shelter. And all animals depend on them for the oxygen they give off as they use the Sun's energy to make food. ■

▲ Kelp is a multicellular alga that can grow to more than 16m in length.

Pond water is just one of many sources of microorganisms that you can observe. In *Microscope* by Eve and Albert Stwertka, you'll find a recipe called a "hay infusion," for growing microorganisms. See if you can get permission to follow the instructions on pages 31–33. In about a week, you should have a cloudy, smelly mess that will be filled with microscopic life.

If all this activity occurs in such a small sample, what does this suggest about the activity on God's planet Earth?

RESOURCE

Protozoan Diseases

In the science fiction movie *The Blob*, the creature looked like a gigantic amoeba that engulfed people, animals, and buildings. Protozoans do not grow as big as that creature and they certainly do not eat people. However, protozoans can be quite dangerous.

Some kinds of protozoans cause diseases by invading the body of another living thing. The living thing that is invaded by the protozoan is called a host. The protozoan is a parasite. When a disease-causing parasite settles in a host, the host is said to have an infection. The disease itself is called an infectious (in fek′shəs) disease. Malaria (mə ler′ē ə), sleeping sickness, and amoebic dysentery (ə mē′bik dis′ən ter ē) are examples of diseases caused by protozoans. Each year, these diseases infect and kill millions of people.

A common and dangerous infectious disease—malaria—is caused by the protozoan *Plasmodium* (plaz mō′dē əm). At one time, people thought malaria was caused by bad air, so they kept their windows closed during outbreaks of malaria. As you study the diagram on page A39, see if you can figure out why this method was partially successful.

Controlling Malaria

Malaria is carried by the *Anopheles* mosquito, which lives in hot, wet areas. The mosquitoes breed in rain pools and ponds that form because of high rainfall. As a result, the best way to control malaria is to control the mosquitoes that spread it. People use insect spray and mosquito netting to protect themselves from adult insects. They also drain ponds or cover them with oil to kill young mosquito larvae.

Unfortunately, destroying the larvae can also harm other organisms that live in or depend on the water. In some places, people are now introducing small fish that eat the mosquito larvae in the infested ponds.

INVESTIGATE FURTHER!

RESEARCH

In the library, read about the cause of sleeping sickness and amoebic dysentery, two diseases caused by protozoans. How are people infected? Where are these diseases most common? How can the diseases be prevented and treated?

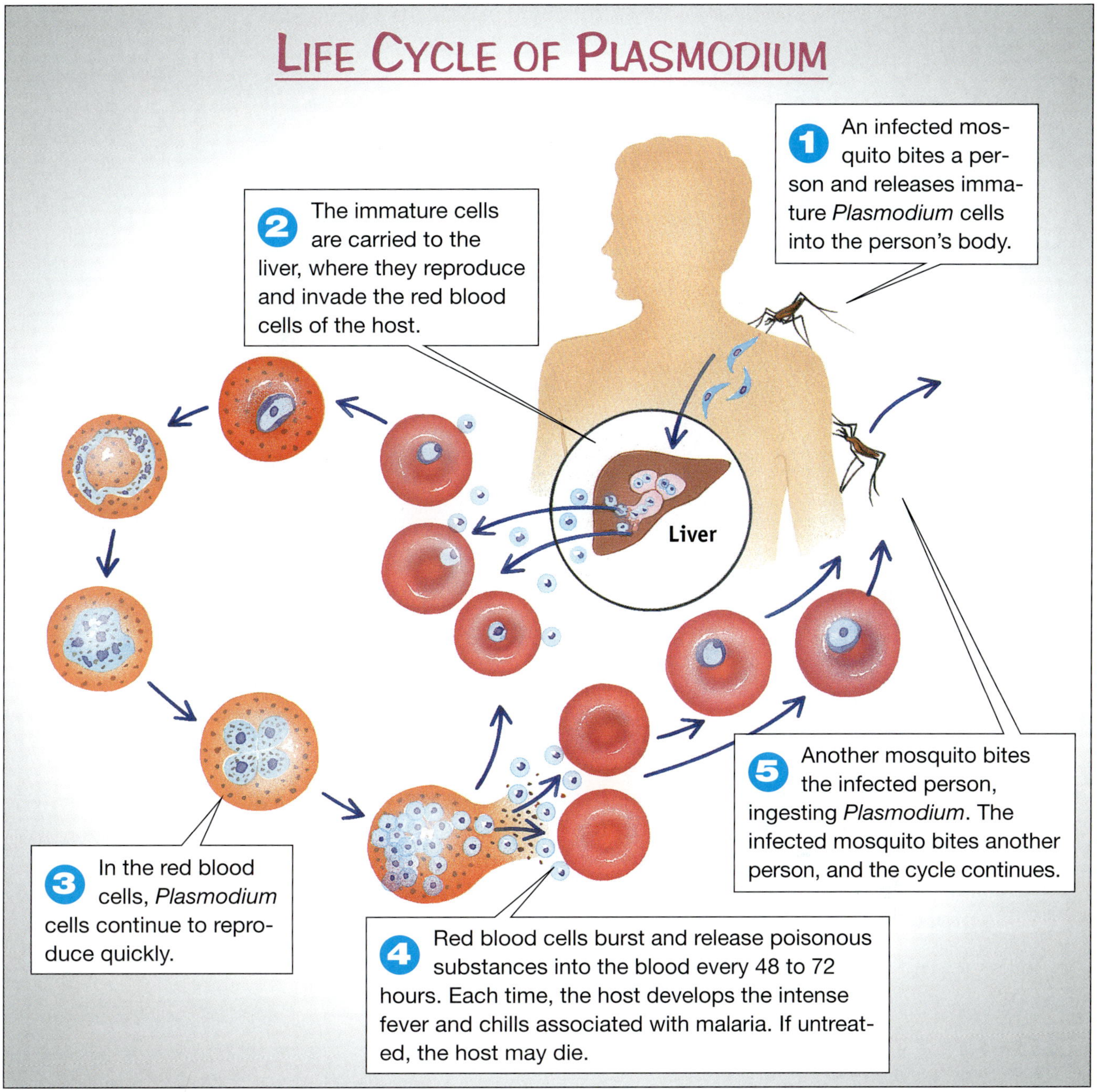

LIFE CYCLE OF PLASMODIUM

1 An infected mosquito bites a person and releases immature *Plasmodium* cells into the person's body.

2 The immature cells are carried to the liver, where they reproduce and invade the red blood cells of the host.

3 In the red blood cells, *Plasmodium* cells continue to reproduce quickly.

4 Red blood cells burst and release poisonous substances into the blood every 48 to 72 hours. Each time, the host develops the intense fever and chills associated with malaria. If untreated, the host may die.

5 Another mosquito bites the infected person, ingesting *Plasmodium*. The infected mosquito bites another person, and the cycle continues.

INVESTIGATION 1

1. A friend of yours insists that all protists are microscopic. Write a letter to that friend, explaining why this statement is not true.

2. Choose one of the protozoans you studied and imagine you are that organism. Write one day's entry in an imaginary journal of that protozoan.

INVESTIGATION 2

WHAT ARE FUNGI?

If somebody told you that you ate a fungus for lunch, you might make a face and say, "No way!" But if you ate a pizza with mushrooms on it, you did eat a fungus—a mushroom is a type of fungus. Find out more about fungi in this investigation.

Activity

Lifestyles of Fungi

You may have gobbled down the mushrooms on a pizza, but you had better stay away from molds on bread and fruit. These fungi can be extremely dangerous if eaten. In this activity you'll investigate bread molds.

MATERIALS
- goggles
- gloves
- marking pen
- 3 sealable plastic bags
- spray bottle filled with water
- 3 pieces of bread
- hand lens
- tweezers
- microscope slide
- microscope
- *Science Notebook*

SAFETY
Wear goggles and gloves. To prevent allergic reactions, keep bags that may contain mold sealed when not in use. Wash your hands in warm soapy water after handling the bags.

Procedure

1. Use a marking pen to label three sealable plastic bags *1, 2,* and *3*.

2. Use a spray bottle to moisten three pieces of bread. Expose the bread to the air for about half an hour. Put one piece of bread into each bag and seal the bags.

3. **Predict** what conditions are best for growing mold. **Test your prediction** by leaving the bags of bread in three different places for several days.

4. Use a hand lens to **observe** the slices of bread through the plastic bags. **Make a drawing** of your observations in your *Science Notebook*.

A40

Step 5

▲ Mold on bread

5. Use tweezers to remove a small piece of mold from the bread. Reseal the bag. Place a small piece of mold on a slide. **Observe** the mold under low power with the microscope. **Make a drawing** of what you observe. **Observe** the mold under high power. **Make another drawing**.

6. **Compare** your results with those of your classmates. Under what conditions did the mold grow the best?

Analyze and Conclude

1. **Describe** what happened to the bread in each sealed bag after a few days. From your observations of the bags, what do you **conclude** about the growing conditions needed by bread mold?

2. **Infer** how mold obtains its food. **Tell what evidence** in the bags and under the microscope supports your inference.

UNIT PROJECT LINK

With your group, choose a specific fungus or protist that you explored earlier and build a model for the Micromenagerie. Use a variety of materials to model the fungus or protist. Brainstorm with your group how your models can be displayed. Then decide how many times larger your model is than the actual fungus or protist.

Yeasts, Bread, and Fuels

The bread you see in the picture has something in common with what may be the car of the future. Each uses a product made from yeast.

Yeasts are single-celled fungi. In a process called **fermentation** (fŭr mən-tā′shən), yeasts feed on sugars and break them down to produce carbon dioxide and a kind of alcohol called **ethanol** (eth′ə nôl).

Ethanol is used in many different products, from drugs and industrial materials to food. The food industry uses ethanol to make products such as olives, pickles, dairy products, and flavorings. It is also used as an antifreeze component and as a raw material for certain manufacturing processes. In addition, the alcohol in wine and beer is produced when sugars found in fruits and grains are fermented.

Scientists are currently working with a number of plant products that can be fermented to produce ethanol. Corn, wheat, wood chips, and grass clippings can be treated with chemicals and placed in fermentation vats. The yeast ferments the sugars in the plant products to produce ethanol. The ethanol is then mixed with other chemicals to produce a fuel that can be used in motor vehicles.

But why make fuel from ethanol? Unlike other fuel sources, ethanol is made from products that are renewable or have been discarded as wastes. Wood chips created when hardwood is cut for lumber are used in ethanol production. Corn plants left in the field after harvesting are also used to make ethanol. In both cases, new plants can be grown to replace the old.

Ethanol, like other fuels, releases carbon dioxide during combustion. Some of this carbon dioxide is used by growing plants. These plants can be used to produce more ethanol fuel. ■

The gas that is produced as a by-product of yeast fermentation causes bread dough to rise. ▶

Fungi— Good and Bad

A quick trip through your refrigerator and kitchen cupboard would probably lead to the discovery of several members of the fungi kingdom. Canned mushrooms, mold growing on old bread, and packets of yeast used for baking are all types of **fungi** (fun′jī).

A mushroom may look like a plant, but mushrooms and other fungi are not plants. Fungi do not have chlorophyll and cannot make their own food by using sunlight. Although most are multicellular, some fungi, such as yeasts, are single-celled organisms.

Kinds of Fungi

Most fungi can reproduce asexually by releasing spores. **Spores** are reproductive cells that develop into new organisms. The spores of fungi are carried in special sacs called spore cases. However, most fungi can also reproduce sexually. The ways that fungi reproduce are used to classify fungi.

▲ Bread mold may be seen on old bread or vegetables. The mold digests the bread or vegetable by releasing a chemical that breaks down organic matter.

One common type of mold, *Rhizopus* (rī′zə pəs), grows on bread. It spreads out over the surface of the bread, forming structures called stolons (stō′länz). As the mold spreads, short extensions called rhizoids (rī′zoidz) grow from the stolons and penetrate the bread. The rhizoids anchor the mold to the bread, produce digestive fluids, and absorb nutrients.

The Roles of Fungi

Most fungi attach to and grow on organic matter. As they feed, fungi break down this matter and return some nutrients to the soil. Without this process, Earth would soon become buried under mountains of dead waste material! Organisms that live on dead or decaying matter, such as molds, mildews, yeasts, and mushrooms, are called **saprophytes** (sap′rə fīts).

Fungi can also be parasitic. Rusts, smuts, and powdery mildews, for example, are fungi that cause tremendous damage to crops. Cereal and vegetable crops are susceptible to infection by rusts and smuts, while apples, roses, and grapes are susceptible to infection by powdery mildew. In most cases, the only way to control the fungus is to destroy the infected plants.

Some fungi, like molds, produce important substances. For example, the antibiotic penicillin is made from a group of molds called *Penicillium* (pen i-sil′ē əm). Discovered in 1928 by Alexander Fleming, penicillin has been used to save millions of lives.

▲ *Penicillium*, which can grow on fruit, is the source of the antibiotic penicillin.

Other fungi, like yeasts, are used to make foods such as bread. What other uses for fungi can you think of? ■

Some fungi, like the corn smut shown in the photograph on the right, are parasites that get food from other living organisms. ▼

INVESTIGATION 2

1. How can fungi and plants be distinguished?
2. Why do fungi not require light in order to survive?

REFLECT & EVALUATE

WORD POWER

algae
diatom
ethanol
fermentation
fungi
multicellular
plankton
protist
protozoan
saprophyte
spore

On Your Own
Write a definition for each term in the list.

With a Partner
Mix up the letters of each term in the list. Provide a clue for each term and challenge your partner to unscramble the terms.

Create a concept map of the protist kingdom. Include some of these words: *protozoan, amoeba, algae, diatom, Euglena,* and *plankton*.

Analyze Information

Study the photo. Then explain if the protist is more like an animal or a plant. Give reasons for your choice.

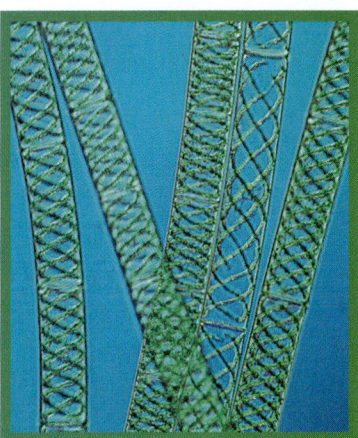

Assess Performance

Design an experiment to test whether you can prevent bread mold from growing on bread. Plan to work with several slices of bread and assorted materials for wrapping. Write a hypothesis about conditions that are best for preventing growth of bread mold. After your teacher has reviewed your plan, carry out your experiment. Describe the results and explain whether they support your hypothesis.

Problem Solving

1. An oil tanker has spilled oil in a region of the ocean. The oil slick floats on top of the water and spreads for miles. How might this spill affect the marine organisms that live deep in the ocean?

2. You've noticed the growth of some mold and mildew along some wood paneling in your basement. How are the fungi getting energy? What steps could you take to get rid of them?

3. Some members of a camping trip have developed stomachaches. These same people drank water from a nearby pond. How might microscopic pond life have contributed to this problem?

A45

CHAPTER 3

BACTERIA AND VIRUSES

"Have you gotten your flu shot?" That's something you hear at the beginning of the flu season. How does a flu shot protect you against this disease? In this chapter you'll answer this question as you explore bacteria and viruses.

Superstar Scientist

Dr. Flossie Wong-Staal is a research biologist on a mission to save countless lives. She leads a dedicated team of scientists who are working to make a drug that will prevent HIV, the virus that causes AIDS, from reproducing.

As a research biologist, Dr. Wong-Staal is held in high esteem by other scientists. They use her AIDS research findings in their own research work.

Dr. Wong-Staal encourages her 9-year-old daughter to like science. They go to the lab together on weekends and do simple science experiments. What questions would you ask Dr. Wong-Staal about her research work or her life as a scientist?

Coming Up

INVESTIGATION 1

WHAT ARE BACTERIA AND VIRUSES?
............A48

INVESTIGATION 2

HOW DO BACTERIA AND VIRUSES AFFECT OTHER LIVING THINGS?
............A56

Dr. Flossie Wong-Staal answering questions about HIV and AIDS. ▼

INVESTIGATION 1

WHAT ARE BACTERIA AND VIRUSES?

You may not realize it, but you are surrounded by, and even home to, millions of organisms that you cannot see. In fact, these one-celled organisms, called bacteria, are just about everywhere. You'll find out about bacteria and even tinier life forms, viruses, in this investigation.

Activity

Classifying Bacteria

MATERIALS
- Science Notebook

Bacteria may be everywhere, but they are too small to see with the unaided eye. In this activity you'll examine several different types of bacteria in photographs taken through a microscope.

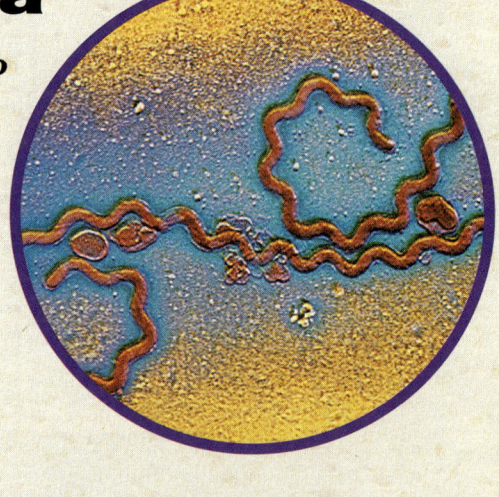

Procedure

1. The photographs on these two pages show some different kinds of bacteria. **Study** each photo and **write your observations** in your *Science Notebook*.

2. Based on your observations, **brainstorm** with your group how to **classify** the types of bacteria that you see. Give reasons for your method of classification.

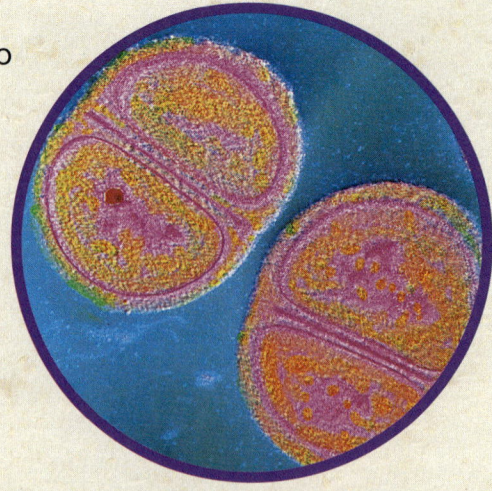

Analyze and Conclude

1. Compare your system of classification with that of another group. How do the two systems compare? **Discuss** any changes you may want to make in your classification system with the members of your group.

2. Biologists classify bacteria according to shape. Generally, bacteria have one of these shapes: rod-shaped (bacillus), spherical (coccus), and spiral (spirillum). How does your classification system compare with that of biologists?

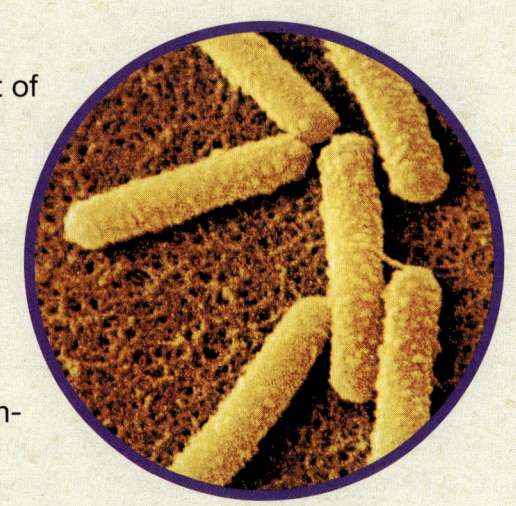

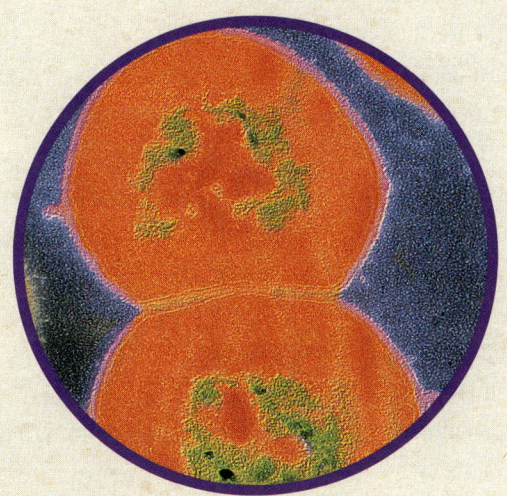

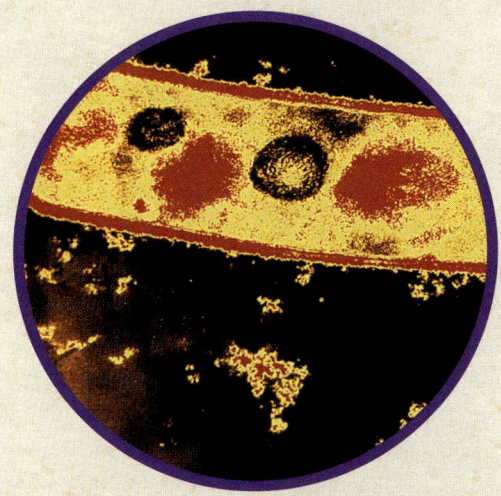

▲ How would you classify the bacteria on these pages?

UNIT PROJECT LINK

Rod-shaped and spherical bacteria can form clumps or chains. Research one of these types of bacteria in a biology text. Work with classmates to create a model of a bacterium. Use a variety of materials, such as modeling clay, construction paper, plastic, foam, toothpicks, beads, wire, and tape.

A49

Bacteria and Viruses

There are millions of kinds of organisms in God's creation. Most of those familiar to you are classified into the plant kingdom or the animal kingdom. You've also learned about organisms in two other kingdoms, the protists and the fungi. But Earth is home to another kingdom of creatures—the kingdom Monera.

The Moneran Kingdom

A **moneran** (mə nēr'ən) is a one-celled organism that does not have a nucleus. Monerans are among the smallest and simplest organisms in the world. They exist everywhere that life can be found, from the ocean depths to the tops of mountains.

A moneran cell is different from the cells you studied in Chapter 1. It not only lacks a nucleus and most of the cell parts typically found in plant or animal cells, it also is smaller than plant or animal cells. Although monerans cells have a cell wall, it's made of different materials from the cell wall found in plant cells.

Kinds of Monerans

There are more than 10,000 kinds of monerans. Scientists divide monerans into two large groups, the bacteria and

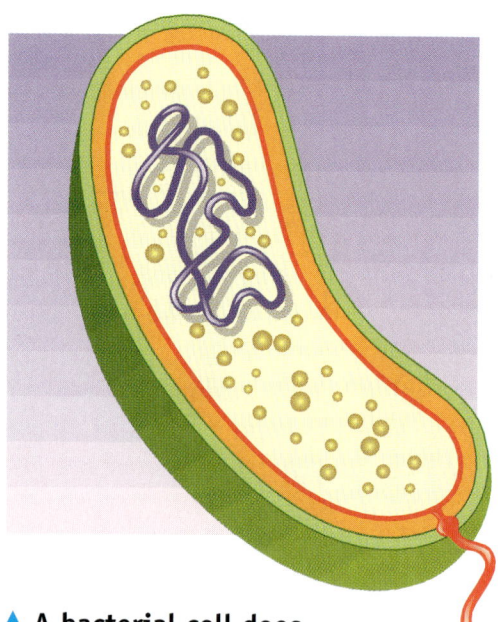

▲ A bacterial cell does not have a nucleus.

Bacteria are classified by shape: rod-shaped, spherical, and spiral. Identify each shape below. ▼

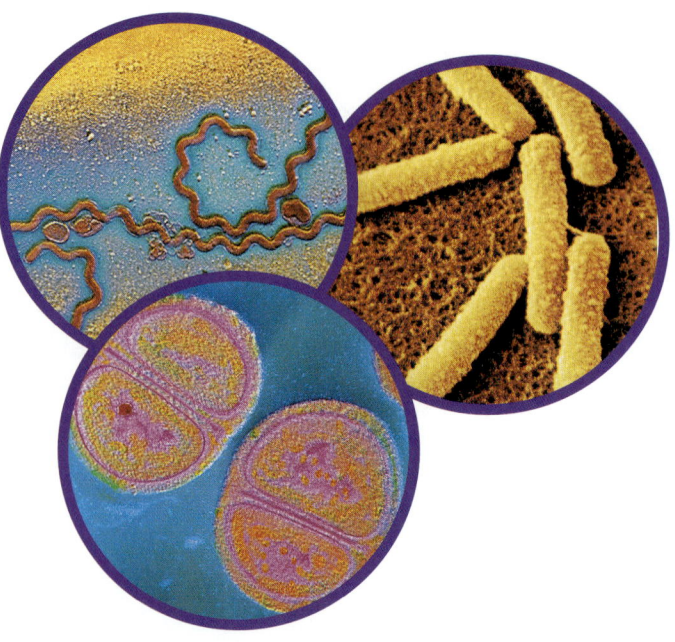

A microscope might reveal the pond scum (*left*) to be Oscillatoria (*right*), a blue-green bacteria.

the blue-green bacteria.

Bacteria are monerans that feed on dead organic matter or on living things. They occur in water, soil, and air, as well as on and in the bodies of other organisms. Most live as single cells, but they may join into pairs, chains, or clusters.

What features did you use to classify bacteria when you did the activity on pages A48 and A49? Scientists classify bacteria into three groups according to shape. These groups are bacillus (rod-shaped), coccus (spherical), and spirillum (spiral).

Blue-green bacteria are monerans that contain chlorophyll. Like plants, they carry out photosynthesis and make their own food. Blue-green bacteria can live in a variety of places—in salt water, in fresh water, and on land. Some live in the very hot water of natural springs. Others grow on snow in the Arctic and Antarctic.

Reproduction in Monerans

Monerans reproduce by splitting to form two identical cells. This process is called **fission**. First, the genetic material in the cytoplasm of the cell reproduces itself. Then the cell wall pinches inward and divides the cell, forming two new cells. Then each new bacterial cell has its own copy of the genetic material.

Under ideal conditions, bacteria can reproduce every 20 minutes. That means that in 24 hours, a single bacterium could produce a mass of cells equal to 2 million kg (4.4 million lb). Fortunately, this could never happen because the environment would not be able to provide enough nutrients for this large a mass of bacteria.

Viruses: Alive or Not Alive?

Smaller even than monerans are the viruses. If you were to use a very powerful microscope to examine viruses, you wouldn't see anything you would recognize as an organism. What you would find would be that some viruses are round, some are tube-shaped, and still others appear to be shaped like sticks and spools.

Not only do viruses have unusual shapes, they also have some unusual characteristics. Unlike bacteria, a virus doesn't have a cell wall, a cell membrane, or cytoplasm. In fact, a virus isn't a cell at all! A **virus** is a tiny fragment of genetic material—either DNA or RNA—wrapped inside a capsule of protein.

For years, scientists have debated whether viruses are alive or not. A virus can reproduce itself, but only within a cell of a host organism. Although a virus contains genes, it cannot obtain or use energy on its own. So viruses seem to fall between the living world and the nonliving world. They are not organisms, but they have some characteristics of organisms.

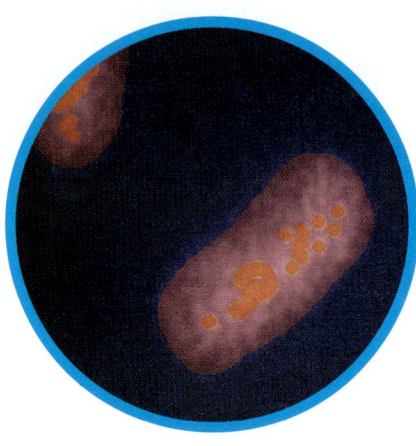

Pretty, isn't it? It's the virus that causes one kind of flu! ▶

SCIENCE AND FAITH

Sin is like a virus. It causes suffering and death. While scientists spend much time and money to find ways to stop viruses, the only cure for sin has already been found. What is it?

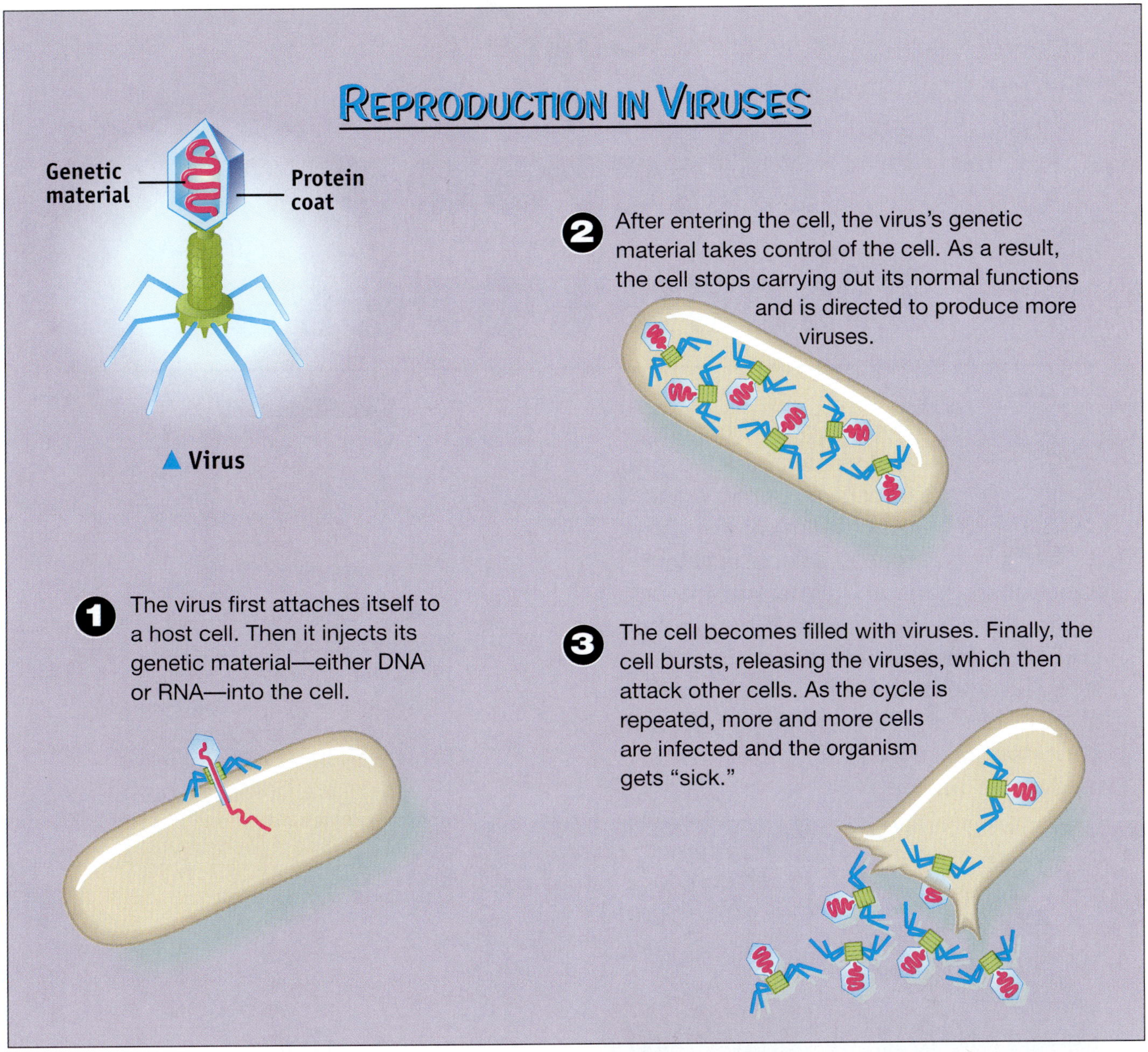

Reproduction in Viruses

Virus — Genetic material, Protein coat

1 The virus first attaches itself to a host cell. Then it injects its genetic material—either DNA or RNA—into the cell.

2 After entering the cell, the virus's genetic material takes control of the cell. As a result, the cell stops carrying out its normal functions and is directed to produce more viruses.

3 The cell becomes filled with viruses. Finally, the cell bursts, releasing the viruses, which then attack other cells. As the cycle is repeated, more and more cells are infected and the organism gets "sick."

Viruses are active only within the cells of living things. It is this ability to reproduce within cells that makes them dangerous. Many diseases, including the flu, polio, and AIDS, are caused by viruses. A virus takes control of the chemistry of the cell it infects, damaging and even destroying the cell. The diagram above explains this process. ■

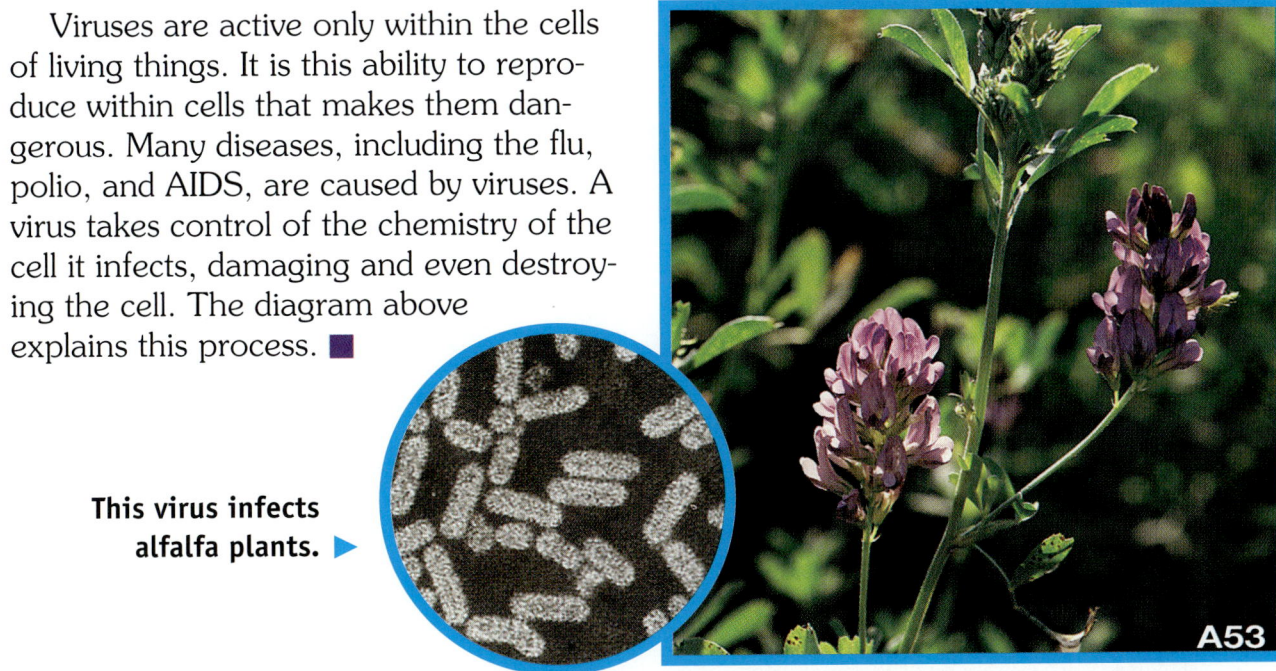

This virus infects alfalfa plants. ▶

Microbe Discoverers

Some kinds of bacteria and viruses have harmful effects on humans and other animals. For this reason scientists often focus on bacteria and viruses when looking for causes of diseases. When trying to find cures for diseases, scientists also study how these microbes react to different substances. Here are just a few of the important discoveries scientists have made over time.

Daniel Hale Williams, United States
Williams, using the discoveries of Pasteur and Lister, performs the first surgeries under sterile conditions. His methods result in fewer bacterial infections and a high survival rate.

1880s

Louis Pasteur, France
Pasteur suggests that bacteria can cause disease. He invents pasteurization, a process that uses heat to kill bacteria in milk.

1867

Edward Jenner, England
Jenner discovers that injecting people with the cowpox virus prevents them from getting the disease smallpox.

1796

1880
Fannie Hess, Germany
Hess shows that bacteria can be cultured, or grown, in a material called agar.

1857
Joseph Lister, England
Lister shows that infections in open wounds come from bacteria. He develops sterilization techniques.

A54

Sir Alexander Fleming, England
Fleming shows that penicillin, an antibiotic, can be used to treat bacterial diseases.
1928

Jonas Salk, United States
Salk develops a vaccine for polio, a disease caused by a virus that can cause paralysis.
1954

1983
Dr. Robert Gallo, United States and Dr. Luc Montagnier, France
Gallo and Montagnier identify the virus, HIV, that causes AIDS.

1945
Jane Wright, United States
Wright graduates from medical school with honors. Dr. Wright becomes a pioneer in cancer research. She supports the theory that some cancers are caused by a virus or viruses.

1881
Carlos Finlay, Cuba
Finlay correctly hypothesizes that the virus that causes yellow fever is transmitted by mosquitoes.
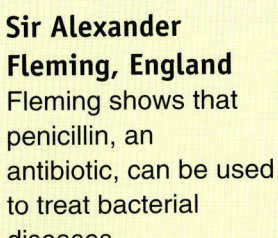
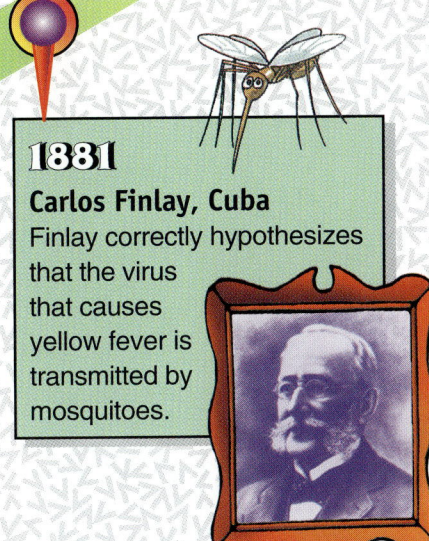

INVESTIGATION 1

1. A person looks at a cell through a microscope and thinks it's a plant cell. You look and see that it's a bacterial cell. Explain to the other person the features of the cell that allow you to draw your conclusion.

2. Describe how viruses affect living cells.

A55

How Do Bacteria and Viruses Affect Other Living Things?

You've probably had a cold. But have you ever had chickenpox or pneumonia? These and other illnesses are caused by viruses or bacteria. In this investigation you'll find out how bacteria and viruses affect people and other living things.

Activity

Warm Milk

Young people are advised to drink milk for good health. But the sugars and other nutrients in milk can also help bacteria to grow and reproduce. What evidence can you find that bacteria are numerous in a sample of milk?

MATERIALS
- goggles
- 2 plastic soda bottles (1 L)
- milk
- 2 corks
- Science Notebook

SAFETY
Wear goggles. Do not drink the milk.

Procedure

1. Half-fill two soda bottles with milk. Use a cork to tightly seal each bottle.

2. Predict what will happen to the milk in each bottle if one is kept in the refrigerator and the other is kept at room temperature for two days. **Record** your prediction in your *Science Notebook*.

3. Place one bottle in a refrigerator and keep the other bottle at room temperature.

Step 1

4. After two days, **observe** the milk in each bottle. Can you see any difference between the milk in the two bottles?

5. Follow your teacher's instructions for observing the smell of the milk in each bottle. **Compare** the smell of the milk in each bottle. **Record** your observations.

Step 5

Analyze and Conclude

1. Describe any differences that you observed between the two samples of milk.

2. **Hypothesize** the causes of any changes you observed in either sample of milk.

3. What do you think prevented the milk in the other bottle from undergoing changes?

INVESTIGATE FURTHER!

EXPERIMENT

Make yogurt. Slowly heat one quart of milk, but do not let it boil. Stir in a packet of freeze-dried bacteria culture. Pour the mixture into a wide-mouthed thermos that has just been warmed and cover it. Let the mixture sit in the thermos, without disturbing it, for 5 to 10 hours. Then chill the thickened yogurt in the refrigerator for at least 12 hours. How do you think the bacteria you added to the milk caused the changes you observed?

Bacterial and Viral Diseases

Bacterial and Viral Diseases

Some bacteria and viruses can cause infectious diseases. A **communicable** (kə myōō′ni kə bəl) **disease** is one in which the disease-causing organism can be passed from one host to another.

When disease-causing bacteria enter the body, they multiply there. The bacteria usually produce **toxins**, or chemical poisons that are harmful to the body. These toxins may kill cells or interfere with cell activities.

As you already know, viruses harm cells by reproducing within the cells and eventually bursting them. You've probably had a viral disease sometime during your life. A cold is caused by a virus. The flu, or influenza, is a serious viral disease, particularly in young children and in the elderly.

BACTERIAL DISEASES			
Disease	**Symptoms**	**Transmission**	**Vaccine**
anthrax	sores	infected animal	yes
cholera	diarrhea, dehydration	fecal matter	yes
diphtheria	swollen throat	inhalation, contact	yes
leprosy	skin lesions, nerve damage	cut or wound	no
bacterial meningitis	rash, fever	inhalation, contact	yes
pneumococcal pneumonia	fever, headache, paralysis	inhalation, contact	yes
syphilis	sores	sexual contact	no
tetanus	fever, jaw stiffness, muscle paralysis	contact with soil, cut or wound	yes
tuberculosis	inflamed lungs	inhalation, contact	no
whooping cough	rapid coughing	inhalation	yes

VIRAL DISEASES

Disease	Symptoms	Transmission	Vaccine
AIDS	weakened immune system	blood, sexual contact	no
bronchitis	deep cough, wheezing, fever	inhalation, contact	no
chickenpox	fever, bumps, itching	inhalation, contact	yes
cold	runny nose, cough	inhalation, contact	no
encephalitis	high fever, convulsions, coma	inhalation, contact	no
hepatitis B	fever, jaundice	contact, contaminated food	yes
herpes	sores	contact	no
influenza	fever, chills, cough	inhalation, contact	yes
laryngitis	hoarseness, temporary loss of voice	inhalation, contact	no
measles	rash, fever	inhalation, contact	yes
viral meningitis	fever, headache, nausea, stiff neck, drowsiness, unconsciousness	inhalation, contact	no
mononucleosis	enlarged lymph nodes, fever, sore throat, fatigue	inhalation, contact	no
mumps	swollen glands, fever, pain when chewing and swallowing	inhalation, contact	yes
rabies	fever, convulsions, death	bite of infected animal	yes
smallpox	chills, fever, rash	inhalation, contact	yes
yellow fever	fever, aches, jaundice	mosquito bite	yes

Fighting Disease

God created a line of defense to protect people against infection--the white blood cells of the **immune system.** Some white blood cells actually eat bacteria. Others produce proteins called **antibodies**, which can attach to bacterial cells or to viruses and destroy them. White blood cells also destroy body cells that are infected with viruses.

Medicines called **antibiotics**, which are substances that stop the growth and reproduction of bacteria, are also used to fight infection. Many antibiotics are produced from other microbes and from fungi. A **vaccine**, which is usually made with weakened or dead disease-causing microbes, can cause the body to produce antibodies. Thus a vaccine is usually given to prevent a person from contracting a disease.

AIDS
Searching for a Cure

What do you know about AIDS? There are newspaper and magazine articles written about it all the time. The letters in AIDS stand for **A**cquired **I**mmune **D**eficiency **S**yndrome. Everyone has an immune system to protect the body from disease. Most of the time the body's immune system works so well that invading bacteria and viruses are destroyed before they can make a person sick.

However, if a person has a weak immune system, he or she can get sick very easily. Infections and diseases that the immune system normally would fight can be very harmful and even deadly.

HIV is the virus that causes AIDS. If it infects a person, it attacks the immune system and weakens the body's defenses against infection. As a result, the person can get sick from many diseases.

HIV can sometimes live in someone's cells for years before it begins to destroy the immune system. It also tends to evolve, or change, very quickly. This makes it difficult to find a cure or a vaccine for AIDS.

Some researchers are trying to find drugs that will rob the AIDS virus of its ability to reproduce in human cells. Another approach being investigated is to insert HIV genetic material into another virus. The altered virus would then be injected into a host, and the host would develop an immunity to both the virus in which the HIV genetic material was placed and to the HIV itself.

These are just some of the ways scientists are working to find a cure for AIDS or a vaccine against the disease. Look back to the first page of this chapter. What is Dr. Flossie Wong-Staal working on to fight this disease? ■

As you read at the beginning of this chapter, one of the leaders in the fight against AIDS is Dr. Flossie Wong-Staal. ▶

Helpful Bacteria

We all know the harm some bacteria can do by causing diseases. However, most kinds of bacteria are harmless, and some kinds of bacteria are even helpful. For example, the production of foods such as cheese, pickles, butter, yogurt, and chocolate requires certain kinds of bacteria. Think about it. Without bacteria, pizza would not be possible! Then there are bacteria that are absolutely necessary for human life—without them we would die.

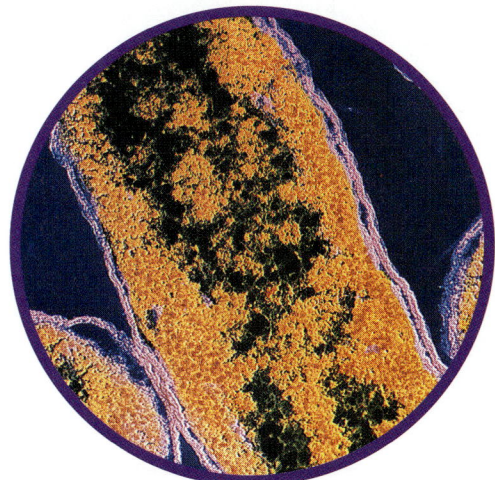

▲ The *E. coli* bacteria in your intestines help you to make certain vitamins. However, when present in the food you eat or the water you drink, *E. coli* can cause severe food poisoning and death.

How Bacteria Can Help

The dependency two organisms have on each other for survival is called **symbiosis** (sim bī ō'sis). For example, many grazing animals have a symbiotic relationship with certain kinds of bacteria. These animals depend on bacteria in their intestines for digestion of the plant materials that they eat.

Plants may also have symbiotic relationships with bacteria. Some plants depend on bacteria in their roots to make compounds with nitrogen. The plants need these compounds to grow.

Every autumn, millions of leaves fall from trees. Over a ton of leaves may fall in just a small portion of forest. Some bacteria help break down these dead leaves as well as other dead plant and animal materials. By doing so, bacteria also return nutrients to the soil so that new plants can use them.

INVESTIGATE FURTHER!

RESEARCH

With your group, research the use of bacteria in food production. Select one type of food that has been produced using bacteria and make a chart of the process.

◀ Trees are constantly absorbing nutrients from the soil. When a tree dies and finally falls to the ground, bacteria in the soil help to break down the wood, returning nutrients to the soil for use by other plants—another example of God's recycling plan.

Imagine what our world would be like if bacteria did not break down garbage or dead plants and animals. Land and water would quickly become polluted with waste and the remains of millions of dead plants and animals. This material could not be used and it would never be decomposed.

Because bacteria are so useful in breaking down materials, people have found many ways to use them. Bacteria are sometimes used in sewage treatment plants to break down sewage. Bacteria may even be used to break down the oil in oil spills. Bacteria can be helpful in many different ways. ■

INVESTIGATION 2

1. How does a person's body fight bacterial and viral attacks? What type of medicine can be used to treat bacterial infections if the body's immune system is not successful?

2. Give two examples of ways that God made bacteria helpful.

REFLECT & EVALUATE

WORD POWER

antibody
antibiotic
bacteria
blue-green bacteria
communicable disease
fission
immune system
moneran
symbiosis
toxin
vaccine
virus

 On Your Own
Review the terms in the list. Then use each term in a different sentence that shows its meaning.

 With a Partner
Write a clue for each term in the list. Then design a crossword puzzle, using the terms. Trade puzzles with your partner.

Make a labeled diagram to show the reproduction cycle of a virus.

Analyze Information

Look at the photographs of bacteria below. Identify each one as either spirilla, coccus, or bacillus.

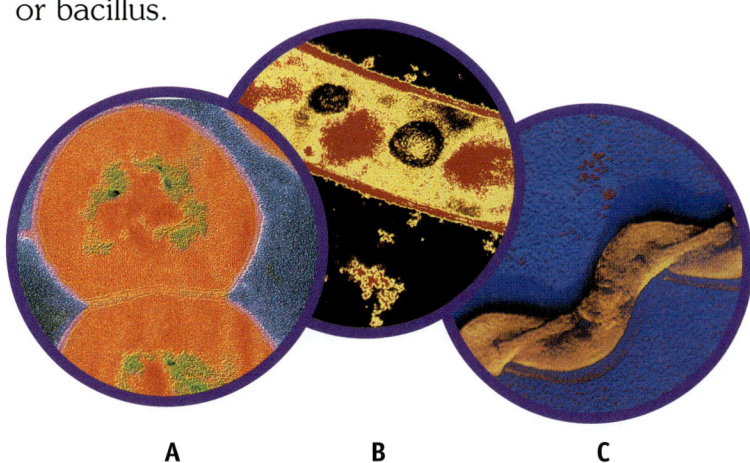

A   B   C

Assess Performance

Design and conduct an experiment to determine whether an opened can of soda will spoil if it is not refrigerated. Hypothesize about the reason some food items must be refrigerated, but others do not require refrigeration.

Problem Solving

1. Scientists have debated whether viruses should be considered a form of life. Compare viruses to other forms of matter. How do viruses resemble forms of life? How do they differ from most forms of life?

2. Compare the ways that viruses and bacteria cause diseases in humans. Also describe how the body responds to these invaders.

3. Describe several ways that scientists are using bacteria to help people by taking advantage of the ability of bacteria to break down substances.

UNIT A INVESTIGATE FURTHER!

Throughout this unit, you've investigated questions related to cells and microbes. How will you use what you've learned and share that information with others? Here are some ideas.

Hold a Big Event to Share Your Unit Project

It's opening day at the Great American Microscopic Zoo! And you are the official zoo keeper. Invite friends, relatives, classmates, even complete strangers to see the fantastic fungi, to observe the beautiful bacteria, to quake in fear at the sight of the villainous viruses. Challenge your classmates to see who can make the largest model, the most beautiful model, the most creative and imaginative model, and then hold a "beauty" contest judged by your teacher.

Experiment

Explore the role of fungi as agents of decay in the environment. Design an experiment in which you can test for the ability of fungi to dispose of materials in the environment. You might want to try using slices of different kinds of fruits as the basis for your experiment. After you have designed your experiment and gotten approval from your teacher, have your classmates predict which fruits will be broken down the fastest by fungi. Perform your experiment to test the predictions.

Research

Research into the cause and treatment of bacterial and viral diseases has involved dedicated detective work, great risks, and incredible triumphs. Research the work of one of the great researchers such as Jenner, Fleming, Pasteur, Salk, Sabin, or Wong-Staal. Then write a play about the individual. Cast the play, rehearse it, and present it to your class.

THE CHANGING EARTH

Theme: Models

Get Ready to Investigate! B2

1 Cracked Crust B4

Investigation 1   Do Continents Really Drift About? B6
Investigation 2   What Do the Locations of
                   Volcanoes and Earthquakes Tell Us? B16
Investigation 3   What Does the Sea Floor
                   Tell Us About Plate Tectonics? B22

2 Tectonic Plates and Mountains B34

Investigation 1   Why Do Tectonic Plates Move? B36
Investigation 2   How Does the Motion of Tectonic Plates
                   Build Mountains? B42

3 Shake, Rattle, and Roll B52

Investigation 1   What Causes Earthquakes, and
                   How Can They Be Compared? B54
Investigation 2   What Happens to Earth's Crust During
                   an Earthquake? B62
Investigation 3   How Are Earthquakes Located and Measured? .. B68

4 Volcanoes B82

Investigation 1   Where Do Volcanoes Occur, and
                   How Are They Classified? B84
Investigation 2   How Do Volcanic Eruptions Affect Earth? B94
Investigation 3   In What Other Places Can Volcanoes Occur? ... B100

Investigate Further! B112

GET READY TO

OBSERVE & QUESTION

How do volcanic eruptions affect Earth?

This beautiful sunset occurred after a volcanic eruption in the Philippines. How might a volcano erupting in the Philippines affect other places on Earth?

EXPERIMENT & HYPOTHESIZE

How are earthquakes located and measured?

Create your own mini-earthquake and then record the tremor. Later, find out how you can locate the epicenter of an earthquake.

INVESTIGATE!

RESEARCH & ANALYZE

As you investigate, find out more from these books.

- **Volcanoes and Earthquakes** by Basil Booth (Silver Burdett Press, 1991). Besides learning all about volcanoes and earthquakes, you'll find out what fumaroles and hot springs are!

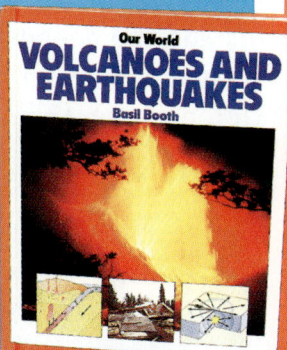

- **Earthquake at Dawn** by Kristiana Gregory (Harcourt Brace, 1992). Daisy Valentine watches in horror as San Francisco is rocked by an earthquake in 1906.

- **Surtsey: The Newest Place on Earth** by Kathryn Lasky (Hyperion Books for Children, 1992). The wonderful photographs in Lasky's book take you on an adventurer's tour of a newly formed island.

WORK TOGETHER & SHARE IDEAS

Is an earthquake likely to occur where you live?

Working together, you'll have a chance to apply what you've learned. With your class you'll explore the geologic events of your state and town. You'll find out whether you're likely to experience an earthquake or a volcanic eruption. Finally, you'll find out how to prepare for these events.

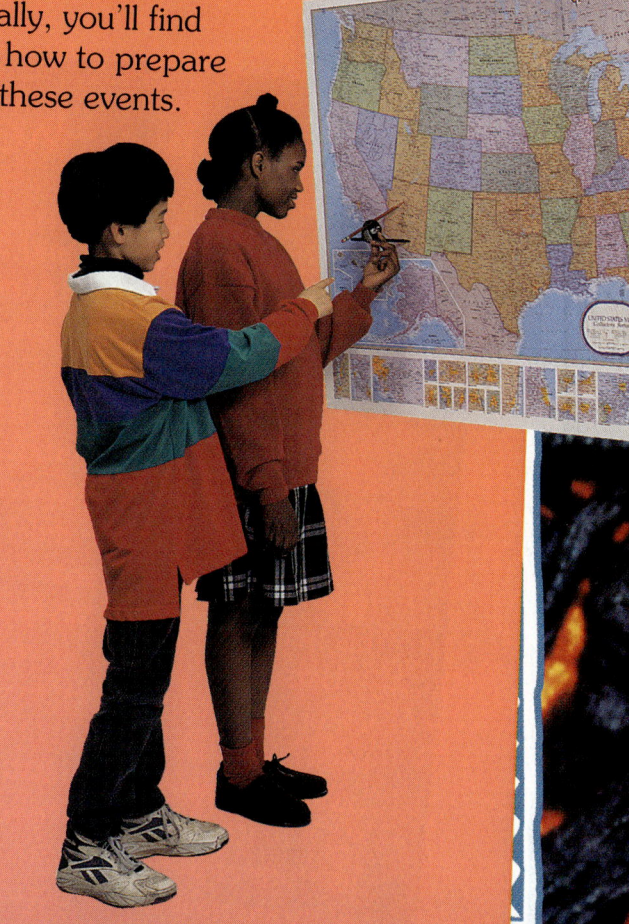

CHAPTER 1

CRACKED CRUST

Beneath the oceans are the highest mountains and the deepest trenches on Earth. Here molten rock erupts along underwater mountain ranges. The eruptions are part of the constant change taking place on the ocean floor.

Mapping the Ocean Floor

Few will ever see firsthand the impressive mountains and valleys below the surface of the oceans. The best view has been through sonar maps produced by ocean-floor surveys done from ships.

Now scientists in California and New York have used satellite information to produce an improved map of the ocean floor. Radar equipment on the satellite measured the distance from the satellite to Earth's surface, providing a map of the surface of the oceans. But how does this help map the ocean floor?

Because of gravity, ocean water piles up around underwater mountain ranges. Less water is found over the deep trenches. This means that the surface of the ocean has hills and valleys that imitate the contours of the ocean floor. So a map of the *surface* of the ocean provides a picture of its *floor* at the same time. Why is it important to have an accurate map of the ocean floor?

Coming Up

INVESTIGATION 1
Do Continents Really Drift About?
.... B6

INVESTIGATION 2
What Do the Locations of Volcanoes and Earthquakes Tell Us?
.... B16

INVESTIGATION 3
What Does the Sea Floor Tell Us About Plate Tectonics?
.... B22

◀ Improved maps show that the sea floor has features as varied as those on land.

B5

Investigation 1: Do Continents Really Drift About?

About 80 years ago, Alfred Wegener suggested that at one time all the continents were joined together in one large landmass that he called Pangaea. Further, he suggested that the continents split apart and drifted to their current locations. Other scientists laughed at him. Could he have been right?

Activity

The Great Puzzle

Take a look at a map of the world. You may notice that the continents fit together like the pieces of a jigsaw puzzle. Can you reconstruct the "supercontinent" of Pangaea from today's continents?

MATERIALS
- scissors
- outline map of the continents
- sheet of paper
- glue
- map of the world
- *Science Notebook*

Procedure

1. Using scissors, cut out each of the continents from the outline map. Cut along the dark outlines.

2. Arrange the continents on a sheet of paper so that they all fit together, forming one supercontinent.

3. After you have obtained your best fit, make a map by gluing the pieces onto the sheet of paper in the pattern that you obtained. Keep your map in your *Science Notebook*.

4. Use a map of the world to find the name of each continent on your map. **Label** the continents.

Step 1

▲ Outline map of the continents

Analyze and Conclude

1. How well did the continents fit together to make a single supercontinent?

2. Compare the map that you made with one showing the present locations of the continents. What can you **infer** about Earth's continents if both maps are accurate?

3. In your reconstruction, what continents border on the continent of North America?

4. What evidence, besides the shapes of the continents, might scientists look for to confirm the idea that continents were once joined in a supercontinent?

INVESTIGATE FURTHER!

RESEARCH

Look in a world atlas, such as *Goode's World Atlas*, to find a map that shows Earth's landforms. Use this information to explain why Wegener thought Earth's landmasses were once joined as a supercontinent.

Alfred Wegener
and the Drifting Continents

The year was 1911. Nabisco introduced its cream-filled chocolate cookie called Oreo. Marie Curie won a Nobel Prize for her isolation of pure radium. The National Urban League was founded. Sunday schools were growing rapidly.

That same year, Alfred Wegener read a scientific paper that changed his life. The paper presented evidence that many years ago a land bridge may have connected South America with Africa. To Wegener the evidence suggested that the two continents were at one time a continuous landmass. Further, he thought that *all* of Earth's continents might once have been joined. But he dropped the idea when he couldn't explain how such vast landmasses had moved.

In 1912, Wegener gave a scientific talk about his ideas on moving continents. He suggested that the landmasses were once joined and had since drifted apart. Nearly all who attended the talk, as well as others in the scientific community, thought Wegener's idea was ridiculous. Wegener still held on to his hypothesis.

In 1915 he published a book explaining how Earth's continents and oceans might have formed and changed over time. His evidence came from many fields of science. Wegener noted that the continental shelves fit together like the pieces of a puzzle. A continental shelf is an underwater part of a continent that extends under shallow water from the edge of the land down to a steeper slope. He noted that the fossil remains of certain species of plants and animals were found on widely separated continents. The plants and animals that left these fossils could not have crossed the oceans.

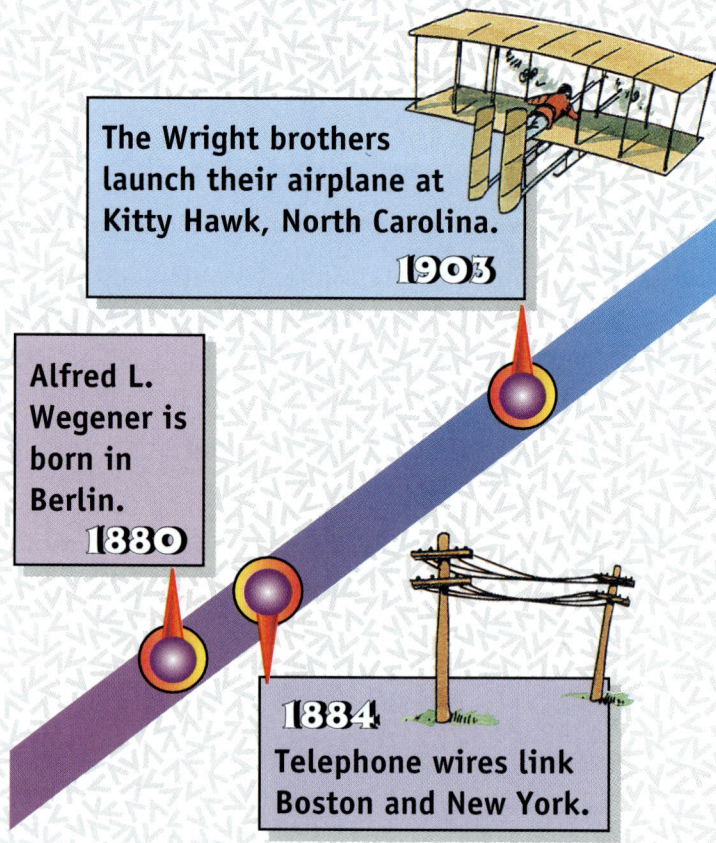

The Wright brothers launch their airplane at Kitty Hawk, North Carolina.
1903

Alfred L. Wegener is born in Berlin.
1880

1884
Telephone wires link Boston and New York.

B8

Alfred L. Wegener proposes his idea of continental drift. 1912

Motion pictures with sound ("talkies") are shown. 1926

Alfred Wegener dies in Greenland. 1930

1967 Scientists show renewed interest in theory of continental drift. Today the idea is accepted.

1914 World War I begins.

1906 San Francisco experiences its worst earthquake to date.

Finally, Wegener produced evidence that the climate of many parts of the world has changed dramatically over time.

Wegener used this evidence to reconstruct a supercontinent that he called **Pangaea** (pan-jē′ə), or "all land." Wegener hypothesized that this giant landmass existed long ago. He proposed that over time the landmass broke apart, and he concluded that continents are still moving. Wegener's hypothesis on the movement of continents is called continental drift. Despite all the evidence cited, it wasn't until the 1960s that scientists took Wegener's hypothesis seriously. ■

200 million years ago

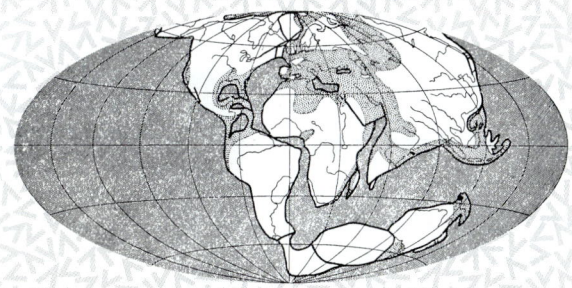
140 million years ago

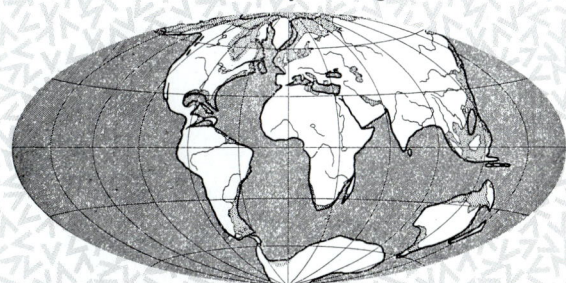
60 million years ago

▲ **Wegener's maps of drifting continents** What problem do the dates present to Bible-believers?

Evidence for Continental Drift

Alfred Wegener proposed the theory of continental drift. Wegener was a meteorologist--a scientist who studies weather. However, his interest in many fields of science led him to create this theory. His knowledge of weather and climate helped him support the theory with other scientific explanations.

Once Wegener had published his ideas about continental drift, he began to refine the theory. By the time he had published the third edition of his book, he had found additional evidence that made the theory more believable. Many of the rocks that made up mountains in Argentina were identical to those found in South Africa. In addition, he found that diamond-rich rocks in South Africa were very similar to diamond-rich rocks in Brazil. And a thick red sandstone layer crossed continental boundaries from North America to Greenland, Britain, and Norway.

Wegener used the evidence he had gathered to hypothesize about a supercontinent that he named Pangaea. He hypothesized that Pangaea was a single landmass that existed long ago. Over time, he proposed, the landmass broke apart and the continents drifted to their present positions on Earth's surface. Look at the map shown below. What pieces of evidence support the theory of continental drift?

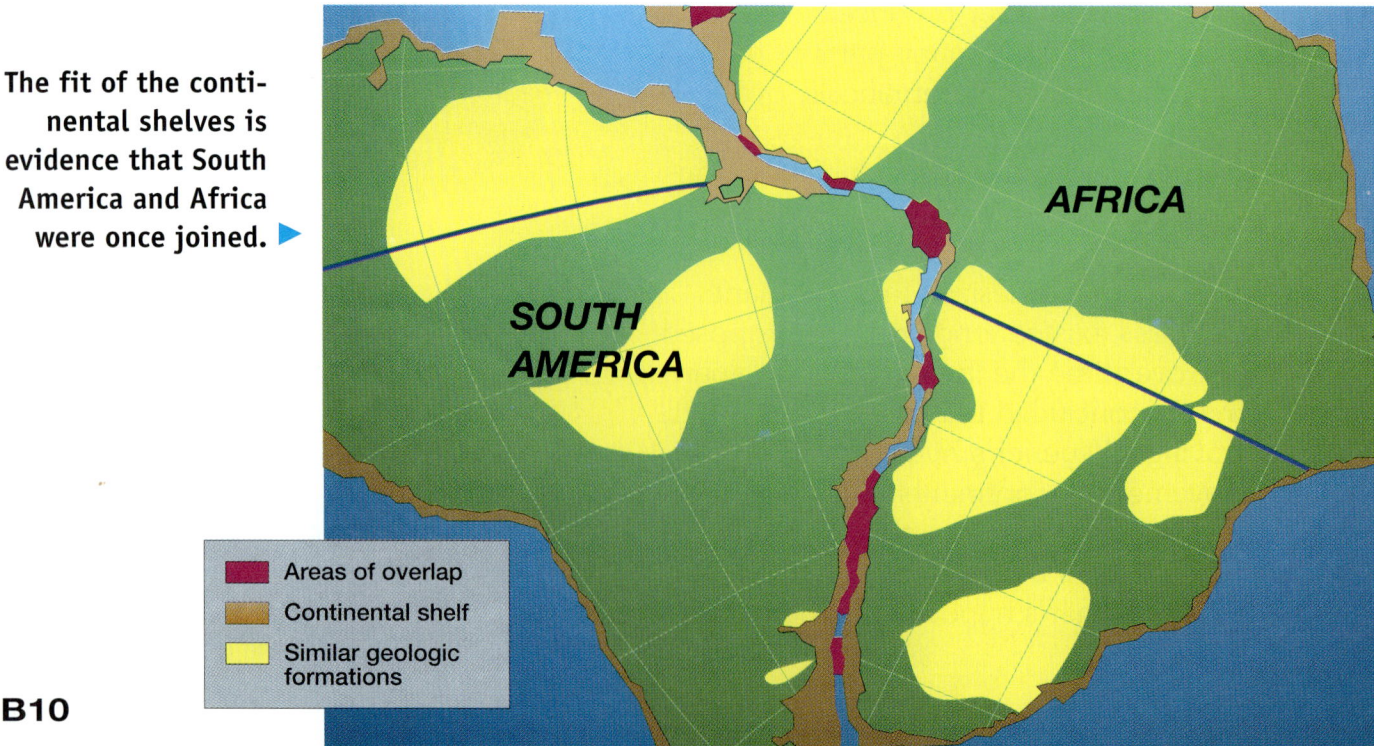

The fit of the continental shelves is evidence that South America and Africa were once joined. ▶

Wegener also noted that certain fossils were preserved in similar rocks on different continents. He argued that the remains of these once-living organisms were so similar that they must have been left by the same kinds of organisms. One of these creatures was a small reptile called *Mesosaurus*, which lived its life in fresh water. Other fossils found in rocks that were very far apart were those of *Glossopteris*. Remains of this plant had been discovered in South America, Australia, India, and Africa. How, Wegener asked, could this plant have survived the different climates of these four landmasses?

Because of his training as a meteorologist, much of Wegener's evidence included information about climate. You probably already know that Earth can be divided into three major climate zones. The tropics are located near the equator and extend to about $23\frac{1}{2}°$ north and south of the equator. The temperate zones lie between the tropics and the polar zones. The polar climatic zones extend from about $66\frac{1}{2}°$ north and south to the poles.

Wegener noted that fossils of beech, maple, oak, poplar, ash, chestnut, and elm trees had been found on a small island named Spitsbergen, near the North Pole. These trees generally grow only in temperate areas. Today, however, the island is covered for much of the year with snow and ice because it has a very cold climate—a polar climate.

Coal forms in swampy marshes that receive a lot of rain each year. Today coal beds are forming in areas near the equator and in some temperate regions. Wegener proposed that coal beds in the eastern United States, Europe, and Siberia formed when the continents were joined and were located closer to the equator.

Wegener used all of these different lines of evidence to reconstruct the supercontinent he called Pangaea. He hypothesized that this single landmass existed about 200 million years ago. Over time, he proposed, the landmass broke apart and the continents drifted to their present positions on Earth's surface.

◀ A variety of *Glossopteris*, a plant with fossil remains found in widely separated continents.

Another variety of *Glossopteris* ▼

◀ *Mesosaurus*. Fossil remains of this reptile were found on widely separated continents.

Continents on the Move

Most scientists contend that the continents began to drift apart many years ago. Some scientists, like Wegener, believed that it took many years for the continents to arrive at their present positions. Wegener suggested that it took 180 million years for this to happen. That time span, however, is not supported by the passage of time recorded in the Bible; therefore, other scientists suggest that continental drift was possible on a different time line.

The maps on the next four pages show how some scientists believe landmasses—later Earth's continents—moved over time.

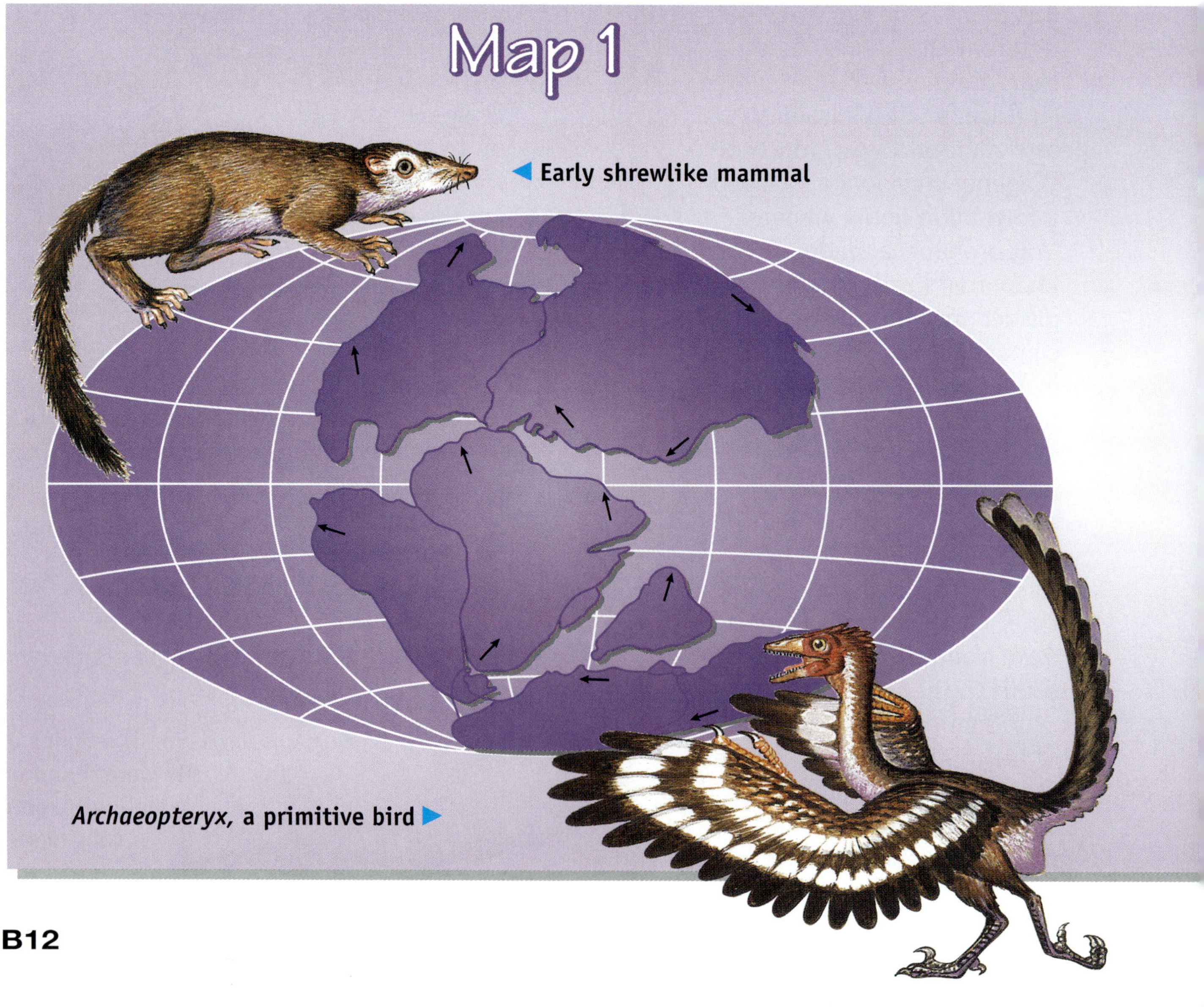

Map 1

◀ Early shrewlike mammal

Archaeopteryx, a primitive bird ▶

Map 2

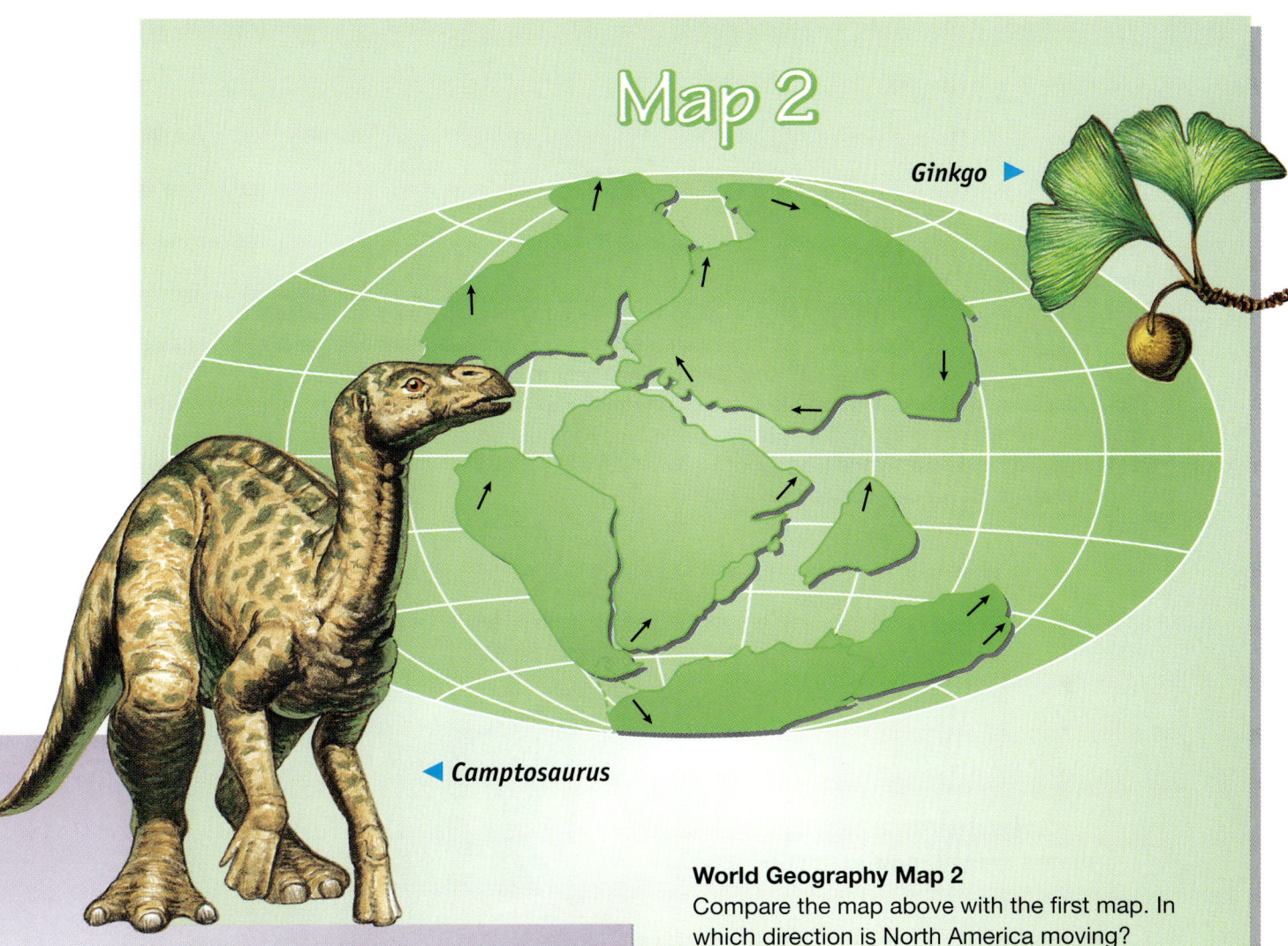

◀ *Camptosaurus*

Ginkgo ▶

World Geography Map 1

North America, Europe, and much of Asia began to split from South America and Africa. India separated from the landmass around the South Pole and started moving northward. Australia and Antarctica drifted to the south and west. The Atlantic and Indian Oceans began to form.

A single event, such as the Great Flood recorded in Genesis 6–8 could have caused enough damage to Earth to split apart the land. Following the Flood, other violent Earth events may also have reshaped the Earth's physical features.

As the landmass divided and drifted, some animals and plants became extinct. Others relocated successfully, perhaps following land bridges to locations of suitable habitat before those bridges disappeared.

World Geography Map 2

Compare the map above with the first map. In which direction is North America moving? How does the location of India compare with that on the first map? In which direction is Australia moving? What has happened to South America and Africa?

Map 3

World Geography Map 3
Scientists are uncertain of exactly what happened. Aside from Noah's experience with the Great Flood, no records exist from eyewitnesses of other possible explanations. Regardless of how and when continents began drifting, if that indeed was the case, God continued to care for His creation. Although many plants and animals did not survive from the beginning until now, God did preserve His finest creation–human beings. Someday, God will destroy the Earth, but He will take all His believers to a new creation to live with Him forever.

Ankylosaurus, a heavily plated animal, now extinct ▶

◀ Cockroach, an insect that inhabited Earth many years ago and today

B14

Map 4

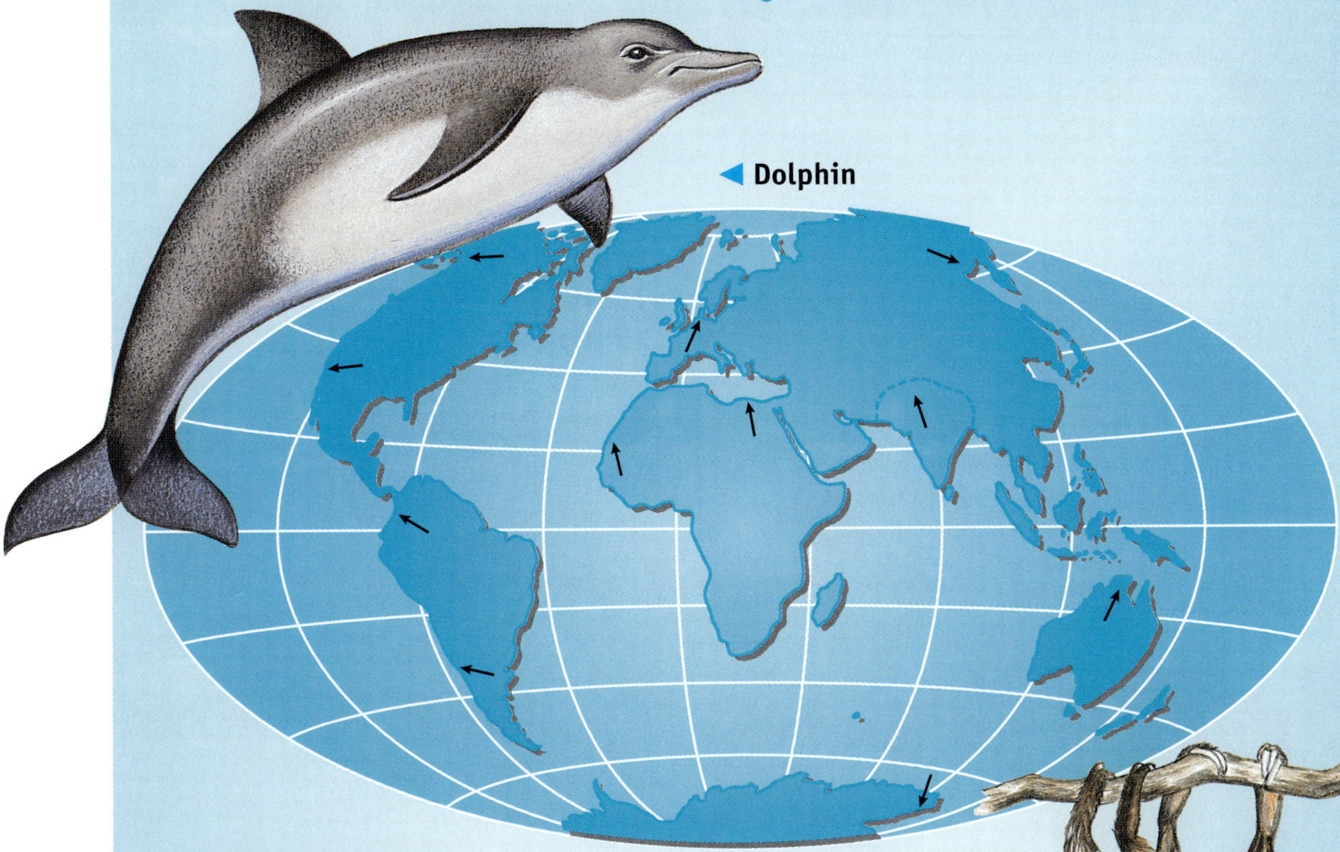

◀ Dolphin

Sloth ▶

World Geography Today Map 4

This is a map of Earth's present-day continents and their locations. What has happened to North and South America? Locate Antarctica and Australia.

Even though many plants and animals disappeared with shifts on Earth's surface, many more still remain. Insects are the most numerous land animals. Birds, mammals, and seed plants are also very numerous life forms. Survivors include fish and some species of mammals that swim in the seas. Starfish, mollusks, corals, algae, and plankton also thrive in today's ocean.

INVESTIGATION 1

1. Evidence of glaciers has been found in many parts of southern Africa! What does this information tell you about the possible location of this continent at some time in the past?

2. Describe the kinds of evidence that Alfred Wegener and other scientists have used to show that the continents move over time.

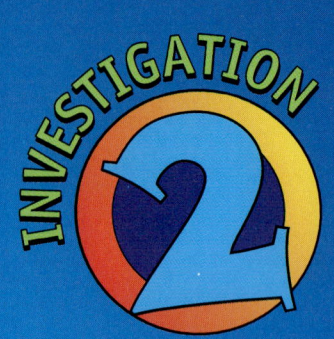

WHAT DO THE LOCATIONS OF VOLCANOES AND EARTHQUAKES TELL US?

INVESTIGATION 2

Earthquakes and volcanoes make our world a bit shaky! Think of all the stories you have heard about earthquakes and volcanic eruptions. Can the locations of these events give us clues about continental drift?

Activity

Earth—Always Rockin' and Rollin'!

Did you ever wonder why earthquakes occur where they do? See if you can find any pattern in the locations of earthquakes.

MATERIALS
- earthquake map of Earth
- tracing paper
- *Science Notebook*

Procedure

1. Study the earthquake map. Every dot on the map represents a place where a strong earthquake has occurred. Look for a pattern that the dots form. **Describe** this pattern in your *Science Notebook*. **Discuss** your observations with your team members.

2. On tracing paper, use your pencil to trace and then darken the pattern formed by the earthquake dots. Work with your team members to decide how to draw the pattern.

3. Think about the way a cracked eggshell looks. Earth's **crust**, which is its outermost, solid layer, is a lot like a cracked eggshell, broken up into large pieces. Look again at the pattern of the earthquake dots. How is the pattern of the dots like the cracks of an eggshell? **Record** your answer.

How is Earth like a cracked eggshell? ▼

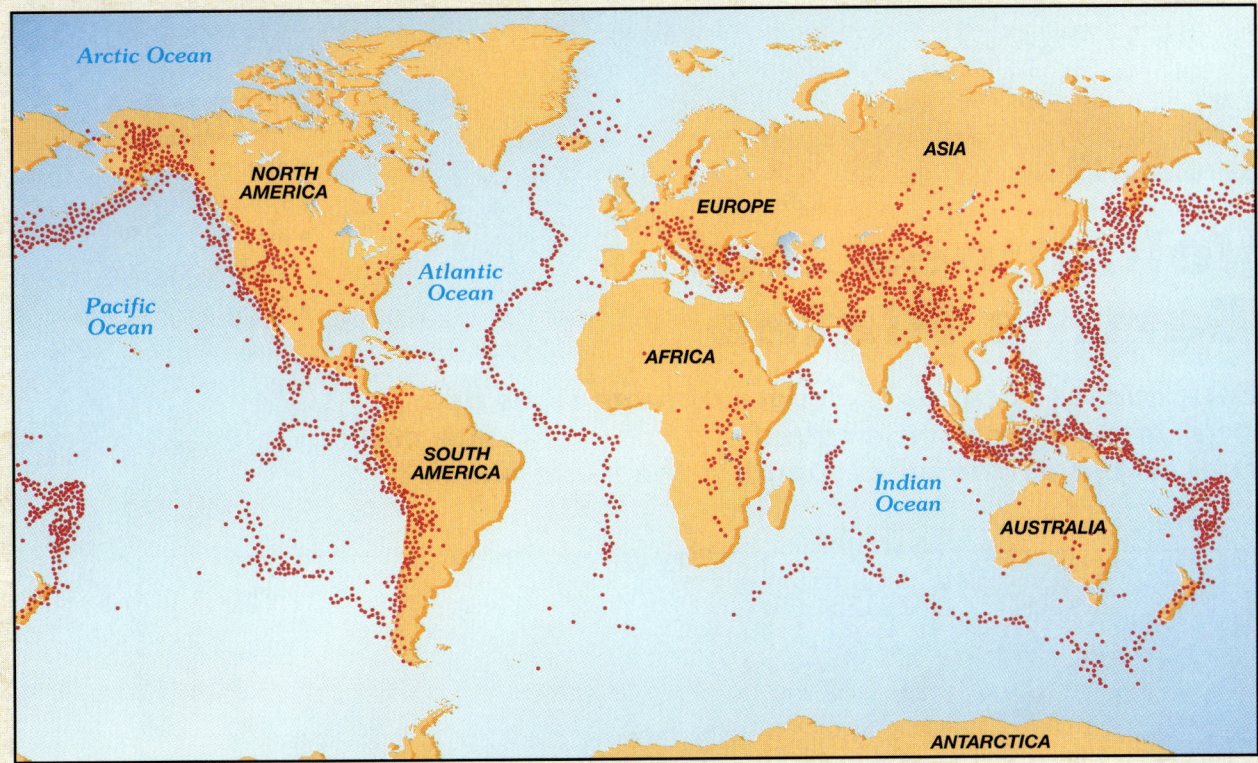

▲ Earthquakes around the world

Analyze and Conclude

1. Earth's crust is broken into large pieces called **tectonic plates**. Use your tracing and the map to locate some of these tectonic plates.

2. Earthquakes occur mostly along cracks in Earth's crust. **Predict** some locations where earthquakes are likely to occur. **Record** your predictions.

UNIT PROJECT LINK

Create a tectonic-plates map that shows your town. Also, show the tectonic plate(s) surrounding the plate that includes your town. How close is your town to the edge of a tectonic plate? Place a map pin where your town is located. Predict how likely your town is to have an earthquake.

As you go through this unit, collect data from news articles about earthquakes and volcanic activity around the world. Place map pins on a classroom map showing where this activity is taking place. Look for relationships between earthquakes, volcanoes, and tectonic plates.

Activity
Volcanoes and Earth's Plates

> **MATERIALS**
> - map of Earth's volcanoes
> - map of Earth's earthquakes (page B17)
> - Science Notebook

Earthquakes occur at the edges of huge slabs of crust and upper mantle called **tectonic plates**. Are volcanoes and earthquakes found in the same places?

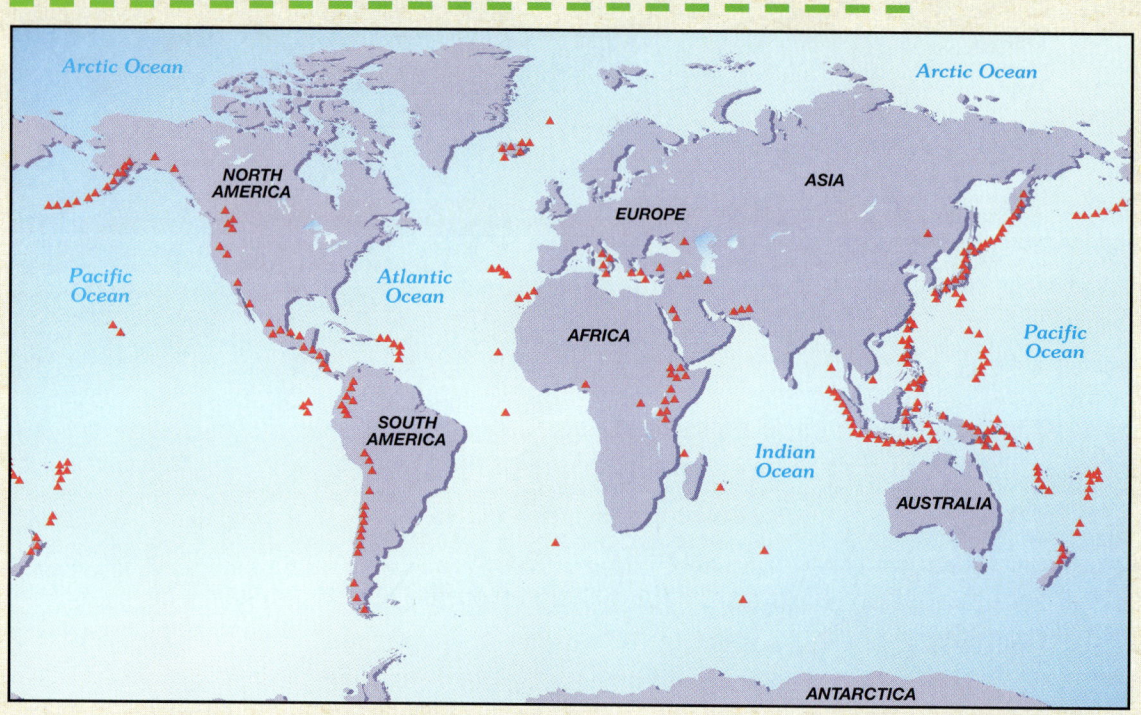

▲ Volcanic activity around the world

Procedure

Study the map of Earth's volcanoes and **compare** it with your map of Earth's earthquakes. In your *Science Notebook*, list the places where volcanoes occur.

Form a hypothesis about the locations of volcanoes, earthquakes, and the edges of Earth's tectonic plates. **Record** your hypothesis. **Discuss** your observations with your group.

Analyze and Conclude

1. Using the maps on B17 and B18, **describe** where both earthquakes and volcanoes occur.

2. How do the locations of earthquakes and volcanoes help identify Earth's tectonic plates?

The Cracked Crust: Tectonic Plates

Floating Plates

Sometimes you'll hear the expression "It's as solid as a rock." This expression means that whatever is referred to is solid, permanent, and dependable. We may like to think that rock is solid and permanent, but even large slabs of rock move. Actually, nothing on the surface of Earth is permanent and unmoving. Even the continent of North America is moving. The movement is very slow, but it is movement, just the same. The slow movement of North America and the continents can be explained by the theory of plate tectonics.

In the late 1960s, scientists expanded Alfred Wegener's idea of drifting continents and proposed the **theory of plate tectonics**. The word *tectonics* refers to the forces causing the movement of Earth's rock formations and plates.

The theory of plate tectonics states that Earth's crust and upper mantle are broken into enormous slabs called **plates**, also called **tectonic plates**. (The **crust** is Earth's outermost, solid layer. The **mantle** is the layer of Earth between the crust and the core.) The continents are like enormous ships attached to these floating plates. Scientists believe that currents, or slow plastic movements in the mantle, cause the plates to move across Earth's surface. The currents are caused by differences in temperature in Earth's interior regions.

This theory is one of the most important theories about Earth's geologic history. It has guided scientists in the way they think Earth might have looked millions of years ago. Plate tectonics has helped them reconstruct the ways the continents might have moved.

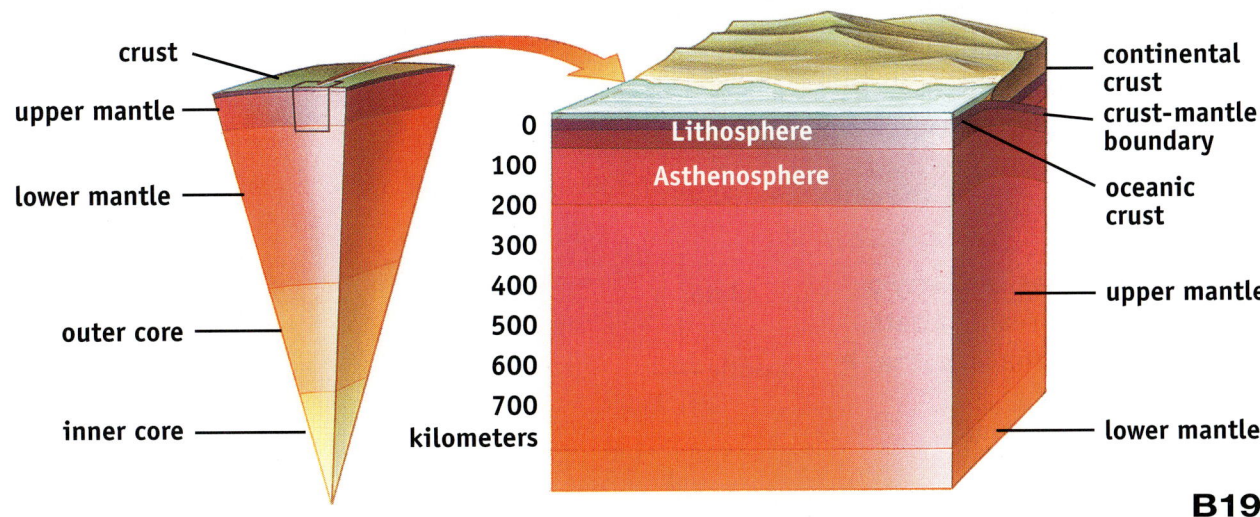

A wedge showing Earth's layers (*left*); a section of the crust and upper mantle (*right*)

EARTH'S TECTONIC PLATES There are seven major plates and several minor ones. Many of the plates are named after the major landmasses that are parts of the plates. The plates act like rafts that carry Earth's crust and upper mantle around on a layer of semisolid material. Study the map shown to the right. You will see that most of the United States is located on the North American Plate. In what direction is this plate moving? In what direction is the Pacific Plate moving?

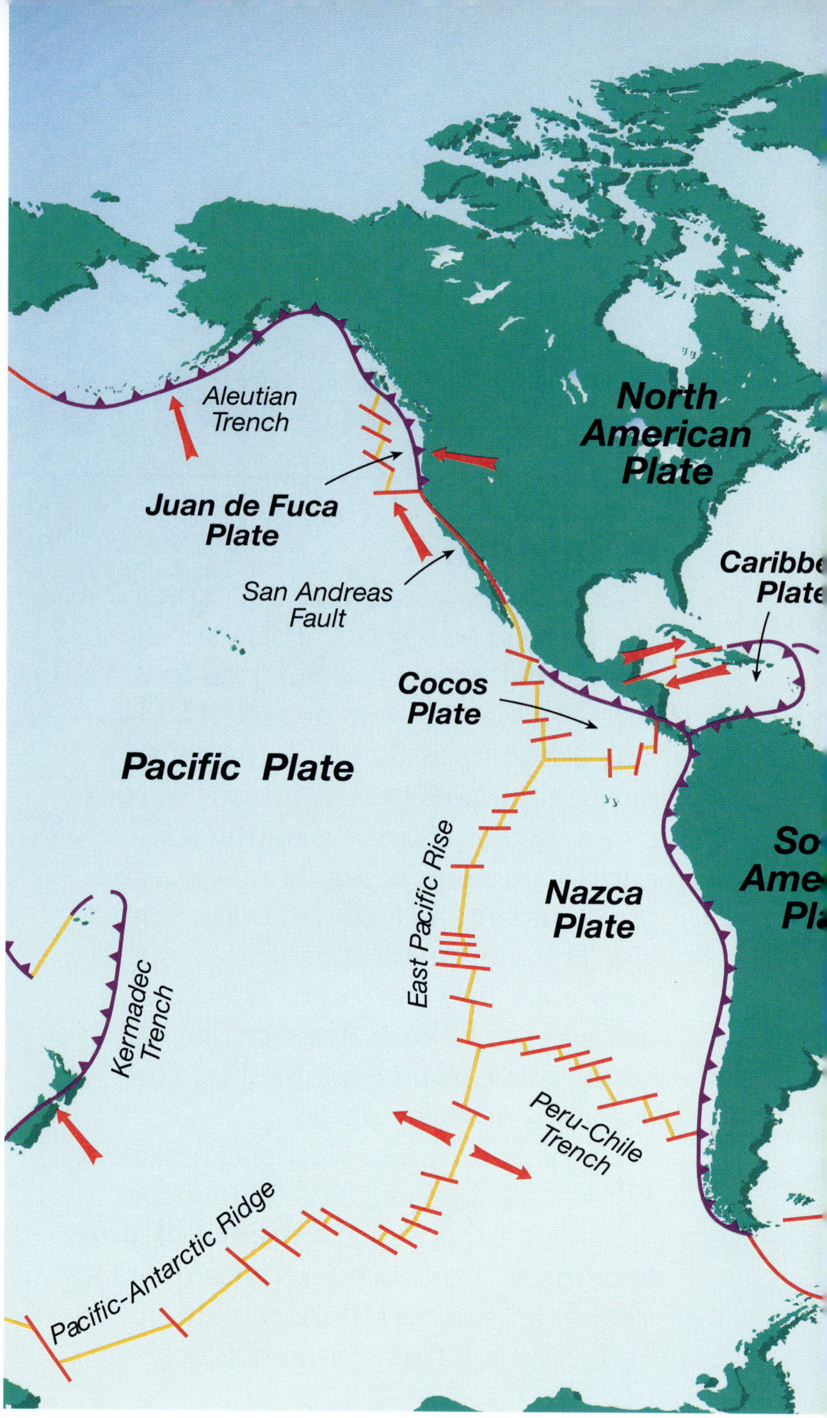

Makeup of the Plates

What do the tectonic plates consist of? Each plate is formed of a thin layer of crust, which overlies a region called the upper mantle. In a plate that carries a continent, the crust can be 40 to 48 km (25 to 30 mi) thick. In a plate that is under an ocean, the crust can be only 5 to 8 km (3 to 5 mi) thick. The drawing at the bottom of this page shows the makeup of a tectonic plate.

Interacting Plates

Plates can interact in three ways: (1) They can come together, (2) they can move apart, and (3) they can slide past one another. Places where plates interact are called **plate boundaries**. As you probably know by now, earthquakes and volcanoes occur along plate boundaries. In Chapter 2 you will find out much more about what happens along these boundaries. ■

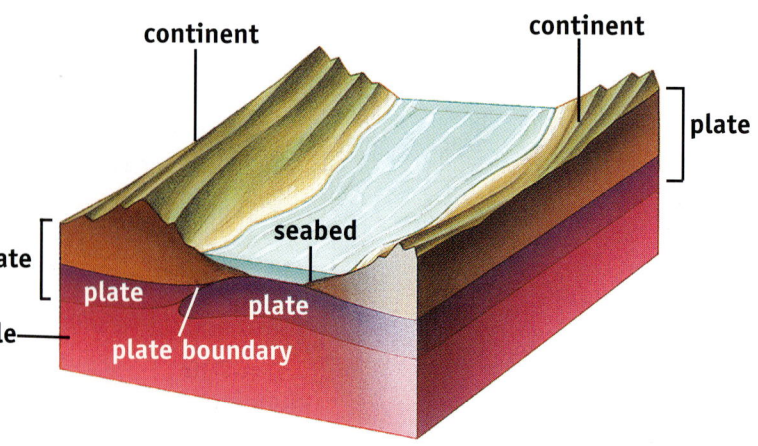

Tectonic plates can carry a continent, an ocean, or both a continent and an ocean. ▶

B20

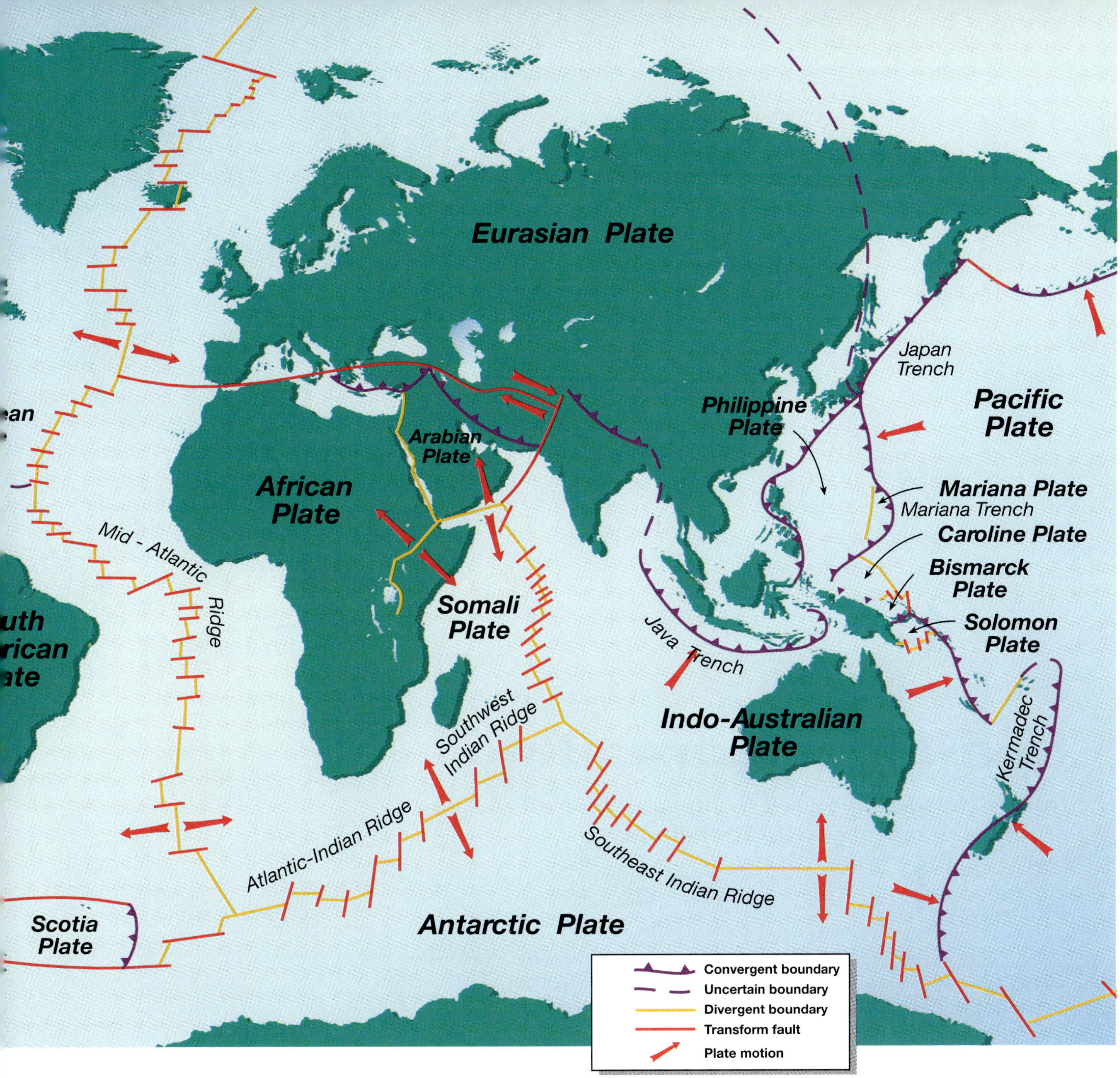

INVESTIGATION 2

1. Predict what might happen in the future to Los Angeles (on the Pacific Plate) and San Francisco (on the North American Plate) if the two plates carrying these cities continue to move in the direction in which they are now moving.

2. What is the connection between earthquakes, volcanoes, and tectonic plates? Give evidence to support your answer.

INVESTIGATION 3

WHAT DOES THE SEA FLOOR TELL US ABOUT PLATE TECTONICS?

How do scientists know what the sea floor looks like? Is there evidence for plate tectonics hidden beneath the waters? Find out in this investigation.

Activity

Sea-Floor Spreading

New rock is being added to the sea floor all the time. Model this process in this activity.

MATERIALS
- sheet of paper with 3 slits, each 10 cm long
- 2 strips of notebook paper, each 9.5 × 27 cm long
- metric ruler
- scissors
- pencil
- *Science Notebook*

Procedure

Prepare a sheet of white paper as shown in the top drawing. Draw mountains. The middle slit represents a very long crack in the ocean floor, called a **mid-ocean ridge**.

Pull strips of notebook paper up through the middle slit and down through the side slits, as shown. These strips represent magma that is flowing up through the ocean ridge and then hardening. The strips are a model of the way the ocean floor spreads. This process is often called **sea-floor spreading**.

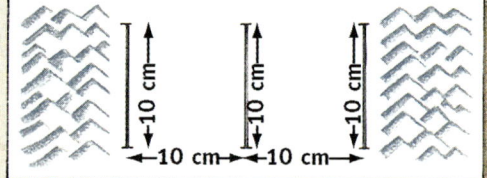

Analyze and Conclude

Consider that the magma coming up through the ridge is hardening into rock. What can you **infer** about the age of the rock along each side of the ridge? **Record** your ideas in your *Science Notebook*. Where do you think the oldest rock on the sea floor is?

Activity
Building a Model of the Ocean Floor

The sea floor is much like the dry land. Tall mountains and deep valleys exist there. You can build your own model of these structures.

MATERIALS
- modeling clay
- shoebox with lid
- metric ruler
- grid
- pencil
- tape
- *Science Notebook*

Procedure

1. Place modeling clay along the bottom of a shoebox until the clay is about 2.5 cm (1 in.) deep in all places.

2. Add enough clay to mold an underwater valley, mountain, and an uneven surface.

3. Tape the grid to the lid of the shoebox.

4. Use your pencil to punch holes in the grid and lid wherever there are small circles on the grid. Put the lid on the shoebox.

Analyze and Conclude

1. Which ocean floor features does your model illustrate? **Record** your answer in your *Science Notebook*.

2. How could someone determine the shape of the "ocean floor" without looking inside the shoebox?

INVESTIGATE FURTHER!

RESEARCH

Find out the height and extent of underwater mountains. Where are the highest underwater mountains? Are these mountains related in any way to Earth's plates?

Steps 2 and 4

Activity

Mapping the Ocean Floor

MATERIALS
- coffee stirrer
- fine-tip marker
- plastic straws
- scissors
- shoebox model of ocean floor, including grid taped to shoebox lid
- metric ruler
- *Science Notebook*

The water is too deep to swim through, and there's no light. So how do scientists figure out the shape of the ocean floor? Use the ocean floor structures that you built in the last activity to model one way scientists do it!

Procedure

1. Cut a coffee stirrer so that it is the same length as the height of the shoebox. Beginning at one end of the stirrer, mark each centimeter along its length.

2. The stirrer is a model for a sound beam from a ship's sonar system. After a ship's sonar transmits a "ping," it "hears" (receives and records) an echo from the ocean bottom a short time later. The length of time needed for the echo to return to the ship is related to the depth of the ocean at that point. Each hole in the grid on top of the shoebox represents the location on the surface of the ocean from which a ship's sonar has sent out a sound beam or "ping."

3. Locate hole *A1* on the grid taped to the shoebox lid. Place your stirrer into this hole, inserting the 1-cm end first. In your *Science Notebook,* set up a chart for recording the depth to the surface of the clay below each hole. **Record** the depth for the hole at *A1*. **Measure** and **record** the depth to the surface of the clay under each hole on the grid.

4. Cut a piece of straw to match the depth that you measured under each point on the grid. For example, if you measured a depth of 4 cm, cut a straw piece that is 4 cm long.

Hole	Depth (cm)
A1	
A2	
A3	
A4	

Hole	Depth (cm)
B1	
B2	
B3	
B4	

Hole	Depth (cm)
C1	
C2	
C3	
C4	

5. Now stick a piece of straw in the hole to match the depth you measured under that hole. For example, if you measured 4 cm at *A1*, stick a 4-cm straw into hole *A1*. Next, *push the piece of straw through the shoebox lid* so that the straw hangs down below the lid. Tape the top end of the straw in place so that it is even with the shoebox lid. Insert a length of straw in each hole on the grid until every hole has a straw hanging from it. These straws represent sonar beams that are sent down to the ocean bottom. What do you think the lid represents?

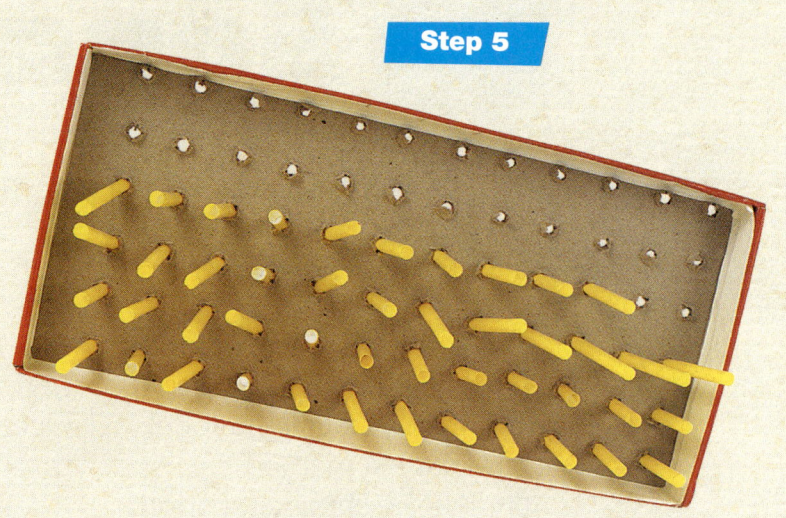

Step 5

Analyze and Conclude

1. Remove the lid, cut away one side of the shoebox, and replace the lid. Look at all the straws. How well does the pattern of the straws match the highs and lows of your ocean floor?

2. Would your straw model be more accurate if you had taken more depth readings? Why?

Analyze and Conclude, #1 ▼

INVESTIGATE FURTHER!

RESEARCH

Find out where the deepest ocean trench is located and how deep that trench is. How did oceanographers determine the depth of that trench?

B25

Sonar: Mapping the Sea Floor

Did you try the activity on pages B24 and B25? If you did, then you built a model of sonar—a method for finding the shape and depth of the ocean floor. *Sonar* stands for *so*und *na*vigation *a*nd *r*anging.

British naval scientists first developed sonar in 1921. During World War II (1939–1945), sonar was used to detect enemy submarines. Scientists realized that sound could be used to measure the distance from a ship on the surface of the water to the bottom of the ocean. A sonar device sends out a sound and then listens for an echo to return. By using sonar, scientists can measure the time between sending out a sound and receiving the echo of that sound. Then, by knowing this time and the speed at which sound travels through sea water, they can compute the depth of the ocean at that point. In the activity "Mapping the Ocean Floor," the straws you pushed through each hole in the grid represented a sound impulse that might have been sent out by a ship carrying a sonar device.

As a ship with sonar moves along the surface of the ocean, it sends out frequent sound impulses. The sound impulses travel down through the sea water, strike the ocean floor, and then send back an echo. Each echo arrives at a receiver

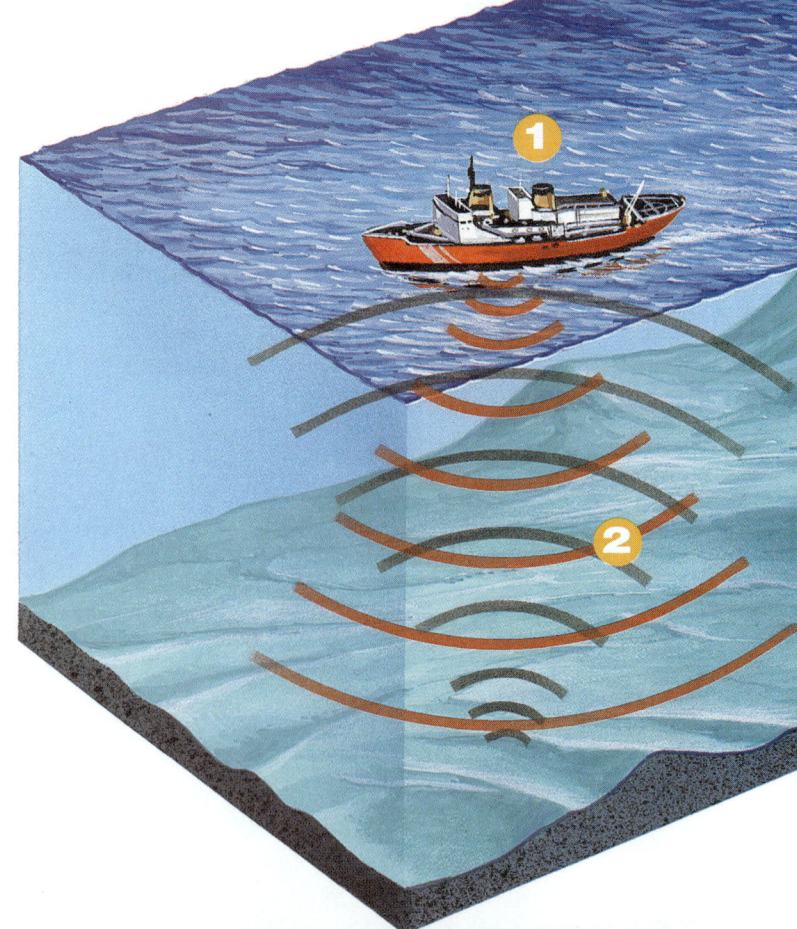

① Ship sending out signals from sonar device

② Sound sent out by sonar device and returning echo

③ Sea floor

How sonar is used to map the sea floor ▶

back at the ship and is recorded on a recording chart. The sonar device records the length of time required for the echo to return from the ocean floor. It then computes the depth of the ocean floor at that point. Finally, the depth is registered on a scale.

If the total time for a sound to travel from the ship to the ocean floor and back is 6.60 s, and sound travels through sea water at 1,530 m/s, the sound has traveled a total of 10,098 m. The distance from the ship to the ocean floor is half the total, or 5,049 m. By assembling all the measurements taken as the ship moves through the water, scientists can produce a map of a section of the ocean floor. The more readings they take, the more accurate their map will be. Sonar has allowed scientists to discover many new features of the ocean floor. For example, they have found some places that are over 10,600 m (6.3 mi) deep. That's over 10 km! They also have found undersea mountains higher than Mount Everest, which is 8,848 m (29,028 ft) high!

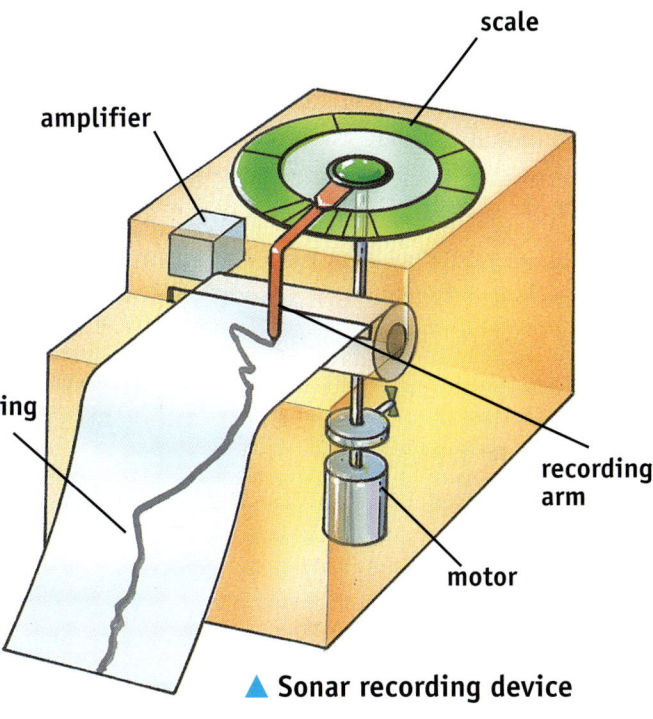

▲ Sonar recording device

Probing the Land with Sonar

Sonar can also be used on land. Sound pulses can be sent through the ground, and the returning echoes can be used to identify different layers of soil and rock as well as to locate deposits of natural gas and oil. ■

RESOURCE

Magnetism
Tells a Story

You have probably used magnets many times. Perhaps you used one to pick up a string of paper clips or to hold notes on the refrigerator door. How is Earth like a magnet?

A magnet is an object that attracts certain metals, including iron, steel, and nickel. A magnet has two ends, or poles. When hung from a string, the pole that turns toward north is called the *north pole* of the magnet. The pole that points south is the *south pole* of the magnet. A **magnetic field** is the area around a magnet where the effects of magnetism are felt.

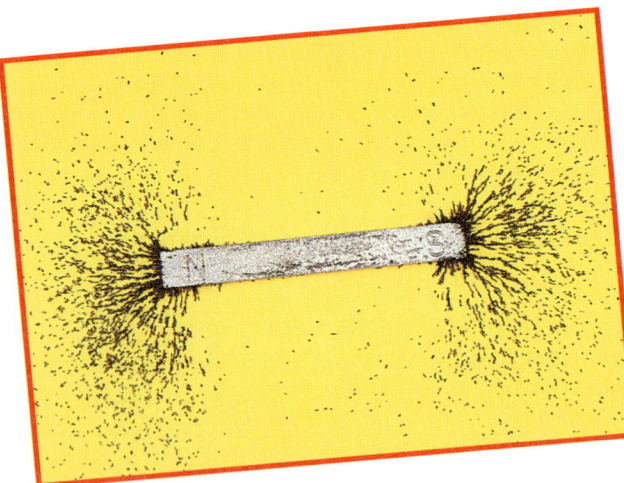

▲ Iron filings show the magnetic field around a magnet.

Earth is like a giant magnet, and it has two magnetic poles. These poles are inclined, or tilted, about 11° from the geographic poles. The magnetic field around Earth is thought to be due to movements within Earth's fluid outer core, which is composed mainly of iron and nickel. For reasons unknown, Earth's

▲ The earth is like a giant magnet surrounded by a magnetic field.

magnetic field reverses, or flips, from time to time. Such a change in the magnetic field is called a **magnetic reversal**.

At present, the magnetic field is said to be normal. This means that the north-seeking needle of a compass will point toward Earth's north magnetic pole. What do you think will happen when the field is reversed?

You probably know that some of Earth's rocks contain iron. When these rocks formed from magma, the particles in the iron lined up with the magnetic field of the time, much as a compass needle lines up with Earth's magnetic field. Scientists can use this lining up of iron particles to find the direction of Earth's magnetic field at the time the rock formed.

Scientists use a device called a magnetometer (mag nə täm′ət ər) to detect magnetic fields. This device can show how particles of iron line up within rock. Magnetometers have been used by oceanographers to study the magnetic fields of rock on the ocean floor. What the scientists found surprised them!

When the scientists studied the sea floor at mid-ocean ridges and on either side of the ridges, they found a magnetic pattern. There were long stretches of rock in which iron particles were lined up in one direction. Then there were other stretches of rock, parallel to the first, in which the iron particles lined up in the reverse direction. This pattern of reversals continued from the mid-ocean ridge outward, away from the ridge. A further finding was that the pattern on one side of the ridge was exactly the same as the pattern on the other side of the ridge.

The drawing below helps explain the magnetic patterns on the ocean floor. At the center of the drawing is a mid-ocean ridge. Magma flows up from below the ridge and then hardens into rock on the sea floor. Only when iron-containing rock is fluid can the iron particles line up in a magnetic field. Once the rock hardens, the iron does not change its direction. The arrows show the magnetic directions of the iron in the rock at the mid-ocean ridge and on either side of the ridge. Note the repeating pattern.

Scientists have found that rocks closer to mid-ocean ridges formed more recently than rocks farther from the ridge. The magnetic patterns in the sea-floor rocks and the different ages of the rocks led scientists to a startling conclusion. New sea floor is continually being formed along underwater mountain chains, or mid-ocean ridges! As two plates separate along a ridge, magma fills the separation. As it is carried away from the ridge due

Sea-floor spreading. Magma bubbles up and flows out along the ridge. When it hardens, it forms rock. On either side of a mid-ocean ridge are layers of magnetized rock. Each arrow represents a magnetic reversal. ▼

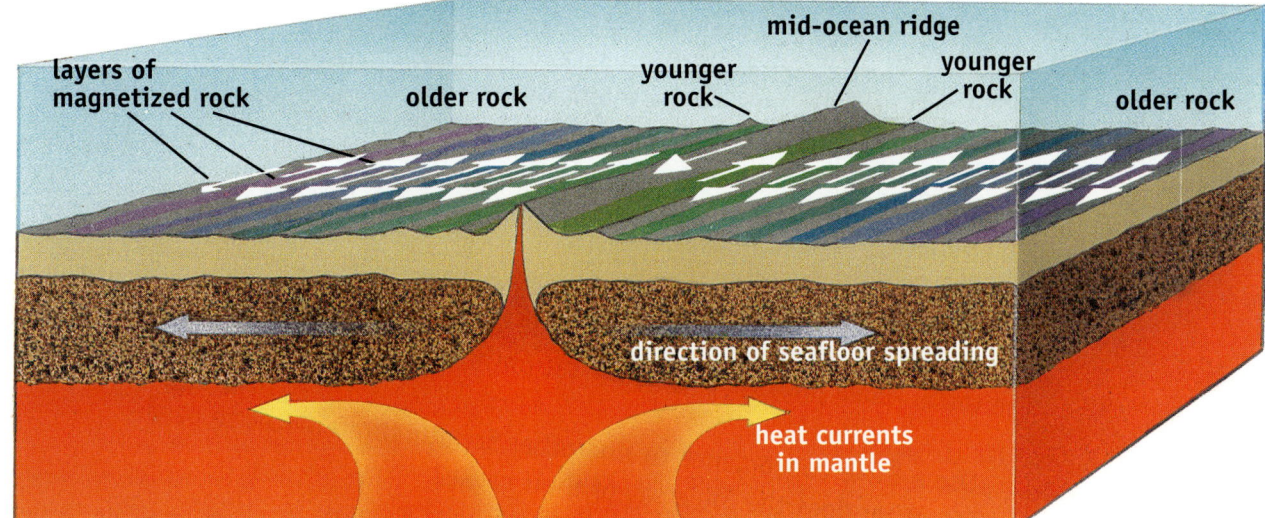

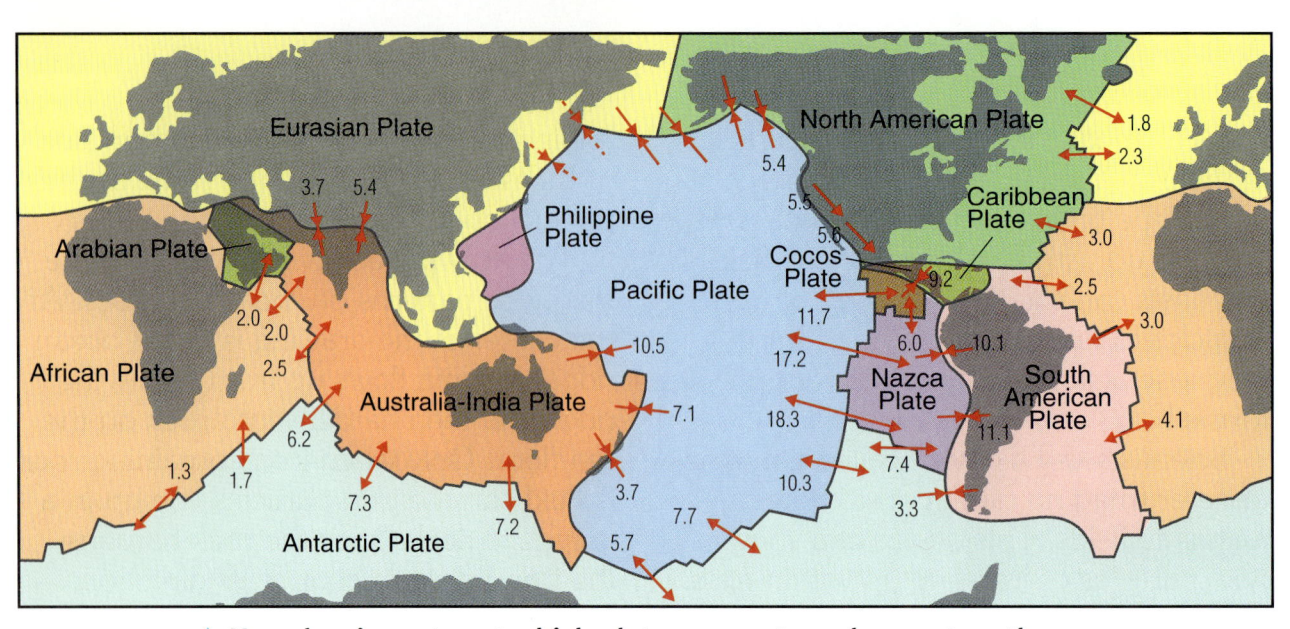

▲ Map showing rates at which plates separate and move together. The rates are in centimeters per year.

to convection currents in the mantle, the magma cools. As it cools, the iron in the magma lines up with Earth's magnetic field. This process by which new ocean floor is continually being added is called **sea-floor spreading**. Recall that you constructed a model of sea-floor spreading on page B22. Sea-floor spreading is strong evidence for the theory of plate tectonics.

Look at the map above that shows rates of sea-floor spreading along the Mid-Atlantic Ridge. Where is spreading the fastest? Where is it the slowest? ■

SCIENCE AND FAITH

The Bible speaks of earthquakes in many places. Two of the most important earthquakes are recorded in Matthew. "At that moment the curtain of the temple was torn in two from top to bottom. The earth shook and the rocks split. The tombs broke open and the bodies of many holy people who had died were raised to life. They came out of the tombs, and after Jesus' resurrection they went into the holy city and appeared to many people. When the centurion and those with him who were guarding Jesus saw the earthquake and all that had happened, they were terrified and exclaimed, 'Surely He was the Son of God!' " (Matthew 27:51-54). Read these verses. What do you think caused these earthquakes?

The second reference is Matthew 28:2 which says "There was a violent earthquake, for an angel of the Lord came down from heaven and, going to the tomb, rolled back the stone and sat on it."

Use a Bible concordance to find other Scriptural references to earthquakes. What does the Bible say of their cause?

Heating Up Iceland

In Iceland, some families don't need ovens to bake their bread; they simply place the dough inside a hole in the ground. Do they have underground ovens? Yes, but these ovens are created by natural processes taking place inside Earth. Below ground, but still close to the surface, there are very hot rocks. These rocks are heated by magma that bubbles up from deep inside Earth. Icelanders use these heated rocks to bake things in their underground ovens.

Helpful Shifting Plates

Movement of Earth's plates can cause trouble. Earthquakes and volcanic eruptions often occur along the edges of moving plates. But there are regions where plate movement can be helpful. In Iceland, for example, moving plates produce underground ovens that use an inexpensive kind of energy—geothermal energy.

Why It Is Hot

Iceland lies on the Mid-Atlantic Ridge, a chain of mountains running through the middle of the Atlantic Ocean. This small country is also located on the edge of two plates—the North American Plate and the Eurasian Plate. As these two plates move away from each other, hot

◀ A geothermal plant in Iceland

A geyser formed by the heating of water within Earth ▼

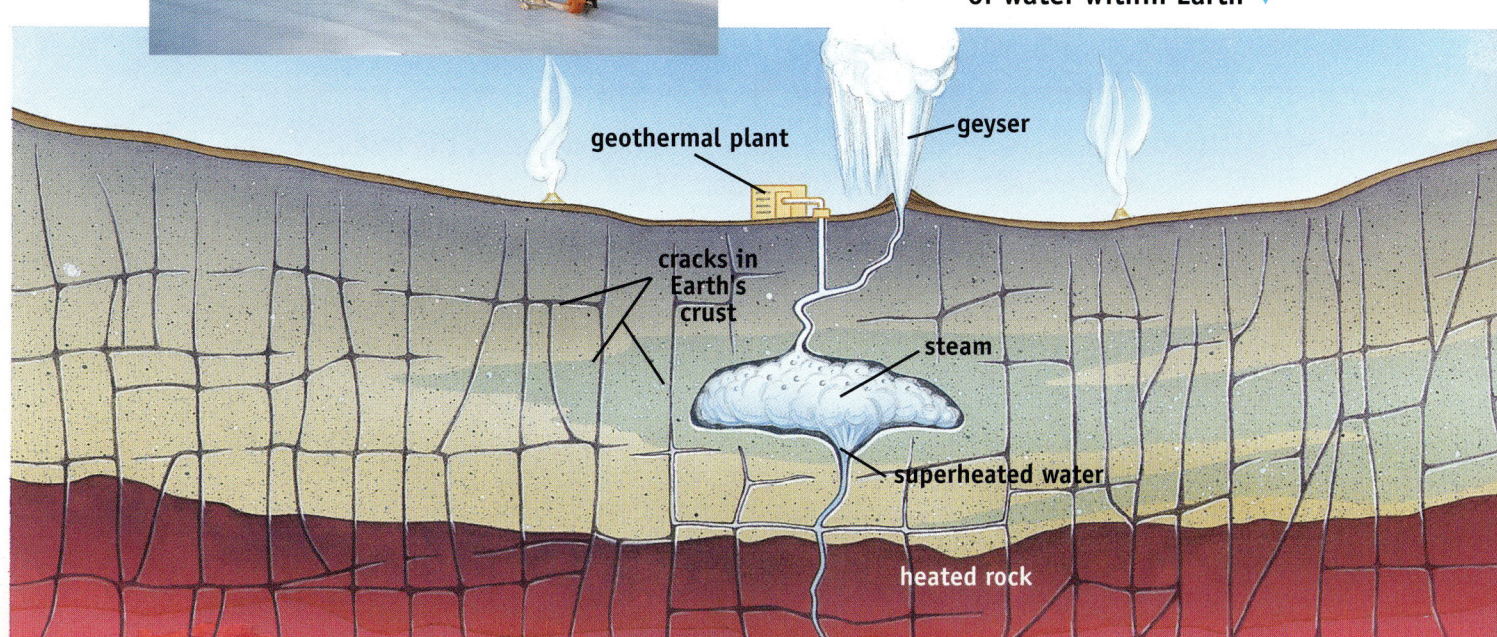

magma rises up from inside Earth, heating the underground rock. The heated rock in turn heats any nearby ground water, changing it to steam. Some of this steam spurts out of the ground in the form of huge geysers.

Energy From Earth

Icelanders use this heated underground water as geothermal ("hot earth") energy. This energy, which comes from heat produced inside Earth, is used by the Icelanders to heat their homes, businesses, swimming pools, and greenhouses. The steam produced by the heated water runs generators that produce electrical energy.

Value of Geothermal Energy

Compared to other forms of energy, geothermal energy has many advantages, as you can see in the table below. Which form of energy is used where you live?

Geothermal energy is used now in several parts of the world besides Iceland—such as in Italy, Japan, Australia, New Zealand, Russia, and the United States. Some of the same processes that can lead to a volcanic eruption can also be turned to useful purposes. The use of geothermal energy in Iceland shows that processes inside Earth can provide people with the heat and electricity they need every day.

Comparison of Forms of Energy

Energy	Advantages	Disadvantages
Fossil fuels	no toxic waste	nonrenewable, polluting
Geothermal	less polluting than fossil fuels or nuclear energy	produces sulfur, boron, and ammonia wastes
Hydroelectric	cheap form of energy; renewable, nonpolluting	dams cause flooding of valuable land
Nuclear	cheap, renewable, powerful	toxic waste; risk of radiation leaks
Solar	renewable, nonpolluting	expensive development and maintenance

INVESTIGATION 3

1. You are planning a TV program about the mysteries at the bottom of the sea. How would you explain sea-floor spreading to your viewers?

2. Describe some of the most important features you might find along a mid-ocean ridge. Explain how these features are formed.

REFLECT & EVALUATE

WORD POWER

crust
mantle
magnetic field
magnetic reversal
mid-ocean ridge
plate boundaries
sea-floor spreading
tectonic plates
theory of continental drift
theory of plate tectonics
Pangaea
plates

On Your Own
Review the terms in the list. Then write one new thing you learned about each term.

With a Partner
Use the terms in the list to make a word-search puzzle. See if your partner can find the hidden terms and tell you what each one means.

Write a story that tells what you would see if you were the pilot of a research submarine that dived around a mid-ocean ridge.

Analyze Information
The maps on pages B17 and B18 show the location of earthquakes and volcanoes. Why are there so many earthquakes and volcanoes located around the shores of the Pacific Ocean?

Assess Performance
The two strips of paper in the model on page B22 represent the spreading sea floor. Make a similar model and use it to show how magnetic reversals occur on each side of a mid-ocean ridge. Write an explanation of how your model shows what happens at mid-ocean ridges.

Problem Solving

1. Oceanographers have found a large mountain range that runs down the middle of the South Atlantic Ocean between Africa and South America. Careful measurements show that South America is moving away from Africa at about 3 to 5 cm each year. How would you explain this?

2. Explain how the same kinds of rock could be found in Norway, Scotland, and parts of eastern Canada and the eastern United States.

3. Dinosaur skeletons have been found in Antarctica, but they could not have lived in such a cold climate. How could they possibly be there?

CHAPTER 2
TECTONIC PLATES AND MOUNTAINS

The Himalayas, the Andes, and other great mountain ranges have existed for many years. The largest of all mountain ranges is actually beneath an ocean. How do mountains form? Do mountains on land and beneath the ocean form in the same way?

The Strangest Volcano

The West Antarctic ice sheet stretches for hundreds of kilometers across the continent of Antarctica. This seemingly unchanging land with its 1.6-km thick (1-mi thick) ice holds a secret that reminds us of how highly active Earth is.

Donald Blankenship and Robin Bell are both geophysicists (jē ō fiz′i sists), scientists who deal with Earth's weather, wind, earthquakes, and so forth. Blankenship and Bell were flying over the West Antarctic ice sheet when they noticed a caved-in area that measured 48 m deep and 6.4 km across. What could cause such a strange hole in the thick ice?

Using radar to see through the ice, the researchers discovered a 630-m mountain—a volcano. Imagine finding a volcano under a thick sheet of ice!

Coming Up

INVESTIGATION 1

WHY DO TECTONIC PLATES MOVE?
.... B36

INVESTIGATION 2

HOW DOES THE MOTION OF TECTONIC PLATES BUILD MOUNTAINS?
.... B42

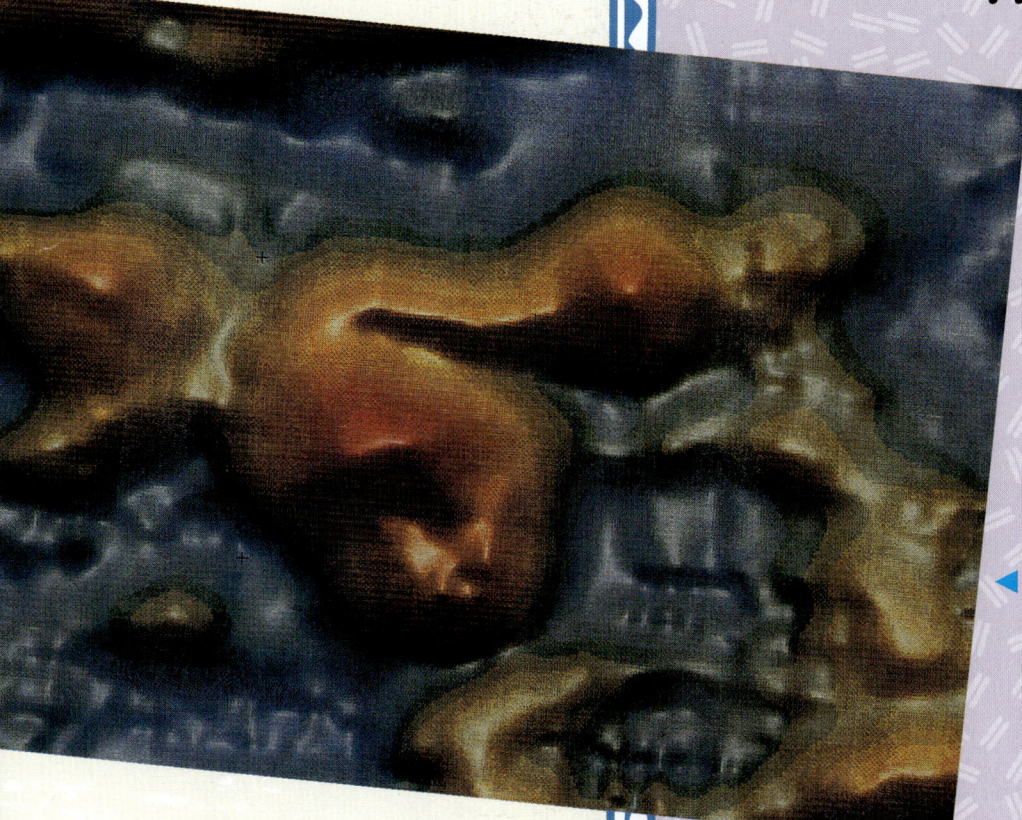

◄ Map showing presence of volcanic rock under the ice sheet.

INVESTIGATION 1

WHY DO TECTONIC PLATES MOVE?

Wegener's hypothesis on continental drift helped to explain why the continents appear to be just so many pieces of a jigsaw puzzle. However, his hypothesis didn't explain why the continents moved. What force can move such huge plates of rock?

Activity
The Conveyor

Heat is a form of energy. Energy can do work. How can heat energy from Earth's interior move tectonic plates? In this activity you'll construct a model that shows what moves tectonic plates.

MATERIALS
- aquarium
- cold water
- milk carton (0.24 L)
- 2 lengths of string (60 cm)
- duct tape
- measuring cup
- hot water
- food coloring
- scissors
- metric ruler
- paper towels
- *Science Notebook*

Procedure

1. Fill an aquarium with cold water.

2. Punch a 5-mm hole in the side of a milk carton, near the bottom. Punch another hole near the top of the carton.

3. Place a length of string over the hole near the bottom so that it extends down 2.5 cm below the hole. Cover the string and hole securely with a strip of duct tape, as shown.

4. Repeat step 3, this time covering the hole near the top of the carton.

Step 3

B36

5. Using a measuring cup, fill the milk carton with hot water colored with food coloring. Seal the carton with duct tape.

6. Place the carton in the middle of the aquarium. **Predict** what will happen when the holes in the carton are opened. **Record** your predictions in your *Science Notebook*.

7. Have a group member hold down the milk carton while you carefully pull the strings to peel the tape off the holes. Watch what happens. **Record** your observations.

8. Form a **hypothesis** on how the movement in the aquarium is a model of the movement of material in Earth's crust and upper mantle. **Discuss** your hypothesis with your group.

Analyze and Conclude

1. What happened in step 7 when you removed the tape from the holes?

2. Did the hot water do what you predicted it would do? Compare your predictions with what actually happened.

3. If the hot and cold water represent the layer of Earth known as the mantle, which is just below the crust, how might the mantle move tectonic plates?

INVESTIGATE FURTHER!

EXPERIMENT

Predict what would happen if you floated a small piece of paper directly over the milk carton before you opened the holes. Then try it and compare your prediction with what actually happened.

Moving Plates

Recall from Chapter 1 that Earth's crust and upper mantle are broken into seven large slabs and several small ones. The slabs are called tectonic plates. These plates move over Earth's surface an average of several centimeters a year. Just what keeps these enormous slabs in motion?

Tectonic plates make up a part of Earth called the lithosphere. The word part *litho-* means "rock." You probably know that *sphere* means "ball."

The **lithosphere** (lith′ō sfir), then, is the solid, rocky layer of Earth. It is about 100 km (62 mi) thick. This part of Earth includes the crust, with the oceans and continents, and the rigid uppermost part of the mantle.

Have you ever slowly pulled on some silicon putty? What happened to the putty as the result of the force you applied? It stretched, didn't it? Suppose you gave the putty a quick, sharp tug. What would happen? The putty would snap and break. What do these two activities tell you about the putty? The putty has properties of both liquids and solids. Like a liquid, it flows when the force is applied slowly. Like a solid, putty snaps when the force is applied quickly.

(Left), Pulling slowly on silicon putty
(Right), Giving silicon putty a sharp tug

ASTHENOSPHERE The layer just below the lithosphere, in the upper mantle, is the asthenosphere. It is made up of rock that is hot, soft, and slightly fluid.

LITHOSPHERE Earth's rigid outer layer is the lithosphere. It includes the crust and solid upper part of the mantle.

▲ Layers of Earth's crust and upper mantle

The **asthenosphere** (as then′ə sfir), the layer of Earth below the lithosphere, is not rigid.

The upper part of the asthenosphere is made of rock that behaves like a plastic and is much like silicon putty when the putty is gently stretched. The rock in the lower asthenosphere is partially melted.

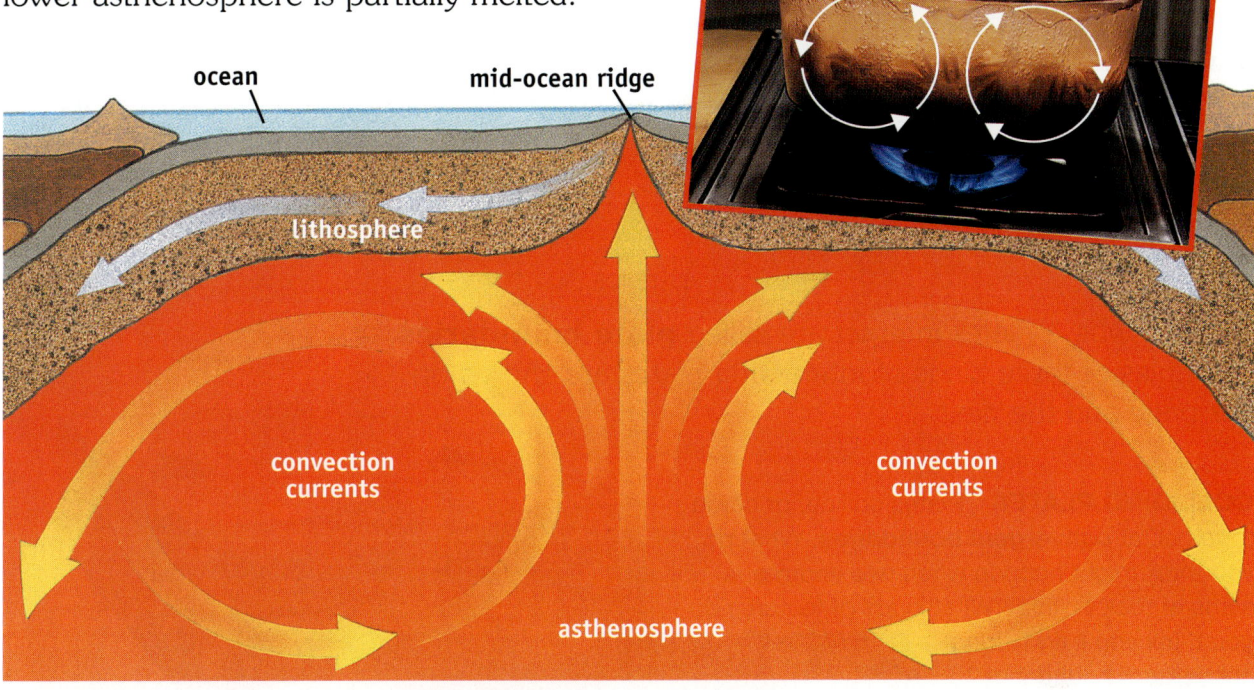

Convection currents in a pot of boiling pasta ▼

▲ Convection currents in the asthenosphere are thought to drive the movement of the tectonic plates.

Heating and Cooling Rock

Scientists think that Earth's plates move over its surface because of convection in the asthenosphere. **Convection** (kən-vek′shən) is a process by which energy is transferred by a moving fluid. Convection occurs when a fluid is placed between a hot lower surface and a cold upper surface. A **convection current** is the path along which the energy is transferred.

You are probably familiar with several kinds of convection currents. Have you ever watched rice or pasta whirl around in a pot of boiling water? Convection currents are set in motion when water or air is heated. The heated fluid then rises because it is less dense than the surrounding fluid. In a pot of rice or pasta, when the heated water reaches the top of the pot, it cools and flows back down to begin another journey around the pot. When you did the activity on pages B36 and B37, you saw the effect of convection currents as you watched the movement of the hot and cold water in the aquarium.

Convection in the Mantle

How does convection occur in Earth's mantle? The partly melted hot rock in the asthenosphere rises because it is less

B39

dense than the surrounding materials. It slowly makes its way toward the lithosphere. When the melted rock reaches the cooler lithosphere, the melted rock begins to cool and harden. The cooler rock then moves horizontally along the bottom of the lithosphere. When the rock reaches the edge of a plate, it sinks down under the plate into the mantle. As the rock moves down into the asthenosphere, it begins to melt, and the cycle starts again.

Moving Tectonic Plates

Today scientists generally agree that convection currents in the asthenosphere are the force that moves tectonic plates. Recall from Chapter 1 that Alfred Wegener, despite all his evidence, could not explain what caused the continents to move over Earth's surface. Thus, his idea of continental drift was a hypothesis, or a guess based on observations. In the 1960s the theory of plate tectonics was

HOW PLATES INTERACT

Places where plates interact are called **plate boundaries**. Examples of three kinds of interacting plates are shown on this page and the next.

COLLIDING PLATES Plates collide, or come together, at **convergent boundaries**. What do you think might happen when two enormous slabs of rock collide? What kinds of features do you think you'll find along convergent boundaries?

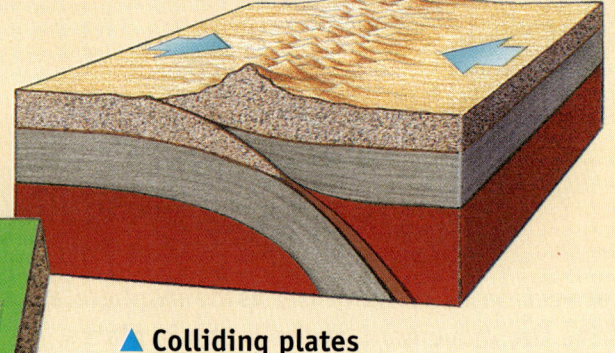

▲ Colliding plates

SEPARATING PLATES Plates move away from one another at **divergent boundaries**. Most divergent boundaries are found on the ocean floor. These boundaries are places where new oceanic crust forms through the process of sea-floor spreading. The photograph shows a divergent boundary.

▲ The walls of this riverbank in Iceland are on plates that separated.

proposed. A theory carries more weight than a hypothesis because a theory is an idea that is supported by evidence. And a theory can be used to make accurate predictions about future events. The **theory of plate tectonics** states that Earth's crust and upper mantle are made up of a series of rigid or nearly rigid plates that are in motion. The map on this page shows these plates and the direction in which they move. ■

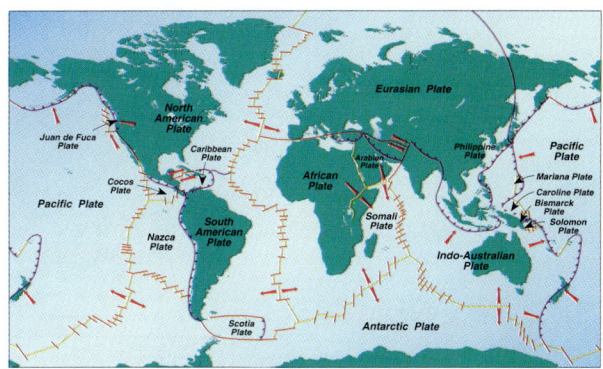

▲ This map shows the location of Earth's major tectonic plates. A full-size map is on pages B20 and B21.

SLIDING PLATES Plates move past one another at **transform-fault boundaries**. A fault is a very large crack in Earth's rocks, along which movement has taken place. The photograph shows the San Andreas Fault, found in the western United States. This fault, one of the longest and most famous in the world, is the site of many earthquakes.

▲ San Andreas Fault, California, as seen from an airplane

INVESTIGATION 1

1. Can convergent and divergent plate boundaries be considered opposites? Write a paragraph comparing these two kinds of plate boundaries.

2. Define the term *tectonic plate* and explain what might cause tectonic plates to move.

B41

INVESTIGATION 2

How Does the Motion of Tectonic Plates Build Mountains?

The tectonic plates that make up Earth's surface are large, thick, and massive. When they move, something has to give! Find out what "gives" in Investigation 2.

Activity

Colliding Plates

MATERIALS
- sheet of cardboard
- tectonic-plates map
- Earth-features map
- *Science Notebook*

Plates are enormously big and heavy. What might happen when one plate runs into another? In this activity you'll demonstrate a simple model of colliding plates.

Procedure

1. Imagine that the sheet of cardboard is a tectonic plate and that a wall is another tectonic plate. **Predict** what will happen when the two plates collide. **Record** your predictions.

2. Take the sheet of cardboard and press one edge of it firmly against a wall and push.

3. In your *Science Notebook*, **record** what happens to the cardboard.

4. Your map of the tectonic plates shows the edges of tectonic plates and the directions in which the plates are moving. Study your map and find one or more places where the boundary between plates is a convergent boundary.

Step 1

▲ Earth-features map

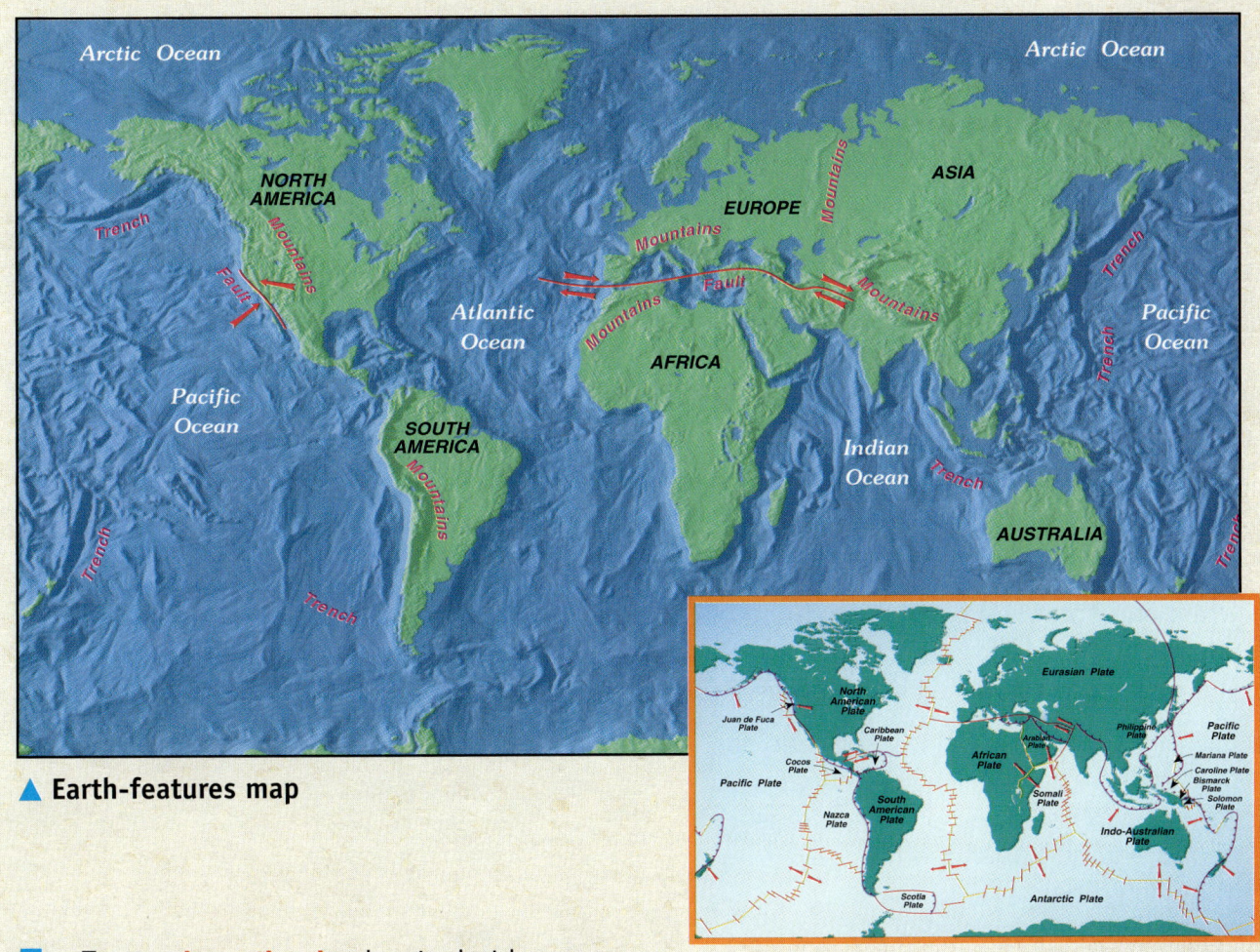

▲ Tectonic-plates map. For the full-size map, see pages B20 and B21.

5. Form a **hypothesis** about what happens when two plates meet at a convergent boundary.

Analyze and Conclude

1. What feature forms when two plates collide at a convergent boundary? Locate several such features on the Earth-features map.

2. In what parts of the world are two plates now colliding? **Infer** how these regions may change in the future.

UNIT PROJECT LINK

After several earthquakes shook California in the 1990s, the Sierra Nevada range became more than 0.3 m (1 ft) taller. What other mountains in the world are still growing? Use newspapers and magazines to find out about earthquakes and volcanoes that have recently lifted mountains. Find out what form of mountain building caused the uplift. Use a map to identify the location of the growing mountains.

Activity
A Big Fender Bender

MATERIALS
- 2 cellulose sponges
- water
- *Science Notebook*

Think about what happens when two cars collide. What happens to the metal? What do you think happens when two continents collide? You'll use a simple model to find out.

Procedure

1. Form a **hypothesis** about what you think will happen when one continent bumps into another. **Discuss** your hypothesis with other members of your group. **Record** your hypothesis in your *Science Notebook*.

2. Moisten two cellulose sponges so that they are flexible. **Predict** what will happen if you place the sponges end to end and push them slowly into each other.

Step 2

3. Then place the sponges end to end and push them into each other. **Record** your observations.

Analyze and Conclude

1. What did you observe?

2. Did the sponges do what you predicted they would do? If not, what was different?

3. Explain how the moist sponges are a model of continents colliding. How is this model related to what you did in the preceding activity?

INVESTIGATE FURTHER!

RESEARCH

Some scientists speculate that when North America collided with North Africa to form part of Pangaea, a large mountain range was thrust upward on the North American Plate. Find out which mountains they were and what has happened to them.

Mountain-Building

Have you ever gone mountain climbing? A mountain is any feature that rises above the surrounding landscape. So whether you've climbed the steep slopes of the Rocky Mountains or just hiked a local hill, you've gone mountain climbing!

Mountains form as the result of four basic processes: folding, faulting, doming, and volcanic activity—so mountains can be classified as folded mountains, fault-block mountains, dome mountains, or volcanoes. Three of these kinds of mountains—folded, fault-block, and volcanic—result from plate movements.

Folded Mountains

Have you ever made a paper fan? If you have, then you've squeezed paper to make a series of pleats, or folds. If you were to look at the folded edge of the fan, you would see a series of crests, or high points, and troughs, or low points. Folded mountains form when masses of rock are squeezed from opposite sides. In the activities on pages B42 to B44, you saw that folded mountains form when two plates collide. The Appalachians, the Alps, the Urals, and the Himalayas can be classified as folded mountains. Locate these mountain ranges on a globe of Earth.

FOLDED MOUNTAINS These form when two tectonic plates collide.

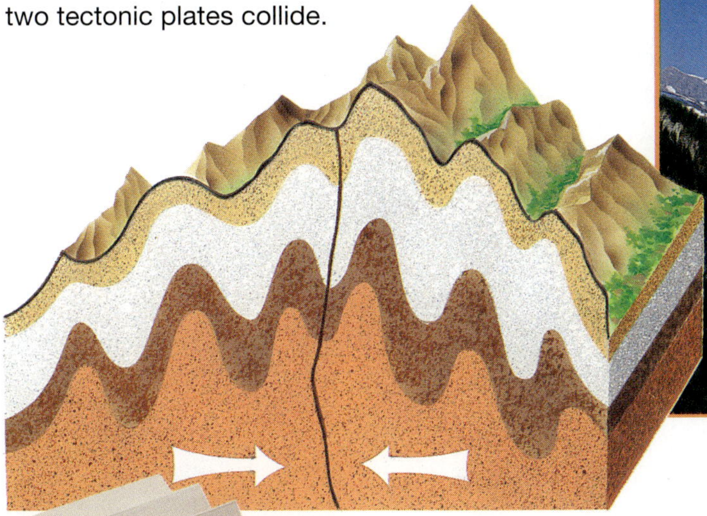

▲ The Swiss Alps, a range of folded mountains

◀ A folded paper fan, showing crests and troughs

B45

Fault-block Mountains

Recall that a fault is a large crack in Earth's rocks, along which movement has taken place. Forces produced by moving plates can move rock along faults. When blocks of rock move up or down along a fault, a mountain can form.

Examples of fault-block mountains include those in the Dead Sea area, the Grand Tetons in Wyoming, and those in the Great Rift Valley of Africa. Among the mountains in the Great Rift Valley, scientists have unearthed some of the oldest known human fossils.

Dome Mountains

Have you ever heard of Pikes Peak? This granite summit in the Colorado Rockies is 4,341 m (14,110 ft) tall! It was explored in 1806 by Zebulon Pike. Although the peak was eventually named after him, Pike never even reached its summit! Pikes Peak is a dome mountain that formed millions of years ago when forces deep within Earth pushed magma toward the surface, where it cooled and hardened. Although dome mountains have an igneous core, sedimentary rocks can border such mountains. But erosion often strips away the sedimentary rocks to reveal the harder igneous core.

Other dome mountains in the United States are the Sangre de Cristo Mountains, the Bighorn Mountains, the Black Hills, and Longs Peak. Find these dome mountains on a map of the United States. Are any of them in your state or in nearby states?

SCIENCE AND FAITH

Genesis 1 reveals no specific mention of mountains. By the time more than 10 centuries pass, we hear of high mountains swallowed by the waters of the Great Flood. Did God originally create those mountains, or did they form according to the principles of earth science? The Bible doesn't say, but the Ararat Range in eastern Turkey formed a cradle for Noah's Ark–a symbol of our own salvation–from which to release its cargo.

FAULT-BLOCK MOUNTAINS These mountains form when masses of rock move up or down along a fault.

▲ Wasatch Range, Utah, fault-block mountains

DOME MOUNTAINS These mountains form when the surface is lifted up by magma, forming a broad dome, or bulge. Wind and rain erode the dome, stripping away layers of sedimentary rock and exposing the igneous rock below.

▲ Pikes Peak, Colorado, a dome mountain

INVESTIGATE FURTHER!

EXPERIMENT

Use a few different colors of modeling clay to demonstrate how folded mountains form. Then use the clay and a plastic knife to show how fault-block mountains form. USE CARE IN HANDLING THE KNIFE. Make sketches of your models in your *Science Notebook*.

B47

Volcanoes

Have you ever opened a bottle of warm soda and had it spray all over you? The spraying of the soda is a bit like the eruption of magma when a volcano forms. **Volcanoes**, a fourth type of mountain, are common along convergent and divergent plate boundaries. They form when magma, or molten rock, erupts from an opening in Earth's surface. Sometimes the eruption is quiet; at other times it is quite forceful.

Mount St. Helens is a volcano in the Cascade Range. This mountain chain extends from northern California to British Columbia, in Canada. On May 18, 1980, Mount St. Helens blew its top and threw dust, ash, and volcanic rocks 18,000 m (59,400 ft) above the ground! As the ash rained back down to Earth, it blanketed some places with as much as 2 m (6.6 ft) of fine material. In some places the ash was so thick that it looked like midnight when it was actually noon! You will learn much more about volcanoes in Chapter 4. ■

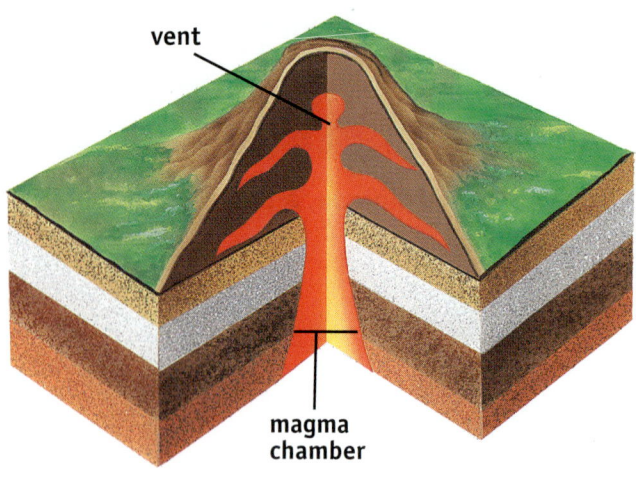

▲ A typical volcano

Mount St. Helens, Washington State. (*Top*), before the 1980 eruption; (*middle*), during the eruption; and (*bottom*), after the eruption.

Life at the Top

You now know that folded mountains are formed by the interactions of tectonic plates. The Himalaya Mountains, for example, were formed long ago when the plate carrying India, then a separate continent, rammed into the plate carrying Asia. This enormous collision of plates crumpled the crust and lifted up sediment from the ocean floor, forming the Himalayas. In some places the sediment was raised up thousands of meters, forming folded mountains.

People used to living at low altitudes experience problems as they move up into higher country. Climbers of very high mountains—the Himalayas, for example—can experience many difficulties. Newcomers experience problems with breathing. The lower air pressure at higher altitudes means that less oxygen is taken in with each breath. A lack of oxygen can affect vision and make walking dangerous. Heart rate quickens sharply, and the heart tries to supply more oxygen to the body. Climbers often have to stop to rest every few meters.

People in Nepal, a country in the Himalayas, have adapted to living high

The world's highest mountains, compared to the Empire State Building ▼

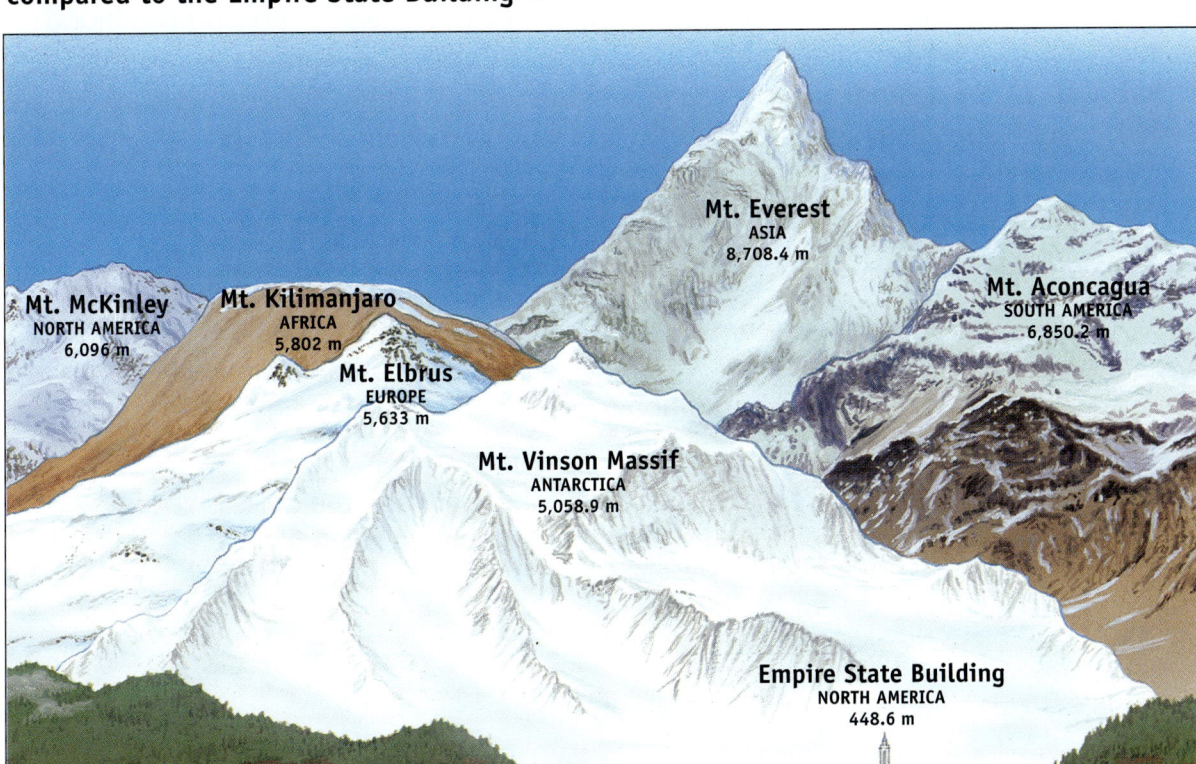

▲ Tenzing Norgay climbed Mount Everest.

▲ Sherpa women in their mountain village

up in the mountains. Nepal is the home of the highest mountain peak in the world—Mount Everest, which towers 8,848 m (29,028 ft) above sea level.

The Sherpas, a people of Tibetan ancestry who live mainly in Nepal, are known for their ability to live and work in the high terrain of their country. How have the Sherpas adapted to their life high in the mountains?

Because the Sherpas have lived all their lives in the mountains, their blood contains more oxygen-carrying red blood cells than that of most other people. So, with each breath the Sherpas take, they can absorb more available oxygen and pump it throughout their bodies. The ability to move enough oxygen throughout the body prevents many problems. In fact, Tenzing Norgay, a Sherpa, was one of the first two men to climb to the top of Mount Everest!

Visitors to the high mountains adapt to the lower air pressure after several weeks. What happens? Like the bodies of the native peoples, their bodies produce more of the oxygen-carrying red blood cells. In time, newcomers to the high mountains can also pump more oxygen throughout their bodies. ■

INVESTIGATION 2

1. How are folded mountains like fault-block mountains? How are the two kinds of mountains different? Write a paragraph comparing and contrasting these kinds of mountains.

2. Describe the relationship between the collision of plates and the formation of mountains.

CHAPTER 2 REVIEW: REFLECT & EVALUATE

WORD POWER

asthenosphere
convection
plate boundary
volcano
dome mountain
lithosphere
convection current
convergent boundary
divergent boundary
fault-block mountain
folded mountain
theory of plate tectonics
transform-fault boundary

 On Your Own
Define each term.

 With a Partner
Scramble the letters of each term in the list. With terms of two or more words, keep the scrambled letters separate for each word. Exchange scrambled terms with your partner. Who can unscramble them first?

Collect photos of mountains. Classify them as folded, fault-block, dome, or volcano. Make a poster of your collection.

Analyze Information

The map below shows a convergent boundary between two tectonic plates. Describe what features you might see along this convergent boundary.

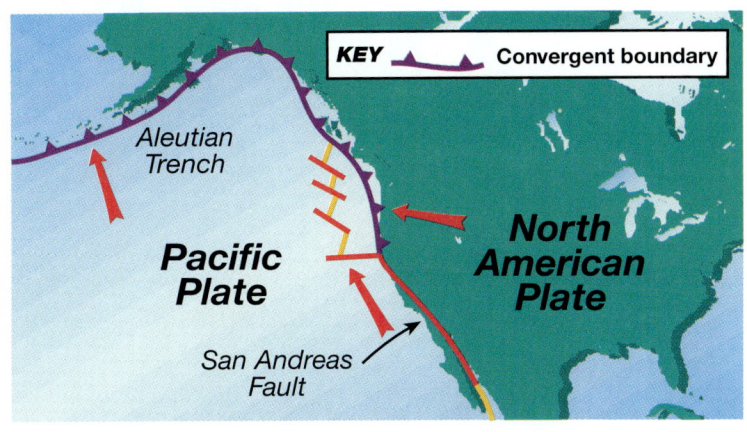

Assess Performance

Make a double-decker peanut-butter-and-jelly sandwich. Cut it in half and use it to show how fault-block mountains are formed.

Problem Solving

1. Imagine that you are in a special kind of submarine that has entered Earth's upper mantle. The submarine is riding along in the convection currents. Describe your journey.

2. You skid on a small rug into a wall. How is what happens to the rug like tectonic plates building mountains?

3. The San Andreas Fault in California is a transform-fault boundary between the North American Plate and the Pacific Plate. Describe and model how the plates are moving along this boundary.

CHAPTER 3

SHAKE, RATTLE, AND ROLL

Many men and women in science try to solve problems that affect people's daily lives. Earthquakes have terrified people throughout history, and they continue to threaten loss of life and property today. How can science help?

Scientists on the Scene

Among the first people to investigate an earthquake are the seismologists (sīz mäl′ ə jists). These scientists study how and why earthquakes happen. Waverly Person is the chief of the National Earthquake Information Service in Denver, Colorado. He and his staff monitor movements in Earth's crust, using seismographs and other technology.

Seismologists examine the strength of each earthquake, how long it lasts, and where it is located. They exchange ideas about *why* an earthquake has happened. Over the years, seismologists have developed hypotheses about where future earthquakes will happen. How might such predictions be useful?

Coming Up

INVESTIGATION 1
WHAT CAUSES EARTHQUAKES, AND HOW CAN THEY BE COMPARED?
............B54

INVESTIGATION 2
WHAT HAPPENS TO EARTH'S CRUST DURING AN EARTHQUAKE?
............B62

INVESTIGATION 3
HOW ARE EARTHQUAKES LOCATED AND MEASURED?
............B68

◀ Waverly Person checking a seismograph

INVESTIGATION 1

WHAT CAUSES EARTHQUAKES AND HOW CAN THEY BE COMPARED?

Picture two railroad cars rolling by each other on side-by-side tracks. Could they get past each other if their sides were touching? Some tectonic plates are a little like these trains. This investigation is about the sudden changes that can occur when plates that touch move past one another.

Activity

A Model of Sliding Plates

MATERIALS
- 2 blocks of wood
- coarse sandpaper
- 4 rubber bands
- tectonic-plates map
- Earth-features map
- *Science Notebook*

Did you ever try to slide a heavy box over a rough sidewalk and have the box get stuck? Tectonic plates have rough surfaces, too. What happens when the plates keep pushing but the rocks don't slide?

Procedure

1. Cover two blocks of wood with coarse sandpaper. Use rubber bands, as shown, to hold the sandpaper on the blocks of wood.

2. Predict what will happen if you hold the sandpaper surfaces tightly against each other and then try to slide the blocks past each other. **Record** your prediction in your *Science Notebook*.

Step 1

B54

▲ Tectonic-plates map. For a larger map, see pages B20 and B21.

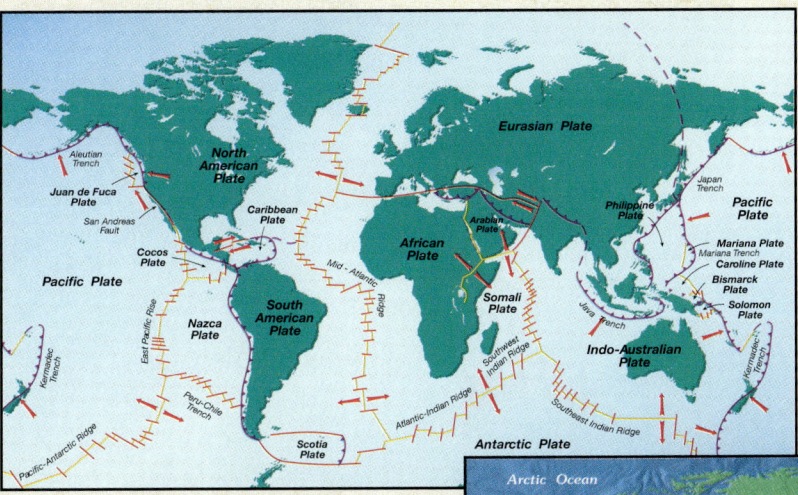

▲ Earth-features map. For a larger map, see page B43.

3. Try sliding the blocks past each other. (Hold together the surfaces on which there are no rubber bands.) **Observe** what happens and **record** your observations.

4. Explain how this action might be like two tectonic plates passing each other.

5. Now list the places shown on your tectonic-plates map where plates are sliding past each other. For example, note that the Pacific Plate and the North American Plate are sliding past each other near the west coast of the United States.

6. Find the same places on the Earth-features map. List any features you find in those places that seem to be related to the motion of the plates.

Analyze and Conclude

1. Think about the places you identified in steps 5 and 6. Have you read or heard anything about either of these locations that might involve changes in Earth's crust? What do you conclude might happen when two tectonic plates slide past each other?

2. Did you find anything that looks like it might be caused by the sliding of two plates? If so, what did you find?

INVESTIGATE FURTHER!

EXPERIMENT

Find two bricks. Slide one over the other. Do they slide easily? What do you hear? What do you feel? What happens when two smooth rock surfaces slide past each other?

Sliding Plates

It was a little after 5:00 A.M. on April 18, 1906. Many San Franciscans were awakened by a deep rumbling of the ground beneath them. Homes, stores, offices, hotels, churches, and bridges collapsed. Sergeant Jesse Cook, a police officer, observed, "The whole street was undulating [waving]. It was as if the waves of the ocean were coming toward me."

An editor from the *Examiner* newspaper noted that trolley tracks were twisted like wriggling snakes and that water and gas spurted high into the air.

Scientists estimate that the earthquake that struck San Francisco in 1906 would have had a reading of about 8.3 on the Richter scale. (You'll read more about the Richter scale in "Our Active Earth" on pages B58 and B59.) The earthquake

▲ City Hall after the 1906 San Francisco earthquake; a 1906 newspaper headline

Gold is discovered at Sutter's Mill.
1848

Cable cars climb the hills of San Francisco for the first time.
1873

lasted for only a little over a minute. But its effects were enormous. About 500 people died, and nearly 250,000 were left homeless. Water mains were destroyed. Fires due to broken gas lines raged throughout the city for days. More than 28,000 buildings were destroyed by the fires.

Shortly after the quake, San Franciscans began to rebuild their destroyed city and their disrupted lives. By December 1906, many new buildings stood where others had collapsed. Within about three years, 20,000 buildings had been constructed to replace those lost to fire and to the quake itself.

Today, just as in 1906, people ask "What are earthquakes? Why do these tremors happen in some places and not in others?" An earthquake is a vibration of the Earth, caused by a sudden release of energy stored in the crust. Most earthquakes occur along tectonic plate boundaries, places on Earth where vast slabs of rock separate, collide, or slide past one another.

Faults

The 1906 earthquake occurred when blocks of rock deep within Earth's surface began to move along a crack called the San Andreas Fault. A fault is a large crack in layers of rock along which movement has occurred. The San Andreas Fault runs through much of California and separates the North American Plate from the Pacific Plate. The 1906 San Francisco earthquake wasn't the first "earth-shaking" event to occur along the San Andreas Fault and it wasn't the last. Many large earthquakes have struck that region since 1906. A major earthquake struck the San Francisco Bay area in October 1989. That quake, measuring 7.1 on the Richter scale, caused $7 billion in damage and 63 deaths. Scientists predict that a much larger earthquake—the "Big One"—is yet to come. ■

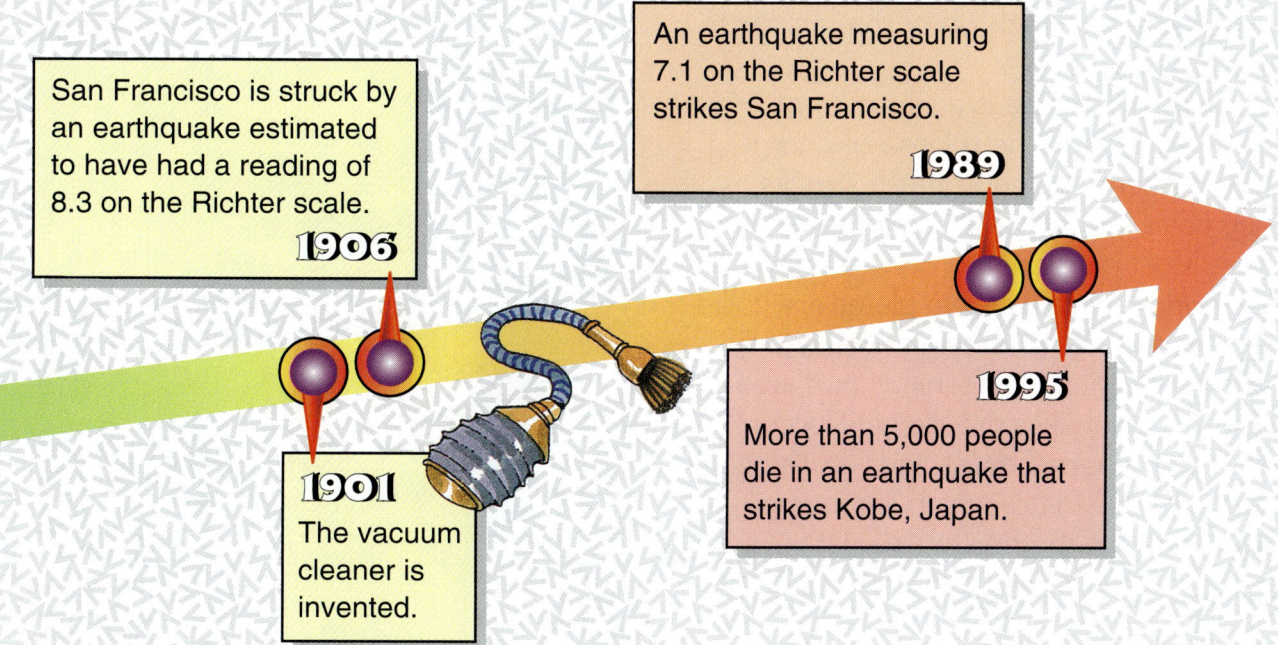

San Francisco is struck by an earthquake estimated to have had a reading of 8.3 on the Richter scale.
1906

1901
The vacuum cleaner is invented.

An earthquake measuring 7.1 on the Richter scale strikes San Francisco.
1989

1995
More than 5,000 people die in an earthquake that strikes Kobe, Japan.

Our Active Earth

Earth is an ever-changing planet. Some changes happen in a matter of seconds or minutes. Other changes occur over months or years. Soils are eroded by water, wind, and gravity. Mountains take hundreds, thousands, or even millions of years to form and just as long to be worn away. And some changes, such as those caused by earthquakes, occur suddenly and violently.

Earthquakes

Earthquakes usually last for only a few minutes. But it takes many years to build up the energy that is released during an earthquake. As blocks of rocks move past one another along faults, friction prevents some sections of rock from slipping very much. Instead, the rocks bend and change shape, until the force becomes too great. It is only when the rocks suddenly slide past each other that an earthquake occurs.

An **earthquake** is a vibration of Earth, caused by the release of energy that has been stored in Earth's rocks as they have ground past one another over time. Most earthquakes occur in parts of the world where tectonic plates are colliding, separating, or moving horizontally past each other. California is one area where earthquakes are likely to occur. Part of southern California is on the edge of the Pacific Plate, which is moving slowly toward the northwest.

The San Andreas Fault

During the history of the San Andreas Fault in California, hundreds of earthquakes and many thousands of aftershocks have occurred along its length of 1,200 km (720 mi). An **aftershock** is a shock that occurs after the principal shock of an earthquake. Recall that one of these tremors nearly destroyed the city of San Francisco in 1906.

A more recent earthquake, which was centered in Loma Prieta, California, in October 1989, was felt as far away as Oregon and Nevada. This earthquake caused more than 60 deaths and registered 7.1 on the Richter scale.

Damage caused by the Loma Prieta, California, earthquake in October 1989. ▼

The Richter Scale

If you've ever listened to or read a news report about an earthquake, you've heard the term *Richter scale*. The **Richter scale**, with numbers ranging from 1 to 10, describes the magnitude, or strength, of an earthquake. The **magnitude** of an earthquake is the amount of energy released by the quake. The Richter scale is named after the American seismologist Charles Richter.

Minor earthquakes have magnitudes of 4 or less. The largest recorded earthquakes have magnitudes of about 8.5.

Each increase of 1.0 on the Richter scale represents a difference of about 30 times more energy than the previous number. For example, an earthquake measuring 5.0 on the Richter scale releases about 30 times more energy than a quake measuring 4.0. Likewise, an earthquake measuring 5.7 on the

The Pacific Plate and North American Plate border the San Andreas Fault. In which directions do the plates move? ▼

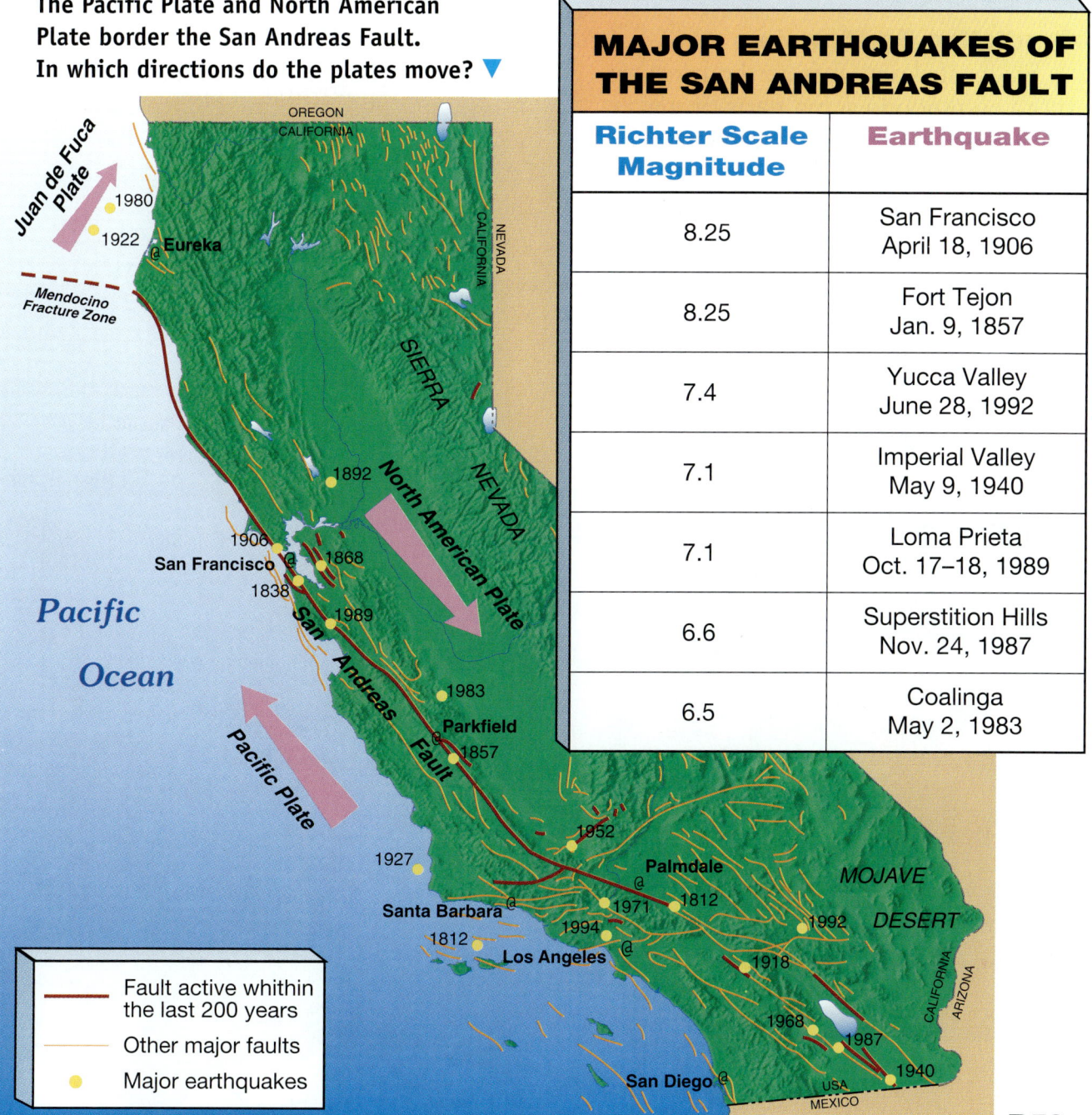

MAJOR EARTHQUAKES OF THE SAN ANDREAS FAULT

Richter Scale Magnitude	Earthquake
8.25	San Francisco April 18, 1906
8.25	Fort Tejon Jan. 9, 1857
7.4	Yucca Valley June 28, 1992
7.1	Imperial Valley May 9, 1940
7.1	Loma Prieta Oct. 17–18, 1989
6.6	Superstition Hills Nov. 24, 1987
6.5	Coalinga May 2, 1983

Richter scale releases about 30 times less energy than an earthquake measuring 6.7 on the scale.

Now study the table and map on page B59, showing some of the earthquakes that occurred along the San Andreas Fault over the past century. Where along the San Andreas did most of the quakes occur? Where did the strongest earthquakes occur? Then look at the map below. Where is the strongest quake likely to occur in the future?

Predicting Earthquakes

Scientists know that earthquakes are more common in some parts of the world than in others. Yet the actual timing of these Earth movements is difficult to predict. Seismologists, scientists who study earthquakes, have no sure way of knowing when or where an earthquake will strike or how strong it will be. They can only give estimates of the probability that an earthquake will strike in a certain place within a certain span of years.

Once in a while, seismologists are accurate in predicting earthquakes. In 1988, seismologists of the United States Geological Survey predicted that Loma Prieta, California, was likely to have an earthquake. Loma Prieta is along the San Andreas Fault. On October 17, 1989, a severe earthquake struck Loma Prieta and nearby San Francisco and Oakland.

Seismologists have found that there are changes in Earth that come before most earthquakes. Knowing this, the seismologists closely watch instruments that measure and record these changes. Seismologists are especially careful to

A map of California showing how likely it is that the "Big One" will strike in different parts of the state ▼

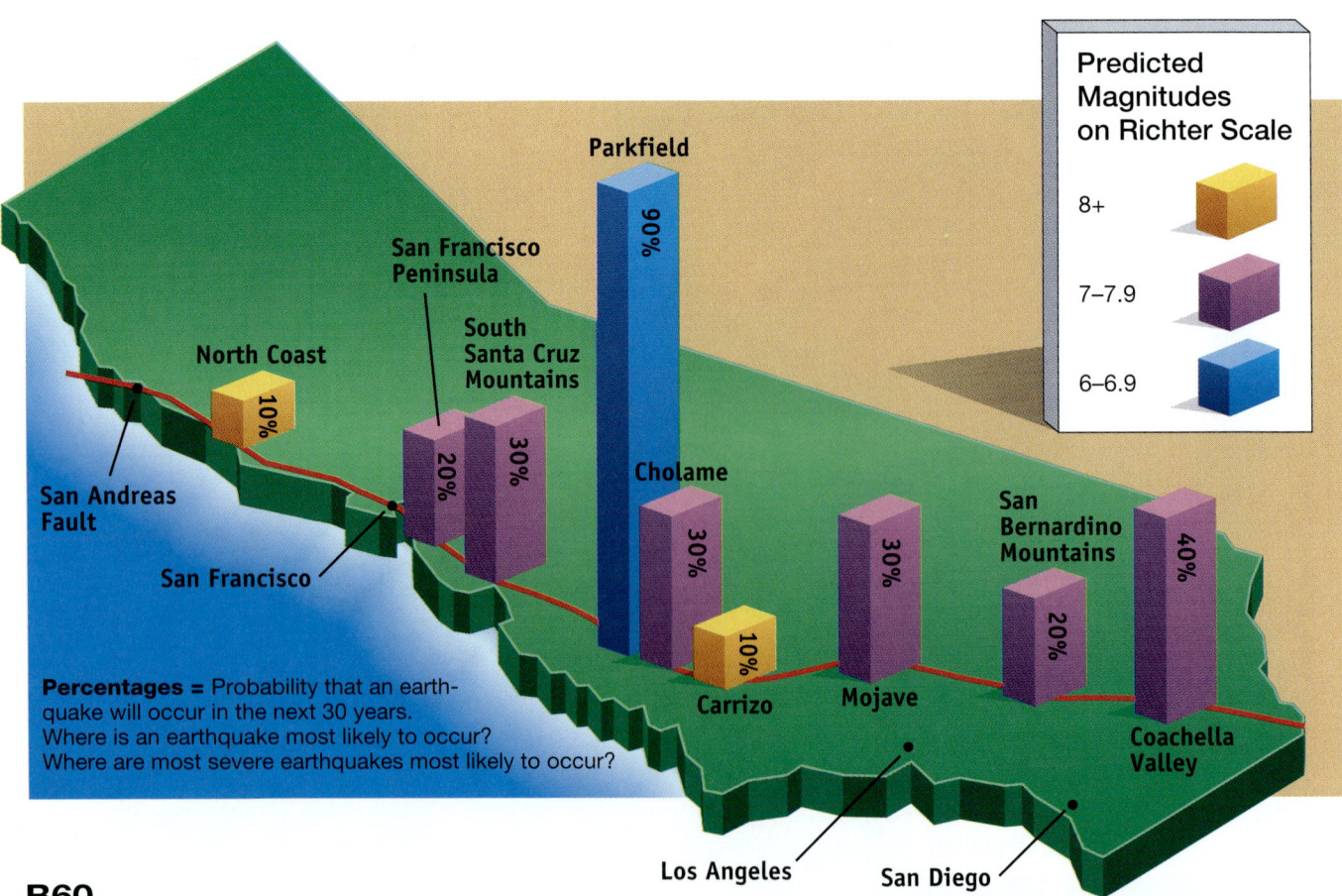

watch the instruments in regions where earthquakes are likely to occur. For example, changes in the tilt of slabs of rock below ground can indicate that an earthquake is brewing. Studies have shown that rock formations will swell before an earthquake. Changes in Earth's magnetic and gravitational fields can mean an earthquake is soon to strike. Increases in the amount of a radioactive gas called radon from within Earth often come before an earthquake. Micro-earthquakes, or minor tremors, can also indicate that a more intense earthquake will strike an area.

Just how accurate are these warnings? Some scientists argue that watching changes in various instruments can lead to the prediction of earthquakes. Eleven days before the 1989 Loma Prieta earthquake, an instrument in the area recorded natural radio waves from Earth that were nearly 30 times stronger than usual. Just a few hours before the earthquake struck, these radio signals became so strong that they shot off the scale of the instrument.

A study by scientists at the Southern California Earthquake Center suggests that in the next 30 years there will be a severe earthquake in southern California. Exactly when and where it will strike is anyone's guess. ■

▲ Laser beams are being used to monitor Earth's movements and to predict quakes.

INVESTIGATE FURTHER!

RESEARCH

Some people believe that animals are very sensitive to the changes that occur before events such as storms and earthquakes. Find out about this hypothesis concerning animal behavior before an earthquake as a possible warning sign for people. What do you think about this idea?

INVESTIGATION 1

1. You are writing a news report on an earthquake that has just occurred. Tell your readers where and why the quake occurred, which plates were involved, and how severe it was.

2. Explain how the movement of tectonic plates and the occurrence of earthquakes are related.

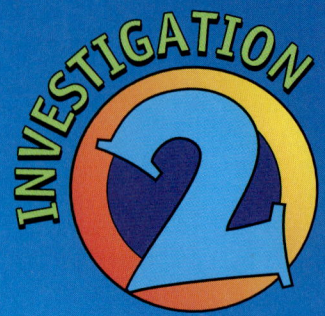

INVESTIGATION 2

WHAT HAPPENS TO EARTH'S CRUST DURING AN EARTHQUAKE?

Have you ever pushed a desk across a floor? Sometimes the desk starts to vibrate, and you can feel the vibrations in your hands and arms. In this investigation you'll find out how this experience is similar to what happens during an earthquake.

Activity

Shake It!

In this activity you'll make a model for observing what can happen to buildings during an earthquake. In your model you'll make the vibrations.

MATERIALS
- small block of wood
- clear plastic bowl, filled with sand
- water
- measuring cup
- clear plastic bowl, filled with gelatin
- *Science Notebook*

Procedure

1. Think of a block of wood as a building and a bowl filled with sand as the surface of Earth. Stand a block of wood in a bowl full of sand.

2. Predict what will happen if you shake the bowl. **Record** your predictions in your *Science Notebook*.

A highway toppled during the 1995 earthquake in Kobe, Japan. ▶

B62

3. Shake the bowl rapidly by sliding it back and forth. **Observe** what happens to the block and the surface of the sand. **Record** your observations.

4. Pour water over the sand until the water is at the same level as the sand. Again stand the wooden block on the sand. **Predict** what will happen to the block if you shake the bowl with the wet sand. Repeat the shaking, **observe** what happens, and **record** your observations.

5. Now **predict** what will happen when you set the block on the gelatin and shake the bowl. Try it; then **record** your observations.

Step 4

Analyze and Conclude

1. During the "earthquake," what happened to the dry sand? the wet sand? the gelatin? What, do you think, did the dry sand, wet sand, and the gelatin represent?

2. What happened to the "building" as it stood on the different surfaces?

3. Which model showed the most damage to the "building"? What evidence supports your conclusions?

UNIT PROJECT LINK

At 5:30 P.M. on March 27, 1964, the most powerful earthquake to hit North America struck Anchorage, Alaska. More than 130 people in Alaska and 12 people in Crescent City, California, were killed by the tsunami that followed the quake. (You'll find out about tsunamis on pages B76–77.) Use a map to trace how far the tsunami traveled. Then compute the distance that the tsunami traveled. Look at an earthquake map of the world. Outline in red those North American coastlines that might experience tsunamis.

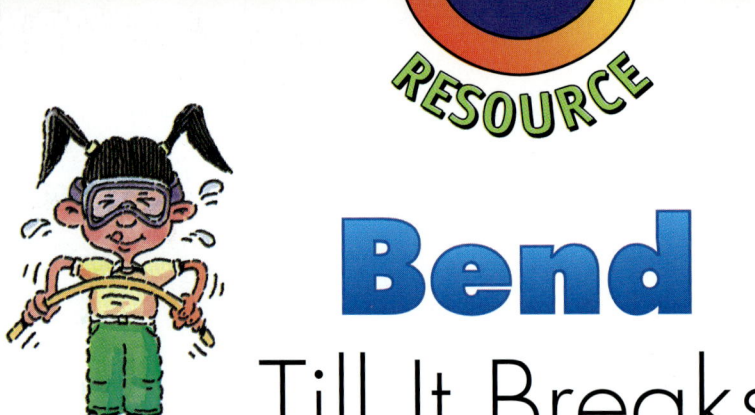

Bend
Till It Breaks

Imagine that you are holding a flexible wooden stick that is about 2 cm wide and 1 m long. You are holding one end in each hand and are gently bending the stick. If you stop bending the stick, it will return to its original shape. What will happen if you keep on bending it? Eventually it will snap!

Forces and Faults

Although Earth's rocks are hard and brittle, in some ways they can behave like the bending wooden stick. You probably know that a force is a push or a pull. If a pulling force is applied slowly to rocks, they will stretch. But like the wooden stick, the rocks will break or snap if the

Movement Along Faults

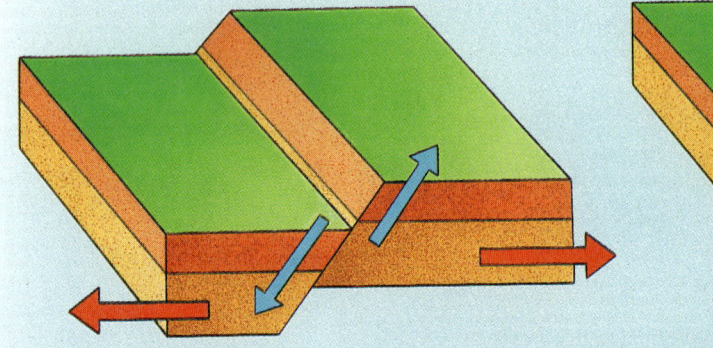

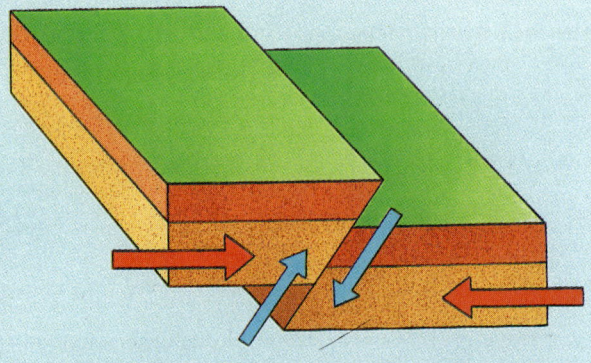

NORMAL FAULT The rock slabs are pulling apart, and one slab has moved up, while the other has moved down along the fault.

REVERSE FAULT The rock slabs are pushing together, and one rock slab has pushed under the other along the fault.

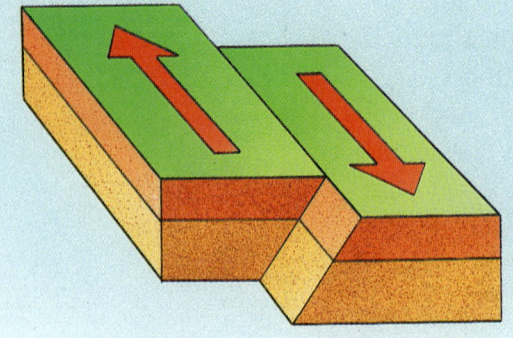

STRIKE-SLIP FAULT Slabs of rock are moving horizontally past each other along a fault. This type of fault is produced by twisting and tearing of layers of rock. The San Andreas Fault is an example of a strike-slip fault.

force on them is too great. A break in rocks along which the rocks have moved is called a **fault**.

What do you think would happen if rocks are squeezed together from opposite sides? If pushing forces are applied to rocks, they bend, or fold. But, just as with pulling forces, pushing forces will eventually cause rocks to break. So, pushing forces also create faults in rocks. You can see the effect of these pushing forces in the drawing of the reverse fault on page B64.

Movement Along Faults

Forces may continue to be applied to slabs of rock that contain faults. The forces, which may be either up-and-down or sideways, may continue for many years. The three drawings on page B64 show examples of the main kinds of movement along faults. In time, the forces on the rocks become so great that the slabs overcome the friction that has held them together. Then the rock slabs move violently along the fault.

Earthquakes and Faults

Imagine that your two hands are the two rock walls on either side of a fault. Picture rubbing your hands together when they are in soapy water. Then picture rubbing them together when they are dry. Sometimes the movement of rocks along a fault is quick and smooth, like the rubbing together of soap-covered hands. But at other times, as with dry hands rubbed together, the movement can be slow and rough. As the movement causes rocks to lock and bend, energy builds up in the rocks, much as energy builds up in a flexed wooden stick. When the energy in the rocks is released, an earthquake occurs.

You know that an earthquake is a vibration of the Earth produced by the quick release of this stored energy. The point at which an earthquake begins is the **focus** of the earthquake. Most earthquakes begin below the surface. The point on Earth's surface directly above the focus is called the **epicenter** (ep′ə sen tər) of the earthquake.

Earthquakes can begin anywhere from about 5 km (about 3 mi) to 700 km (about 430 mi) below Earth's surface. Scientists have found that most earthquakes are shallow—they occur within 60 km (about 35 mi) of the surface. The most destructive earthquakes seem to be the shallow ones. The focus of the 1906 San Francisco earthquake was no deeper than about 15 km (about 9 mi).

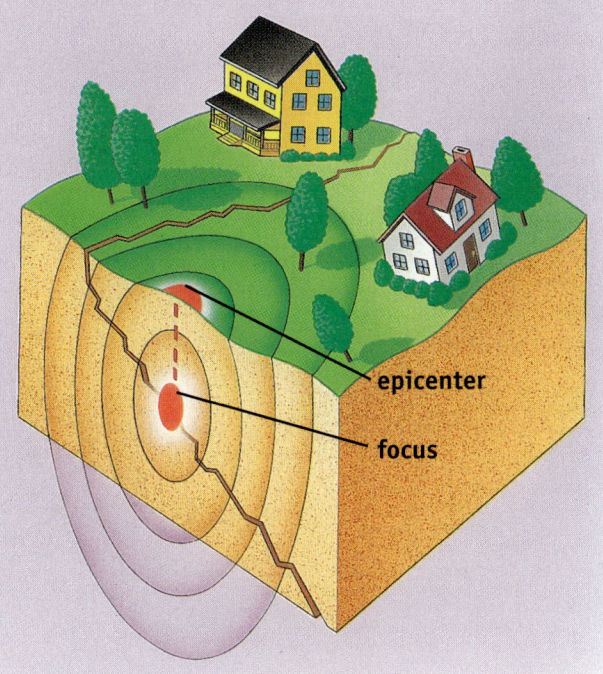

Earthquake Focus and Epicenter

Waves are sent out in all directions from the focus of the earthquake. Notice that the epicenter is the spot on the surface of Earth that lies directly above the focus. ▼

Earthquakes Around the World

When earthquake locations are plotted on a world map, patterns emerge. From the map on page B17 you can see that earthquakes occur along certain belts, or zones. Do these zones look familiar? They should! Most earthquakes occur along tectonic plate boundaries. Many occur near the edges of the Pacific Ocean.

Japan, the western United States, Chile, and parts of Central America are just a few of the areas around the edges of the Pacific Ocean that experience earthquakes.

Where do most earthquakes occur in the United States? Even without looking at a map, you probably could have guessed that most earthquakes in the United States happen in California. Now look closely at the map on page B17. Some earthquakes have occurred in the eastern part of the country—far away from the San Andreas Fault. Is your area at risk for an earthquake? Although most earthquakes occur in California, earthquakes are possible anywhere in this country. What is the risk that your state or surrounding states will experience an earthquake?

Earthquake Waves

Have you ever stood in a pool, lake, or ocean and felt water waves break against your body? Have you ever "done the wave" at a sporting event? What do all waves have in common? A wave is a

Scientists and other professionals constantly seek ways to minimize risks and protect lives threatened by earthquakes. While they have developed and applied many progressive methods of accomplishing their goals, earthquakes continue to claim lives and property, often with little warning.

Earthquakes are a result of sin in the world; therefore, they will continue to threaten people. After Jesus returns to end the world, earthquakes will never again threaten us. Thanks to Jesus, who removes all sin, we will live forever in safety, comfort, and happiness.

rhythmic disturbance that carries energy. The energy released by an earthquake travels in all directions from the earthquake's focus. There are three kinds of earthquake waves: P waves, S waves, and L waves. The drawings below show how these waves differ. ■

Earthquakes can severely damage property. ▶

P WAVES P waves move out in all directions from the earthquake focus. The primary waves push and pull the rocks causing them to vibrate in the same direction in which the wave is traveling.

S WAVES S waves move out in all directions from the earthquake focus. The secondary waves cause the rocks to move at right angles to the direction in which the wave is traveling.

L WAVES When the P and S waves punch into Earth's surface, they cause the formation of L waves or surface waves. L waves move along the surface causing rocks to move up and down. These are the most destructive earthquake waves.

INVESTIGATION 2

1. Describe and make drawings of the changes taking place in Earth's crust during an earthquake. Explain the forces that caused these changes.

2. What is the connection between a fault and the production of an earthquake? Give a well-known example of such a connection.

B67

INVESTIGATION 3

HOW ARE EARTHQUAKES LOCATED AND MEASURED?

The newscaster read, "The earthquake last night in Prince William Sound, Alaska, measured 8.4 on the Richter scale. It was a BIG one!" What tools and methods do scientists use to measure how strong an earthquake is or where it began?

Activity

Shake It Harder!

The energy of an earthquake is measured with a device called a seismograph. In this activity you'll build a working model of a seismograph and then test how it works as you create your own small "earthquake."

MATERIALS
- string
- chair
- metric ruler
- 2 heavy books
- masking tape
- fine-point marker
- table
- shelf paper (2 m long)
- Science Notebook

SAFETY
Be careful not to push or shake the chair off the tabletop while doing this activity.

Procedure

1. Tightly wrap several lengths of string around the seat of a chair in two places (about 10 cm apart), as shown on page B69.

2. Tightly wrap string around two heavy books in two places (about 6 cm from each end of the books).

3. Tape a fine-point marker to one of the short edges of the books. The tip of the marker should hang about 3–4 cm below the edges of the books.

4. Place a length of shelf paper on the top of a table. Place the chair with the string wrapped around the seat on the table, above the shelf paper. Make sure the legs of the chair don't touch the shelf paper.

Steps 1–4

5. Using string, suspend the books from the chair so that the tip of the marker just touches the surface of the shelf paper. Make sure that the books are parallel to the paper.

6. You have just built a simple seismograph. You'll use it to measure an "earthquake" that you'll create by gently shaking the table from side to side. The shelf paper will become the seismogram, or record of the earthquake.

7. **Predict** what will be shown on the seismogram if you shake the table gently. **Record** your predictions in your *Science Notebook*.

8. Place your hands against the side of the table and gently shake it as another member of your group slowly pulls the paper under the pen.

9. Repeat step 8. This time, shake the table a little harder (move the table farther but not faster).

Analyze and Conclude

1. How did your prediction in step 7 compare with what actually happened?

2. How did changing the energy with which you shook the table change the seismogram? How did the record on the seismogram for the first "earthquake" differ from that for the second "earthquake"?

3. How do you think a real seismograph is like the one you built? How might it be different?

INVESTIGATE FURTHER!

EXPERIMENT

Does the seismograph work as well if you shake the table in the same direction in which the paper is being pulled? What would this mean with a real seismograph? Is there any connection between the length of the strings and the working of the seismograph?

Activity

Locating Earthquakes

The point on Earth's surface directly above the origin of an earthquake is called the epicenter. The location of the epicenter can be found by comparing the travel times of two kinds of energy waves (called P waves and S waves) at different locations.

MATERIALS
- metric ruler
- Earthquake Travel Time graph
- map of the United States
- drawing compass
- *Science Notebook*

Data

The table below shows the times (in Pacific Daylight Saving Time) at which shock waves reached three cities in the United States after the earthquake in California on October 17–18, 1989. You'll use this information to find the exact location of the epicenter of that earthquake.

Procedure

1. In your *Science Notebook*, set up a table like the one shown. For each city, **calculate** the difference in arrival time between the P wave and the S wave. **Record** your results.

City	P Wave Arrival Time (hr: min: sec)	S Wave Arrival Time (hr: min: sec)	Difference in Arrival Time (hr: min: sec)
Tucson, AZ	5:06:35	5:08:50	
Billings, MT	5:07:10	5:10:00	
Houston, TX	5:09:10	5:13:35	

ARRIVAL TIMES OF P WAVES AND S WAVES

2. Place a sheet of paper along the y-axis of the Earthquake Travel Time graph provided by your teacher. On the sheet of paper, mark the time interval between the arrival of the P wave and the S wave in Tucson. For example, if the time difference was 4 minutes, you would make a mark next to "0" and a mark next to "4."

3. Keep the edge of the paper parallel to the *y*-axis. Move the paper to the right until the space between the marks matches the space between the S-wave curve and the P-wave curve.

4. The point on the *x*-axis directly below (or along) the edge of the paper is the distance from Tucson to the epicenter of the quake. **Record** this distance.

5. Repeat steps 2 through 4 for Billings and Houston.

6. On a United States map, use a drawing compass to draw a circle around each city in the chart. Use the calculated distance from the quake as the radius of each circle. The point at which the circles intersect is the epicenter of the October 1989 earthquake.

Step 6

Analyze and Conclude

1. What is the distance from each of the cities to the epicenter?

2. Where was the epicenter of the October 1989 earthquake?

3. What is the lowest number of reporting locations necessary to locate an epicenter? Explain your answer.

4. Compare your results with those of other members of your class. Account for any differences you find.

INVESTIGATE FURTHER!

TAKE ACTION

Contact or visit an office of the U.S. Geological Survey for more information about locating earthquakes. You may write to the U.S. Geological Survey at Distribution Branch, Box 25286, Federal Center, Denver, CO 80225.

Activity
Be an Architect

The competition is stiff! You and your teammates will build an "earthquake-proof" building. Then you will create a mini-earthquake and test your building. Will it remain standing? Which team will have the most earthquake-proof building?

MATERIALS
- several small cardboard boxes
- masking tape
- large aluminum pan
- clay
- sand
- soil
- dowels
- timer with a second hand
- *Science Notebook*

Procedure

1. With other members of your team, **design** a high-rise "building" that will not tip over in an earthquake. The building must be made of cardboard boxes and any other materials, such as clay, sand, soil, and dowels, that your teacher provides for you. You will subject this building to an "earthquake" that you create by shaking your desk or table. **Draw** your design in your *Science Notebook*.

2. With the rest of your class, **design** a standard that describes when a building is considered earthquake-proof. Make sure the standard will clearly separate good designs from poor designs following an earthquake.

3. Construct your building on top of your desk or table.

4. Predict how well your building will withstand an earthquake. **Discuss** your prediction with other members of your group.

Step 1

5. With the rest of your class, determine how long the earthquake will last and how strongly you'll shake the table. Note the length of time the building remains standing during the earthquake. Note whether the building undergoes any kind of damage during the earthquake. Use the standard to determine if your building is earthquake-proof. **Record** all observations.

6. Compare your results with those of other groups of students in your class.

Analyze and Conclude

1. How closely did your results agree with your prediction of how well your building could withstand an earthquake?

2. How did your design compare with those of other teams of students?

3. Which design best stood up to the earthquake? What was important about that design?

INVESTIGATE FURTHER!

EXPERIMENT

After you've had your classroom competition, decide how to improve your design. Redesign, reconstruct, and retest your building. How can you make a tall building earthquake-proof?

The Seismograph

Energy from an earthquake travels outward from the focus in all directions, much in the way that energy is released when a pebble is dropped into a pond. Seismic waves travel at different speeds through Earth's crust and upper mantle. P waves are the fastest; S waves are the slowest. These waves are recorded by an instrument called a **seismograph** (sīz′ mə graf).

One of the earliest seismographs used bronze balls to detect earthquake waves.

This Chinese earthquake detector is known as Chang Heng's seismoscope. This early version of a seismograph was used to detect earthquakes. ▼

The dragons on this Chinese earthquake detector clenched the bronze balls in their mouths. When the ground vibrated, one or more balls fell from the dragons' mouths. The balls landed in the mouths of waiting metal toads around the base of the instrument. The noise the balls made when they reached the toads' mouths alerted people that the ground had shaken. The direction from which the waves came was determined by the direction in which the dragons' empty mouths pointed.

A modern seismograph is a device that generally includes a frame (mounted to bedrock), a weight, a pen, and a rotating drum. You built a model of a seismograph on pages B68 and B69. With seismographs, either up-and-down or side-to-side Earth movements can be measured.

A pendulum seismograph consists of a support frame, a heavy weight to which a pen is attached, and a rotating drum. This type of seismograph measures side-to-side Earth movements. A spring seismograph measures up-and-down Earth movements. The drawings on the facing page show you all the parts of these earthquake-recording devices.

Parts of the Seismograph

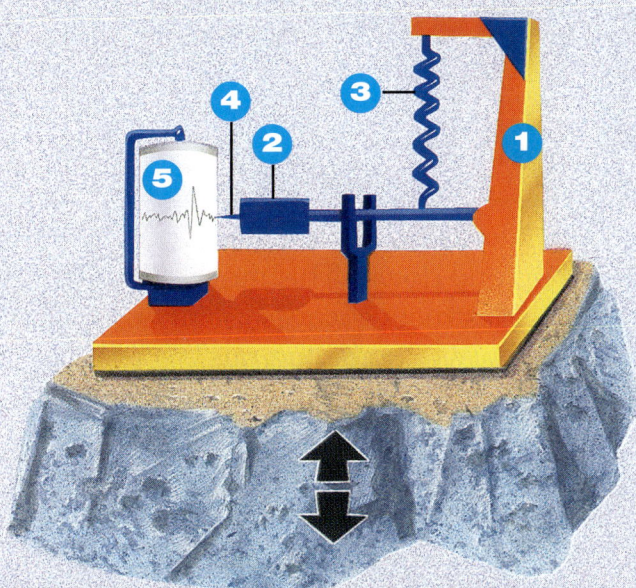

Spring Seismograph

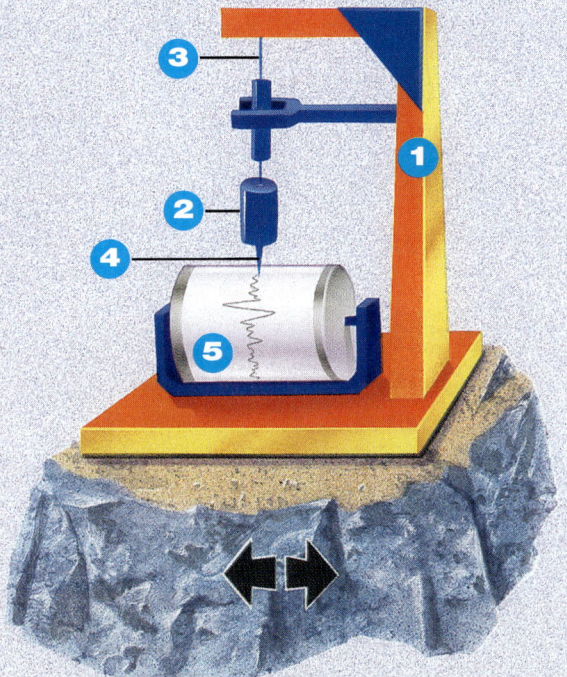

Pendulum Seismograph

1 SUPPORT FRAME
The frame is anchored to solid rock, deep beneath the soil.

2 WEIGHT
The weight of a seismograph is essentially motionless. The magnet reduces the motion of the weight.

3 WIRE OR SPRING
In the spring seismograph, the spring supports the weight. In the pendulum seismograph, the metal wire keeps the weight suspended above the rotating drum.

4 PEN
The pen, which touches the rotating drum, records movements caused by seismic waves.

5 ROTATING DRUM
The drum rotates, or turns, all the time. If there are any movements of Earth, the pen touching the drum records these movements.

INVESTIGATE FURTHER!

RESEARCH

Find out about early seismographs. How are they like modern ones? How are they different from modern ones?

Earthquakes
On the Sea Floor

Tsunamis—What Are They?

You have probably heard the term *tsunami* (tsoo nä'mē). This Japanese word means "harbor wave." You may have heard such waves incorrectly called tidal waves. A **tsunami** has nothing to do with ocean tides. Rather, this seismic sea wave forms when an earthquake occurs on the ocean floor. The earthquake's energy causes the sea floor to move up and down. This movement can produce destructive waves of water. Why are these waves so dangerous?

Most tsunamis are related to the earthquakes that occur around the edges of the Pacific Plate. In these areas massive slabs of rock are being forced down into the mantle. Often, when the plates collide, they lock, allowing energy to build up. Eventually this energy is released as

1 TSUNAMI FORMING
In the open ocean, tsunamis are barely detectable. In deep water, where a tsunami generally forms, the wave's height is only about a meter (about 3 ft).

2 TSUNAMI TRAVELING
In the open ocean, the distance between two crests or troughs can be about 100 km (62.1 mi). A tsunami is often unnoticed in the open ocean, even though it can be traveling close to 800 km/h (496 mph)!

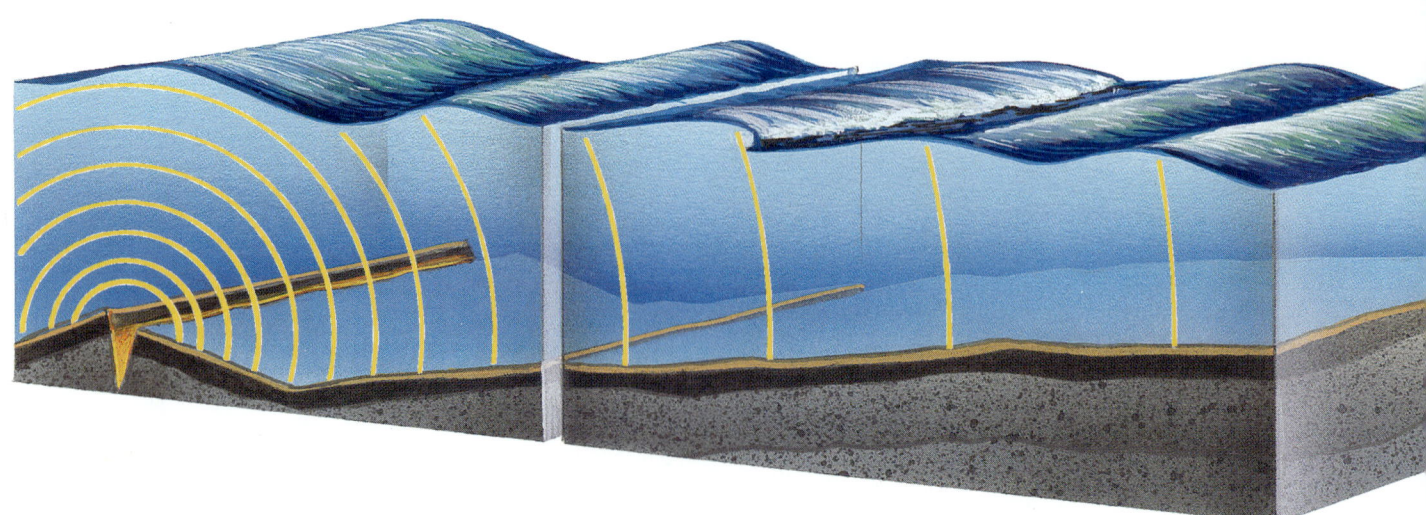

▲ A tsunami

an earthquake, which raises and lowers the nearby ocean floor. This movement sets a tsunami in motion.

Destructive Walls of Water

Most tsunamis are caused by earthquakes. But landslides on the ocean floor and volcanic eruptions can also cause tsunamis. Fortunately, tsunamis only occur about once a year. Study the table on page B78. What was the cause of the 1993 tsunami that began off the coast of Japan?

As with earthquakes, tsunamis cause destruction where they begin as well as along their paths. The tsunami that began with the 1964 Alaskan earthquake, for example, struck the Alaskan coastline and then Vancouver Island in Canada. Waves also struck California and the Hawaiian Islands. The seismic sea waves finally lost their energy at the Japanese coast—over 6,400 km (about 4,000 mi) from their point of origin!

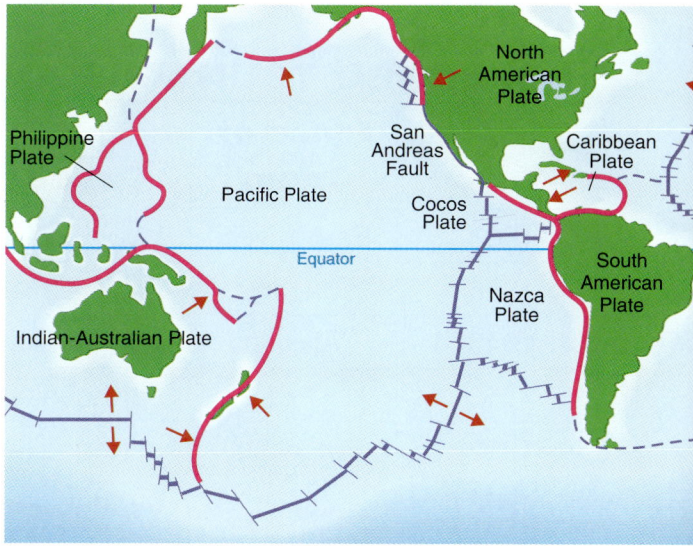

▲ Tsunamis are common along the shores close to the edges of the Pacific Plate.

③ TSUNAMI NEARING SHORE

As the wave makes its way toward shore, it slows down due to friction between the advancing water and the ocean floor. But as the water becomes shallower, the height of the wave increases.

④ TSUNAMI STRIKING SHORE

Close to shore a tsunami can reach a height of tens of meters! On March 2, 1933, a tsunami struck the Japanese island of Honshu. It reached a height of 14 m (46 ft).

SELECTED TSUNAMIS AND THEIR EFFECTS

Year	Place of Origin	Cause	Height of Water (m)	Deaths
1883	East Indies	volcano	>40 m	>36,000
1896	Japan	earthquake	38 m	26,000
1946	Alaska	earthquake	>30 m	164
1960	Chile	earthquake	6 m	144
1992	Indonesia	earthquake	10 m	71,000
1993	Japan	earthquake	32 m	120

Predicting Tsunamis

Unlike earthquakes and volcanic eruptions, some tsunamis can be predicted. In 1946 the Tsunami Warning System was established to forewarn people in the areas surrounding the Pacific Ocean of these destructive events.

There are two tsunami warning centers in the United States. One center is near Honolulu, Hawaii; the other is just north of Anchorage, in Palmer, Alaska. Scientists at these centers use satellites to gather seismic data from more than 20 countries that border the Pacific Ocean. If earthquakes registering more than about 6.5 on the Richter scale are found, warnings are sent to other centers.

Recall that in the open ocean, tsunamis are hardly detectable at the surface of the water. So in addition to the warning centers, scientists with the National Oceanic and Atmospheric Administration are studying the usefulness of tsunami sensors that rest on the ocean floor. These devices look promising. In water 4,000 to 5,000 m deep, the sensors can detect a change in sea level of less than a millimeter!

Tsunami sensors are flexible metal tubes that are weighted down on the ocean floor. Each tube measures the mass of the water column above it. When a wave passes over the tube, the mass of the water column increases, causing the tube to straighten. After the wave has passed, the tube coils up again. The straightening and coiling of the tubes record changes in water pressure—and the presence of large waves. Such changes can show the presence of tsunamis. ■

Huge waves from a tsunami strike the shore. ▼

Designing For Survival

 Much of the damage done during an earthquake is caused by the earthquake's L waves. Recall that these waves move in two directions—up and down and back and forth. These destructive waves cause the foundations of most buildings to move with the passing waves. The buildings themselves, however, tend to resist the movements.

Because of the damage earthquakes can do, building codes in the western United States and in other earthquake-prone areas of the world have been

CONVENTIONAL FOUNDATION With this foundation, the ground movement is exaggerated on upper floors. The building "drifts," and a lot of damage occurs. Upper floors can collapse onto lower floors.

EARTHQUAKE-RESISTANT FOUNDATION This foundation is built of steel and rubber around columns with lead cores. Since the frame is flexible, the floors can move from side to side, and the building isn't badly damaged.

Pillars such as this one support the building and flex during an earthquake. ▶

changed. The new codes deal with the design of new buildings that will help to withstand earthquakes. The building codes also suggest ways to prevent damage in older buildings. Drawings in this resource show some ways that structures are strengthened against earthquakes. ■

Damage to the Golden Gate Freeway, following an earthquake in California in 1989. ▼

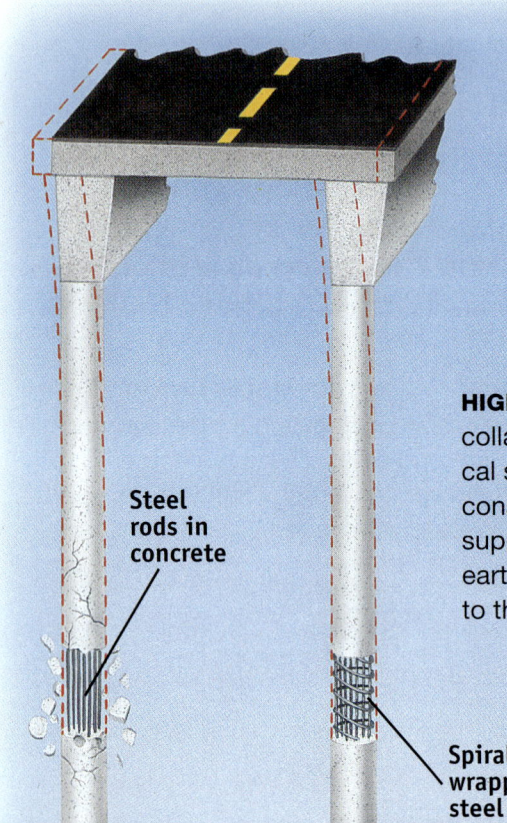

Steel rods in concrete

Spiral-wrapped steel rods in concrete

HIGHWAY SUPPORT The column at the left will probably collapse in an earthquake. The column at the right has vertical steel rods that are spiral-wrapped in steel. This kind of construction could prevent collapse during a quake. Blocks supporting the columns should be able to move with the earthquake. At the same time, they must be firmly anchored to the columns.

INVESTIGATION 3

1. Compare the effects of an earthquake in which the focus is under the ocean with one in which the focus is under the land.

2. Nearly everyone knows that earthquakes can be dangerous. Explain why some people still choose to live in earthquake-prone areas.

REFLECT & EVALUATE

WORD POWER

aftershock
earthquake
epicenter
fault
focus
magnitude
Richter scale
seismograph
tsunami

 On Your Own
Write a definition for each term in the list.

 With a Partner
Mix up the letters of each term in the list. Provide a clue for each term and challenge your partner to unscramble the terms.

Draw a diagram that shows one way an earthquake is produced. Label each part of your diagram.

Analyze Information

What is shown in the drawing below? Describe what might occur at such a location.

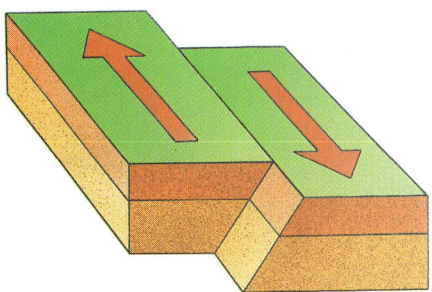

Assess Performance

Work with two or three of your classmates to design and build a model that shows how tsunamis are produced. Describe what each part of your model represents.

Problem Solving

1. Why are strong earthquakes more common on the west coast of the United States than on the east coast?

2. The 1993 earthquake near Los Angeles registered about 7.5 on the Richter scale. The 1964 earthquake near Anchorage, Alaska, registered 8.4 on the Richter scale. Compare the energy released in the two earthquakes.

3. Assume that you live in an area that experiences strong earthquakes. What could you do to protect yourself and your family during an earthquake? What could you do to prepare for an earthquake?

CHAPTER 4

VOLCANOES

Never trust a volcano! Millions of people live near active volcanoes. And over the past 20 years, sudden volcanic eruptions have killed over 28,000 people. Volcanoes have always been unpredictable and dangerous.

Predicting Eruptions

What if scientists could predict the onset of a volcanic eruption? Think of the lives that could be saved by knowing several days in advance that a volcano is about to blow! Barry Voight, a geoscientist at Pennsylvania State University, has come up with a way of making such a prediction.

Voight and his science team have placed monitoring devices on the slopes of Merapi, on the island of Java in Indonesia. Merapi is an active volcano that erupted suddenly in 1930, taking the lives of 1,300 people.

The team uses the monitoring devices and a laser to continually measure the distance to the volcano. Team members who are kilometers away can detect movements of about 2 cm on the surface of the volcano. What do you think such movement on the surface of the volcano tells geoscientists?

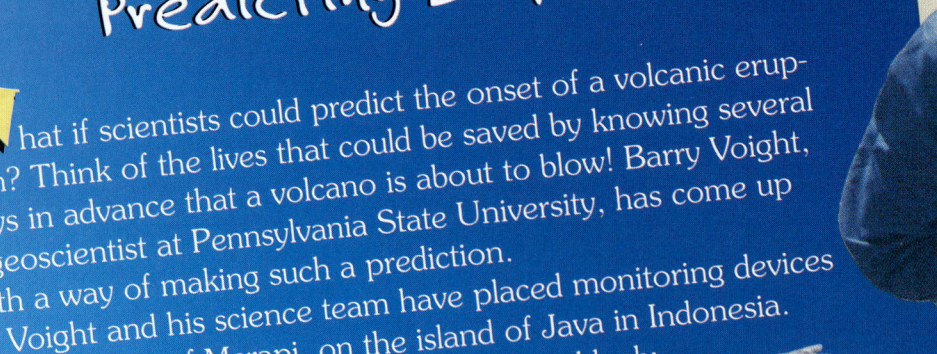

Coming Up

Where Do Volcanoes Occur, and How Are They Classified?
.... B84

How Do Volcanic Eruptions Affect Earth?
.... B94

In What Other Places Can Volcanoes Occur?
.... B100

◀ Barry Voight and another geoscientist installing a monitoring device on Merapi

Investigation 1

Where Do Volcanoes Occur, and How Are They Classified?

Volcanoes form when magma erupts from an opening in Earth's surface. Where are most volcanoes found in relation to tectonic plates? In this investigation you'll locate volcanoes and find out how they are compared and classified.

Activity
Worldwide Eruptions

You can plot volcanic eruptions in the news to figure out how they relate to Earth's tectonic plates.

MATERIALS
- wall map of the world
- table of eruptions
- world almanac
- red map pins
- yellow map pins
- map of tectonic plates
- *Science Notebook*

Procedure

1. Break up into teams of researchers. Each team will research the location of active volcanoes during a six-month period in the last two years. Your teacher will make sure that no two groups are researching the same six months. The goal of all the teams is to collect news articles about active volcnoes throughout the world during the past two years.

2. In your *Science Notebook*, **record** the date of each eruption, the name of the volcano, and the location. Also list whether each volcano is on a spreading ridge, on a plate margin near a descening plate, on a transform fault, or in the middle of a plate. **Record** how each volcano erupted: Was it a quiet lava flow, did it explode, or did it belch heavy clouds of ash?

Step 3

| SELECTED MAJOR VOLCANIC ERUPTIONS ||||
Date	Volcano	Area	Death Toll
79	Vesuvius	Pompeii, Italy	16,000
1169	Etna	Sicily, Italy	15,000
1669	Etna	Sicily, Italy	20,000
1793	Unzen Island	Japan	50,000
1883	Krakatoa	Java, Indonesia	36,000
1902	Pelee	St. Pierre, Martinique	28,000
1919	Kelud	Java, Indonesia	5,500
1980	Saint Helens	Washington State	62
1985	Nevado del Ruis	Armero, Colombia	22,000
1991	Pinatubo	Luzon, Philippines	200
1993	Mayon	Legazpi, Philippines	67

3. Use a world almanac to find the sites of major volcanic activity over the last 500 years.

4. Tack a large world map to your bulletin board. Using the data gathered by the teams, the data from the almanac, and the data in the table, mark the locations of volcanoes. Stick a red map pin on the map at the site of any volcanic eruption; stick a yellow map pin at the site of any active volcano.

5. Throughout the school year, keep adding to your records and to the world map. **Record** new volcanic activity and new eruptions as they occur. Note how the location of volcanoes is related to Earth's tectonic plates.

Analyze and Conclude

1. How many volcanic eruptions did you find in the news during the six months your team researched? What was the total number of eruptions found by your class during the two-year period?

2. Where on tectonic plates were the volcanoes located?

3. Were any of the volcanic eruptions on a mid-ocean spreading ridge? What kind of an eruption did they have?

4. **Hypothesize** about the relationship between volcanic eruptions and Earth's tectonic plates.

INVESTIGATE FURTHER!

RESEARCH

Get a world atlas from the library. Look for islands that are in the same locations as mid-ocean ridges. Find out as much as possible about the islands. Are they volcanic? If they are, what kinds of volcanoes are they?

Volcanoes and Plate Tectonics

Volcanoes

What comes to mind when you hear the word *volcano*? Probably you think of a large mountain spewing red-hot lava and other material high into Earth's atmosphere. Some volcanoes are, in fact, towering mountains that throw rock, molten material, dust, and ash into the air. But a **volcano** is *any* opening in Earth's crust through which hot gases, rocks, and melted material erupt.

Have you ever opened a can of cold soda that has been dropped on the floor? Soda probably squirted into the air above the can. More soda bubbled out and flowed down the side of the can. Now, what do you think would happen if you opened a can of warm soda that had been dropped? The release of the warm soda from the can would be even *more* violent. Volcanoes are like cans of soda. Some erupt violently; others have more gentle eruptions.

The high temperatures and pressures deep within Earth can cause rock to melt. This melted rock is called **magma**. Because it's less dense than surrounding material, magma slowly makes its way toward Earth's surface. As it travels toward the surface, the magma melts surrounding material to form a central pipe, which is connected to the magma chamber. Eventually this hot melted material escapes through an opening in the crust called a volcanic vent. When magma reaches Earth's surface, it is called **lava**.

When a volcano erupts, different kinds of materials can be spewed out. Lava is magma that reaches Earth's surface. When lava flows from a volcano, its temperature can be higher than 1,100°C

Structure of an erupting volcano ▼

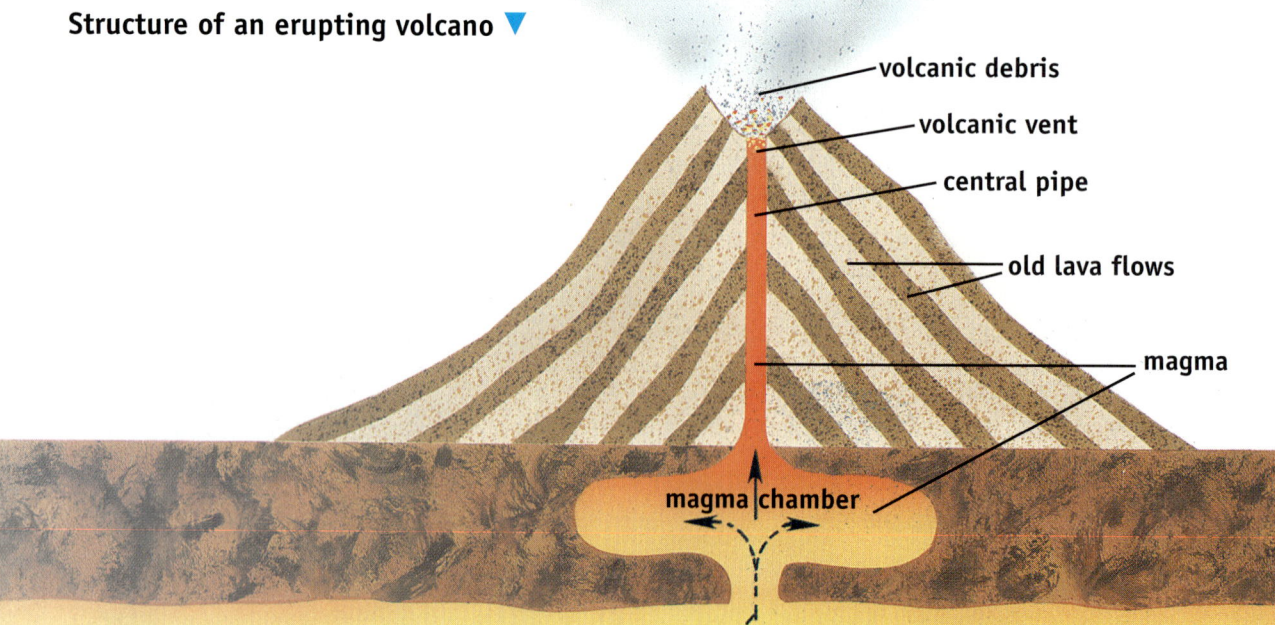

- volcanic debris
- volcanic vent
- central pipe
- old lava flows
- magma
- magma chamber
- mantle

▲ Mount Tolbackik erupts in former U.S.S.R.

▲ Mount Kilauea erupts in Hawaii.

(2,012°F)! Solid volcanic debris includes bombs, cinders, ash, and dust. Bombs are volcanic rocks the size of a baseball or bigger. Large bombs can weigh nearly 100 metric tons (1,100 short tons). Volcanic dust and ash, on the other hand, range in size from about 0.25 mm to 0.5 mm (0.009 in. to 0.02 in.) in diameter and can be carried hundreds or thousands of kilometers from a volcano.

Volcanism and Plate Tectonics

Like earthquakes, volcanoes occur along certain plate boundaries. From the map to the right, you can see that many volcanoes occur around the edges of the Pacific Plate in an area that scientists have named the Ring of Fire. Between 500 and 600 active volcanoes make up the region called the Ring of Fire.

Volcanoes in the Ring of Fire were formed in subduction zones. In a subduction zone, plates collide and one plate descends below the other. The descending plate melts as it descends slowly into the mantle. The magma then rises to the surface, forming a chain of volcanoes near the boundaries of the two plates.

Lava also erupts at divergent plate boundaries. Find the purple faults on the map. These indicate divergent plate boundaries, where new ocean floor is formed as magma wells up between the separating plates.

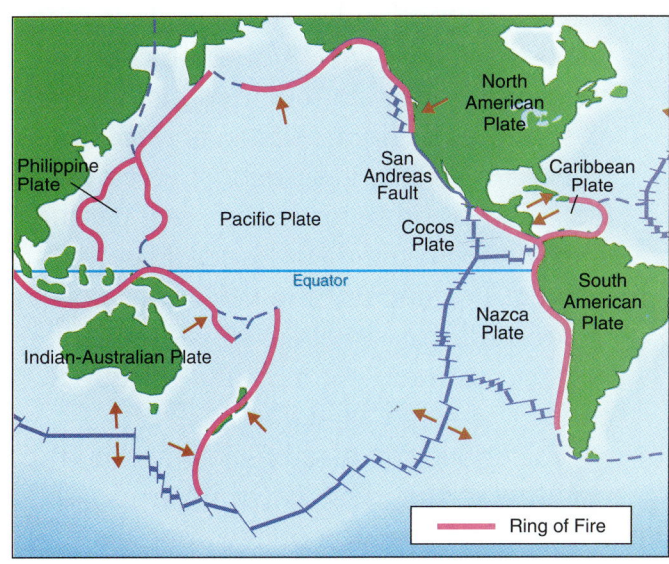

▶ Hundreds of active volcanoes are located in a region known as the Ring of Fire.

CINDER-CONE VOLCANO Paricutín, in Mexico (*left*); drawing of a cinder-cone volcano. Notice the very steep slopes (*below*).

Classifying Volcanoes

Volcanoes can be classified in different ways. One classification system is based on how often eruptions occur. An *active* volcano is one that erupts constantly. Some volcanoes that make up the Hawaiian Islands are active volcanoes. *Intermittent* volcanoes are those that erupt on a regular basis. Mount Vesuvius, in Italy, is an intermittent volcano. Volcanoes that haven't erupted in a while but could erupt in the near future are called *dormant* volcanoes. Mount Lassen, in the California Cascade Range, is a dormant volcano. Volcanoes that have not erupted in recorded history are classified as *extinct* volcanoes. Mount Kenya, in Africa, is an extinct volcano. Go back to the records you have been keeping from the "Worldwide Eruptions" activity. For each of the volcanoes you have listed, classify it as active, intermittent, or dormant. Would any of the volcanoes be listed as extinct?

Volcanoes can also be classified by the way they erupt. The way they erupt depends on the type of lava that is spewed from the volcano. One kind of lava is highly fluid. Fluid lava erupts quietly. Another kind of lava is very sticky. This sticky lava erupts violently. The kind of lava that pours from the volcano affects the shape of the volcano that is formed. These two pages show the main kinds of volcanoes—cinder cone, shield, and composite-cone—which are based on their shapes.

Cinder-Cone Volcanoes

Cinders are sticky bits of volcanic material that are about the size of peas. A **cinder-cone volcano** is one made of layers of cinders. The cinder cone forms around a central vent containing magma.

These volcanoes are produced by explosive eruptions. Generally, cinder cones are small volcanoes, less than 300 m (984 ft) tall, with very steep slopes. There is usually a bowl-shaped crater. Cinder cones often form in groups. Paricutín, which is a dormant volcano just west of Mexico City, and Stromboli, a very active volcano off the coast of Italy, are cinder-cone volcanoes.

Shield Volcanoes

Shield volcanoes form when lava flows quietly from a crack in Earth's crust. What kind of lava do you think makes up shield volcanoes? Because of the composition of the lava, shield volcanoes are large mountains that have very gentle slopes. Mauna Loa, the largest volcano on Earth, is a shield volcano. Mauna Loa, which is a part of the island of Hawaii, towers over 4,100 m (13,448 ft) above sea level. The rest—about 5,000 m (about 16,400 ft)—of this vast volcano is below the waters of the Pacific Ocean.

COMPOSITE-CONE VOLCANO Mount Fuji, in Japan (*top*); a drawing of a composite volcano. This type of volcano has steep slopes near its top and gentle slopes near its base (*bottom*).

SHIELD VOLCANO Mauna Loa (*top*); a drawing of a shield volcano. Notice the very gentle slopes (*bottom*).

Composite-Cone Volcanoes

Composite-cone volcanoes are those that form when explosive eruptions of sticky lava alternate with quieter eruptions of volcanic rock bits. Composite cones are also called stratovolcanoes. A composite cone has very steep slopes near its top but gentle slopes closer to its base.

Composite cones are the most explosive of all volcanoes. Their eruptions often occur without warning and can be very destructive. Mount Vesuvius, a once-dormant volcano in Italy, erupted in A.D. 79 and killed thousands of residents in Pompeii and nearby cities. This same volcano still erupts from time to time. You will learn more about Mount Vesuvius on page B92. ■

Surtsey

▲ Surtsey, a young volcanic island, begins to form.

▲ Living things begin to populate the new island of Surtsey.

In 1963 off the southern coast of Iceland, a sailor on a fishing boat observed a pillar of smoke in the distance. He ran to alert his captain that he had spotted a ship that was on fire. Soon the odor of sulfur filled the salty air. The crew of the fishing vessel measured the water's temperature. It was much warmer than usual. The captain soon informed his crew that the smoke in the distance wasn't a burning ship at all. The smoke and fire signaled that one of the youngest volcanic islands on Earth was beginning to rise from the icy waters. Named after the Norse god Surtur, a giant who bore fire from the sea, Surtsey started to form as lava spewed from a long, narrow rift on the ocean floor.

Within a couple of weeks, an island nearly half a kilometer wide rose about 160 m (528 ft) above the water's surface. And after spewing lava, gases, and bits of rock debris from its vent for almost four years, Surtsey became inactive—geologically, that is. Scientists then had Surtsey designated as a nature preserve in order to study how living things inhabit a newly formed area. Surtsey is now home to 27 species of plants and animals. Among the first organisms to inhabit the island were plants called sea rockets. Seeds from faraway places were carried to the island by birds and the wind. A few varieties of grasses and mosses painted colorful splotches against the black rock of the island. In the spring, seals now crawl up the black beaches to have their young.

Few people are allowed to visit this volcanic island. The Surtsey Research Council allows only a few scientists to visit the island to study the living things growing there. The impact of the few human beings that visit the island is very small. Only natural forces, such as wind and rain, have acted upon the land and its inhabitants. Erosion has shrunk the island to about three fourths of its original size. Unless it erupts again, the effects of wind and water will eventually make Surtsey disappear. ■

INVESTIGATE FURTHER!

RESEARCH

In 1973 a volcanic eruption occurred on Heimaey, an island off the southern coast of Iceland. Find out how much destruction was done as a result of this eruption. Look also for ways that the eruption benefited the island. Compare the eruption on Heimaey with the eruption on Surtsey.

SCIENCE AND FAITH

God designed a recovery process for places devastated by sin's destructive forces. The island of Surtsey is a good example of God's loving care for His creation.

What other examples of God's recreative power can you see in events around you?

Mount Vesuvius

Time Capsule

Over the past 2,000 years or so, Mount Vesuvius, a cinder-cone volcano in southern Italy, has erupted about 50 times. Before its eruption in A.D. 79, Vesuvius was a picturesque cone-shaped mountain, towering over 1,000 m (3,300 ft) above the Bay of Naples. Vineyards and orchards crept nearly halfway up the mountain's slopes. Most historians think that very few people knew that Vesuvius was a volcano—until the terrible morning of August 24 in the year A.D. 79.

During the early morning hours of that day, an earthquake rumbled through the area. By early afternoon loud thunder ripped through the air, and red-hot ash rained from the skies. Within 24 hours the twin Roman cities of Pompeii and Herculaneum were destroyed.

In Pompeii more than 2,000 people were buried beneath about 5 to 8 m (16 to 26 ft) of volcanic ash. Because the ash was so hot and fell so quickly, it preserved many of the city's residents doing what they normally did in their day-to-day lives. By studying the remains of people, animals, utensils, and decorations found in Pompeii, archaeologists have learned a lot about the people who lived at this time. Archaeologists are scientists who study ancient cultures by digging up the evidence of human life from the past.

The city of Herculaneum, which was several kilometers from Pompeii, met its destruction not from the volcanic ash but from a mudflow. A mudflow is a mixture of wet materials that rushes down a mountainside and destroys everything in its path. Volcanologists, or scientists who study volcanoes, think that flowing hot volcanic debris swept over the city and covered it to depths of over 20 m (66 ft)!

The eruption of Mount Vesuvius in A.D. 79 is probably most famous because

Cast of man buried by the eruption of Mount Vesuvius (*far left*); **nuts buried and preserved by the eruption** (*left*)

it perfectly preserved the people and customs of ancient Rome. However, it was not the last nor the worst eruption in the area. In the summer of 1631, earthquakes once again shook the area. By winter, molten rock filled the volcano. On December 16, 1631, ash was spewing from the mountain. By the next day, red-hot lava raced down the volcano's slopes. The destructive toll of this eruption included 15 villages. At least 4,000 people and 6,000 animals died.

Since the 1631 eruption of Mount Vesuvius, the volcano has erupted every 15 to 40 years. The ash and rock fragments have made the soil very fertile. Farmers successfully grow grapes, citrus fruits, carnations, beans, and peas in this region. But the threat of losing it all to the volcano is always there. ■

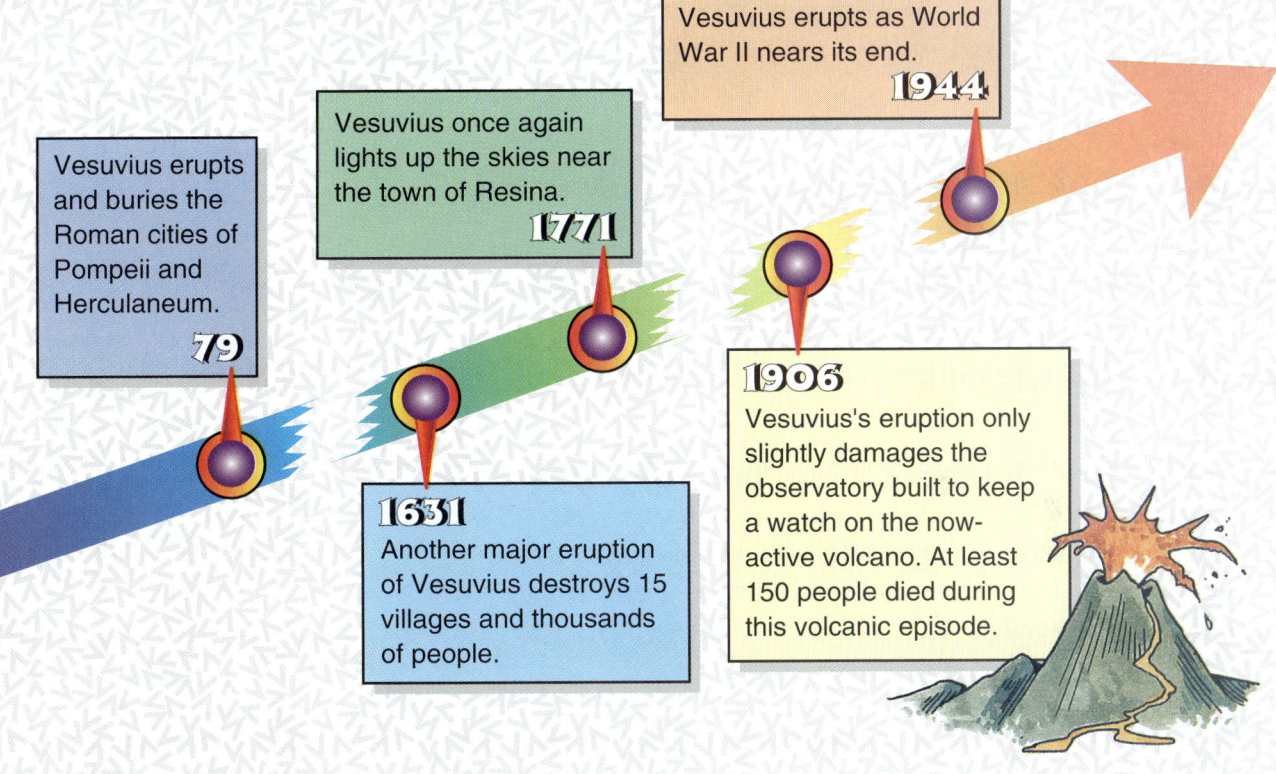

INVESTIGATION 1

1. Describe how most volcanoes form.

2. Make a chart that compares and contrasts cinder cones, shield volcanoes, and composite cones. In your chart, include a sketch of each type of volcano. Label the parts of each volcano.

How Do Volcanic Eruptions Affect Earth?

In March 1980, a strong earthquake rocked Mount St. Helens, in the state of Washington. For the next two months steam and ash blew out. Then in May, the volcano exploded with great violence. In this investigation you'll find out what you can expect before, during, and after a volcanic eruption.

Activity

Volcanoes You Can Eat!

How is an erupting volcano like a pot of cooking oatmeal? Volcanoes erupt because liquids, solids, and gases are forced out of a hole, called a vent. Can you see a vent in a pot of oatmeal?

MATERIALS
- goggles
- measuring cup
- quick oats
- saucepan
- water
- hot plate
- mixing spoon
- oven mitt
- Science Notebook

SAFETY
Do this activity only under the direct supervision of your teacher. Wear goggles.

Procedure

1. Use the measuring cup to **measure** quick oats and water.

2. Put the oats and water into a saucepan and mix together.

3. Place the saucepan on a hot plate and set the hot plate on *Medium High*.

Step 4

4. After the hot plate has warmed up, stir the oats and water constantly for one minute.

5. Carefully **observe** the top surface of the oatmeal as it cooks. **Record** your observations in your *Science Notebook*.

6. After one minute, remove the oatmeal from the heat and turn off the hot plate.

Analyze and Conclude

1. What did you observe on the surface of the oatmeal as it cooked?

2. How is cooking oatmeal like an erupting volcano? How is it different?

UNIT PROJECT LINK

Have you ever dreamed of living on your own island paradise? Locate the Ring of Fire on a map and identify those islands created by volcanic activity. Predict where future volcanic islands might rise out of the ocean; indicate these areas on your map. Draw a small picture of your island paradise and describe where you think your island will emerge.

Mount Pinatubo

Mount Pinatubo, which towers over 1,900 m (6,232 ft) above sea level, is only one of about 13 active volcanoes in the Philippines. This volcano, which is located on the island of Luzon, is a composite cone. At times when it erupts, there is a sticky lava flow. At other times a combination of ash, dust, and other volcanic rock bits erupt from the volcano.

Mount Pinatubo and the other volcanoes in the Philippines formed as a result of tectonic activity. The Philippine Islands are a part of the Ring of Fire.

You already know that at some convergent plate boundaries, one oceanic plate collides with another oceanic plate. At such boundaries, one plate goes down deep into Earth's mantle. As the plate is dragged down, it bends, and a deep canyon, or ocean trench, forms. As this oceanic plate descends into the asthenosphere, parts of the plate melt, forming magma. The magma then rises and forms a chain of volcanoes called **island arcs**. The islands that make up the Philippines are a mature island arc system that formed long ago when two oceanic plates collided.

There She Blows!

After being dormant for over six centuries, Mount Pinatubo began to erupt in mid-June of 1991. As the eruption began, brilliant lightning bolts colored the skies above the volcano. Within minutes, these same skies were black because of the enormous amounts of ash, dust, and gases that spurted from the mountain. Scientists estimate that the mountain's violent eruption had a force equal to that of 2,000 to 3,000 exploding atomic bombs! The ash clouds produced by the eruption polluted the air so much that astronauts out in space in the space shuttle could not get a clear view of Earth's surface!

This period of volcanic activity lasted for several months and stopped in early September 1991. The first eruption

Two oceanic plates colliding at their boundaries ▼

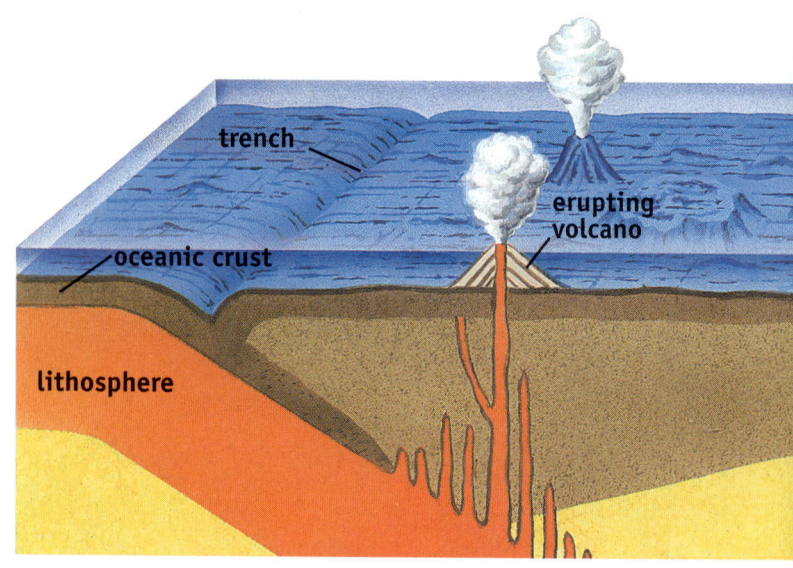

destroyed about 42,000 houses and nearly 100,000 acres of farmland. Over 900 people died. Much of the damage and many of the deaths were caused by flowing mud and hot volcanic material. Also, masses of gas, ash, and igneous rock called pumice covered many villages at and near the base of Mount Pinatubo.

The cause of the 1991 eruption of Mount Pinatubo is not completely understood. It is likely that many months prior to the eruption, magma began forcing its way up through the lithosphere. Slowly the magma made its way toward the surface. As it snaked along its path, the magma increased temperatures and pressures beneath the mountain. In some places the magma crept into cracks in the bedrock, causing the bedrock to swell. On June 15, 1991, the mountain erupted, sending clouds of gases and tons of lava to Earth's surface.

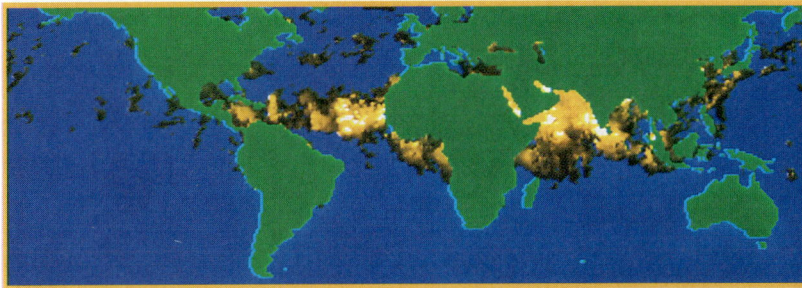
JUNE 19-27, 1991

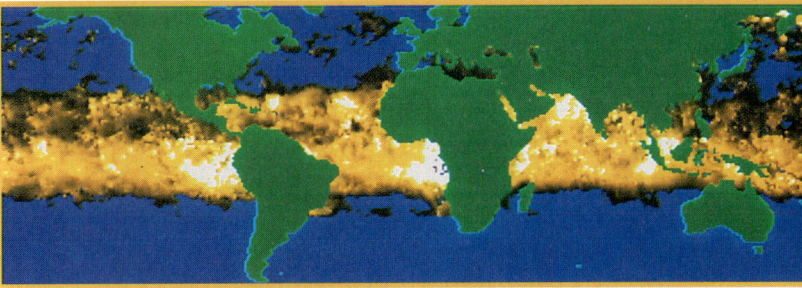
AUGUST 8-14, 1991

▲ Effect of the eruption of Mount Pinatubo. The yellow band shows how volcanic debris travels around the globe and extends over time.

Mount Pinatubo's Warning Signs

Earthquakes and volcanoes are more common in some parts of the world than in others. Both are closely related to the movements of tectonic plates. Scientists monitor earthquake- and volcano-prone areas for changes. But the exact time of volcanic eruptions can be difficult to predict accurately. Fortunately, in the case of Mount Pinatubo, the mountain "cooperated." There were many warnings of its explosive 1991 eruption.

First, there was an earthquake that shook the area in July 1990. There is

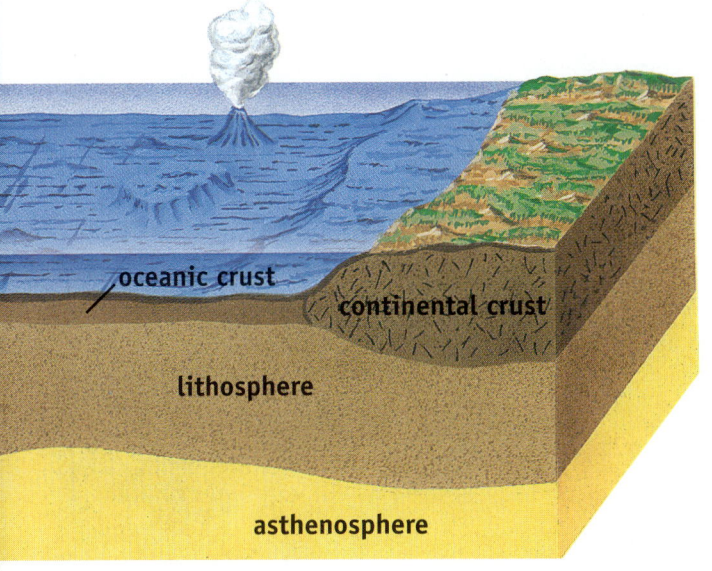

INVESTIGATE FURTHER!

RESEARCH

Find out about another famous volcano in the Philippines called Mount Mayon. Where is it located? How do you think this volcano formed? When did it last erupt? What kind of volcano is it?

B97

◀ Clouds and gases rise from Mount Pinatubo.

often a relationship between earthquake activity and later volcanic activity. In April 1991, small clouds of smoke and ash were forced from cracks along the mountain's slopes. These clouds prompted earth scientists from the Philippines and the United States to more closely monitor the majestic Pinatubo.

Watching Pinatubo

Two kinds of measuring devices—seismometers and tiltmeters—were put into place near the mountain and then connected to computers. A **seismometer** is an instrument that detects Earth's movements. These movements can indicate that a volcano is preparing to blow its top! A tiltmeter measures any change in the slope of an area. Installing these devices allowed scientists to note any bulges in the mountain's slopes. Such bulges indicate the presence of magma and/or gases welling up into the volcano. In fact, Mount Pinatubo did bulge before

the 1991 eruption. Its lava dome, a bulge that is produced when sticky lava is slowly squeezed from a volcano's vent, had doubled in size in a little over two months!

Because the volcano gave these warning signs, many lives were saved. For several months before the explosion, scientists explained what the mountain was doing and urged people to leave the area. Over 200,000 people had been safely evacuated before the explosion.

What Goes Up Must Come Down—But When?

Before the eruption, instruments aboard weather satellites monitored the atmosphere above the volcano. These instruments were looking for increases in the amount of sulfur dioxide in the air around the composite cone. About two weeks before the explosion, the amount of sulfur dioxide was ten times what it

Evacuation of people before the eruption of Mount Pinatubo ▶

had been the month before. This increase was another warning that Mount Pinatubo might erupt.

These same instruments measured the amount of sulfur dioxide that had been spewed out into the air during the eruption. About 15 to 20 million tons of this gas blew nearly 40 km (about 25 mi) into the air! This gas combined with other gases in the air and formed a thin layer of sulfuric acid droplets that circled the globe within about three weeks.

Mount Pinatubo, like other active volcanoes, is a source of pollution. The dust, gases, and ash spewed out in 1991 had several effects on Earth and its atmosphere. First, vivid sunsets colored the skies in many places far removed from the Philippines.

Second, the sulfuric acid droplets remained above the planet for a few years following the eruption. The droplets reflected back into space about 2 percent of the Sun's energy that normally reached Earth's surface. This in turn led to a global cooling of about 1°C (1.2°F). This short period of cooling reversed a global warming trend for a short time. The warming

▲ Sunset after the 1991 eruption of Mount Pinatubo

trend is caused by the collection of gases that trap the Sun's heat. This effect, called the greenhouse effect, is the result of natural climatic changes and human activities, such as burning fossil fuels and cutting down forests.

Another effect of the 1991 eruption of Mount Pinatubo is that the 30 to 40 million tons of sulfuric acid added to the air may speed up the breakdown of Earth's ozone layer. The ozone layer in the upper atmosphere protects you and Earth's other inhabitants from harmful solar rays. ■

INVESTIGATION 2

1. Using Mount Pinatubo as your example, explain how volcanic eruptions can have long-term effects on the planet.

2. Describe some of the events that may occur and some measurements that may be taken to alert scientists to a coming volcanic eruption.

In What Other Places Can Volcanoes Occur?

So far, you have learned that volcanoes can occur along mid-ocean ridges and where one tectonic plate is descending under another. In this investigation you'll explore two other kinds of places where volcanoes can occur.

Activity

How Hawaii Formed

Geologists have a hypothesis that magma rising from a large chamber of molten rock—called a hot spot—deep below the Pacific Plate has built the volcanic islands that make up the state of Hawaii. In this activity you'll examine some of their evidence.

MATERIALS
- metric ruler
- map of the Hawaiian Islands, showing volcanoes
- calculator
- *Science Notebook*

What assumption do scientists make when they date material at millions of years old?

Procedure

1. **Measure** the distance between the center of the island of Hawaii and the center of each of the other islands. **Record** this information in your *Science Notebook*. Use the map scale to find out how far apart the centers are.

2. The table on this page tells you the age scientists have ascribed to the rock on each island. **Record** the youngest island and the oldest island.

3. **Make a chart** that shows the age difference between Hawaii and each of the other islands.

THE HAWAIIAN ISLANDS	
Island	Estimated Age of Rock
Maui	1.63 million years
Molokai	1.84 million years
Oahu	2.9 million years
Kauai	5.1 million years
Hawaii	375,000 years
Lanai	1.28 million years
Niihau	5.5 million years
Kahoolawe	1.03 million years

B100

▲ The Hawaiian Islands

Analyze and Conclude

1. Based on your measurements, how far apart are the Hawaiian Islands?

2. Which island is the latest? Which is the earliest?

3. If the hot spot under the islands stayed in the same place and the Pacific Plate moved over it, the hot spot may have created one island after another. In which direction does this show the Pacific Plate moving?

4. Based on the dates of formation of Hawaii and Kauai, what was the speed of the plate's movement?

5. Would you say that the Pacific Plate moves at a nearly constant speed, or does its speed change from time to time? What evidence supports your conclusion?

INVESTIGATE FURTHER!

RESEARCH

Look at a map of Earth's surface features. Observe the northwestward underwater extension of the Hawaiian Islands. Notice that there is an abrupt northward bend where the Hawaiian chain meets the Emperor Seamount chain. What do you think this bend means?

An Island in the Making

Hot Spots

Recall that the theory of plate tectonics states that slabs of Earth's crust and upper mantle move slowly over the planet's surface. Convection currents in the partly melted mantle, or asthenosphere, are thought to drive plate motion.

Most of Earth's volcanoes are found along convergent and divergent plate boundaries. But recently, scientists discovered that volcanoes can also form in the middle of a tectonic plate. **Hot spots** are extremely hot places deep within Earth's mantle. The magma that forms at these spots slowly rises toward the surface because the magma is less dense than the surrounding material. Scientists have evidence that most of the 120 known hot spots don't move. Rather, as a plate moves over a hot spot, the magma wells up and breaks through the crust to form a volcano, as shown in the drawings on this page.

Formation of the Hawaiian Islands

Pele is the mythical goddess of Hawaiian volcanoes. Native legends state that volcanic eruptions along the island chain are caused when the goddess is angry. She supposedly takes her Pa'oa, a magic stick, and pokes it into the ground, unearthing the fires below. The

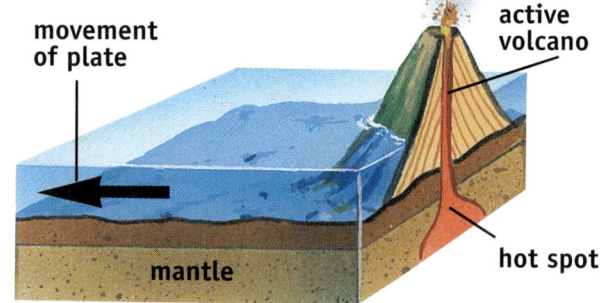

1 As a plate passes over a hot spot, a volcano is formed.

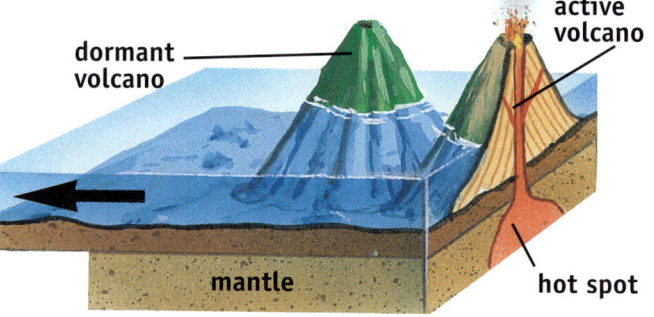

2 When the plate moves, the old volcano becomes inactive and a new volcano forms over the hot spot and becomes active.

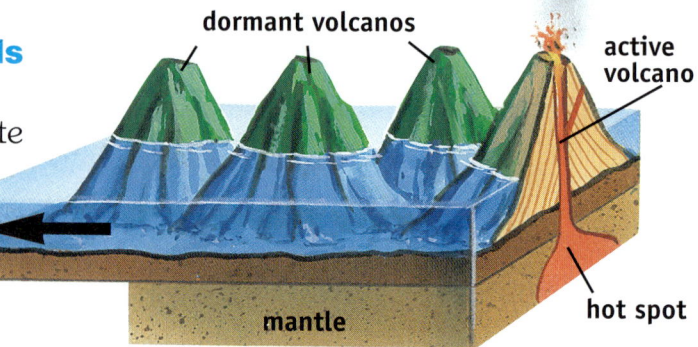

3 The plate keeps moving and the process continues.

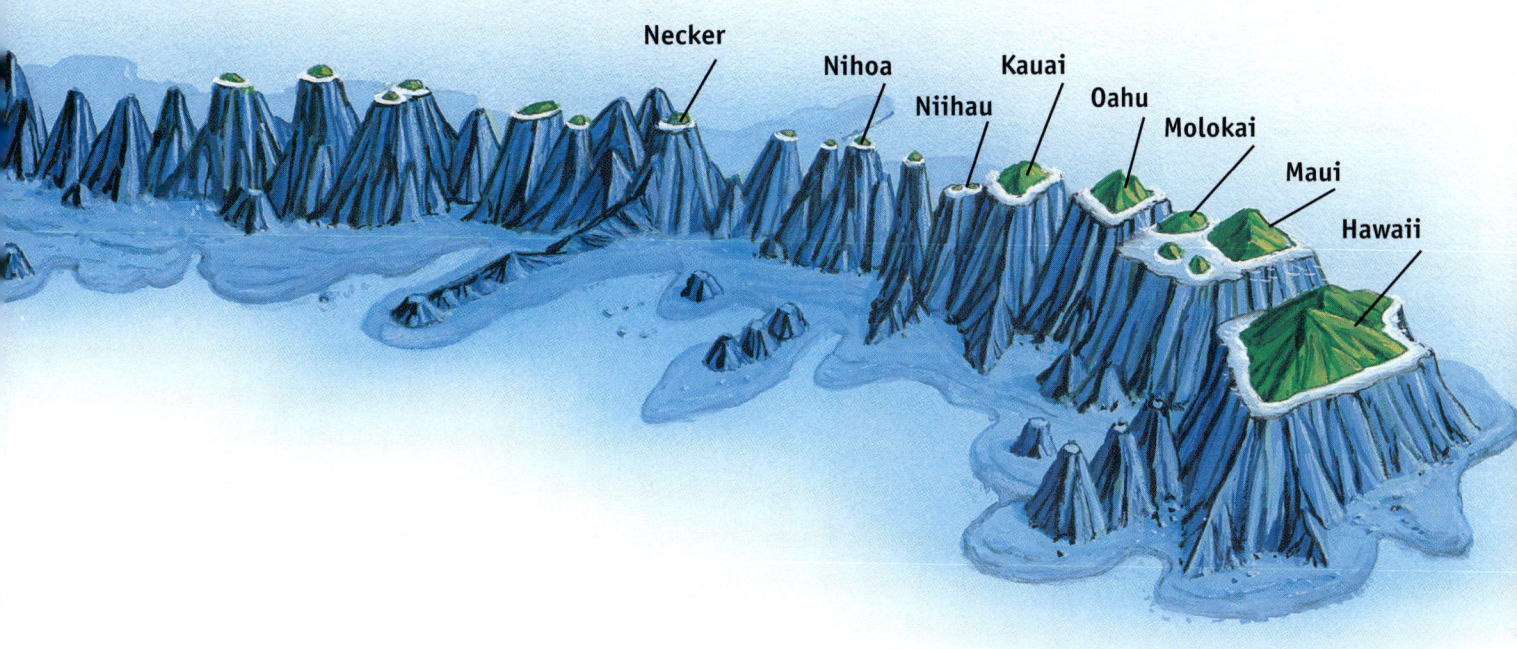

▲ Pele

islands are said to have been formed when Pele and her sister, Namakaokahai, had a bitter argument. As the sisters quarreled, Pele moved from island to island and dug fire pits—the Hawaiian volcanoes themselves. Pele is said to have first used her Pa'oa on Kauai. Then she fled to Oahu, Molokai, Maui, and finally to the "Big Island," Hawaii. Legend says that Pele now lives at the summit of Kilauea on Hawaii. How is this legend similar to the data you worked with in the activity "How Hawaii Formed"?

Scientists have evidence that the Hawaiian Islands formed as the Pacific Plate slowly moved northwestward over a hot spot beneath the Pacific Ocean. A chain of volcanic islands, each developing as the plate moved over the hot spot on the ocean floor, formed over many years. This chain of islands, which is made up of over 80 large volcanoes, is called the

▲ The chain of Hawaiian islands. The islands are the tips of volcanoes that have slowly built up from underwater eruptions.

Hawaiian Ridge–Emperor Seamount Chain. A seamount is a volcanic peak that rises at least 1,000 m (3,300 ft) above the ocean floor. The Emperor Seamounts, which now lie beneath the ocean's surface, were once islands. They have been eroded by wind and waves.

The Hawaiian Ridge–Emperor Seamount Chain stretches northwest from the island of Hawaii and then north to the Aleutian Trench, off the coast of Kamchatka. The Hawaiian Ridge segment alone, which includes the Hawaiian Islands, is about 2,560 km (1,590 mi) long! Scientists estimate that the amount of lava thrust out to form this volcanic ridge was enough to cover the entire state of California with a blanket of lava 1.6 km (1 mi) thick!

◀ **DSV *Sea Cliff*, used to study underwater volcanoes**

Loihi—A New Island in the Making

The Hawaiian hot spot, which lies deep beneath the Pacific Ocean floor, currently feeds the volcanoes Mauna Loa and Kilauea on the island of Hawaii.

Recently a new seamount was discovered, forming off the southern coast of Hawaii. This underwater volcano, or seamount, is called Loihi (lō ē'hē).

Loihi towers about 3,300 m (10,820 ft) above the ocean floor. Only about 1,000 m (3,280 ft) of salty water covers this young volcano. Scientists don't expect Loihi to poke above the water's surface anytime in the near future. To study the newly emerging member of the Hawaiian volcanic chain, scientists have used a submarine, the DSV *Sea Cliff*, to take pictures of the events as they unfold.

Photographs of Loihi taken by cameras aboard the submarine show fresh pillow lavas and talus blocks. Pillow lava is lava formed when there is an undersea eruption. The rock formed is rounded, looking somewhat like piles of pillows. Pillow lavas form when the extremely hot lava erupts into the cold ocean waters, which quickly cool the lava. Talus blocks, which are also linked with "fresh" eruptions, are large angular pieces of rock that slide down a mountain's slope and pile up at the base of the structure.

Maps made of the area surrounding the new volcano show that Loihi is similar to some of its sister volcanoes—Mauna Loa and Kilauea. It is gently sloping and has a flat top. A **caldera**, or large circular depression, with a diameter of about 5 km (3 mi) lies within the volcano's summit. Cracking, followed by the formation of new ocean crust, is occurring along the sides of the volcano. The exact age of this new volcano is not yet known. Scientists have hypothesized, though, that the volcano is only a few hundred years old.

Within a few years, scientists are hoping to get an even better view of Loihi. They plan to use optical cables to monitor the eruptions taking place as they happen. These cables will connect an underwater observatory with an onshore observatory. The cables will then transmit

The caldera of a volcano ▶

information from the various instruments monitoring the volcano. Seismometers will also be put in place near the volcano. Perhaps even a small submarine rover will crawl around the ocean floor to witness history in the making!

Risk of Eruptions

Because the eruptions of the Hawaiian volcanoes are quiet flows, scientists have been able to study these volcanoes at close range without much danger. In fact, the volcanoes that make up the islands of Hawaii are probably some of the most closely studied volcanoes in the world. Look at the map showing the risk of volcanic eruptions in Hawaii. Which part of the Big Island seems to be the most dangerous? Why?

Perhaps because they are two of the most recent and most active volcanoes in the Hawaiian Ridge chain, Mauna Loa and Kilauea are closely watched. Study the bar graphs below. Which of the two volcanoes has erupted more often? ■

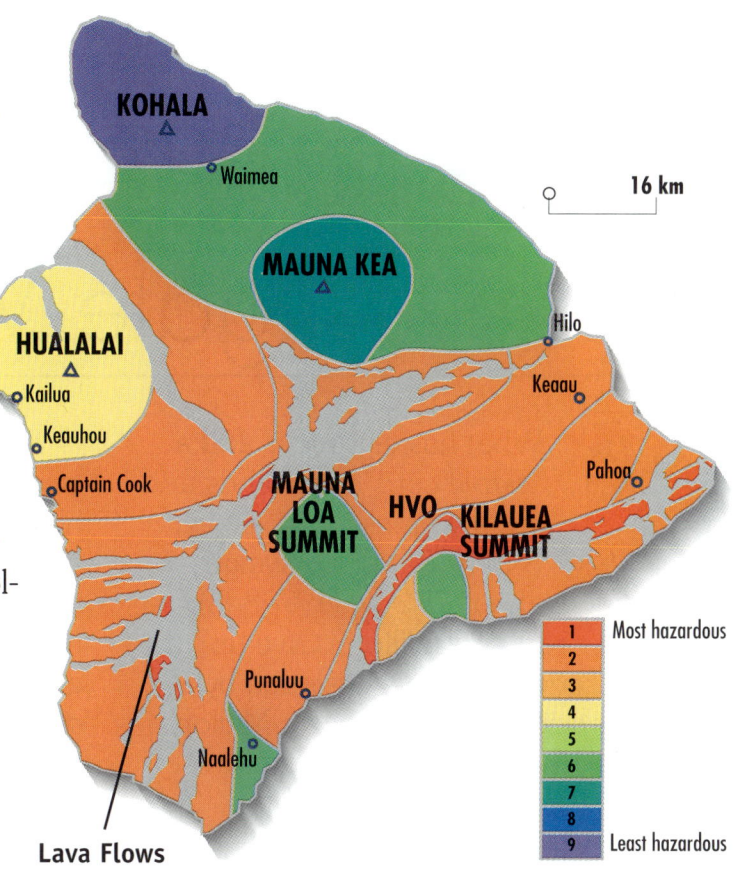

▲ Map of Hawaii, showing risk of volcanic eruptions

Eruptions of Mauna Loa and Kilauea compared ▼

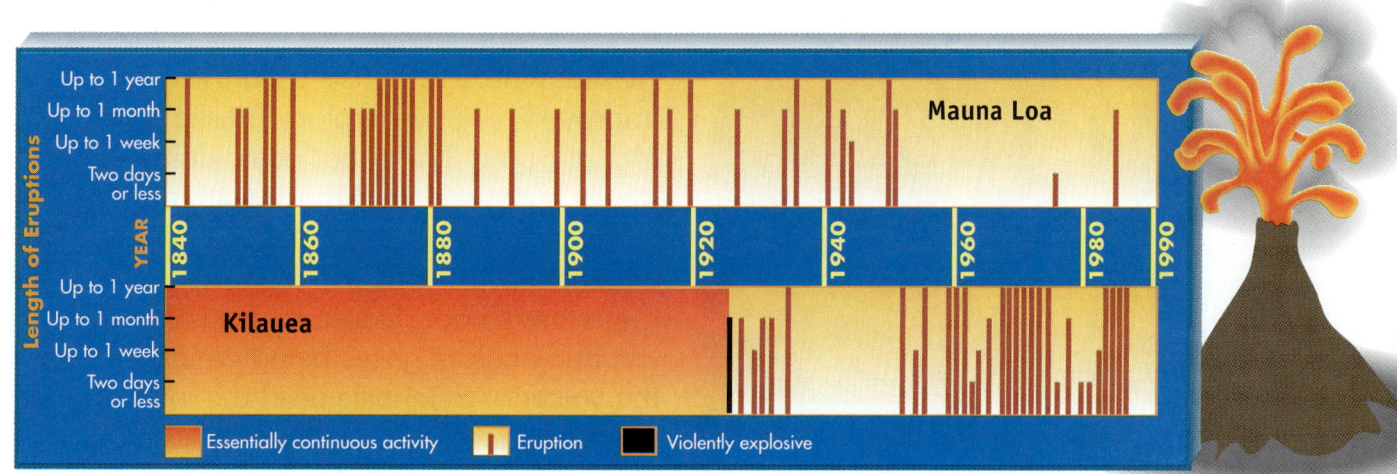

Using Robots to Investigate Volcanoes

What has eight legs and a "nerve cord" that sends and receives messages, is over 3 m (9.84 ft) tall, weighs about 772 kg (1,698 lb), and costs nearly $2 million? Give up? It's Dante, a series of robots designed by computer scientists at Carnegie-Mellon University, in Pittsburgh, Pennsylvania.

Dante II exploring a volcano in Anchorage, Alaska ▼

Dante was named after a fourteenth-century poet who wrote a poem in which he spends some time traveling through fiery regions deep within Earth. During a part of his mythical journey, Dante is led by a ghost named Virgil. Because the scientists send their robots into the fiery depths of volcanoes, they thought it appropriate to name the robots Dante. A transporter robot called Virgil carries Dante along some stretches of its journeys.

The first version of Dante was designed to help volcanologists explore one of the most active volcanoes on Earth—Mount Erebus, a smoldering 3,790-m (12,431-ft) volcano on Antarctica. A kink in one of the robot's cables, however, stopped the robot from going deeper than 6 m (about 20 ft) into the volcano. Although it couldn't complete its mission, Dante proved that it could tackle similar future assignments.

Dante II made its debut in Anchorage, Alaska, where scientists used this improved robot to explore Alaska's active Mount Spurr. The robot could descend slowly but surely 100 m (330 ft) into the volcano. It was able to produce a three-dimensional map of the rugged terrain of the crater's floor. Dante II could also collect and analyze gases being emitted from the volcano. Scientists used the information to infer that Mount Spurr will probably remain dormant for some time.

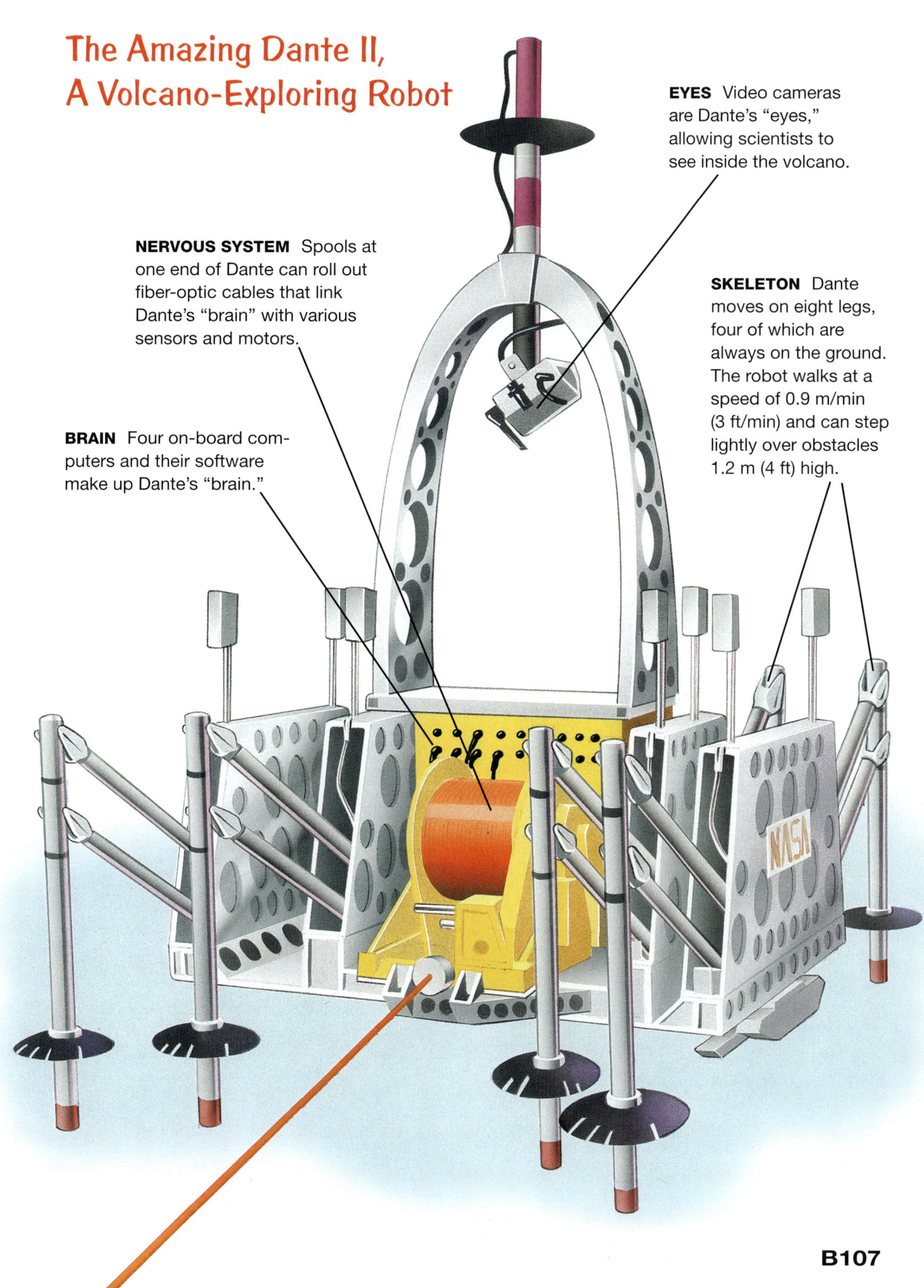

Great Rift Valley of Africa

Rifting

What happens if you slowly pull on some silicon putty? The putty stretches, sags, and often breaks. The process of rifting is similar to your stretching the putty.

Rifting is a process that occurs at divergent plate boundaries. As two plates separate, hot magma in the asthenosphere oozes upward to fill the newly formed gap. In general, rifting occurs along mid-ocean ridges deep beneath the oceans. Rifting along mid-ocean ridges leads to the process of sea-floor spreading. Some rifting, however, occurs where two continental plates are moving apart. When rifting occurs on land, the continental crust breaks up, or splits. Study the drawings on these two pages. What eventually forms when rifting occurs in continental crust?

The Great African Rift System

Over time, continental rifting has been pulling eastern Africa apart—at the rate of several centimeters per decade. Jokes a Djibouti geologist, "[We are] Africa's fastest-growing nation!" Three rifts—the East African Rift, one in the Gulf of Aden, and a third in the Red Sea—form a 5,600-km-long (3,472-mi-long) system known as the Great Rift Valley. The place where the three rift systems meet is called the Afar Triangle, named after the people who live in the region.

The Great Rift Valley may be the place

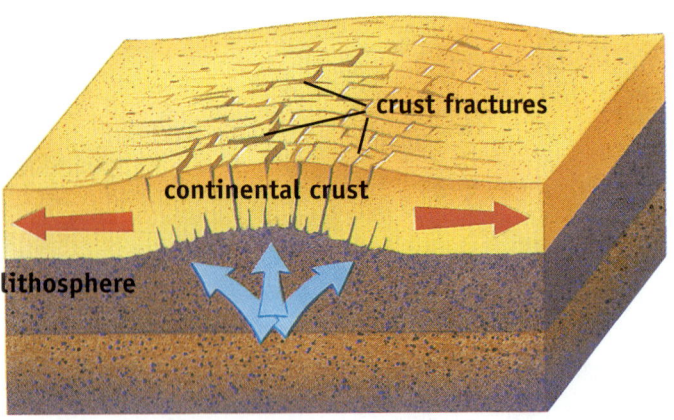

① Magma produced by Earth's mantle rises through the crust, lifts it up, and causes fractures in the crust.

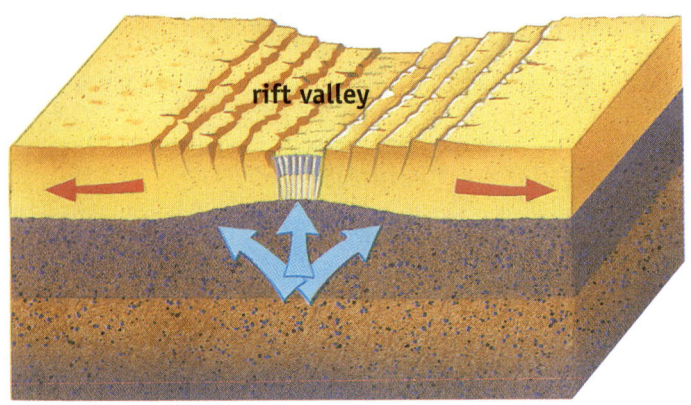

② The crust pulls apart, faults open, and blocks of crust fall inward. Volcanoes begin to erupt. A rift valley forms.

where humans had their first encounters with volcanoes. In fact, it is because of volcanic eruptions that anthropologists today are finding very old human remains. Some humans living in the Afar region of Africa were buried under the volcanic debris of an eruption that occurred many years ago! Their fossil remains continue to be unearthed and provide important information about early human history.

Found along the Great Rift Valley are some of the world's oldest volcanoes—including Mount Kenya and Mount Kilimanjaro. Mount Kilimanjaro, a volcano that towers nearly 5,900 m (19,352 ft) above the surrounding land, is Africa's highest peak.

Rifting along the Great Rift Valley—which runs through Mozambique, Zambia, Zaire, Tanzania, Uganda, Kenya, and Sudan, up into the Ethiopian highlands and down into the Djibouti coastal plains—has produced some of Earth's deepest lakes as well as some of the high-

▲ **Mount Kilimanjaro, one of Earth's oldest volcanoes**

est volcanic mountains. Lake Tanganyika, the longest freshwater lake on Earth, is the second deepest lake in the world. It formed many years ago when two tectonic plates shifted horizontally.

All along the Great Rift Valley, as with any rift zone, earthquakes and volcanoes are common. Study the map on page B110. Notice that along the East African Rift, the Somali Plate is moving away from

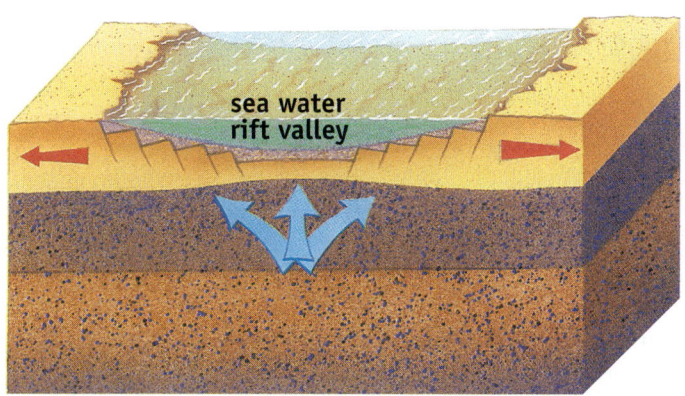

③ The rift valley widens, allowing sea water to fill the basin that has formed.

④ A new rift begins in the middle of the ocean basin that was formed. This rift is known as a mid-ocean ridge.

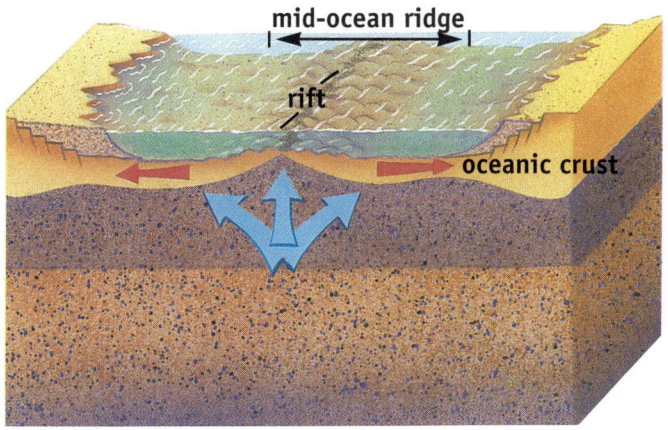

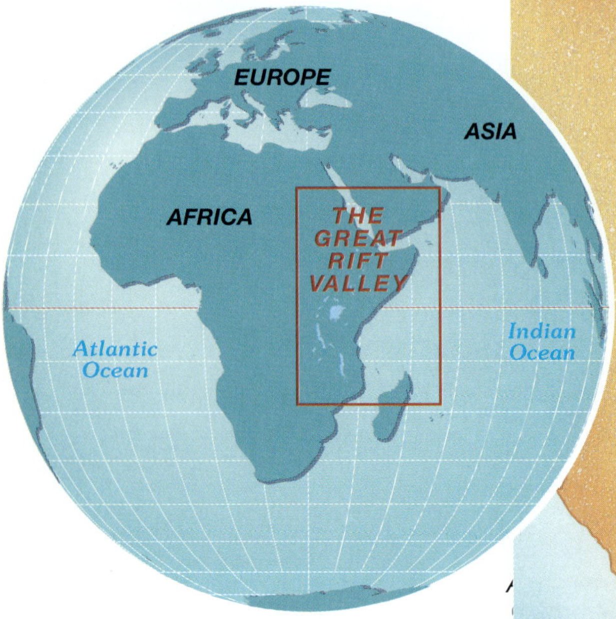

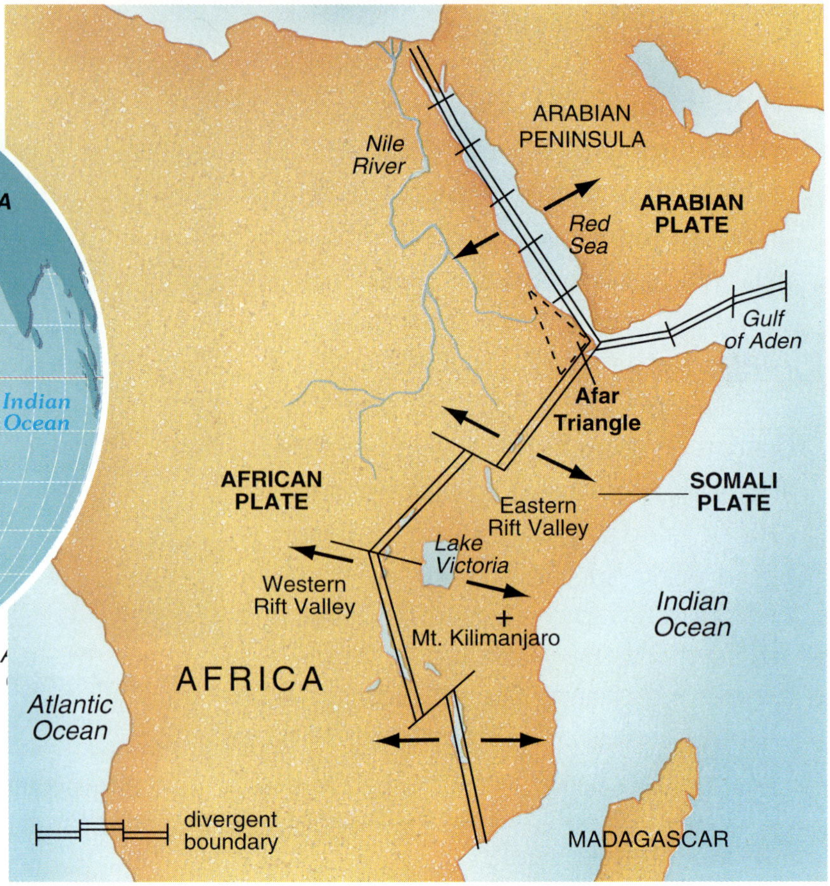

Map of the Great Rift Valley
At some time in the future, the Somali Plate may break away from the rest of Africa. ▶

the African Plate. Along the Gulf of Aden arm of the rift, the Somali Plate is moving southwestward relative to the Arabian Plate. How might this area look in the distant future if rifting continues?

As with most volcanic areas, fertile soils cover much of the land in the Great Rift Valley. In Kenya, for example, rich red soils blanket the land. Trona, a mineral in the local volcanic ash, is used to make glass and detergents.

Near the Afar Triangle, where Earth's crust is only 25 km (15.5 mi) thick, steam from the many volcanoes spouts into the air. Someday, perhaps, the volcanoes of the rift system will provide electricity from geothermal energy to Africa's millions of residents. ■

INVESTIGATION 3

1. Volcanoes occur on Earth's surface—the crust. Yet scientists study volcanoes to find out about the planet's mantle. Explain why.

2. Using the Hawaiian Islands as an example, describe how volcanic islands can occur in places other than at the boundaries of tectonic plates.

REFLECT & EVALUATE

WORD POWER

caldera
cinder-cone volcano
composite-cone volcano
hot spot
island arc
lava
magma
rifting
seismometer
shield volcano
volcano

On Your Own
Write a definition for each term in the list.

With a Partner
Make a labeled drawing or model of one of the three types of volcanoes.

Search through magazines and newspapers. Make photocopies of pictures of each of the three kinds of volcanoes.

Analyze Information

Use the drawing below to help explain how the Hawaiian Islands show the direction in which the Pacific Plate is moving.

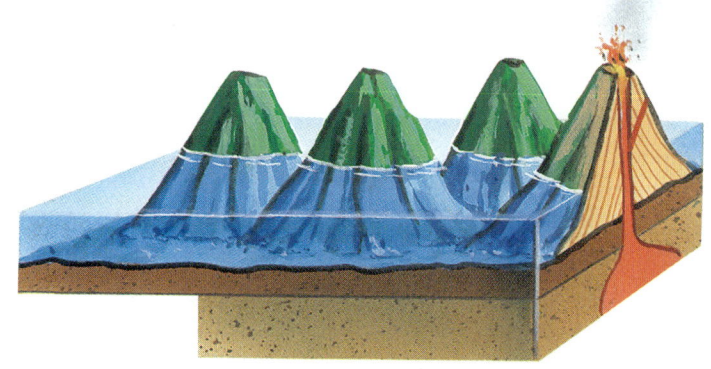

Assess Performance

Locate the Hawaiian Islands on a world map. Then locate them on a tectonic-plates map. Name the plate on which they are located and the direction in which the plate is moving.

Problem Solving

1. How are volcanoes on spreading ridges and rift zones different from those above descending edges of ocean plates?

2. On a map of Earth's tectonic plates, show where volcanoes are most likely to occur. Identify five active volcanoes throughout the world.

3. Explain how a satellite map could demonstrate that a volcano has erupted. How might that map change in a couple of months?

B111

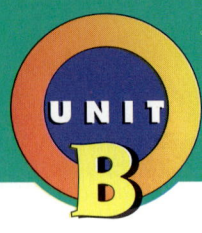

INVESTIGATE FURTHER!

Throughout this unit you've investigated questions related to the changing Earth. How will you use what you've learned and share that information with others? Here are some ideas…

Hold a Big Event to Share Your Unit Project

Imagine that you live in a part of the world where earthquakes occur frequently or where a volcano erupts from time to time. You are part of a team that is developing a guide—Preparing for an Earthquake and for Volcanic Activity. Your guide should give people information on protecting themselves against earthquakes and volcanic eruptions. It should prepare people for emergency measures, such as evacuation procedures. Be sure to include maps, tables, and other ways to communicate ideas clearly. Include suggestions for spiritual preparations, too.

Experiment

Plan a long-term project based on this unit. Monitor newspapers and/or news broadcasts for at least two months. Record reported incidents of earthquakes and volcanoes. On a world map, place colored labels at those sites that experience seismic or volcanic activity. Note any patterns in the incidents: on fault lines, near the Ring of Fire, and so on. What conclusions can you draw about geologically active areas? What predictions would you make on the basis of your conclusions?

Take Action

If areas in your state are geologically active, find out what kinds of structures and industries are nearby. What safety precautions are in place in the event of earthquakes or volcanic activity? Write your local newspaper or government officials. Express your views about the quality of safety standards at these sites. Report your recommendations and any responses to your class.

THE NATURE OF MATTER

Theme: Scale

Get Ready to Investigate! C2

1 Characteristics of Matter C4
Investigation 1   How Can You Describe Matter? C6
Investigation 2   What Makes Up Matter? C16
Investigation 3   How Does Energy Affect Matter? C22

2 Kinds of Matter C30
Investigation 1   How Can Matter Be Classified? C32
Investigation 2   What Is a Mixture? C44
Investigation 3   What Are Liquid Mixtures Like? C52

3 How Matter Changes C62
Investigation 1   How Can Matter Change? C64
Investigation 2   What Are Acids and Bases? C78
Investigation 3   What Do Chemists Do? C86

Investigate Further! C96

GET READY TO

OBSERVE & QUESTION

What are liquid mixtures like?

What holds a bubble together? Why does ice feel cold? As you learn more about matter, you'll find yourself asking questions about things you never really thought about before.

EXPERIMENT & HYPOTHESIZE

What do chemists do?

Analyze some unknown powders. Create a substance and study its behavior. These and similar hands-on activities will help you understand what chemists do and how they do it.

INVESTIGATE!

RESEARCH & ANALYZE

As you investigate, find out more from these books.

- **Kitchen Chemistry** by Robert Gardner (Julian Messner, 1988). Your kitchen contains all the equipment and materials you need to do dozens of experiments. This book will tell you what they are and how to use them.

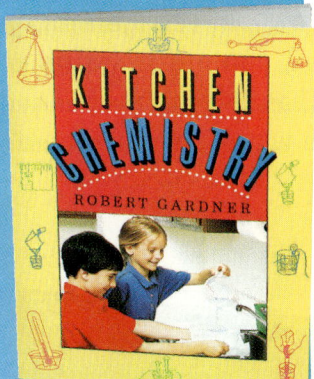

- **Eyewitness Science: Chemistry** by Dr. Ann Newmark (Dorling Kindersley, 1993). This book contains fascinating information about the study of matter through the ages.

WORK TOGETHER & SHARE IDEAS

How can you use what you know about matter to put on a magic show?

Working together, you'll have a chance to creatively apply what you've learned about matter to develop and master a few magic tricks. Then you and your group will perform your tricks in a magic show.

CHAPTER 1

CHARACTERISTICS OF MATTER

When you take ice cubes from the freezer of your refrigerator, you are removing solid chunks of water. Yesterday, you put in liquid water. Besides becoming cold and solid, how else has the water changed? Have the mass, density, and volume of the water been affected?

The Ice Man

Erik Blake surveys the bleak, white landscape around him. Without his dark glasses, he would be virtually blinded by the glare of sunlight upon the seemingly endless sheet of ice. As a **glaciologist** (glā shē äl′ ə jist), or scientist who studies glaciers, he is exploring the vast Hubbard Glacier in Canada's rugged Yukon Territory.

A glacier is a giant mass of ice, 90 m (300 ft) to 3,000 m (10,000 ft) thick, that moves slowly over land. The Hubbard Glacier, which is 140 km (87 mi) long, is among the largest in North America. The glacier is a natural laboratory for Blake. He seeks to understand how it moves and the kinds of wildlife found in this harsh environment.

Where a glacier meets the ocean, great mountains of ice break off and fall into the sea. Yet these massive ice mountains float! What questions would you like to ask about how glacial ice differs from liquid water?

Coming Up

INVESTIGATION 1
How Can You Describe Matter?
.... C6

INVESTIGATION 2
What Makes Up Matter?
.... C16

INVESTIGATION 3
How Does Energy Affect Matter?
.... C22

◀ Erik Blake, glaciologist

How Can You Describe Matter?

Suppose you were asked to compare a building brick and a basketball. List the characteristics you would use to describe each object. Could another person identify both objects based on your lists?

Activity

A Matter of Mass

MATERIALS
- 3 sealed containers, labeled *A*, *B*, and *C*
- balance and masses
- *Science Notebook*

A golf ball and a table-tennis ball are about the same size. Which contains more matter? How can you measure the amount of matter in an object?

Procedure

1. Look at the three containers. Without picking them up, **compare** their sizes and shapes. **Record** your observations in your *Science Notebook*.

2. Now pick up each container, but don't shake it. Based on the way the containers feel, arrange them in order from heaviest to lightest.

3. **Make a chart** like the one shown here.

Container	Mass (g)	Contents
A		
B		
C		

Step 2

C6

4. Using a balance, **measure** in grams the mass—the amount of matter—of each container. **Record** the results in your chart.

5. Each container is filled with a different material—one with sand, one with water, and one with cotton. Based on your observations, **infer** the contents of each of the three containers. In the *Contents* column of your chart, write the name of the material you think is in each container. Then open the containers and check your inferences.

Step 4

Analyze and Conclude

1. By studying and handling the containers, what can you **infer** about the amount of space taken up by each of the materials?

2. What did you learn about the amount of matter in each container? How did you learn this?

3. **Describe** what you learned about mass and matter by doing this activity.

God tells us about Himself in His Word. From the Bible we learn that God is a spirit – a personal being without a body. What characteristics can you learn about God from these verses?

- "Do I not fill the heaven and earth?" declares the LORD. (Jeremiah 23:24)
- I the LORD do not change. (Malachi 3:6)
- God made Him who had no sin to be sin for us so that in Him we might become the righteousness of God. (2 Corinthians 5:21)
- God so loved the world that He gave His one and only Son, that whoever believes in Him shall not perish but have eternal life. (John 3:16)

Activity
A Matter of Space

Does a softball take up more space than a shoe? Try to describe the amount of space each of these objects takes up. Does the amount of matter an object contains affect how much space it takes up?

MATERIALS
- goggles
- 2 plastic bags
- sand
- cotton balls
- spoon
- balance and masses
- metric measuring cup
- *Science Notebook*

SAFETY
Wear goggles during this activity.

Procedure

1. If you placed some cotton in one container and an equal mass of sand in another container, **predict** which material will take up more space.

2. Fill a plastic bag with cotton balls. Place as much cotton as you can in the bag without squashing it down.

3. Place the bag of cotton on the balance and **measure** its mass in grams. **Record** this measurement in your *Science Notebook*.

4. Remove the masses. Place a second plastic bag on the empty pan. Add sand to the bag until it has the same mass as the bag of cotton.

5. Pour the sand from the plastic bag into the measuring cup. **Measure** and **record** how many milliliters of sand were in the bag. Then pour the sand back into its original container.

6. Take the cotton balls from the bag and push them down into the cup. **Record** how many milliliters of cotton you have. You may have to fill the measuring cup more than once.

Step 2

Step 5

Analyze and Conclude

1. Which bag contained more mass, the bag of cotton or the bag of sand?

2. Which material took up more space, the cotton or the sand?

3. Can an object's volume be determined just from its mass? Explain your answer.

Activity
Checking for Purity

Imagine a sphere and a cube, each about the same size. One is made of pure gold; the other is a mixture of gold and some other lighter material. How could you tell which was which?

MATERIALS
- clay cube
- clay ball
- balance and masses
- metric measuring cup
- water
- *Science Notebook*

Procedure

1. Study the ball and the cube carefully. One is made of pure clay. The other is made of clay and some lighter material. You may handle them, but do not do anything to change either object's shape or size. **Make inferences** about the mass and volume of each object and **record** your inferences in your *Science Notebook*.

Step 1

2. Measure and **record** the mass of each object.

3. Add water to a measuring cup until it is half full. **Record** the volume of the water in milliliters.

4. Carefully place the ball in the measuring cup. **Observe** what happens to the water level. **Record** the new volume reading. **Calculate** the volume of the ball. Then remove the ball, shaking any excess water into the measuring cup.

5. Repeat step 4 with the cube.

Analyze and Conclude

1. What did you **infer** about the mass and volume of the two objects in step 1?

2. How did the masses of the ball and cube compare?

3. What did the changing water level in the measuring cup tell you about each object?

4. Hypothesize which object is made of pure clay. Give evidence to support your hypothesis.

Measuring Mass and Volume

Which package would you rather be holding? ▼

It's a cold, windy day, and you and a friend are standing at a bus stop. You've been shopping, and you each have a package to hold. One package is quite heavy, and the other is lighter but is larger and more bulky. Which package would you choose to hold?

Like everything in God's visible creation, the packages are made up of matter. **Matter** is anything that has mass and volume. In fact, the problem of which package is easier to hold involves these two physical properties—mass and volume. As you learned in the activities on pages C6 and C8, these properties can be measured. To review and practice your measuring skills, read pages H12–H16 in the Science Handbook.

Mass

The heaviness of each package is directly related to its mass. **Mass** is a measure of how much matter something contains. Weight is a measure of the force of gravity acting on a mass. So the more matter an object contains—the greater its mass—the more it will weigh.

When you weigh yourself on a bathroom scale, the scale measures the effect of Earth's gravitational force on the mass of your body. So how could you find the mass of your body? You would have to compare the unknown mass of your body to some known mass. For example, you could sit on one end of a seesaw and have someone add objects of known mass to the other end. When the seesaw

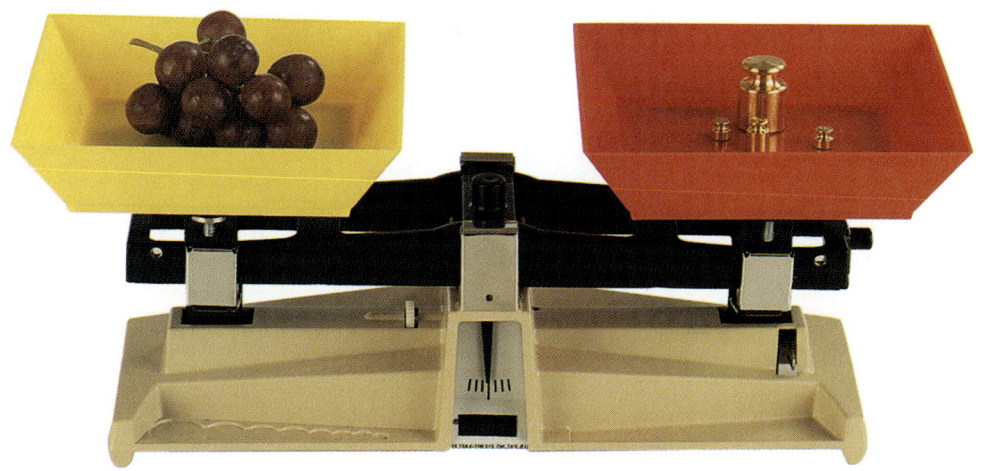

▲ **Finding the Mass of an Object**
The mass of an object is found by placing the object in one pan of a balance and objects of known mass in the other.

balanced, you'd know that your mass was the same as the total mass of the objects. Now you can see why the instrument used to measure the mass of an object is called a balance.

The most common metric units used to measure mass are grams (g) and kilograms (kg). A penny has a mass of about 2 g. A kilogram is one thousand times as large as a gram. A large cantaloupe has a mass of about 1 kg.

Other units are also used for measuring mass in the metric system. For example, the mass of a very light object could be measured in milligrams (mg). One milligram is equal to one thousandth ($\frac{1}{1000}$) of a gram. Very heavy objects can be measured in metric tons. A metric ton is equal to 1,000 kg.

Volume

The **volume** of an object is the amount of space it takes up. For example, an inflated balloon takes up more space—has greater volume—than an empty balloon. Volume can also be used to express *capacity*—that is, how much material something can hold. A bathtub can hold a lot more water than a teakettle.

The basic unit of volume in the metric system is the liter (L). A liter (lē′tər) is slightly larger than a quart. Many soft drinks are now sold in 2-L containers. Units used to measure smaller volumes include the centiliter (cL), which is one hundredth of a liter, and the milliliter (mL), which is one thousandth of a liter.

An instrument called a graduated cylinder, or graduate, is used to measure liquid volumes. Using a graduate is similar to using a measuring cup.

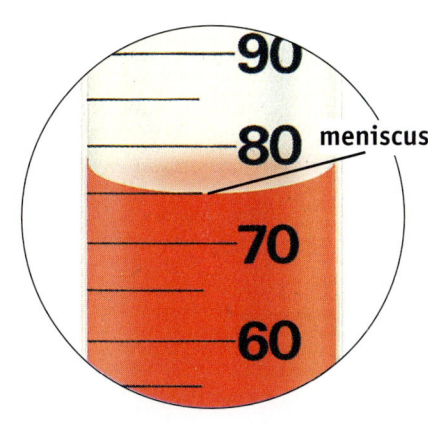

▲ **Reading a Graduate**
Notice that the surface of the liquid in the graduate curves upward at the sides of the glass. This curved surface is called a meniscus (mə nis′kəs). To find the volume of the liquid, read the mark that lines up with the bottom of the meniscus.

Suppose you want to know how much water is in a container of some kind. First you pour the water from the container into a graduate. Then you measure the level of the liquid against the scale marked on the side of the graduate. Graduates come in many sizes. This makes it possible for you to measure small volumes, large volumes, and all volumes in between.

There are two methods for finding the volume of a solid. One method is used for finding volumes of solids that have regular geometric shapes, such as cubes, spheres, and rectangular blocks. For any solid with a regular shape, you can measure such dimensions as length, width, height, and diameter. Then you can calculate the volume of the solid by substituting the measurements into a mathematical formula. For example, the volume of a rectangular block can be found by multiplying its length times its width times its height. The formula for this calculation is below.

$$V = l \times w \times h$$

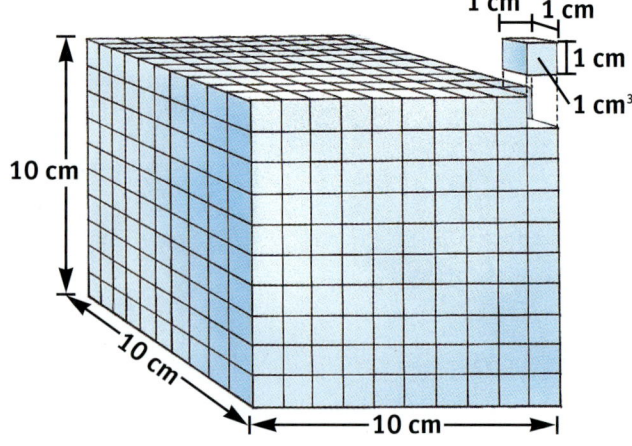

▲ **Finding the Volume of a Regular Solid**
Volumes of regular solids are often expressed in cubic centimeters (cm^3). A cubic centimeter is the volume of a cube 1 cm long on each edge. One cm^3 is equal to 1 mL.

Many solids do not have a regular shape. A rock, for example, is likely to have an irregular shape. The volume of these kinds of solids can be found by using the water displacement method.

The first step in using the water displacement method is to find a graduate large enough to hold the object. Then you follow the procedure shown below. ■

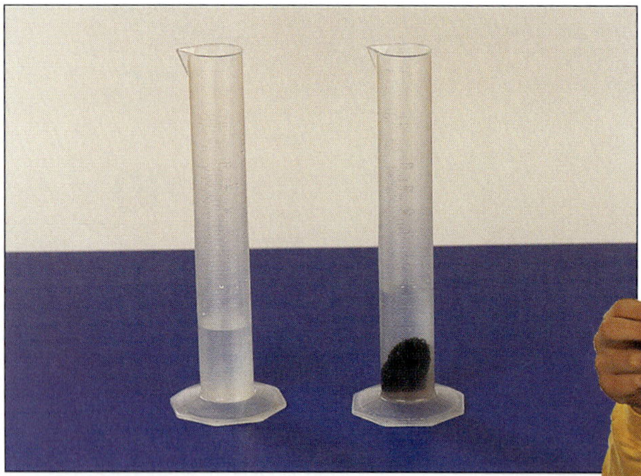

▲ **Finding the Volume of a Rock**
The volume of water in the graduate is 30 mL. When the object being measured is lowered into the water, the water level rises to 45 mL. What is the volume of the object?

C12

Density

Imagine yourself in this situation. You have just packed and sealed two identical boxes. One box contains a down pillow and the other box contains books. The problem is, you have forgotten which box contains which item. Since the two boxes look exactly alike, how can you solve this problem without opening one of the boxes?

You can probably think of an easy solution. All you have to do is pick up each box. The box containing books will be much heavier than the one containing the pillow.

Density

You solved your problem by comparing the masses of two objects (cartons) having equal volumes. You may not have realized it, but you used a very important property of matter—density—to solve your problem.

Density refers to the amount of matter packed into a given space. In other words, **density** is the amount of mass in a certain volume of matter. To get an idea of what density is, look at the objects on the balance shown in the photograph below.

What will happen if the block on the left is replaced with another block made of the same stuff, but equal in size (volume) to the block on the right? The balance will tilt to the left. The block on the left has the greater density.

You can calculate the density of any sample of matter if you know two things—its mass and its volume. You can find the density of the sample by dividing its mass by its volume. The formula for finding density is below.

$$D = m/v$$

For example, suppose you are working with a piece of metal that has a volume of 2.0 mL and a mass of 9.0 g. Using the formula, the density of that metal is determined here.

$$D = 9.0 \text{ g}/2.0 \text{ mL} = 4.5 \text{ g/mL}$$

Notice that density measurements always include mass and volume units.

Understanding Density
Since the two blocks balance each other, they must have the same mass. But the block on the left is obviously smaller than the one on the right—its volume is less. Thus the block on the left has a greater density than the block on the right. ▶

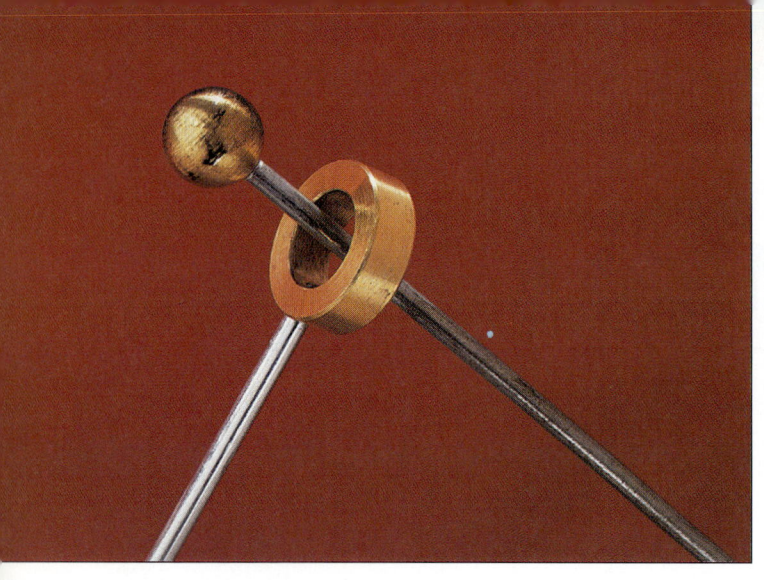
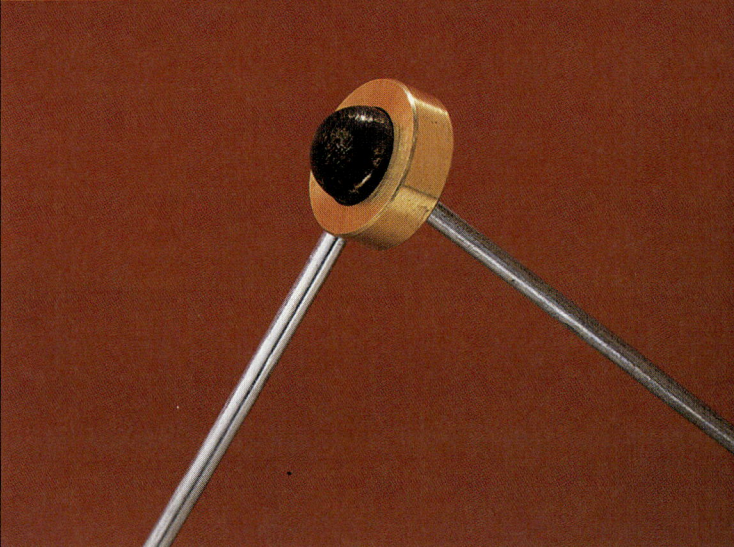

The ball and ring are both made of brass. When they are at the same temperature (*left*), the ball fits easily through the ring. How does heating the ball affect its volume (*right*)?

Using Density to Identify Materials

Density is a characteristic property of all matter. This means that a particular kind of matter always has the same density, regardless of where the matter comes from or where it is measured. For example, the density of pure water is 1.0 g/mL. This means that a milliliter of water always has a mass of 1 g. The table below gives the densities of some common materials.

Since every substance has a definite density, this property can be used to identify materials. For example, suppose you measure the mass and volume of an object and find its density is 7.9 g/mL. Could you make a reasonable guess as to what material the object is made of? You could if you had a table of densities like the one on this page. Use the table to find what the object is most likely made of.

Density and Temperature

Notice that the table lists the densities of the materials at a particular temperature—in this case, 20°C. This is done because temperature affects density. As a general rule, matter expands when it

DENSITIES OF SOME COMMON SUBSTANCES AT 20°C

Substance	Density (g/mL)	Substance	Density (g/mL)
gold	19.3	water	1.0
mercury	13.6	ice	0.92
lead	11.3	oil	0.90
silver	10.5	wood (oak)	0.7
copper	8.9	wood (pine)	0.4
iron	7.9	oxygen	0.0014
aluminum	2.7	helium	0.0002

gains heat and contracts when it loses heat. In other words, the volume of a material increases as its temperature goes up and decreases as its temperature goes down.

How does a change in volume affect density? Look again at the formula for density: $D = m/v$. If the mass of a material doesn't change and the volume of the material increases, its density decreases. On the other hand, if the volume of a material decreases and its mass stays the same, its density increases.

Float or Sink?

Density can be used to predict whether an object will sink or float in water. The density of water is 1.0 g/mL. Any material with a density less than 1.0 g/mL will float in water. Anything with a density greater than 1.0 g/mL will sink. How might such information be useful?

Imagine you're going to boil some eggs for breakfast. You want to make sure the eggs you're using aren't spoiled. The density of a fresh egg is about 1.2 g/mL.

The density of a spoiled egg is about 0.9 g/mL. If you place an egg in water and it floats, what does this tell you about the egg?

Density in Calculations

Density can also be used to answer questions about the purity of a material. Suppose you have a chunk of metal with a volume of 10 mL. You're told that the metal is pure silver. How could you find out for sure?

You could start by looking up the density of silver, which is 10.5 g/mL. This tells you that 1 mL of silver has a mass of 10.5 g. So, 10 mL of pure silver will have a mass of 10×10.5 g, or 105 g. Now all you have to do is measure the mass of your chunk of metal. ■

INVESTIGATE FURTHER!

EXPERIMENT

Design an activity for finding the density of an object that floats in water, such as an irregularly shaped piece of wood. Carry out your activity and record all your observations and measurements.

INVESTIGATION 1

1. By measuring density, mass, and volume, we learn about the materials God created. Why does density provide a more useful description of a material than does either mass or volume by itself?

2. A cube and a sphere each have a mass of 10 g. The cube floats in water; the sphere does not. What can you infer about the volume of each object? Explain the reasoning behind your inference.

INVESTIGATION 2

WHAT MAKES UP MATTER?

Think about what happens when water is spilled on a kitchen countertop. If you wipe the countertop with a dry sponge, where does the water go? How is the sponge different from the countertop? In this investigation you'll find out how the particles that make up matter give matter its properties.

Activity

Always Room for More

When you add sugar to a glass of iced tea, where does the sugar go? How does the sugar "fit" into the full glass?

MATERIALS
- goggles
- 2 plastic jars
- marbles
- spoon
- sand
- water
- beaker
- sugar
- *Science Notebook*

SAFETY
Wear goggles during this activity.

Procedure

1. Fill a jar to the brim with marbles. Is the jar full, or is there room for more matter? **Record** your inference in your *Science Notebook*.

2. Using a spoon, carefully add sand to the jar. Gently tap the sides of the jar as you add the sand. Continue until no more sand will fit in the jar. What can you **infer** about the space in the jar now?

3. Slowly and carefully pour water into the jar until no more water can be added.

4. Fill a second jar with water. Carefully add a spoonful of sugar and stir. **Record** your observations.

Step 1

C16

Step 3

Step 4

Analyze and Conclude

1. Was any matter in the jar before you added the marbles? If so, what happened to it?

2. Why could the jar full of marbles still hold sand and water?

3. How would this activity have been different if you had started by filling the jar with water?

4. Use your observations of the first jar to **infer** what happened to the sugar that was added to the second jar. How does the sugar "fit" in the water?

5. Make a sketch of what you think the mixture of sugar and water would look like if you could see how the two materials fit together.

INVESTIGATE FURTHER!

EXPERIMENT

Repeat steps 1–3 of this activity, using modeling clay instead of the marbles. Explain the difference in your final results.

Activity
Racing Liquids

A paper towel soaks up water, but do other types of paper? Paper strips can help you model how particles are packed in different materials.

MATERIALS
- goggles
- paper towel
- brown paper bag
- typing paper
- waxed paper
- filter paper
- metric ruler
- scissors
- tape
- wire coat hanger
- large shallow pan
- water
- food coloring
- hand lens
- **Science Notebook**

SAFETY
Wear goggles during this activity. Handle scissors with care.

Procedure

1. Cut a strip 2.5 cm wide and 15 cm long from each kind of paper. Cut one end of each strip to form a point.

2. Tape the strips, points down, to the bottom of a coat hanger so that the points of the tips hang the same distance below the hanger.

3. Pour water in the pan and add a few drops of food coloring to the water. Hold the coat hanger above the pan so that the tips of the paper strips touch the water.

4. **Predict** which paper strip the water will move through most quickly. **Observe** as the water "races" up the strips. When the water reaches the top of one strip, remove the hanger and lay all five strips of paper on a flat surface.

Analyze and Conclude

1. Based on the distances that water traveled through the strips, **list** types of paper in order from fastest to slowest.

2. Study dry samples of each kind of paper with a hand lens. Describe how they are different. How could the type of paper affect the movement of water through it?

3. Imagine that you could observe the water and paper through an extremely high-powered microscope. **Make a sketch** showing how you think the water moves through the paper.

4. Do samples of matter contain "empty" spaces? **Give evidence** to support your conclusion.

Step 3

C18

Structure of Matter

▲ Even in still air, specks of dust dance and dart about.

Picture yourself sitting in your room on a quiet summer afternoon. You're home alone, there's nothing to do, and you're *bored*! You're so bored that you begin staring at the specks of dust dancing in a sparkling beam of sunlight. Even with all the doors and windows closed and no hint of a breeze, you notice that the tiny specks dart about as if they were being stirred by an invisible hand. What could be moving the dust around?

Particles in Motion

The moving specks of dust offer evidence of the structure and nature of matter. God constructed matter of very tiny particles that are constantly in motion. The particles that make up matter are much smaller than the tiniest speck of dust. These particles are so small, in fact, that they can't be seen, even with the best microscope your school owns.

Air is made up of such particles, moving through space. As the particles of air move about, they collide with each other and with everything in your room, including the specks of dust. The movements of dust specks are caused by particles of air bouncing the specks of dust around!

It's easy to see the effects of moving air particles. Inflated objects, such as balloons and basketballs, provide evidence that air is made up of particles. When you put air in a container, the moving air particles continuously bang against the sides of the container. It's these collisions that keep objects inflated.

C19

Air, of course, is a gas. Actually it's a mixture of several different gases. Because gases are invisible, it's easy to think of them as being made up of tiny moving particles. But what about other forms of matter? What evidence do we have that liquids and solids are made up of moving particles? Look at the pictures on this page.

Like the air in a room, the water in the pictures seems calm. Yet the water and the colored liquid mix together on their own. This mixing indicates that liquids, like gases, are made up of moving particles. As the particles of water and colored liquid bump into each other, the particles spread out and mixing occurs.

So evidence indicates that gases and liquids are made up of tiny moving particles. What about solids? It's hard to visualize something as hard and unchanging as a rock or your desk being made up of moving particles. But it's true! You'll find out about evidence that supports this idea as you read on.

The photographs show Ⓐ a colored liquid being added to water, Ⓑ the mixture 5 minutes later, and Ⓒ 10 minutes later. ▼

States of Matter

Think about some kinds of matter that you see every day, such as air, water, ice, iron, wood, syrup, sugar, and cloth. As different as these materials are, they can all be classified into one of three major categories, or states. The three common **states of matter** are solid, liquid, and gas. Study the drawings and descriptions of these states on page C21.

As you have just read, solids, liquids, and gases are all made up of tiny particles in constant motion. The particles that make up a substance are attracted to each other to some degree. The forces of attraction among particles are called chemical forces. The state in which a substance is found depends on two things: how fast the particles are moving and how strongly the particles are attracted to each other.

The forces of attraction among particles are different for different substances. For example, particles of helium gas barely attract each other at all. These particles fly around even when they are moving at fairly slow speeds.

Particles of water have slightly stronger attractions to each other. These particles have to be moving at a pretty good speed before they actually separate and fly around. The chemical forces between particles of iron are very strong. These particles have to be moving at very high speeds before they overcome the forces of attraction and fly around.

The state in which a substance is found depends on the nature of its particles and the speed at which they are moving. As you will discover, the motion of the particles can be changed. ■

Solids
In a solid chemical forces hold the particles in place. The particles vibrate back and forth, but don't leave their positions. This is why a solid keeps its shape.

Liquids
In a liquid particles move faster and farther apart than particles in a solid. The particles in the liquid can slip and slide past each other. This is why liquids have no definite shape.

Gases
In a gas the particles move so fast that chemical forces can't hold them together. So, particles of a gas spread out to fill their container. This is why gases have no definite shape or volume.

INVESTIGATION 2

1. Why do solids have a definite shape while liquids and gases do not?

2. Iron expands when it is heated. Draw a sketch of how the particles of a piece of iron might look at 10°C and at 50°C.

3. How do the three states of matter remind you of the three persons in the Trinity?

Investigation 3

How Does Energy Affect Matter?

What happens when you put some hard kernels of corn in a pan, hold the pan over a fire, and shake it? A few minutes later you have popcorn! In this investigation you'll find out how energy changes matter in different ways.

Activity

Cooling Race

Suppose you are enjoying a glass of lemonade on a hot day. What happens to your drink when you add ice cubes? How do the ice cubes change? Can these changes be described in terms of energy?

MATERIALS
- water
- 2 plastic jars
- 2 thermometers
- 2 small plastic bags
- ice cubes
- balance and masses
- spoon
- crushed ice
- timer
- *Science Notebook*

Procedure

1. Make a chart in your *Science Notebook* like the one shown.

	WATER TEMPERATURE					
	Start	3 Min	6 Min	9 Min	12 Min	15 Min
Water + Ice Cubes						
Water + Crushed Ice						

2. Half-fill two plastic jars with water. Put a thermometer in each jar. **Record** the water temperature under *Start* in your chart.

Step 3

3. Put two ice cubes in a plastic bag and set them on one pan of a balance. Place a second bag on the other pan. Use a spoon to add crushed ice to this bag until the pans balance.

4. Add the ice cubes to one jar and the crushed ice to the other jar.

5. At three-minute intervals, **measure** and **record** the temperature of the water in each jar. Continue for 15 minutes.

Analyze and Conclude

1. Describe how the ice in each jar changed.

2. In which jar did the ice change faster?

3. In which jar did the water cool more quickly? What difference between the ice cubes and the crushed ice might explain why the water in one jar cooled faster?

4. Heat energy is needed to melt ice. **Suggest a hypothesis** to explain where the heat energy came from. **Give evidence** to support your hypothesis.

5. The water contained more heat energy at the start of the activity than it did at the end. **Hypothesize** what happened to this heat energy. Support your hypothesis.

INVESTIGATE FURTHER!

EXPERIMENT

Predict the changes that would occur if you added an equal number of ice cubes to both a glass of cold water and a glass of warm water. Try the experiment and check your predictions.

Activity
Speeding Up Change

Wet your finger and hold it up in the air. How does it feel? Does the feeling change when you blow on the finger? What does energy have to do with these changes?

MATERIALS
- dropper
- water
- 4 small dishes
- timer
- plastic toothpick or stirrer
- *Science Notebook*

Procedure

1. Use a dropper to place a small drop of water in a dish. Place a drop of the same size in a second dish. Set one dish in direct sunlight and the other in a cool, shaded spot. **Predict** what will happen to the two drops of water.

2. Allow the dishes to stand undisturbed, checking on the water drops every few minutes. Each time you check, **record** your observations and the time in your *Science Notebook*.

3. Between observations, **brainstorm** with members of your group. Try to think of ways to make a drop of water evaporate faster. List your suggestions in your *Science Notebook*.

4. Put identical drops of water in two dry dishes. Leave one drop alone. **Experiment** with the other drop to see if you can make it evaporate.

5. Repeat step 4 for each technique you try. **Record** each technique and **describe** your results.

Step 4

Analyze and Conclude

1. Which drop of water from step 1 evaporated more quickly? **Suggest a hypothesis** to explain your results.

2. What techniques were successful in causing a drop of water to evaporate faster? Explain why you think each technique was successful.

3. **Make a general statement** about what causes water to evaporate.

▲ Water is rare in the universe as a whole. Yet, God has made this resource – essential to life – common on our planet.

Particle Energy

Picture in your mind a sample of iron. What do you see? You probably see a hard, grayish solid. This is the state in which iron is usually found. But under the proper conditions, iron can also exist as a liquid. It can even exist as a gas!

Most forms of matter can exist in all three states—solid, liquid, and gas. Perhaps the best example of a substance in all three states is water. You are familiar with water as a solid (ice), a liquid, and a gas (water vapor).

You have also seen water change from one state to another. You have seen ice melt, puddles "dry up," and water vapor change to a liquid and fog up a mirror. Materials change state when energy is added to them or taken away from them. These changes can be understood by thinking about the motion of the particles that make up all matter.

Energy and Temperature

You know from experience that a thrown ball or a falling rock has energy. These objects have energy due to their motion. This energy of motion is called **kinetic energy**. Even the particles that make up matter have kinetic energy because they're moving.

Look back at the drawings on page C21, which show the relative motion of particles in the three states of matter. Would you like to know how fast the particles of a material are moving? Take the material's temperature! **Temperature** is a measure of the average kinetic energy of the particles in a material.

The term *average* indicates that not all particles in a material are moving at the same rate of speed. Some are traveling (or vibrating) a little bit faster or slower than most of the particles.

Temperature and Heat

Many people think that temperature and heat are exactly the same. While temperature is related to heat, the two are quite different. To help you understand the difference, study the two beehives in the drawing.

Now think of a glass of hot water and a bathtub full of water at the same temperature. Just like the bees, the particles of water in each container would have the same average speed. But because there are more particles in the tub, that water would have more heat energy.

Heat energy includes the total kinetic energy of the particles in a material. So a large sample of matter will have more heat energy than a smaller sample of the same matter, even though both samples have the same temperature.

What would happen if you added five or six ice cubes to the hot water in the glass and in the bathtub? The ice cubes in the bathtub would melt more quickly than those in the glass because the water in the tub has more energy.

This example helps to define heat. **Heat** is energy that flows from warmer to cooler regions of matter. Here energy travels from warm water to cool ice.

Energy and Change of State

Energy is always involved in a change of state. When heat energy is added to a solid at its melting point or a liquid about to evaporate, the temperature does not increase. However, the heat does overcome the forces holding the molecules in solid or liquid form. In the reverse reactions, heat is given back, allowing a liquid or a solid to form.

Water is the best substance to study to learn about changes in state. Study the pictures on page C27 as you read about energy and changes of state.

▲ **Average Versus Total Energy**
The bees in both of these hives have energy—they are buzzing around. The average speed of the bees in each hive is the same. But the bees in the larger hive have more total energy because there are more bees.

WATER CHANGES STATE

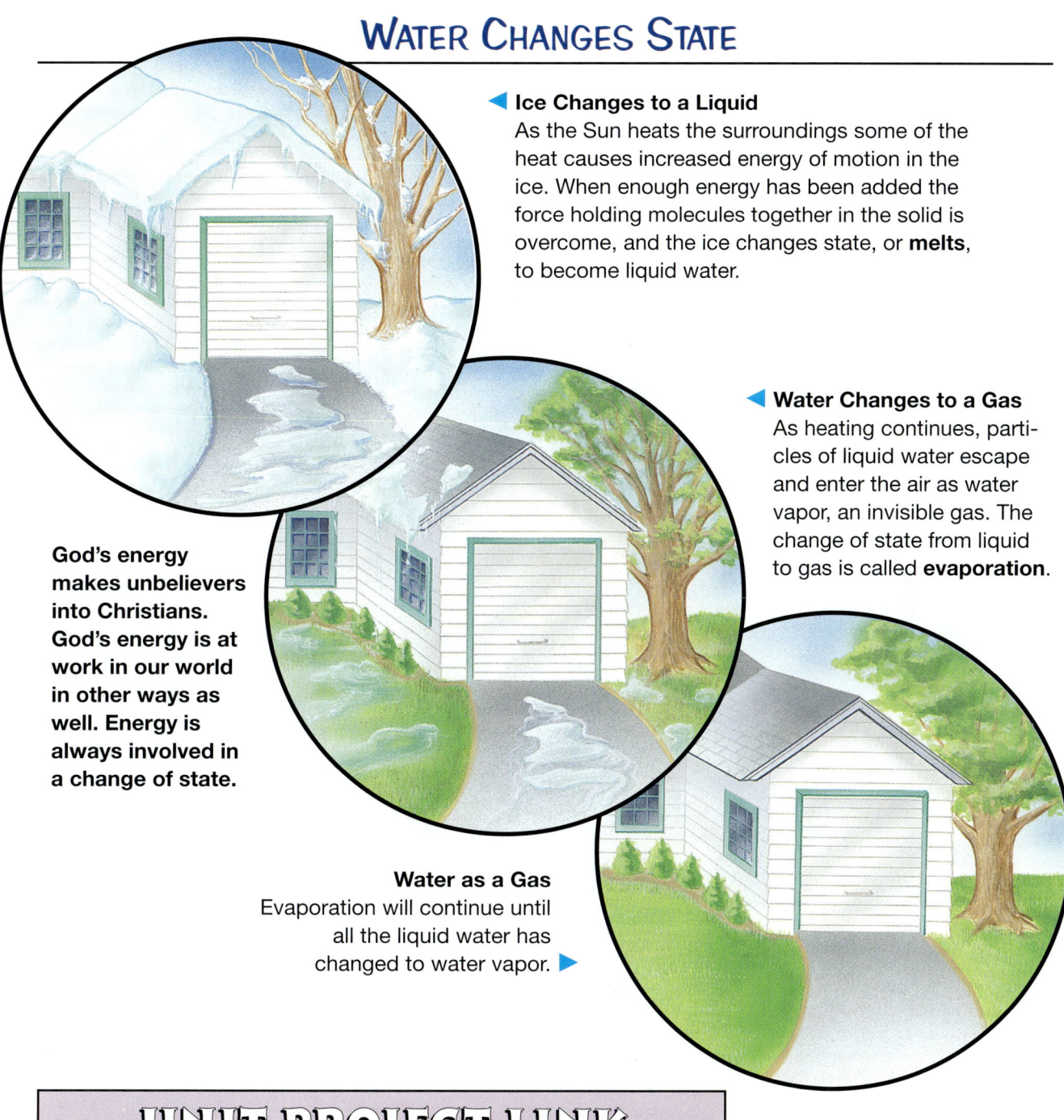

◀ **Ice Changes to a Liquid**
As the Sun heats the surroundings some of the heat causes increased energy of motion in the ice. When enough energy has been added the force holding molecules together in the solid is overcome, and the ice changes state, or **melts**, to become liquid water.

◀ **Water Changes to a Gas**
As heating continues, particles of liquid water escape and enter the air as water vapor, an invisible gas. The change of state from liquid to gas is called **evaporation**.

God's energy makes unbelievers into Christians. God's energy is at work in our world in other ways as well. Energy is always involved in a change of state.

Water as a Gas
Evaporation will continue until all the liquid water has changed to water vapor. ▶

UNIT PROJECT LINK

Choose one of the following magic tricks to master.
1. The Disappearing Liquid. What happens when you mix two different liquids and some liquid disappears?
2. The Great Tissue Bust. Can a tissue be stronger than you are? Find out, when the tissue is part of the trick. Be sure you can use what you learn in this unit to explain why your trick works.

Evaporation occurs over a wide range of temperatures and takes place only at the surface of liquid water. If enough heat is added to liquid water, the water will eventually boil. When this happens, bubbles of water vapor form throughout the liquid. These bubbles will rise through the liquid and escape into the air.

A Change in Direction

Changes in state also take place when heat is removed from water. If enough heat is removed from a gas, it will change to a liquid. This process is called **condensation**. If enough heat is then removed from the liquid, it will change to a solid in a process called **freezing**. ■

▲ Boiling is rapid evaporation that takes place throughout a liquid at high temperatures.

▲ When liquid water freezes, forces between water particles hold them in definite, fixed patterns called crystals.

INVESTIGATION 3

1. Describe the changes that take place in a sample of water as it changes from water vapor to liquid water to ice.

2. If you hold an ice cube in one hand and a hot muffin in the other, one hand feels cold and the other feels hot. Explain these feelings in terms of movement of heat.

3. How does the material studied in this chapter help us to give God glory?

CHAPTER 1 REVIEW

REFLECT & EVALUATE

WORD POWER

condensation
density
evaporation
freezing
heat
kinetic energy
states of matter
temperature
mass
matter
melting
volume

 On Your Own
Write a definition for each term in the list.

 With a Partner
Use the terms in the list to make a word-search puzzle. See if your partner can find the hidden terms and tell what each means.

Make a chart that compares the characteristics of water in its three states. Include drawings that show the arrangements of particles.

Analyze Information

Study the drawings. Then in your own words explain how you would determine the volume of each object.

Assess Performance

Design and carry out an experiment to find out if quarters, nickels, and dimes are made of the same kind of metal.

Problem Solving

1. A 20-mL sample of grayish metal has a mass of 54 g. What is the density of the metal? After you've found its density, use the table of densities on page C14 to identify the metal.

2. Hypothesize why a piece of wood can float in water but not in air. Use your hypothesis to explain why a balloon filled with helium floats in air.

3. God designed water as a common substance. But water is unusual in that it expands when it freezes. Use this information to explain why ice cubes float in liquid water.

CHAPTER 2

KINDS OF MATTER

Sometimes people remove things from water to make it safe to drink. At other times, people add things to water, as is the case when they make iced tea. What is it about the nature of water that allows people to do these things?

Don't Drink the Water

Water is the most important liquid on Earth. Humans and other living things need fresh water. Yet, of all the water on Earth, only 3 percent is fresh water. Ocean water, which makes up 97 percent of Earth's water, is too salty to drink.

How can we increase our supply of fresh water? This is a question that conservationists (kän sər vā′shən ists) and managers of water districts ask. Some believe that desalination (dē-sal ə nā′shən) is part of the answer. In a desalination plant, salt water is heated until it turns to steam. This leaves the salt behind. The steam is cooled until it condenses into fresh water, which is collected and stored for later use.

A different process is used in Yuma, Arizona, where the problem is salt in water used for irrigation. The salty water is pumped under high pressure over membranes that act as superfine filters. These membranes allow water molecules, but not salt and other impurities, to pass through. As you explore the kinds of matter in this chapter, you'll learn why we are able to separate salt and water.

Coming Up

INVESTIGATION 1

HOW CAN MATTER BE CLASSIFIED?
............C32

INVESTIGATION 2

WHAT IS A MIXTURE?
............C44

INVESTIGATION 3

WHAT ARE LIQUID MIXTURES LIKE?
............C52

◀ Only a small percentage of the water on Earth's surface is fit for people to drink.

INVESTIGATION 1

How Can Matter Be Classified?

If you were asked to organize all the matter in the world into groups, how many groups do you think you'd need? What characteristics would you choose to identify each group? In this investigation you'll classify matter into two groups: kinds of matter that cannot be broken down and kinds that can.

Activity

Testing Your Metal

Aluminum and copper are kinds of matter. This activity will help you decide which group they belong in.

MATERIALS
- goggles
- samples of aluminum
- samples of copper
- *Science Notebook*

SAFETY
Wear goggles during this activity.

Procedure

Obtain samples of aluminum and copper. In your *Science Notebook,* **list** some properties of each of these metals. **Brainstorm** with members of your group to think about things you can do to change these samples. **Make a list** of your ideas and, after getting your teacher's approval, carry out your plans. **Describe** each of your actions and **record** all changes in the samples caused by the actions.

Analyze and Conclude

1. Based on your observations, what properties do copper and aluminum have in common? How are the two metals different?

2. Did any of the changes you caused produce any new materials? Explain your answer.

C32

Activity

A Change for the Wetter

Sugar is a kind of matter. Can sugar be broken down into other materials? Heat some sugar and find out.

MATERIALS
- goggles
- sugar
- black construction paper
- hand lens
- metal spoon
- candle
- shallow dish
- potholder
- tongs
- glass square
- *Science Notebook*

SAFETY
Wear goggles. Be very careful when working around open flames. Secure loose clothing and tie back long hair. Avoid melted candle wax and heated sugar. They can cause painful burns.

Procedure

1. Sprinkle a small amount of sugar on a sheet of black paper. Examine the grains of sugar with a hand lens. Make a sketch of a sugar grain in your *Science Notebook*.

2. Obtain about a half spoonful of sugar. Place a candle in the center of a shallow dish and ask your teacher to light the candle. Using a potholder, hold the spoon over the candle so that the flame just touches the bowl of the spoon.

3. While you heat the sugar, have your partner use tongs to hold a glass square 2–3 centimeters above the sugar.

4. Watch the sugar and the glass square carefully. Continue heating the sugar until the white crystals have all disappeared. **Record** your observations of the sugar and the glass.

Step 2

Analyze and Conclude

1. What was the first sign that a change was taking place?

2. **Compare** the appearance of the material in the spoon at the end of the activity with the sugar you started with. What evidence is there that you've produced different kinds of matter from the sugar?

3. What appeared on the glass square? **Infer** where this material came from.

C33

Elements

Look at the familiar materials in the photographs on this page and the next. These materials are all different, yet they have at least one thing in common—they are all matter.

Matter can be identified by its properties, or characteristics. **Physical properties** are characteristics that can be measured or detected by the senses. Color, size, odor, and density are examples of physical properties. **Chemical properties** describe how matter changes when it reacts with other matter. The fact that paper burns is a chemical property of paper.

Given time, you could probably list hundreds or even thousands of kinds of matter. Yet scientists are able to classify all matter into two large groups—substances and mixtures. These two groups can be divided into smaller groups, as shown in the graphic organizer on page C35.

A **substance** is a material that always has the same makeup and properties, wherever it may be found. Of the materials shown in the photographs below, gold, aluminum, sugar, and water are all substances.

Milk is a mixture. A **mixture** is a combination of two or more different kinds of matter that can be separated by physical means. You will learn about mixtures later in this chapter.

There are two kinds of substances—elements and compounds. An **element** is a substance that cannot be broken down by simple means into any other substance. In the activity on page C32, you weren't able to change aluminum or copper into simpler kinds of matter. Copper and aluminum are elements.

A **compound** is a substance made up of two or more elements that are chemically combined. Water and sugar are examples of compounds. In the

What properties can be used to identify these different materials? ▼

C34

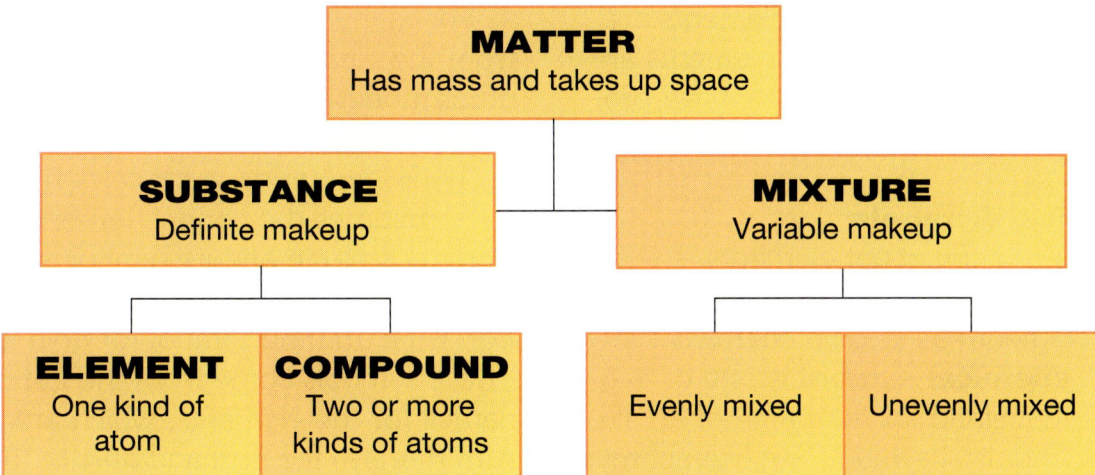

activity on page C33, sugar was changed into simpler substances. One was water. The black material remaining in the spoon was an element, carbon.

Identifying Elements

Elements have been described as the building blocks of matter. All matter, regardless of its form, is made up of one or more elements. What, then, are elements made of?

Recall that all matter is made up of very tiny particles. Think about cutting a small piece of aluminum in half, and then cutting one of the halves in half. Now imagine dividing the aluminum into smaller and smaller pieces. Eventually you would have a particle so small that it could not be divided anymore and still be aluminum.

The tiny particle would be a building block of aluminum—an aluminum atom. An **atom** is the smallest particle of an element that has the chemical properties of the element.

All the atoms that make up a particular element are the same. Gold, for example, is made up only of gold atoms; aluminum is made up only of aluminum atoms. Gold atoms differ from aluminum atoms and from the atoms of all other elements.

Today scientists know of 109 elements. Each element is made up of only one kind of atom. This means that there are 109 different kinds of atoms.

Ninety elements are found in nature. These elements include many familiar substances, such as iron, copper, iodine, aluminum, and tin. But many unfamiliar elements exist too, such as ruthenium (roo thē′nē əm), francium (fran′sē-əm), and xenon (zē′nän). From these 90 elements are built the many kinds of matter that make up the whole universe!

aluminum

Nineteen of the known elements are not found in nature. These elements are known only because scientists have produced them artificially in the laboratory.

Chemical Symbols

When writing about elements, scientists use a kind of shorthand in which each element has its own chemical symbol. A **chemical symbol** is one or two letters that stand for the name of an element. Chemical symbols are like abbreviations for the names of elements.

For many elements, the symbols come from the elements' names in English or other modern languages. Some examples of such symbols include O for oxygen, H for hydrogen, and Ca for calcium.

Sometimes the connection between an element's name and its symbol is not so obvious. For example, the symbol for iron is Fe and the symbol for gold is Au. These symbols come from the Latin names for the elements, which are *ferrum* (fer′əm) for iron and *aurum* (ô′rəm) for gold.

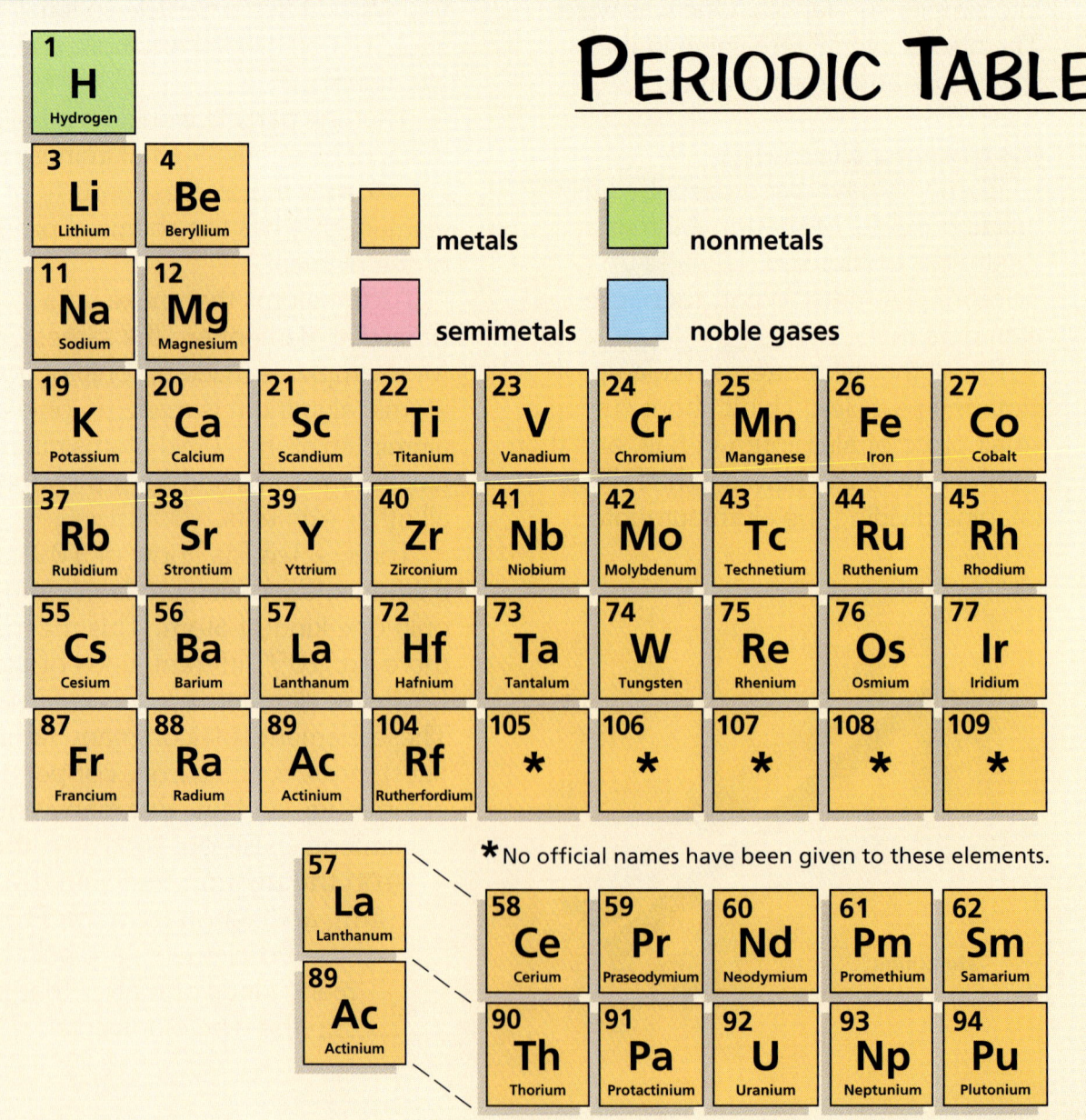

The Periodic Table

The idea that there are certain basic kinds of matter—elements—is an old one. Some early scientists thought there were four elements—fire, earth, air, and water. However, by the seventeenth century, scientists had identified a number of elements. By the nineteenth century, more than 50 elements were known.

In 1869 the Russian chemist Dmitri Mendeleev published a table of the 63 elements known at that time. Mendeleev organized the elements into a table according to the weights of their atoms and their properties. The elements in each column of the table had similar properties. The table below is a modern version of Mendeleev's table. It is called the Periodic Table of Elements.

Each block of this periodic table includes information about a particular element. For example, hydrogen is the simplest element. That is, hydrogen atoms have the simplest structure. For this reason, hydrogen is listed first and it is given the atomic number 1.

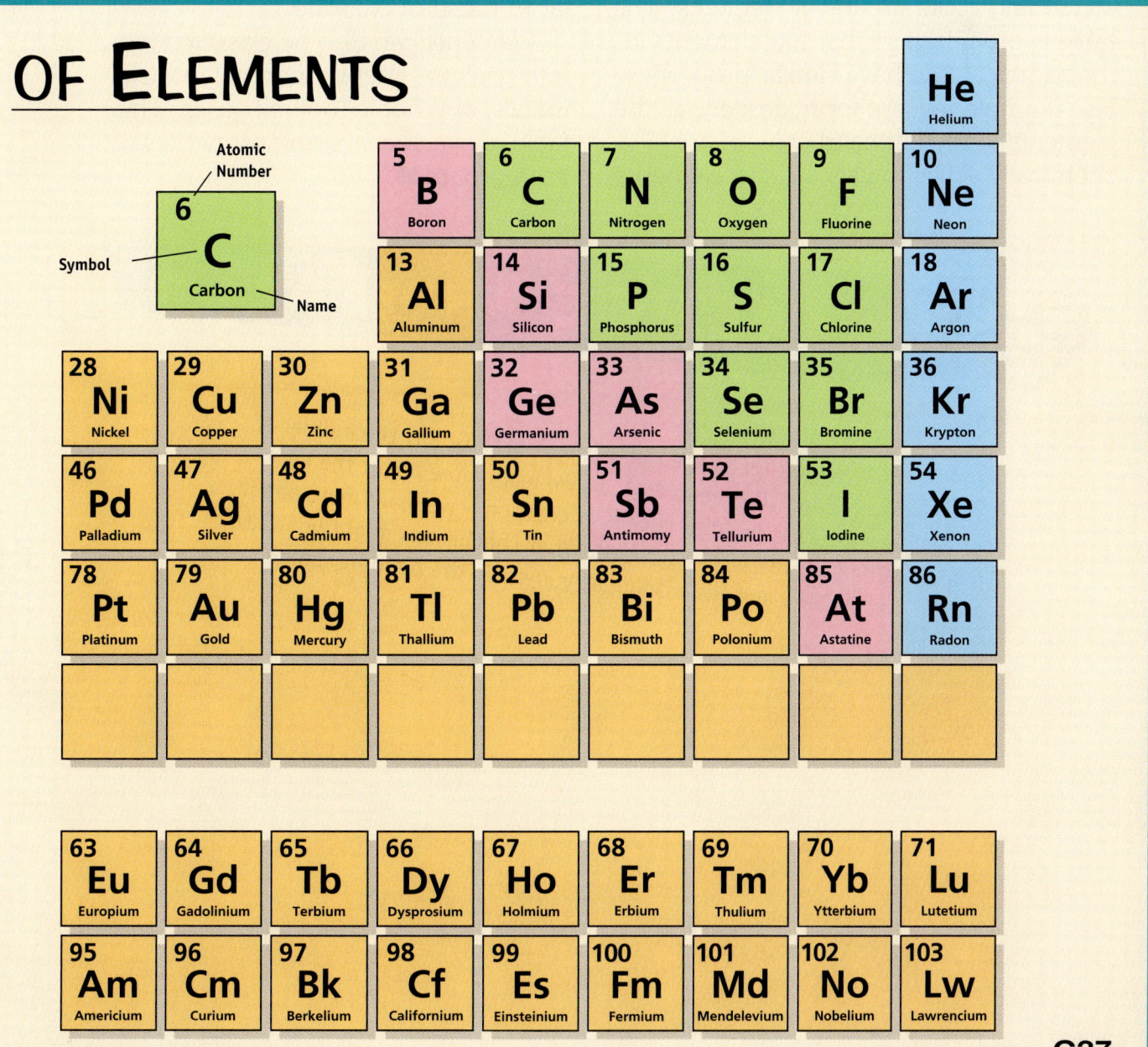

Group	Examples	Properties
Metals	iron, copper, aluminum	Usually shiny; can be formed into sheets and wire; good conductors of heat and electricity
Nonmetals	sulfur, carbon, chlorine	Dull; cannot be easily shaped; poor conductors of heat and electricity; some are gases
Semimetals	silicon, boron	Have some properties of both metals and nonmetals
Noble Gases	helium, neon, radon	Do not combine readily with other elements

Using the Periodic Table

In addition to information about each element, the periodic table tells you something about groups of elements. The table is organized so that the elements in the same column have similar properties. For example, except for hydrogen, all the elements in the left-hand column are chemically active metals. All the elements in the right-hand column are inactive gases. Use the table on page C37 to find out which elements have properties similar to those of chlorine.

Elements can also be classified into four groups—metals, nonmetals, semimetals, and noble (nō′bəl) gases. The table above shows some properties of each group.

The writer to the Hebrews records, "God is the builder of everything" (Hebrews 3:4). As we learn more about the elements – the building blocks of creation – we learn more about God the Creator of all things. What conclusions might you draw about God and His wisdom as you study the periodic table?

Compounds

One of the most beautiful materials found in the laboratory is a reddish-orange powder sometimes known as red precipitate (prē sip'ə tit). The photographs show what happens to this powder if you heat a small amount of it in a test tube.

In the photographs you can see the contents of the test tube change from a reddish-orange solid to a dark powder and then to a shiny liquid on the sides of the test tube. What you can't see is the gas escaping from the mouth of the test tube. How can you tell that red precipitate is *not* an element?

The Composition of Compounds

Red precipitate is a compound of mercury and oxygen. Its scientific name is mercuric (mər kyoor'ik) oxide, and it forms when when the elements mercury and oxygen combine. When elements combine to form a compound, their atoms become chemically linked, or joined. In most compounds the linked atoms form **molecules** (mäl'i kyoolz). In some compounds, such as salt, or sodium chloride, the atoms are held together in hundreds or thousands of units, forming crystal-like structures.

When elements join to form compounds, the elements lose their original properties and take on new ones. For example, mercury is a shiny liquid metal. Oxygen is a colorless, invisible gas. But as you have seen, the compound made up of these elements, mercuric oxide, is a reddish-orange powdery solid.

The photographs show mercuric oxide as it is heated to seperate it into mercury and oxygen. ▼

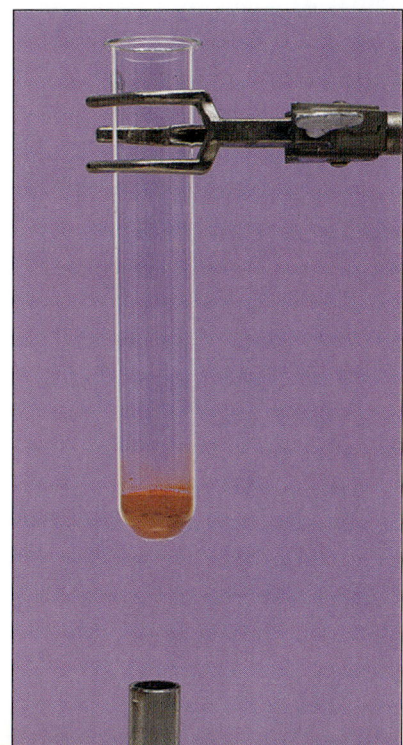
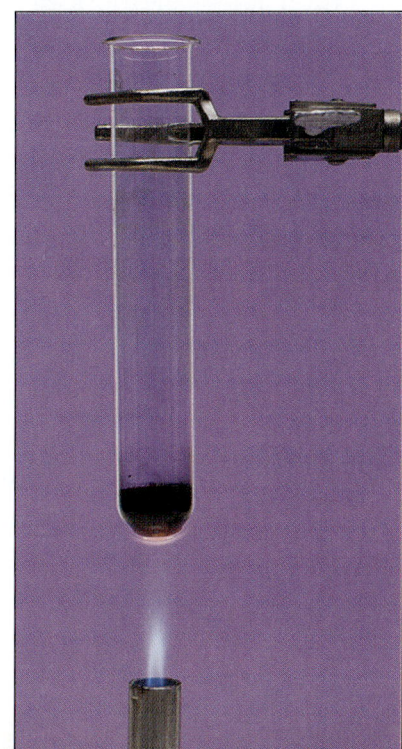
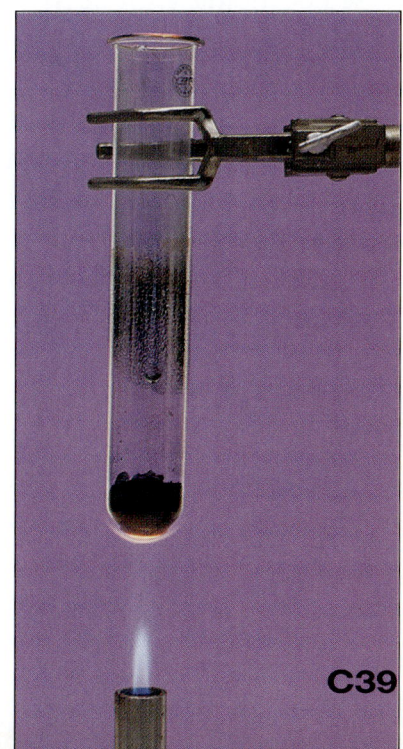

▲ Sodium is a soft metal that reacts explosively with water.

▲ Chlorine is a poisonous, greenish-yellow gas.

Water and salt are two common substances that show how much elements can change when they combine to form compounds. Water is a compound made up of the elements hydrogen and oxygen, which are both colorless gases. Hydrogen burns with a very hot blue flame. Oxygen helps other substances to burn but does not itself burn.

So what are the properties of the compound that is made when these two gases combine with each other? Water is a liquid that does not burn. In fact, it can be used to put out fires!

Sodium chloride is made up of sodium and chlorine. The photographs above show what these elements are like. It's hard to believe that the white crystals you sprinkle on your popcorn are made up of such dangerous elements!

Chemical Formulas

Just as chemical symbols are used to represent elements, chemical formulas are used to represent compounds. A **chemical formula** is a group of symbols that shows the elements in a compound. For example, the chemical formula for water is H_2O. This formula shows that a single molecule of water is made up of 2 hydrogen atoms and 1 oxygen atom.

In the formula for water, look at the number 2 after the symbol for hydrogen. A number written to the right of and below a symbol in a chemical formula is called a *subscript* (sub'skript). A subscript shows how many atoms of an element are present in a single molecule or the simplest unit of a compound.

No subscript is written to show a single atom. So if you don't see a subscript in a formula (as with the O in H_2O), you can assume that the subscript is 1. The formula for sulfuric acid, for example, is H_2SO_4. This formula shows that each unit of sulfuric acid contains 2 atoms of hydrogen, 1 atom of sulfur, and 4 atoms of oxygen.

Compounds of Carbon

Many compounds found in nature are very complex. This is especially true of compounds of carbon. Carbon is an element that is found in all living things. An entire field of chemistry, called organic chemistry, is devoted to the study of carbon compounds.

The table sugar you put on your cereal in the morning has the chemical formula $C_{12}H_{22}O_{11}$. How many atoms make up a single molecule of this compound? Does this sound like a giant, complex molecule? Not when it's compared with a particle of cholesterol (kə les′tər ôl).

Cholesterol is a compound found in the cells of many living things. Although cholesterol plays some important roles in living organisms, an excess of the compound can cause serious health problems, such as heart disease, in humans. The chemical formula for cholesterol is $C_{27}H_{45}OH$.

How many atoms are present in a single molecule of cholesterol? You would probably agree that this molecule is, indeed, complex. But carbon is a very "linkable" atom. The number of different carbon compounds is seemingly endless. And many of these compounds are more complex than cholesterol. ■

UNIT PROJECT LINK

Here are some more suggested magic tricks. Choose one to work on with your group.
1. "What Color Is Blue Ink?" Is ink a mixture or a compound?
2. "The Invisible Force." Can an index card be used as a cap to keep a glass full of water from spilling?
3. "The Leakproof Strainer." How can one liquid keep another liquid from passing through the holes in a strainer?

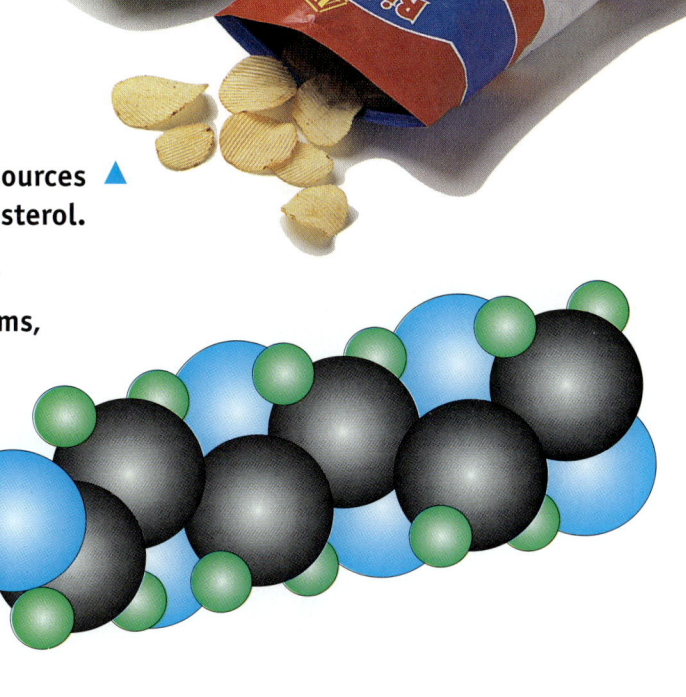

Eggs and fried foods are sources ▲ of cholesterol.

A molecule of sugar, or sucrose, is made up of 45 atoms—12 carbon atoms, 22 hydrogen atoms, and 11 oxygen atoms. What is its formula? ▼

C41

RESOURCE

Ancient Elements

Chemistry got its start in the Middle Ages with the alchemists (al′kə mists). The alchemists spent much effort trying to change iron and lead into gold and searching for a substance that could give everlasting life. We know, of course, that eternal life is God's free gift to us by grace through faith in Jesus.

Though many of the ideas of the alchemists were wrong, God worked much good from their efforts. Alchemists discovered at least five elements and identified many chemicals. They helped pave the way for modern chemistry.

The term *element* is coined by Plato, a famous Greek philosopher. The Greeks consider the four basic kinds of matter, or elements, to be fire, water, air, and earth.

400–300 B.C.

1550 B.C.
Plows made of bronze are used in Vietnam.

3200 B.C.
Copper is mined on a large scale in Egypt. Copper is used in the making of bronze during the Bronze Age.

The earliest metal objects are made. In the Middle East, small jewels and tools are carved or cut from gold, copper, and silver.
EARLY YEARS

Dmitri Mendeleev, a Russian scientist, develops a periodic table of the elements.

1869

1803
English chemist John Dalton proposes his atomic theory.

1661
English chemist Robert Boyle (1627–1691) re-introduces the idea of basic types of matter called elements.

A.D. 700-1300
Science declines in Europe and thrives in the Arab world. Chemistry develops into an experimental science through the efforts of the alchemists. They learn many things about how elements behave and combine with each other. At least five new elements are discovered.

INVESTIGATION 1

1. What do elements and compounds have in common? How do they differ?

2. The chemical formula for carbon dioxide is CO_2. The formula for sulfur trioxide is SO_3. The formula for carbon tetrachloride is CCl_4. From the information in the formulas, infer the meanings of the prefixes *di-*, *tri-*, and *tetra-*.

3. What good did God bring from the misdirected efforts of the alchemists?

INVESTIGATION 2

What Is a Mixture?

Perhaps the two most common kinds of matter at Earth's surface are rocks and ocean water. Neither is a substance. Both kinds of matter are made up of different elements and compounds mixed together. Find out about mixtures in this investigation.

Activity

Working With Mixtures

How can you tell if something is a mixture? With some things, such as chocolate chip ice cream or vegetable soup, it's easy to tell. With others, such as vanilla ice cream or salt water, it's more difficult.

MATERIALS
- goggles
- aluminum foil
- copper foil
- sugar
- 2 clear jars with lids
- aquarium gravel
- hand lens
- sand
- scissors
- spoon
- *Science Notebook*

SAFETY
Wear goggles. Be careful working with scissors.

Procedure

1. Cut a piece of aluminum foil and a piece of copper foil into small pieces. Add the pieces to a clear jar.

2. Add 2 or 3 spoonfuls of sugar to the jar. Place the lid on the jar and shake the jar vigorously. **Predict** whether the properties of any of the materials in the jar will be changed by being mixed together.

Step 2

C44

3. Use a hand lens to examine the contents of the jar carefully. In your *Science Notebook*, **describe** the contents of the jar and tell how you would separate the parts of this mixture.

4. Add 2 spoonfuls each of aquarium gravel and sand to another jar. Cover the jar and shake it vigorously.

5. Brainstorm with your partner to **plan an experiment** for separating the sand-gravel mixture. After showing the plan to your teacher, obtain the necessary materials and carry out your plan.

6. Return the sand and gravel to the jar. Add 2 spoonfuls of sugar to the jar and repeat step 5 for this mixture.

Analyze and Conclude

1. Were any properties of the aluminum, copper, or sugar changed by being mixed together? How do you know?

2. What can you **infer** about the differences between a mixture and an element? a mixture and a compound?

3. **Describe** your method for separating the mixture of sand and gravel. Were you able to use the same method to separate the mixture of sand, gravel, and sugar? Why or why not? If not, **describe** the method you used to separate this mixture.

INVESTIGATE FURTHER!

EXPERIMENT

Mix a spoonful of sand and a spoonful of iron filings. Think of a property of iron that you could use to help separate this mixture. Write up a plan for separating the mixture. Show the plan to your teacher. If the plan is approved, carry it out.

Activity
Racing Colors

Is black ink a substance or a mixture? Find out if you can separate it into parts.

MATERIALS
- water
- wide-mouth jar
- scissors
- filter paper
- water-based marker
- rubber band
- *Science Notebook*

SAFETY
Handle scissors with care.

Procedure

1. Add water to a jar to within a few millimeters of its rim.

2. Cut a small hole in the center of a piece of filter paper. Use a water-based marker to make a circle of round dots near the hole in the filter paper, as shown.

Step 2 — marker dot, hole

3. Stretch the filter paper over the mouth of the jar and hold it in place with a rubber band.

4. Cut a second piece of filter paper in quarters. Roll up one of the quarters to make a cone. Insert the tip of the cone through the hole in the filter paper, as shown. The tip of the cone should touch the water.

5. **Predict** what will happen as water moves up the cone and past the marker spots. **Record** your prediction in your *Science Notebook*.

6. **Observe** the setup until the water has passed the marker spots. **Record** your observations.

Step 4

Analyze and Conclude

1. **Describe** what happens to each marker spot.

2. Is ink a substance or a mixture? What evidence can you give to support your answer?

Activity

A Mixed-Up State

Some mixtures behave like a liquid. Some behave like a solid. The behavior of some mixtures, as you will discover, is not easy to describe.

MATERIALS
- goggles
- cornstarch
- spoon
- shallow dish
- dropper
- food coloring
- water
- plastic jar
- plastic knife
- marbles
- *Science Notebook*

SAFETY
Wear goggles during this activity.

Procedure

1. Place four or five spoonfuls of cornstarch in a dish. **Predict** how the cornstarch will change if you add water to it.

2. Add several drops of food coloring to some water in a plastic jar. Add this colored water, a few drops at a time, to the cornstarch. Stir with a plastic knife until you have a wet ball of cornstarch.

3. Describe the material you have created. Pick some up and **observe** its properties. **Record** your observations in your *Science Notebook*.

4. Try cutting the material with a plastic knife. Try rolling it into various shapes. Place marbles on the material and describe what happens.

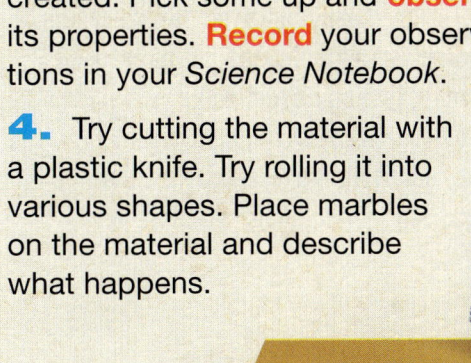

Step 2

Analyze and Conclude

1. Why is the material produced in this activity a mixture?

2. **Describe** the ways that the material acts like a liquid. Like a solid.

3. Do you think the mixture can easily be separated into its original materials? Explain your answer.

C47

Mixtures

The chemical formula for water is H_2O. This formula tells you that water is made up of 2 parts hydrogen and 1 part oxygen. Is water a mixture of hydrogen and oxygen? This question may confuse people who are just beginning to study chemistry. The answer to the question is no. About the only thing that compounds and mixtures have in common is that each is made up of two or more different kinds of matter.

Keeping Their Properties

In the activity on pages C44 and C45, you mixed aluminum, copper, and sugar together in a jar. Even after shaking the jar, you were still able to recognize the different parts of the mixture.

This activity gave you a clue as to how mixtures are different from compounds. All the substances in a mixture keep their original properties. When substances combine to form a compound, the properties of the substances that make up the compound are gone. The properties of these substances are replaced by the unique properties of the compound.

Suppose you were to mix iron filings with salt. No matter how thoroughly you mixed the two substances, you would still have iron and salt. Both substances would still have their original properties. For example, one physical property of iron is that it is attracted to a magnet. Mixing the iron with salt has no effect on this property, as the photograph below shows.

◀ Iron is magnetic and it keeps this property in a salt-iron mixture.

▲ Is this fruit punch a mixture or a compound?

When substances combine to form a compound, the substances change. Water, for example, is nothing like the hydrogen and oxygen that combine to make up the water. And water's properties are very different from those of hydrogen and oxygen.

The Makeup of a Mixture

Ice cream is a mixture—perhaps one of your favorite mixtures. There are many varieties (flavors) of ice cream, and each contains different ingredients.

Mixtures, including the various flavors of ice cream, don't have chemical formulas. The reason is that two mixtures of the same materials can be quite different in makeup. This explains why the same flavor of ice cream may taste different from brand to brand.

To understand how mixtures of the same materials can differ, think about two bowls of fruit punch made with the same ingredients. One person might mix two bottles of orange juice, one bottle of club soda, some strawberries, some cherries, and a cut-up orange. Using the same ingredients, someone else might mix one bottle of orange juice, two bottles of club soda, and the same kinds of fruit but in different amounts.

You both would have mixtures of liquids and fruit, but the mixtures would not be the same throughout. So a single formula could not accurately represent the makeup of such a mixture.

Unlike a mixture, a compound *always* has the same composition. For example, no matter where it comes from, salt always contains one part sodium and one part chlorine. Water always contains two parts hydrogen and one part oxygen. That's why you can use a chemical formula to represent a compound. The chemical makeup of a given compound never changes.

Some Common Mixtures

Most matter in the world around you exists as mixtures. You just have to look out the window to see evidence of this. In fact, the glass in your classroom windows is a mixture. Most window glass is made up of silicon dioxide (sil'i kän dī äks'īd), sodium oxide, and perhaps some other substances.

Most glass is pretty much the same. However, the amount of each substance that is used to make glass can vary a little from sample to sample without affecting the properties of the glass.

Beyond your classroom window you can probably see a variety of materials, such as bricks, cement, and asphalt (as'fôlt). All these building materials are mixtures. As you observe these mixtures, you are looking through, and are surrounded by, a very important natural mixture—air.

Air is a mixture of gases. This mixture consists of about four-fifths nitrogen gas and one-fifth oxygen gas. But air also contains small amounts of other gases, such as carbon dioxide and water vapor. The percentages of these gases vary from place to place and from time to time.

You don't have to look outside the classroom to find mixtures. In fact, you don't even have to look outside your own body. Everyone's body contains many different mixtures. Blood, sweat, tears, and saliva are a few examples of mixtures that make you what you are.

Separating Mixtures

The different materials in a mixture can almost always be separated from

▲ The composition of air changes from time to time and place to place. Polluted air is a mixture that evidences one effect of sin in our world.

each other by some physical means. For example, think of the methods you used to separate different mixtures in the activity on pages C44 and C45.

As you learned, the method used to separate a mixture depends on some difference in the physical properties of the materials in the mixture. One important property used in separating a mixture is the size of the pieces making up the mixture. Suppose, for example, you had a pocketful of coins—pennies, nickels, dimes, and quarters. You could easily separate this mixture by hand.

Now suppose you get a job in a store. At the end of the week, you are asked to separate a shopping bag full of coins. You could do this by hand, but it would take quite a while. A sorting machine like the one shown would make the job of separating the coins easier.

A mixture of salt and sand would be more difficult to separate than a mixture of coins. It would be almost impossible to separate the materials by hand. And a sorting machine wouldn't work, because the pieces of salt and sand are similar in size. So you have to find another method for separating the mixture.

Think about salt and sand. Do either of these materials have some property you could use to separate them? Yes; salt

▲ What properties of coins does this machine use to separate a mixture of coins?

What property or properties could you use to separate a mixture of coins? ▶

dissolves in water and sand does not. If you add water to a mixture of salt and sand, the salt will dissolve in the water. You can then pour off the salt water and collect the sand, which remains behind. How might you get the salt back from the salt water? ■

INVESTIGATION 2

1. Explain why a mixture is not a substance and cannot be represented by a chemical formula.

2. Suppose you had a mixture of iron pellets, pebbles, and small wood spheres, all about the same size. How would you separate this mixture?

3. Name a mixture that you regard as a special blessing from God.

INVESTIGATION 3

WHAT ARE LIQUID MIXTURES LIKE?

What do milk, soft drinks, and ocean water have in common? Your first thought may be that they are all liquids. But if you consider it more carefully, you'll realize that they are all liquid mixtures. Study the properties of these mixtures in this investigation.

Activity

Mixing Solids into Liquids

When you mix sugar and water, the sugar dissolves in the water and seems to disappear. What factors affect how fast the sugar disappears?

MATERIALS
- goggles
- 3 plastic jars
- water
- marker
- sugar cubes
- stirring rod
- timer
- spoon
- Science Notebook

SAFETY
Wear goggles during this activity.

Procedure

1. In your *Science Notebook*, **make a chart** like the one shown on page C53.

2. Fill one jar with ice-cold water, a second jar with water at room temperature, and a third jar with warm water. Use a marker to label the jars as shown here.

Step 2

3. Predict in which water a sugar cube will dissolve most quickly. Then add a sugar cube to each jar. Time how long it takes for each sugar cube to dissolve. **Record** the times in your chart.

Conditions	Time
Cold Water	
Water at Room Temperature	
Warm Water	
Warm Water + Stirring	
Warm Water + Crushed Sugar + Stirring	

4. Pour out the water and rinse the jars. Refill one jar with warm water and add a sugar cube. This time, stir the mixture until the sugar cube dissolves. **Record** the time.

5. Use a spoon to crush a sugar cube. Repeat step 4 using the crushed sugar. **Record** the time.

Step 4

Analyze and Conclude

1. How did the temperature of the water affect the rate at which the sugar dissolved in it?

2. What effect did stirring have on the rate at which the sugar dissolved in water?

3. What effect did crushing the sugar into small particles have on the rate at which the sugar dissolved?

4. What can you **infer** about the size of the sugar particles that are dissolved in a mixture of sugar and water?

5. Suggest a hypothesis that relates the effects of water temperature, stirring, and smaller pieces of sugar to the rate at which sugar dissolves.

INVESTIGATE FURTHER!

EXPERIMENT

Why is ocean water salty? Once salt is dissolved in water, how can you get the salt back? Design an experiment to get the salt out of salt water.

Activity
To Mix or Not to Mix

Shake that bottle of salad dressing before you pour it on your salad. If you don't, you may get only part of the mixture.

MATERIALS
- clear bottle with screw-on lid
- water
- dropper
- blue food coloring
- mineral oil
- *Science Notebook*

Procedure

1. Add water to a bottle until it is about one-third full.

2. Add a few drops of food coloring to the water. Swirl the bottle around until the water is evenly colored throughout.

3. Add the same amount of mineral oil to the bottle as you did water. Screw the lid tightly on the bottle.

4. Shake the bottle several times and stand it on the table. **Observe** what happens to the liquids in the bottle. **Record** your observations in your *Science Notebook*.

5. Turn the bottle upside down and hold it that way. **Observe** what happens to the liquids and **record** your observations.

Step 3

Analyze and Conclude

1. Does water mix with food coloring? **Give evidence** to support your answer.

2. Do water and oil mix? **Give evidence** to support your answer.

3. What happened when you turned the bottle upside down?

4. Based on your observations, what can you **infer** about the ability of different liquids to mix?

Step 4

Activity
Making Water Wetter

What happens if you try to clean a greasy dish with plain water? The water runs off the dish. The water doesn't seem to wet the dish. Can you mix something with water to make it "wetter"?

MATERIALS
- wax paper
- 3 droppers
- unidentified blue liquid
- unidentified red liquid
- toothpick
- water
- *Science Notebook*

Procedure

1. Spread a sheet of wax paper on the table.

2. Use a dropper to carefully place one drop of either colored liquid on the paper. Use a toothpick to probe the drop and **observe** how it behaves. In your *Science Notebook*, **record** your observations, including the color of the drop and what shape the drop takes.

3. Using a clean dropper, place a drop of the other colored liquid on the paper. Use the toothpick to probe the drop and **observe** how it behaves. **Record** your observations.

4. Repeat step 3 with a drop of water.

Step 3

Analyze and Conclude

1. Describe the shapes of the two colored drops and **compare** their behavior when you probed them with a toothpick.

2. One colored liquid is plain water mixed with food coloring; the other is water mixed with food coloring and detergent. **Infer** which is which. **Give evidence** to support your inference.

3. Which liquid seemed to "wet" the waxed paper better?

4. **Suggest a hypothesis** to explain how detergent in water helps clean grease.

C55

What's the Solution?

When viewed from space, Earth is a lovely planet. Satellite photographs of our planet show cloud patterns, oceans, and continents—in other words, air, sea, and land. These three nonliving parts of our planet are mixtures. Air is a mixture of gases. Rocks are mixtures of minerals. And seawater is a mixture of water and different minerals, mainly salts.

More Mixing

Look back at the graphic organizer on page C35. Notice that mixtures are divided into two groups—unevenly mixed and evenly mixed. Most mixtures fall into the unevenly mixed group.

Suppose you added equal amounts of sand, salt, and sugar to a container. You could try everything to mix the materials evenly, but some parts of the mixture would be just a little different from the other parts. One part of the mixture would contain a few more grains of salt or sugar than another part, for example. Now think of the sugar-water mixture you made in the activity on page C23. Recall that the sugar and water mixed so completely that the solid sugar seemed to disappear. If you had taken samples from different parts of the mixture, you would have found that every part was exactly the same as every other part.

When sugar mixes with water, the sugar spreads evenly throughout the water and seems to disappear. ▼

C56

◄ Salad dressing is an example of a suspension. A suspension is a liquid mixture in which some particles are temporarily suspended in the mixture.

Even after it is shaken, the salad ▶ dressing is not a solution. If the bottle is left to stand, the dressing separates into its different parts.

Solutions Are Not Puzzling

A mixture in which the different particles of matter are spread evenly throughout is called a **solution**. A solution has two main parts. The **solvent** (säl′vənt) is the material that is present in the greater amount. The **solute** (säl′yo͞ot) is the material present in the smaller amount.

You are probably most familiar with solutions formed when a solid solute, such as sugar, dissolves in a liquid solvent, such as water. You might be surprised to learn that there are other types of solutions. For example, bronze (bränz) is a solution of two metals, tin and copper.

Factors Affecting the Rate of Solution

Which dissolves faster in water—a sugar cube or a spoonful of loose sugar grains? Dissolving takes place only on the surface of the sugar, where the water is in contact with the sugar. Sugar grains dissolve faster than a sugar cube. The drawing below shows why.

Temperature also affects the rate at which things dissolve. For example, sugar dissolves faster in hot water than in cold water. The particles of hot water are moving faster and have more energy than the particles of cold water. The fast-moving particles bump into the sugar harder and more frequently, helping to break the sugar into smaller pieces.

Stirring a mixture also helps speed up the rate at which things dissolve. Stirring causes the particles of solute to mix more quickly with the particles of solvent. ■

▲ This sugar cube has six sides. Each side has a surface area of 4 cm². The total surface area of this cube is 6 × 4 cm² = 24 cm².

◄ This is the same amount of sugar. The total surface area of 1 small cube is 6 × 1 cm². There are 8 small cubes. So the total surface area of 8 cubes is 8 × 6 cm² = 48 cm².

Bubbles

Matthew 14 records that Jesus walked on top of the water. Jesus can walk on water because He is true God. But have you ever seen a water strider? A water strider is an insect that is able to walk on water! How does the water strider manage to stay on the water's surface? If you look closely at the surface, it seems to be covered with a very thin skin. The shape of the insect's feet allow it to glide across this skin without breaking it.

A force of attraction called cohesion exists among water particles. This force produces an effect called surface tension, which is responsible for the "skin" on the water's surface.

Have you ever tried to produce large bubbles like the one shown, using plain water? It's not possible. But if you add a little soap to the water, you can form delicate bubbles that float in the air.

When soap is added to water, it reduces the cohesion among water particles. Surface tension is also greatly reduced. If the water strider stepped onto the surface of soapy water, the insect would enjoy a swim rather than a stroll.

▲ The reduced cohesion makes it possible for the soap-water mixture to be stretched out into a thin film, or bubble. Some soap bubbles are no more than one or two particles in thickness.

Alloys

Question: When is a metal not an element? Answer: When it's an alloy. An **alloy** is a solution of two or more metals with properties of its own. For example, stainless steel is an alloy of iron, chromium, carbon, and nickel. Stainless steel is stronger than iron, lighter than iron, and resists rusting.

An alloy is made by melting two or more metals and mixing them together. The mixture is then allowed to cool and harden to a solid. In its final form an alloy consists of a solution in which the metal components are thoroughly mixed with each other.

Some Important Alloys

Alloys have been important to humans for thousands of years. One of the first alloys ever prepared was bronze, a mixture of copper and tin. Some bronzes also include small amounts of zinc.

The earliest bronze items have been dated back to about 3500 B.C. The introduction of bronze was such an important event that a whole period in human history—the Bronze Age—has been named after this alloy.

▲ God's Old Testament people used a portable altar overlaid in bronze (Exodus 27:2). God told Moses to place a bronze snake on a pole (Numbers 21:9) to heal the people who trusted in God. Jesus later compared this bronze snake to Himself (John 3:14). The artifacts pictured above are made of bronze.

Alloy	Composition	Use
Brass	70% Cu, 30% Zn	Hardware, plumbing
Bronze	90% Cu, 10% Sn	Artwork, domes of buildings
Gold alloy	70% Au, 15% Ag, 10% Cu, 1% Pt, 1% Zn, 1% Pd	Dentistry, Jewelry
Pewter	85% Sn, 7% Cu, 6% Bi, 2% Sb	Cups, candlesticks
Solder	60% Pb, 40% Sn	Connecting metal pieces together
Stainless Steel	74% Fe, 18% Cr, 8% Ni	Cutlery
Steel	99% Fe, 1% C	Bridges, Buildings
Sterling Silver	93% Ag, 7% Cu	Jewelry, tableware

The table above lists some common alloys and tells what metals they contain and how they are used. Refer to the periodic table on pages C36 and C37 for the names of the metals whose chemical symbols are given.

Alloys are useful because their properties are different from those of the metals from which they are made. For example, alloys of gold are much harder and less expensive than pure gold. A unit called a karat (kar′ət) is used to express the purity of a sample of gold.

Amalgams (ə mal′gəmz) are alloys that contain mercury. An amalgam used in dental work consists of 70 percent silver, 18 percent tin, 10 percent copper, and 2 percent mercury. The mercury makes the amalgam soft enough for a dentist to work with it.

Some alloys have unusual properties. For example, Wood's metal is an alloy of bismuth (biz′məth), lead, tin, and cadmium (kad′mē əm). This alloy has a melting point of 70°C. It will melt on your stove at a relatively low temperature setting. Can you think of any use for such an alloy?

Another interesting alloy is misch (mish) metal, which is made of cerium (sir′ē əm), lanthanum (lan′thə nəm), and other metals known as "rare earth" elements. Misch metal has the unusual property of giving off sparks when it is rubbed. Because of this property, misch metal is used in the manufacture of flints used for lighting butane stoves. ∎

INVESTIGATION 3

1. Explain why salad dressing is not a solution.

2. Why is an alloy both a mixture and a solution?

3. Explain why the ability to make alloys is a great blessing from God.

REFLECT & EVALUATE

WORD POWER

alloy
atom
compound
element
mixture
chemical property
chemical symbol
chemical formula
physical property
molecule
solution
solute
solvent
substance

On Your Own
Review the terms in the list. Then use as many terms as you can to write a brief summary of the chapter.

With a Partner
Make a quiz using all the words in the list. Challenge your partner to complete the quiz.

Make a chart with three columns. Use the headings Elements, Compounds, and Mixtures. Under each heading, list ten examples of materials that belong in that group.

Analyze Information

Study the section of the periodic table shown. Use the section to determine which elements God designed to be more similar in chemical and physical properties—copper and zinc or copper and silver. How do you know?

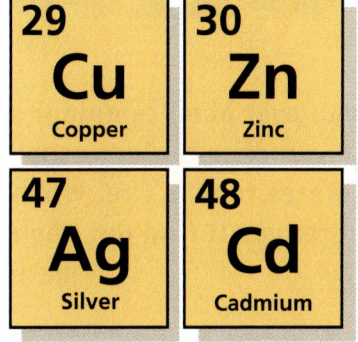

Assess Performance

Design and carry out an experiment to find out how temperature affects the amount of sugar that can be dissolved in 50 mL of water.

Problem Solving

1. Explain why all the elements that appear in the same column of the periodic table are commonly referred to as a family.

2. Suppose you had a can filled with brass tacks and iron tacks. How could you quickly separate this mixture of objects?

3. Explain why salt cannot be removed from a salt-water mixture by pouring the mixture through a paper filter.

CHAPTER 3

HOW MATTER CHANGES

Have you ever been camping? A good campfire may have helped warm you. A campfire builder usually has to cut large pieces of wood into smaller pieces for the fire. When this wood burns, it leaves only ashes. In this chapter you'll find out about the physical and chemical changes that matter undergoes.

Nature's Medicines

Petrona Rios collects plants and insects in the rain forests of Costa Rica. As a bioprospector (bī ō prä'spek tər), she gathers these specimens so that chemists can analyze them for their potential use in developing new medicines.

Along with other bioprospectors, Petrona Rios continually crisscrosses the rain forest, gathering plant and insect specimens. The collected specimens are processed at INBio (Instituto Nacional de Biodiversidad) and sent to the University of Costa Rica. There, chemists make samples of the materials and send them to a major drug company. Chemists at the drug company thoroughly test the samples, looking for substances that can be used in new medicines.

As the samples are tested, they go through many chemical and physical changes. What chemical and physical changes do you see every day?

Coming Up

INVESTIGATION 1 — How Can Matter Change? C64

INVESTIGATION 2 — What Are Acids and Bases? C78

INVESTIGATION 3 — What Do Chemists Do? C86

◀ Petrona Rios (*center*) with student assistants

How Can Matter Change?

INVESTIGATION 1

You can tear a piece of paper into hundreds of smaller pieces. Yet each piece, no matter how small, is still paper. You could recycle the small pieces and make new paper from them. But what would you have if you were to burn the paper? Find out about changes that matter can undergo in this investigation.

Activity

Balloon Blower

Blowing up a balloon can be a lot of work. How would you like to have a balloon that blows itself up? In this activity you can combine some materials and make an automatic balloon inflator with the changes that result.

MATERIALS
- goggles
- balloon
- funnel
- measuring spoon
- baking soda
- vinegar
- narrow-necked glass bottle
- Science Notebook

SAFETY
Wear goggles during this activity.

Procedure

1. Blow up a balloon and let the air out several times. This action will stretch the rubber, making the balloon easier to inflate.

2. Place the stem of a funnel in the neck of the deflated balloon. Pour two spoonfuls of baking soda into the balloon. Gently shake the balloon to make sure the baking soda settles to the bottom of the balloon. Remove the funnel from the balloon.

3. Add several spoonfuls of vinegar to a narrow-necked bottle.

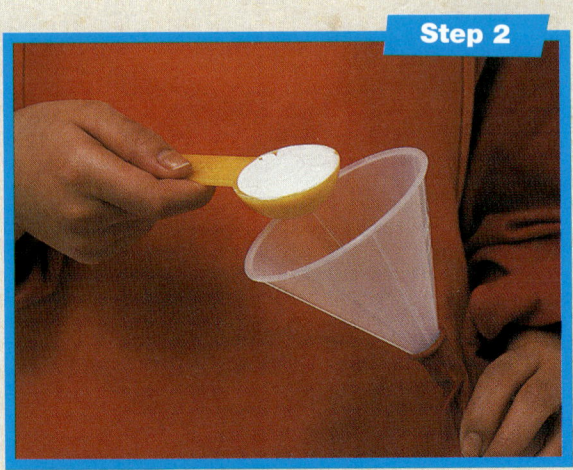

Step 2

4. Stretch the opening of the balloon over the mouth of the bottle, as shown in the picture. Make sure no baking soda escapes from the balloon.

5. Lift the balloon and hold it above the bottle so that the baking soda falls into the bottle.

Step 4

6. Observe the changes that take place when the baking soda mixes with the vinegar. **Record** your observations in your *Science Notebook*.

Analyze and Conclude

1. Describe what you observed happening inside the bottle after the baking soda dropped into the vinegar. A chemical change involves the formation of new substances. What evidence is there that a chemical change took place?

2. What happened to the balloon? From your observation, what can you **infer** about one of the substances produced when vinegar and baking soda reacted?

3. Hypothesize about the action of the baking soda and vinegar. Are they both still present, or have they changed into new types of matter? **Give evidence** to support your hypothesis.

INVESTIGATE FURTHER!

RESEARCH

Look up the ingredients in baking soda in a cookbook and find out some of its uses. What does baking soda do when a food containing it is cooked? What kinds of foods include baking soda as an ingredient?

Activity
Making a Fire Extinguisher

In the last activity a chemical change produced a gas. In this activity you can see why this gas makes a useful fire extinguisher.

MATERIALS
- goggles
- measuring spoon
- vinegar
- 2 plastic jars
- baking soda
- candle
- shallow dish
- 2 long fireplace matches
- *Science Notebook*

SAFETY
Wear goggles during this activity. Be very careful when working around open flames. Secure loose clothing and tie back long hair. Avoid melted candle wax. It can cause painful burns.

Procedure

1. Add three spoonfuls of vinegar to one jar and one spoonful of baking soda to another jar.

2. Place a candle in the center of a shallow dish and ask your teacher to light the candle. Ignite a fireplace match by holding it at the end and placing the tip of the match in the candle flame.

3. Insert the burning match first into the jar containing baking soda and then into the jar containing vinegar, as shown in the picture. Do not allow the flame to touch the contents of the jars. Look for any changes in the flame, and **record** your observations in your *Science Notebook*. Blow out the match.

4. Hold the jar containing baking soda firmly on the tabletop while you carefully pour the vinegar into this jar. **Describe** what happens.

5. Light another match by holding it in the candle flame and then blow out the candle. Insert the tip of the burning match into the jar containing the vinegar and baking soda. **Observe** what happens and **record** your observations.

Analyze and Conclude

1. Oxygen must be present for burning to take place. **Infer** whether oxygen was present inside the jars above the baking soda and the vinegar before you mixed them. **Explain** what your inference is based on.

2. What **inferences** can you make about the gas released when you mixed the vinegar and the baking soda? **Give evidence** to support your inferences.

Step 3

Activity
Solids From Liquids

MATERIALS
- goggles
- unknown liquids *A* and *B*
- *Science Notebook*

SAFETY
Wear goggles during this activity. Avoid letting chemicals come in contact with your skin. Do not put any chemicals in your mouth.

You've made a solid from a liquid if you have ever frozen water into ice. In this activity you'll make a solid from two liquids by causing a chemical change.

Procedure

1. Obtain samples of unknown liquids *A* and *B*. Study the liquids and **record** your observations in your *Science Notebook*.

2. Mix the two liquids by carefully pouring the contents of one container into the other container.

Step 2

3. Observe the mixture for five minutes. **Record** any changes you observe.

Analyze and Conclude

1. What did you **observe** happening when you mixed the two liquids together?

2. What evidence indicates that the change you observed taking place was a chemical change?

3. Hypothesize whether liquids *A* and *B* are the same material or different materials. Support your hypothesis.

Physical and Chemical Change

Picture yourself in this situation. You're getting ready to go to a party. You're all dressed except for your favorite wool sweater, which just came from the cleaners. You take the sweater from its protective plastic and pull it on. But it's too small—much too small!

You take the sweater off and hold it up. It's about half the size it's supposed to be! At first you think the cleaners gave you the wrong sweater. But the name tag sewn inside tells you it's your sweater. What went wrong?

Changing but Staying the Same

The case of the shrunken sweater is an example of a physical change. A **physical change** is a change in the size, shape, or state of a material. No new matter is formed during a physical change. The wool of the sweater is still the same. It just takes up less space now!

You see physical changes every day. When you sharpen a pencil or rub chalk on the board, you cause physical changes to take place. The pencil shavings and the chalk dust produced by your actions are different from the objects they came from. But the shavings are still made up of wood, and the dust is still made up of chalk.

In nature, physical changes can turn one kind of landscape into another. For example, over millions of years a river can carve its way down through solid rock to form a deep canyon. Pounding waves can transform rock cliffs into fine sand. In both cases, the rocks may be changed in size and appearance, but they are still made of the same substances.

Water is a good substance to use when studying physical changes. Many substances dissolve in water. The act of dissolving is a physical change. Changes in state—melting, freezing, evaporation, and condensation—are physical changes.

How can you tell when milk has turned sour? ▼

Changing but *Not* Staying the Same

Have you ever smelled milk that has turned sour? Do you think that sour milk is the same as fresh milk? Whole milk is a mixture. When bacteria from the air digest part of the mixture, changes occur and a new substance (lactic acid) is produced. This change is similar to the one you observed when you mixed two liquids together in the activity on page C67. Any change in which one or more new substances are formed is a **chemical change**.

Water can also be changed chemically. Recall that water is a compound made up of the elements hydrogen and oxygen. The drawing shows how water can be changed into its component elements.

▲ Plants use energy from sunlight to change water and carbon dioxide gas into sugar. Plants use the sugar as food.

▲ Animals use plants as food. Chemical changes occur when food is digested. These chemical changes release energy that animals need to grow and be active.

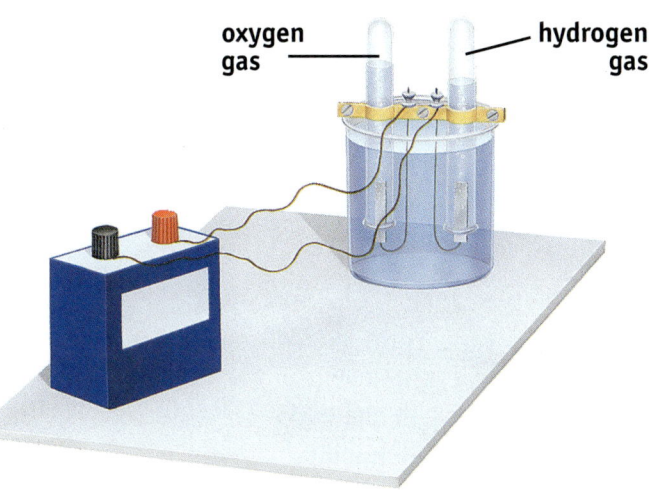

▲ An electric current can be used to separate water into oxygen gas and hydrogen gas. The gases can be collected in test tubes.

Chemical changes are common in nature. The rusting of iron is one example of such a change. Rust is produced when oxygen from the air combines with iron. The product is neither iron nor oxygen, but a new substance called iron oxide, or rust.

▲ Some chemical changes are not helpful. For example, rusty parts on a bicycle don't move smoothly and may even crumble.

C69

Describing Chemical Changes

Chemical changes are triggered by chemical reactions. In a chemical reaction, one or more substances interact to form new substances. When describing what happens during a chemical reaction, scientists often use symbols and formulas to write "chemical sentences." These sentences are written in the form of equations, much like those used in math problems.

Suppose you wanted to describe the reaction in which water is broken down into hydrogen and oxygen. The chemical equation for this reaction is shown here.

$$2H_2O \rightarrow 2H_2 + O_2$$

If you wanted to express this reaction in words, you would say that two molecules of water break down to produce two molecules of hydrogen gas and one molecule of oxygen gas. In this equation, the plus sign is read as *and* and the arrow is read as *produce*.

Let's look at the formula for the reaction in which iron and oxygen combine to produce iron oxide, or rust.

$$4Fe + 3O_2 \rightarrow 2Fe_2O_3$$

How would you write this chemical sentence in words?

Changes occur every second of the day. Many changes, such as the freezing of water to form ice, are physical. No new substances are formed. Other changes, such as those that occur when a fuel is burned, or a piece of iron rusts, result in new substances being formed. Such changes are chemical changes. ■

SCIENCE AND FAITH

In his <u>Addresses to the Communicants for a Third Service</u>, Joseph Priestly, chemist and clergyman, wrote, "The true Christian lives as seeing God who is invisible. In all the works of nature he rejoices in the God of nature. In every human being he sees a child of the same parent as himself, an object of the same parental care and bounty, a scholar in the same school of discipline, and as he may hope, an heir to the same immortal life, revealed to him in the Gospel." What change does Priestly, the discoverer of oxygen, describe taking place in those who belong to God by faith in Jesus?

Atomic Structure and Chemical Change

Imagine that the marbles in the picture are elements. Suppose you were asked to arrange the marbles to make as many different substances as possible. You are told that a substance can have as few as one element and as many as five. How many different substances can you make in two minutes?

Now think about the 109 known elements. How many different substances can be made from these elements? Now you have some idea about how it is possible to have so many different kinds of matter on Earth.

What Is a Model?

All chemical changes involve atoms. So if you want to understand what's happening when a match burns, when iron rusts, or when milk sours, you need to know more about atoms.

Atoms, of course, are much too small to be seen, even with the most powerful microscope. How then do scientists learn about atoms? Just about everything known about atoms has been learned from indirect evidence. This evidence is gathered by studying how matter behaves in all kinds of chemical reactions.

Based on this evidence, scientists have developed various models of the atom. In science, a **model** is a way to represent an object or to describe how a process takes place. Models are often used to describe things that are too big or too small to be studied directly. For example, a globe is a model of Earth.

What Is an Atom Like?

Modern scientific models of the atom describe it as being made up of several different tiny parts. These tiny parts are called protons (prō′tänz), neutrons (n$\overline{oo}$′tränz), and electrons (ē lek′tränz).

Most of the mass of an atom is contained in a dense, central core called a **nucleus** (n$\overline{oo}$′klē əs). This nucleus contains protons and neutrons. A **proton** is a particle with a positive electric charge. A **neutron** is a particle with no electric charge.

Traveling around the nucleus, at some distance from it, are one or more electrons. An **electron** is a particle with a negative electric charge.

C71

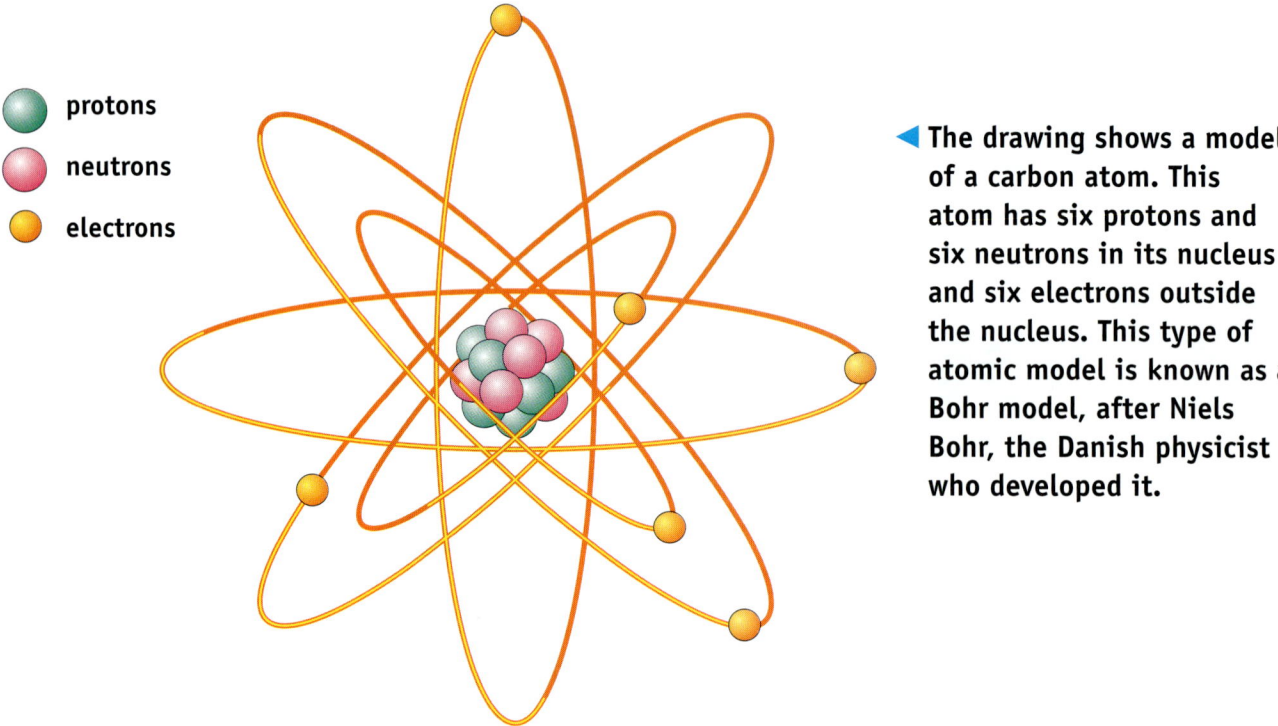

◀ The drawing shows a model of a carbon atom. This atom has six protons and six neutrons in its nucleus and six electrons outside the nucleus. This type of atomic model is known as a Bohr model, after Niels Bohr, the Danish physicist who developed it.

Two Models—Old and New

Look at the Bohr models of a helium atom and a lithium (lith′ē əm) atom below. Notice how the electrons are shown moving around the nucleus in paths called orbits. This model is also called the planetary model of the atom. Why do you think this is so?

Bohr suggested his model in 1913. As scientists learned more about atoms, they found that electrons do not travel in definite orbits. Rather, they "swarm" around the nucleus, much like bees swarm around a hive.

Because electrons travel so fast, they can be thought of as a "cloud" surrounding the nucleus. The drawing below shows a model of the atom known as the electron cloud model.

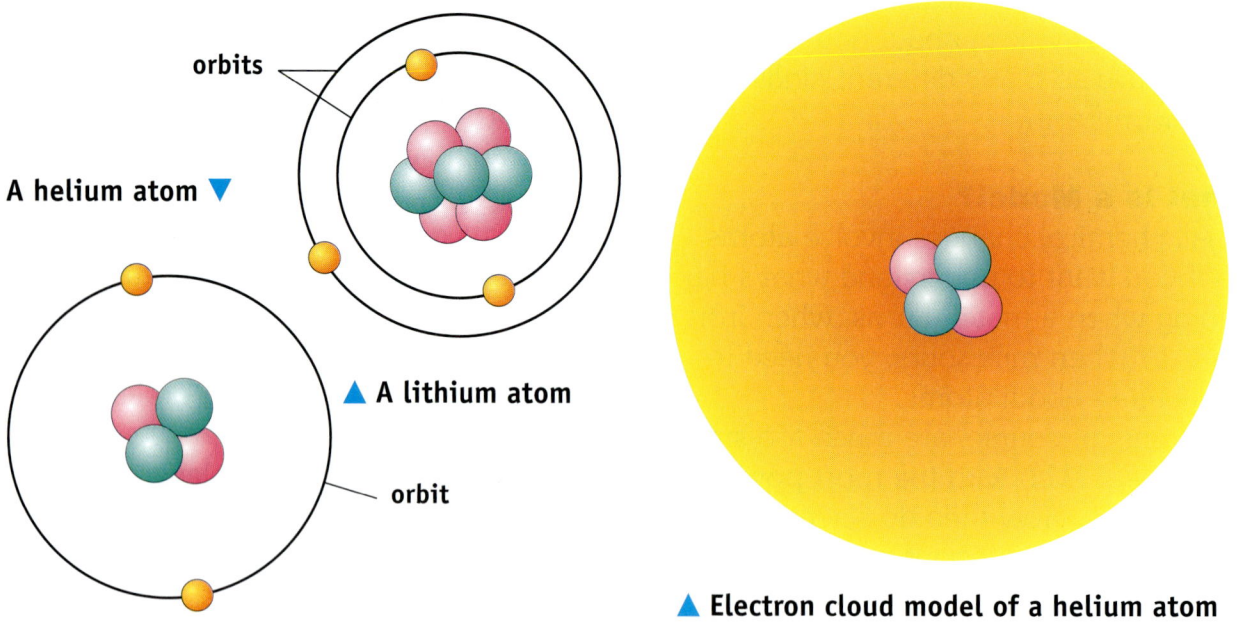

▲ Electron cloud model of a helium atom

Roles of Protons and Electrons

The number of protons in the nucleus of an atom gives the atom its identity. An atom of hydrogen has one proton. An atom of oxygen has eight protons. That's what makes hydrogen what it is and oxygen what it is.

Recall from the periodic table on pages C36 and C37 that every element has a different atomic number. The **atomic number** of an element is the number of protons in an atom of that element. The atomic number of hydrogen is 1. What is the atomic number of oxygen?

Electrons are the smallest and lightest of the three types of atomic particles. Yet, because electrons move around outside the nucleus, they determine how an atom reacts with other atoms. In other words, the electrons surrounding a nucleus give an atom its chemical properties.

When an atom loses electrons, it becomes a positive ion. ▼

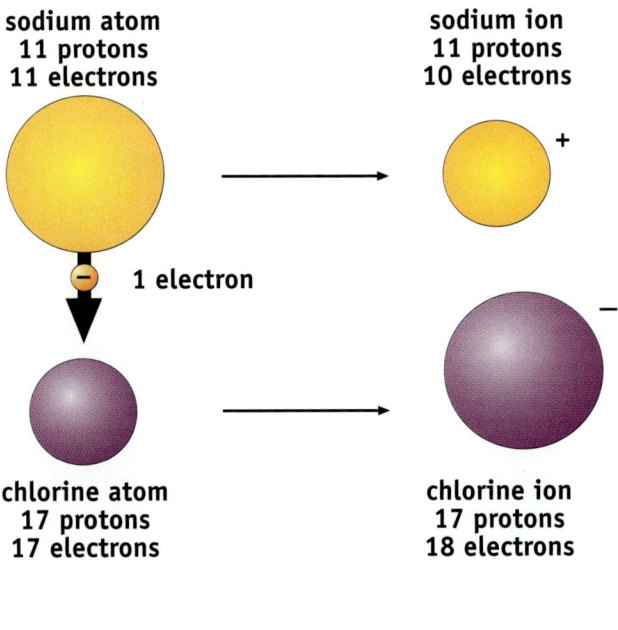

▲ **When an atom gains electrons, it becomes a negative ion.**

Atoms With a Charge

Usually the number of protons in an atom equals the number of electrons. So the positive and negative charges balance each other. This balance leaves the atom electrically neutral.

Sometimes, however, an atom may capture one or more electrons from another atom. When this happens, both atoms become electrically charged. An electrically charged atom is called an **ion** (ī′ən). The drawing shows how positive and negative ions are formed.

Because they have opposite charges, positive and negative ions attract each other. If the attraction is strong enough, the ions are held tightly together and form an ionic compound. Perhaps the most familiar compound formed in this way is table salt, or sodium chloride.

Ionic compounds are not made up of molecules. Instead, the basic unit of any ionic compound is made up of one or more positive ions and one or more negative ions.

Sodium chloride is made up of positive sodium ions (*yellow*) and negative chlorine ions (*violet*). ▼

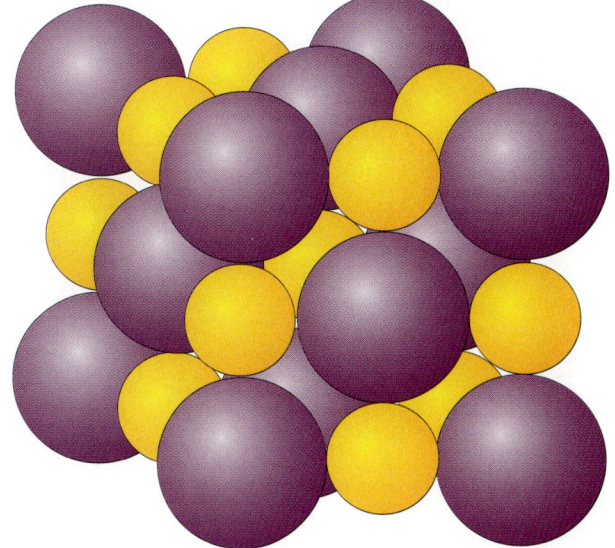

Atoms and Molecules

Many compounds, such as water, are made up of molecules. In forming molecules, atoms don't gain or lose electrons. Instead they share electrons. For example, when hydrogen reacts with oxygen to form water, two hydrogen atoms and one oxygen atom join up by sharing electrons, as shown in the drawing.

It is as if the oxygen atom is holding hands with two hydrogen atoms. Think of each hand as an electron. And think of each pair of clasped hands as a chemical bond between the atoms. Chemists call this type of compound a covalent compound.

Making and Breaking Bonds

Energy is always involved in the making or breaking of chemical bonds. Usually when bonds form between atoms, energy is given off. However, sometimes a little energy must be added to get such a reaction started. For example, a little spark is needed to get hydrogen to combine with oxygen. But once the reaction starts, energy is given off rapidly, as shown in the photograph.

Energy is also involved in breaking chemical bonds. Recall the description on page C69 of how water can be broken down into hydrogen and oxygen by passing electricity through it. The electricity provides the energy needed to break the bonds between the hydrogen atoms and oxygen atoms that make up water.

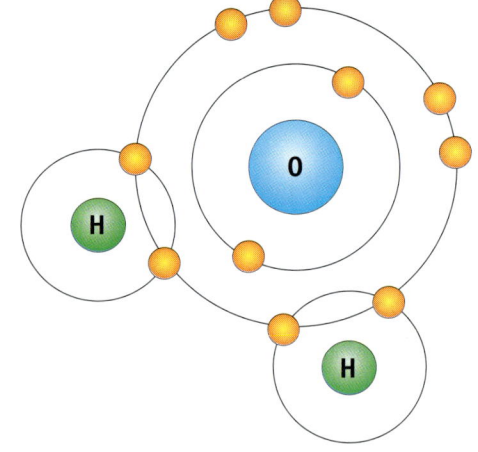
▲ Chemical bonds in a water molecule

In 1937, disaster struck the hydrogen-filled *Hindenberg*, the best-known airship in the world. A spark ignited the ship's hydrogen, and energy was released as the hydrogen combined with oxygen in the air. How can God work good even in disasters such as this?

Conservation of Mass

When a piece of wood burns, the mass of the ashes that remain is less than the mass of the original piece of wood. On the other hand, when a piece of tin is heated, it gains mass. Three hundred years ago, these and similar observations led scientists to wonder: Is matter destroyed when wood burns? Is matter created when tin is heated?

Over the years the work of many scientists provided answers to these and other questions about matter. For example, when wood burns, some of its mass goes into gases that are produced. These gases escape into the air. Today we know that matter cannot be created or destroyed by any chemical reaction. This statement of fact is known as the law of conservation of mass.

Working independently, two scientists — Joseph Priestly and Karl Wilhelm Scheele — discover oxygen.

A.D. 1774

Albert Einstein publishes his Theory of Relativity, which includes the equation $E = mc^2$. This theory establishes the relationship between mass and energy.

1905

1890–1910
Marie Curie's work with radium leads to a better understanding of radioactivity.

1789
Antoine Lavoisier, a French chemist, discovers that when matter such as tin burns, it combines with oxygen. This discovery leads to the law of conservation of mass.

450 B.C.
Greek philosophers Leucippus (lōō sip′əs) and Democritus (di mäk′rə təs) first state the ideas set forth in the law of conservation of mass.

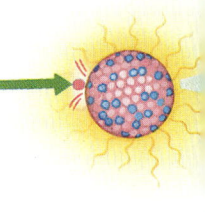

Radioactive Elements

On March 1, 1896, French scientist Henri Becquerel wrapped a sheet of photographic film in paper that light couldn't penetrate. He placed the package in a desk drawer, together with a few small rocks, and closed the drawer.

A few days later, Becquerel developed the film, expecting to see an unexposed white negative. Instead he was shocked to see darkened areas on the film. Something had changed the chemicals on the film—but what?

▲ Becquerel discovers radioactivity.

Nuclear Radiation

Becquerel's film had been exposed to nuclear radiation (rā dē ā′shən), invisible energy that came from the rocks. The rocks contained the radioactive element uranium (yo͞o rā′nē əm). A **radioactive element** is made up of atoms whose nuclei break down, or decay, into nuclei of other atoms.

When a radioactive element decays, it changes into a different element. This happens because some of the radiation released by the decaying nucleus is in the form of protons and neutrons. And when an atom loses protons from its nucleus, its atomic number changes.

Recall that an element is identified by its atomic number. The drawing shows how a uranium nucleus decays to form a thorium (thôr′ē əm) nucleus.

When a nucleus decays, large amounts of energy are released. This energy travels in the form of invisible high-energy rays called gamma (gam′ə) rays.

Using Energy From Atoms

Radioactive elements occur naturally. However, scientists have also learned

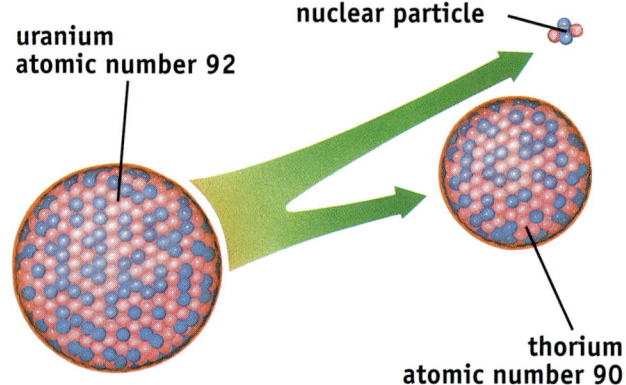

▲ When a uranium nucleus decays, it loses 2 protons and 2 neutrons, leaving a nucleus with 90 protons. The element with atomic number 90 is thorium.

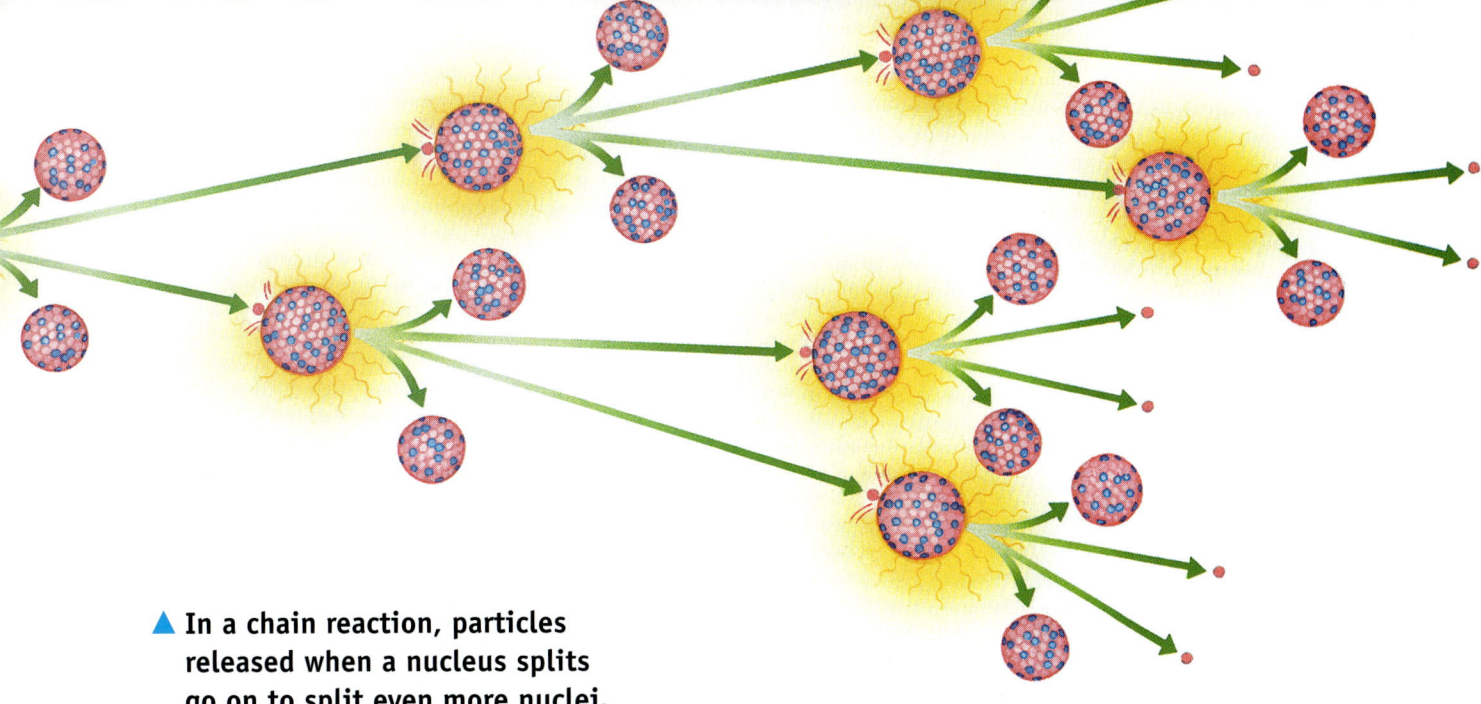

▼ In a chain reaction, particles released when a nucleus splits go on to split even more nuclei.

how to split the nuclei of atoms of some elements by bombarding them with neutrons. This reaction is called **nuclear fission** (no͞o′klē ər fish′ən). *Fission* means "to split."

The drawing above shows how neutrons are used to split nuclei of uranium atoms. Each time a nucleus splits, particles and energy are released. Some of the released neutrons collide with and split other nuclei, producing a chain reaction.

An uncontrolled nuclear chain reaction releases energy so fast that an explosion takes place. A nuclear reactor is a device in which a nuclear chain reaction is controlled. In a controlled chain reaction, energy is released slowly.

Radiation—Helpful and Harmful

Nuclear reactors provide energy that is used to generate electricity. Reactors are also used to make radioactive forms of many elements. These elements are used in medical research and in the treatment of certain illnesses.

Nuclear radiation can also be dangerous. For example, gamma rays can pass through human tissue, damaging cells along the way. This damage can cause serious illness or even death.

Clearly, nuclear energy has many beneficial uses. But if radioactive materials are not handled safely or if they get into the environment by accident, they can present serious health problems. ■

INVESTIGATION 1

1. How does heating sugar in a spoon differ from dissolving it in a cup of hot water?

2. Suppose two neutrons escape the nucleus of an atom. What effect would this event have on the atomic number of and total electric charge on the atom? Explain your answer.

3. What effects of radiation evidence the consequences of sin in our world? What effects evidence God's love and grace?

INVESTIGATION 2

WHAT ARE ACIDS AND BASES?

Vinegar, orange juice, soap, baking soda, and antacid tablets are all things you can probably find around your home. Some of these materials are acids, and some are bases. In this investigation you'll find out what acids and bases are and how to use some simple tests to tell the difference.

Activity

Cabbage-Juice Science

Some substances, called indicators, are one color in an acid and a different color in a base. In this activity you can see for yourself how an indicator works.

Procedure

1. In your *Science Notebook*, prepare a chart like the one shown on page C79.

2. Half-fill four small plastic jars with red cabbage juice, and number the jars with a marker.

3. Use a dropper to add a few drops of vinegar to the cabbage juice in jar 1. Use a clean dropper to add a few drops of lemon juice to jar 2. **Record** in your chart any changes that you observe.

Step 3

MATERIALS
- goggles
- 6 small plastic jars
- red cabbage juice
- marker
- 2 droppers
- vinegar
- lemon juice
- baking soda
- powdered lime
- pineapple juice
- liquid soap
- *Science Notebook*

SAFETY
Wear goggles during this activity. Do not touch or taste any chemicals.

4. Add a small amount of baking soda to jar 3 and a small amount of powdered lime to jar 4. **Record** any changes that you observe.

Step 4

5. Predict what would happen if you tested red cabbage juice with pineapple juice and with liquid soap. Carry out the tests in clean jars and check your predictions.

6. Predict what would happen if you added vinegar to the jar containing baking soda. Carry out the test. **Record** your results.

	Red Cabbage Juice
Vinegar	
Lemon juice	
Baking soda	
Powdered lime	

Analyze and Conclude

1. In which plastic jars did chemical changes occur? How do you know?

2. Cabbage juice is an indicator. What evidence is there that the substances you tested are acids? Bases?

3. Infer which of the chemicals is the most similar to vinegar. **Give evidence** to support your inference.

4. Classify all the substances you tested into two groups, based on how they react with the cabbage-juice indicator.

INVESTIGATE FURTHER!

EXPERIMENT

Use additional cabbage juice to test different liquids, including plain water and carbonated water. Group the liquids by the color changes they produce.

Activity
The Litmus Test

Litmus paper is an indicator. Blue litmus paper turns red in an acid. Red litmus paper turns blue in a base. See if you can identify the acids and bases in this activity.

MATERIALS
- goggles
- 3 pieces of red litmus paper
- 3 pieces of blue litmus paper
- 3 liquids in containers—one labeled A, one labeled B, and one labeled C
- *Science Notebook*

SAFETY

Wear goggles during this activity. Do not touch or taste any of the chemicals used in this activity.

Procedure

1. In your *Science Notebook*, make a chart like the one shown here.

Solution	Red Litmus Paper	Blue Litmus Paper
A		
B		
C		

2. Place a piece of red litmus (lit′məs) paper and a piece of blue litmus paper beside each container. Remember, blue litmus paper turns red in an acid; red litmus paper turns blue in a base.

3. Dip a piece of blue litmus paper and a piece of red litmus paper in each liquid. Leave each piece of litmus paper beside the container in which it was dipped.

4. Check each piece of litmus paper for any change in color. In your chart, **record** your observations.

Step 2

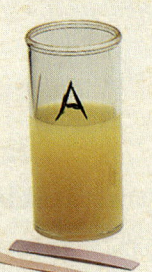  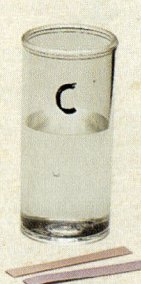

Step 3

Analyze and Conclude

1. Which liquids were acids? How do you know?

2. Which liquids were bases? How do you know?

3. Write a rule for using litmus paper to identify a solution that is neither an acid nor a base.

Acids, Bases, and Salts

It's a brutally hot day, and you've just finished mowing the lawn. Now you're looking forward to a cool, refreshing drink of lemonade. You take the pitcher from the refrigerator, pour yourself an ice-cold glass, and take a deep gulp. Immediately your mouth puckers and your eyes begin to water. It's not lemonade—it's lemon juice! And is it sour!

Although you didn't mean to, you just discovered a telltale property of an important group of chemical compounds—acids. And you used a test that you wouldn't be able to use in the laboratory—the taste test.

Telltale Colors

Different compounds have certain properties that can be used to classify the compounds. Acids and bases are two important groups of compounds. As the picture below shows, these compounds are found in many household products.

One property of acids and bases is the effect they have on indicators (in'di kāt-ərz). An **indicator** is a substance that changes color when mixed with an acid or a base. You used cabbage juice as an indicator in the activity on pages C78 and C79.

As you saw in the activity on page C80, paper treated with an indicator called litmus is used to test for acids and

BASES A base is a compound that turns red litmus paper to blue. ▼

▲ **ACIDS** An acid is a compound that turns blue litmus paper to red.

bases. As the pictures on page C81 show, the effects of acids and bases on litmus can be used to define these compounds.

Some Properties of Acids and Bases

As you would learn if you drank some lemon juice, acids have a sour taste. Some acids, like the natural acids in foods, are weak. Vinegar and citrus fruits are foods that contain acids. Boric (bôr′ik) acid is safe enough to be used in eyewash solutions.

Strong acids, such as sulfuric (sul-fyoor′ik) acid, are dangerous—they are poisonous and can burn the skin. Many acids, even some weak ones, are *corrosive*—they eat away metals and other substances. Digestive juices produced by your stomach contain a strong acid. However, the acid is very dilute (di loot′). This means that small amounts of the acid are mixed with large amounts of water. Diluting strong acids helps to reduce their harmful effects.

Bases taste bitter and feel slippery. Like acids, some bases are weak and some are strong. Examples of weak bases include baking soda, which is used in cooking, and antacid tablets, which are used for upset stomachs.

Strong bases, like strong acids, are poisonous and can burn the skin. Sodium hydroxide (hī dräks′īd), commonly known as lye, is an example of a strong base. Sodium hydroxide is used in soap-making and in drain cleaners.

The pH scale ▼

▲ pH Paper

The Strong and the Weak

Acids and bases are usually found dissolved in water. If you add a small amount of acid to a large volume of water, the solution won't be very acidic. On the other hand, if you add a large amount of acid to a small volume of water, the solution might be very acidic.

Is there a way to measure how acidic or how basic a solution is? The answer is yes. The acidic or basic strength of a solution is measured on a scale known as the pH scale. (Keep in mind that a material such as lemon juice is a solution of substances in water.)

The pH scale has units from zero to 14. The smaller the unit, the more acidic a solution is. The larger the unit, the more basic it is. So a solution with a pH of 1 or less would be very acidic. On the other hand, a solution with a pH near 14 would be very basic. Solutions with a pH near the middle of the scale are neutral. Pure water has a pH of 7.

How can you find the pH of a solution? Indicator paper made with special dyes is used for this purpose. The paper turns different colors depending upon how acidic or basic the solution is that's being tested.

Canceling Out Each Other

Have you ever heard someone complain of having acid indigestion, or heartburn? This condition occurs when the stomach produces too much acid, resulting in a burning sensation.

Antacid tablets, which are weak bases, are often used to relieve this condition. The *ant* in the word *antacid* comes from the prefix *anti-*, which means "against" or "opposed to." The base in the tablet reacts with the acid and cancels out, or neutralizes (no͞o′trə līz əz), its effects.

The reaction between an acid and a base is called **neutralization** (no͞o trə lī-zā′shən). When an acid and a base come together, two substances—water and a salt—are produced. A **salt** is a compound that can be formed when an acid reacts with a base. The properties of water and salt are much different than those of the acids and bases that react to produce them. ■

UNIT PROJECT LINK

Work to perfect one of these tricks for your magic show.

Crystal Creation. Make crystals appear in a glass containing liquid.

Great Burnout. Make a flame go out as if by magic.

Parting Pepper. Make pepper grains scatter across the surface of a liquid without disturbing the liquid.

Dissolving Pictures. Use a magic solution to transfer a picture from a newspaper onto another piece of paper.

Acid Rain

A gentle wind blows constantly across the land. As the wind travels, it sweeps across cities, villages, factories, and power plants like an invisible broom. And like a real broom, the wind carries all sorts of dirt along with it. This dirt includes soot, dust, and smoke. It also includes a number of harmful gases.

Pickup and Delivery

When the wind moves over farm areas, it picks up dust and may pick up traces of fertilizers or chemicals used to control weeds and insects. Over cities and industrial regions, the wind picks up gases produced by the burning of gasoline, coal, and oil. These gases include compounds of sulfur and of nitrogen.

Where acid rain is "born" ▼

Acids From the Sky

As sulfur and nitrogen compounds mix with water in the air, they react to produce two strong acids—sulfuric acid and nitric acid.

At first these acids are dissolved in tiny droplets of water that remain in the air, part of the clouds that form and drift across the sky. However, over time these droplets begin to collect into larger and larger drops. Eventually the drops are too big to stay in the air, and they begin to fall as rain, snow, sleet, or hail.

If you were to measure the pH of this precipitation, you might discover readings as low as 2.0. Acid solutions that strong can do serious damage to both living and nonliving things. People in many parts of the world have suffered from lung, skin, and eye irritations related to acid precipitation.

Modern windmills use clean wind energy to generate electricity. ▶

The stone and metal of famous statues and well-known buildings have been damaged or eaten away by acids from the sky. Forests and lakes in many regions of the world have been severely affected by acid rain. In Germany's Black Forest, acid rain has killed trees covering an area of more than 5,000 km^2. In Sweden, thousands of lakes have become so acidic that most plants and many species of fish can no longer live in them. Similar events and conditions have been reported in many areas of the world, including the United States and Canada.

What can be done to stop the destruction caused by acid precipitation? The obvious answer is to reduce air pollution. The major source of air pollution is the burning of fossil fuels—coal, oil, and gas. These are the fuels we use to run our cars, heat our homes, produce our electricity, and power our factories.

Scientists and engineers worldwide are seeking ways to reduce our dependency on fossil fuels. Many promising alternate sources of energy are being developed. These sources include hydroelectric plants, which use the energy of moving water to generate electricity. Other sources of clean energy being explored are wind energy and solar energy.

In cases where fossil fuels are commonly used—such as in power plants, factories, and automobiles—methods have been developed to keep pollutants from escaping into the air. Various measures for reducing air pollution are being used in many countries. After all, lemon juice—or its acidic relatives—belongs in a container, not in a cloud. ■

INVESTIGATION 2

1. What properties do acids and bases have in common? How are they different?

2. You test the pH of a solution and find it to be 11. What effect would this solution have on litmus paper? How would you neutralize this solution?

3. How do we show our love for Jesus in our regard for the environment?

INVESTIGATION 3

WHAT DO CHEMISTS DO?

Suppose you read about a mysterious material beneath the Antarctic icecap that has been discovered by scientists. How would you learn about such a material? A chemist would study it to learn about its chemical and physical properties. You can do the same thing.

Activity
Testing a Tablet

Imagine you are given a small disk-shaped object and are told that it is made of the mystery material described above. How would you test its properties?

MATERIALS
- goggles
- mystery tablet
- test tube
- water
- sheet of black construction paper
- hand lens
- small plastic jar
- fireplace match
- *Science Notebook*

SAFETY
Wear goggles during this activity. Be very careful when working around open flames. Secure loose clothing and tie back long hair. Do not put any materials in your mouth.

Procedure

1. Observe the tablet carefully. **Record** in your *Science Notebook* any properties you can observe just by looking at the tablet and handling it. Then break the tablet into four pieces of about the same size.

2. Add one piece of the tablet to a test tube half full of water. **Observe** what happens and **record** your observations in your *Science Notebook*.

3. Hold the bottom of the test tube in one hand. Cover the opening of the test tube with your thumb. **Describe** what you feel.

Step 1

4. Place a piece of the tablet on a sheet of black paper and crush it. Examine the small pieces carefully with a hand lens. **Describe** what you see.

5. Place another piece of the tablet in a small jar and add a small amount of water.

6. Have your teacher light a fireplace match for you. While the tablet is still reacting, dip the flame into the beaker, keeping it above the surface of the liquid. **Observe** what happens and **record** your observations.

Step 4

Analyze and Conclude

1. Describe what happened when the tablet was added to water.

2. In step 3, how did the bottom of the test tube feel? What did you feel with your thumb?

3. What can you **infer** about the gas that was produced during the reaction? **Give evidence** to support your inference.

4. Make a list of the physical and chemical properties of the tablet. What do you think the tablet might be?

Step 6

INVESTIGATE FURTHER!

EXPERIMENT

Think of some other properties you might test for. Design your own experiment. After your teacher reviews your design, use the remaining piece of the tablet to test for these properties.

Activity
Mystery Powders

Now you have another mystery. Imagine that you find six jars, each containing a different powder. On the floor you find six labels—sugar, salt, baking soda, cornstarch, powdered milk, and plaster of Paris. How will you test the powders to identify them?

MATERIALS
- goggles
- mystery powders in jars labeled A through F
- black construction paper
- hand lens
- aluminum foil
- 3 droppers
- water
- toothpicks
- plastic spoons
- vinegar
- tincture of iodine
- *Science Notebook*

SAFETY
Wear goggles during this activity. Do not touch or taste any of the chemicals in this activity.

Procedure

1. Study the following table. It contains information about how six materials look, how they behave in water, and how they react with two other materials.

2. In your *Science Notebook*, **make a chart** like the table below. Use the same headings across the top and list the letters of the 6 mystery powders down the side. Don't fill in the chart.

	Appearance	Water	Vinegar	Iodine
Sugar	white; grains of different shapes	dissolves forming clear solution	no reaction	no reaction
Salt	white; small crystal cubes	dissolves forming clear solution	no reaction	no reaction
Baking Soda	small grains of different shapes	dissolves forming clear solution	bubbles form	no reaction
Cornstarch	white powder; tiny particles	forms gooey mixture	no reaction	turns dark blue
Powdered milk	white powder; tiny particles	forms cloudy mixture	no reaction	no reaction
Plaster of Paris	white powder; tiny particles	cloudy, warm mixture forms, which hardens after sitting a while	no reaction	no reaction

3. Sprinkle a sample of one powder on a sheet of black construction paper. Examine it with a hand lens. **Record** how the powder looks. Repeat this step for each mystery powder.

4. Place three small samples of one mystery powder on a piece of foil. Add a few drops of water to one sample and stir the mixture with a toothpick. **Record** your observations. Add vinegar to the second sample and iodine to the third. Mix and **observe** each sample and **record** your observations.

5. Repeat step 4 for each mystery powder.

Step 4

Analyze and Conclude

1. Study your chart and **compare** it with the table on page C88. Based on the properties you observed, **identify** each powder. Write the names on the chart.

2. Which test or tests did you find were most helpful for identifying the powders? Explain your choices.

INVESTIGATE FURTHER!

EXPERIMENT

Think of a powder you did not use in this activity. Check with your teacher to be sure that your choice is safe. Then have your classmates test your mystery powder and describe their observations. Have them tell which of the six powders studied in this activity is most like your mystery powder.

Activity
"Slime" Time

Look around you. Many objects in your classroom are made of materials that were "invented" by chemists working in laboratories. Plastics and synthetic fibers are good examples of such materials. In this activity you'll make some "slime." Is this a good name for your substance?

MATERIALS
- goggles
- water
- white glue
- large bowl
- food coloring
- plastic spoon
- white powder
- *Science Notebook*

SAFETY
Wear goggles during this activity. Do not put any of the materials in your mouth.

Procedure

1. Study the materials you are going to mix together in this activity and list them in your *Science Notebook*. **Describe** the appearance of each material and **list** as many properties of each material as you can.

2. Add equal amounts of the water and white glue to a large bowl. Add a few drops of the food coloring and stir the mixture thoroughly with a plastic spoon.

3. Observe how the mixture looks. If you wish, you may keep adding more food coloring until the mixture is the color you want.

4. Gradually add the white powder to the mixture while you stir it. **Observe** and **record** any changes in the appearance of the mixture.

5. Add powder until no more liquid is visible. Touch the mixture and describe how it feels. You can adjust the amount of powder to give your slime exactly the slimy feeling you want it to have.

Step 4

Analyze and Conclude

1. Pick up and handle your slime. **Describe** as many of its properties as you can.

2. Compare the properties of your slime to the properties of the materials you mixed together to make it.

3. Think of some possible uses for your slime. **Describe** the uses in your *Science Notebook*.

Polymers and Plastics

At one time, scientists believed that compounds containing carbon could only be produced by living things. Because living things are called organisms, compounds containing carbon were called organic compounds. The study of these compounds was, and still is, called organic chemistry.

Carbon, the Supercombiner

All elements are not created equal. Scientists have identified about 11 million different compounds. Of these, more than 10 million contain carbon.

One of carbon's unique properties is its ability to join, or form bonds, with other atoms. Recall that chemical bonding was described in an earlier section as electrons that are holding hands. Because of the arrangement of its electrons, a single carbon atom is able to hold hands with as many as four other atoms.

This bond-forming ability makes it possible for long chains of carbon atoms to form. Each carbon atom in a chain can also form bonds with atoms of other elements. For example, there are hundreds of ways that compounds can form from the elements carbon and hydrogen.

Not all organic compounds are complex. A molecule of methane (meth′ān), the simplest organic compound, is made up of only five atoms. A model of a methane molecule and examples of two familiar organic compounds are shown below.

Vitamin C—$C_6H_8O_6$ ▼

Fructose, or fruit sugar—$C_6H_{12}O_6$ ▼

A methane molecule—CH_4 ▼

Polymers—Chemical Giants

The next time you sprinkle sugar on your cereal, think of its formula.

$C_{12}H_{22}O_{11}$

Every molecule in those sugar crystals contains 45 atoms! Sounds pretty impressive, doesn't it? Now look at the model of a small part of a protein molecule. Proteins are the building blocks from which your body is made. They are probably the most complex organic compounds found in nature.

Proteins are polymers (päl′ə mərz). A **polymer** is an organic compound made up mainly of a very long chain or chains of carbon compounds. The word *polymer* means "many parts."

▲ Some useful products made of plastic

Part of a protein molecule ▼

Try to imagine how different your life would be without plastics. Plastics are synthetic polymers. To make a polymer, chemists start with a simple organic molecule. This molecule is one "part" of the polymer. Hundreds or even thousands of these parts are put together to form the carbon chain. At the same time, other molecules are added to the sides of the carbon chain.

The side chains of a polymer determine its properties. For example, side chains can make a polymer hard, flexible, or tough. Just think of all the different kinds of plastics there are and the wide range of properties they exhibit. ■

INVESTIGATE FURTHER!

EXPERIMENT

You can make your own model of a polymer by using paper clips of different sizes and colors, as shown here. Work with a partner to create a paper-clip polymer. When you're finished, describe its properties.

What Chemists Do

Chemistry is the study of matter—what it's made of and how it behaves. Now think back to the title of this unit—"The Nature of Matter." The title could have been "An Introduction to Chemistry." So all this time you have been studying chemistry and doing some of the things chemists do!

Analysis and Synthesis

The things that chemists do can be divided into two large categories—analysis (ə nal'ə sis) and synthesis (sin'thə sis). In simple terms, *analysis* means "taking things apart" and *synthesis* means "putting things together".

Many of the materials you use in everyday life are products of chemical research. Research chemists are constantly inventing and testing new drugs and medicines. The making of polymers, as described in the last resource, is an excellent example of synthesis.

Types of Chemical Reactions

In conducting their research, chemists observe different types of chemical reactions. Most of those reactions can be classified into one of four major groups—synthesis, decomposition (dē käm pə-zish'ən), single replacement, and double replacement. Let's take a closer look at these reactions. It might surprise you to know that many of the changes you observed during the activities you performed involved these reactions.

A chemist at work in the laboratory ▼

C93

SYNTHESIS Recall that *synthesis* means "putting things together." The reaction in which hydrogen gas and oxygen gas combine to produce water is an example of a synthesis reaction in which a water molecule is "put together."

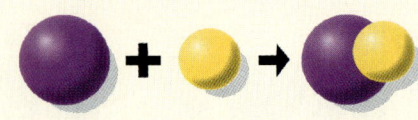
synthesis

DECOMPOSITION Decomposition involves the breaking down of a substance into simpler substances. In the activity on page C33, you heated sugar, causing it to break down into simpler substances—carbon and water.

decomposition

SINGLE REPLACEMENT In this type of reaction, one of the elements in a compound is replaced by another element. Such a reaction can be used to coat a piece of metal, such as copper, with a thin layer of another metal, such as silver.

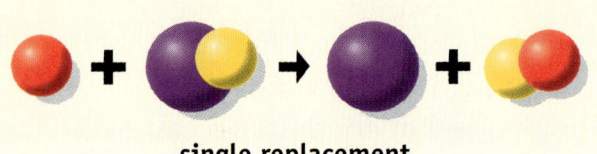
single replacement

DOUBLE REPLACEMENT In this type of reaction, elements from two different compounds change places, something like two couples changing partners at a school dance. Such a reaction produced the solid from two clear liquids in the activity on page C67.

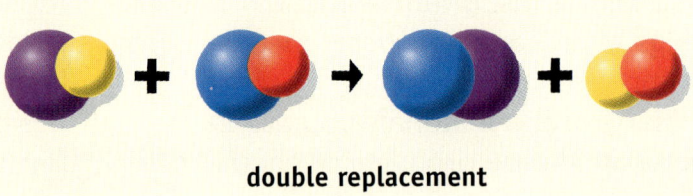
double replacement

Now you know a lot more about matter than you did at the beginning of this unit. You know what matter is made up of. You know what happens when things change. You know what to look for and how to tell whether a change is chemical or physical. And you have an idea of what causes things to change. So, congratulations! You are officially a beginning chemist in good standing. ■

INVESTIGATION 3

1. Compare and contrast synthesis and analysis.

2. Why are there so many more compounds of carbon than of any other element? Use your knowledge of elements and the periodic table to hypothesize which group of elements forms the fewest compounds.

REFLECT & EVALUATE

WORD POWER

acid
base
electron
indicator
ion
polymer
neutron
model
proton
nucleus
atomic number
salt
chemical bond
chemical change
neutralization
physical change
radioactive element
nuclear fission

On Your Own
Write a definition for each term in the list.

With a Partner
Mix up the letters for each term in the list. Provide a clue for each term and challenge a partner to unscramble the terms.

Use magazine pictures to make an illustrated chart that classifies common substances as acids, bases, or salts.

Analyze Information

Study the photographs. Then use the photographs to explain what happens during a physical change and a chemical change.

Assess Performance

Design a plan to use litmus paper to check the results you obtained using cabbage juice in the activity on page C78. Show your plan to your teacher. After getting approval, carry out your tests.

Problem Solving

1. Tungsten is an element with 74 protons and 109 neutrons. What is tungsten's atomic number? How many electrons does a tungsten atom have?

2. Sodium (an element) reacts with water (a compound) to produce sodium hydroxide (a compound) and hydrogen gas (an element). What kind of chemical reaction is this? Explain how you know.

3. Your community is considering building a nuclear power plant. From your viewpoint as a Christian, would you support such a project? Explain your position.

C95

INVESTIGATE FURTHER!

Throughout this unit, you've investigated questions about the nature of matter. How will you use what you've learned and share that information with others? Here are some ideas.

Hold a Big Event to Share Your Unit Project

Put on a magic show. Set up your materials on tables around the room. You may wish to decorate the classroom and create magician costumes. Write a brief script so that each member of your group can describe his or her trick. Invite other classes to watch the show, and dazzle your audience with your magic tricks and your knowledge of matter, its properties, and behavior. You might want to challenge the audience to explain how or why each trick works.

Experiment

Plan a project based on an activity or activities in this unit. For example, you might want to try to separate various liquid mixtures into their component parts, as you did in the activity on page C46. If so, you will want to read about paper chromatography in a reference book or chemistry textbook. Or, you might have another idea for a project. Set up a plan for your investigation and show it to your teacher before you begin.

Take Action

Acid rain is produced when certain chemicals in the air react with water in the atmosphere. Find out if your area receives acid rain. Collect rainwater in a clean container and test it with litmus paper or pH paper. Check the pH of the water in local ponds and lakes. Record your data and prepare a report on your findings.

CONTINUITY OF LIFE

Theme: Constancy and Change

Get Ready to Investigate! D2

1 Reproduction D4
Investigation 1   What Is Asexual Reproduction? D6
Investigation 2   What Is Sexual Reproduction? D18

2 Heredity D28
Investigation 1   What Are Inherited Traits? D30
Investigation 2   How Are Traits Inherited? D38

3 Change Through Time D50
Investigation 1   What Do Fossils Tell Us About Life—
                  Past and Present? D52
Investigation 2   What Evidence Do Scientists Have
                  That Species Change Over Time? D64
Investigation 3   How Do Changes In Species Occur? D72

Investigate Further! D80

GET READY TO

OBSERVE & QUESTION

What do fossils tell us about life— past and present?

How can you study the past? The man pictured here died 5,000 years ago. His body was preserved in ice. It has been carefully studied to give us answers about how life was lived long ago.

EXPERIMENT & HYPOTHESIZE

What are inherited traits?

The boy in the photo below can roll his tongue. Can you? The activities in this unit will help you find out why, and what the ability to roll (or not to roll) tells us about ourselves!

INVESTIGATE!

RESEARCH & ANALYZE

As you investigate, find out more from these books.

- ***What Makes You What You Are: A First Look at Genetics*** by Sandy Bornstein (Julian Messner, 1989). This book explains in detail why you are exactly who you are, and offers short activities so that you can see for yourself what makes you what you are.

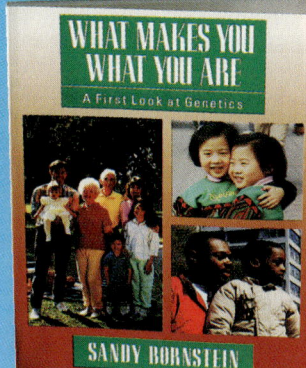

- ***What Happened to the Dinosaurs?*** by Dr. Philip Whitfield (Viking, 1991). This book gives you answers to all sorts of questions about dinosaurs—and more! Reading this book, you'll feel as if you are actually witnessing the lives of these creatures!

WORK TOGETHER & SHARE IDEAS

How would you debate why—or why not—a certain endangered species should be saved?

Working together, you will have the chance to apply what you have learned. In a class debate, you'll get the chance to stand up for an endangered species—or explain why you don't think it should be saved from extinction. Look for the Unit Project Links for ideas on how to gather the information you will need.

CHAPTER 1

REPRODUCTION

An oak tree, a human being, and bacteria can do something that a rock can't do. They can reproduce and grow because they are alive. All living things can reproduce. By God's grace and in the environment He provides, life will continue through the offspring of the organisms.

Right From the Start

Vina Isaac is carrying on a family tradition. Like her father, she is a medical doctor. Her specialty is obstetrics. She cares for women before and after they give birth.

There is a big difference between obstetrics now and obstetrics in the time of Dr. Isaac's father. Today, doctors know much more about babies before they are born. Here are some new discoveries about babies.

- People once thought that babies could not see until they were several weeks old. Today we know that babies open their eyes two months before they are born! A baby sees light as a reddish glow.
- The unborn baby can hear, too. Doctors have found that loud noises make the baby's heart beat faster.
- Photographs of babies still inside their mothers have even shown them happily sucking their thumbs!

As you read this chapter, think about the scientific discoveries made in this century. What have we learned about the way life begins?

Coming Up

INVESTIGATION 1

WHAT IS ASEXUAL REPRODUCTION?
............D6

INVESTIGATION 2

WHAT IS SEXUAL REPRODUCTION?
............D18

◀ A baby is born: Dr. Vina Isaac helps her patient ensure the continuity of life.

INVESTIGATION 1

WHAT IS ASEXUAL REPRODUCTION?

One morning you discover that the water in your fish tank has turned green over night. You think that the green color comes from algae, but how could algae reproduce so quickly? In this investigation, you'll find out.

Activity

Divide and Conquer!

Reproduction is the life process by which living things produce more of their own kind. How do some microorganisms reproduce?

MATERIALS
- 2 prepared slides of parameciums
- microscope
- *Science Notebook*

Procedure

1. A paramecium is a protist. It is a one-celled organism. Place the first prepared slide of paramecium on the microscope stage.

2. **Observe** the parameciums under the microscope. Then study one paramecium closely. In your *Science Notebook*, **describe** and **draw** what you see.

3. Place the second prepared slide of paramecium on the microscope stage.

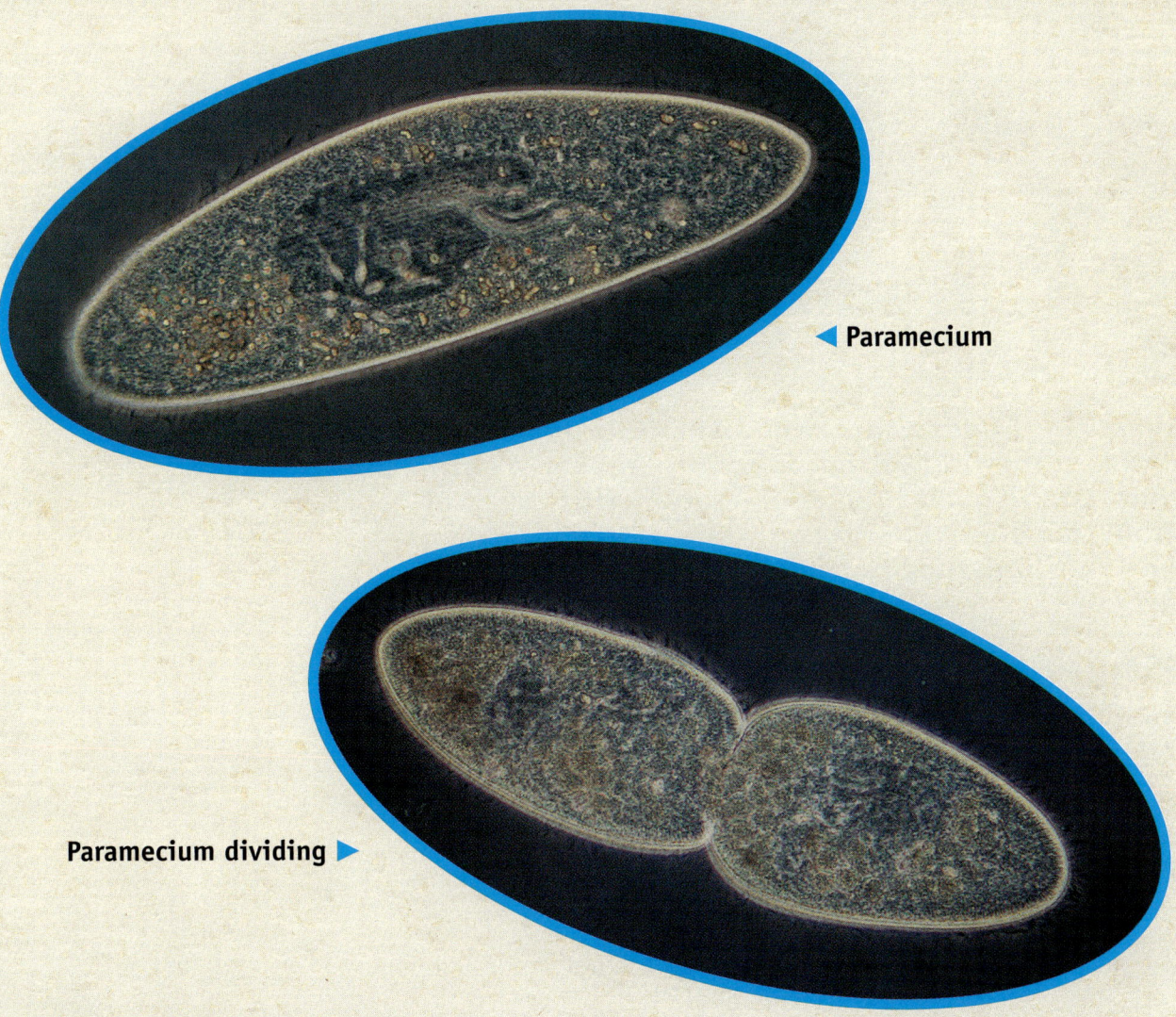

◀ Paramecium

Paramecium dividing ▶

4. Choose one specimen to study closely. **Describe** and **draw** what you see.

5. Look again at both prepared slides. **Compare** what you saw on the slides with the photographs of parameciums on this page. **Record** your comparisons.

6. **Suggest a hypothesis** to explain the differences between the first and second slides.

Analyze and Conclude

1. How would you describe the shape of a paramecium?

2. How are the shapes different in the two slides?

3. What evidence is there that the paramecium on the second slide is reproducing?

4. On the second slide, you saw a paramecium dividing. **Hypothesize** what will happen to the two new cells after division is complete.

INVESTIGATE FURTHER!

RESEARCH

Using resources from the library, research how other protists reproduce.

Activity

The "Budding" System

Yeasts and hydras are organisms that have an unusual method of reproduction. Yeasts are fungi that can be used to make bread. Hydras are animals that live in pond water. Do this activity to find out how they reproduce.

MATERIALS
- goggles
- dropper
- yeast culture
- microscope slide and cover slip
- microscope
- paper towels
- lens paper
- prepared slide of a hydra with bud
- *Science Notebook*

SAFETY Wear goggles during this activity.

Procedure

1. Place one drop of yeast culture in the center of a clean slide. Gently add a cover slip.

2. Using your microscope, **observe** the yeast under low power. In your *Science Notebook*, **describe** and **draw** what you see. How many yeast cells do you see? Note any differences among the yeast cells.

3. Change to high power and **observe** the cells more closely. Look for a cell that seems to have a smaller cell attached to it. Based on your observations, **infer** what is happening to such cells.

4. Wash and dry the slide and cover slip and be sure that the microscope stage is clean before you look at the slide of a hydra.

5. Using the microscope, **observe** the prepared slide of a hydra. **Describe** and **draw** what you see.

Step 1

D8

Analyze and Conclude

1. A yeast cell can reproduce by forming a bud. What evidence of budding did you observe?

2. A yeast cell that forms a bud is called a parent cell. **Infer** what eventually happens as the bud develops from the parent cell.

3. What evidence did you observe that the hydra reproduces by budding?

4. **Infer** how a hydra bud is like a yeast bud. How are they different?

5. Reproduction involving only one parent is called asexual reproduction. Is budding a form of asexual reproduction? Explain your answer.

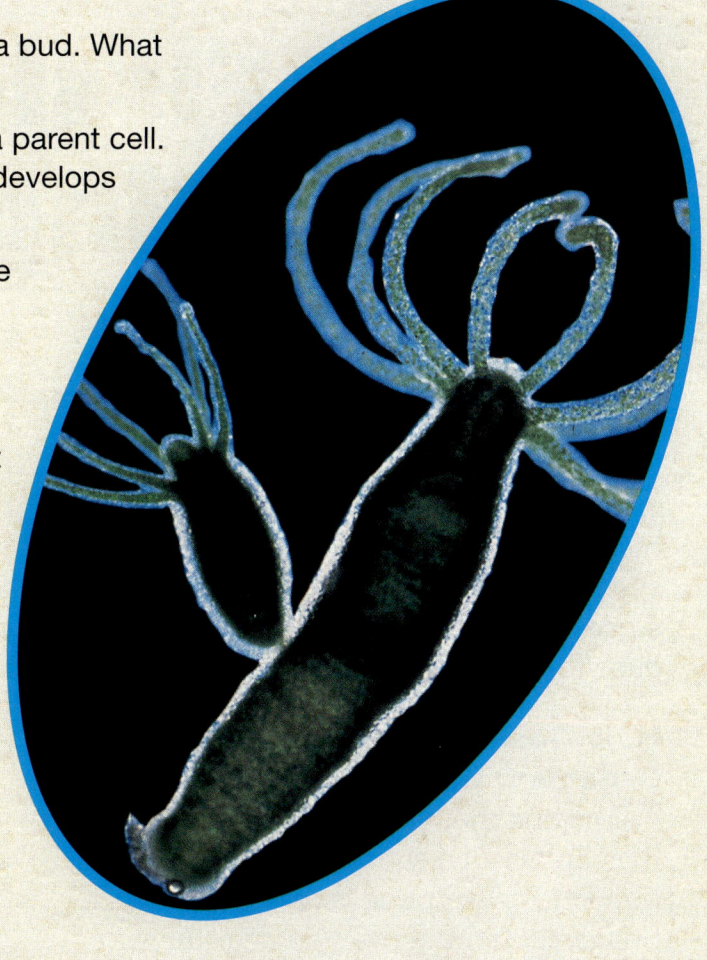

▲ Hydra: What is it doing?

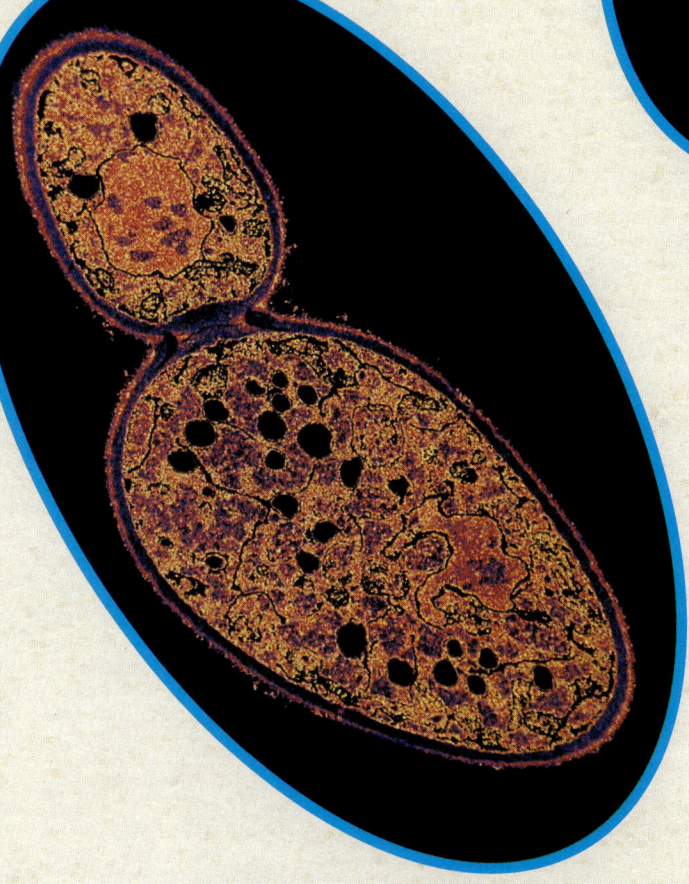

▲ Yeast: What is it doing?

INVESTIGATE FURTHER!

RESEARCH

Now that you have seen how yeast reproduces, do research in the library to find out how yeast budding is important to certain industries. Report on how scientists prepare and store yeasts for use in these industries.

D9

Fission: Splitting Heirs

On pages D6 and D7, you learned that **reproduction** is the life process God put into place at the beginning by which organisms produce more of their own kind. Not every organism in a species has to reproduce—but at least some members of a species must reproduce for the species to survive.

How Does a One-Celled Organism Reproduce?

Imagine that you are 1 cm tall and are the captain of a submarine sent to study how one-celled pond dwellers reproduce. Suddenly, right above you near the surface of the pond, you see some amoebas. When you get closer, you notice that a few of the amoebas seem to be splitting apart. What's going on here?

Many one-celled organisms, including animal-like protists such as parameciums and amoebas, reproduce by splitting in half. When the split is complete, two identical cells result. This process is known as **fission** (fish′ən). Fission is a form of **asexual** (ā sek′shoo əl) **reproduction** because it involves a single parent producing an offspring that is exactly like the parent.

Fission is the simplest kind of asexual reproduction. Before it can take place, certain changes must occur within the parent cell.

All organisms, even single-celled ones, contain a chemical code that controls the life processes of the cell. Before a single-celled organism can undergo fission, it must copy the chemical code that is necessary for life. One copy of this code will become part of one new cell that is formed during fission; the other copy will become part of the second new cell that is formed during fission. Once the two copies of the chemical code are produced, the parent cell begins to divide.

Now imagine that you're back in your submarine, observing the amoebas. Study the diagrams on the next page to see what you would see.

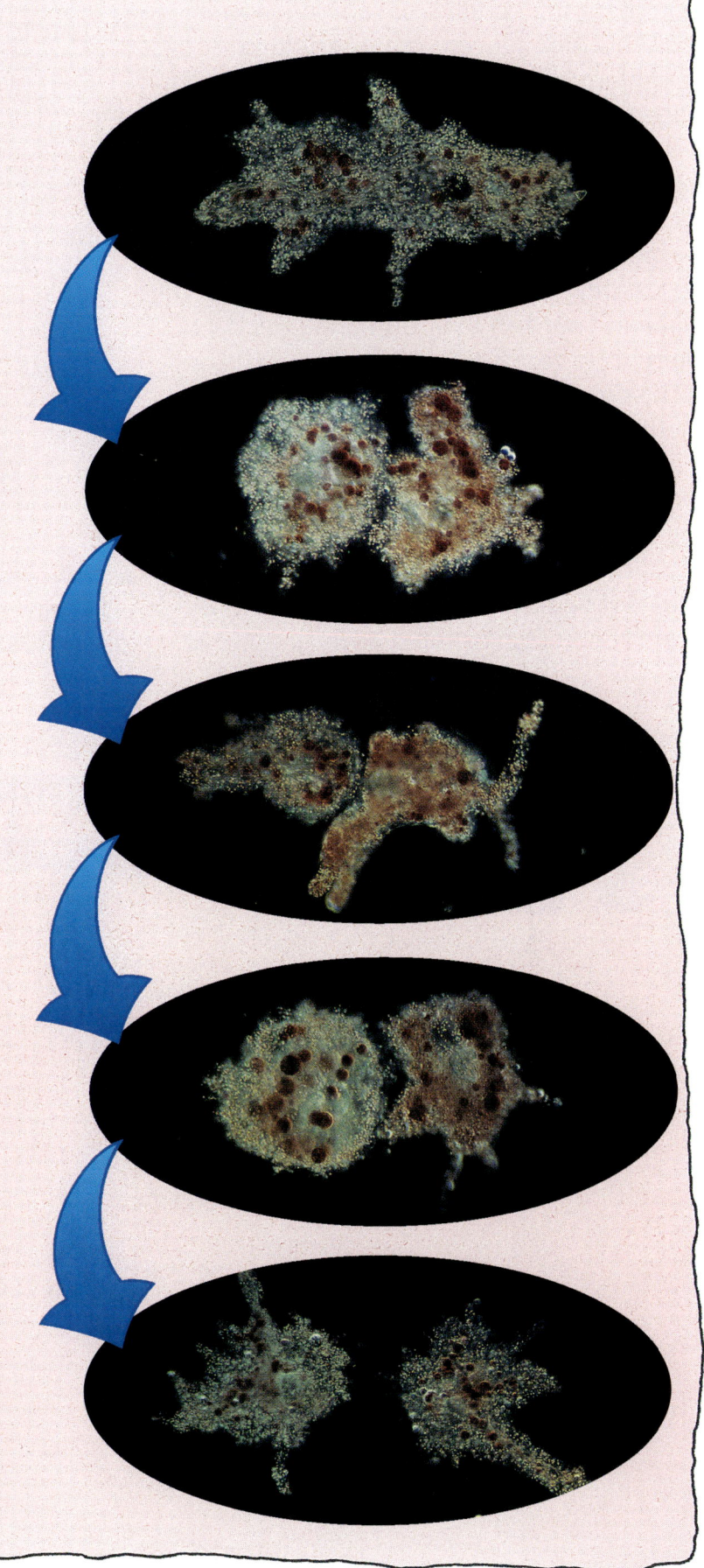

1 The cell material in an amoeba begins to stretch out toward the opposite ends of the cell.

2 Gradually, the center of the cell begins to pinch inward, as if the cell were developing a "waist."

3 The waist of the parent cell becomes a dividing line between the two sections of cell material. If you got a little closer in your submarine, you'd begin to see a line forming along the waist of the cell.

4 Once the cell material is about evenly divided between the two newly forming cells, the waistline becomes thicker. In fact, this waistline is actually a new cell membrane forming between the two new cells.

5 Look at that! The cell membrane has completely formed, and the two new "daughter" cells have completely separated. The parent cell no longer exists. In its place are two identical daughter cells.

One of the benefits of reproduction by fission is that it's very rapid. The two daughter cells shown on the previous page will be ready to reproduce in 24 hours. In four days, four generations of amoebas could be produced.

Bacteria also reproduce by fission. This is one reason bacterial diseases can be so devastating. This is also the process the algae in your fish tank on page D6 go through to reproduce so quickly!

Fission is a quick and efficient method of asexual reproduction. But like all forms of asexual reproduction, fission results in offspring that are exactly like the parent. Thus a factor in the environment that is harmful to one of the organisms will be harmful to all—resulting in a population crash as rapid as its growth. ■

▲ Sixty years produces four generations of humans—and *21,900* generations of amoebas!

SCIENCE AND FAITH

From God's Word we know that God created each person special and unique and that He has a plan for each of us that predates the creation of the world.

Explain the following verses
- You created my inmost being; You knit me together in my mother's womb. I praise You for I am fearfully and wonderfully made. Your works are wonderful. I know that full well. (Psalm 139:13-14)
- [God] chose us in [Christ] before the creation of the world to be holy and blameless in His sight. In love He predestined us to be adopted as His sons through Jesus Christ in accordance with His pleasure and will.
(Ephesians 1:4-5)

Reproduction by Budding

Some organisms reproduce asexually by fission. Other organisms use a form of asexual reproduction called budding. **Budding** begins with the development of a tiny bump, or bud, on the parent's body. Although the bud initially looks like a pimple, it's the beginning of a new organism. As the tiny bump grows, it begins to take on a recognizable shape. It starts to look exactly like its one parent.

Yeast and some other single-celled organisms reproduce asexually by budding. The yeast bud grows out from the parent cell and eventually pinches off.

In the activity "The 'Budding' System," on pages D8 and D9, you saw that the hydra also reproduces by budding. So this form of asexual reproduction is not limited to single-celled organisms. A projection, or bud, appears on the hydra's body. As the bud becomes bigger, one part begins to look like the "stalk" part of the hydra's body. The tip of the bud starts to grow what look like long, wild hairs. These will continue to develop, becoming the tentacles with which the mature hydra will catch its food.

The hydra bud will contain all the features that the hydra needs to live as an adult, independent hydra. Then it breaks free of its parent's body to start life on its own.

Budding in a hydra ▼

Some plants reproduce by budding. For example, bryophyllum (brī ə fil'əm), commonly called the air plant, produces buds on the edges of its leaves, as shown in photo 1 below. The buds develop into tiny copies of the parent plant, complete with leaves and roots. When the buds are sufficiently developed, they fall off the parent's leaf and begin their own individual lives. The new plants will then begin the cycle of reproduction by budding once again.

Budding, then, is like fission, in that it produces a population of copies in a rapid fashion. In budding, though, the parent organism remains intact after the duplicate organisms have begun their own lives. In fact, the parent continues to produce offspring by the process of budding. ■

BUDDING IN BRYOPHYLLUM

1. Bryophyllum buds grow on the edges of leaves. ▶

▲ **3.** The cycle is complete: the buds look just like their parent and are ready to begin life on their own.

▲ **2.** The buds begin to resemble the parent.

New Plants From Old

Have you ever visited a friend or neighbor who had a beautiful houseplant that you wished you had? Maybe your friend offered to give you a cutting from the plant. Perhaps she snipped off some of the plant stem, including some leaves, and told you how to plant the cutting to grow a plant of your own. Growing a new plant from a part of a parent plant is called **vegetative propagation**. Vegetative propagation is a kind of asexual reproduction, because a new plant is generated from a part of only one parent—the original plant.

Vegetative propagation occurs naturally, too. For example, when a willow branch bends so that it touches the ground, roots may grow into the soil from a part of the branch. The roots then send up the shoots of a new willow tree. Other examples of how vegetative propagation occurs in nature are shown on the next two pages.

Professional gardeners use vegetative propagation to grow new plants. ▼

Growth resulting from stem damage

Sometimes a plant stem or tree trunk is damaged or completely cut in two. New plants, identical to the original, may grow out of the stem or stump.

Growth from existing root systems

Roots of some plants, such as the poplar tree, may develop tiny sprouts beneath the soil. The sprouts produce shoots that worm their way up out of the soil and roots that push down into the soil, producing many identical poplars very rapidly.

Runners

Some plants, such as strawberry plants, produce runners—stems that snake along the ground away from the parent plant. At some point, a runner begins to grow roots into the ground. A new strawberry plant grows out of the runner above these roots.

Rhizomes

Ever wonder why crabgrass is such a problem? Crabgrass reproduces itself by growing a spreading network of underground stems, called rhizomes, that send down roots and send up shoots. Rhizomes can spread and propagate new plants very rapidly.

Tubers

Potatoes, which are tubers (meaning that they grow from the knobby bulges on the underground stems of the plant), have "eyes," or indentations from which new potato plants sprout. Potato farmers cut up "seed" potatoes so that each piece contains an eye. Each eye will grow a new potato plant that produces tubers—the potatoes we eat.

Grafting

Stems of two plants—two different apple trees, for example—are joined to create a new plant that has characteristics of both parents. The single plant that results produces two different kinds of apples. Grafting—a kind of asexual reproduction controlled by people—is used to improve the number of crops that can be grown in one area.

INVESTIGATE FURTHER!

RESEARCH

George Washington Carver, the African American botanist who developed products from peanuts, had revolutionary ideas about how to grow plants. Research and share his ideas on grafting and vegetative propagation.

▲ This illustration of George Washington Carver appeared on a recent stamp honoring him.

INVESTIGATION 1

1. What are the advantages of asexual reproduction? What benefits are there to species that reproduce in this way?

2. Why might a gardener choose to use vegetative propagation rather than planting a garden with seeds?

3. George Washington Carver is reported to have said, "Nature is an unlimited broadcasting station, through which God speaks to us every hour." What did Carver mean?

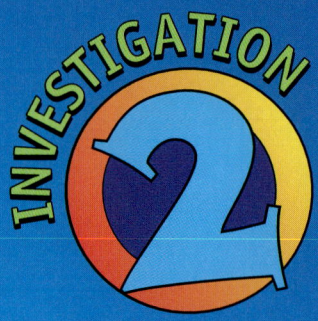

WHAT IS SEXUAL REPRODUCTION?

The chemical code that controls life processes is found in cells on structures called chromosomes. In sexual reproduction the offspring receives chromosomes from two different cells. How does this happen?

Activity

Splitting Pairs

The cells involved in sexual reproduction are called sperm and egg. Find out how they differ from other body cells in this activity.

MATERIALS
- large sheet of paper
- colored pencils
- scissors
- yarn of 2 different colors
- metric ruler
- removable tape
- Science Notebook

Procedure

1. On a large sheet of paper, use colored pencils to **draw** and **label** two large circles and four small circles, as shown on the next page. The sperm cells and the egg cells are formed by cell division, called meiosis, from the cells called immature sex cells. Make a copy of these cell drawings in your *Science Notebook*.

2. Cut six pieces of yarn of one color. Two pieces should be about 2 cm long, two should be about 4 cm long, and two should be about 6 cm long.

3. These pieces of yarn represent three pairs of chromosomes. Place them on the sheet of paper in the circle labeled *immature female sex cell*.

4. Repeat step 2 with the yarn of another color. Place these chromosomes on the sheet of paper in the circle labeled *immature male sex cell*.

5. **Draw** the chromosomes of the female and male immature sex cells in the cells in your *Science Notebook*.

6. Take the two long pieces of yarn from the female cell, and place one in each of the circles labeled *egg cell*. Repeat with the other pieces of yarn. Put an *X* through the immature sex cell you drew to show that it has divided to form new cells.

7. Add the chromosomes of the egg cells to the drawing in your *Science Notebook*.

8. Repeat step 6 with the yarn from the male cell, placing one piece of yarn from each pair into each of the circles labeled *sperm cell*.

9. Repeat step 7 for the sperm cells in your drawing.

10. Tape the chromosomes in place and save the large sheet of paper for the next activity.

Analyze and Conclude

1. In your model, how many pairs of chromosomes are there in each immature male sex cell and each immature female sex cell? How many chromosomes are there in each cell?

2. How are the paired chromosomes in the immature sex cells alike?

3. The sperm cells and the egg cells, produced from immature sex cells, are called sex cells. How many chromosomes are there in each sperm cell and each egg cell?

4. Are there any pairs of chromosomes in the sperm and egg cells?

5. **Infer** from what you have observed how immature sex cells differ from sperm cells and egg cells.

6. **Hypothesize** as to the amount of chemical code in each sperm cell and in each egg cell compared with the amount in immature sex cells.

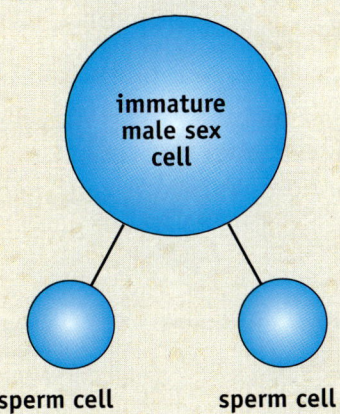

INVESTIGATE FURTHER!

RESEARCH

Human sex cells have 23 chromosomes. Do other animals' sex cells have this number of chromosomes? Research your favorite animal in the library (or talk to a veterinarian or local zoo) to find out.

Activity
Combining Cells

Sexual reproduction involves the joining of a sperm cell and an egg cell. Find out what happens to the chromosomes when these cells join.

MATERIALS
- colored pencils
- large sheet of paper and yarn from the activity "Splitting Pairs"
- *Science Notebook*

Procedure

1. Study the cells you drew on the large sheet of paper in the previous activity. **Predict** what will happen to the number of chromosomes when an egg cell and a sperm cell combine. **Record** your prediction.

2. Draw one circle below the sperm cell and the egg cell that are the closest together, as shown in the diagram on the next page. **Label** the circle *zygote*. A zygote is the first cell of the offspring of the combination of the sperm cell and the egg cell. Also add a circle to the drawing in your *Science Notebook*.

Step 2

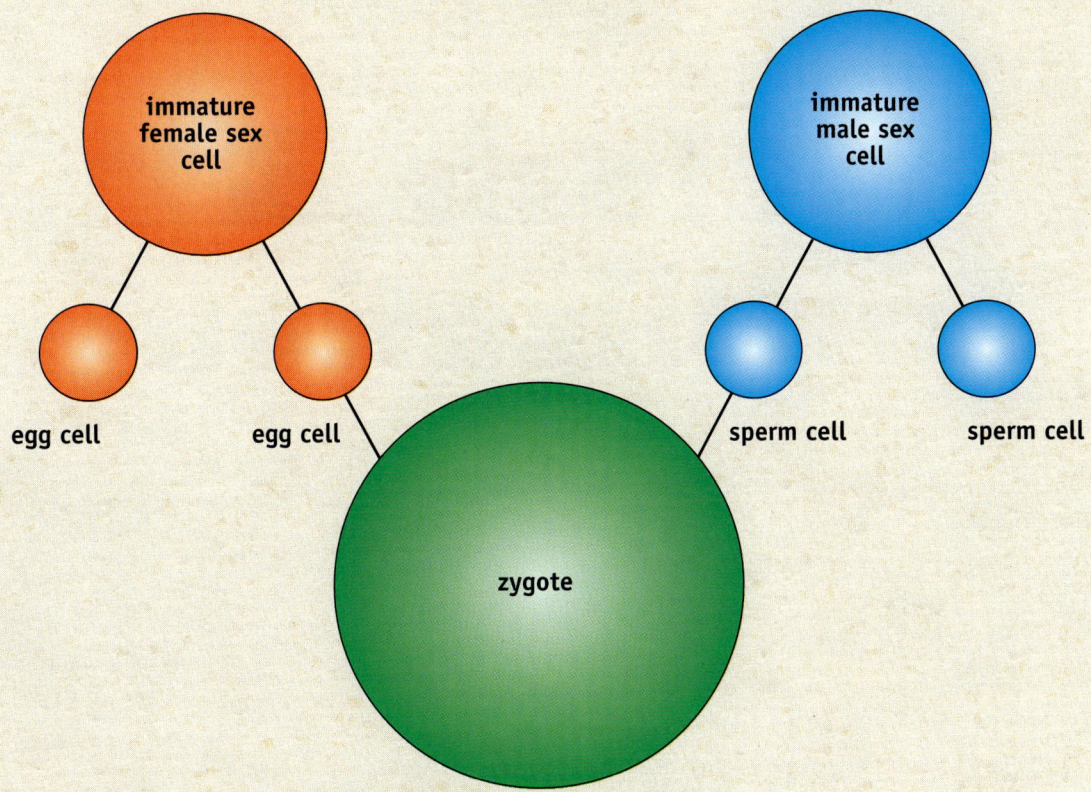

3. Remove the tape that held the yarn in the first activity. Move the yarn chromosomes from one egg cell and one sperm cell into the circle labeled *zygote*. Make sure that the yarn chromosomes are matched in pairs by color and size. Then count the chromosomes in the zygote and **record** them.

4. Add these chromosomes to the drawing in your *Science Notebook*.

Analyze and Conclude

1. How many chromosomes did the zygote have? How does this compare with your prediction?

2. How many pairs of chromosomes did the zygote have?

3. How does the number of chromosome pairs that the zygote has compare with the number of pairs in each male and female immature sex cell at the beginning of the activity on pages D18 and D19? **Infer** what has happened.

4. The joining of a sperm cell and an egg cell is called fertilization. How do meiosis and fertilization keep a species' chromosome number the same from generation to generation?

INVESTIGATE FURTHER!

RESEARCH

Down syndrome can result when meiosis occurs imprecisely. Research Down syndrome and other conditions that can result from problems in meiosis.

Meiosis & Fertilization

Your body is still growing—even as you're reading this! So your body cells must be reproducing for growth to occur. Your bone cells are making more bone cells; your skin cells, blood cells, and many other specialized cells are reproducing as you grow. This cell reproduction will continue as you become an adult and throughout the rest of your life.

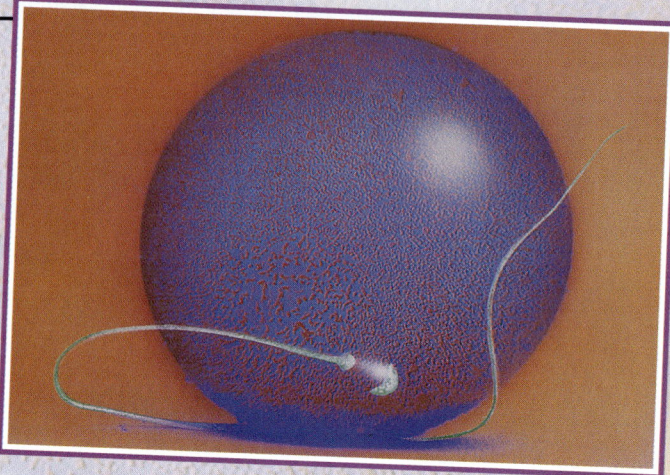

▲ Sperm cell and egg cell

Body Cells

In the activity on pages D20 and D21, you learned that a zygote contains pairs of chromosomes. Each human body cell contains 23 pairs of chromosomes, or 46 chromosomes. **Chromosomes** are stringlike packets of chemical information that are in a cell's nucleus. The information, coded by the chemicals, controls everything that a cell does.

When one of your body cells, such as a liver cell, reproduces, it first doubles the number of chromosomes it has (from 46 to 92), then divides into two cells. Each of the two newly formed cells has the 46 chromosomes it needs to function properly. The new cells have exactly the same chemical information that the parent cell had.

Solving the Chromosome Problem

Humans, like most multicellular animals and most plants, reproduce sexually. **Sexual reproduction** involves the joining of **sex cells**. The male sex cell is the sperm cell; the female sex cell is the egg cell.

Since sexual reproduction involves the joining of cells, it would seem to pose some peculiar problems with regard to the number of chromosomes. If sperm cells and egg cells were produced in the same way as other body cells, each would have a full set of chromosomes. Then when an egg cell united with a sperm cell, the resulting zygote would contain twice as many chromosomes as it should.

However, this problem does not occur in nature. Through a complex type of cell division called **meiosis** (mī ō'sis), sex cells develop that contain only half the number of chromosomes as body cells. So instead of having 46 chromosomes, human sex cells contain only 23 chromosomes. To make meiosis a bit easier to understand, follow the steps in the process in the drawing on the facing page.

THE PROCESS OF MEIOSIS

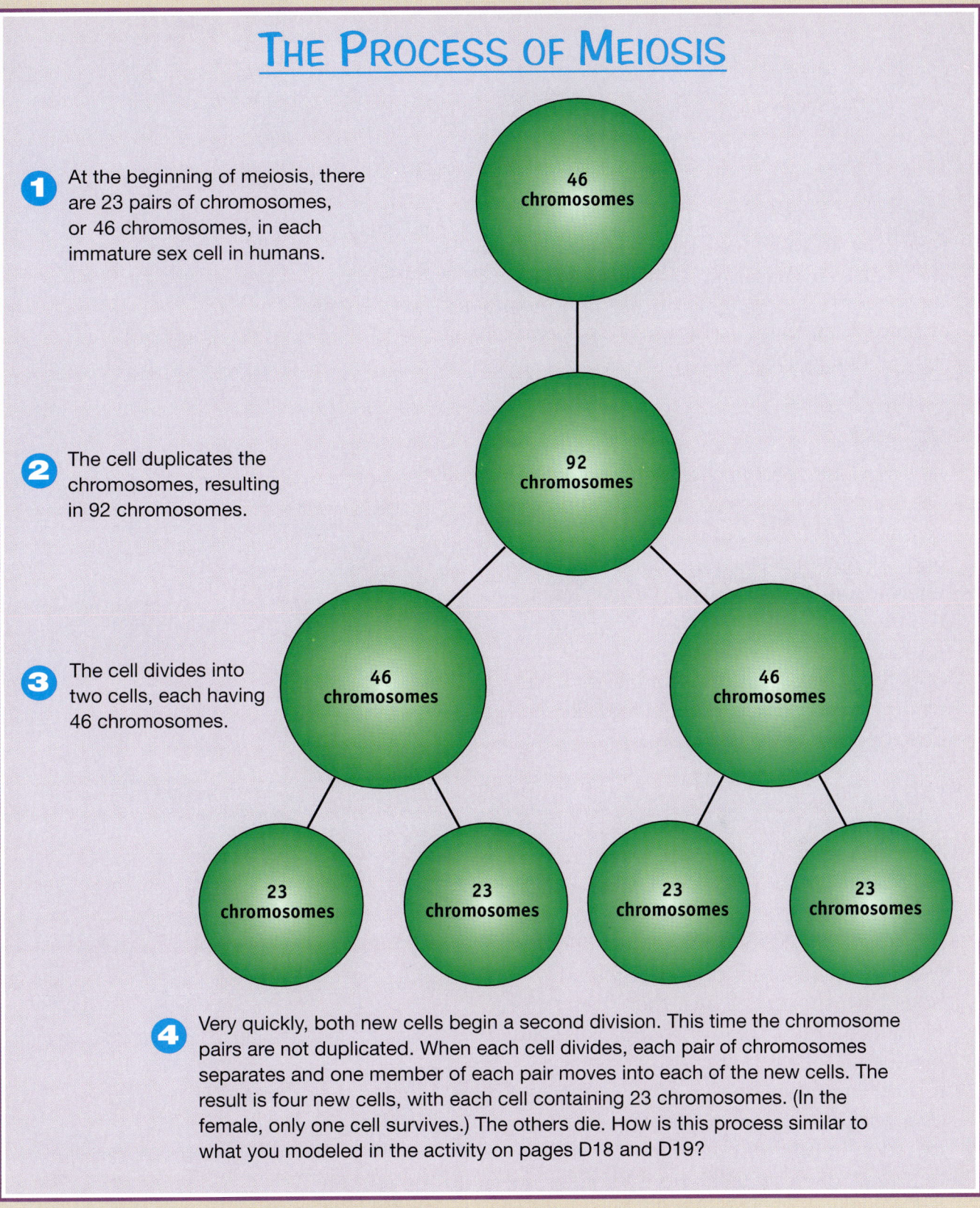

1 At the beginning of meiosis, there are 23 pairs of chromosomes, or 46 chromosomes, in each immature sex cell in humans.

2 The cell duplicates the chromosomes, resulting in 92 chromosomes.

3 The cell divides into two cells, each having 46 chromosomes.

4 Very quickly, both new cells begin a second division. This time the chromosome pairs are not duplicated. When each cell divides, each pair of chromosomes separates and one member of each pair moves into each of the new cells. The result is four new cells, with each cell containing 23 chromosomes. (In the female, only one cell survives.) The others die. How is this process similar to what you modeled in the activity on pages D18 and D19?

The process of meiosis is complete. What happened was that an immature sex cell with a normal number of body cell chromosomes doubled that number. The cell then divided into two cells, each with the normal number of chromosomes. These two cells then divided, producing four sex cells. ■

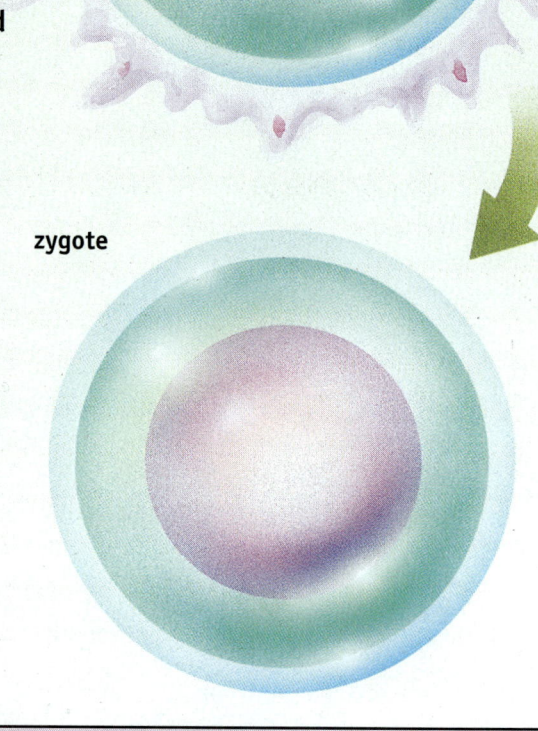

sperm cell egg cell

zygote

[God said,] "Listen to Me...you whom I have upheld since you were conceived" (Isaiah 46:3).
The zygote *(below right)* is the result of the process of conception, which occurs when the sperm cell and egg cell unite *(above right)*.

Fertilization

When the sperm cell and the egg cell are united, the egg is fertilized. This process is called **fertilization**. The fertilized egg cell now has the normal number of chromosomes, half of which it gets from the male and half of which it gets from the female. Thus, the fertilized cell, or **zygote**, uses the chemical information it has from all 46 chromosomes to begin to divide and develop into a new organism.

Sexual Reproduction and Nature

Millions of kinds of organisms reproduce sexually. Yet different organisms have different numbers of chromosomes. For example, the body cells of a common housefly have 12 chromosomes. (How many chromosomes do you think a housefly's sperm cell has, then?)

All organisms that reproduce sexually produce sex cells by meiosis. Sexual reproduction has one great advantage over asexual reproduction—it results in variation in offspring. Among organisms that reproduce sexually, no two offspring are exactly alike. Some individuals may be better adapted to a particular environment than other individuals. As you will see, this variation is important in understanding the history of life. ■

UNIT PROJECT LINK

Find out whether any species that reproduce asexually are endangered. What advantages or disadvantages could asexual reproduction give a species? Think about possible relationships between an organism's method of reproduction and its risk of being endangered. Write a short report explaining your views. Share your report or place it in a journal for reference during the debate.

Saving Species

◀ The peregine falcon: saved from extinction

GLOBAL views

Reproduction is supposed to ensure the survival of a species. But sometimes the survival of a species is threatened by the actions of other organisms. Before Europeans settled in North America, there were approximately 75 million American bison roaming the Great Plains. In less than two decades in the mid-1800s, settlers systematically slaughtered the bison. There were so few bison left that this symbol of the American West would have become **extinct,** or no longer exist, had it not been for the efforts of the New York Zoological Society. Concerned scientists at the Society's Bronx Zoo rescued the few remaining bison and began breeding them at the zoo. This was one of the first examples of zoos helping to save endangered wildlife. Today the American bison has returned to many western states.

An **endangered species** is a species whose population has become so low that it is in danger of extinction. Species become endangered for many reasons, but in modern times, human destruction of natural habitats has become a common cause. The peregrine falcon became endangered because its eggs were harmed by pesticides humans produced.

Sometimes, scientists try to save a species by capturing some or all of the remaining animals of that species. These animals are cared for in zoos or wildlife

One example of the mismanagement of God's creation--in the 1800s bison were hunted nearly to extinction. ▶

D25

▲ A California condor and its zookeeper

centers. If conditions are right, the animals will breed. New generations can then be returned to the wild. Breeding programs at zoos, such as at the San Diego Zoo, helped save the California condor. The San Diego program began when four eggs were taken from one of the few condor nests found in the wild. The eggs were carefully incubated. When the chicks hatched, they were fed by zookeepers who wore "condor costumes" over their arms. The costumes were worn so that the chicks would not become attached to their human captors.

Even though zoos try to create conditions like those of an animal's natural habitat, some species do not breed well, if at all, in captivity. Even when captive breeding is successful, it is not a complete victory until the animal can be released back to its natural home. Scientists are hard at work trying to preserve the native habitats of many endangered species. If a new suitable habitat is found or if a degraded habitat can be restored, scientists must convince people not to disturb it. Only then can the endangered animal be released into the habitat.

For example, black-footed ferrets lived on the Great Plains and hunted prairie dogs. In the nineteenth century, many prairie dogs were poisoned by ranchers. The ferrets starved and nearly became extinct. Eventually some ferrets were captured and bred at a wildlife center. Scientists found an unspoiled place where the ferrets might survive and where prairie dogs still lived. The scientists convinced ranchers not to disturb the area, and some ferrets were released back into their natural home. ■

▲ A black-footed ferret

INVESTIGATION 2

1. Imagine that you are a zoologist who has discovered a new organism, the xanaxana. Describe how it reproduces—sexually or asexually? If it reproduces sexually, does meiosis occur? How many chromosomes does it have? What does its offspring look like?

2. What are the advantages and disadvantages of sexual reproduction?

REFLECT & EVALUATE

WORD POWER

budding
extinct
fertilization
fission
asexual reproduction
chromosomes
endangered species
sexual reproduction
vegetative propagation
meiosis
reproduction
sex cells
zygote

On Your Own
Review the terms in the list. Then divide them into two lists to show which are associated with asexual reproduction and which are associated with sexual reproduction.

With a Partner
Make up a quiz, using all the terms in the list. Challenge your partner to complete the quiz.

Write the phrase *Methods of Reproduction* in a circle. Make a word web, using Word Power terms.

Analyze Information
Study the photograph. Then identify and describe the process that is taking place.

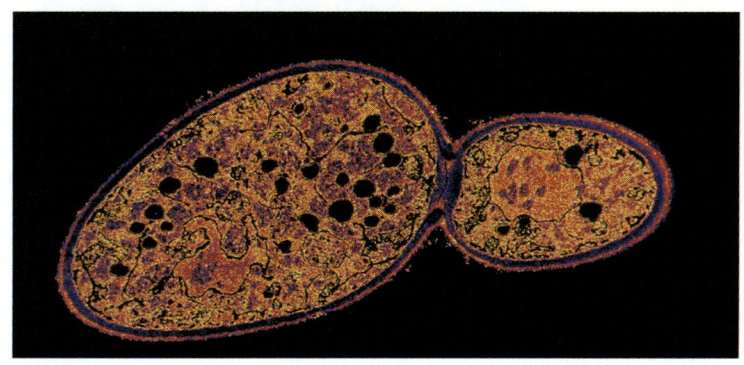

Assess Performance
Use the information about tubers in the chart on pages D16 and D17 to grow your own potatoes. You will need a potato with several eyes, a plastic knife, several small containers, potting soil, and water.

Problem Solving

1. A type of bacteria reproduces by fission every 20 minutes. At this rate of reproduction, how many bacteria will be present after 1 hour?

2. An organism reproduces sexually. This organism normally has 26 chromosomes in each body cell. How many chromosomes will be present in the sex cells of this organism? How many chromosomes will be present in a zygote that forms from the sex cells?

3. God has designed organisms such as people that reproduce sexually to be better able to resist certain diseases than organisms that reproduce asexually. Explain.

CHAPTER 2

HEREDITY

Why are some roses red and others yellow? How can one puppy in a litter have golden fur when all the others and both its parents are black? You could think of the traits an organism inherits from its parents as items in a salad bar. Each salad that is made is unique, because the vegetables are combined in a different way. In the same way, combinations of inherited traits create unique individuals.

Trait Maker

Jack Hearn is a plant geneticist (jə net'ə sist). He works with a team at the U.S. Horticultural Research Laboratory in Orlando, Florida. Researchers at the laboratory develop new fruits and vegetables by fertilizing one plant species with pollen from another, similar species. The tangelo, a cross between a tangerine and a grapefruit, was made in this way.

Recently Jack Hearn and his team fertilized tangelos with pollen from a type of sweet orange. The result? A new citrus fruit called the Ambersweet. From the tangelo the Ambersweet inherited a tangerine's loose skin and a grapefruit's size. From the orange, the Ambersweet inherited its dark orange pulp.

As you do the investigations in this chapter, think about how parents affect the traits that an individual inherits. What else besides parents influences the traits of living things?

Coming Up

WHAT ARE INHERITED TRAITS?
.... **D30**

HOW ARE TRAITS INHERITED?
.... **D38**

◀ Jack Hearn, plant geneticist, with some of his Ambersweets

INVESTIGATION 1

WHAT ARE INHERITED TRAITS?

When you describe how someone looks—the person is short or tall, has blue eyes or brown eyes—you are often talking about the traits that the person inherited from his or her parents. Can these traits be changed? Find out in this investigation.

Activity

What Can You Do?

MATERIALS
- mirror
- *Science Notebook*

You have learned to do many things. But some things are impossible to learn because they are inherited traits. What kinds of traits are inherited?

Procedure

1. You and your classmates will collect data on three traits. First, stick out your tongue and try to roll up the edges to form a tube. With the help of your partner, look in a mirror to see if you can do this.

Step 1

D30

2. After everyone in the class has had a chance to check this trait, **make a chart** in your *Science Notebook* to **record** the class data.

3. Next, fold your hands together and see which thumb naturally falls on the top. Are you left-thumb superior (left thumb on top) or right-thumb superior? (See the photographs below.) **Record** the class data on this trait.

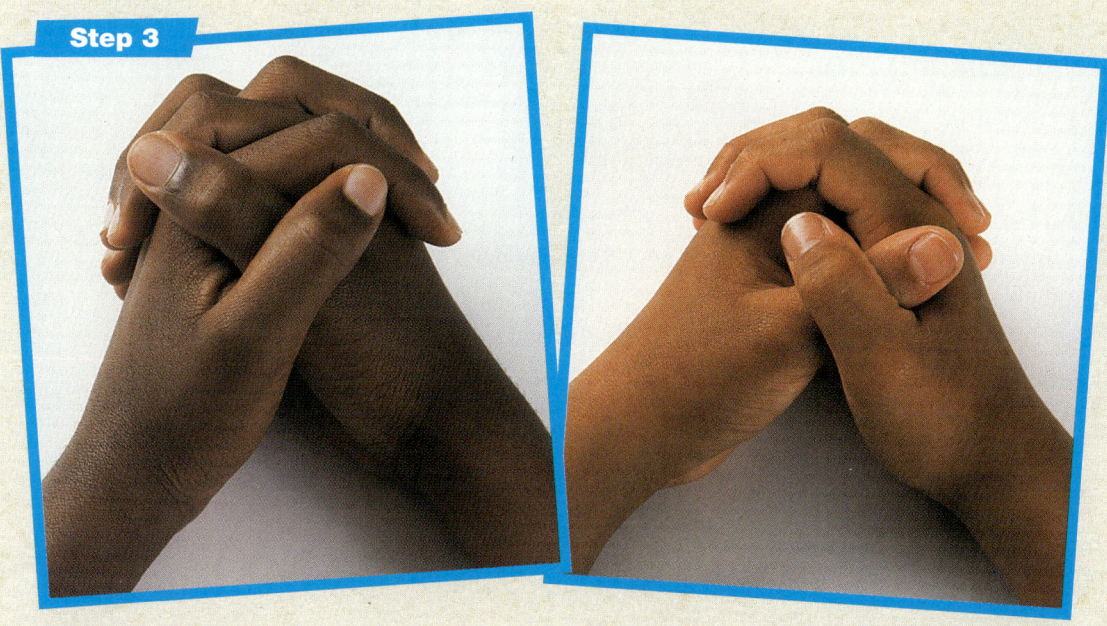

▲ Left-thumb superior   ▲ Right-thumb superior

4. Finally, are you left-handed or right-handed? **Record** the class data in your chart.

Analyze and Conclude

1. Were there more tongue rollers or nonrollers in your class? Were more people left-thumb superior or right-thumb superior? Were there more lefties or righties? **Make a bar graph** to show the number of people with each trait. Color the graph and **compare** the incidence of each trait.

2. If these three traits are inherited traits, what can you **infer** about the incidence of these traits in the general population? Use the bar graph you created as a guide.

3. **Hypothesize** whether nonrollers can learn to roll their tongues. Can a person change which thumb naturally falls on top when the hands are folded? Can righties learn to be lefties and vice versa? Explain your hypotheses.

INVESTIGATE FURTHER!

EXPERIMENT

Poll a random group of 25 people—members of a school club or sports team—and see whether they are tongue rollers or nonrollers, left-thumb or right-thumb superior, or right-handed or left-handed. Draw a bar graph and compare it to the one you drew of your class data.

D31

Activity
Environmental Influence

Many inherited traits are influenced by an organism's environment. Explore the effects of the environment in this activity.

MATERIALS
- goggles
- masking tape
- marker
- three small flowerpots or paper cups
- "eyes" of a potato
- soil
- water
- metric ruler
- plastic spoon
- watering can
- *Science Notebook*

SAFETY
Wear goggles during this activity.

Procedure

1. With masking tape and a marker, label three flowerpots *A*, *B*, and *C*. Put the same amount of soil in each pot. Plant one potato "eye" in each pot. (New plants will sprout from the "eyes" of the potato.) The "eye" should be just under the surface of the soil. Water the soil. Be sure to give all plants the same amount of water.

2. With your group, **brainstorm** a list of environmental conditions that plants need to grow well. (For example, most plants need light.) Plan to give potato eye *A* all of these conditions. This plant is the control for the experiment. Then choose two of the conditions to test. Potato eye *B* will have all the same conditions as potato eye *A* except for one of the conditions you will test. Potato eye *C* will have all the same conditions as potato eye *A* except for the other condition you will test.

Step 1

3. Make a copy of the chart shown. **Record** the conditions given to each plant. **Predict** how each plant will grow. **Record** your predictions in your *Science Notebook*.

Date	Conditions	Plant A Observations	Plant B Observations	Plant C Observations

4. Carry out your plan. Each day for a week, take a look at the three plants and **record** your observations in your chart.

Analyze and Conclude

1. What conditions did you test?

2. How did the variations in environmental conditions affect the potato eyes?

3. **Compare** the results of this activity with what you predicted.

4. How can you be sure that any differences you saw were caused by the conditions under which you grew the plants, and not by differences in the traits of the plants?

5. From your observations, **tell what evidence** there is that indicates that the environment can influence hereditary traits.

INVESTIGATE FURTHER!

EXPERIMENT

Can changing a plant's environment a second time cause a new change? Predict what will happen if you give plants *B* and *C* the same conditions that plant *A* has. Test your prediction. Report your results, and record them in a chart like the one above.

D33

Genes, Traits, and Environment

When friends and family see a new baby for the first time, they may make comments such as "She has her father's eyes" or "Look at that curly hair—just like his mother's!" Are such similarities coincidence, or do parents somehow pass traits to their offspring? And why does a baby look like one parent in some ways, and like the other parent in other ways?

The Secret in the Cell

Inherited traits are traits that are passed on from parents to offspring, from generation to generation. These traits are determined by a chemical code found inside cells. As a baby develops, the code causes cells to develop into the tissues that make up the body's organs and systems. Some cells become heart muscle, for example. Others become part of the body's bones.

This chemical code, called DNA, is transferred from generation to generation by the egg cells and sperm cells that join to form the zygote. If you haven't already guessed it, it is this code that controls the hereditary characteristics of the baby that will develop from the zygote. DNA controls eye color, skin color, and hair color, as well as thousands of other characteristics of the new baby. Therefore, it makes sense to look closely at how DNA is passed from parents to offspring.

CHROMOSOMES, GENES, AND DNA Just how unique are you? It all comes down to DNA! Each chromosome (*left*) is made up of message units called genes (*center*). And each gene is defined by a unique combination of DNA! (*right*)

D34

Passing on DNA

Remember that the chromosomes in a cell are duplicated before the cell divides. These chromosomes carry the code that controls the structure and function of each cell. Tiny message units, called **genes**, make up the chromosomes. The genes themselves are made of DNA. So when a cell reproduces by meiosis, half of each gene pair is passed on to each sperm cell or egg cell.

Each chromosome is like a chain made up of many genes. As shown in the illustration on page D34, each gene is a small piece of the cell's total DNA. For example, one gene might carry a code for hair color, another might carry a code for skin texture, and a third might carry a code for tongue rolling.

Genes: A Gift From Your Parents

Genes, too small to be seen even with a microscope, are the units from which your unique inheritance is created. Because half of your genes come from one parent and half from the other, you might have eyes with the shape of your father's and color like your mother's.

But if half your genes and chromosomes come from your father and half from your mother, why don't brothers and sisters in a family all look identical? It's because each new offspring has a new combination of chromosomes and genes. During meiosis, chromosomes are reshuffled, mixing the genetic information, and ensuring that different combinations of the parents' genetic information will be passed on. Therefore, each offspring has a unique set of genes. Genes make sure you have all the right parts doing the right jobs. They also make sure that you are a designer original—not like anyone else.

Is the World Series in Your Genes?

It would be simple if all traits were determined totally by genes! From the moment of fertilization, your traits would be set in stone—your final height, your health, your intelligence, even how long you will live.

Identical twins share the same exact inherited traits. Fraternal twins do not. Who's who in this picture? ▼

But this would be like saying that the look of a new house is the result of only the architect's blueprint. Many factors actually affect the final look of a new house. The blueprint determines the structural features, but the builder may use cheaper or more expensive materials in constructing it. And the new owner will determine the colors and type of wallpaper. Two houses built from identical blueprints may look—and be—very different when finally completed.

If you think about it, it's pretty obvious that some traits aren't simply the result of orders from genes. The ability to learn to speak is an inherited trait but the language you speak (and how well you speak it) is determined by where you are born and what language your parents speak. Language is a **learned trait**—a trait that is not passed on in DNA. Can you think of other learned traits?

Sometimes it's difficult to determine to what extent inherited traits are influenced by the environment. For example, did Ken Griffey, Jr., inherit the way he plays baseball from Ken Griffey, Sr.? Or did he inherit certain muscle structure, coordination skills, and other traits from his father, and then learn from his father to love the game and practice hard at it?

Who's in Charge?

God helps people develop many traits resulting from the interaction of genes and environment. Genes provide the opportunity for certain traits to develop. The environment in which you live influences the way in which many of the traits you inherit will develop. In the activity on pages D32 and D33 you probably gave some young plants a dark environment. All the plants had the genes that enable

God uses both genes and environment in our development. What traits did Ken Griffey, Jr., inherit from his father, and what habits did he learn from him?

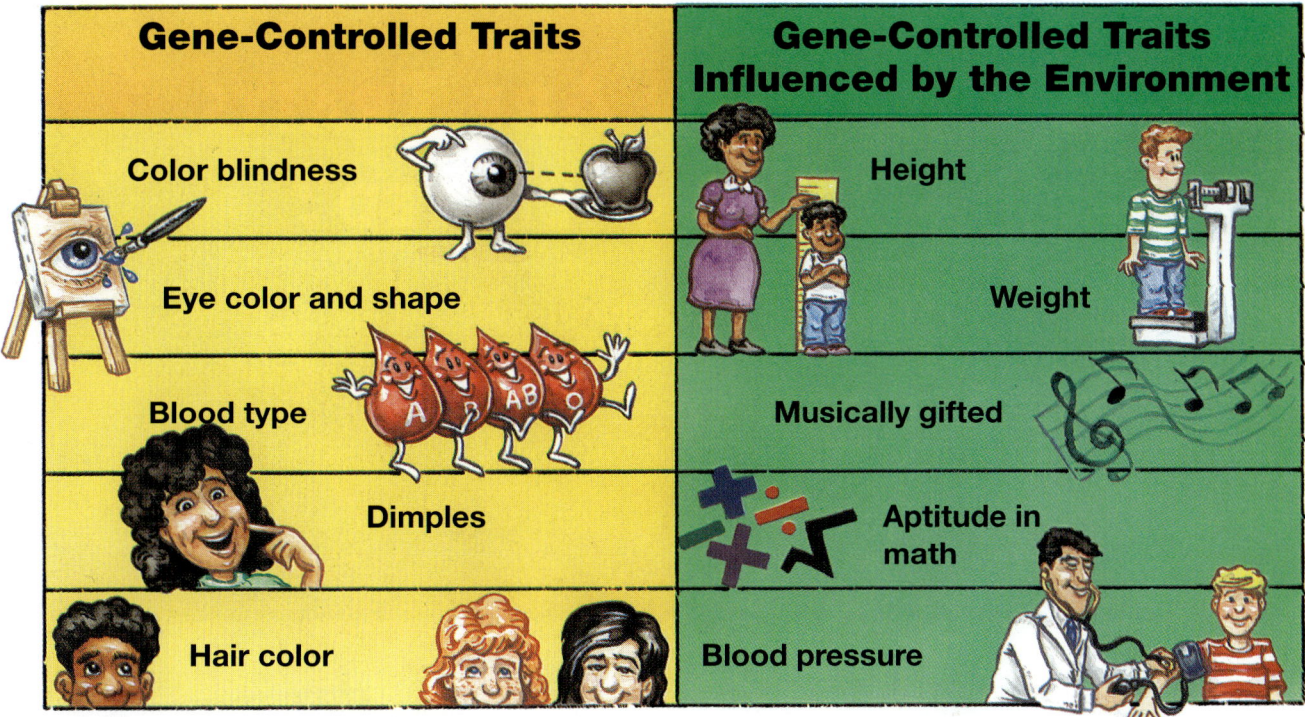

them to grow green leaves. But those plants in a dark environment produced leaves that were colorless or light green. Without light, plants can't develop chlorophyll, the pigment that makes leaves green and that traps the Sun's energy.

Use the diagram above to help you see how genes and environment interact. Some traits, like eye color, are controlled entirely by genes. Musical ability, however, may be passed from generation to generation, but the ability can only thrive in an environment that teaches a love for music.

For many traits, genes and environmental factors interact in complex ways. For example, genes may give you an ability to burn food quickly. Your tendency would be to remain lean. But overeating may cause you to be overweight despite this tendency.

It's good to know that you can affect certain traits by modifying your environment. For example, you can increase your chances of having a long life by eating properly, getting enough rest, and avoiding dangerous behaviors.

INVESTIGATION 1

1. Name two inherited traits that can be influenced by the environment. Explain how these traits might be influenced.

2. Consider two sisters with the same parents. One becomes a champion long-distance runner, the other a lead dancer in a major ballet company. Explain their similarities and differences in terms of heredity and environment.

INVESTIGATION 2

HOW ARE TRAITS INHERITED?

Juan's mother has brown eyes and his father has green eyes. Both grandfathers have blue eyes, while one grandmother has brown and the other has green. How did Juan inherit blue eyes?

Activity
Scrambled Genes

Brothers and sisters in a family get their genes from their parents. How do genes combine to create individuals distinct from one another?

MATERIALS
- 2 paper cups
- 2 sets of disks of 4 different colors
- marker or pencil
- large sheet of paper
- *Science Notebook*

Procedure

1. Divide the disks into two sets, each with the same four colors. One set will represent genes for four different traits from a male parent, the other, genes for these same traits from a female parent.

2. The two sides of each disk represent a gene pair, with each gene controlling a different form of the trait (such as brown eyes and blue eyes). Mark one side of each disk with the marker or pencil so that the two forms can be told apart.

3. **Label** one paper cup *male* and the other *female*. Place one set of the gene pairs in the *female* cup. Place the second set of gene pairs in the *male* cup.

4. On a large sheet of paper, **draw** three circles. **Label** one of the circles *sperm cell*; another, *egg cell*; and the third, *zygote*.

5. Prepare a data chart like the one shown. You will record the color of the disk, and *H* for head side (the marked side) or *T* for tail side (the unmarked side).

Trial 1			
Disk color	Female gene	Male gene	Zygote

Step 6

6. Hold one hand over the cup marked *female* and gently shake it. Empty the disks into the circle labeled *egg cell*. You will see one gene from each pair. **Record** the genes in your data chart. Repeat with the cup marked *male*, but empty the disks into the circle labeled *sperm cell*.

7. Match up the same-colored disk pairs from the egg cell and the sperm cell. Do not turn any of the disks over. Slide the matched pairs of genes into the circle labeled *zygote*. **Record** the combination of genes in the zygote.

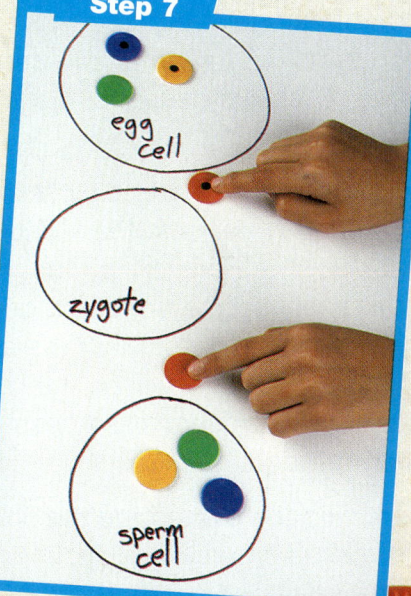

Step 7

8. Predict what the combination of genes would be if you did steps 6 and 7 again. **Record** your prediction. Then put the disks back into the cups and test your prediction. Repeat steps 6 and 7 a total of five times. **Record** the results of your trials. Recopy the data chart each time.

Analyze and Conclude

1. Identify and **describe** the processes you were modeling when you shook the cups and emptied the disks onto the paper and then moved the disks into the circle labeled *zygote*.

2. If the six "zygotes" were people, how would they be related? How would they be different?

UNIT PROJECT LINK

The traits of some animals make them "specialists": animals that specialize in using one kind of resource efficiently to survive. For example, black-footed ferrets eat prairie dogs almost exclusively. Do some research and find out about some endangered plants or animals that are specialists. Decide whether specialists are more likely to be endangered than organisms called generalists, which use many kinds of resources. Organize your data in a poster or large chart.

Activity
Inheriting Traits

MATERIALS
- marker
- disk
- *Science Notebook*

Parents often differ for particular traits. As a result their offspring may vary for the trait. Why?

Procedure

1. In this activity, the sperm and egg cells can carry either a dominant gene or a recessive gene. If present, a dominant gene controls the trait in an offspring, masking the recessive gene. If two recessive genes for a trait are passed on, that trait is present in the offspring.

2. Copy the chart below into your *Science Notebook*. Mark one side of your disk *A*. This will be the "head" side, representing the dominant gene for right-handedness. Mark the other side of your disk *a*. This will be the "tail" side and will represent the recessive gene for left-handedness.

3. Flip the disk to run the first trial. If the head side comes up, **record** the dominant gene (*A*) in the space for the sperm cell in the chart you copied. If the tail side comes up, **record** the recessive gene (*a*) in the space for the sperm cell.

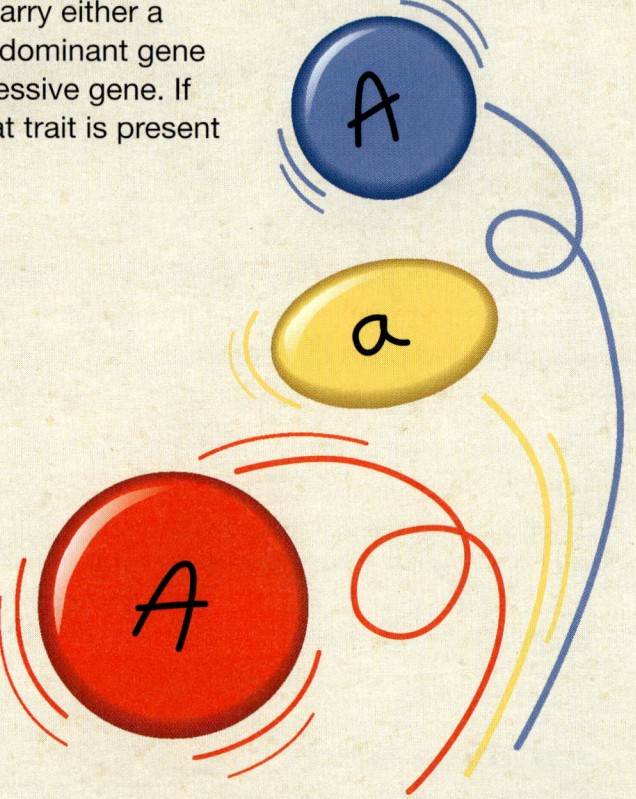

	Sperm cell	Egg cell	Zygote
Trial 1			
Trial 2			
Trial 3			
Trial 4			
Trial 5			
Trial 6			

4. Repeat the trial five more times for the sperm cell, **recording** each time whether the flip of the disk gives you the dominant or recessive gene. Then run the trial a total of six times for the egg cell.

5. Record the combination of genes in the zygote that would result from a union of the sperm and egg cells in each trial.

Step 3

Analyze and Conclude

1. Which zygotes carry one or more dominant genes? Which carry one or more recessive genes?

2. In your *Science Notebook*, indicate whether each offspring would be right-handed or left-handed.

3. Suggest a hypothesis to explain how two parents who are both right-handed could have a left-handed child.

INVESTIGATE FURTHER!

TAKE ACTION

Do you realize—maybe from personal experience—that people who have certain traits have a bit of difficulty in this world of ours? For example, left-handed people have trouble using right-handed scissors. Nearsighted people have trouble seeing far, so without corrective lenses they might have trouble seeing the chalkboard. See what you and your friends can do to adjust your thinking and find ways to help people who have these and other traits that might limit how they can participate in activities.

Activity
All in the Family

The inheritance of traits in a family can be recorded in a pedigree chart. Find out how one works in this activity.

Procedure

1. The pedigree chart shown here has information about ear lobes in a family. Ear lobes may be attached or free, depending on whether the individual has genes for attached ear lobes or genes for free ear lobes.

2. On this pedigree chart, circles represent females, and squares represent males. The horizontal lines connect two parents. The vertical and diagonal lines connect parents to children.

MATERIALS
• Science Notebook

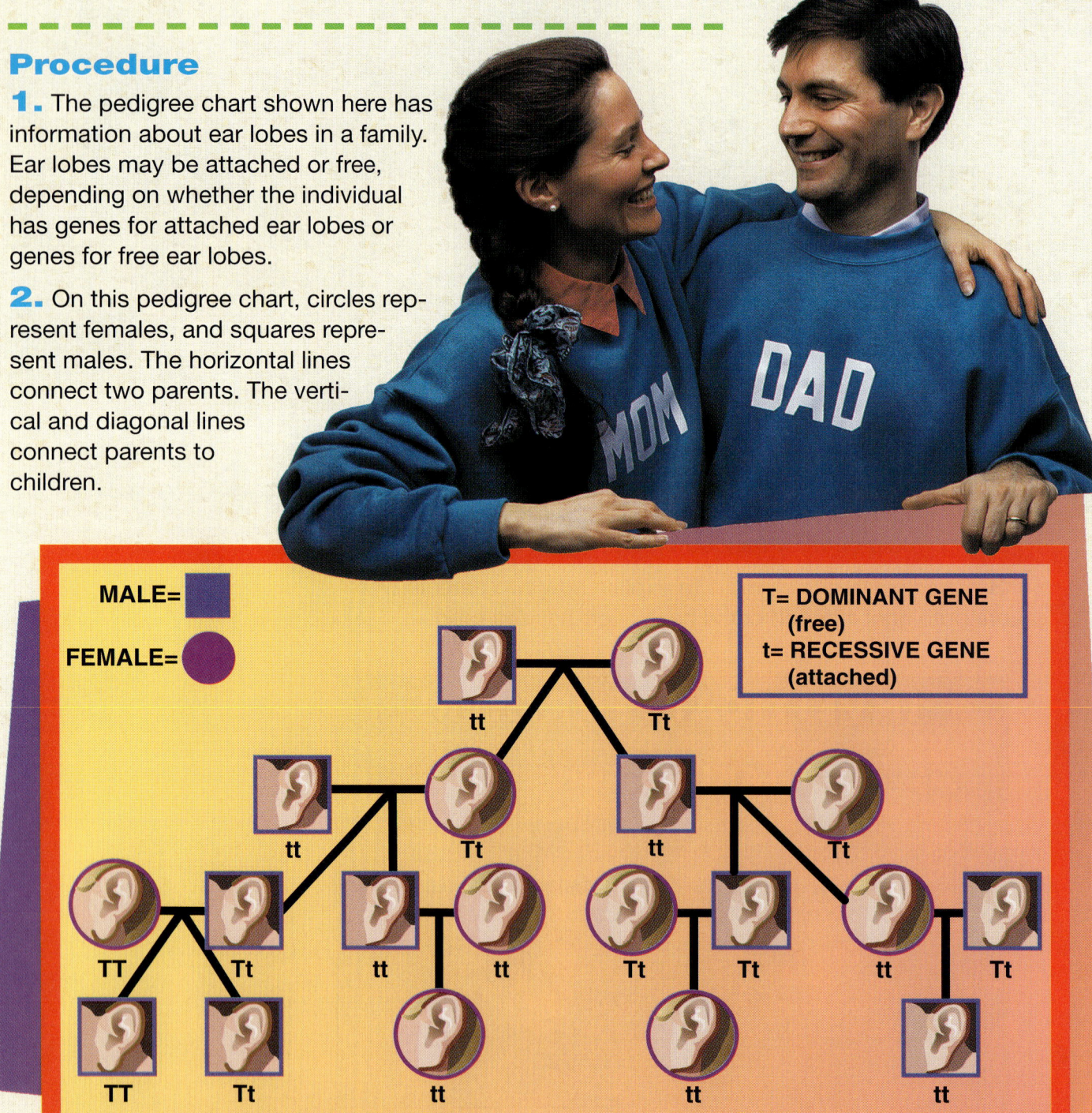

3. Look at the pedigree chart and **identify** the members of the family who have attached ear lobes. Then **identify** the members who have free ear lobes. In your *Science Notebook*, **record** your observations about the ear lobes of each individual in the chart.

Analyze and Conclude

1. Can two parents with attached ear lobes have children with free ear lobes? Explain your answer.

2. Can two parents with free ear lobes have children with attached ear lobes? Explain your answer.

3. Look for patterns in the way ear lobes are inherited. **Write a hypothesis** to explain how attached or free ear lobes are inherited.

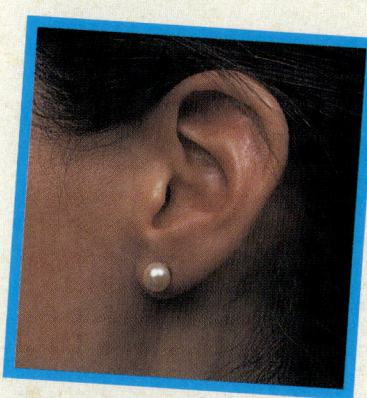

▲ Free ear lobe

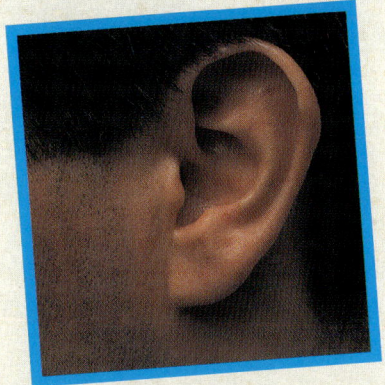

▲ Attached ear lobe

SCIENCE AND FAITH

When God gave His people the Ten Commandments He said, "I the Lord your God am a jealous God punishing the children for the sin of the fathers to the third and fourth generation of those who hate Me, but showing love to a thousand generations of those who love Me and keep My Commandments" (Exodus 20:5-6).

How do the sins of parents lead to similar or other sins in the lives of children? How has God's love reached a "thousand generations"? Talk with your parents about how God has blessed your family. Identify those in your family who profess faith in Jesus as their Savior.

D43

Laws of Heredity

A cat may have eight kittens, and each will be different from the others. How can that possibly be the case? In the activity on pages D38 and D39, what did you observe? Are the same combinations of genes always passed on when egg cells and sperm cells form? When an egg cell and a sperm cell are joined, the offspring receives a full set of chromosome pairs (and genes), but that set is different from the chromosomes of either parent. The recombining of genetic information leads to a unique instruction manual for building the next organism. You may be wondering whether there is any way to determine which traits an offspring will inherit. Will a brown-eyed parent and a blue-eyed parent have children with blue, brown, or green eyes?

If you wanted to look for a pattern in the way traits are passed from one generation to the next, what sort of experiment would you set up? How would you decide on the traits to observe? These are questions a monk named Gregor Mendel asked a century and a half ago.

Minding Your Peas and Questions

Mendel's love of plants and mathematics led him to discover how traits are passed on. As he worked in the monastery gardens, he noticed that certain traits of pea plants were passed from generation to generation. Curious, he set up experiments to find out why.

At the time, no one knew about genes or chromosomes. Mendel just knew he was looking for "something" that controlled how traits are passed. He made some very smart—and fortunate—decisions that would give him good data:

- He chose to observe just a few traits and observed only one at a time.
- He chose traits that were clear-cut and easy to observe.
- He worked carefully and kept good records.
- He used thousands of plants, not just a few.
- He carried out experiments at least to the second generation.

The Tall and the Short of It

One trait Mendel observed was tallness. Pea plants usually self-pollinate; male and female cells are produced by the same plant. Mendel noted that some pea plants always produced tall offspring; others always produced short offspring. He described these plants as being "pure" for the trait of height.

Mendel wondered what would happen if pure tall plants were crossed with pure short ones. He found out by hand-pollinating plants to be sure one parent was tall and one short. You might expect the offspring of a tall parent and a short parent to be medium in height. Instead, all the offspring were tall! Mendel hypothesized that each parent contributed one unit of heredity for tallness. He called these units T (tall) and t (short). (Today we refer to these units as genes.) He used the term **dominant trait** (T) to describe the trait that was expressed. The trait that was not expressed was the **recessive trait** (t). He reasoned that the offspring must have a Tt combination. Mendel allowed the Tt offspring to self-pollinate. The drawing and table below—known as a Punnett square—will help you understand what happened.

Notice that one fourth of the offspring of Tt plants were short, and three fourths were tall. The two possible genes that each parent may pass on appear at the top and side of the table. The squares in the table show the combinations of genes the offspring may have.

You can see there are three possible combinations of genes and the combina-

MENDEL'S METHOD When Mendel crossed pure tall plants with pure short plants, all of the offspring were tall! When this generation was allowed to self-pollinate, both tall and short offspring occurred, in a ratio of 3 tall to 1 short.

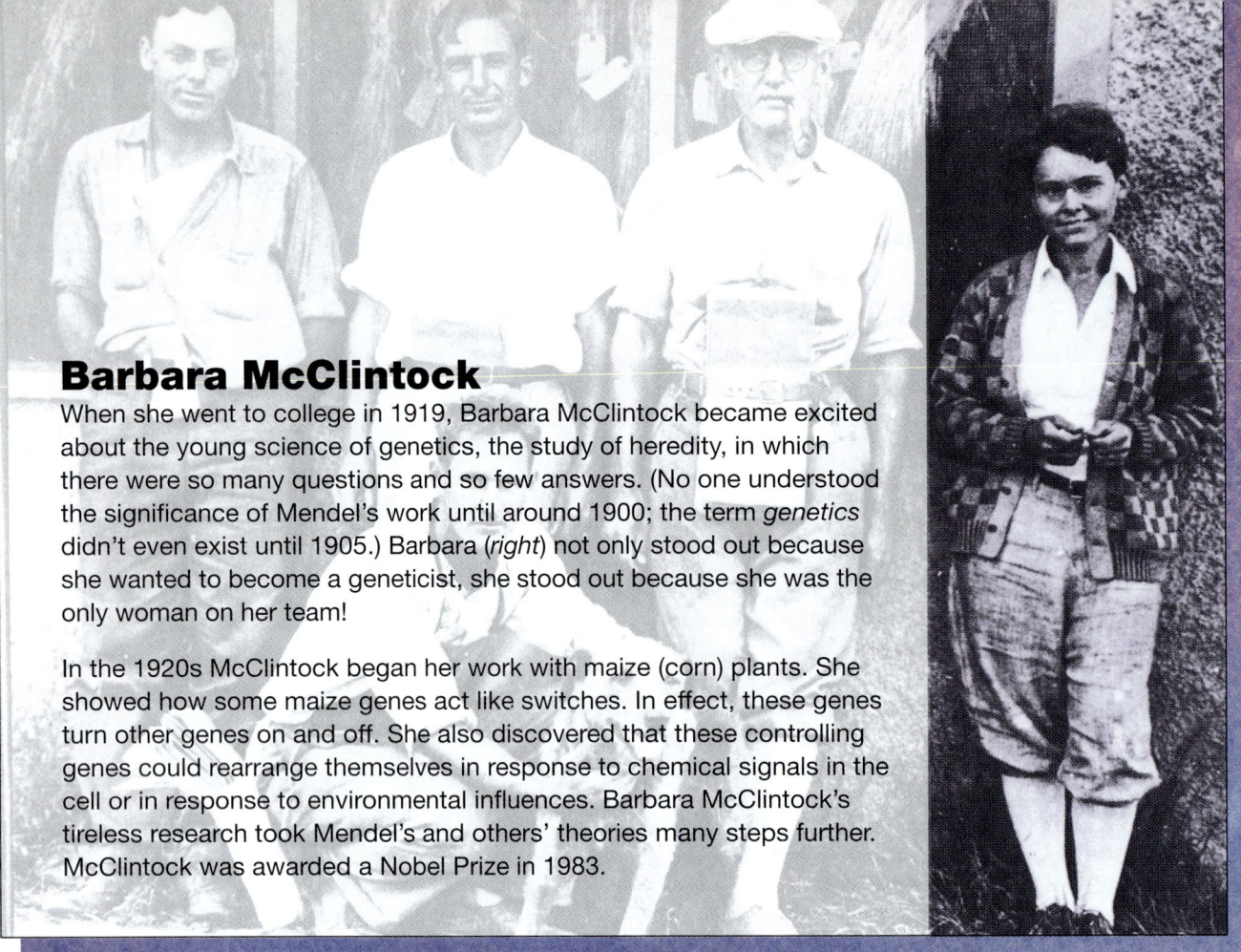

Barbara McClintock

When she went to college in 1919, Barbara McClintock became excited about the young science of genetics, the study of heredity, in which there were so many questions and so few answers. (No one understood the significance of Mendel's work until around 1900; the term *genetics* didn't even exist until 1905.) Barbara (*right*) not only stood out because she wanted to become a geneticist, she stood out because she was the only woman on her team!

In the 1920s McClintock began her work with maize (corn) plants. She showed how some maize genes act like switches. In effect, these genes turn other genes on and off. She also discovered that these controlling genes could rearrange themselves in response to chemical signals in the cell or in response to environmental influences. Barbara McClintock's tireless research took Mendel's and others' theories many steps further. McClintock was awarded a Nobel Prize in 1983.

tion Tt occurs twice. So, on average, three zygotes out of four will inherit a dominant gene (T). Sure enough, three out of the four pea plants proved to be tall. Mendel's results show clearly that a dominant gene masks the effect of a recessive one (t) when both are present. Only plants with two recessive genes for shortness (tt) were short.

Black and White, or Gray?

For some traits there are two different dominant genes, and both can be expressed to a varying degree. For example, the four o'clock flower may have red flowers (RR—two genes for red flower color) or white flowers (WW—two genes for white flower color). When red and white are crossed, the offspring have pink (RW) flowers. In this case, neither gene is masked; both are expressed in a way that produces a blended effect. This is known as **incomplete dominance**.

Multiple Genes

Is inheritance always so simple? Of course not. Many traits have more than two variations and, therefore, more than two forms of the gene for that trait. Eye color is one such trait. There are several genes for *eye color* ranging from brown, which is most dominant, to blue, which is most recessive. In between are genes for hazel, green, gray, and violet. An individual has only a pair of genes for *eye color*—but it can be any combination of these! Some traits are influenced by two or more pairs of genes. Skin color is determined not by a single pair of genes but by many pairs. Thus, skin color in humans is quite varied and its inheritance very complex.

Designer Genes

The researchers who unlocked the secrets of genes opened a world of possibilities and raised more exciting questions than were even dreamed of years before. Today, genes can be altered and even transferred from one organism to another, a process called **genetic engineering**. One important example of genetic engineering is the use of microorganisms to produce medicines needed by humans.

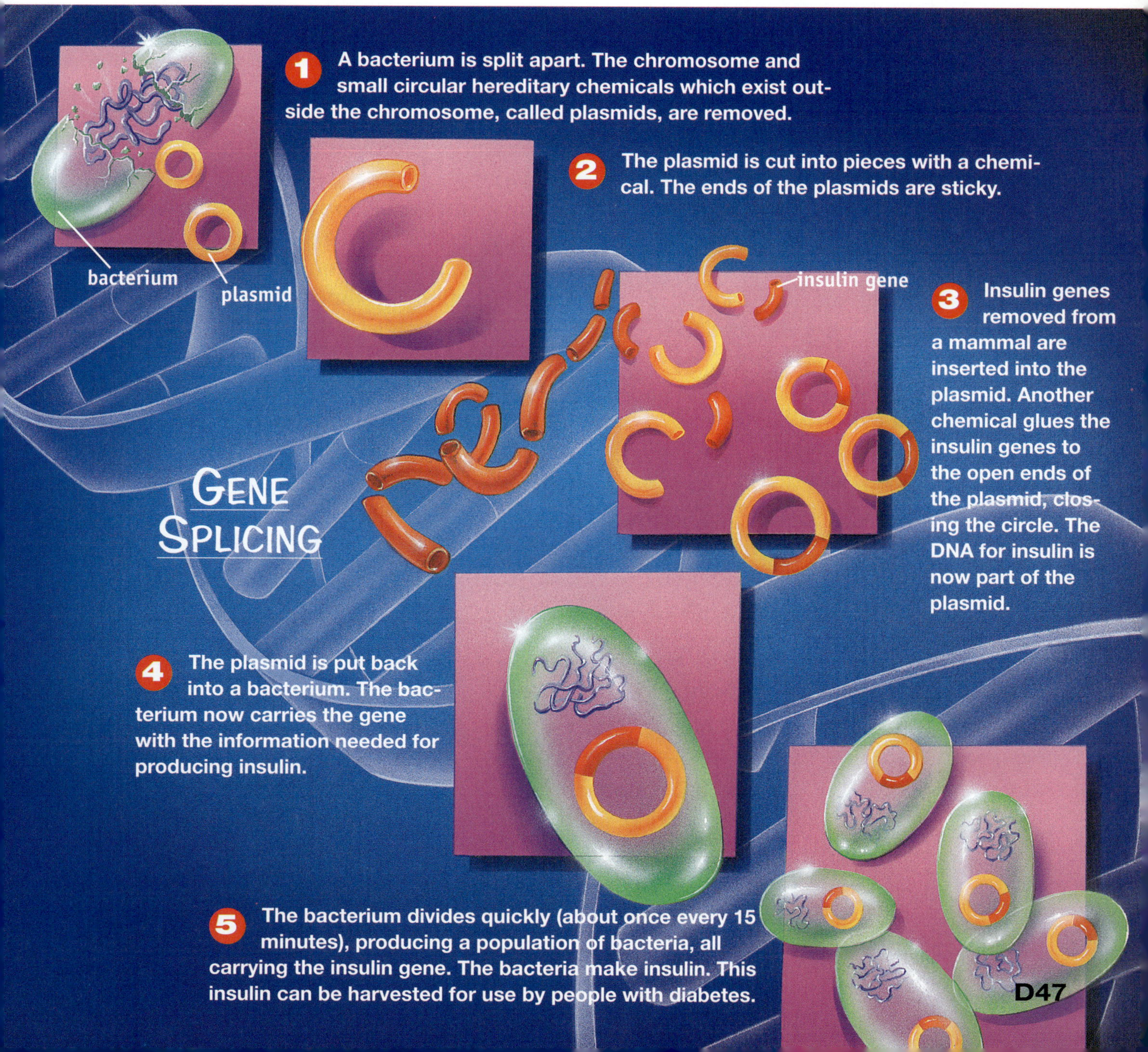

Gene Splicing

1 A bacterium is split apart. The chromosome and small circular hereditary chemicals which exist outside the chromosome, called plasmids, are removed.

bacterium | plasmid

2 The plasmid is cut into pieces with a chemical. The ends of the plasmids are sticky.

insulin gene

3 Insulin genes removed from a mammal are inserted into the plasmid. Another chemical glues the insulin genes to the open ends of the plasmid, closing the circle. The DNA for insulin is now part of the plasmid.

4 The plasmid is put back into a bacterium. The bacterium now carries the gene with the information needed for producing insulin.

5 The bacterium divides quickly (about once every 15 minutes), producing a population of bacteria, all carrying the insulin gene. The bacteria make insulin. This insulin can be harvested for use by people with diabetes.

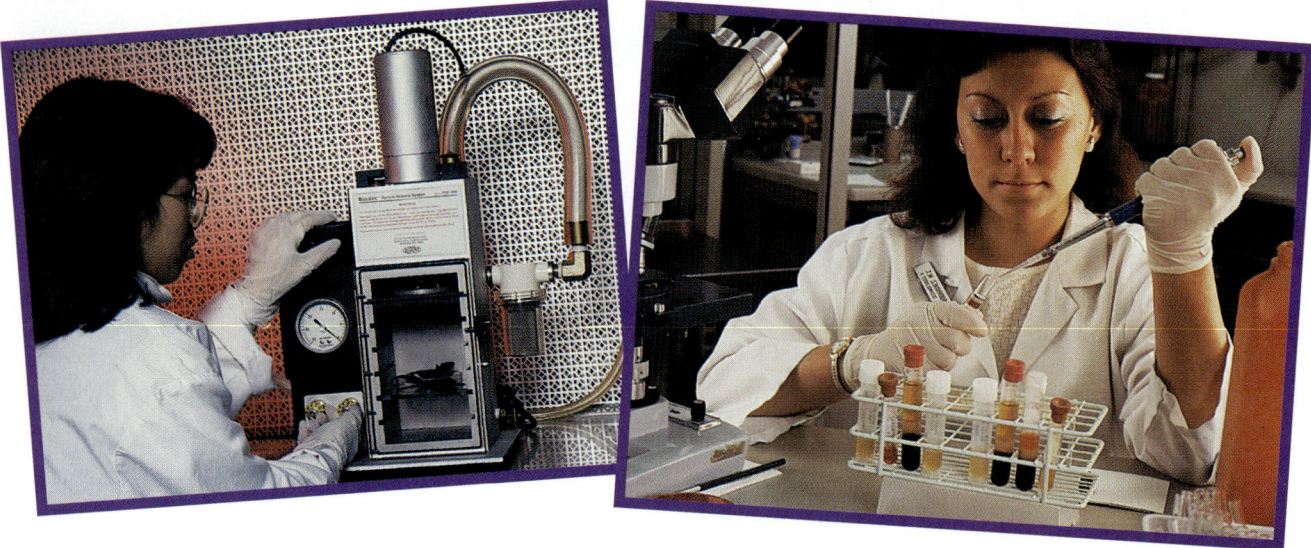

▲ Scientists use genetic engineering to try to discover cures for diseases.

Diabetics, for example, need the chemical insulin, which their bodies have stopped producing. Today, bacteria are used to produce human insulin.

How can a gene for producing insulin be removed from one organism and transferred to a bacterium? Think of a precise, delicate operation carried out in the world's smallest operating room. The diagram on page D47 will help you understand this operation, called **gene splicing**.

What Are the Possibilities?

What would make the process of transplanting genes easier and more useful? What if we could just insert the new genes right into a human cell? This would involve identifying the location of each gene on all 46 human chromosomes, a project currently under way.

Several new techniques of transplanting genes show great promise. The ability to transplant genes directly into human cells has created the field of gene therapy. For example, a gene that produces a cancer-fighting substance can be injected right into a tumor.

Genetic engineering opens a world of fascinating possibilities. Scientists can now turn cells into living factories that can produce medicines, hormones, and drugs. They might one day be able to correct genetic defects before birth. What other possibilities do you see? ■

INVESTIGATION 2

1. Distinguish between dominant genes and recessive genes for a trait.

2. Mendel crossed tall plants (gene combination TT) with short plants (tt). Use a Punnett square like the one on page D45 to show the possible gene combinations in the offspring. Describe each type.

3. Genetic technology can be used to the glory of God for the benefit of others. Explain.

REFLECT & EVALUATE

WORD POWER

dominant trait
genes
gene splicing
genetic engineering
incomplete dominance
inherited traits
learned trait
recessive trait

On Your Own
Review the terms in the list. Then use as many terms as you can in a paragraph about the importance of genes.

With a Partner
Make a word web and show how the words on the list relate.

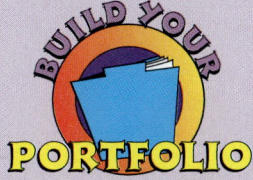

Pick an animal. Cut out photos from magazines that show all the variations in coat color that you can find. Make a poster to explain the variations you found.

Analyze Information

The incomplete Punnett square below shows a cross between a female guinea pig with black fur and a male guinea pig with white fur. Determine the possible gene pairs and fur colors in the offspring. What percent of the offspring are likely to have white fur?

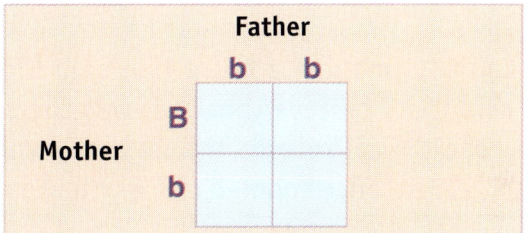

Assess Performance

Construct a pedigree for an imaginary family for a specific hereditary trait and explain how that trait is transmitted through the generations.

Problem Solving

1. Sickle-cell anemia is an inherited disease in which red blood cells cannot carry oxygen because of their shape. How might gene splicing someday help in treating this disease?

2. If you were a chicken farmer, how might keeping records of egg size and production help you to develop the best egg-laying chickens?

3. Wolfgang Mozart was born to a musical family. He became one of the world's great musical geniuses. Explain Mozart's talent in terms of learned and inherited traits.

4. Is faith in Jesus inherited or learned?

D49

CHAPTER 3

CHANGE THROUGH TIME

Can you imagine a horse that's no bigger than a beagle? Some scientists believe that that was the size of horses many years ago! Fossil records tell us that some types of animals that once roamed the earth are no longer alive.

That's About the Size of It

Fossil evidence shows that dinosaurs, like horses, once existed in various sizes. Although many were very large, other dinosaur fossils show mature dinosaurs the size of sheep. Dinosaurs of this size could well have survived the flood, together with other animals inside Noah's ark.

Some scientists have attempted to create what they think may have been the atmospheric conditions of the pre-flood world. In a climate with increased oxygen and air pressure, they are able to grow cherry tomatoes the size of a grapefruit. These conditions could explain why ancient animals grew to such great size.

Coming Up

INVESTIGATION 1
WHAT DO FOSSILS TELL US ABOUT LIFE—PAST AND PRESENT?
.... **D52**

INVESTIGATION 2
WHAT EVIDENCE DO SCIENTISTS HAVE THAT SPECIES CHANGE OVER TIME?
.... **D64**

INVESTIGATION 3
HOW DO CHANGES IN SPECIES OCCUR?
.... **D72**

◀ Though now found only in a few zoos in Europe, Przewalski's horse lived wild in Asia until the 1960s.

INVESTIGATION 1

WHAT DO FOSSILS TELL US ABOUT LIFE —PAST AND PRESENT?

Scientists search for clues about organisms that lived long ago. Such clues may include fossil remains, footprints, and other traces, and, in rare cases, the organism itself! What do these fossils tell us about life long ago.

Activity
Examine a Fossil

Fossils are the remains and traces of organisms that lived long ago. What can a fossil tell you about organisms from the past?

MATERIALS
- 2 fossils
- metric ruler
- hand lens
- *Science Notebook*

Procedure

1. Examine one of the fossils. Note its size, shape, structure, and texture. Use a metric ruler to take measurements of the fossil. In your *Science Notebook*, **record** your observations.

2. Use a hand lens to get a closer look at the fossil. **Record** any details you see that you could not see before.

Step 2

D52

3. Make a drawing of the fossil, including all the details you see. **Label** any parts you can identify.

4. Examine the second fossil, repeating steps 1 through 3. **Compare** this fossil with the first one you studied.

Analyze and Conclude

1. Infer what the fossils are made of.

2. How are the two fossils similar? How are they different?

3. What organism do you think each fossil is the remains of? Give reasons for your answers.

4. Based on your observations of the fossils, **infer** what you can about the environments in which the organisms lived.

Step 3

INVESTIGATE FURTHER!

RESEARCH

Use books and other sources to try to identify the fossils in this activity as well as the fossils pictured below. Try to find out when each organism lived, what its diet was, and where it might have lived.

Use reference books to identify these fossils. ▼

D53

Activity

Make a Model Fossil

If you put your hand in wet sand, it will leave an outline of your hand. Some fossils formed in a similar way when they were pressed into layers of sediment, which then hardened into a rock. You can make a model of these types of fossils to see how they formed.

MATERIALS
- goggles
- modeling clay
- paper cup
- metric ruler
- scissors
- shell
- petroleum jelly
- spoon
- water
- plaster of Paris
- jar
- *Science Notebook*

SAFETY
Wear goggles during this activity. Wash hands after handling plaster of Paris. Do not inhale plaster of Paris dust.

Procedure

1. Press modeling clay into the bottom of a paper cup. Use scissors to cut off the top of the cup about 5 cm above the level of the clay.

2. Coat the outside of a shell with a thin layer of petroleum jelly and press that side of the shell into the clay. **Predict** what the clay will look like after you remove the shell.

3. Remove the shell and look at the surface of the clay. You have **made a model** of a mold fossil. In your *Science Notebook*, **record** your observations.

4. Use a spoon to mix water and plaster of Paris in a jar. Follow the directions on the package.

5. Pour the plaster of Paris into the cup, over the clay, until the cup is almost full.

6. Let the plaster of Paris harden overnight. Peel away the paper cup. Gently separate the layer of clay from the layer of plaster. You have **made a model** of a cast fossil. **Record** your observations.

Step 2

Step 6

Analyze and Conclude

1. How does a mold fossil differ from a cast fossil?

2. How is your mold fossil like the shell? What can you learn about an organism from a mold fossil of it?

3. How is your cast fossil like the shell? What can you learn about an organism from a cast fossil of it?

4. How is your cast fossil different from the original object? What kind of information about an organism can you *not* learn from its cast fossil?

5. **Infer** why a cast fossil might form in one instance and a mold fossil in another.

UNIT PROJECT LINK

As part of your project, make a cast or mold "fossil" of a footprint from an endangered animal you've learned about. Get a field guide to animal tracks from your teacher or librarian. Then find an illustration and a description of the animal's footprint. Assemble all the materials you will need, such as clay and modeling tools. Now use these materials and the illustration of the animal's footprint to create your own "fossil."

How Fossils Form

Have fossils ever been discovered in your area? **Fossils** are the remains and traces of organisms that lived long ago. Most fossils are found in sedimentary rock, such as sandstone or limestone. This kind of rock formed when sediment—bits of rock and minerals—built up in layers. The tiny particles of sediment on the bottom were squeezed together as layers of sediment formed above them. Over many years, the particles slowly hardened into rock layers.

Molds and Casts

The remains of animals and plants that have died can become preserved as fossils in sedimentary rock in several ways. Sometimes after an organism dies, sediments collect and harden around its body. As the organism decays or dissolves, an open space that has the shape of the organism remains in the sedimentary rock. A hollowed space in the shape of an organism or one of its parts is called a **mold fossil**. When you pressed a shell into clay, you modeled how a mold fossil forms.

Minerals from the rock surrounding a mold fossil may slowly move into the space left when the organism decayed.

This dinosaur's remains began as bones in sediment. Over many years the bones became petrified. ▼

These minerals harden into the shape of the original organism, forming a **cast fossil**. By using plaster of Paris to fill in a mold, you modeled the formation of a cast fossil.

Sometimes living things leave behind traces of their activities instead of fossils of their bodies. Some animals, including dinosaurs, walked through soft mud that dried in the sun before the footprints were buried by sediment. These fossilized imprints are a type of mold fossil, and the prints tell us much about the animals and their lives. For example, the size and shape of a dinosaur footprint might give a scientist clues about how large the dinosaur was, how it moved, and even what kinds of foods it ate.

Cast in Stone

Another kind of fossil can form from the hard parts of organisms, parts such as bones and wood. For example, a tree may fall into water and be quickly buried in the mud at the bottom. Water and minerals seep into the wood. As the wood decays, the minerals replace the wood, taking the shape of the wood and hardening into stone. The changing of the hard parts of a dead organism to stone is called **petrification**. You may have seen petrified wood that is hard as a rock but still shows the rings of the original tree. The fossilized skeletons of dinosaurs and other animals are often petrified remains. Such remains preserve fine details of these organisms.

Cross section of a tree trunk turned to stone ▼

▲ Petrified Forest National Park, in Arizona, is known for its vast number of trees turned to stone.

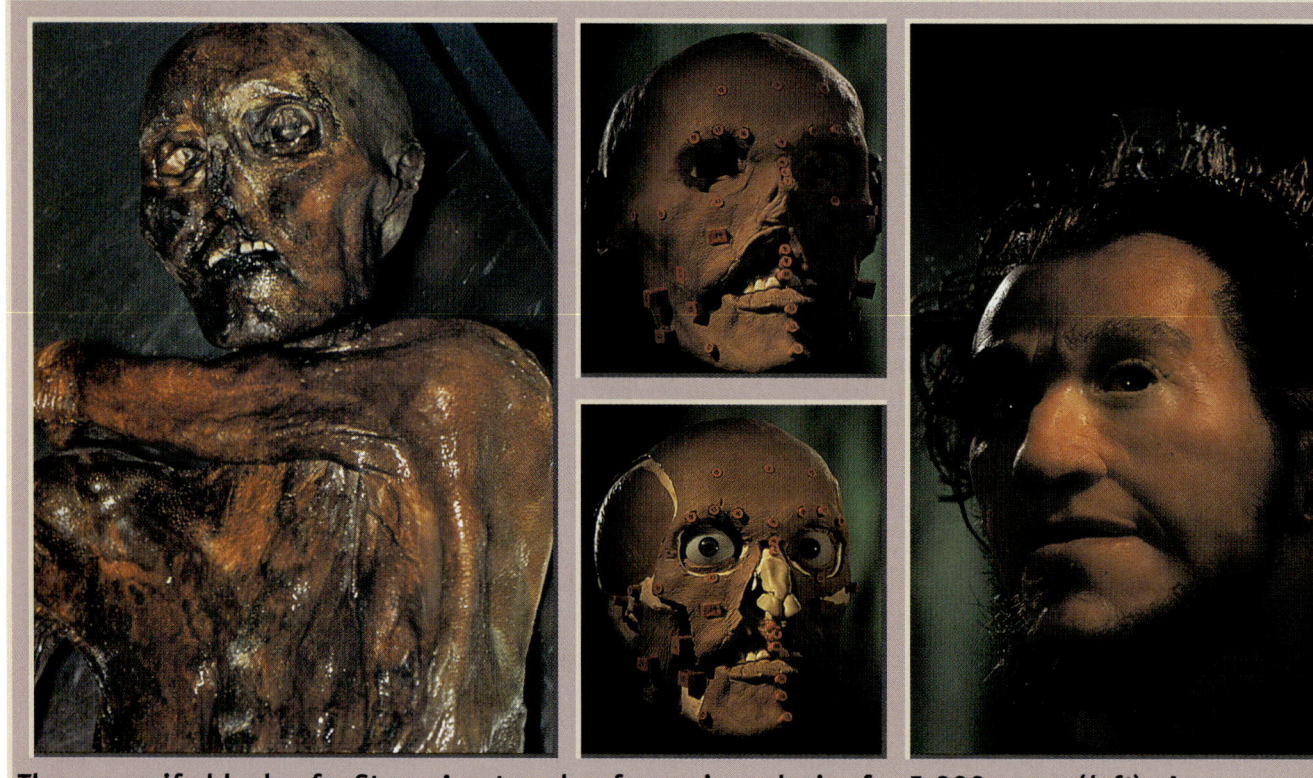

The mummifed body of a Stone Age traveler, frozen in a glacier for 5,000 years (*left*). A reconstruction was made (*center*) so that scientists could learn more about him (*right*).

Entombed Fossils

Do you think you'd like to wear a fossil as jewelry? Many people do. Amber is fossilized tree resin. Resin is a sticky kind of tree sap. If you've handled pine cones or pine branches, you know how sticky resin can be. Insects that became stuck in resin were sometimes preserved as the resin hardened into the clear, golden material we call amber. Some pieces of amber contain whole insects, and others contain only bits and pieces. One piece of amber was found with a tiny tree frog preserved inside!

How can food be preserved for many months? You can put it in a freezer. Occasionally, whole animals were accidentally trapped and preserved in ice. In recent times, as the ice melted, the remains of some of these ancient creatures were revealed. A number of woolly mammoths, uncovered in Siberia, had not decayed at all! Even more amazing was the discovery in 1991 of the frozen, mummified body of a hunter! Scientists estimate that he froze to death along what is now the Austria-Italy border 5,000 years ago!

Fossils as Evidence

Scientists called **paleontologists** (pā lē ən täl'ə jists) study fossils of ancient life. By digging carefully, they work to uncover the history of life on Earth.

Fossils suggest that many species from the past are similar to species alive today—similar but not identical. Many scientists have concluded that living species are related to and descended from species that lived in the past. The idea that new species develop from earlier species is called **evolution**. The fossil record is one of the most important pieces of evidence used to support the idea that species evolve.

The Geologic Time Scale

By analyzing the different kinds of fossils found in layers of rock, some scientists speculate that life on Earth has changed drastically over time. They have divided the time since Earth was formed into four large spans of time. The earliest span is known as Precambrian (prē kam′brē ən) time. Next are the Paleozoic (pā lē ō zō′ik), Mesozoic (mes ō zō′ik), and the most recent, the Cenozoic (sē nə zō′ik) **eras**.

Evolutionists believe that nine tenths of Earth's history occurred during the span of time known as the Precambrian.

The three eras following Precambrian time have been divided into shorter time spans called **periods**, as illustrated on the next two pages.

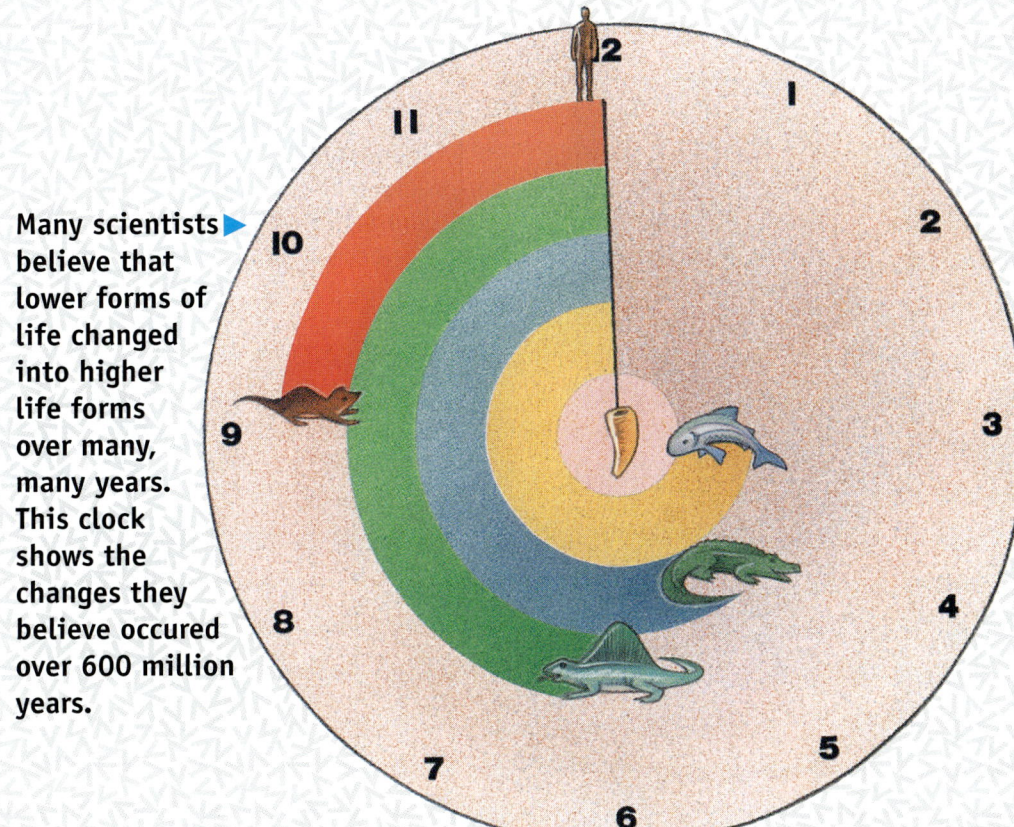

▶ Many scientists believe that lower forms of life changed into higher life forms over many, many years. This clock shows the changes they believe occured over 600 million years.

◀ Trusting in God's Word, we believe that the universe was not developed in 600 million years, but rather in 6 days. And we believe that the theory of evolution is a belief system based on ideas and interpretations which are subject to errors. By faith we see that complexities of the universe are so great that they cannot be derived simply from change over time, but must be directed by divine wisdom and power – by the action of God Himself.

The Bible teaches that God created the world in 6 days. Genesis 1 records that God made plants on day 3 (vv.9-13), birds and water animals on day 5 (vv.20-23), and land animals on day 6 (vv.24-28). God made all things good. God could not have used evolution to create higher level organisms including people because He tells us in His Word that He made all things in 6 days, not millions of years. Plus, there was no death until Adam

PALEOZOIC ERA
600 million to 230 million years ago (mya)

Cambrian Period (600 mya)
Life exploded into great varieties of forms in Earth's oceans. Many creatures with hard shells are preserved as fossils. There were many life forms and most of them have no counterparts today. They simply died out.

Silurian Period (435 mya)
Land plants and such animals as scorpions appeared. The first fish with jaws evolved during this period.

Carboniferous Period (360 mya)
Tropical climates resulted in swamps that would become coal beds millions of years later. The earliest insects and reptiles appeared. Amphibians thrived.

Ordovician Period (500 mya)
Fish, the first vertebrates, or animals with backbones, appeared. An ice age occurred, causing the extinction of much ocean life during this period.

Devonian Period (410 mya)
As Earth's land masses drifted and ocean conditions changed, many kinds of ocean life became extinct. Many new fish and the first sharks roamed the seas. Amphibians and ferns populated the land.

Permian Period (290 mya)
Earth's climate became drier, and more and more species lived on land. Reptiles thrived. Toward the end of the Permian Period, many species, particularly in the sea, became extinct, perhaps due to environmental changes.

and Eve sinned. There, no plants and animals could have died to form fossils until after sin entered the world. As the chart on these pages shows, evolutionists believe life forms changed into other life forms after millions of years.

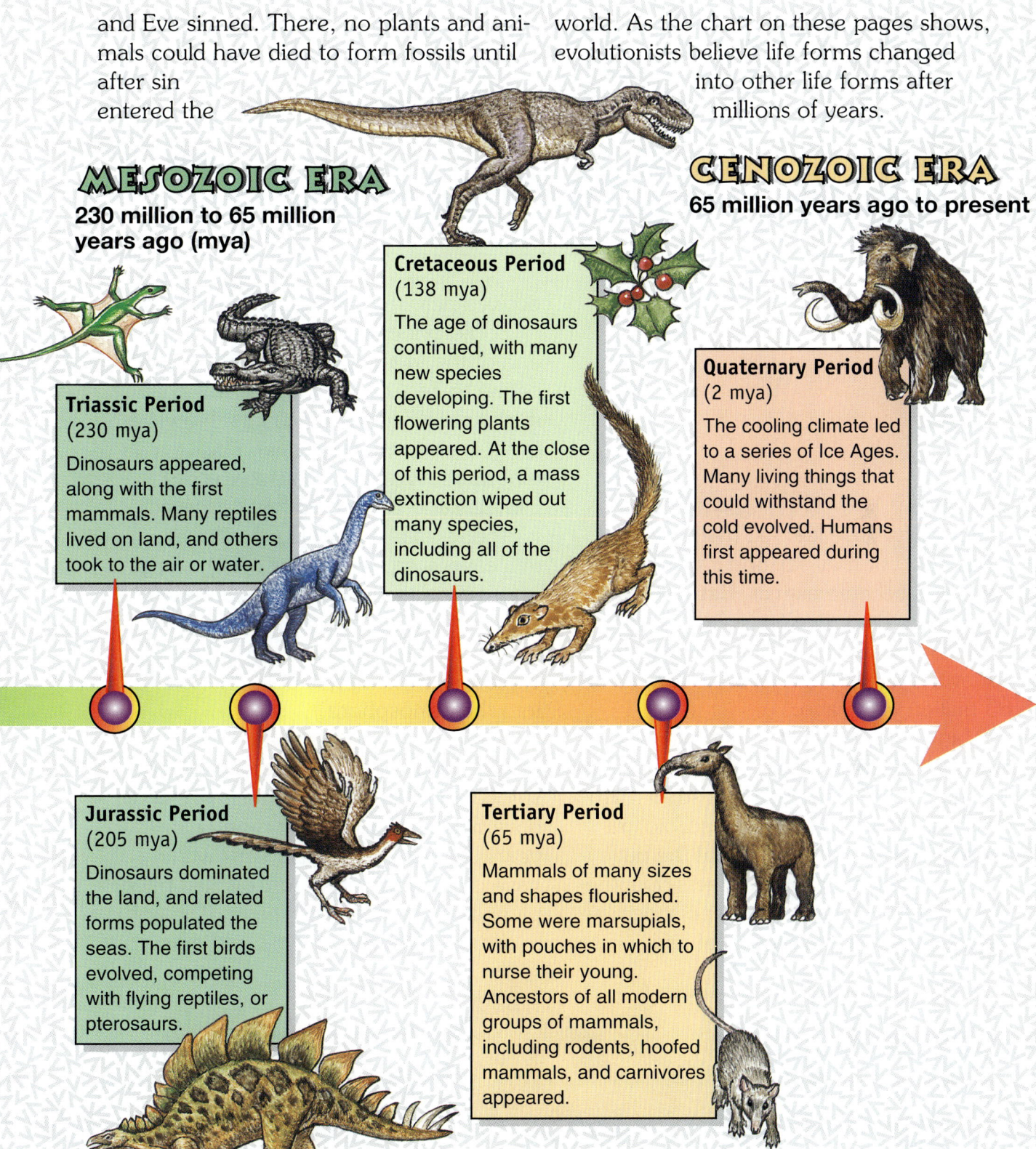

MESOZOIC ERA
230 million to 65 million years ago (mya)

Triassic Period (230 mya)
Dinosaurs appeared, along with the first mammals. Many reptiles lived on land, and others took to the air or water.

Cretaceous Period (138 mya)
The age of dinosaurs continued, with many new species developing. The first flowering plants appeared. At the close of this period, a mass extinction wiped out many species, including all of the dinosaurs.

Jurassic Period (205 mya)
Dinosaurs dominated the land, and related forms populated the seas. The first birds evolved, competing with flying reptiles, or pterosaurs.

CENOZOIC ERA
65 million years ago to present

Quaternary Period (2 mya)
The cooling climate led to a series of Ice Ages. Many living things that could withstand the cold evolved. Humans first appeared during this time.

Tertiary Period (65 mya)
Mammals of many sizes and shapes flourished. Some were marsupials, with pouches in which to nurse their young. Ancestors of all modern groups of mammals, including rodents, hoofed mammals, and carnivores appeared.

What Happened to the Dinosaurs?

Scientists have learned much about dinosaurs, but they still don't know why dinosaurs became extinct. **Extinction** means that a species no longer exists. Evolutionists claim that the dinosaurs died out at the end of the Mesozoic Era, about 65 million years ago.

Many hypotheses have been suggested to explain the extinction of the dinosaurs. Some scientists proposed that small mammals also living during the Mesozoic Era ate so many dinosaur eggs that the huge creatures became extinct. Others hypothesized that the dinosaurs were poisoned by eating the flowering plants that had evolved near the end of the Mesozoic Era.

Some evidence suggests that at the end of the Mesozoic Era, Earth's climate began to cool down and that this change in climate killed the dinosaurs. However, there is also evidence that some dinosaurs were well-adapted to cool climates and thus could have survived.

Today, many scientists think that dinosaurs were wiped out when a large asteroid collided with Earth. An asteroid is a chunk of rock that orbits the Sun. An asteroid that struck Earth would have exploded, sending millions of tons of dust into the atmosphere.

Such a collision could have greatly disturbed the climate. Thick clouds of black smoke and dust in the atmosphere could have blocked sunlight for months or even years. Without sunlight, plants would have died and temperatures would have plunged. The loss of plants on land and in the ocean could have caused many

▲ Artists have imagined what an asteroid's impact on Earth might have looked like.

▲ Iridium: some speculate it offers a clue as to what happened to the dinosaurs.

food webs to collapse. The plant eaters and the meat eaters would have starved to death eventually.

Some say the asteroid hypothesis is supported by the discovery of the metal iridium (ī rid′ē əm) in the rock layers said to have formed about 65 million years ago, at the end of the Mesozoic Era. Iridium is very rare on Earth, but it is common in asteroids and other objects in space. It is reasoned that if an asteroid collided with Earth 65 million years ago, it could have showered the land with iridium. Evidence for this hypothesis is that the rock layer said to have formed at the close of the Mesozoic Era has 30 times more iridium than is found in other layers.

Although many scientists support the asteroid hypothesis, others say the evidence is not strong enough. Many Christians believe that large dinosaurs died during the Great Flood, speculating that small dinosaurs could have survived with Noah and his family inside the ark. Perhaps climatic changes after the flood made it impossible for them to survive. ■

INVESTIGATION 1

1. Describe two ways by which fossils can form.

2. The petrified remains of complete skeletons of animals are rare. Why do you think is this so?

3. Archeologists claim to have discovered dinosaur and human footprints in the same layer of rock. Does this finding support or contradict the theory of evolution? Why?

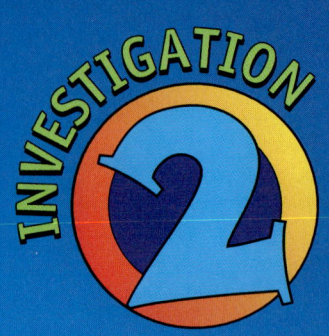

INVESTIGATION 2

WHAT EVIDENCE DO SCIENTISTS HAVE THAT SPECIES CHANGE OVER TIME?

The shape and structure of each living thing give scientists clues as to how organisms are related. What other clues to evolution do scientists have?

Activity
Out on a Limb

Your arm bones and leg bones are similar to those of your classmates. Do other animals have bone structures similar to those in humans? Find out!

MATERIALS
- illustrations of animal limbs
- newspaper
- modeling clay in 4 different colors
- *Science Notebook*

Procedure

1. Study and **compare** the drawings of the front limbs of four animals—a lizard, a bird, a cat, and a chimpanzee. Look for ways in which they are different and ways in which they are similar. **Record** your observations in your *Science Notebook*.

Step 1

2. Working on newspaper, use clay to **make models** of the bones of the lizard's front limb. Use one color for the upper limb, a second color for the lower limb, a third color for the small wrist bones, and a fourth for the hand and fingers. Arrange the bones on a piece of paper.

3. Using the colors in the same way, **make models** of the bones of the bird's wing. Also **make models** of the bones of the cat's front limb and the chimpanzee's front limb.

4. **Compare** and **contrast** the models of the limb-bone structures of these animals. **Record** your observations.

Analyze and Conclude

1. How did the structures of the limbs compare?

2. Did the same bones occur in more than one of the models? Which bones were they?

3. Which bones were not found in all three models?

4. What do you think the similarities among the models mean to those who believe in evolution?

5. What do you think the differences among the models mean to those who believe that God had a master plan for the world He made?

INVESTIGATE FURTHER!

EXPERIMENT

Which of the models has a limb most like your arm? To find out, use a picture of a human skeleton. Make a model of the bones of the human arm and then compare all the models you made.

Your Family Tree

In 1836 an American named Constantine Rafinesque thought over what he had learned in his study of living things. He concluded, "All species might have been varieties once." He was suggesting that living things all began as varieties of the same species. He thought that gradually, overtime, living things evolved into separate species.

In the activity on pages D64 and D65, you noted similarities among the front limbs of four animals. If you compared these limbs with the bones in a human's arm, you saw more similarities. In fact, all vertebrates, or animals with backbones, have the same basic bones in their front limbs. The term *vertebrates* includes mammals as well as dinosaurs, birds, reptiles, amphibians, and fish.

Differences in the sizes and shapes of bones in the front limbs enable different vertebrates to fly, swim, dig, hang from trees, and applaud their favorite sports heroes. Note that in bats, the bones of the wrists and fingers are long, delicate supports for the wings. In a dolphin's flipper, you can see that these bones as well as the arm bones are very short.

The differences in bone structure among kinds of animals hint at the detailed design from which almighty God made all living things so that they could live and interact with one another in similar yet different ways. Imagine Adam's delight when he first met the animals God made and named them.

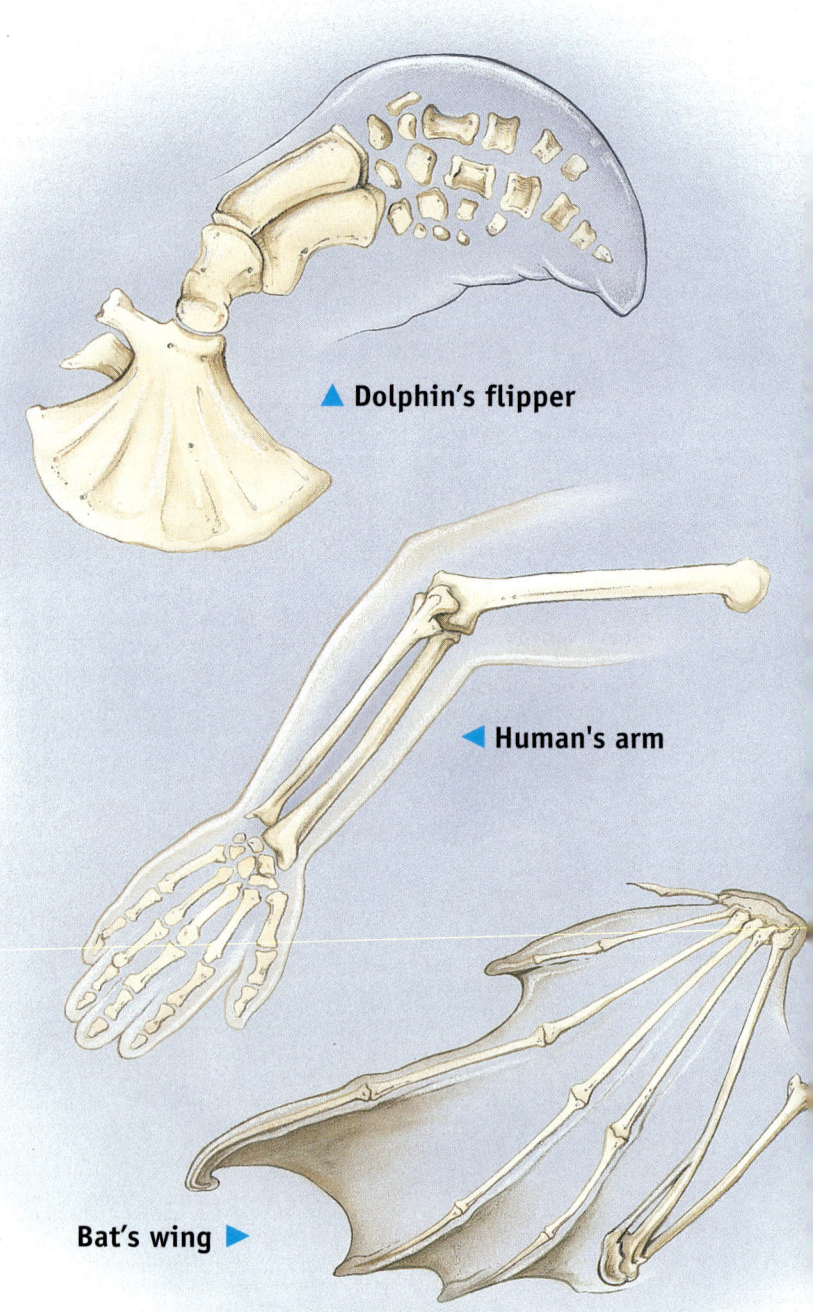

▲ Dolphin's flipper

◀ Human's arm

Bat's wing ▶

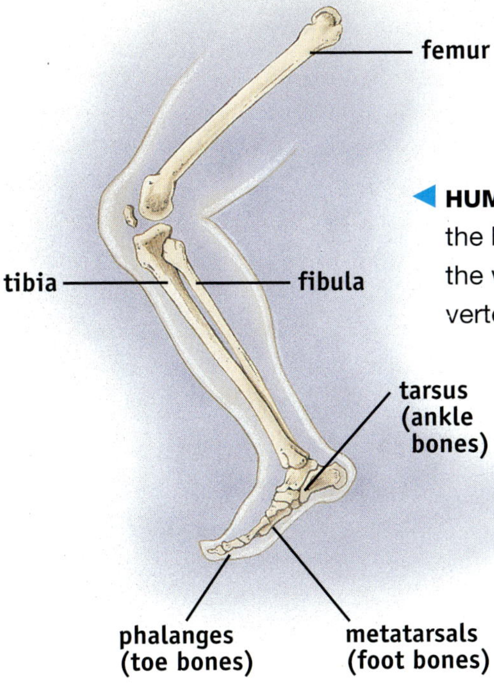

◀ **HUMAN LEG** Compare in the illustrations the bones of the human's leg and foot with the leg and foot bones of the wolf and the bird. Again, you can see that different vertebrates have the same basic set of bones.

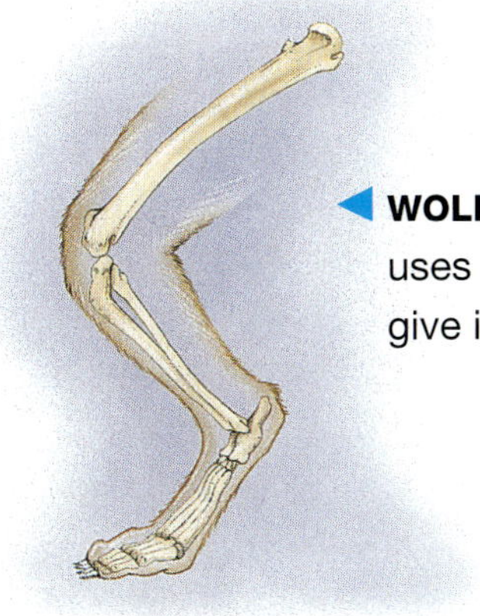

◀ **WOLF LEG** The wolf walks on its toes and uses its long metatarsals (met ə tär′səlz) to give itself an extra push when it runs.

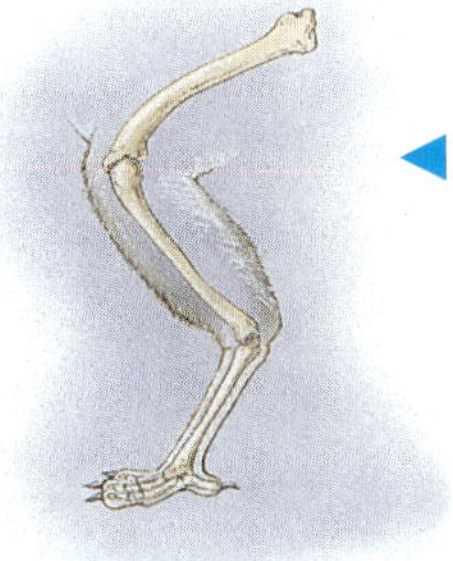

◀ **BIRD LEG** The bird does not have a fibula and has only one metatarsal.

SCIENCE AND FAITH

Psalm 104 is a hymn of praise to the Creator. Think about the many animals in creation as you read these words:

How many are Your works, O LORD! In wisdom You made them all; the earth is full of Your creatures. There is the sea, vast and spacious, teeming with creatures beyond number—living things both large and small...These all look to You to give them their food at the proper time. When You give it to them, they gather it up; when You open Your hand, they are satisfied with good things. (Psalm 104:24-25, 27-28)

Darwin's Voyage

Charles Darwin's nose almost cost him the most important job of his life. The captain of the ship that Darwin wanted to work on believed he could read a person's character in the shape of his or her head. To him, Darwin's nose showed that he lacked energy and determination.

The year was 1831, the ship was a British sailing vessel called H.M.S. *Beagle*, and the captain turned out to be quite wrong. Darwin had applied for a full-time job as a sea-going naturalist, to study nature and gather samples on a voyage around the world. None of this work was easy, but the 22-year-old Darwin got the job and did it well.

▲ Charles Darwin

Before the *Beagle* sailed from London, Darwin had studied for the ministry. But his real love was nature—especially beetles! His enthusiasm for collecting beetles was so strong that he once stuck one in his mouth to hold it while he caught two more. By squirting a bitter liquid on Darwin's tongue, the captive beetle got itself spit out—and got away!

What Did Darwin Find?

H.M.S. *Beagle* sailed west from England, down the east coast of South America, up the west coast, then west again until it had gone all the way around the globe. All the while, the crew was

H.M.S. *Beagle*'s path through the Galápagos Islands ▼

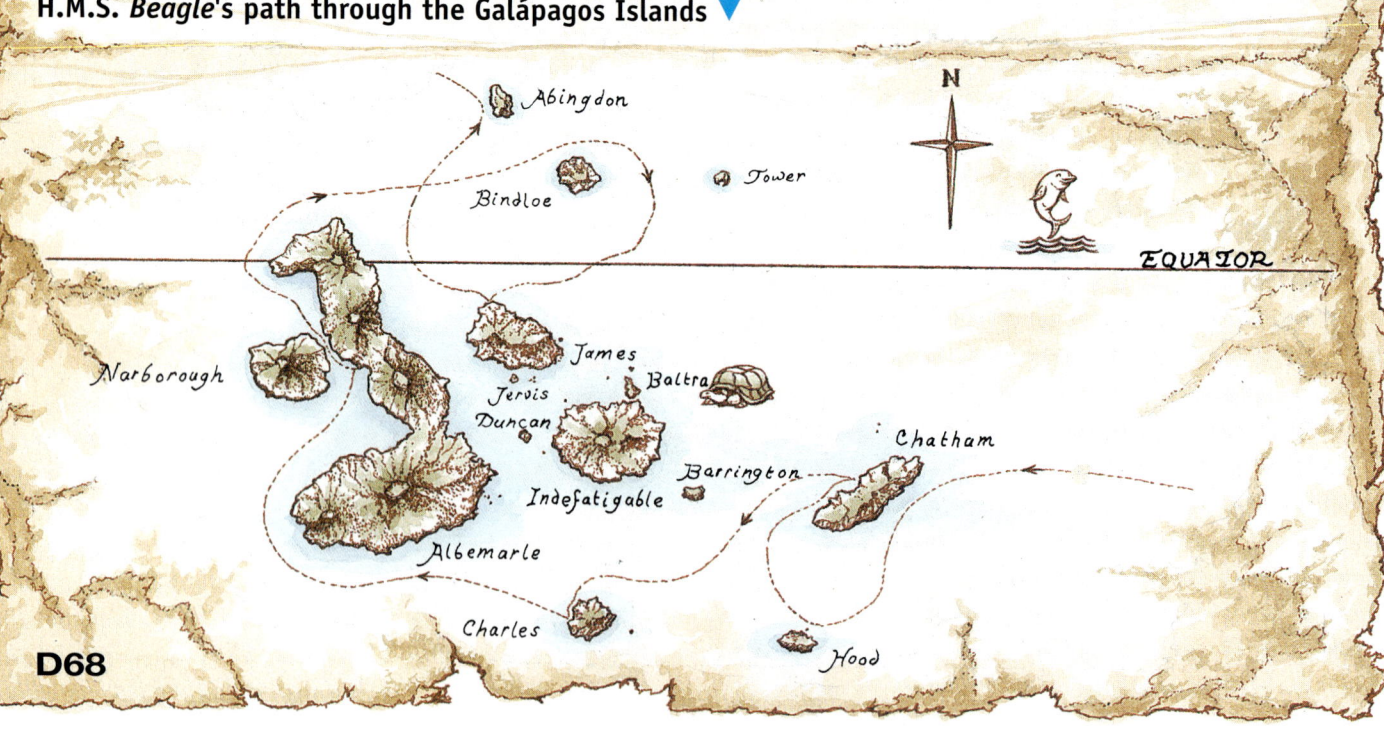

▲ Thirteen finches, 14 islands: Darwin studied similarities and differences between their beaks.

mapping the lands the ship visited. Off the coast of Ecuador, at a group of islands called the Galápagos (gə lä′pə-gōs), Darwin discovered an incredible treasure trove of plants, fossils, and living animals.

- Darwin found the world's only sea-dwelling lizards. These sea iguanas looked like tiny dinosaurs and fed on seaweed growing on underwater rocks. They had blunt snouts, and their strong claws helped them cling to the rocks.
- A short distance inland Darwin found land-dwelling lizards. They were iguanas, too, but they never mated with the sea iguanas. These iguanas lived in trees and ate cactus plants. The sea iguanas had partially webbed toes and rather flat tails; the land dwellers had normal toes and round tails. Darwin noted, however, that the two species were alike in many ways, as well.
- Darwin's most famous discovery was what he called "a most singular group of finches," birds found throughout the world. Darwin noted 13 varieties of finches on the Galápagos, and each variety was adapted to a different way of life. Some finches ate insects and some ate plants. The tool-using finch even hunted food by holding a cactus spine in its beak and chipping holes in bark. The finches in each group had their own characteristics that were well-suited to the ways they lived. For example, the beaks of plant eaters were different from the beaks of insect eaters.

Charles Darwin certainly found his share of adventure aboard the *Beagle*, yet he found something that to him was a lot more important. He found thousands of unique plants and animals—more than most people of his day and age knew anything about. As he studied his notes and samples, Darwin speculated that many of the species he had found and studied seemed to be related. He theorized that these species evolved from a common ancestor.

Darwin proposed his theory of evolution by natural selection to attempt to explain these relationships. You will learn more about Darwin's theory in the next investigation. ■

Selective Breeding

Long before Charles Darwin sailed around the world, people had discovered that they could tame some wild animals if they caught the animals when they were very young. By breeding such animals, people produced new generations of **domesticated**, or tamed, animals that could be controlled and used by humans. Horses, for example, were tamed and used as pack animals and for transportation.

Other animals were also domesticated—the elephant and the water buffalo in India, the camel in Africa, the reindeer in Lapland. The musk ox, which is actually a member of the sheep-goat family, was domesticated as recently as the 1950s. It is now raised by native Alaskans for its fine cashmerelike wool.

Along Comes Selective Breeding

But people did not stop with domestication alone. They realized that they could actually direct the development of certain characteristics in plants and animals by breeding individuals that had those characteristics. In this way the farm animals with which we are most familiar came into barnyards. Domestic sheep were developed around 7,000 years ago from a long-horned, hairy beast called the Asiatic mouflon. The modern pig was bred from the wild boar. Such breeding of living things to produce offspring with desirable characteristics is called **selective breeding**.

Through the generations, people developed gentler elephants, hardier camels, and faster horses. People domesticated the dog many years ago to help with hunting. Since then, more selective breeding has produced hundreds of different kinds of dogs. Yet despite the astonishing variety, each kind is still a dog.

People practiced selective breeding of plants, too. By 3600 B.C., the native people of North America had developed plants that yielded small ears of corn, most likely from a grasslike plant. Other native tribes in

A sheep (*right*) and its ancestor, an Asiatic mouflon (*left*)

▲ Corn is an example of a product that has been selectively bred and grown in the Americas for centuries.

North and South America developed tomatoes, potatoes, and tobacco.

Back to the Wild Again!

Charles Darwin already knew about selective breeding when he returned to England from his journey. But as Darwin studied his notes and samples, he recognized that the plants and animals he'd seen had evolved from one form to another in the wild, with no help from humans.

He then decided to learn all he could about selective breeding. He wanted to compare what had been discovered by others with the new things he'd learned. Immediately, he began tracing the wild origins of a number of domesticated plants and animals. These included sheep, cattle, pigs, rabbits, pigeons, chickens, dogs, cats, peacocks, canaries, goldfish, bees, and silk moths. He also studied cabbages, peas, potatoes, fruit trees, beans, roses, pansies, and dahlias. (Along the way, Darwin even became a pigeon breeder himself!)

It took 20 years, but Charles Darwin at last understood how the plants and animals in the wild had changed through a natural form of selective breeding. ■

INVESTIGATION 2

1. How do structural similarities among living things support the idea that living things are related?

2. What characteristics do you think early breeders found in the wolf that they bred into the domesticated dog?

3. How has God blessed us through the knowledge of selective breeding?

How Do Changes In Species Occur?

You saw in Investigation 2 that there is evidence that changes occur in organisms over time. But how do these changes occur? In this investigation you'll find out some of the answers scientists have for this question.

Activity

A Variety of Peanuts

Differences among organisms of a single species are important in helping them survive in a variety of environments. Sometimes these variations are easy to see. You can study variations in peanuts and draw some conclusions about how those variations are helpful to the plant.

MATERIALS
- 40 peanuts
- metric ruler
- small bowl or other container
- graph paper
- *Science Notebook*

Procedure

1. Look through the peanuts. Use a metric ruler to find the longest peanut and the shortest peanut. **Record** these values in your *Science Notebook*. Place these two peanuts in a container.

Investigate Further!

2. Find the difference in length between the longest and the shortest peanut. **Record** the data. Set up a graph, with the *X*-axis marked in 1-mm intervals in the range from the shortest length to the longest length. The *Y*-axis will show the number of peanuts.

3. Place an *X* in the square above the number for the length of the shortest peanut. Place an *X* in the square above the number for the length of the longest peanut. Recording your data in this way will produce a bar graph. **Predict** the length that will be measured most often.

4. **Measure the length** of another peanut. Locate this length value on your graph and place an *X* in the square above that value. Place the peanut in the container.

5. Repeat step 4 for the rest of the peanuts. Some peanuts will have the same length as others. When a value is repeated, place an *X* in the square above the last X for that value.

Analyze and Conclude

1. What length did you predict would be found most often? Why did you choose this length?

2. Were the lengths of the peanuts evenly distributed, or was there some other pattern to the lengths?

3. Each peanut is a seed that can develop into a new peanut plant. Most of the peanut is stored food for the baby plant. Why might forming large peanuts be helpful?

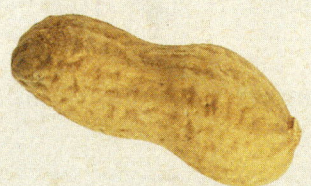

4. Why might forming large peanuts be harmful?

INVESTIGATE FURTHER!

EXPERIMENT

If your class has a balance that can measure the mass of an object as light as a peanut, find the mass of each of the peanuts. Set up a graph, as you did in the activity, to record the masses. Before you begin, hypothesize whether you will find any correlation between peanut length and peanut mass. Did your hypothesis match your results?

Natural Selection, Variation, and Mutation

Think about a giraffe. What do you picture? Do you think about the animal's big brown eyes? Its soft fuzzy ears? Not likely! Chances are you think of the giraffe's long neck. That long neck fits very well into this animal's way of life. The giraffe feeds on tree leaves that no other animal can reach from the ground. How might this strange specialization have come about?

Winners and Losers

Think back to Charles Darwin's studies of selective breeding. He knew that people could breed plants and animals selectively to get the best characteristics in their offspring. Two fast-running horses could be mated and produce a colt that could run fast, too.

Darwin also suspected that a similar process worked in nature without any selection by humans. He suspected that the natural version of this process worked very slowly. People might breed two swift horses together and hope to get a faster horse right away. Nature might produce a similar result, but more slowly. Darwin also realized that while people had many reasons for selecting certain plants or animals to breed, nature had only one reason for

Natural selection, variation, and mutation are at work in all biomes, including the African savanna. ▼

selection—survival. Thus nature would favor faster horses over slower horses only if speed could help them survive. As it happens, a horse is better made for flight than for fight, so it first tries to run away when it senses trouble. Over thousands of years, more of the faster horses with longer legs survived and passed on the trait for speed. Meanwhile, slower horses with shorter legs were more likely to become dinner for predators. On average, slower horses died sooner and produced fewer young.

This example shows Darwin's theory of evolution through the process he called **natural selection**. In a population, more of the most fit organisms live longer and have more offspring. These offspring inherit the survival characteristics of their parents. Many of the less fit organisms die young, so they have fewer offspring. As a result, over long periods of time the characteristics that favor survival become common, and the less favorable characteristics die out.

Now, perhaps, you can understand how the giraffe's neck got to be so long. Of all the giraffes born over the years, those with longer necks had more success in reaching food, especially food that no other animals could reach. That meant better survival rates than those of giraffes with shorter necks. So in each generation more and more giraffes inherited longer and longer necks until that characteristic was seen in all giraffes.

Natural selection is at work as organisms interact with their environments. For example, as a pond or lake dries up, fish get stranded. Many fish die, but some kinds of fish are able to breathe air for a time and thus survive. Some of these fish may have longer and stronger bones in their fins, which would help them move on to the next pond or lake. So in some environments, natural selection favors the survival of fish with lungs!

The Theory of Evolution

When Charles Darwin published his theory of how species evolved—his theory of evolution through natural selection—nobody knew what a gene was. He hypothesized how natural selection took place even though he didn't know all the details.

Changes in DNA

Although sexual reproduction produces a new combination of genes with each new individual, it doesn't change the DNA in the genes. But sometimes genes do change. A change in the gene's DNA is called a **mutation**. Mutations may be caused by chemicals or radiation in the environment. Some mutations happen for reasons scientists haven't identified. Many are harmful and may make the individual less likely to survive. Some mutations are so severe that the individual quickly dies.

Sometimes, however, a mutation is beneficial. It helps the individual to survive better. Evolutionists suggest that mutations over many generations changed horses from tiny, short-legged animals to the horse of today.

Though accepted by many, Darwin's work remains a theory—an idea used to explain a concept or occurrence. Scientists know that organisms change due to natural selection and environmental changes. These occurrences are referred to as micro-evolution. However, no scientific evidence exists showing one type of organism evolving into another kind of animal as those who believe in macro-evolution claim.

Evolutionary thinking denies God who created people in His image. It also suggests that with the passing of time things progressively improve. God's Word teaches that since the fall into sin all creation "has been groaning" under its fallen condition (Romans 8:22). But God's Word also promises that Jesus our Savior and friend will come once again to bring all who love and trust in Him to a forever-perfect home in heaven.

Fossil evidence suggests that an ancient horse, (*right*) **the** *Hyracotherium* (*left*), **was the size of a small dog!**

Competition and Isolation

After his voyage on H.M.S. *Beagle*, Charles Darwin worked for 20 years to be absolutely sure of his two most important conclusions. First, a struggle for existence goes on all the time in nature—day by day, year by year, century by century. Second, in that struggle the most fit are likely to survive and reproduce.

You have already seen how the most fit are defined by natural selection. But **competition**—or lack of competition because of isolation—also plays a big role. On the surface, competition in nature may even resemble the rivalry between tennis players or baseball teams. But competition in nature is not friendly, and often it is a matter of life or death.

Competition in Nature

You see competition at work in nature every time you go outside. The branches of trees spread wide, allowing as many leaves as possible to be in the sunlight. Small bushes below reach out to whatever sunlight passes through the trees. Nearby, grass blades are turned sideways, also to catch sunlight.

But what you see in an ordinary yard is just the beginning. Plants and animals have thousands and thousands of variations on basic ways of competing with one another for sunlight, food, water, and everything else needed for survival.

Throughout the entire world, different plants and animals grow in every possible place—from dark forests to ocean floors; from mountaintops to deep valleys; from dry deserts to soggy swamps; from desert sands to frozen tundra. In all these places, different species live in slightly different environments. Each species seems to have the best characteristics to survive in its environment. Thus trees grow tall, and ferns are adapted to a shady environment around the bases of trees.

But individuals within a species compete with their own kind, perhaps by growing bigger and stronger as fast as

▲ Competition for scarce resources favors the most fit organisms.

they can. You may not see it happening, but as plants grow, they block each other and send out huge root systems. These are adaptations to obtain as much light and water as possible. When you pull weeds and find the roots of plants all tangled together, you know they were fighting for the same minerals in the same soil!

Where Does Isolation Fit In?

Each of the Galápagos Islands visited by Darwin is isolated from the others by strong winds and rough waters. When he arrived, Darwin found that isolation had produced an unusual cast of characters. Huge 227–kg (500-lb) tortoises, with shells like upturned bathtubs, grazed like cattle in the fields and lived 100 years. Many of the islands had populations of such tortoises. On each island, the population differed from those on the other islands. In fact, each island had a different species of tortoise—all closely related.

The finches on the different islands and in the different environments taught Darwin the most. Though they apparently had the same ancestor, they had not interbred for centuries. Thus they had developed different kinds of beaks for eating different kinds of food. There were also small, medium, and large versions of each kind of beak, to match the birds' food sources. And they had developed brilliant colors to attract each other in order to mate, for they had nothing to hide from. From these and similar studies, scientists have concluded that when two populations of the same species are isolated, or separated, over time they tend to become separate species. ■

Some scientists believe that isolation leads to the rise of new species, such as the giant tortoise. ▼

INVESTIGATION 3

1. How did Darwin's theory of natural selection explain how varieties of species came to be?

2. How was the work of Mendel influential in explaining Darwin's theory?

REFLECT & EVALUATE

WORD POWER

competition
era
evolution
extinction
cast fossil
domesticated
mold fossil
natural selection
paleontologist
petrification
selective breeding
fossils
mutation
periods

On Your Own
Write a definition for each term in the list.

With a Partner
Write each term in the list on one side of an index card and the definition on the other side. Use the cards to quiz your partner.

Make a poster showing how similarities in the limbs of certain organisms showing how these organisms differ in how they use their limbs.

Analyze Information
Explain how God expanded His creative work of days 1, 2, and 3 on days 4, 5, and 6.

Assess Performance
Some species generate many generations in a short period of time. Although changes occur through selective breeding, science has never observed an organism change into a different kind of organism. Use your imagination to create an improved orange through selective breeding.

Problem Solving

1. Explain the differences in the way each of these fossils form: dinosaur skeleton; insect encased in amber; shell preserved in rock.

2. If the earth would become hot, dry, and barren, what kinds of organisms might be able to survive?

3. How do many who believe in evolution regard God and others?

Investigate Further!

Throughout this unit, you've investigated questions related to evolution. How will you use what you've learned about evolution as it relates to the teachings of God's Word? Here are some ideas.

Hold a Big Event to Share Your Unit Project

Get ready to stand up for your ideas! To prepare for the debate, study the information you have collected about evolution and the influence of evolutionary thinking.

- On society as a whole
- On those who profess Jesus as their Savior

Create a display showing how evolutionary thinking can lead people away from God and His free gift of salvation.

Research

Study what God's Word says about God the creator and preserver of all things and about our role as managers of His creation.

Take Action

Consider ways to preserve and protect endangered species. Or, look for ways you and your class can help those for whom Christ died who are not likely to survive due to the threat of abortion or euthanasia.

OCEANOGRAPHY

Theme: Systems

Get Ready to Investigate! E2

1 Ocean Water E4
Investigation 1   What Makes Up Ocean Water? E6
Investigation 2   What Are the Properties of Ocean Water? E12
Investigation 3   What Living Things Are in Ocean Water? E22

2 The Ocean Floor E28
Investigation 1   What Features and Sediments
                  Occur on the Ocean Floor? E30
Investigation 2   How Do Scientists Study the Ocean Floor? E40

3 Moving Ocean Water E50
Investigation 1   What Causes Ocean Currents? E52
Investigation 2   What Causes Ocean Waves? E62
Investigation 3   What Causes Tides? E68

4 Ocean Resources E74
Investigation 1   What Resources Can the Oceans Provide? E76
Investigation 2   How Does Pollution Affect the Oceans
                  and Their Resources? E88

Investigate Further! E96

GET READY TO

OBSERVE & QUESTION

What makes up ocean water?

If you jump into a body of water and don't try to swim, will you sink or float? In this unit you'll find out why knowing the properties of water might affect your answer to that question.

EXPERIMENT & HYPOTHESIZE

How does pollution affect the oceans and their resources?

Why is an oil spill such a major problem? Doesn't the oil eventually just get washed away? The activities in this unit will help you answer this and many other questions about the oceans.

INVESTIGATE!

RESEARCH & ANALYZE

As you investigate, learn more from these books.

- ***The Illustrated World of Oceans*** by Susan Wells (Simon & Schuster Books for Young Readers, 1991). Use this book to enter the oceans, the least explored part of Earth's surface.

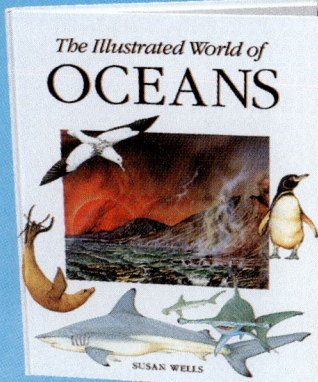

- ***Sharks: The Perfect Predators*** (Silver Burdett Press, 1995). Are we justified in our fear of sharks? Discover the world of sharks and you may be surprised at what you find.

- ***The Black Pearl*** by Scott O'Dell (Dell Publishing, 1967). The oceans hide incredible mysteries that form the basis for many wonderful legends. Enter this world with caution and beware of the monster Manta ray.

WORK TOGETHER & SHARE IDEAS

What would you do if you were asked to market and promote a brand new vacation site—an undersea lodge?

Working together, apply what you have learned about properties of ocean water, organisms living in the oceans, the ocean floor and its features, motions of ocean water, and ocean pollution. Plan and develop the advertising material for this new vacation adventure. Look for the Unit Project Links for ideas on how to develop the advertising campaign.

CHAPTER 1

OCEAN WATER

God created the oceans to be a vast resource with a rich abundance of life. Yet, the exploration of the oceans has really just begun. What would you like to find out about the ocean waters?

Exploring Down Under

Rose Petrecca says she wanted to learn more about the ocean ever since she watched the television program *Sea Hunt* as a young girl. Now she is a marine biologist and the lead scientist on LEO-15—the Long-Term Ecosystem Observatory. The LEO-15 is one of the world's few underwater laboratories. It is being built off the New Jersey coast in 15 m (49.5 ft) of water. Petrecca and other oceanographers will use the permanent lab to study ocean conditions over a long period of time. Using video cameras and vehicles operated by remote control, the scientists will observe daily life in the ocean. They will check on how pollution is affecting the sea robins, black sea bass, starfish, and surf clams in the water around the LEO. What questions would you ask Rose Petrecca about her work?

Coming Up

WHAT MAKES UP OCEAN WATER?
.... E6

WHAT ARE THE PROPERTIES OF OCEAN WATER?
.... E12

WHAT LIVING THINGS ARE IN OCEAN WATER?
.... E22

▲ Rose Petrecca works on LEO-15.

WHAT MAKES UP OCEAN WATER?

You probably know that ocean water is not the same as the water that comes from a faucet in your home. What makes ocean water different from the water you drink each day?

Activity

A Closer Look at Ocean Water

How can you use observations to help you infer what's in ocean water?

MATERIALS
- goggles
- sample of ocean water
- clear container or saucer
- dropper
- microscope slide
- cover slip
- microscope
- hand lens
- water
- *Science Notebook*

SAFETY
Wear goggles during this activity. Never taste unknown substances.

Procedure

1. Your teacher will give you a sample of ocean water in a clear glass container. Examine the sample and test for any odor. **Record** your observations in your *Science Notebook*.

2. Use the dropper to place a drop of ocean water on the slide. Place the cover slip over the drop and examine the slide through the microscope. **Record** your observations.

3. Use the dropper to stir the ocean water sample. Then place several dropperfuls of the sample in the clear container. Place the container in sunlight and allow the water to evaporate. **Predict** what you will see as the water evaporates. **Record** your prediction. Then **observe** the container periodically as the water evaporates. **Record** your observations.

Step 3

4. When evaporation is complete, use the hand lens to **observe** any material left behind in the container. **Record** your observations.

5. Add tap water to the container and **observe** what happens. **Record** your observations.

Analyze and Conclude

1. Infer from your observations what was left behind when the water evaporated. **Explain** your inference.

2. What can you **conclude** about ocean water?

3. Why was evaporation important to the results of this activity?

INVESTIGATE FURTHER!

EXPERIMENT

Predict how your observations would differ if you were using fresh water instead of ocean water. Obtain a sample of fresh water and repeat the activity to check your predictions. Record your data.

What's in the Water?

▲ Water covers two thirds of Earth's surface—from the vast oceans to small mountain streams.

Someday you may have the opportunity to peer from the window of a spacecraft and see Earth floating in space. You'll see a brilliant sphere shining blue, green, brown, and white. But mostly you'll see blue—the blue of Earth's oceans covering two thirds of its surface.

A Salty Story

God created bodies of water on the third day. Some of the water was in fresh water lakes and rivers, but most of the water was in salt water oceans and seas. When you think of the ocean, what characteristic first comes to mind? Do you think of the ocean as being salty? In the activity on pages E6 and E7, you probably inferred that ocean water contains salt and some other substances.

Ocean water is a mixture of the compound water (H_2O) and several salts. The most common salt in ocean water consists of two elements—sodium and chlorine. These two elements are combined as sodium chloride, which you use as table salt.

In nature, sodium chloride, potassium chloride, and magnesium chloride are all salts that are present in rocks and soils. When rainwater flows over the land, it carries away traces of the salts as well as other elements and compounds. The rainwater drains into rivers and streams and then into the ocean. Each year about 364 billion kilograms (400 million tons) of dissolved salts and other substances are washed into the ocean. Some of these substances stay dissolved in the water. Those that don't form sediments, which drift down to and settle on the ocean floor.

Measuring Salt Content

When water evaporates, any solid substance dissolved in the water is left behind. So when ocean water evaporates, sodium chloride and other compounds are left behind. How much salt would you expect to find in the oceans of the world? On average, 1 kg of ocean water contains 35 g of salts. Thus, 3.5 percent of ocean water is dissolved salts.

The total amount of dissolved salts in ocean water is called **salinity** (sə lin′ə tē). Because the ocean is so huge, its overall salinity changes very slowly. However, salinity does vary in different parts of the ocean. Around the world, the salinity of the oceans and seas can range from 33 to 40 grams per kilogram of water.

Near the equator, heavy rainfalls over the ocean increase the amount of fresh water in the ocean, so salinity tends to be lower there. Areas where rivers empty into the ocean also have lower salinity.

In areas of the ocean where rainfall is low, the salinity of the water is higher than normal, since evaporation leaves salts behind. For example, the Red Sea,

In some parts of the world, such as Great Salt Lake and the Dead Sea, the salt content of water has become so great that salt deposits form along the shore (*left*), and a person doesn't need a flotation device to stay afloat (*bottom*).

which is surrounded by deserts, receives little rainfall. Hot, dry winds speed evaporation. As a result, 1 kg of water from the Red Sea contains about 40 g of salt instead of the average 35 g.

Other Dissolved Substances

Ocean water contains other substances. The graph on page E11 shows these substances and their concentrations. Six substances make up about 99% of the dissolved materials. The amounts of these six main compounds tend to remain the same in ocean water everywhere in the world.

As you can see from the graph, all other compounds and elements make up about 1.0% of the dissolved materials in ocean water. In fact, 80 of the 109 known elements have been found in ocean water. The percentage of the rare elements tends to vary from one region to another, depending upon rainfall, evaporation, and outflow of water from rivers and bays.

Dissolved Gases

Ocean water also contains large amounts of dissolved gases, especially nitrogen, carbon dioxide, and oxygen. (The dissolved oxygen is in addition to the oxygen that is part of the water molecules themselves.) The amounts of these gases in the water depend on many factors, including water depth and temperature. For example, near the surface of the ocean, sunlight helps tiny plantlike organisms in the water grow. As they grow, they release oxygen into the water. As a result, water at or near the surface contains much more oxygen than deeper water does.

Gases dissolve more easily in cold water than in warm water, so water in colder regions of the world contains larger amounts of dissolved gases. Near the equator, the water is warmer so the amount of dissolved gases is less.

Both plants and animals depend on the dissolved gases in ocean water. Tiny

Ocean water is a "soup" of living organisms, such as fish, plants, and kelp (*inset*) along with minerals and dissolved gases. ▼

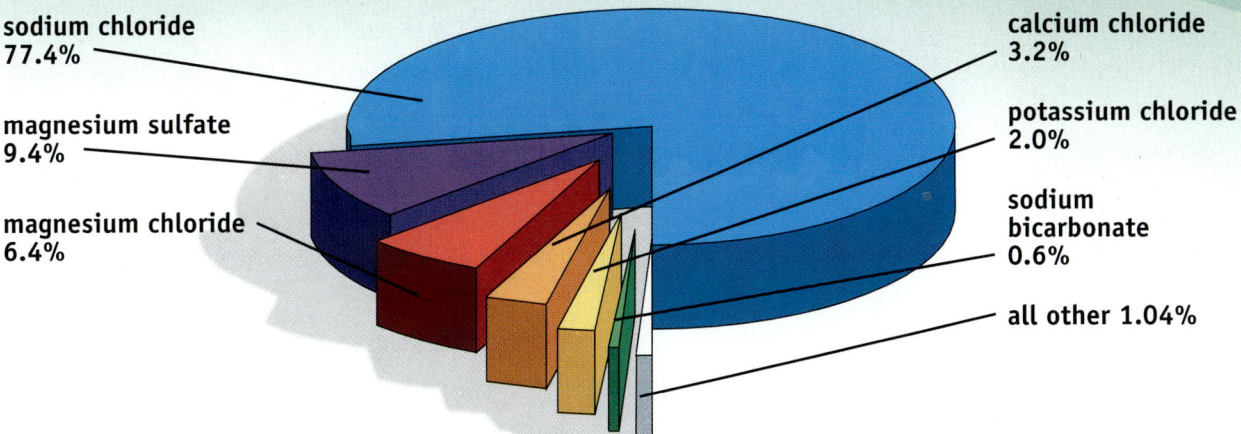

▲ This graph shows the breakdown of substances dissolved in ocean water.

living creatures called **plankton** (plaŋk′tən) float near the surface and drift with the currents. Plantlike plankton, called **phytoplankton** (fīt′ō plaŋk′tən), must have oxygen, carbon dioxide, and certain other dissolved gases and elements to survive. Animal-like plankton, called **zooplankton** (zō′ō plaŋk′tən) feed on the phytoplankton. If a region's water cannot support phytoplankton, the zooplankton cannot survive. If the zooplankton cannot survive, then few other organisms can survive there, either.

Sediments and Pollution

Along with dissolved salts and gases and living plankton, ocean water also contains sediments that have been washed into the ocean or stirred up from the bottom. Sediments might include sand particles, bits of shells, and decaying organisms. Unlike salts, sediments do not dissolve in the water.

Unfortunately, ocean water also includes some harmful substances put there by people. We already know what human-caused pollution is doing to the water along our coasts. Now wastes from many communities are being dumped at sea and are affecting water quality far out in the ocean.

Ocean water is much more than a mixture of salt and water. It's a complex and constantly changing mixture of water, elements, and living things. This carefully balanced mixture provides oxygen and food, which supports other living things in the ocean. They, in turn, support all the organisms living on the land—including us. ■

INVESTIGATION 1

1. What kinds of materials are found in ocean water?

2. You are given two samples of water and told that one is ocean water and one is water from a lake. Without tasting them, how might you determine which is which?

E11

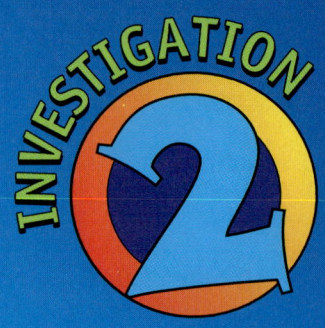

What Are the Properties of Ocean Water?

All matter, including ocean water, has physical properties. When you first stick your foot in the ocean, what physical property determines if you'll dive right in or run back to shore? What other properties does ocean water have?

Activity

Lighting the Water

Living things depend on sunlight that moves down through the water. How does the amount of available light change with depth?

Procedure

1. In your *Science Notebook*, copy the chart below.

2. Fill a bucket with water. Holding the Secchi disk by its string, lower it 10 cm into the water. **Record** how well you can see the disk.

Water's Depth	Observation
10 cm	
20 cm	
30 cm	

MATERIALS
- goggles
- large bucket or trash can
- water
- Secchi disk
- meterstick
- flour
- paper cup
- spoon
- balance
- measuring cup
- *Science Notebook*

SAFETY
Wear goggles at all times. To prevent slipping and falling, immediately clean up any spills.

E12

3. Lower the disk by 10-cm intervals and **record** how well you can see the disk at each depth.

4. Pour 50 g of flour into the water. Mix it with the spoon.

5. Lower the Secchi disk into the water until you can no longer see the disk. Grasp the string at the surface of the water and pull the disk out of the water while you hold this spot. Use the meterstick to **measure** the distance between your fingers and the disk. This measurement represents the depth below the water's surface at which you can no longer see the disk. **Record** the depth.

6. **Predict** the depth to which you would be able to see the Secchi disk if you added 100 g more of flour to the water.

7. **Test your prediction** by adding 100 g of flour and repeating steps 4 and 5.

Analyze and Conclude

1. **Compare** the visibility of the disk at 10-cm intervals beneath the surface.

2. **Suggest a hypothesis** to explain any change in the visibility of the Secchi disk.

3. What can you **infer** about the available light as depth increases in the ocean?

4. If the water in the bucket models ocean water, **infer** what kinds of particles the flour might represent. How do those particles affect how light penetrates the water?

INVESTIGATE FURTHER!

RESEARCH

Work in groups to research the role light plays in determining the color of ocean water. Write a report on your findings.

Activity
Dense Water

Density is a physical property of matter. It can be thought of as how tightly packed the particles are that make up a substance. What factors affect the density of water?

MATERIALS
- waterproof marker
- metric ruler
- plastic straw
- modeling clay
- bottom half of a plastic soda bottle (2 L)
- distilled water
- thermometer
- scissors
- tablespoon
- table salt
- *Science Notebook*

Procedure

	Warm Water	Cold Water	Salt Water
Temperature			
Estimated Length (in cm)			

1. In your *Science Notebook*, copy the chart above.
2. Mark lines at 0.5-cm intervals along the straw.
3. Pack one end of the straw with clay to a length of 3 cm.
4. Half fill the bottle with water. Place the thermometer in the bottle. **Record** the water temperature in your chart.
5. Place the clay-filled end of the straw in the water so that it floats straight up. (You may need to cut off the open end of the straw 0.5 cm at a time until it floats properly.) Use the lines on the straw to **estimate** the length of the straw that is under water. **Record** the length in your chart.
6. Remove the straw. Place the thermometer in the bottle. Place the bottle in an ice bath.
7. When the temperature of the water drops 5° to 10°C, remove the bottle from the ice bath. **Record** the temperature in your

Step 2

chart. **Predict** how much of the straw will be under water in cold water. **Discuss** your prediction with your classmates and explain why you think your prediction will be correct. Repeat step 5.

8. Allow the water to stand until it warms up to the original temperature. **Record** the temperature in your chart and remove the thermometer. Add 3 tablespoons of salt and stir until it dissolves. **Predict** how much of the straw will be under water in salt water. **Discuss** your prediction with your classmates and explain why you think your prediction will be correct. Repeat step 5.

Analyze and Conclude

1. The deeper the straw sinks, the less dense the water is. Which was more dense, the warm fresh water, the cold fresh water, or the salt water? How do you know?

2. Suggest a hypothesis about how temperature and salinity affect the density of water.

What seems to be a simple cup of water is really an awesome work of God. One cup of water contains eight septillion—that's 8,000,000,000,000,000,000,000,000—molecules, and each molecule is made of two hydrogen atoms and one oxygen atom (H_2O). In addition to the water molecules, salt water also contains several salts. Just think how much God packs into only one cup of water!

What happens when you mix water molecules with God's Word? You get Baptism! Martin Luther said this about Baptism: "It is nothing else than a divine water, not that the water in itself is nobler than other water but that God's Word and commandment are added to it" (Large Catechism IV 14). Through the divine waters of Baptism God welcomes us into His family.

Activity

Under Pressure

If you've ever dived deep into the water, you may have felt some pain in your ears. What physical property of water causes this effect?

MATERIALS
- pencil
- milk carton
- metric ruler
- small ball of clay
- sink or basin
- water
- *Science Notebook*

Procedure

1. Use a pencil to make a hole in the milk carton about 2 cm from the bottom, as shown in the photo.

2. Plug the hole with clay.

3. From the hole measure up 5 cm, 10 cm, 15 cm, and 20 cm. Make a mark at each point.

4. Carefully pour water into the carton up to the 5-cm mark.

5. Hold the carton over a sink or a basin. Your partner should hold the metric ruler below the hole as shown.

6. Unplug the hole and **measure** how far the water squirts out of the carton. In your *Science Notebook*, **record** your results.

7. Replug the hole and fill the carton to the 10-cm mark. Repeat steps 5 and 6.

8. **Predict** how far the water will squirt if you fill the carton to the 15-cm and 20-cm marks. Test your predictions and **record** your results.

Analyze and Conclude

1. When did the water squirt the farthest? Why do you think this happened?

2. Pressure is the amount of force acting on an area. **Infer** from your observations when the water pressure was the greatest in the carton.

3. **Suggest a hypothesis** that relates water pressure and depth.

Steps 5 and 6

The Bends

People who want to explore the ocean depths need to understand the effects of water pressure. Divers using scuba (**s**elf-**c**ontained **u**nderwater **b**reathing **a**pparatus) equipment receive one to eight weeks of instruction on diving safely. Because of the increasing water pressure, most scuba divers venture to depths of no more than 50 m (165 ft). However, some scuba divers have descended to depths of 90 m (300 ft).

The divers wear air tanks and carry depth gauges to tell them how far down they are and pressure gauges to show how much air they have left in their tanks. Some divers now carry tiny computers that figure out how long they can stay at a certain depth.

When divers descend into the water, their bodies naturally adjust to the increasing water pressure. However, after divers spend some time under greater pressure, nitrogen from their air tanks begins to build up in their body tissues. As the divers begin rising to the surface, the decreasing water pressure can cause the nitrogen to form bubbles in their blood and other tissues. This condition, called the *bends*, can cause problems ranging from itchy skin to brain damage or even death.

▲ Scuba equipment has enabled people to explore shallow ocean depths. Those who go too deep and come up too fast may suffer from the bends.

To avoid the bends, divers must rise slowly to allow the nitrogen to be released safely from their bodies through respiration. A diver who has been at 90 m (300 ft) for two hours may need five or six hours to rise safely to the surface.

To avoid this long delay, divers who intend to explore deep waters sometimes breathe a mixture of oxygen and the gas helium. Helium doesn't dissolve as easily in body tissues as nitrogen, so it doesn't build up quickly and require such a slow return to the surface. ■

Ocean Temperatures and Pressure

January 23, 1960—Western Pacific Ocean: For several hours now, Jacques Piccard and Lieutenant Don Walsh of the U.S. Navy have been descending into the inky blackness of the *Challenger Deep* in the Mariana Trench. Inside the deep-diving vehicle *Trieste* the two men have been monitoring the temperature and pressure of the water surrounding them.

Some time ago, the vehicle passed the 9,090-m (30,000-ft) mark. The *Trieste*'s walls creak under the nearly 7 $T/in.^2$ of pressure, and the outside water temperature has dropped well below what would be freezing at a normal surface pressure of 14.7 $lbs/in.^2$. *Trieste* stops at a depth of 10,910 m (35,800 ft)—nearly 7 mi beneath the surface. Piccard and Walsh peer out at the cold dark world surrounding them. Strange-looking fish move slowly through the water and a "snowstorm" of sediment drifts down past the *Trieste*'s lights as they penetrate the total blackness of the water.

Jan. 23
Trieste is readied for the descent into the trench.

Trieste surfaces and awaits pickup by the mother ship.

On that day in January 1960, Jacques Piccard and Lt. Don Walsh descended into the deepest known part of the ocean. And as you read, most of their descent into the trench was through water that was completely black. Without the lights from the *Trieste*, they would have seen nothing at all. But how can that be? If oceans cover two thirds of Earth's surface, then most of the Sun's light that strikes Earth must fall on ocean water.

Think about the activity on page E12. How did the visibility of the disk change with depth? Visibility worsens with depth because the surface water quickly absorbs much of the light. By the time sunlight penetrates 10 m (33 ft) into the water, it's no longer bright and shiny. The water has absorbed most of the visible light rays, leaving only a blue-green light. This blue-green light gives the ocean its color.

No sunlight—and no direct heat from sunlight—penetrates deep into the ocean. Although sunlight can heat the water surface near the equator to the bathtub temperature of 30°C (86°F), water temperatures in the deepest regions of the ocean stay near or below 0°C (32°F). Only the tremendous pressures at those depths keep the water from becoming solid ice.

Just as temperatures decrease in the ocean depths, water pressure increases. In the activity on page E16, you saw for yourself how water pressure increases as the water depth increases. Water pressure can be measured in pounds per square inch. At the ocean's surface, air pressure is 14.7 lbs/in.^{2}, but the water pressure is 0 lbs/in.^{2}. At great depths, water pressure can reach more than 14,000 lbs/in.^{2}. Had the *Trieste* not been specially constructed, the water pressure at the bottom of the Mariana Trench would have crushed it, and everything in it, within seconds. ■

INVESTIGATE FURTHER!

EXPERIMENT

Find out what and where the Dead Sea is and what its water is like. Then infer whether its water is more dense or less dense than ocean water. Explain your inference. Also find out why the water in the Dead Sea is the way it is and report your information to the class.

That's Dense!

▲ If you were to dive below the surface of this water, you would find the water getting colder as you went down.

As ocean water is warmed, it expands slightly. The same volume of water now has less mass. That makes the warm water on the ocean surface less dense than the colder water at the bottom of the ocean. As the water on the surface cools, it contracts, making it more dense. Then the denser water sinks, while any warmer, less dense water below rises to the surface. Water continues to contract until it reaches a temperature of 4°C (39.2°F). Then something strange happens. Water begins to expand. It continues to expand until its temperature reaches 0°C (32°F). Then it freezes. Think about it. Have you ever seen an ice cube sink? Can you now

As an iceberg melts, it releases less dense fresh water that floats on top of more dense salt water. ▼

When Piccard and Walsh descended into the Mariana Trench, they monitored the increasing pressure and decreasing temperature of the water. They also monitored the water's density. When you did the activity on page E16, you observed firsthand that water pressure increases with depth. However, you could not observe or measure any changes in the density of the water.

But how can water become more or less dense? Generally, as a substance becomes colder, it contracts and becomes more dense. As a substance becomes warmer, it expands and becomes less dense.

E20

explain why an ice cube at 0°C floats in water that is substantially warmer?

However, as you read, water at the very bottom of the ocean reaches temperatures near or below 0°C (32°F). But it doesn't freeze. Why? Actually there are two reasons. First, the water is salty. Salt water freezes at a lower temperature than fresh water. Second, along with the contraction caused by the coldness at the ocean depths, the water molecules there are also slightly squeezed together by the weight of the water above them. This squeezing helps increase the water's density. It also helps prevent the water from freezing even though the temperature is near or below 0°C.

The difference in water density between the surface and the deep ocean is not great. When the *Trieste* descended into the Mariana Trench, Piccard and Walsh discovered that the water there was only 7 percent denser than water at the surface.

However, density is greatly affected by the amount of salt and other substances dissolved in the water. Dissolved substances add mass to a given volume of water. Thus, salty ocean water is more dense than the fresh water in rivers.

When fresh water and salt water meet, the less dense fresh water sometimes floats on top of the more dense salt water. For example, Hudson Bay in Canada is almost completely surrounded by land. At one end it's fed by freshwater rivers. At the other end it connects with the Atlantic Ocean.

In the bay, salinity and density increase as the water depth increases. The surface of the bay has a salinity level of only 2 g/1,000 g of water when the current is strong and the ice is melting, thus adding more fresh water. However, about 25 m (80 ft) down, the water's salinity increases to 31 g/1,000 g of water. Differences in density are an important factor in the development of some kinds of ocean currents. ■

INVESTIGATE FURTHER!

EXPERIMENT

Predict how the results of the activity on page E16 would vary if you repeated the experiment with holes punched at 2 cm, 6 cm, and 10 cm. Try it and explain the results observed.

INVESTIGATION 2

1. What are the physical properties of ocean water?

2. What do you think would happen to any organisms found at the bottom of the Mariana Trench if they were brought suddenly to the surface? Explain your answer.

WHAT LIVING THINGS ARE IN OCEAN WATER?

The oceans of the world are teeming with life. Some organisms float with the currents; others swim; still others spend their adult lives crawling on or anchored to the bottom. Find out more about living things in the ocean in this investigation.

Activity

Let the Sun Shine

Living things besides humans affect the oceans. Find out one way plants change ocean water in this activity.

MATERIALS
- goggles
- water
- *Elodea*
- large jar or aquarium
- funnel
- test tube
- paper towels
- *Science Notebook*

SAFETY
Wear goggles. Handle any glass equipment with care. Wipe up any spills immediately.

Procedure

1. Place the large jar in an area where it will be exposed to strong sunlight for several hours each day.

2. Fill the large jar with water to within a few centimeters of the top. Roll up your sleeves.

3. *Elodea* is a freshwater plant that you will use **to model** a marine plant. Place the *Elodea* in the bottom of the aquarium and cover it with the funnel.

4. Completely submerge the jar or test tube in the water. Turn it until it is filled with water. If any air bubbles remain inside, push them out with your finger or a straw. Invert the jar or test tube over the funnel, as shown. Don't let air get into the test tube.

5. After 10 minutes, **observe** and **record** any changes. **Predict** any changes that will occur over 24 hours. **Discuss** with your group any changes you think might occur during that time. Then let the jar sit overnight. The next day, examine the assembly and **record your observations**.

Step 4

Analyze and Conclude

1. Oxygen is produced by organisms that have chlorophyll. What evidence is there that oxygen was produced in this activity?

2. Make a hypothesis as to how the oxygen produced by plants affects other ocean life.

Step 5

UNIT PROJECT LINK

Imagine you are promoting a brand-new, undersea nature lodge. Visitors will get to and from the lodge in a deep-diving vehicle used for ocean research. Your presentation will include a moving picture of what visitors will see, a taped narration, and other materials. Begin preparing by researching how organisms are adapted to different ocean depths. For example, you might focus on phosphorescent fish, which glow in the lightless waters of the deep. How might phosphorescence help the fish survive? Collect or draw pictures of some of these fish. Create "storyboards" for your moving picture.

All Creatures Great and Small

Sea Nettle jellyfish ▼

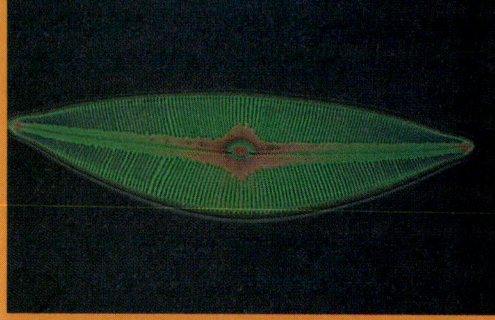

▲ **Phytoplankton and zooplankton make up the very bottom of the ocean food chain.**

Today, more than 200,000 species of plants and animals live in the ocean. These organisms can be divided into three groups—plankton, nekton, and benthos—according to the depth at which they live.

Plankton

Plankton includes organisms that float on or near the surface and drift with the ocean currents. There are two types of plankton, phytoplankton and zooplankton, but there are billions and billions of individual organisms. Although most phytoplankton are too small to see without a microscope, these tiny organisms produce 80 percent of the oxygen on our planet through **photosynthesis** (fōt o-sin′thə sis). Remember that during photosynthesis, organisms containing chlorophyll use the energy in sunlight to produce sugar and oxygen from carbon dioxide and water. The sugar is used for food, and oxygen is used for respiration. Creatures on land and in the ocean could not survive without the oxygen produced by phytoplankton. Because phytoplankton need sunlight for photosynthesis, they must live near the surface of the ocean.

Zooplankton includes some of the young (larval form) of other types of ocean creatures. When they mature, these organisms will no longer be consid-

◀ Common green sea turtle

Nekton includes many varieties of free-swimming organisms like the butterfish (*top*) and red soldier fish (*bottom*).

ered plankton. Instead, they will be lobsters, sea cucumbers, jellyfish, corals, or other organisms.

Nekton

The second main group of organisms, **nekton** (nek′tən), consists of all creatures that swim. It includes invertebrates such as squids and octopuses, all kinds of fish, and mammals such as whales and porpoises. Do you think any plants are considered nekton? Nekton can live at any depth, from near the ocean surface, to the ocean floor. However, each type stays mostly at the ocean depth where the water pressure and other conditions are suitable for its needs.

Benthos

The third group of ocean organisms, the **benthos** (ben′thäs), consists of plants and animals that live on the ocean floor, and do not swim.

The ocean floor starts at the shoreline and goes to the deepest parts of the ocean. Think about the different environments this includes, from waves crashing on the sand to the sea bottom miles beneath the surface. About 98 percent of all the species of ocean life live on the ocean floor. Can you hypothesize why the benthos group contains the greatest variety of ocean life? (Variety is measured

E25

Plants and animals of the benthos (*left*) live attached to the bottom, while nekton (*right*) swim freely in the water.

by the number of different species, as opposed to the number of individuals.) Shellfish, such as clams, oysters, and scallops, are members of the benthos group. So are starfish, sea cucumbers, crabs, barnacles, sea anemones, coral and many types of seaweed.

Most members of the benthos group live in shallow water, where food is more plentiful and the water is warmer. You've probably seen cartoons of a big fish about to eat a small fish that is about to eat a smaller fish that is about to eat an insect that is about to eat a plant. This is an example of a food chain. All food chains in the ocean start with phytoplankton. In one simple food chain, phytoplankton is eaten by krill (a kind of zooplankton that look like tiny shrimp). The krill is then eaten by enormous baleen whales. These whales swim with their mouths open wide, filtering millions of these tiny krill from the water. You've already seen that all creatures need the phytoplankton for oxygen. Additionally, they either eat phytoplankton directly, or they eat another organism that has eaten phytoplankton. ■

INVESTIGATION 3

1. What organisms might you find as part of the plankton, nekton, and benthos groups?

2. Why do you think most plantlike organisms are found in ocean water no deeper than about 9 or 10 m?

E26

REFLECT & EVALUATE

WORD POWER

benthos
nekton
photosynthesis
phytoplankton
plankton
salinity
zooplankton

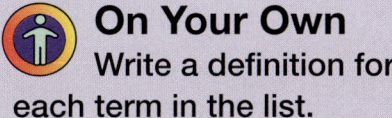 **On Your Own**
Write a definition for each term in the list.

 **With a Partner**
Use the terms in the list to make a word-search puzzle. See if your partner can find the hidden terms and tell you what each one means.

BUILD YOUR PORTFOLIO

Using pictures cut from magazines or drawings, make diagrams that show three possible ocean food chains. Label the organisms in your food chains as examples of plankton, benthos, or nekton.

Analyze Information

Study the photographs. Then classify the organisms in each photograph as nekton or benthos. Explain why you classified each organism as you did.

Assess Performance

Design an experiment to find out if salinity affects the freezing temperature of water. After your plan is approved by your teacher, carry out your experiment.

Problem Solving

1. If you had samples of fresh water and ocean water with the same volume, how could you distinguish the samples using only a balance?

2. Give three reasons why a greater number of organisms are likely to live 5 m below the ocean surface than at 1,000 m below the surface.

3. Many chemicals are water pollutants. If a chemical killed all the phytoplankton in the ocean, how would this affect other ocean organisms? How would it affect land organisms?

4. In what ways are the oceans a sign of God's love for all creation?

E27

CHAPTER 2

THE OCEAN FLOOR

Scientists have much to learn about the bottom of the sea, with its volcanic activity and strange life forms. There will be many surprises for the explorers who venture there. How do scientists gather information about the sea floor?

Space-Age Subs

Graham Hawkes is a marine engineer who is busy designing a new type of submersible to explore the ocean. Unlike existing subs, the new submersible will be light and fast. It will twirl and spin, maneuvering like a dolphin. It will seem to fly rather than float to the bottom of the ocean.

The pilot will lie face down, with little room to move, in the 360-cm (12-ft) long body of the sub. The person operating the new craft will look through a clear dome and will steer with joysticks.

The new submersible will be used in a project called *Deep Flight*. One of the goals of this project is to explore the 10.85-km (35,850-ft) deep Mariana Trench in the Pacific Ocean. The challenge for the marine engineer is to produce a vessel that can withstand the tremendous pressure at that depth. Graham Hawkes and his team will make the new submersible out of a ceramic material, which is light and strong. What else do the designers have to consider as they plan and build this new submersible?

Coming Up

WHAT FEATURES AND SEDIMENTS OCCUR ON THE OCEAN FLOOR?
............E30

HOW DO SCIENTISTS STUDY THE OCEAN FLOOR?
............E40

◀ Graham Hawkes in his experimental submersible; submersibles such as this will someday explore the deepest parts of the oceans.

INVESTIGATION 1

WHAT FEATURES AND SEDIMENTS OCCUR ON THE OCEAN FLOOR?

If you were asked to describe the ocean floor, what would you say? For a long time, people thought the ocean floor was shaped like the bottom of a bathtub. In this investigation you'll see how wrong they were!

Activity

Graphing the Ocean Floor

MATERIALS
- graph paper
- *Science Notebook*

Scientists use sonar to "see" the ocean floor. In this activity you'll make your own ocean floor profile.

Procedure

The table provides depth measurements for an area of the ocean off the east coast of the United States. **Graph the data** on a piece of graph paper. The distance from the coast should be along the *x*-axis and the depth to the ocean floor should be on the *y*-axis. Set up the *y*-axis so that the greatest depth is at the bottom of the *y*-axis.

Analyze and Conclude

1. **Describe** the shape of your graph.
2. What would you call the feature you graphed if it was on land?
3. **Infer** from your profile how the shape of the ocean floor might be like that of the continents.

Distance from coast (in km)	Depth to the ocean floor (in m)
610	-5988
620	-5840
660	-4965
695	-4520
720	-2333
750	-1895
775	-1754
810	-5110
835	-5840
850	-5842

Activity
Modeling Ocean Sediments

Sediments from the land are constantly being washed into the ocean. Where do they end up?

MATERIALS
- goggles
- 2 plastic soda bottles (1L)
- water
- tablespoon
- sediments of various sizes including clay (powdered), silt, fine sand, coarse sand, and fine gravel
- 2 paper cups
- funnel
- 2 bottle caps
- stack of books
- *Science Notebook*

SAFETY
Wear goggles during this activity. To prevent slipping and falling, immediately mop up any spills.

Procedure

1. Fill the bottles with water to within a few centimeters of the top.

2. Pour several spoonfuls of powdered clay into a paper cup. Add a pinch of silt and fine sand and stir.

3. Pour 2 spoonfuls of each of the sediments into a second paper cup. Stir the mixture.

4. Model the washing of clay (soil) into the ocean by using the funnel to slowly pour the clay from the first paper cup into one bottle. Set the bottle to one side and screw on the bottle cap.

5. Model the action of sediments that become suspended in ocean water by first tilting the second bottle until the water is within 1 cm of the top. Then use the funnel to pour the cup of mixed sediment into the bottle. Keeping the bottle tilted, screw on the cap and set it aside. Use books to prop it up.

6. Observe the bottles for several minutes. In your *Science Notebook* **sketch** the results and **record** your observations. Repeat this step after 1 hour.

Step 4

Analyze and Conclude

1. Describe the appearance of the sediments in each bottle after several minutes and after 1 hour. Be sure to **describe** any difference in the way the sediments behaved.

2. Infer from your observations what happens to sediments that wash into the ocean.

Features of the Ocean Floor

People build things up and also tear things down. And sometimes nature tears things down for us. Waves wash away sand castles on the beach, for example, and storm waves may wash away homes, boardwalks, and other structures. So it's nice to know that at least the mountains, the rivers, the valleys, and oceans are forever, right? Wrong! Not even Earth's natural features are forever. Its mountains, its rivers, its valleys, and even its mighty oceans have been altered almost continuously since God created the earth many years ago.

Powerful natural forces pull and wrench at Earth's crust, making constant changes. Earthquakes and volcanoes shift huge masses of rocks on the land and in the sea. Rivers carry weathered rock and deposit it in the oceans. So what natural wonders might you find on the ocean bottoms? Are there features similar to those on dry land?

The Continental Shelf

Let's start where the oceans begin. The **continental shelf**, which covers about 5 percent of Earth's surface,

The ocean basin ▼

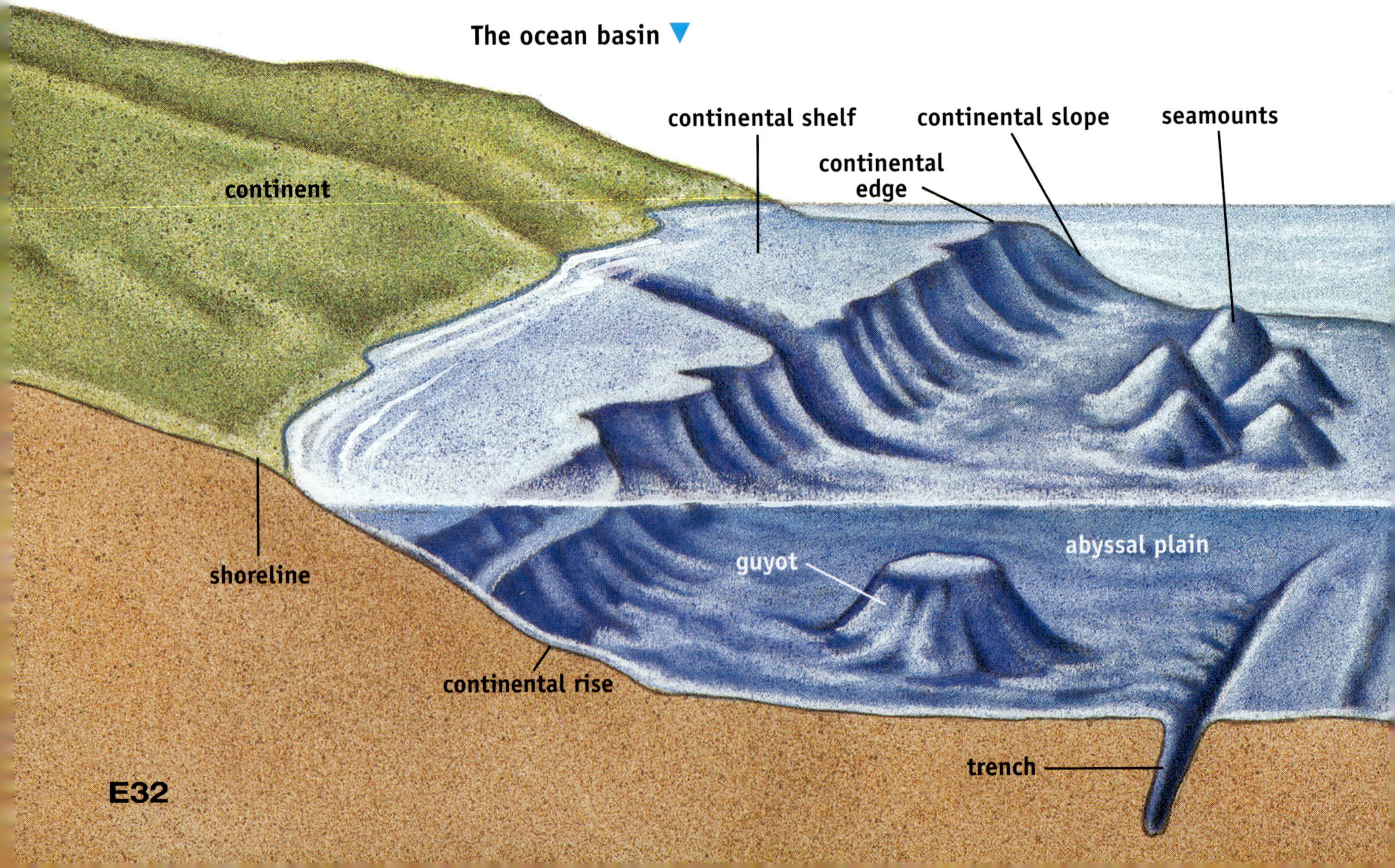

extends in a gentle downward slope from the edges of the continents into the oceans. Throughout the world, when you wade into the ocean, you are walking on the continental shelf. At its deepest it is about 365 m (1,205 ft) below the surface, but its average depth is less than 152 m (500 feet).

Although on average the continental shelf extends less than 80 km (50 mi) from shore, it extends more than 1,120 km (700 mi) off the coast of Siberia. Off the Atlantic coast of North America, the continental shelf extends 144 km (90 mi) out into the ocean. But off the Pacific coast it extends only 29 km (18 mi).

The continental shelf tends to be widest near the mouths of rivers and off coasts that were formed by glaciers. Rocks, sediments, and other materials carried into the ocean by rivers and glaciers have greatly increased the size of the continental shelf in those areas.

The Continental Edge and the Continental Slope

The **continental edge** is the point at which the shelf surrounding each continent begins to angle sharply downward toward the ocean depths. The clifflike drop beyond the continental edge is called the **continental slope**. The continental slope is the true boundary between the deep ocean floor and the continents.

To help you remember these first three features, think of them as parts of a gigantic bowl. The continental shelf is the rim (or the lip) of the bowl; the continental edge is the inner edge of the lip; and the continental slope is the inside wall of the bowl, leading down to the bottom like a gigantic bluff.

The Continental Rise

The **continental rise** stretches from the lower portion of the continental slope to the deepest part of the ocean.

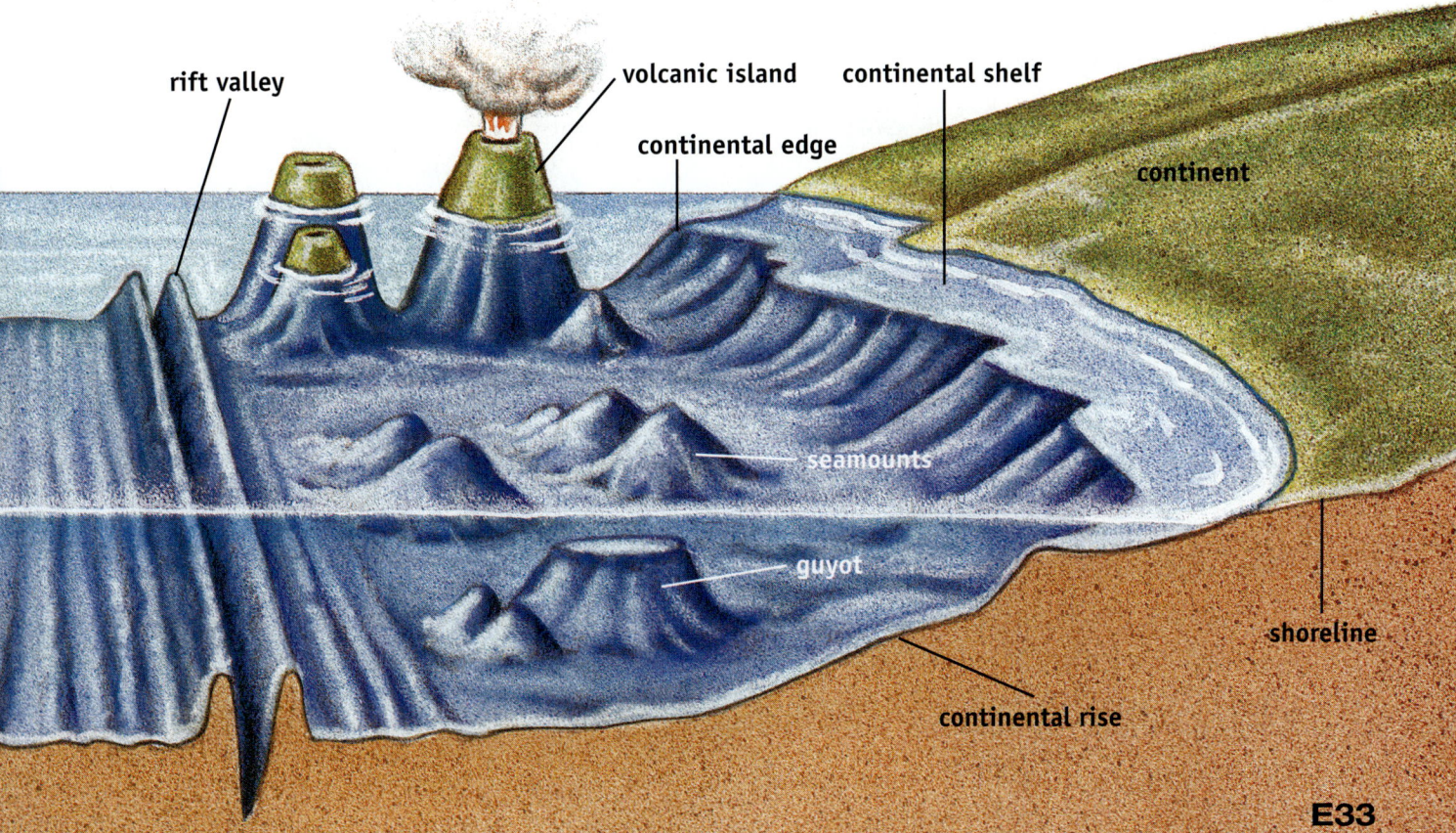

Although the continental rise slopes downward, it is not nearly as steep as the continental slope. The continental rise usually begins at 1,425 to 1,970 m (4,700 to 6,500 ft) under the ocean's surface. If you again think of the ocean as a giant bowl, the rise is the softly curving link between the flat bottom and the steep, near-vertical sides.

The Abyssal Plain

Typically, the continental rise flattens out completely at about 3,630 m (12,000 ft), leading into the vast ocean bottom itself. The bottom is called the **abyssal plain** and covers about 46 percent of Earth's surface.

Parts of the abyssal plain are flat, but for the most part, both the continental rise and the abyssal plain feature caves and deep, steep-walled canyons called trenches. Most of these trenches were formed long ago by undersea rivers and currents, and the cooling, contracting, and pulling apart of Earth's rocky crust. Even today the ocean bottom is undergoing change as undersea volcanoes, earthquakes, and powerful deep-water currents continue to alter and reshape the abyssal plain.

Mountains in the Sea

Perhaps the single most startling feature of the abyssal plain is a colossal chain of underwater mountains called the **Mid-Ocean Ridge**. The Mid-Ocean Ridge is the longest mountain range in the world, extending nearly 60,000 km (36,000 mi) and passing through the Atlantic, Indian, and Pacific oceans.

Free-standing mountains, called **seamounts**, formed by volcanoes also exist in the oceans. They are especially numerous in the Pacific, where thousands of seamounts lie beneath the surface. Their tops, which were once above the surface, have been flattened by wave action. A flat-topped seamount is called a guyot (gē′ō).

Covering the ocean floor is a thick layer of sediments that has built up over many years. ▼

Some seamounts rise above the surface, forming islands. A spectacular example is Mauna Kea (mou'nə kā'ə), a volcano forming the island of Hawaii. Rising from the ocean floor, Mauna Kea climbs more than 5,144 m (16,877 ft) to the ocean surface. Then it rises an additional 4,649 m (15,253 ft) to a total height of 9,793 m (32,130 ft). It is the tallest mountain in the world, almost 1.0 km (.6 mi) taller than Mount Everest!

So, as you can see, the ocean floor certainly doesn't have a flat, bathtub shape. It is made up of some rather spectacular features.

▲ Would you believe that Mauna Kea, not Mt. Everest, is the tallest mountain in the world? Most of it is underwater.

SCIENCE AND FAITH

Can you imagine a time when the entire planet was watery? At the end of God's second day of creation, that's how the Earth looked. Then, on the third day, God separated the waters. Now Earth had both dry land and water. Most of the water went into the oceans, but God also provided inland water--most of it fresh in the form of lakes and river systems. Genesis 1:9 describes it this way: "And God said, `Let the water under the sky be gathered to one place, and let dry ground appear'. And it was so."

By God's command, dry land rose from beneath the water and provided an ideal environment for the life God would place on the planet during the next few days of creation. The environment didn't remain ideal, however. When Eve and Adam introduced sin into the world, God also allowed nature to operate in ways sometimes hostile to life. But in His mercy, God also sent a Savior so that believers could live forever starting here on earth and coninuing later in the perfect environment of heaven.

Sediments
on the Ocean Floor

The ocean has its own snow storm of sorts. It's not a blizzard of snowflakes, however. Instead, it's countless particles of solid material drifting slowly to the bottom of the ocean. As sediment settled day after day, year after year, century after century, it created a heavy blanket covering the ocean floor. The blanket was so thick with particles that it crushed the ones on the bottom and even compressed the rocks and soil underneath until everything sank into the crust.

Tiny particles have been settling on the ocean floor since God created the oceans. Even as you read this sentence, the process continues. The result is a layer of sediments on the ocean floor, forming soft deposits of mud, slime, and decomposed shells that are called ooze. Ooze covers every part of the ocean floor, except where stong currents sweep the bottom bare or where active volcanoes deposit new rock.

Inorganic Sediments

Every time it rains, soil and rock on land are eroded. Some of the particles of soil and rock are washed into the oceans by runoff from the land. Other particles ride the currents of rivers and streams, all of which empty eventually into the oceans.

Other inorganic sediments drifting downward in the oceans include deposits from the thousands of volcanoes rising from the ocean floor. Active volcanoes can contribute great quantities of rock

▲ As this iceberg melts, rocks, soil, and other debris will settle into the ocean as sediments.

and rock particles each time they erupt. But volcanoes need not be spewing lava and blowing off debris to add to the sediment layer. Constant friction by the ocean currents, plus the dissolving actions of the water itself, continually erodes ocean volcanoes.

Other inorganic particles reach the ocean floor by way of glaciers that fringe the northern and southern parts of the oceans. As glaciers move slowly toward the oceans, they pick up rocks, soil, and organic deposits—the remains of living things. When the glaciers meet the oceans, pieces break off, or calve, to form icebergs. Gradually, materials that were carried by the glacier are released by the melting iceberg and settle to the ocean bottom.

Another source of inorganic sediments is the burning of meteors and comets in the atmosphere. Fragments of iron, nickel, and other debris settle eventually to the ocean bottom.

Where inorganic sediments are plentiful, they form muds and clays of various consistencies and colors. They cover about a quarter of the ocean floor and build up in the thickest layers near the mouths of rivers and streams.

Organic Sediments

Organic ooze is found most frequently in the deeper parts of the ocean. Most of the deep-sea ooze is formed from the shells of protists, particularly the remains of single-celled algae. Some ooze is formed from the shells of tiny snails and other small marine animals. Organic ooze covers about half of the ocean floor. Normally, it builds up very slowly, from about 1.3 cm (0.5 in.) to about 10.2 cm (4 in.) in a thousand years.

When organisms in the ocean die, their remains settle to the bottom and become part of the organic sediments. ▼

Chemical and Mineral Deposits

During the nineteenth century, people traveling west across the vast plains and imposing mountains of the United States heard it said that "there's gold in them thar hills!" Well, there's gold in "them thar oceans," too. A cubic mile of seawater contains enough gold to make you rich. Unfortunately, extracting the gold costs more than the gold is worth.

As you know, water moving over the land dissolves vast quantities of chemicals and minerals that eventually end up in the oceans. Many minerals, such as gold, remain suspended in the water. Other minerals build up in the ooze of shallow coastal waters. Although some of the minerals can be mined at a profit, others, like gold and the millions of manganese nodules that litter the ocean floor, aren't yet being reclaimed.

First discovered more than 100 years ago, manganese nodules range in size from 0.5 cm (0.2 in.) to 25 cm (10 in.) across. No one knows for sure how they form, but they appear to grow very slowly from metals dissolved in the water.

Turbidity Currents

Over the open Atlantic basin, the sediment layer is often more than 3,200 m (10,560 ft) thick. Yet it's never more than 303 m (1,000 ft) thick in the Indian and Pacific oceans. The sediment layer also tends to form huge drifts at the bases of mountains and continental slopes.

What causes such differences in the thickness of the sedimentary layer? One possible answer is a **turbidity current** (tʉr bid'i tē kʉr'ənt). These currents, which are still barely understood, seem to occur near the mouths of rivers where heavy sedimentary deposits have built up. In time, the sediments become like layers of unstable snow on hillsides, needing only a slight jolt to send them rolling downhill, like an avalanche. Turbidity currents may cause sediment layers to build up more in some places than in others.

The steep walls of the Hudson canyon were probably carved by the action of turbidity currents. ▼

Ideas About the Past in Sediments

By studying the layers of ocean sediments, scientists try to form ideas about the past. For example, in some places the rare element iridium is hundreds of times more concentrated than normal. Some scientists think that the most likely source for such quantities of iridium would be a single gigantic meteorite or a shower of smaller meteorites striking Earth all at the same time. They use this idea to propose a natural disaster during which dust from the meteorite's impact blotted out the sun, caused plants to die, and caused animals like the dinosaur to starve.

The meteorite idea cannot be proven and remains controversial among scientists. The Bible provides what may be other clues about any history captured in layers of sediment. The Great Flood reported in Genesis 7 changed much on the surface of Earth, and may be responsible for changes in environment and landscape that contributed to the extinction of plants and animals even after the flood waters disappeared. Perhaps ooze-frosted sediment reveals some of that story. ■

▲ Uh, oh!

INVESTIGATE FURTHER!

RESEARCH

Water sometimes deposits sediments on land that look very similar to those deposited in the ocean. Do research in geology or earth science books to find out how such deposits form.

INVESTIGATION 1

1. Draw and describe the features of the ocean floor.

2. Why is looking at the sedimentary layers of the ocean floor like looking at a time line?

E39

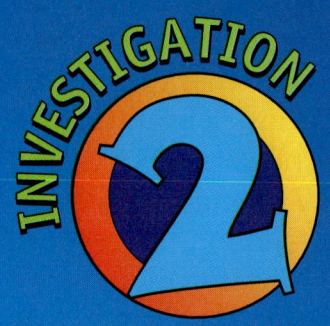

How Do Scientists Study the Ocean Floor?

You've been assigned to investigate something you can't see, touch, or even get near. How do you investigate something under those conditions? That's the question scientists had to answer when they tried to study the ocean floor. Find out how they do it in this investigation.

Activity
Hear the Distance

You can't see the ocean floor from a ship. But maybe you can "hear" it. Make a model of how scientists "hear" the ocean floor in this activity.

MATERIALS
- timer
- calculator
- meterstick or metric tape measure
- *Science Notebook*

Procedure

1. Work with a partner. Stand about 60 m from a large wall made of brick, cement, or metal. Clap your hands and listen for an echo. If necessary, change your position until you hear an echo. Then mark your location.

2. Clap your hands at a steady rate. Keep practicing until you can time each clap to occur just as an echo reaches you.

3. Have your partner use the timer to determine how long it takes to do 20 of these timed claps. **Record** this data in your *Science Notebook*. Divide this time by 20 to **calculate** the time it takes the sound of one clap to travel from you to the wall and back again. **Record** this data.

Step 1

4. **Measure** the distance between your location and the wall and **record** the data. Then **calculate** the speed of sound, using the following equation:

$$\text{speed of sound} = \frac{2 \times \text{distance to wall}}{\text{time for round trip}}$$

5. Now that you know the speed of sound in air, **plan a method** that uses sound to determine distance. Talk with your partner to plan a method, then tell your plan to your teacher. If he or she approves, try your method at different distances from the wall. Then use the meterstick to check the accuracy of your results. **Record** your data each time.

Analyze and Conclude

1. **Infer** how an echo is produced.

2. Sound actually travels through water faster than it does through air. **Hypothesize** how sound might be used to determine the distance from the ocean surface to the ocean floor. **Explain** your hypothesis.

3. How might sound have been used to develop the table you used to graph a profile of the ocean floor in the activity on page E30?

UNIT PROJECT LINK

An important part of your *undersea lodge* promotion is to show where on the ocean floor the lodge would be. At what depth and distance from land would you locate the site, and why? What safety factors would you take into account? Use an ocean map to help you decide where to build. Draw illustrations to show the topography that visitors to the lodge would see. Also, keep gathering data for your taped narration. Remember, your goal is to communicate how unique and interesting an underwater living experience would be.

Activity
Modeling Sonar

Sonar waves are sound waves that can be used to probe the ocean. Find out how scientists collect and use data gathered with sonar.

MATERIALS
- goggles
- spring toy
- length of string
- meterstick
- timer
- calculator
- *Science Notebook*

Procedure

1. Work with a partner. Tie one end of the spring toy to a doorknob and pull the spring so that it is parallel to the floor.

2. Hit the spring sharply with your free hand as close to your other hand as possible. Have your partner **measure** the time it takes the wave motion to travel to the doorknob and back to your hand. **Record** the time in your *Science Notebook*.

3. **Measure** the distance from your hand to the doorknob. **Record** the distance.

4. Repeat step 2 five times and find the average time. To **calculate** the rate of travel, multiply the distance by 2 for the round trip distance and then divide the product by the time. **Record** the rate in your *Science Notebook*.

Step 2

Analyze and Conclude

1. Sonar waves traveling through ocean water bounce off objects and return. How is your model similar to the way sonar waves behave?

2. Suppose it takes 4 seconds for the wave motion in a spring to make a round trip. **Calculate** the distance traveled.

E42

Sonar

Slicing through the water like a living torpedo, a hungry porpoise approaches a school of mackerel. The porpoise follows every movement of the school and soon catches its meal.

Porpoises navigate and track prey by bouncing high-pitched sound pulses off nearby objects. The animal can tell the object's location by the time it takes the sound to return. *Sonar*, meaning "**so**und **na**vigation **r**anging," works on the same principle. The first sonar systems were invented in the 1920s. They were greatly improved during World War II (1939–1945) to help surface ships detect submarines and to help submarines detect surface ships.

After the war, oceanographers adapted sonar techniques to mapping the ocean floor. Modern "side-scan" sonar even works in two directions at once. The system includes a 120-cm (4-ft) metal "fish" with built-in stabilizing fins. The fish is lowered and towed through the water by a ship or a submarine. High-frequency sound pulses go out from the fish and scan the ocean floor. The pulses are also transmitted horizontally through the surrounding water.

The returning sound impulses go to a receiver on the fish itself. Signals then go to a computer on the ship, which prints out visual images on paper. The darkness of the printed image depends on the distance and density of the scanned material. Valleys, rocks, mud, sand, and other underwater features become clearly recognizable. Modern sonar provides a detailed map of the ocean floor that is superior to those obtained in the past. ■

▲ A porpoise's sonar, called *echolocation*, enables the animal to locate and track food.

Underwater Exploration

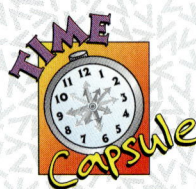

Explorers have always been fascinated with what could be found beneath the ocean waves. Early in the seventeenth century, inventors began developing diving suits and diving chambers. But it wasn't until the nineteenth century that underwater exploration was really taken seriously.

Cornelis Drebbel builds the first working submarine. It actually works for a few hours!

1620

Matthew Fontaine Maury, a landlubber from Tennessee, joins the U.S. Navy and begins gathering information and developing accurate charts of the world's oceans. He becomes the father of modern oceanography.

1825

British scientists and the Royal Navy launch HMS *Challenger* on the most ambitious oceanographic voyage to date. At sea for more than three years, the scientists travel more than 112,000 km (70,000 miles), and collect more than 300 deep sea samples.

1872

1870

Jules Verne's *Twenty Thousand Leagues Under the Sea* revives the ageless dream that safe undersea travel might be possible.

Off Makapu'u Point, Oahu, Hawaii, Sylvia Earle plants the Stars and Stripes at a depth of 378.78 m (1,250 ft), completing the deepest untethered solo dive in history.

1979

1985

Argo, a complex, advanced underwater survey vehicle, locates the *Titanic*. *Jason Jr.*, a tiny robot submarine, sends back hundreds of high-quality video and still pictures from inside the wreck.

1968–83

The *Glomar Challenger* takes up where the HMS *Challenger* has left off. It drills hundreds of deep-water "core samples" from sediment layers all over the world, adding immeasurably to our knowledge of the makeup, age, and natural forces at work in and on Earth.

Exploring the Oceans

Why explore the oceans? Why explore anything for that matter? You might as well ask, "Why eat?" Because, as humans, exploring is something that's in our nature. Soon after we are born, we begin to get curious about our surroundings. So we explore. People have always looked at the oceans and wondered what was under all the water. In recent times people devised some means of finding out.

The first direct observations of what was under all that water began near the end of the nineteenth century. In 1872, the Royal Society of London helped equip the 2,300-ton warship HMS *Challenger* with the most advanced navigating and measuring instruments of the day. During the next three years, the *Challenger* crew sailed about 112,000 km (70,000 miles), measuring ocean depths and collecting deep-sea samples.

What the *Challenger* crew discovered changed the scientific world. In more than 300 locations around the world, the *Challenger* crew dropped a crude dredging device, allowed it to drag along the bottom until it filled with samples, and then hauled it back on deck. A typical drop and retrieval took an entire day. But then, as the dredge was emptied on deck, imagine the scene! Deep into the night, scientists and sailors were still bouncing around on deck, yelling and shaking their heads as they examined by flickering lantern light the day's astonishing finds.

HMS *Challenger* under sail in the Antarctic ▼

A deep-sea lobster brought up by the *Challenger* crew. ▼

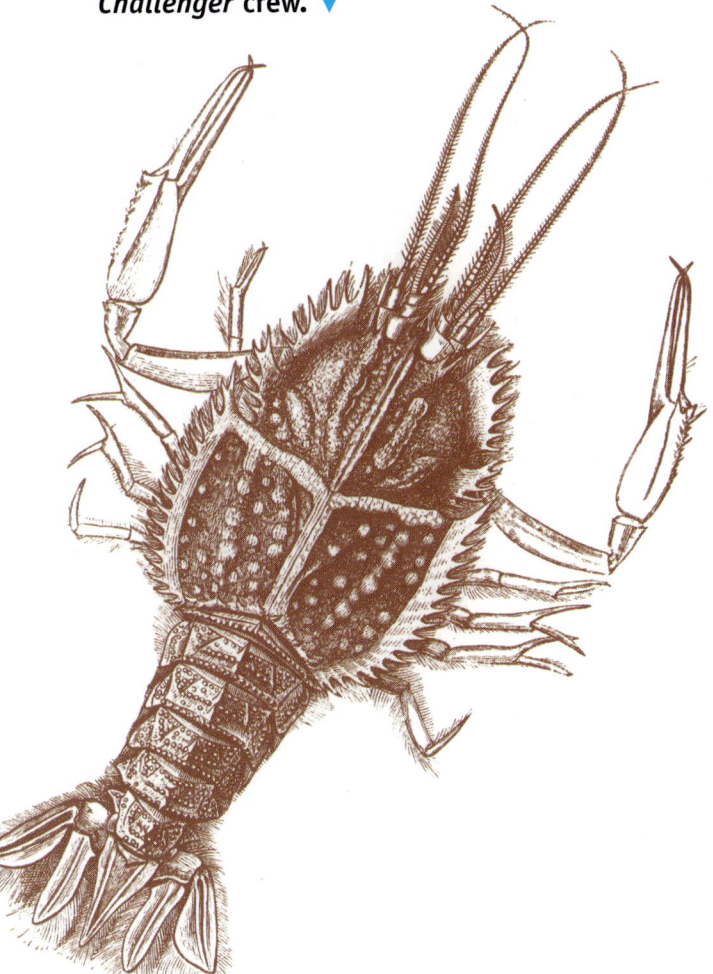

The ocean bottom had been envisioned as empty and barren. Instead, the *Challenger* crew found the ocean to be teeming with life.

The crew of the *Challenger* also took measurements of the ocean depths, using weighted lines. Where they presumed a shallow bottom, the sounding weights fell almost 11.2 km (7 mi) into what became known as the Challenger Deep of the Mariana Trench. At the end of the voyage, the scientists on board the *Challenger* concluded that they had barely begun to explore the oceans.

Almost 100 years later, the *Glomar Challenger* took up the work begun by the first *Challenger*. Between 1968 and 1983 this highly advanced exploration ship bored hundreds of holes into the ocean floor and collected long core samples of the sediments. Some of these sediments were thousands of years old. Such core samples gave valuable information about the water, the life it supports, and the forces that still shape our planet today.

Among many other sophisticated instruments, the *Glomar Challenger* had satellite navigation systems that gave it accurate positioning via on-board computers. In the 1980s, the ship *JOIDES Resolution* took over the job of exploration and continues today. (JOIDES stands for **J**oint **O**ceanographic **I**nstitutions for **D**eep **E**arth **S**ampling.) The *JOIDES Resolution* can probe depths of 8,291 m (27,200 ft), even deeper than the *Glomar Challenger*.

A deep-sea animal-like protist brought up by the *Challenger* crew. ▼

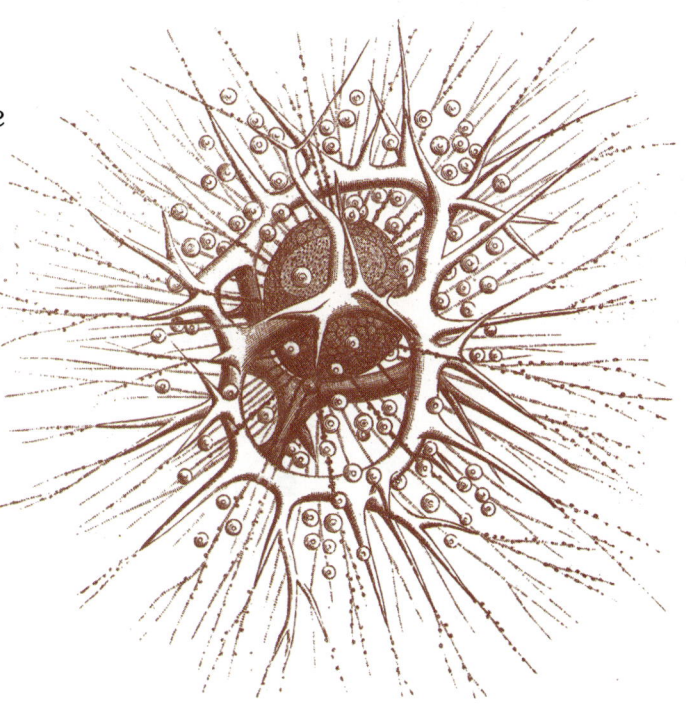

Submersibles, Bathyspheres, and Bathyscaphs

Ocean exploration also has been done by some very daring and brave individuals using a wide variety of specialized equipment. The legendary deep-sea divers with their bulky pressure suits, heavy metal helmets, flexible air hoses, and weighted shoes still exist, and are still in demand for specialized tasks. But much of what such divers once did can now be completed by submersibles.

In modern oceanography a submersible is any self-propelled underwater craft. Most are shaped like submarines, though they are usually smaller. They can carry researchers, but often they carry only robots and sampling equipment controlled by computers and cameras.

An older type of submersible is the bathysphere, such as the one used by Charles William Beebe to descend to 923 m (3,028 ft) in 1934. A bathysphere is usually a heavily reinforced, spherical capsule that is attached to a cable that lowers it into the ocean and brings it back to the surface. However, since the late 1950s, bathyspheres have been replaced by bathyscaphs, such as the *Trieste*. Unlike a bathysphere, a bathyscaph is free-moving. It dives and surfaces like a submarine.

In 1934, Charles Beebe entered this bathysphere and descended further into the ocean than anyone had ever gone before.

Underwater Housing

Once humans began to explore the oceans, it was only a matter of time before someone began thinking about living there. In the 1960s *Conshelf I* was built by Jacques Cousteau and placed 10 m (33 ft) deep off the coast of France. *Conshelf I* housed two researchers for seven days. On the floor of the Red Sea at 11 m (36 ft), *Conshelf II* housed five researchers for 30 days. Within your lifetime, researchers and vacationers will probably have the opportunity to spend time on the ocean floor for research and recreation. ■

INVESTIGATION 2

1. Describe some methods that have been used to explore the ocean floor.

2. Using sonar, a scientist aboard ship notes that for the first five pulses the signal takes longer to return each time. For the next five pulses the signal returns faster each time. What is the ship passing over?

REFLECT & EVALUATE

WORD POWER

abyssal plain
continental edge
continental rise
continental shelf
continental slope
Mid-Ocean Ridge
seamount
turbidity current

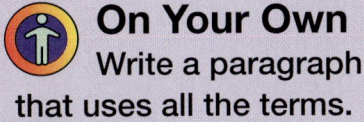

On Your Own
Write a paragraph that uses all the terms.

With a Partner
Mix up the letters of each term. Give a partner one clue to each term.

Imagine you are traveling around the world in a submarine that glides slightly above the ocean floor. Write a short story about your journey that describes at least five features of the ocean floor and some of the organisms you see.

Analyze Information

Study the drawing. Then explain the differences among seamounts, islands, and guyots.

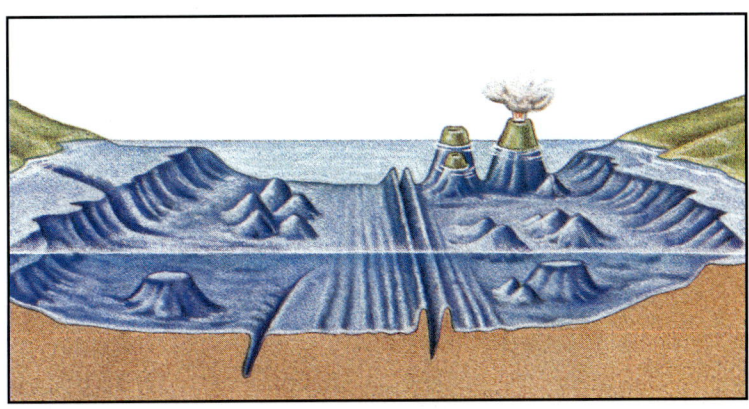

Assess Performance

Make your own core samples. Layer some soil, sand, and clay in different depths in plastic cups. Then carefully push a transparent straw down through the sample. Remove the straw and compare its contents to the layered materials in the cup. Why do scientists find core samples useful?

Problem Solving

1. Sound travels through water at a speed of about 1,531 m per second. If a signal sent from a ship takes 4 seconds to return, how far away is the ocean floor?

2. Give examples of three chemicals or minerals found in ocean water or on the ocean floor. Why do you think many of these substances are not being reclaimed?

3. What advantage do bathyscaphs have over bathyspheres? over human divers?

CHAPTER 3

MOVING OCEAN WATER

The waters of the oceans are constantly in motion. You may have enjoyed watching waves breaking on a beach. While on a boat ride, you may have felt the rhythmic motion of the sea. Yet some waves are powerful enough to alter the course of ships at sea. What do we know about ocean water and how it moves?

Killer Waves

A tsunami (tsōō nä′mē) is an earthquake-generated wave that races across the ocean at 800 km/h (500 mph). As it travels, it can be thousands of feet deep, extending from the ocean floor to the surface, and it can be hundreds of miles long.

A tsunami slowly builds in size as it approaches land, sometimes to a height of 27 m (90 ft) above sea level. When such a wave hits the shore, it can cause great destruction.

Hiroo Kanamori of Caltech in California is a seismologist (sīz mäl′ə jist), a scientist who deals with earthquakes. He seeks to understand how tsunamis are produced. He believes that mild, hardly noticeable, undersea earthquakes slowly move the ocean floor. An enormous amount of water between the ocean floor and its surface is pushed up. Why do you think this would cause tsunami waves to develop on the ocean surface?

Coming Up

INVESTIGATION 1
WHAT CAUSES OCEAN CURRENTS? E52

INVESTIGATION 2
WHAT CAUSES OCEAN WAVES? E62

INVESTIGATION 3
WHAT CAUSES TIDES? E68

◀ Hiroo Kanamori in his lab at Caltech in California

WHAT CAUSES OCEAN CURRENTS?

Thrown overboard by a passenger on a ship, a message in a bottle floats in the ocean for ten years. Then, after being carried thousands of kilometers by ocean currents, it washes onto a lonely shore. How are ocean currents formed?

Activity
Current Trends

A moving stream of air is called wind. In this activity you'll find out how winds and currents are related.

MATERIALS
- goggles
- rectangular pan
- water
- pepper
- straw
- *Science Notebook*

Procedure

1. Wear goggles during this activity. **Record** all observations and responses in your *Science Notebook*.

2. Fill a pan with water to within 1 cm of the top. Sprinkle pepper on the surface of the water.

3. **Predict** what will happen if you gently blow across the surface of the water through a straw. **Record** your prediction in your Science Notebook.

Step 2

4. **Test** your prediction by blowing across the water through a straw. In your *Science Notebook*, **sketch** and **record** your observations.

5. **Predict** what will happen if you blow harder across the surface of the water.

6. Repeat step 4, this time blowing harder.

Analyze and Conclude

1. What did you observe when you blew across the surface of the water?

2. How does a stronger "wind" affect the water?

3. Currents are rivers of water in oceans and other bodies of water. **Suggest a hypothesis** on the role wind plays in producing currents.

INVESTIGATE FURTHER!

RESEARCH

What is the Sargasso Sea and how is it connected to ocean currents? Research and write a report of your findings. Be sure to include any interesting superstitions or tales you discover concerning the Sargasso Sea.

Step 4

Activity

Modeling Density Currents

Recall from Chapter 1 that differences in density cause ocean water to move. In this activity you'll make a model of one kind of density current.

MATERIALS
- large jar
- water
- table salt
- teaspoon
- food coloring
- plastic cup
- plastic straw
- *Science Notebook*

SAFETY
Wipe up any spills immediately.

Procedure

1. Pour water into a jar until it is about three-fourths full. Add 1/2 spoonful of salt. Stir the mixture well with a plastic straw.

2. Half-fill a cup with water. Add 4 spoonfuls of salt. Add several drops of food coloring and stir the mixture well.

3. **Predict** what will happen if you slowly and carefully pour the contents of the cup into the jar. **Test your prediction.**

4. Wait 2 minutes and **describe** what you observe.

5. **Predict** how the liquid will change in 10 minutes. Let the jar of liquid sit for 10 minutes. Then **describe** what you observe.

Step 2

Analyze and Conclude

1. **Describe** what you observed in steps 4 and 5.

2. Which liquid was more dense? How do you know it was more dense?

3. In this activity you made a model of density currents that move water between the ocean's surface and its depths. Based on your observations, **hypothesize** what causes such currents.

Step 3

World Currents

The ocean is never still. It's restless and constantly moving, and it's a partner of the land and atmosphere in shaping Earth's surface. So how do we begin to talk about the restless oceans? Let's start with the great rivers of water that move through them. These rivers, called **currents**, move water through all parts of the ocean. Some currents, deep under the surface, move very slowly. Others, near the surface, move very quickly.

What Causes Currents?

The speed and direction of surface currents is determined by two factors—the wind and Earth's rotation. Remember what happened on pages E52 and E53 when you blew on the water? Moving air produced moving water. The same thing happens in the ocean. When the wind blows, it pushes water in the direction it is blowing. Although these water movements are called surface currents, the wind affects water under the surface as well. A surface current often carries more water than the largest rivers and travels at speeds ranging from 10 to 160 km (6 to 100 mi) a day.

Since the wind produces surface currents, the direction of the wind affects the direction of ocean currents. Let's look more closely at Earth's winds.

Even from high above Earth's surface, the Gulf Stream shows up as a dark blue river flowing north off the eastern coast of Florida. ▼

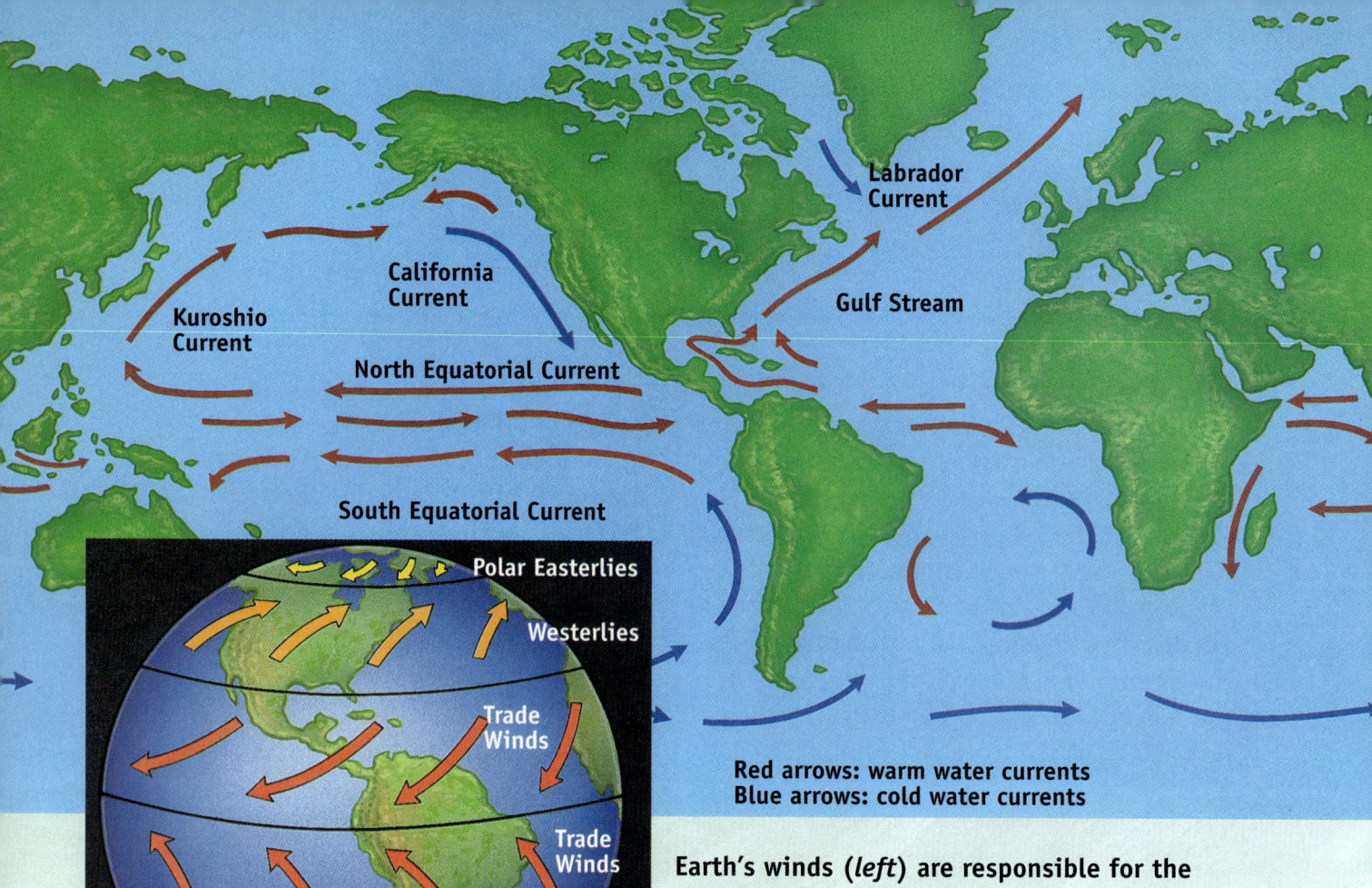

Red arrows: warm water currents
Blue arrows: cold water currents

Earth's winds (*left*) are responsible for the movement of the surface currents in the oceans (*above*).

Examine the diagram of Earth's wind belts. You'll notice that the winds tend to blow across the surface in curved paths rather than in straight lines. In the Northern Hemisphere, Earth's rotation causes the motion of the winds to be bent and shifted in a clockwise direction. In the Southern Hemisphere, Earth's rotation causes the winds to follow counterclockwise paths. The curving motion caused by Earth's rotation is called the **Coriolis effect**. It was named for Gaspard de Coriolis, the French mathematician who explained it.

Some of the winds, called **trade winds**, move from east to west toward the equator. As the trade winds move over the oceans, they push surface currents from east to west. Other winds, called the **westerlies**, blow from west to east, pushing surface currents along with them.

If you examine the two maps above, you will see that the surface ocean currents of the world, like the Gulf Stream and the Kuroshio Current, follow the same general patterns as the global wind belts. The prevailing winds push the water in about the same curving pattern as the wind.

On the maps, notice how the surface currents that begin in warm areas carry warm water, whereas those that begin near the North and South poles carry cold water. How do you think the temperature of ocean currents affect us on land?

How Currents Affect Us

Winds cause currents, and currents influence something that affects us each day—the weather. One current that affects weather in parts of North America and Europe is the Gulf Stream.

The Gulf Stream is one of the Atlantic Ocean's main warm-water surface currents. It moves 100 times more water than all of Earth's rivers combined! The Gulf Stream influences the weather on land by bringing warm water from the equator up the eastern coast of the United States. This water warms the air, producing weather conditions that are milder than they would be without the Gulf Stream, particularly in winter. Then the Gulf Stream crosses the Atlantic and produces the same effects along Europe's western coast.

When the pattern of ocean currents changes, the weather on land can change, too. One country that is greatly affected by changes in ocean currents is India. Twice a year, India's coastal currents are affected when winds, called monsoons, change direction. When this happens, the amount of rainfall and the temperature on land also change. The people of India have come to expect this weather change and depend on it for growing their crops.

Large areas of the world are affected by changes in a surface current called El Niño (el nēn′yō). Trade winds blowing across the Pacific Ocean usually keep warm water away from the coasts of North and South America. When these winds weaken, the warm El Niño current reaches these coasts. This current changes position every two to seven years. When it changes position, it causes dramatic changes in the climate, ranging from drought in some areas to frequent storms in others. ■

Although they are at the same latitude above the equator, Dublin, Ireland (*left*) and Newfoundland (*right*) have very different weather because of the Gulf Stream. Both of these pictures were taken at about the same time in winter.

How Deep Water Moves

Did you know that currents deep in the oceans often move in the opposite direction from surface currents? Deep currents also tend to move more slowly than surface currents, traveling from 91 m to 5 km (300 ft to 3 mi) a day. And deep currents are not formed in the same way as surface currents.

You have learned that surface currents are powered by the winds. For the most part, deep ocean currents are driven by differences in water density. Density refers to the mass of a substance compared to the amount of space it takes up. If you have two samples of water that take up the same amount of space, the sample with the greater mass is more dense. Just as dense air sinks in the atmosphere, dense water sinks in the oceans. It's this sinking of dense water that starts deep water currents moving. The density of ocean water depends on three things: salinity, temperature, and sediment content.

Pass the Salt

In Chapter 1 you found that different parts of the ocean contain different amounts of salt. When you did the activity on page E54, you investigated two water samples with different salinities and saw that salt increases the density of water. In fact, the more salt there is in a body of water, the more dense the water becomes.

▲ At the Strait of Gibraltar, less salty water from the Atlantic flows into the Mediterranean Sea above the saltier water that is flowing out into the Atlantic.

For centuries, sailors and scientists watched water flow constantly into the Mediterranean Sea without increasing the water depth. They couldn't figure out where the extra water went. It wasn't until the late 1600s that a deep density current moving from the Mediterranean Sea into the Atlantic Ocean was discovered.

What causes this current? The hot, dry air above the Mediterranean Sea makes surface water evaporate. The surface water that remains becomes saltier and therefore more dense. This dense, salty water sinks and then flows into the Atlantic Ocean. The less salty water in the Atlantic flows into the Mediterranean Sea on the surface. The result is a surface current and a deep current that move in opposite directions.

Running Hot and Cold

If you poured cold water into a tub of warm water, what do you think would happen? Although some mixing occurs, the cold water would tend to sink below the warm water. That's because cold water is more dense than warm water.

Some deep currents begin in the icy-cold waters near the North and South poles. Water near the poles is very dense, in part because it is so cold but also because it is very salty. When water freezes, as it does near the poles, most of the salt stays behind in the unfrozen water. This dense polar water sinks to the ocean floor and flows under warmer water toward the equator.

Two of these deep currents are shown in the diagram. Notice that the Antarctic Bottom Water flows from the South Pole under the North Atlantic Deep Water, which begins near Greenland. The Antarctic Bottom Water is the coldest, densest water in all the oceans. Some of the water from these deep currents moves slowly toward the equator, warms, and rises slowly toward the surface. Then it begins to flow back toward the pole it came from. However, some of the water stays near the bottom and may circle there for as long as a thousand years!

The area of contact between the Antarctic Bottom Water and the North Atlantic Deep Water is indicated by a light blue wavy boundary. The Antarctic Bottom Water is so cold and dense that most of it is forced to the bottom. However, some of the Antarctic water flows near the surface, warms a little, and flows above the North Atlantic water. ▼

Here in the Antarctic, the coldest, densest water in the oceans sinks to the bottom and begins to flow north. ▼

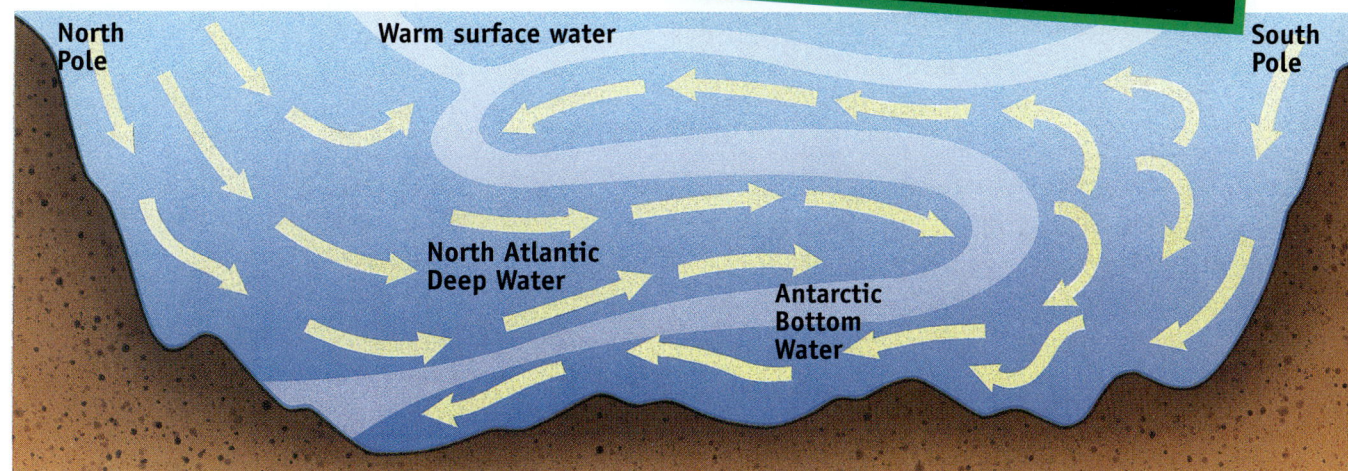

E59

Nutrients, such as zooplankton (*inset*), that are brought to the surface by upwelling currents are eaten by some of the world's largest organisms (*above*).

Water From the Depths

In some coastal areas, winds blow surface water away from the shore. This forces deep currents to flow up and replace the surface water. The rising of deep water to the surface is called **upwelling**.

In the ocean, minerals and detritus—bits of shells and dead organisms—constantly drift down to the ocean floor. An upwelling of cold water carries them back up to the surface where they provide phytoplankton and zooplankton with nourishment. The phytoplankton and zooplankton, in turn, nourish many other kinds of ocean life. This is why areas of upwelling often have abundant sea life.

Upwelling is constant in the Antarctic seas, where cooling surface water sinks and is replaced by warmer water from below. Here, upwelling supports a food chain that begins with phytoplankton, zooplankton, and krill. This food chain goes on to include hundreds of thousands of whales, tens of millions of seals, and hundreds of millions of birds.

Off the coasts of Chile and Peru, upwelling supports the fishing industries by bringing up food for fish. But when the warm El Niño current flows in this area, it prevents the normal upwelling of nutrients since upwelling cannot occur where there is warm surface water. The

UNIT PROJECT LINK

During a stay at the undersea lodge, one-day side trips in the deep-diving vehicle will be offered to visitors. Refer to the world map of ocean currents on page E56. Plan a number of trips from the lodge. Take into account how deep-sea currents affect sea life, visibility, and the stability of the vehicle. Where will you go and what will be seen? Make a map of the routes, using pushpins and labels to explain your choices.

◀ Since the ocean has been used as a dumping ground for wastes, it's important to know how currents are going to move those wastes.

zooplankton have nothing to feed on, so they die. Once the zooplankton die, small fish have nothing to feed on. They leave the coast, and the fishing business is affected until the El Niño shifts again.

Dense Sediment

Have you ever dropped a pebble into a pond? If so, you know it sinks to the bottom. Pebbles, sand, and other sediments are denser than water. When sediment mixes with ocean water, it can sink to form a **turbidity current**.

Turbidity currents form when earthquakes or flood waters flowing from rivers into the ocean send large amounts of sediment into the ocean. As the sediment slides down the continental slope toward the ocean floor, it forms an underwater avalanche that can travel up to 80 km/h (50 mph).

As the turbidity current moves, the swirling sediment erodes the ocean floor. According to some scientists, it's possible that turbidity currents actually were responsible for carving out the steep walls of underwater canyons found on the ocean bottom. Unlike other deep currents, turbidity currents are only temporary. After the turbidity current reaches the ocean floor, it slows down, and the sediment settles out.

Scientists study deep currents to learn how they affect surface currents, ocean life, and weather. Since the ocean floor is being considered as a dumping ground for wastes, the more scientists know about deep currents, the better they will be able to predict the possible movement and spread of those wastes. ■

INVESTIGATION 1

1. What role does wind play in creating currents?

2. How are surface currents and deep currents alike? How are they different?

INVESTIGATION 2

WHAT CAUSES OCEAN WAVES?

You sit on a sandy beach and watch the waves crash against the shore. The next day, the surface of the water is calm, and waves gently lap your feet as you walk along the beach. Why does the force of the waves vary from day to day? How are ocean waves formed?

Activity
Making Waves

You saw in Investigation 1 how steadily blowing winds result in the world's ocean currents. Wind can cause another, more familiar movement of surface water.

MATERIALS
- rectangular pan
- water
- cardboard
- metric ruler
- *Science Notebook*

Procedure

1. Fill a pan with water until the water reaches a level 2 cm from the top.

Step 1

Step 2

2. Hold a piece of cardboard at about a 45° angle to the water's surface. Blow gently down the side of the cardboard. **Record** your observations in your *Science Notebook*.

3. Predict what would happen if you blew harder down the side of the cardboard. **Test** your prediction and **record** your observations.

4. Predict how the waves will be affected if you blow on the water for a longer period of time. **Test** your prediction and **record** your observations.

Analyze and Conclude

1. How were waves produced?

2. How did the waves vary in steps 2, 3, and 4? What caused the variation?

3. Based on your observations, **hypothesize** how the creation of waves differs from the creation of currents.

4. Name two factors that affect the size of ocean waves.

INVESTIGATE FURTHER!

EXPERIMENT

Predict how an island might affect the size of waves. Use a larger or smaller pan and add an "island." Then retry the activity and describe what happens.

Activity
Wave Motion

How do the particles of water move within a wave?

MATERIALS
- goggles
- spring toy
- string
- ribbon
- tape
- meterstick
- *Science Notebook*

SAFETY
Wear goggles during this activity.

Procedure

1. With a piece of string, tie one end of a spring toy to a doorknob.

2. Pull the spring so that it is as taut and parallel to the floor as possible. Have your partner tie a short piece of ribbon to one of the loops in the middle of the spring. Mark the position of the ribbon by placing tape on the floor beneath the ribbon. **Measure** the height of the ribbon knot above the floor.

3. Slowly shake the spring up and down to form a wave. Watch the movement of the ribbon as the wave moves along the spring. **Observe** how the ribbon moves relative to the tape. Form waves of different heights to confirm your observations. Each time, have a student **measure** the height of the wave and **record** these observations in your *Science Notebook* in a chart like the one below. **Sketch** what you observe.

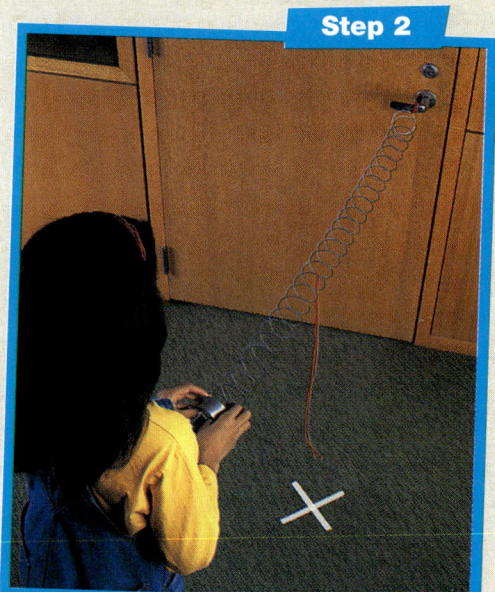
Step 2

Wave Trial	Height	Observations
1		
2		
3		
4		

Analyze and Conclude

1. How did the ribbon move with the wave?

2. **Infer** from your observations how the water particles in a wave move.

3. How did the height of the wave affect the movement of the ribbon?

What Are Waves?

If you've ever jumped into a pool or visited the ocean, you've seen the water's surface move up and down. These up-and-down movements in the ocean are called **waves**.

Measuring Waves

The top of a wave is called the **crest**. A wave's height is the distance from the crest to the level ocean surface. The distance between two successive waves is the **wavelength**. Both height and wavelength can vary for ocean waves.

It is also possible to measure how fast a wave is moving. A **period** is the time it takes for two successive wave crests to pass the same point. The periods for ocean waves usually range from 2 to 20 seconds. This means that the speeds of waves range from 11 to 113 km/h (7 to 70 mph). Most ocean waves travel at about 56 km/h (35 mph).

Movement of Waves

How do the water particles in a wave move? In the activity on page E64, you used a ribbon tied to a spring to model one of these particles. You should have inferred that water particles do not move forward with a wave. Look at the particles represented by circles in the diagram. As the wave passes by, the particles roll in a somersault but end up back where they started. Water particles near the surface turn the biggest somersaults. The motion of the particles decreases as the depth increases.

What controls how big waves get? Think back to when you modeled wind blowing on the ocean on pages E62 and E63. What created the biggest waves?

The harder the wind blows, the higher the waves become. A wind of 48 km/h (30 mph) can cause waves 4.5 m (15 ft) high. The highest wave ever measured

As a wave approaches shore, the wave falls over, or breaks. ▼

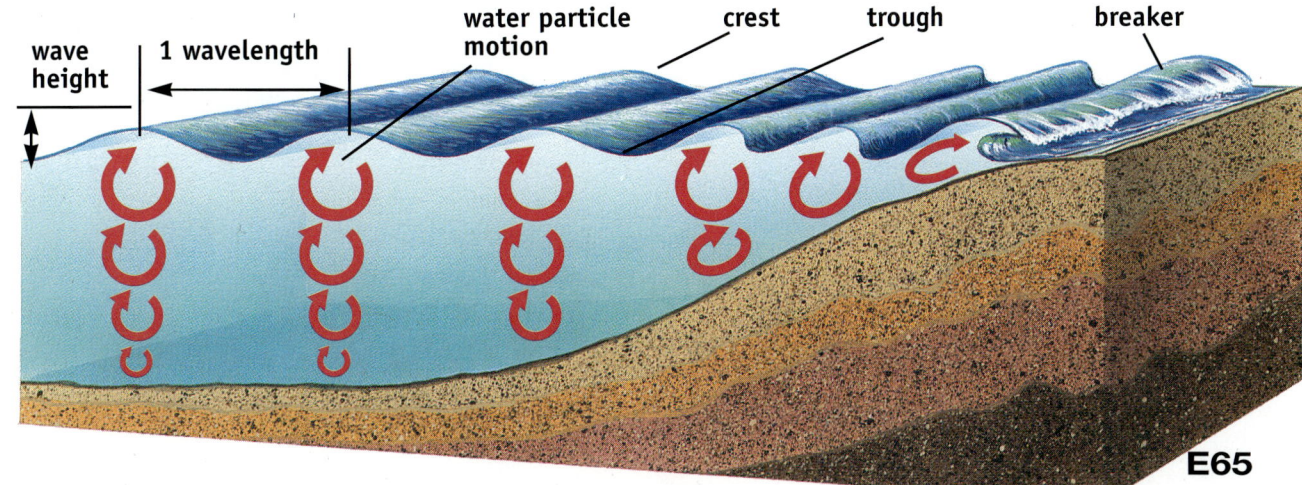

was during a severe storm with winds of more than 88 km/h (55 mph). The wave reached 34 m (112 ft) high, as tall as a ten-story building.

The size of a wave also depends on how long the wind blows and how far it blows. The distance the wind blows over open water is called the **fetch**. The longer the wind blows and the longer the fetch, the bigger the waves become.

When the wind blows hard, the crest of a wave can outrun the lower part. This makes the crest fall forward and break into foam, called a whitecap.

When waves travel from a windy part of the ocean to a calmer area, their crests may become lower and smoother. These waves, called swells, are far apart and can have a wavelength of as much as 1 km (0.6 mi). Swells can travel long dis-

▲ Wind can generate huge storm waves.

tances, even passing from one ocean to another since all oceans are connected.

SCIENCE AND FAITH

Big waves played a role in the lives of God's people on several occasions. The prophet Jonah didn't want to go where God wanted him to go. He didn't want to tell people in the city of Ninevah about God, so he boarded a boat heading in a different direction. Bad choice. A fierce storm tossed the ship mercilessly, and it was Jonah's fault. The sailors threw Jonah overboard to save their lives. The sea became calm once again, and Jonah reconsidered his obedience to God's command (Jonah 1:1–17).

In another incident many years later, Jesus' disciples climbed aboard a boat one evening. There was a stiff wind, and the waves were rough. The disciples rowed for miles when suddenly they saw an amazing sight. It was Jesus walking across the waves! As soon as Jesus stepped into the boat, the waves flattened and the water was calm (Matthew 14:22–33).

Jesus calms the storm of sin that threatens to wreck our

▲ Unless protected, homes near the shoreline are often in danger from storm-generated waves.

Waves and Land

Waves pick up and deposit sediment. Even gentle waves can combine with surface currents to move huge amounts of sand from place to place on beaches. During the winter, strong waves may wash away most of a beach's sand, leaving only gravel. The following summer, the waves slowly replace the sand.

During storms, waves can bring hundreds of tons of water crashing onto the shoreline, greatly eroding it. In France, storm waves once moved a 59,000-kg (65-ton) concrete block 20 m (65 ft). Powerful waves have been known to toss rocks weighing 45 kg (100 lbs).

Waves can be fun for surfing, for swimming, or just for watching. But because of all the energy they carry, they can also be very destructive. Later in this unit you'll find out how we have learned to harness the energy in waves.

INVESTIGATE FURTHER!

RESEARCH

Recall that tsunamis are huge ocean waves that can be extremely destructive as they approach land. Find out where these waves are most likely to occur and how people are warned about them. Report what you find out to the class.

INVESTIGATION 2

1. How are waves formed?

2. Would you expect larger waves to form from a wind with a fetch of 1 km or 3 km? Explain your answer.

WHAT CAUSES TIDES?

What never stops moving, is always going through a phase, is as old as the earth, and yet becomes new again each month? If you know the answer to this riddle, then you know what causes the tides to rise and fall each day!

Activity
Making a Tide Model

What does the Moon's position have to do with the tides?

MATERIALS
- 2 cardboard circles
- tape
- marker or pen
- string
- cardboard sheet
- *Science Notebook*

Procedure

1. Label one side of the larger circle with the numbers 1–4, as shown in the picture.

2. Use the larger circle to model Earth and the smaller circle to model the Moon. Place a sheet of cardboard on a level surface. Then place Earth in the center of the cardboard, with number 1 facing right. Tie the ends of a piece of string together and position it so the string evenly circles Earth. The string represents the ocean water on Earth.

3. Place the Moon outside the string 2–3 cm to the right of number 1. The Moon's gravity pulls on Earth's oceans, causing them to bulge outward on the side where the Moon is located and on

Step 1

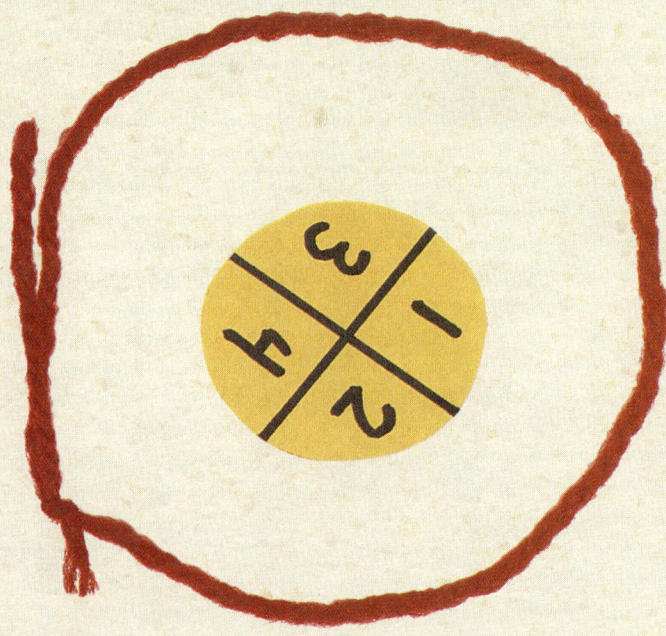

Step 3

the side away from the Moon. What results is that the oceans take on a different shape, shown in the picture. **Model** this by repositioning the string as shown.

4. On which two numbered sides of Earth is the ocean deepest (in other words, bulging out farthest)? **Record** your answer. These sides are experiencing high tide. The two sides where the ocean is shallowest are experiencing low tide.

5. Trace a circle around Earth. Rotate Earth counter-clockwise until 1 moves to the position 3 used to be in. Be careful to keep Earth within the tracing without disturbing the string. You have just **modeled** the passing of about 6 hours in Earth's rotation. Leave Earth in this position.

Analyze and Conclude

1. In step 3, what was the relationship between the Moon's position and the high tides?

2. Describe how the tide changed at position 1 on Earth in step 5.

3. Predict how many high tides position 1, starting from its current location, will experience after one complete rotation of Earth occurs. **Test** your prediction.

4. Suggest a hypothesis to explain how the Moon causes tides.

INVESTIGATE FURTHER!

EXPERIMENT

Now consider the Sun's position. Cut a circle about twice the size of Earth's circle. Make sure it lines up with Earth and the Moon. Infer what the effect will be on Earth's oceans when the Sun is in this position. (Hint: Think about how the Moon causes tides.)

The Moon, Sun, and Tides

The level of the oceans in a given place changes every day. These daily rises and falls in the ocean level are called **tides**. But did you know that tides are connected to the same force that causes falling leaves to drop to the ground?

Tides and the Moon's Gravity

It is the force of gravity that causes tides. In the tide model you constructed on pages E68 and E69, you probably inferred that the Moon's gravity pulls on Earth's oceans. The Moon's gravity pulls on the solid parts of Earth, too, but the effects of the pull are seen only in the rise and fall of water levels. Tides occur not only in oceans but in large rivers and bays as well.

The Moon's gravity pulls most strongly on the water facing the Moon, since this water is closest to the Moon. As a result, a bulge in the ocean called high tide occurs. At the same time, the Moon's gravity pulls Earth itself away from the water on the opposite side of Earth. So a second bulge, or another high tide, occurs at the same time on the opposite side of Earth.

Because Earth rotates on its axis every 24 hours, most shores have two high tides a day. One high tide occurs when the Moon is on the same side of Earth as that shore. The second high tide occurs when the Moon is on the other side of Earth. Notice on the diagram that water is pulled away from the areas between the two high tides. As a result, most shores also have two low tides a day.

Actually, as Earth rotates, the Moon is moving in its orbit. It takes 24 hours and 50 minutes for a particular place in the ocean to pass under the Moon twice. This means that the tide pattern repeats itself every 24 hours and 50 minutes rather than every 24 hours.

The Sun's Role

The Sun's gravity also pulls on Earth. Although the Sun is much bigger than the Moon, it is also much farther away from Earth. Because of this greater distance,

◀ The side of Earth facing the Moon experiences high tide. At the same time, a second high tide occurs on the other side of Earth.

▲ Spring tide

▲ Neap tide

the effect of the Sun's pull is less than that of the Moon's pull in producing tides.

You know that the Moon moves around Earth and Earth moves around the Sun. As a result, their positions are always changing. The Moon, Earth, and Sun line up twice a month—when the Moon is full and when it is new. During this time, the Moon and Sun pull together on Earth's oceans, much like two people pulling on a tug-of-war rope. The result is high tides that are very high and low tides that are very low. These extreme tides are called **spring tides**. (Here, *spring* refers to the "springing up" of the water, not the spring season.)

When the Sun and Moon are at a 90° angle with Earth, they no longer pull in the same direction. The pull of the Sun works against the pull of the Moon. As a result, high tides are not so high and low tides are not so low. These less extreme tides are called **neap tides**. Like spring tides, neap tides occur twice each month, when the Moon is in its first quarter and its third quarter phases. (In the activity you did on pages E68 and E69, how could you have modeled a neap tide?)

People and Tides

Tide charts have been developed to show the times for high and low tides each day at specific shores. Boaters and shell seekers check these charts to find out the best times to launch their boats or visit the beach. Special warnings are

The success of the D-Day invasion was dependent upon landing Allied troops during the lowest possible tide. On June 5 and 6, 1944, those conditions existed. The invasion took place on June 6, 1944.

issued for storms that occur during high tides.

During World War II, the timing of the tides determined the date and time of the D-Day invasion. On June 6, 1944, the Allied forces landed on the beaches at Normandy, France. The invasion was planned for the lowest tide possible. That way, much of the beach would be exposed to make the landing safer.

The difference between the water levels at high tide and low tide is called the tidal range. In the open ocean, the tidal range is about 0.55 m (1.8 ft). When the incoming tide has room to spread out, as in the Gulf of Mexico, the tidal range may be only a few centimeters. Sometimes the incoming tide is forced into a small bay with steep sides. In this case, the water level may rise as much as 18 m (60 ft) during high tide. In addition, the tidal range at one place can change from one season to the next.

Century after century, the tides follow their own schedules, determined by the relative positions of the Moon, the Sun, and Earth. They are one of God's tremendous forces, powerful enough to move entire oceans of water. ■

The tidal range at the Abbey of Mont St. Michel in France is particularly dramatic. Twice a day, the Abbey becomes a secluded island.

INVESTIGATION 3

1. Use a sketch to show how the Moon's gravity causes tides on Earth.

2. How many low tides do most shore areas on Earth have during two days and two nights? Explain your answer.

CHAPTER 3 REVIEW: REFLECT & EVALUATE

WORD POWER

crest
current
fetch
neap tide
period
spring tide
Coriolis effect
turbidity current
tides
trade winds
upwelling
wavelength
waves
westerlies

On Your Own
Review the terms in the list. Then use as many terms as you can to write a brief summary of the chapter.

With a Partner
Use the terms in the list to make a word-search puzzle. See if your partner can find the hidden terms and tell you what each one means.

Write a news report about the water movements and changes you might observe at a beach during a 24-hour period.

Analyze Information
Study the drawing. Then name the ocean feature shown and describe how it forms.

Assess Performance
Design a way of modeling a turbidity current. Outline the materials you would use and the procedure you would follow. After your teacher has approved your outline, create your model.

Problem Solving

1. How can surface currents both aid and hinder the movement of ships?

2. Describe how a toy boat floating on the ocean would move as a wave passed by.

3. Lakes have tides, but we often don't notice because their tidal range is so small. Would you expect a lake's tidal range to be more noticeable during a spring tide or a neap tide? Explain your answer.

4. What do "wave stories" (Jonah 1:1-17; Matthew 14:22-33) tell you about God?

CHAPTER 4

OCEAN RESOURCES

Many useful things come from the oceans—food, valuable minerals, sources of energy, and even fresh water. Yet much of this vast resource is being destroyed by pollution. What can you do to help save the oceans?

Learning About Our Friends

You may be aware of an ocean mammal that is popular with people—the incredible dolphin! People have come to have a special relationship with these playful mammals. Their intelligence and memory rank with the chimpanzees and the elephants.

In the photograph young Steven Clever listens in on "dolphin talk" at the Dolphin Quest Learning Center on the Big Island of Hawaii. The clicks he hears are sonar signals, which enable a dolphin to locate objects at night or in murky water.

Each year thousands of children visit this educational center. They learn that a great number of dolphins face the threat of death from toxic chemicals and garbage that is thrown into the water. This pollution occurs most often near the coastline homes of dolphins. Protecting the ocean helps protect the environment of these fascinating creatures.

Coming Up

WHAT RESOURCES CAN THE OCEANS PROVIDE?
.... E76

HOW DOES POLLUTION AFFECT THE OCEANS AND THEIR RESOURCES?
.... E88

▲ Steven Clever and his new friends at the Dolphin Quest Learning Center

INVESTIGATION 1

WHAT RESOURCES CAN THE OCEANS PROVIDE?

There are many useful things that come from the sea. Did you know that ice cream and pudding contain a product that comes from plantlike organisms in the ocean? There are even farms floating on the sea that may provide some of your food. Find out about resources from the ocean in this investigation.

Activity

What You See From the Sea

Materials made from ocean resources are all around you. How many can you spot?

MATERIALS
- magazines
- newspapers
- scissors
- glue
- markers
- posterboard
- *Science Notebook*

Procedure

Look around the classroom. Do you see anything you use that comes from the sea? Can you think of anything else you use that comes from the sea? Look around the rest of the building and your home. In your *Science Notebook* **make a list** of everything you find that comes from the sea. Be creative and make a poster to present your list.

Analyze and Conclude

1. How many items were you able to think of? How do the items on your list compare with items other students listed?

2. Make an **inference** regarding the importance of the sea to your life, based on all the observations your class made.

E76

Activity
Desalination

The ocean can be used as a fresh-water resource. How difficult is it to remove salt from ocean water?

MATERIALS
- goggles
- sample of ocean water
- glass bowl or beaker
- clear glass plate
- lamp
- *Science Notebook*

SAFETY
Wear goggles during this activity. The lamp will get very hot. Avoid touching the bulb or the lampshade at all times.

Procedure

1. Pour a small amount of ocean water into a beaker. Cover the beaker with a plate.

2. Place the beaker under a lamp so that it is just below the lamp bulb. Turn on the lamp. Be careful not to touch the bulb or the lampshade.

Step 2

3. Leave the lamp on for 30 minutes.

4. Shut the lamp off and allow the setup to cool for 15 minutes. **Record** any changes you observe in the setup.

Analyze and Conclude

1. What collected on the plate? **Infer** how the matter differs from the ocean water and how it got on the plate.

2. How do you think your setup differs from a large-scale method to produce fresh water from ocean water? Could you use your method to efficiently produce fresh water from sea water? Why or why not?

E77

Activity
Obtaining Energy

What kinds of energy might the oceans provide?

MATERIALS
- posterboard
- markers
- construction paper
- cardboard
- wood splints
- glue
- tape
- scissors
- *Science Notebook*

SAFETY
Use care when handling scissors.

Procedure

1. Think of all the ways energy is produced. What raw materials are needed? What kinds of equipment are used to change the raw materials to usable forms of energy? In your *Science Notebook* **list** as many forms of energy as you can.

2. Think about oceans and their resources. **Hypothesize** about what untapped forms of energy there might be in the ocean. Be creative when listing ideas for obtaining energy from the oceans.

3. Choose one energy-source idea and **create a model** or a poster about it. Use any materials available. Be prepared to present your model or poster to the class. **Explain** what you are using from the ocean and how you plan to convert it to energy that people can use.

Step 3

Analyze and Conclude

1. Describe any problems you think your energy source may have that might keep it from being used. For example, is it practical for people living far inland as well as for people living near the ocean?

2. Which idea presented by your classmates do you think is the best idea? **Explain** your answer.

UNIT PROJECT LINK

The oceans provide a great variety of food products, including fish, shellfish, and seaweed. Research which life forms thrive near the site of your undersea lodge. Could some of these forms of life provide ocean farming products? Which ones? Why do you think so? Add pushpins and labels to your map to show possible areas for ocean farms. Also, diagram an idea you have for aquaculture technology. For example, you might show where and how young fish can be confined and fed until they mature.

Treasures From the Sea

With some practice, most people can learn to catch a fish. All you have to do is stand in the water, wait until a big one swims by, and scoop it up. That's how bears catch salmon in Alaska; it's also how ancient people caught fish.

Food from the Sea

Today commercial fishing is much different from what it was in the past. If you were the captain of a modern fishing boat, you'd use sonar to find a school of fish, such as herring. The crew would spread huge nets in the water and then haul the whole school on board at once. No fuss, no muss—your ship could catch up to 36,400 kg (about 40 T) in one grab, enough to make fish dinners for 40,000 people! That school of herring has met its match!

What's the point? Well, seafood is probably the single most important resource we obtain from the ocean. In fact, more than half the protein eaten in Japan comes from the ocean.

Although some countries, such as the United States, may not depend on the ocean quite so heavily, the ocean is still an important source of food. What different kinds of seafood did you include on your list in the activity on page E76?

Modern fishing methods, like sonar, have almost made us *too* good at fishing. Many species of sea life have been overfished putting those species in danger of becoming extinct. Today, many fishing countries are reducing the amount of fish taken to protect this food resource before some species are gone.

▲ Humans are not alone in harvesting the treasures of the sea. We share what is available with a wide variety of plants and animals.

▲ Increasing demand for food worldwide has created a need for fish farming.

▲ As world population increases, the need for fresh water will probably force us to rely on desalination plants.

In addition to reducing the rate at which some species are being depleted, scientists hope to find alternative methods of obtaining ocean resources for food. A method called **aquaculture** (ak′wə kul chər), or ocean farming, will help the world meet growing food needs without overfishing. Aquaculture involves raising animals and seaweed in closed-off areas of the oceans and other waters. Organisms being farmed include lobsters, salmon, kelp, oysters, and mussels.

"Water, water everywhere, nor any drop to drink."

As Earth's population continues to increase, the rate at which fresh water is being used also is increasing. That's why, with so many oceans surrounding us, getting fresh water from salt water seems like a reasonable goal.

Obtaining fresh water from salt water is called **desalination** (dē sal ə nā′shən). However, only a few nations currently operate desalination plants. In the activity on page E77, the method that you used to remove salt from water was not very efficient. Large-scale operations are more efficient but they involve tremendous start-up and running costs. Often the cost of the energy needed to desalinate the ocean water would make the fresh water too expensive.

There is another possible source of fresh water in the oceans. Of all Earth's water, less than 3 percent is fresh, and 77 percent of this water is locked up in icecaps and glaciers. So it might make sense to attach cables to icebergs, tow them to where the water is needed, and pump the ice ashore as slush.

Common Chemicals from the Sea

In addition to water, what other chemicals do the oceans provide? About 30 percent of the world's salt supply comes directly from sea water. Giant factories along some coasts extract it by evaporating the ocean water.

More than 99 percent of the world's supply of bromine comes from the oceans. It's used in the manufacture of gasolines, dyes, medicines, and metals.

Even ocean food sources provide more than just food. For example, seaweed and kelp have been important foods in the Far East for hundreds of years. But seaweed provides other valuable products, too. Red seaweed yields agar, a product that dissolves in boiling water to make a clear gel. As a food additive, agar is used in canned meat, cake icing, candy, pet food, and any number of other foods. It's good for coating pills and for making cosmetics and is used in medical laboratories to grow bacteria, molds, and tissues. Brown seaweed produces alginic acid, which is used as a thickener in ice cream, jellies and pie fillings, salad dressings, shampoos, fabric dyes, plastics, rubber, and paints.

Animals from the sea make many nonfood contributions. Blowfish toxin is a perfect example. If eaten, it can kill in 30 minutes. Yet when used medically, it is an extremely powerful painkiller. Another substance, produced by sea cucumbers, reduces tumors and may someday be used to fight cancer. The inedible parts of fish, including bones, are ground up for use in fertilizers and livestock feed.

Minerals and Fossil Fuels

Even the mud and ooze on the bottom of the oceans and seas are rich in resources. The floor of the Red Sea is covered with mud that contains tons of iron, zinc, copper, and silver, worth billions of dollars. Although these resources can't yet be mined because of the expense, scientists are researching ways to remove these materials cheaply.

When you ride in a car, you may be using another ocean resource. More than 20 percent of the world's oil and gas reserves are located under the ocean floor. From offshore oil rigs, workers drill down through sediment and rock to reach reserves of these fossil fuels. In addition to gasoline, chemicals taken from oil are used to make more than 3,000 products, including heating oil, plastics, detergents, and shampoos.

Think back to the list you created in the activity on page E76. How many of the treasures from the sea mentioned here did you include on your list? ■

▲ Alginic acid, which is obtained from brown kelp (*inset*), is used in the manufacture of products such as those shown here.

◀ Agar, which is obtained from red kelp (*inset*), is used in the manufacture of products such as those shown here.

Treasures Through Time

You may enjoy eating fish or even wearing jewelry made from shells. But did you know that people have been mining the oceans for thousands of years? Ocean resources have been considered valuable treasures for a very long time! Explore some of them in this time line.

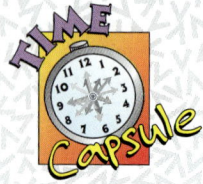

100 B.C.
Native American women in the Pacific Northwest gather foods from the sea floor.

By carrying large stones that make them sink to the sea floor, divers gather pearls in the Mediterranean Sea.
1000 B.C.

30 A.D.
Jesus recruits fishermen to "fish" for people.

1400 A.D.
Early forms of aquaculture are practiced along the coast of Indonesia.

2700 B.C.
Poisonous fish are used as medicine in China.

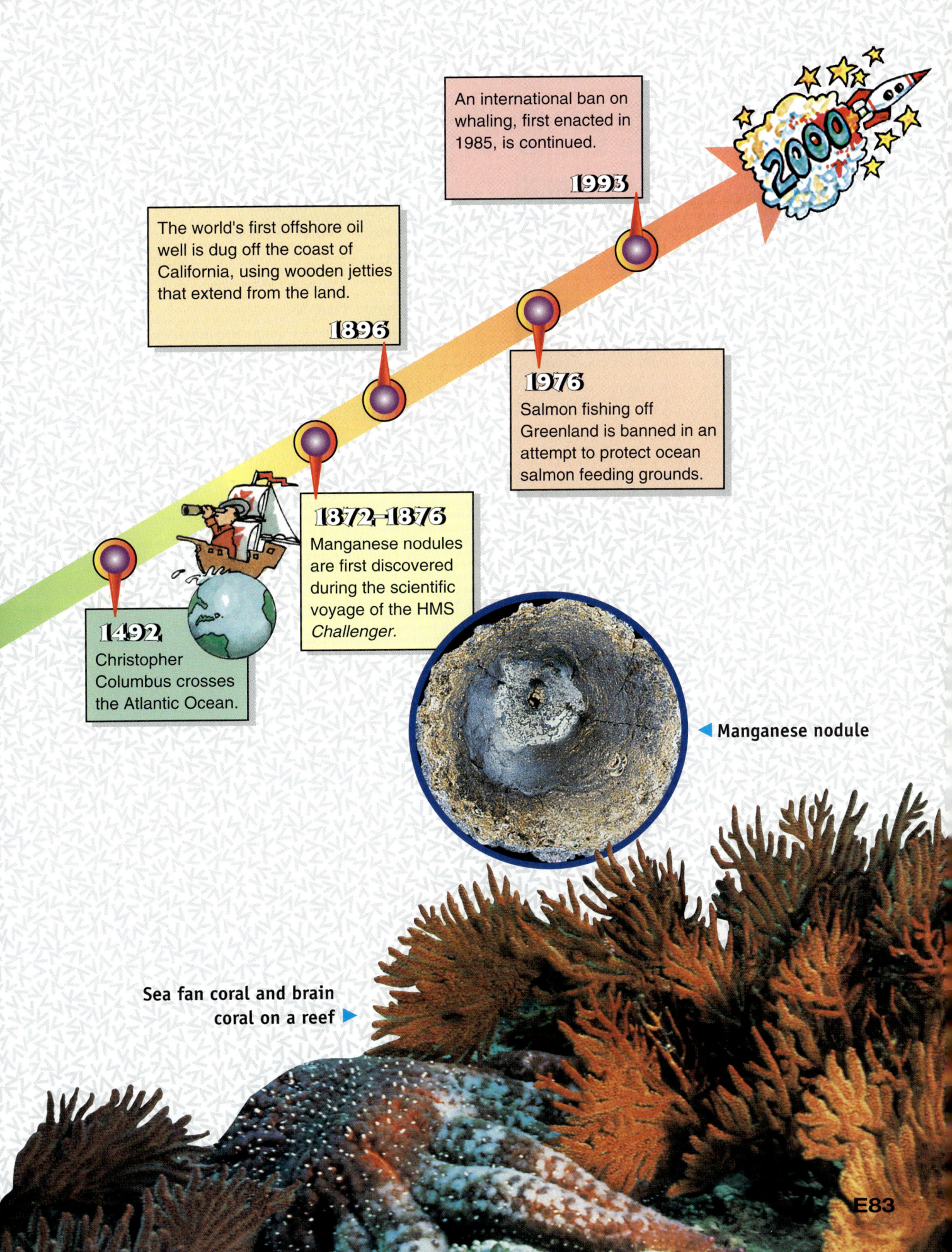

Energy and the Sea

▲ Just standing in a breaking wave can give you an idea of the tremendous energy that waves contain.

For centuries people have stood on the ocean shore, marveled at the majesty of the waves, and dreamed of using that raw power. But other energy sources were cheaper and easier to use. Over the last few decades, however, the prices of coal, oil, and gas have soared, and some people have started looking to the sea for new sources of energy.

Power from the Waves

The Sun, winds, and oceans all produce enormous amounts of energy. So how do we harness all of this power? Recall that waves form when ocean water receives energy from the wind. If you have ever been swimming in the ocean, you know about the energy and power of waves. Water in a breaking wave can knock you over! So it makes sense to conclude that there is usable energy in waves.

Modern computers can calculate how much energy a moving section of ocean water should be able to provide.

① **The ducks** ride the ocean surface, with the angled sides facing incoming waves. A rounded bottom dangles beneath the surface.

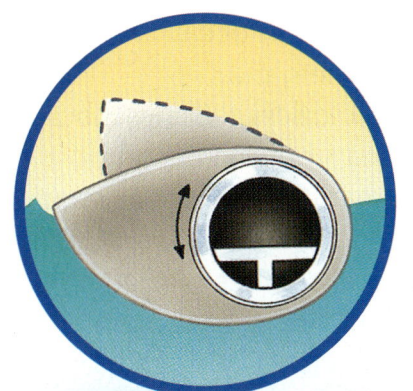

2 **Incoming waves** hit the hollow, concrete ducks; the angled sides tilt up, absorb the wave's energy, and then drop back down. So much of the wave's energy is absorbed that calm water is left behind the ducks. The energy of the bobbing movement turns a shaft running through a line of ducks.

Salter's Ducks

3 **Inside the shaft**, the absorbed energy moves oil through an engine, driving an electric generator. An 800-m (0.5-mi) string of ducks could supply energy for a city of 85,000 people.

The energy stored in 1 m (3 ft) of a typical wave in the Atlantic Ocean could provide about 70 kilowatts (kW) of power, enough to run 70 electric heaters. But several problems must be solved before that energy can be used.

First, obtaining energy from waves is 10 to 20 times more expensive than obtaining energy from other sources. Second, waves are rarely of a constant size for long periods of time, so their power is never constant. Additionally, even in calm areas of the ocean, storms can create waves capable of destroying even the strongest of energy collection devices in just a few minutes or hours. Third, no one has yet thought of a way to store wave energy for later use.

Nevertheless, many ideas for harnessing wave energy are being tested. A promising one involves Salter's ducks, devices named after their inventor, Stephen Salter. Study the diagrams to see how these devices work.

E85

OTEC

Other devices now being tested can take advantage of relatively small differences in ocean water temperatures. The method of using temperature differences to get energy from ocean water is called Ocean Thermal Energy Conversion, or OTEC.

In tropical areas the Sun may heat the ocean surface water to 27°C (81°F). But ocean water found at a depth of 610 m (2,000 ft) or more may be much colder. As shown in the drawing, the difference in temperature between the water at the ocean's surface and the deep water can be harnessed to power an engine that produces electricity.

Methane

As you have learned, the oceans are a major source of oil and natural gas. These fossil fuels are found in sediments and rocks below the ocean floor. But another kind of gas may be obtained from organisms living in ocean waters. This gas is called methane.

Methane is a colorless, odorless, burnable gas produced from the decomposition of organic matter. Rotting seaweed (such as kelp) and other kinds of algae are especially good sources of methane gas, since they are rich in hydrogen and carbon, the components of methane.

A Navy scientist, Howard Wilcox, has come up with a plan for growing kelp for use in making methane gas. He proposes that kelp be grown in open-ocean farms anchored on a series of plastic lines up to 31 m (102 ft) below the ocean surface. Wilcox believes that up to 50 percent of the energy in the kelp can be turned into methane fuel. An ocean farm of about 400 km^2 (154 mi^2) could provide enough methane gas to power a city of 500,000 people.

Think back to the activity you did on page E78. Did you think of any methods

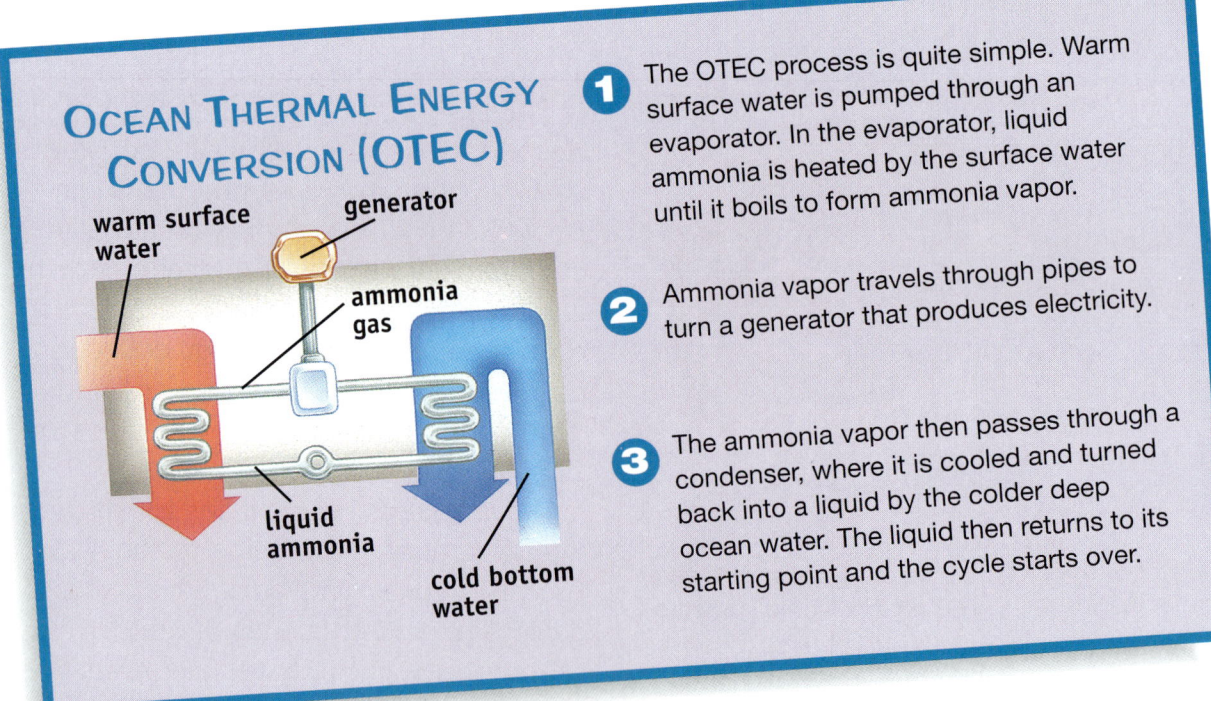

OCEAN THERMAL ENERGY CONVERSION (OTEC)
- warm surface water
- generator
- ammonia gas
- liquid ammonia
- cold bottom water

1. The OTEC process is quite simple. Warm surface water is pumped through an evaporator. In the evaporator, liquid ammonia is heated by the surface water until it boils to form ammonia vapor.

2. Ammonia vapor travels through pipes to turn a generator that produces electricity.

3. The ammonia vapor then passes through a condenser, where it is cooled and turned back into a liquid by the colder deep ocean water. The liquid then returns to its starting point and the cycle starts over.

▲ As you can see in these pictures, the power of water cannot be overestimated. How can tidal energy be harnessed?

for obtaining energy from the ocean that are similar to the ones mentioned here?

Tidal Energy

An ancient myth tells of a king who thought he had grown so powerful he could command the seas. So he went to the ocean's edge, told the tide to stop moving . . . and drowned.

Unlike the king, modern scientists know they can't control the tides. But they have made astonishing progress toward finding ways to use tidal energy. If there is at least a 4.6-m (15-ft) difference between low and high tide, scientists think that the ebb and flow can be harnessed to produce usable energy.

The best-known tidal energy project is a power plant built at the mouth of the Rance (räns) River in France. Known as the Rance Tidal Power Station, the plant consists of 24 separate tunnels, each facing the sea and built into a dam stretching 702 m (2,303 ft) across the river. As the tide moves upriver, the tidal water flows through the tunnels and builds up behind the dam. At peak high tide the water is released and flows back to the sea, turning turbines connected to massive generators.

The Rance Power Station can generate up to 608 million kilowatt-hours (kWh) of electrical energy a year. However, the plant didn't pay its way at first and was almost shut down. Then in the 1970s, rising energy prices made its production costs seem more reasonable. ■

INVESTIGATION 1

1. Name six resources that come from the oceans.

2. Would tidal energy be a good source of energy for the town you live in? Why or why not?

INVESTIGATION 2

How Does Pollution Affect the Oceans and Their Resources?

You now know that the oceans are a very large and very valuable resource. Now consider that pollution is damaging large parts of that resource. Explore the effects of ocean pollution in this investigation.

Activity

Investigating Oil Spills

What problems do oil spills create? To find out, observe how oil affects water and a feather.

Procedure

1. Work with a partner. Half-fill one container with water.

2. **Predict** what will happen if you place a small drop of oil in the water. **Record** your prediction in your *Science Notebook*.

3. **Test your prediction**. Using a spoon, place a small drop of oil in the water. How does the oil behave? **Record** what you observe.

Step 1

MATERIALS
- goggles
- 3 small, clear plastic containers
- water
- cooking oil
- spoon
- lids for containers
- feather
- hand lens
- paper towels
- *Science Notebook*

SAFETY
Wear goggles. Clean up any spills immediately.

4. Place several more drops of oil in the water. Put the lid on the container, then carefully shake the container so that the water moves around. How do the oil and water interact? **Record** your observations. Save this container for the activity on page E90.

Step 4

5. Use a hand lens to examine a feather. **Record** your observations.

6. Fill another container with water. Soak the feather in the water for 1 minute. Remove it and blot it dry with a paper towel. Repeat step 5, using this feather.

7. Fill another container with oil to a depth of 1 cm. Soak the feather in the oil for 1 minute. Remove it and blot it dry with a paper towel. Repeat step 5, using this feather.

8. Dispose of the oil and water as directed by your teacher. Do not pour the oil and water down the drain.

Analyze and Conclude

1. From your observations, **infer** why it might be important to begin cleaning up an oil spill as soon as possible. What problems might a delay create?

2. What effect might an oil spill have on coastal birds?

3. Based upon your observations, **infer** why it is important to properly dispose of the oil used in this and the next activity. Why shouldn't you just pour it down the drain?

INVESTIGATE FURTHER!

EXPERIMENT

Predict the effect an oil spill might have on bird eggs in nests along the coast. Then test your prediction by soaking a hard-boiled egg in oil for 20 minutes. Remove the egg and blot it dry with a paper towel. Peel the egg and record your observations. Do not eat the egg.

E89

Activity
Cleaning Up the Mess

You've seen some of the problems oil spills create. What is the best way to clean up an oil spill?

MATERIALS
- container of oil and water from previous activity
- spoon
- cooking oil
- drinking straw
- plastic container
- paper towels
- cotton balls
- fabric scraps
- any other absorbant materials
- *Science Notebook*

SAFETY
Clean up any spills immediately.

Procedure

1. Use the container of oil and water from step 4 of the previous activity as your model oil spill. Add a few more drops of oil to the water.

2. Hypothesize as to a method you might use to clean up the oil. **Record** your hypothesis in your *Science Notebook*.

3. Experiment to test your cleanup method. Begin by describing the procedure in detail. Then use any of the materials available to test your method.

4. As you test your method, place any oil or oily materials in the empty container. **Report** on how effective your method was.

5. Repeat steps 2 and 3 two more times, using either different materials or procedures. If needed, add more oil to the water.

Analyze and Conclude

1. Describe how difficult it was to clean up the oil spill.

2. Which method worked best? Why?

3. Infer how difficult it might be to use your method or one similar to it to clean up an oil spill in the ocean.

Step 3

RESOURCE

Pollution of the Oceans

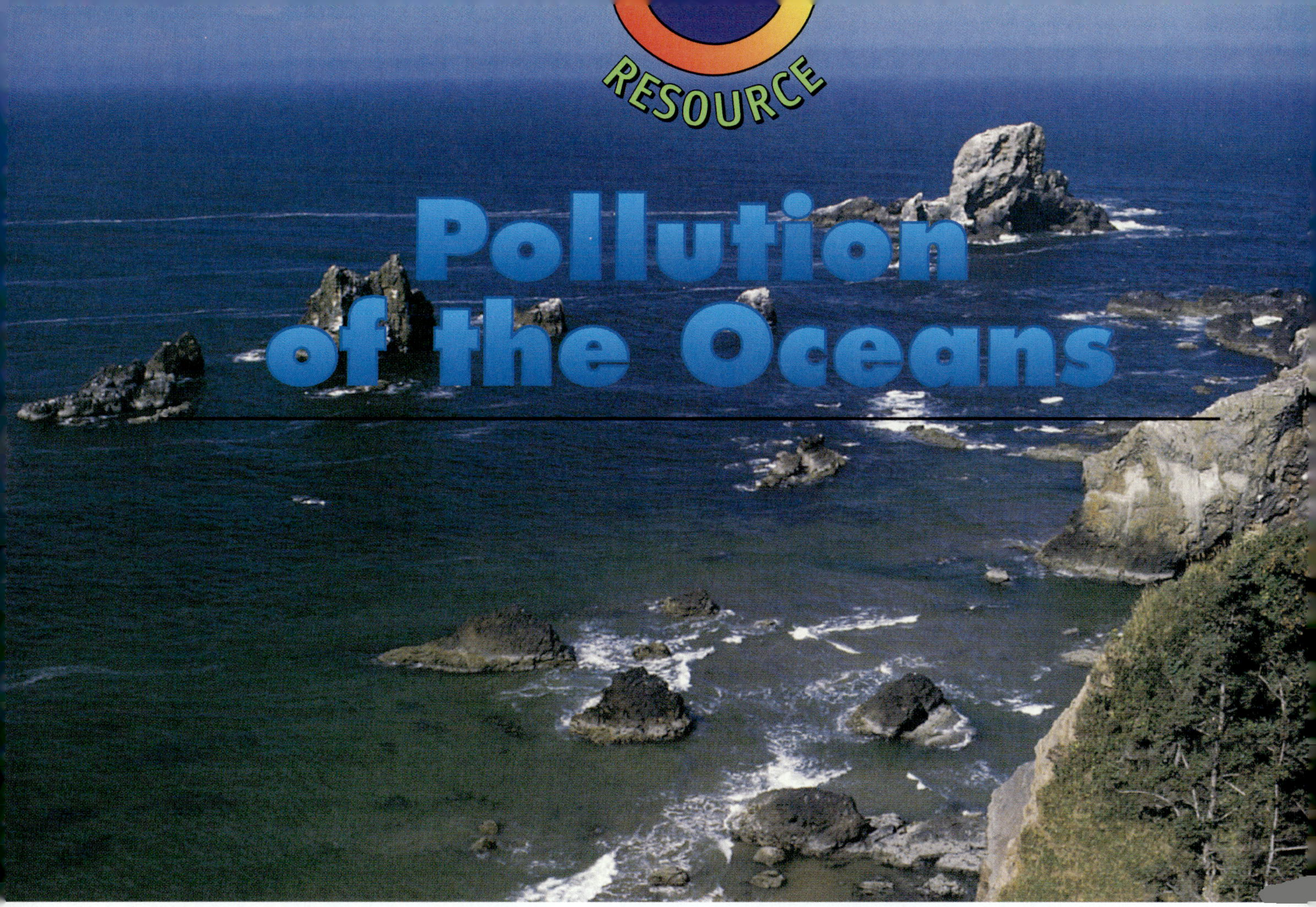

▲ This water may look pure, but the chances are very good that this water is polluted to some extent.

Pollution is the contamination of the environment with waste. When you realize that the water in practically every lake, river, and stream in the world eventually reaches the sea, it's not hard to figure out how our oceans become polluted.

For thousands of years, wastes, both liquid and solid, have been dumped into bodies of water. Even the waste thought to have been safely buried has found its way into underground streams and eventually to the oceans.

Since the nineteenth century, when people began mass-producing most goods, wastes from manufacturing have

Not all pollution is this obvious. Sometimes pollution is dissolved in the water and is impossible to see. ▼

been dumped into the oceans in larger and larger amounts. As a result, the oceans and the life forms in them have been disturbed in very serious ways.

The Chain of Ocean Life

The oceans contain important ecosystems, in which all organisms and the wastes of some varieties of life are used by other organisms. At the beginning of the ocean food chain are microscopic organisms called phytoplankton. They float in the ocean and use sunlight to produce energy, absorbing carbon dioxide from the ocean water and the water itself in the process. Microscopic animal-like organisms, called zooplankton, eat the phytoplankton, and then are eaten in turn by small fish and some whales. The small fish are consumed by larger fish, which may then be consumed by even larger fish, seals, dolphins, some whales, birds, and humans.

Pollutants taken in by some ocean organisms can be passed to others through the ocean's food chains. Thus the harmful effects spread through ocean ecosystems.

Pollution Sources

There are many different sources and kinds of ocean pollution. Ordinary people

God never wanted people to abuse His creation. Yet Earth abuse continues. Like other forms of abuse, polluting the oceans has serious consequences not only for marine life but also for humans. Many local and worldwide agencies and individuals have dedicated themselves to preventing pollution by urging adoption of laws. Others rush to help wildlife and to clean up after pollution disasters like oil spills.

One additional way every Christian can help with problems of pollution is by praying. We can ask God to bless the Earth with people who know how to use resources responsibly. We can also ask Him to bless people with ideas and skills to clean up pollution. The God who sent His Son to clean up our sins will also help us to clean up our environment.

▲ This photo, taken in Spring 1991 by shuttle astronauts 256 km (138 mi) above the Strait of Hormuz, dramatically shows the extent of oil spilled during the Gulf War. The light sheen on the water is oil that has been dumped into the Strait.

are responsible for pollution, for all towns and cities produce sewage, both treated and raw. Few, if any, major industries in the world are entirely nonpolluting—almost all generate waste. Even farmers contribute dangerous chemicals in the form of pesticides and fertilizers that eventually make their way into the oceans by way of streams and rivers.

Toxic pollutants are poisonous chemicals that can cause sickness or death. In the 1950s mercury was dumped from a factory into the ocean near the fishing village of Minamata, Japan. Contaminated fish that were caught and eaten by people of the village caused brain damage, physical deformities, and birth defects.

The effects of ocean pollution were never more terrible than in Minamata, Japan, where mercury pollution caused brain damage and physical deformities. ▼

E93

Ocean Oil Spills

Seemingly worst of all—but only because they are so much more visible than most forms of pollution—are the gigantic ocean spills of oil. When you modeled an oil spill on page E88, you inferred how oil spills can affect oceans.

Between 1967 and 1989, the 15 largest oil spills in the world spewed more than 14 million barrels of oil into the oceans. Most of the oil came from huge tankers rupturing on rocks or reefs. The best known occurred in 1989, when the *Exxon Valdez*, in a navigational error, ripped itself open on a reef in a huge, unspoiled bay in Alaska. Thousands of birds, fish, sea otters, whales, and dolphins died almost immediately by swallowing the oil. Others died slow deaths caused by respiratory distress or contamination of their fur or feathers.

Reducing Pollution!

Thankfully, many of the antipollution laws passed since the 1960s have had good results. Many industries have become extremely careful about adding more pollution to the oceans after realizing how serious the problem was. Now many areas along ocean shores, once badly polluted, are free of waste contamination. The pollution problem is not hopeless, though at times the outlook may seem bad.

As many people have noted, the only good way to deal with ocean pollution is to make sure it never happens. ■

Much of the pollution resulting from the *Exxon Valdez* accident has been cleaned up through the efforts of volunteers.

INVESTIGATION 2

1. Name three kinds of pollution that affect the oceans.

2. Describe why you do or do not think ocean pollution threatens the quality of all life on Earth.

REFLECT & EVALUATE

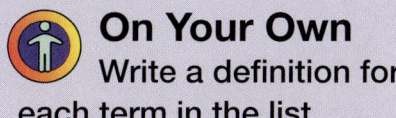

aquaculture
desalination
pollution

On Your Own Write a definition for each term in the list.

With a Partner Mix up the letters of each term in the list. Provide a clue for each term and challenge your partner to unscramble the terms.

Draw diagrams or create models showing ocean resources being obtained and later used. You might also create a display of different ways in which ocean resources are used.

Analyze Information

The photograph below shows one event involving pollution that might affect ocean life. Predict how this event might affect the entire food chain.

Assess Performance

Use the materials from the activities on pages E88 through E90 to design a method for limiting the spread of an oil spill during a cleanup operation. Be sure to take into account all the ways that the oily water might move throughout the ocean.

Problem Solving

1. If you were trapped on a deserted island, how might you use a variety of ocean resources in order to survive?

2. How might toxic ocean pollution and overfishing have a similar effect on ocean life?

3. Compare and contrast the way we use ocean resources today with the way people in the past used ocean resources.

4. What happens after pollution is cleaned up or when people stop polluting? What does this say about God's care of Earth?

INVESTIGATE FURTHER!

Throughout this unit you've investigated questions related to oceanography in these four chapters. How will you use what you've learned, and how will you share that information with others? Here are some ideas.

Hold a Big Event to Share Your Unit Project

Get ready to promote your vision of the undersea nature lodge. Cut a large opening in a big piece of cardboard. This will be the "picture window" that enables travelers in the deep-diving vehicle to observe the ocean environments. Use your knowledge of the oceans to create a "moving picture" of various kinds of ocean life, the effects of waves and currents, and the features of the ocean bottom as seen from inside the vehicle as it descends deeper into the ocean. Draw or paint the storyboards and tape them together in order. Next, prepare a taped narration to accompany the moving pictures. Set up on easels other posters and maps you have made. Now you're ready to go! As your classmates and guests watch, unroll the pictures and turn on the tape.

Research

In the past, many of the ocean food chains were harmed by the actions of humans. However, in recent years, people have been doing things to prevent further damage and to reverse the damage that has already been done. Read library books and magazine articles to find out what actions are being taken to protect the oceans and their food chains. Then present a report on the most appropriate and most effective.

Take Action

Substances on Earth's surface often end up being washed by rain into rivers, which then flow into the ocean. For one week, record everything on your small surface of Earth—your neighborhood—that may end up in the ocean. For example, you might include trash, oil spills, weed killer, or fertilizer. Combine your record with your classmates' records. Which substances from your community threaten the ocean? How? Create a poster ad to educate people about what they can do to protect the ocean.

FORCES AND MOTION

Theme: Scale

Get Ready to Investigate! F2

1 Moving On F4
Investigation 1   How Do You Describe Motion? F6
Investigation 2   How Do You Measure Speed? F12
Investigation 3   How Do You Describe Changes in Motion? F18

2 Getting a Grip on Gravity F28
Investigation 1   How Can the Force of Gravity Be Measured? F30
Investigation 2   Do All Objects Fall at the Same Rate? F36
Investigation 3   How Does Air Change the Rate at Which an Object Falls? F42

3 Making and Measuring Motion F52
Investigation 1   How Are Objects at Rest and Objects in Motion Alike? F54
Investigation 2   How Do Forces Affect Motion? F62
Investigation 3   How Does Friction Affect the Motion of Objects? .. F70

4 Forces in Pairs F78
Investigation 1   What Property Do All Moving Objects Share? F80
Investigation 2   How Do Actions Cause Reactions? F88
Investigation 3   How Are Action-Reaction Forces Used? F96

5 Real-World Forces F104
Investigation 1   How Do Heavy Things Fly? F106
Investigation 2   How Do Rockets Use Action-Reaction Forces? .. F114
Investigation 3   How Do Things Float? F120

Investigate Further! F128

GET READY TO

OBSERVE & QUESTION

How do you describe changes in motion?

Have you ever ridden a water slide? How would you describe what you feel on a water slide? What forces do you think affect you as you speed down a water slide? In this unit you will learn about the forces affecting motion.

EXPERIMENT & HYPOTHESIZE

How are objects at rest and objects in motion alike?

What do you think would happen to a wooden block sitting on the back of a truck when the driver suddenly hits the brakes? Activities in this unit will help you understand what happens and why.

INVESTIGATE!

RESEARCH & ANALYZE

As you investigate, find out more from these books.

- **Liftoff! An Astronaut's Dream** by R. Mike Mullane (Silver Burdett Press, 1995). Think you might like to experience what an astronaut experiences? This book will tell you what it's really like.

- **Eyewitness Science: Force and Motion** by Peter Lafferty (Dorling Kindersley, 1992). What keeps the planets circling the Sun? Read this book and find out.

- **The River** by Gary Paulsen (Dell Publishing, 1993). Moving is more than just motion. As you travel down the river on a raft, you'll find out why knowing direction and distance of motion can be a matter of life or death.

- **The Wright Brothers: How They Invented the Airplane** by Russel Freedman (Holiday House, 1991). In less than 100 years, we've gone from the first powered flight to landings on the Moon. Through actual photos taken by the Wright Brothers, this book will give you a peek at the early days of powered flight.

WORK TOGETHER & SHARE IDEAS

What would you do if you were asked to design an amusement park?

Working together, you'll have a chance to apply what you have learned about Newton's Laws of motion, gravity, and inertia. Using toy cars, ball bearings, plastic tubes, ramps, and other materials find out if your group can build a roller coaster that will go faster or a water slide that splashes more than anyone else's. Look for the Unit Project Links for ideas on how you can build your own amusement park.

CHAPTER 1

MOVING ON

People today are fascinated with how fast things can go. We give trophies and money to the owners of the fastest cars and swiftest horses. Bicyclists compete for prizes. Quick-footed athletes are in demand. What do you need to know to make a bicycle go really fast?

"Moto" Through the Mud

There are 100,000 BMXers in the United States. BMX, short for "bicycle motocross," involves young people on dirt bikes who race over hills of mud and try not to get knocked off. This is one tough race!

Betsy Edmundson of Temecula, California, is a BMX grand champion, winning the 1992 American Bicycle Association's grand national race. The win at age 11 gave her the right to display "#1" on her bike.

Betsy's preparation for the event involved training every day after school and doing uphill sprints with her bike. She practiced getting out of the starting gate 30 times a day. She knew that she had to get a quick jump out of the gate to win the race. What would you do to increase your speed so as to win a motocross race?

Coming Up

INVESTIGATION 1
How Do You Describe Motion?
.... F6

INVESTIGATION 2
How Do You Measure Speed?
.... F12

INVESTIGATION 3
How Do You Describe Changes in Motion?
.... F18

◀ Betsy Edmundson and her Grand-champion trophy

How Do You Describe Motion?

The terms *up, down, backward, forward, right,* and *left* all describe directions in which an object can move. In this investigation you'll find out that you also need to measure to describe the motion of an object.

Activity

The Ant Maze

Compass points can describe direction. In this activity you'll see how measuring is also essential to describe the motion of an object.

MATERIALS
- 1 sheet of graph paper
- 2 colored pencils, in different colors
- metric ruler
- Science Notebook

Procedure

1. **Draw** an ant inside the bottom left-hand square of your graph paper. **Label** the top of your graph paper *North*, the bottom *South*, the right side *East*, and the left side *West*.

2. Using a colored pencil, plot a path for the ant to follow square to square—up, down, across, diagonally—and finally off the paper. The path should include three turns.

3. With a metric ruler, **measure** the length of the path in each direction.

4. In your *Science Notebook,* write a description of the ant's path. Indicate the distance and compass direction for each part of the path.

Step 2

5. Exchange directions with your partner. Do not look at his or her graph paper.

Step 6

6. Using a different-colored pencil, **draw** the path of your partner's ant on your sheet of graph paper.

Analyze and Conclude

1. Compare your drawings with those of your partner. How well did the drawings match?

2. If the drawings did not match, **hypothesize** what you think went wrong.

3. What two factors did you have to include in your directions to describe the path of the ant?

4. Decide whether it is easier to take directions or to write them. When taking or writing directions, which are you more likely to make mistakes with—compass directions or distances?

INVESTIGATE FURTHER!

EXPERIMENT

Using compass directions and distance measurements in meters, write directions for going to a specific place in your school or on the playground. Give a classmate a starting place and your directions to see if your classmate can find the place.

From Feet
To Fathoms

"Why, when I was your age, I had to walk to school. It was three miles, uphill each way, through snow 30 inches deep!"

Have you ever heard something like this from an older relative who was teasing you about how easy you have it today? If you have, you've probably wanted to respond with a statement to prove that you don't have it quite that easy after all. Well, next time, try this: "That's nothing! When I walk to school, I have to walk 4.8 kilometers, uphill each way, through snow 76.2 centimeters deep!" Do you think your teasing relative can figure that out? Can you figure it out?

How far do you live from your school? If you had to give someone directions to your school, what information would you have to provide? Think about the "ant maze" activity for a moment. Just as in the directions for that activity, your directions to your school should include distances and compass directions.

The compass directions you would use would be the same as anyone else's. But the distances might be very different, depending upon how far you are from the school and what system of measurement you decide to use. Students who live near their schools could possibly answer this question in feet or yards. Students who live farther away might answer the question in miles. A science teacher might use an entirely different unit of measurement—the meter or the kilometer—to express the distance from home to school. How would you answer?

Units of Measurement

People use many kinds of units to make measurements of distance: inches, feet, yards, miles, millimeters, centimeters, meters, and kilometers, to name a few. The unit of measurement that a person chooses depends on what is being measured. It makes sense to measure the length of a pencil in centimeters or inches but not in kilometers or miles. On the other hand, you would probably use kilometers or miles instead of centimeters or inches to describe the distance from New York City to Los Angeles.

If you were talking about distances from Earth to the other planets in our solar system, you could use kilometers or miles. However, most astronomers measure these distances in astronomical units (AU). An astronomical unit is equal to the average distance from Earth to the Sun, or about 150 million km (93 million mi). How far in kilometers from Earth is Pluto if Pluto averages 39.3 AU from the Sun? What unit of measurement do you think should be used for describing the distance from Earth to a star?

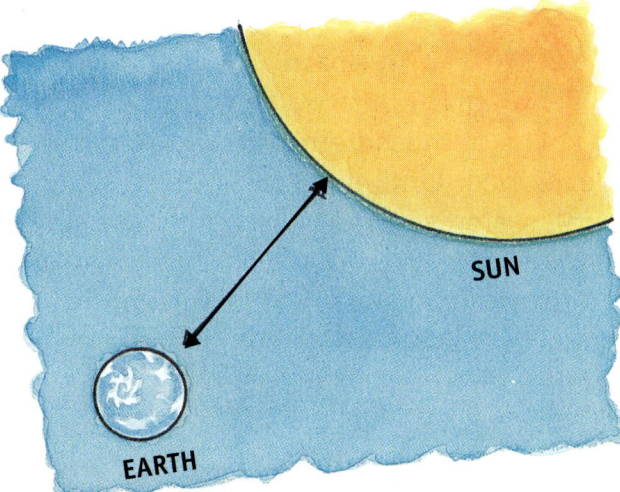

▲ One astronomical unit (AU)

What would you do if you didn't have a system by which to measure distance? Imagine that you and a classmate are stranded on an island. After several days you both become bored, so you decide to map the island. You have food, water, shelter, a small notebook, two pencils, a compass, and matches. But you have no ruler, no tape measure, not even a meterstick! How are you going to map something without being able to measure distances? After some thought, you and your fellow castaway come up with a reasonable solution. You decide to use the length of your stride as the unit for measuring distance. Now that you can measure distance, what else do you need to know to map your movements on the island? Where can you get that information?

Inventing Measuring Units

Just as a system of measurement had to be invented by the castaways on the imaginary island, all existing systems of measurement were invented out of need. The English system of measurement is used by most people in the United States. Yards, feet, inches, pounds, gallons, and pints are all examples of English units.

Many units in the English system originated at a time when there was no consistent system of measurement. In trying to develop a system of measurement that would be convenient, people invented units based upon body parts. For example, one early English measurement—the *yard*—was equal to the distance from the tip of the nose to the tip of the extended forefinger. What do you think happened if people had arms of different lengths?

Another unit is the fathom, often used to describe the depth of water. The fathom is about 6 ft. The term *fathom* origi-

▲ One yard (Old English)

nally comes from the Old English word *faethm,* meaning "two arms outstretched to embrace." Therefore, a fathom came to mean the distance from the tip of a person's left forefinger to the tip of the

F9

▲ One fathom (Old English)

Now back to the island. You have just about finished mapping it when you and your partner discover that you are not alone. There are two more people on the island, and they too have been mapping it. But when you compare your distances with those of the other people, you find differences. Can you make your two systems of measurement agree?

The Metric System

Throughout history, many different systems of measurement have been developed. Until the late eighteenth century, systems of measurement were very confusing.

Every nation, and sometimes every town or village had its own unique system of measurement. If you moved from

right forefinger when the arms are fully extended to the sides. How many different values for a fathom can you find among your classmates?

SCIENCE AND FAITH

On occasion, God used the Bible to reveal the size of objects such as Noah's Ark or the Temple. We sometimes find distances mentioned in the Bible too.

Measurement of length usually involved a portion of the arm or hand. For example, a **cubit** was the length from the elbow to the finger tips (usually about 445mm). Six cubits were combined into a measurement called a **reed**. People also measured by the length of an index **finger** (about 19mm), across the **palm** of the hand (about 76mm), and by the **span** created from little finger to thumb with the fingers spread (about 230mm).

In the New Testament, distance was measured by the **orgyia**, about the same as a fathom (1.85m), the **stadion** (185m), and the **milion** (1,478m or about 1,000 paces).

Do you know what the longest distance known to humans is called? It's the extent of our **forgiveness** according to Psalm 103:12. "As far as the east is from the west, so far has He removed our transgressions from us."

France to England, you had to learn a whole new system of measurement. In addition, a unit of measurement did not always mean the same thing to everyone within a country. A fathom might be one distance in London and another in York.

To solve this problem, in the 1790s the French National Assembly ordered the development of a new system of measurement, which came to be known as the **metric system.** The units of measurement in the metric system include the meter, kilometer, centimeter, liter, gram, and kilogram. These units are based on standards that don't vary. So, regardless of whether you are in France, Mexico, or Japan, if you are given directions to go south for 2 km, you can be sure that you know exactly how far to move.

Using metric and English measures ▼

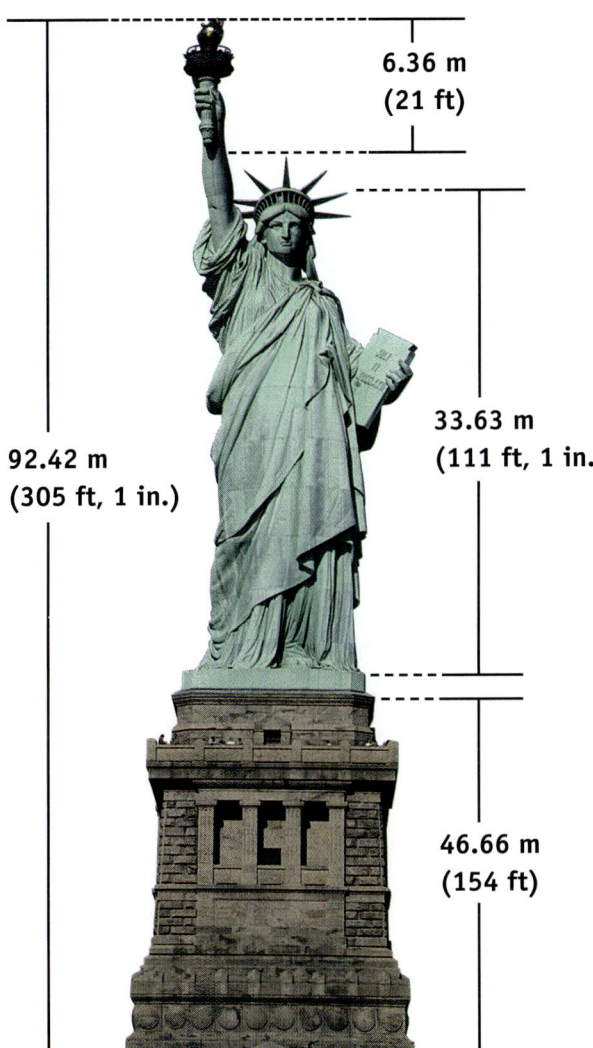

6.36 m (21 ft)

33.63 m (111 ft, 1 in.)

92.42 m (305 ft, 1 in.)

46.66 m (154 ft)

Metric Units

Measurement	Unit
Length and Distance	meter
Mass	kilogram
Volume	liter

Metric Conversions For Length

1,000 m	1 km
100 cm	1 m
10 mm	1 cm

INVESTIGATION 1

1. Write directions from your school to your home. What two factors must be contained in your directions?

2. How does having a set of standards make a system of measurement more reliable?

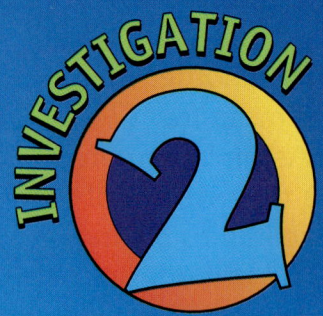

INVESTIGATION 2

How Do You Measure Speed?

In addition to compass direction and distance, motion is also described by how fast the object is moving. Suppose a car's speed is 55 miles per hour. What two measurements are needed to describe the speed?

Activity

Speeding Marbles

How fast can you roll a marble? Your answer must include two measurements. Find out how to measure a marble's speed.

MATERIALS
- 3 marbles
- metric tape measure
- chalk
- stopwatch
- pencil
- *Science Notebook*

SAFETY
Be sure to pick up all the marbles to prevent falls.

Procedure

1. In a hallway of your school, use a metric tape measure to identify a distance of 25 m from a wall. With chalk, mark a line at that point on the floor.

2. Stand 2 m behind the chalk line. While your partner holds a stopwatch, roll a marble at the wall. When the marble crosses the

Step 2

chalk line, your partner should start the stopwatch. When the marble hits the wall, your partner should stop timing. Record your time in a chart similar to the one below.

Trial Number	Distance of Roll	Elapsed Time	Speed (Distance/Time)
1	25 m		
2	25 m		
3	25 m		
4	25 m		
5	25 m		
6	25 m		
7	25 m		
8	25 m		
9	25 m		

3. Roll a second marble, then a third marble, trying to roll each one at about the same speed.

4. Repeat steps 2 and 3, this time trying to roll each of the three marbles at a consistently *slower* speed than in the first three trials. **Predict** how elapsed time will vary as the speed of the marbles is changed. **Record** your prediction.

5. Repeat steps 2 and 3, this time trying to roll each of the three marbles at a consistently *faster* speed than in the first three trials.

6. For each of the trials, **calculate** the speed by dividing the distance the marble had to roll (25 m) by the time it took for the marble to hit the wall. **Record** the speed for each trial in meters per second (m/s).

Analyze and Conclude

1. Which trial had the fastest speed? Which trial had the slowest speed? What was the average speed of all the trials?

2. How would the speed be affected if the distance were decreased, but the time remained the same?

3. How would the speed be affected if the time were increased, but the distance remained the same?

4. What two factors, or measurements, are used to express an object's speed?

INVESTIGATE FURTHER!

RESEARCH

Which ride at an amusement park is the fastest? Contact an amusement park or theme park and ask for fact sheets on the most popular rides. Report the top speed of each ride.

Bicycle Cyclometers

How far did you go on your last bicycle trip? How fast did you go? A bicycle cyclometer can give you this information. A cyclometer is a small device that is attached to a bicycle's handlebars. A wire connects the cyclometer to a sensor on your bike frame. A tiny magnet fits on a spoke of a wheel.

CYCLOMETER The cyclometer multiplies the number of times the wheel has gone around by the distance around the outside of the wheel (the wheel's circumference). The answer is the distance that you have traveled. (Each time your wheel goes around, your bike moves forward one circumference of the wheel. Wheels come in different sizes, so you must set the cyclometer for the exact circumference of your wheel.)

CABLE The sensor sends this information through a cable as an electric current to the cyclometer.

SENSOR To measure the distance, the sensor counts the number of times the magnet goes around on the wheel as you ride.

Some cyclometers keep track of the total distance you have ridden on your bicycle as well as the distance you have ridden on a particular trip. The cyclometer also keeps track of the total riding time. To figure out average speed, the cyclometer divides distance traveled by the total riding time.

What Is Speed?

▲ Traveling at 1,183.466 km/h, this car went faster than the speed of sound.

The expression "Faster than a speeding bullet" does not only apply to Superman. It can also be used to describe the amazing speeds reached by today's fastest racing cars.

Racing Speed

One of the first automobile races took place in 1909 between Count Gaston de Chasseloup-Laubat of France and Camille Jenatzy of Belgium. Jenatzy was clocked at 105.26 km/h (65.79 mph) in that contest. Less than ten years later, a speed of 165.69 km/h (103.56 mph) was recorded by Louis Rigolly of France.

In almost every year since that time, speed records have been broken on speedways around the world. Cars racing in the Indianapolis 500 have no trouble exceeding speeds of 352 km/h (220 mph). Drag racers attain even faster speeds on tracks that have no curves. In fact, Jenatzy's 1909 winning speed is close to what is now the posted legal speed limit on many interstate highways.

Just how fast do you have to be going to be the fastest? As of 1990, the fastest official time recorded for a land vehicle was 1,183.466 km/h (739.666 mph). That record was set by Stan Barrett in a jet-powered car driven at Edwards Air Force Base in California. Barrett's car, which looked like a rocket on wheels, was shaped so it had very low wind resistance.

Edwards Air Force Base was selected for the record-breaking attempt because

F15

8 km/h 32 km/h	104 km/h 112 km/h 192 km/h

the land is so flat and smooth. There, the speed a car reaches depends entirely on the car and not on any uphill or downhill slope of the land. For similar reasons, another popular site for attempts at breaking the land speed record is the Bonneville Salt Flats in western Utah. Like Edwards Air Force Base, the salt flats are level and smooth, making it possible to reach the highest possible speeds.

Defining Speed

What is speed and how is it measured? In the activity, what factors did you use to determine the speed at which the marbles rolled?

Speed is defined as the distance moved in a certain amount of time. If you are able to walk 4.8 km (3 mi) in an hour, you are moving at a speed of 4.8 km/h (3 mph). Suppose you continue to walk for another two hours. In the second hour you walk 3.2 km (2 mi), but by the third hour you're really getting tired and you walk only 1.6 km (1 mi). What is your average speed for the three-hour walk? See if you can figure your average speed, using the table and formula in the next column.

Hour	Distance Walked (km)
1	4.8
2	3.2
3	1.6

$$\text{Average Speed} = \frac{\text{Total Distance}}{\text{Total Time}}; \text{ or}$$

$$\text{Average Speed} = \frac{D}{T}$$

What was your average speed for the three-hour walk? Obviously, you attained a relatively low average speed for your three-hour effort. However, the formula that you used to calculate your speed would be the same regardless of how fast you were going.

So how fast is fast? A fast human might reach 32 km/h (20 mph) running. When swimming, the best a human can hope for is about 8 km/h (5 mph). By comparison, a running cheetah can attain a speed of 112 km/h (70 mph), and a sailfish can reach speeds of 104 km/h (65 mph)!

Some speeds are actually too fast to

320 km/h	360 km/h	1,184 km/h	4,800+ km/h	28,800+ km/h

imagine. If you enjoy playing with numbers, try figuring out how far a jet, a space shuttle, and light travel in just a minute or just a second. How long does it take for each of the entries in the table to travel one kilometer?

Imagine riding in an object that can travel faster than the speed of sound. How do you think travel at these speeds would affect you? People who have traveled at these tremendous speeds describe feeling as if a great weight were pressing down on them as they sped up and then slowed down.

High speeds can place great stress on the human body. As you accelerate, forces on your body may compress your chest, making breathing difficult. Your arms and legs will feel very heavy, and you will have difficulty lifting your head off the back of your seat. In addition, your heart will have difficulty pumping enough blood to your head, and you may feel as if you're going to black out.

Moving at such high speeds can be extremely exciting, but it also can be quite uncomfortable. People such as race-car drivers, jet pilots, and astronauts must be in very good physical condition to handle these speeds. In fact, jet pilots and astronauts wear special suits that help them counteract the pressures experienced when flying at such tremendous speeds.

Now can you answer the question, how fast is fast? How fast do you want to go? ■

INVESTIGATION 2

1. If you want to measure the speed of a car, what two factors do you need to know?

2. Approaching you is a car that appears to be traveling very fast. How might you figure out the speed of the car?

How Do You Describe Changes in Motion?

INVESTIGATION 3

You're leaving for vacation, and you're riding in the back seat of the car. You can't see the dashboard dials or the steering wheel, but you certainly know when your motion changes. In this investigation you'll find out how to describe those changes.

Activity
Swinging Speeds

In this activity you'll observe and then try to describe changes in the motion of swinging washers.

MATERIALS
- goggles
- 2 chairs or 2 ring stands
- string (about 75 cm long)
- metal washer
- scissors
- metric ruler
- *Science Notebook*

SAFETY
Wear goggles throughout the procedure. Do not swing the washer violently.

Procedure

1. Place two chairs or ring stands about 30 cm apart and tie a piece of string between them. The string should be pulled tight between the two chairs or ring stands.

2. Take a second piece of string. Tie one end of it around a washer. Tie the other end to the string that is connecting the chair legs or ring stands.

Step 2

3. Predict how the speed of the washer will change as it swings back and forth. Pull the washer back as shown and release it. Notice how its speed changes as it swings.

4. In your *Science Notebook*, **draw** the washer swinging. Label the place where the washer has the greatest speed. Then label the place where the washer is traveling the slowest.

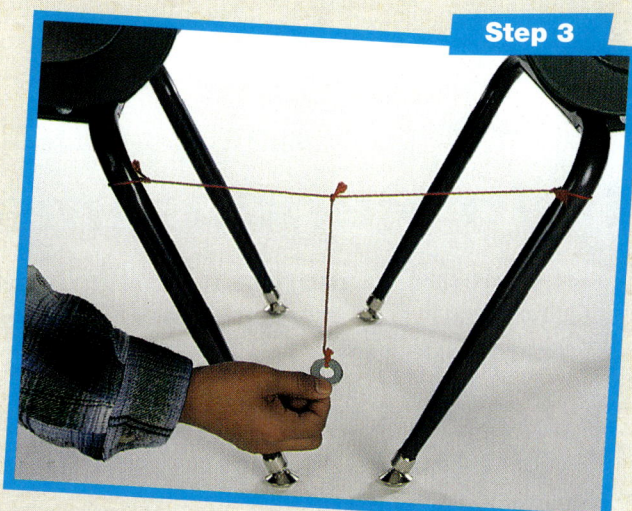

Analyze and Conclude

1. At what point in its swing is the washer gaining speed? Why do you think the washer is gaining speed?

2. At what point in its swing is the washer losing speed? Why do you think the washer is losing speed?

3. At what point in its swing is the washer changing its direction of motion? How do you know it is changing its direction of motion?

4. *Accelerate* means "to change speed or direction." As the washer swings, when is it accelerating? Explain your answer.

UNIT PROJECT LINK

You can investigate forces and motion by building a miniature amusement park for marbles. The first thing you should do is draw a Marble Park map. Leave room for all the rides, games, and restaurants that a big theme park has. Transfer your drawing to large sheets of heavy posterboard. Now design and build some ways to move your marbles around the park. Include a train that circles the park. Design a chair lift using tiny drink cups, string, and straws. Each chair should be able to carry at least one marble across the park. Design walkways that lead from one ride to another.

Activity

Twin Pendulums

What changes in motion would you observe if you were to hang two pendulums from the same horizotal string and swing one of them?

MATERIALS
- same as those of "Swinging Speeds" activity
- additional 30 cm of string
- additional washer
- *Science Notebook*

SAFETY
Wear goggles throughout the procedure. Do not swing the washer violently.

Procedure

1. Make two pendulums of exactly the same length—about 15 cm each.

2. Attach both pendulums to the horizontal string so that they are about 5 cm apart.

3. Start one pendulum swinging while holding the other still.

4. **Predict** what would happen to the still pendulum if you released it. Stop the moving pendulum. Pull back one pendulum and release it. **Record** what happens to the second pendulum.

5. Repeat this experiment twice. **Observe** carefully and **record** your observations.

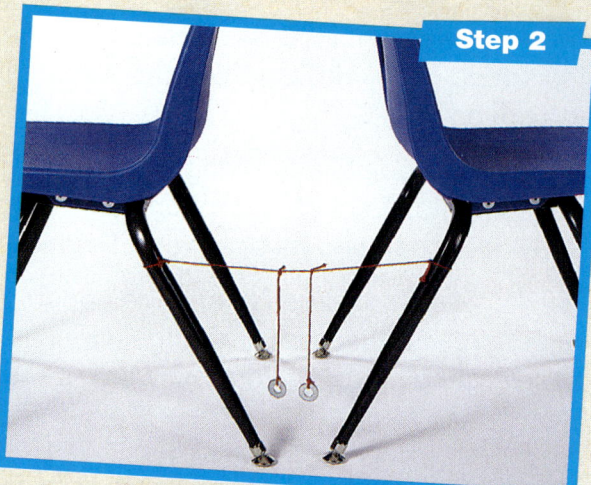
Step 2

Analyze and Conclude

1. How was the second pendulum affected by the swing of the first?

2. Describe how the speed of both pendulums changed. In which pendulum did the speed increase? In which pendulum did it decrease?

3. How can the motion of one pendulum affect the other if the pendulums never touch each other?

4. Did both pendulums accelerate? Explain your answer.

Step 3

Acceleration

Go Faster!

At the top of the hill, you look down the steep slope to the bottom. Your stomach tightens just a little as the sense of impending thrill builds inside you. Then you push off. Skimming over the thin film of water, you speed through twists and turns, going faster and faster until you splash down in the pool at the bottom of the hill. Whether it's the thrill of a water slide, a roller-coaster ride, or a ski run, the increase in speed that you experience can be exciting!

Scientists use the term **velocity** to describe speed and direction. Thus, your velocity down the water slide would be described by both your speed and your direction.

To describe the rate at which velocity changes, scientists use the term **acceleration.** But acceleration varies according to the circumstances. On a steep water slide, your speed will increase quickly; you will accelerate rapidly. On a water slide with a gentler hill, your speed will not increase as quickly. Therefore, your acceleration is less. And even when your speed is constant, you are accelerating if you are changing direction. How would you describe the acceleration of the pendulums in the activity?

Examples of Acceleration

The acceleration you experience when sliding down a hill is only one example of acceleration. Your

F21

muscles accelerate your body when you run, ride a bike, skate, or even walk. A baseball pitcher uses muscles to accelerate a ball toward home plate.

Chemical reactions can also cause objects to accelerate. When sitting on its launch pad, the velocity of a space shuttle is zero. When the shuttle's engines fire, fuel begins to burn and there is an increase in velocity—slowly at first, then faster and faster. The shuttle accelerates because of chemical changes taking place in its engines as the fuel burns.

Units of Acceleration

Imagine that you are riding a bicycle at a speed of 10 km/h (6.25 mph). You decide to gradually increase your speed, and one minute later, you are riding at 15 km/h (9.38 mph). How fast did you accelerate? To figure out your rate of acceleration, you must first answer two questions.

- How much did your speed increase?
- How long did it take you to make that increase?

Your rate of acceleration is equal to your change in speed divided by the time it took you to accelerate.

$$a = \frac{s_2 - s_1}{t}$$

In this example, your increase in speed was 5 km/h (15 km/h − 10 km/h). The time you took to make that increase was 1 minute. Your rate of acceleration, then, was

$$a = \frac{(15 \text{ km/h} - 10 \text{ km/h})}{1 \text{ minute}} ; \text{or}$$

$$a = 5 \text{ km/hr/min}$$

▲ In the few moments after liftoff, the shuttle is accelerating to speeds that will place it in orbit around Earth.

When a diver hits the water, he or she decelerates rapidly because the water is much more dense than the air. ▼

The units of acceleration can seem confusing. But the units simply describe how speed is changing with time. In the example, the speed in kilometers per hour is changing per minute. You can read the answer as "5 kilometers per hour per minute."

Deceleration

Objects that gain speed usually slow down because of gravity or friction. For example, your speed on the water slide is reduced quickly once your body encounters the friction of the water in the pool. This decrease in speed is sometimes called **deceleration**. But since any change in speed or direction is defined as an acceleration, deceleration is just a type of acceleration.

Many things can cause an object to decelerate. In a car, for example, brakes are applied to decelerate. Gravity also can cause deceleration. A ball thrown upward begins to decelerate because of both gravity and friction of the air. Of course, on the way down, gravity causes the ball to accelerate. ■

INVESTIGATE FURTHER!

RESEARCH

From the earliest days of the space program, acceleration related to launch and reentry has been known to produce incredible stress on the human body. Find out what the astronauts experience during launch and reentry, and report on how it is related to acceleration.

Stopping Power

▲ An early attempt at developing brakes

Humans have long understood something very basic about moving heavy objects—that is, it's just not easy to push or pull a heavy object over the ground. And if you happen to be pushing or pulling that object up a hill, the job becomes almost impossible.

At some point in history, someone discovered a way to make the job of moving heavy objects much easier. Perhaps this discovery was accidental, or perhaps it was the result of careful consideration. No one will ever know. But at some point, humans discovered that when a heavy object was pushed or pulled over a narrow log, the log rolled and the object moved more easily. The wheel had been invented!

The wheel is the most commonly used device for reducing friction and increasing the speed of an object. Unfortunately, heavy objects rolling on wheels are not always easy to stop once they start moving, so brakes had to be invented to slow and stop wheels once they started turning. Brakes are used to decelerate cars, bicycles, trains, and most other objects that have wheels.

How Brakes Work

Many kinds of brakes exist, but almost all brakes work on the same principle. Some stationary object is brought into contact with a rotating wheel. Friction between the stationary object and the rotating wheel causes the wheel to slow down and come to a stop.

Most cars today have disc brakes. A car with disc brakes has a large metal disc attached to each wheel. As a wheel turns, so does the metal disc attached to it. Suspended above the disc is the metal housing that holds the rest of the brake system. This part of the system contains the brake fluid, a set of pistons, and the brake shoes.

When a driver wants to stop a car, he or she depresses the brake pedal. This action increases pressure on the brake fluid. That pressure forces the pistons to push the brake shoes against the sides of the rotating discs. Brake linings, or pads, on the face of the brake shoes rub against the discs and slow their speed of rotation. As the discs slow down, so do the wheels to which they are attached.

When a driver pushes forcefully on the brake pedal during a panic stop, normal brakes clamp down hard on the discs. The possible result is locked brakes and a dangerous, uncontrollable skid. To prevent this, engineers designed an anti-lock braking system. If a car has this kind of braking system, the driver can push forcefully on the brake pedal for a panic stop, but a computer controls the amount of pressure exerted by the brake pads on the rotating discs. The computer causes the brake pads to pulse rapidly on and off the rotating disc. This pulsing action prevents brake lockup and enables the driver to bring the car to a safe stop.

Braking Distance

Brakes do not work instantaneously. It takes time for them to bring a bicycle, a

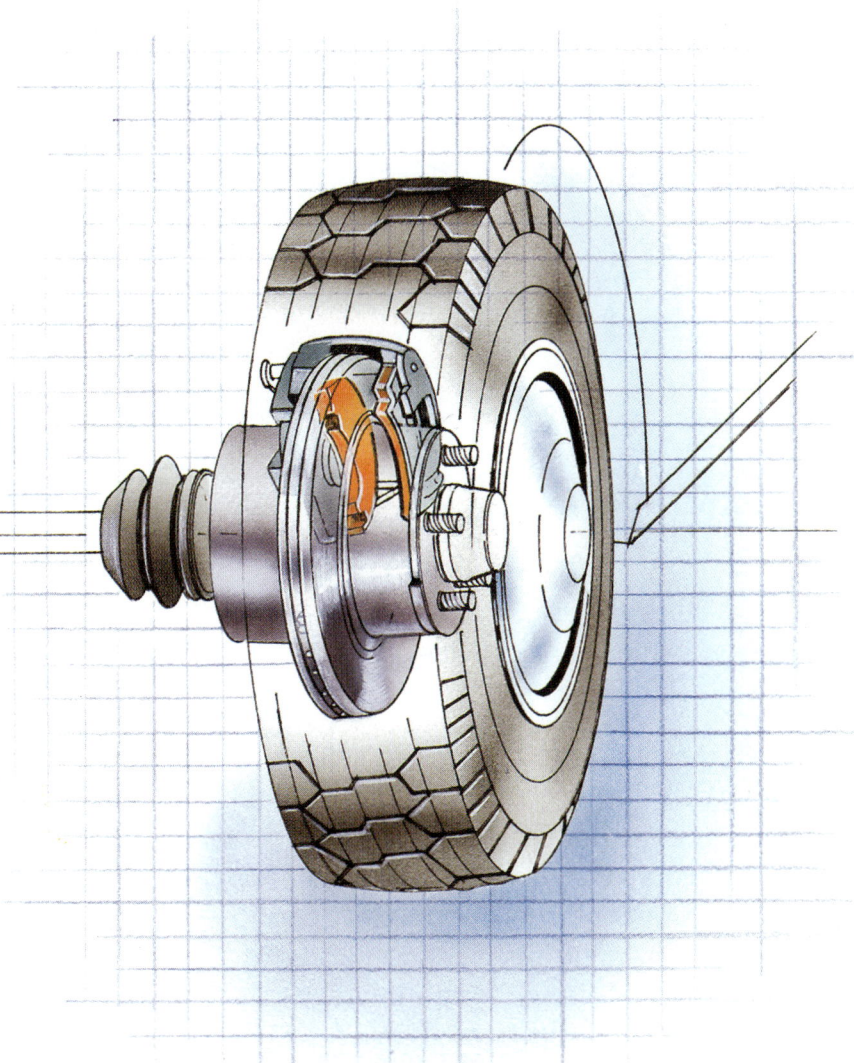

▲ On most automobiles built today, disc brakes are installed at least on the front wheels. They provide an efficient system of stopping a car.

car, or a train to a complete stop. The time it takes for this to happen is called the braking time. The distance needed to stop an object completely is called the braking distance.

Braking distance for a car depends on several factors.
- the reaction time of the driver
- the condition of the road surface
- the kind of tire
- the speed of the car

Reaction time is the time that elapses between the moment the driver realizes that brakes must be applied and the

▲ As speed increases, so does the braking distance.

moment when the brakes are actually applied. What do you estimate would be your own reaction time for an emergency stop if you were driving a car?

The braking time is longer for cars that are traveling fast. The table shows the braking distance for an average-sized car traveling at different speeds. Construct a graph for these figures. What does the graph show about the relationship between car speed and braking distance?

Suppose the average car is 5.0 m long. How many car lengths should you stay behind the car in front of you when traveling at 30 km/h? at 60 km/h? at 90 km/h? How does your reaction time affect your answers to these questions? ■

Car Speed (km/h)	Braking Distance (m)
30	8
45	18
60	32
75	50
90	72

INVESTIGATION 3

1. When is an object accelerating?

2. You observe a ball bouncing down a long staircase. In what ways is the ball accelerating?

REFLECT & EVALUATE

WORD POWER

speed
velocity
acceleration
deceleration
metric system

On Your Own
Write a definition for each term and then use the term in a sentence.

With a Partner
Using all the terms, write a short science fiction story about a space probe traveling to a star in another part of the galaxy. Present your story to the class.

Make a chart, listing the speeds of different things you have observed. Start with the slowest and end with the fastest. On average, how fast or how slow are things in your world moving? Decorate the chart with colorful art work.

Analyze Information

Study the metric conversion chart below. What number is the metric system based upon? How are all the units related to each other? How many times larger is a centimeter (cm) than a millimeter (mm)? How many times smaller is a hectometer (hm) than a kilometer (km)?

Metric Conversion Chart For Length	
10 mm = 1 cm	10 m = 1 dam
10 cm = 1 dm	10 dam = 1 hm
10 dm = 1 m	10 hm = 1 km

Assess Performance

Design a project to determine which student in your class has the fastest average speed for the 50-m dash. What procedure will you use and what materials will you need? Prepare a data collection sheet to record the results. For the analysis of data, decide what formula you will use to determine the average speeds.

Problem Solving

1. You've been given a treasure map. At the bottom it says, "Left for 15, then right for 8. Then go right 15 more, and right for 8." Where, do you think, is the treasure?

2. A hill near you is very popular for sledding. What do you do to figure out how fast you can go down the hill?

3. You have been asked to design a racetrack for model cars and to develop a way to measure the cars' speeds. What would you do?

F27

CHAPTER 2

GETTING A GRIP ON GRAVITY

It certainly seems that what goes up, must come down—birds, planes, and all manner of balloons. Even a basketball player on a slam dunk can't stay in the air forever. What do you know about the force that God provides to bring you back down to the ground?

The Last Dance of Extra 260

Do you like to do gymnastics? Perhaps you are good at somersaults, back flips, and dramatic dismounts. Imagine what it would be like to do moves similar to these with an airplane! Patty Wagstaff, an aerobatic pilot, flies her Extra 260 aircraft through breathtaking maneuvers. In 1991, Patty became the first woman to win the United States National Aerobatic Championship. In 1993, Patty Wagstaff watched her famous airplane become part of the National Air and Space Museum in Washington, D.C. This was a tribute, both to the airplane and its history-making pilot. What do you think Patty had to know about forces that act on an aircraft in order to do her dramatic flying?

Coming Up

INVESTIGATION 1
How Can the Force of Gravity Be Measured?
.... F30

INVESTIGATION 2
Do All Objects Fall at the Same Rate?
.... F36

INVESTIGATION 3
How Does Air Change the Rate at Which an Object Falls?
.... F42

◀ Patty Wagstaff and the Extra 260

How Can the Force of Gravity Be Measured?

You've had the experience many times. An object slips from your hand. Wouldn't you be amazed if it floated to the ceiling? But it doesn't. It falls toward the ground. Gravity wins again. In this investigation you'll find out how to describe and measure the force of gravity.

Activity

Measuring Gravity's Pull

How strong is the force that holds you to Earth's surface? Is the force of gravity the same on all objects? Take some measurements and find out.

MATERIALS
- balance and masses
- mesh bag
- objects of different sizes and masses
- spring scale calibrated in newtons
- *Science Notebook*

Procedure

1. Hold each object separately in your hand. Which object feels the heaviest?

2. Place the object that you think is the heaviest on the balance and determine its mass in kilograms. In your *Science Notebook*, **record** the balance reading under *Mass* in a chart similar to the one on the next page.

3. Repeat this procedure with each object.

4. Now place the object you think is the heaviest in the mesh bag and hang the mesh bag from the scale. **Record** the scale reading under *Force of Gravity*.

Step 1

5. Repeat this procedure with each object.

6. Calculate the ratio of the force of gravity acting on each object to the mass of that object by dividing the force of gravity by the mass. **Record** this information in your chart.

Name of Object	Mass (kg)	Force of Gravity (newtons)	Fraction = Force of Gravity/Mass

Analyze and Conclude

1. Compare the effects of the force of gravity acting on objects of differing masses.

2. Is there a pattern in the relationship of an object's mass to the force of gravity acting upon it? Explain. What do the numbers in the right-hand column represent?

3. Convert your own weight to kilograms (1 kg = 2.2 lb). **Calculate** the force of gravity on your body. **Record** this information in your table.

INVESTIGATE FURTHER!

EXPERIMENT

Invent a scale. Use rubber bands, rulers, hooks, and any other equipment you think is necessary. Use the same mesh bag and objects you worked with in this activity. Experiment with a way to get readings similar to those obtained with the spring scale. Wear safety goggles.

Weighing In

Want to lose weight? Walk to the top of the nearest mountain. Want to gain weight? Walk to the bottom of the nearest valley. Does this sound crazy to you? It probably does, but it works. To understand how this method of weight loss or weight gain works, you have to understand what scientists mean when they use the terms *weight* and *mass*.

Mass

The term *mass* describes the amount of "stuff" in an object or objects. Think about a pile of 400 large gold coins. The mass of the gold is the amount of gold in the pile. The mass of an object is usually measured in grams (g) or in kilograms (kg) in the metric system. Let's say that each gold coin has a mass of 0.25 kg. This pile of gold has a total mass of 100 kg. If you placed the gold on a scale, you'd discover that it weighs 980 N. That much gold is about equal to the mass of an average-sized National Football League quarterback and would be worth about $1 million!

Now let's say you think this particular pile of gold simply has too much mass.

You decide to move the pile to the top of a mountain because you've heard somewhere that things lose weight if you take them to the top of a mountain. You might want to use something with wheels to make this move. The job will be a lot easier.

Once you get the load all the way to the top of the mountain, what do you think the mass of the gold will be? Remember, *mass* describes the amount of stuff in an object. Has the amount of gold decreased? You count the coins. There are still 400 coins. You place a coin on a balance and its mass is 0.25 kg. There is still the same mass of gold as at the bottom of the mountain.

Even on the Moon, on the planets, or in outer space, the bag of gold would still have the same mass: 100 kg. The mass of an object does not change if you change the location of the object.

Weight

But wait. Amazingly, someone has left a scale at the top of the mountain. So you move the pile of gold coins over to the scale and weigh it. The scale reads slightly less than 980 N. Someone stole my gold, you think. So you open the bag and count the coins again. The bag still has 400 beautiful, large, shiny gold coins. What's going on here?

Mass and *weight* both describe something about the "stuff" in an object. **Mass** describes how much stuff there is in the object. **Weight** describes the force with which gravity is pulling on that stuff. In science, the term **force** means a push or a pull. **Gravity** is the attractive force exerted by a body or object on all other bodies or objects.

Large bodies like the Sun, Earth, the Moon, and the planets exert strong gravitational (grav i tā′shən əl) forces on other objects. They act on objects almost as a magnet acts on a piece of iron. For example, when you throw a ball into the air, Earth pulls the ball back down. When an apple falls off a tree, it falls downward, not upward, because of Earth's pull on it. Objects near Earth's surface are pulled toward the surface by gravitational force.

The term *weight*, then, is just another way of expressing the gravitational force exerted on an object by Earth or some other large body. The most common units for measuring weight are the pound (lb) in the English system and the newton (N) in the metric system. But what about the "missing" weight of the gold?

Mass Compared to Weight

Mass and weight are closely related to each other. People sometimes use one word when they mean the other. But mass and weight are different in some important ways. Think about the following situation.

As you were pulling and tugging and sweating, trying to get your gold to the top of the mountain, your best friend walked by, carrying a large, bulging bag that was easily the size of your pile of gold. Is your friend extremely strong or are you extremely weak? Several hours later, you reached the top of the mountain to find your friend stretched out on the ground, sound asleep, resting comfortably on a bag of goose feathers.

Although your friend's bag of goose feathers and your pile of gold are about the same size, your gold obviously has a much larger mass than the bag of goose feathers. The bag of goose feathers might have a mass of about 1 kg. The

SCIENCE AND FAITH

What is the heaviest thing that you can think of? How much would the tallest building in the world weigh? How many tons would describe Mt. McKinley?

Now think of the lightest things. What objects can you name what would be hard to weigh because of their size? Does anything weigh nothing?

If you were under Mt. McKinley, could you ever get up? What would it feel like to weigh nothing?

The Bible says, "Our offenses and sins weigh us down, and we are wasting away because of them. How then can we live?" (Ezekiel 33:10). By God's mercy and love, Jesus came into the world to lift the weight of sin from us. The day is coming when we too will soar into heaven, uplifted by God's grace.

▲ The same amount of two different substances can have very different masses and weights.

gold's mass is 100 times the mass of the feathers.

At Earth's surface, the gold would also weigh more than the feathers. Objects with more mass experience a stronger pull of gravity than do objects with less mass. In this example, the weight of the feathers is only about 49 N—twenty times less than the weight of the gold.

Now let's go back to the top of the mountain. On the way up the mountain, the mass of the gold and the mass of the feathers do not change. Mass never changes, no matter where you go. But the weight of the gold and of the feathers does begin to change.

As you go up the mountain, you move farther from Earth's center. Earth is not able to pull as strongly on the gold and the feathers as it did at the bottom of the mountain. Mass doesn't change, but the weight of the gold and of the feathers decreases. You've solved the mystery of the missing weight of gold. ■

INVESTIGATION 1

1. What is the difference between mass and weight?

2. Your 400 gold coins were stolen, but the police may have found them in Death Valley. When asked how much your gold weighs, you answer, "980 N." The officer says, "Sorry, this gold weighs more than that." What has happened?

F35

Do All Objects Fall at the Same Rate?

Which is heavier, a pound of lead or a pound of feathers? Yes, it's an old joke, but if both the pound of lead and the pound of feathers were dropped from a 20-m tower, would they fall at the same rate?

Activity

The Great Gravity Race

Suppose a heavy object and a light object fall to Earth from the same height. Which will reach the ground first?

MATERIALS
- heavy ball and light ball (table-tennis ball and golf ball, for instance)
- spring scale and mesh bag
- **Science Notebook**

SAFETY
Don't throw the balls or bounce them in the classroom.

Procedure

Using the spring scale and mesh bag, weigh each ball and **record** each value in your *Science Notebook*. Place both balls on the edge of a table or cabinet. **Predict** which ball will hit the ground first if they both roll off the table together. Try it. **Record** your observations. Repeat the activity several times.

Analyze and Conclude

1. If all objects fall the way these two balls do, what kind of rule could you write about falling objects?

2. Imagine sky divers jumping from a plane at the same time and falling through the sky before they open their parachutes. Will they fall at the same rate? Explain.

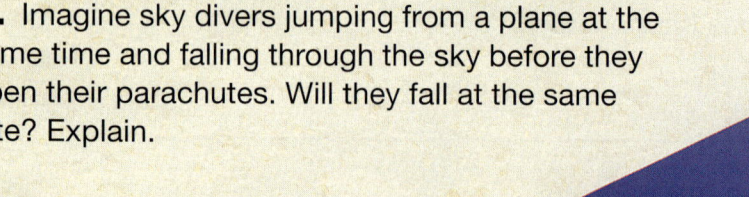

Activity
Falling Together

MATERIALS
- 2 pennies
- quarter
- index card
- *Science Notebook*

If two pennies are at the same height and one is dropped straight down while the other is tossed across the room, which hits the ground first?

Procedure

1. Fold an index card in half lengthwise. Then fold each long edge toward the center fold.

2. Place the card on the edge of a table as shown and put a penny on each side of the center fold.

3. **Predict** which penny will hit the ground first if you flick the long edge of the card with your finger.

4. Flick the long edge of the card and listen for the sounds of the pennies hitting the floor. In your *Science Notebook*, **record** which penny hits the ground first.

5. Repeat the experiment three times.

6. Replace one penny with a quarter. Repeat the experiment. Then put the quarter in the other position and repeat the experiment.

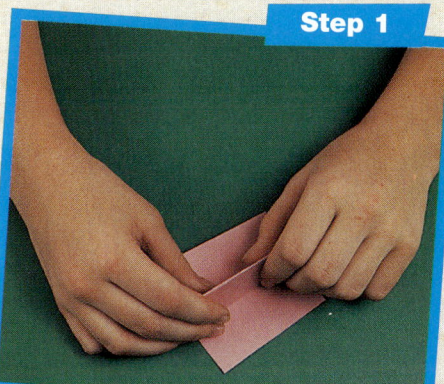
Step 1

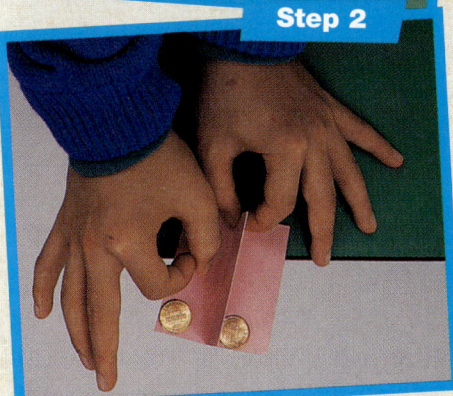
Step 2

Analyze and Conclude

1. How do you know that gravity is pulling both pennies toward the floor?

2. Does the sideways motion of a falling object have an effect on the rate of its fall?

3. Does the weight of the falling object have an effect on the rate of its fall?

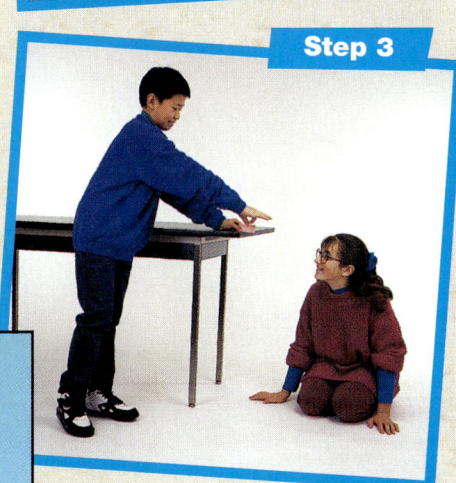
Step 3

INVESTIGATE FURTHER!

EXPERIMENT

Drop pairs consisting of two different objects. Observe when they hit the ground. How do the results compare with the conclusions you reached in the activity?

F37

Galileo's Great Gravity Discovery

A basketball is heavier than a soccer ball. If you drop both at the same time from the same height, which will hit the ground first? If you answered "the basketball," you're in agreement with the Greek philosopher Aristotle (ar' is tät'l), one of the greatest thinkers of all time. However, you are wrong! About 350 B.C., Aristotle taught that Earth was the center of the universe and that the heavier an object is, the faster it will fall toward Earth.

For nearly 2,000 years, Aristotle's teachings went almost unchallenged. Then, in the late sixteenth century, an Italian scientist named Galileo Galilei (gal′i lē′ō gal i lē′ē) decided to test Aristotle's theory that heavy objects fall faster than light objects. Legend has it that Galileo simply climbed to the top of the Leaning Tower of Pisa, held a large cannonball and a small cannonball at arm's length, and dropped them at the same time. An observer, wisely standing well out of the way at the bottom, observed that the cannonballs hit the ground at the same time! While Galileo may not have actually done *this* experiment, he did experiments that showed that objects fall at the same rate.

It wasn't long before other scientists began supporting Galileo's findings. About 1665, Sir Isaac Newton discovered that the force keeping Earth in its orbit around the Sun is the same force that causes all objects to fall at the same rate. That force is gravity! ■

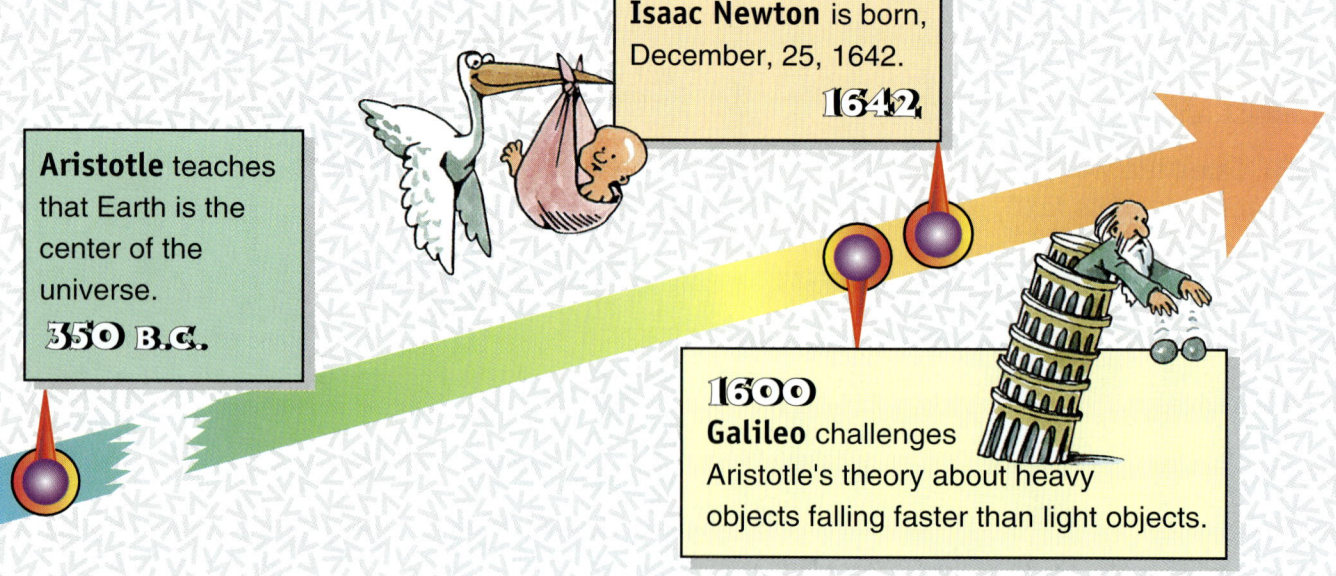

Aristotle teaches that Earth is the center of the universe.
350 B.C.

Isaac Newton is born, December, 25, 1642.
1642

1600
Galileo challenges Aristotle's theory about heavy objects falling faster than light objects.

How High?

▲ How does gravity affect the hitting and catching of a baseball?

"Two out; bases loaded; bottom of the ninth; everything's tied up, two all. Ramirez steps up to the plate and Johnson looks in for the sign. Ramirez needs only a single to put this game away. Johnson goes into the stretch, and here's the pitch. Ramirez swings and smashes a hanging curve! The runners are going, and that ball is almost out of sight! Jefferson is looking for it. He's all the way back at the center-field wall. He's going up. He's got it! Half over the wall, he pulls it back in and robs Ramirez of a grand slam! What a catch! That ball must have been coming down like a rocket! At the end of nine, this game is all tied up and we're going into extra innings!"

If you have ever listened to a baseball announcer call a game, you may have heard commentary like this. Think for a moment about the player who caught the ball. How fast was the ball moving as it came down toward the player? How hard did the ball hit the player's glove?

Graphing Acceleration

The graph below shows the distance an object that is dropped from above Earth's surface falls in a given amount of time. The line on this graph is curved instead of straight. A straight line would indicate that the distance an object falls increases at a steady rate. A line that curves upward indicates that during each successive second, the object falls farther than in the previous second. What distance did the object fall during the first second? How about a second later? during the third second? the fifth second?

The graph also shows that the force of gravity causes an object to accelerate as it falls from any spot above Earth's surface. Each second the object falls, it gains speed. Each second, it will be traveling faster than it did the previous second.

Making Predictions About Falling

The information on the graph is accurate for any place on Earth. You can use the graph in two ways. If you know how much time it has taken an object to fall,

▲ With the help of a teacher or other adult, you could launch your own rocket.

you can find the distance it has fallen. If you know how far the object has fallen, you can determine how much time it took to fall. For example, suppose you want to know how far an object has fallen five seconds after it was dropped. Read across the horizontal (time) axis to 5. Then read up the 5 line until you come to the curve (blue arrow). Next, read to your left across the graph to the vertical (distance) axis (red arrow). You should find

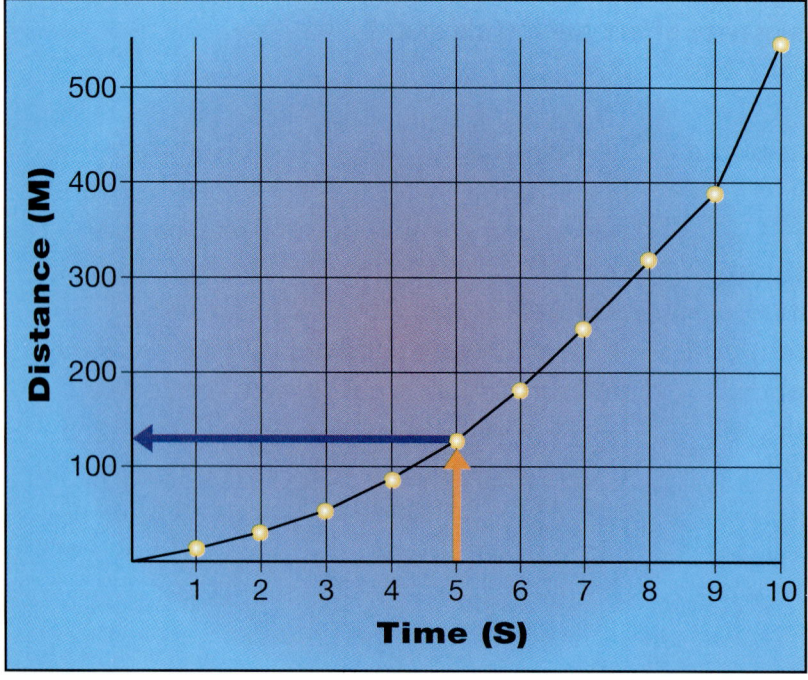

UNIT PROJECT LINK

Design two different roller coasters for your amusement park. Then build a three-dimensional model of each that will fit on your posterboard. Be sure each coaster can carry at least one marble. Experiment to determine how fast the coaster can go. Then, beside each coaster, give its name and information about how high and how fast it goes.

▲ Using a stop watch and the graph on the previous page, you can calculate how high a model rocket goes by how long it takes to come down.

a distance of about 120 m (400 ft). How far would the same object have fallen after six seconds?

Scientists can use a graph like this to calculate distances that might be difficult to measure otherwise. Suppose, for example, that a rocket is fired straight up and then falls back to Earth. You know that the rocket took eight seconds to come down after reaching its maximum height. How far must the rocket have fallen in those eight seconds? Use the graph on the previous page to answer this question.

You also can use this graph to find the time it takes for an object to fall. How long would it take for a baseball to fall the 170 m (about 560 ft) from the top of the Washington Monument? Do you think catching a ball dropped from the top of the Washington Monument is a good test of a baseball player's ability? Explain your answer. ■

INVESTIGATION 2

1. Would the graph on page F40 be useful in predicting the fall of both a marble and a baseball? Why or why not?

2. An astronaut standing on the Moon and a scientist standing on Earth drop identical hammers from identical heights at exactly the same moment. Which will hit the surface first? Explain your answer.

INVESTIGATION 3

HOW DOES AIR CHANGE THE RATE AT WHICH AN OBJECT FALLS?

An acorn and a leaf both fall from the same branch at the same moment. What prediction would you make concerning which one will hit the ground first? In this investigation find out about a force you must consider when making your prediction.

Activity
Paper Race

MATERIALS
- 2 sheets of notebook paper
- spring scale
- *Science Notebook*

Can an object fall at different rates at different times? It doesn't take slight of hand to make it happen.

Procedure

1. Crumple up a sheet of paper into a small ball. Leave the other sheet flat.

2. Using a spring scale, weigh each sheet of paper. **Record** the weights in your *Science Notebook* in a chart similar to the one below.

Step 1

	Weight	Description of Results
Crumpled paper		
Flat paper		

F42

3. Predict what will happen if both sheets of paper are dropped from the same height at the same time. **Test your prediction**.

4. Record which one reaches the ground first.

5. Repeat the experiment three times and **record** your results.

Analyze and Conclude

1. Which sheet of paper experiences a stronger gravitational pull? How do you know?

2. How can the difference between the open paper and the paper ball be used to explain your results?

3. How might the results of this activity have been different if you had dropped both pieces of paper in a vacuum (a space containing no matter)?

Step 3

INVESTIGATE FURTHER!

EXPERIMENT

Trees release seeds every year. These seeds have different shapes. Collect seeds of different shapes and compare the ways they fall. How do the shapes seem to affect the rates of fall? How might these different rates be advantageous for the trees?

Activity
Parachuting

How does the design of a parachute affect the rate at which it falls?

MATERIALS
- thin plastic garbage bags (for parachute material)
- string
- tape
- small action figure
- stopwatch
- *Science Notebook*

Procedure

1. Cut two parachute shapes from the garbage bag as shown in the diagram. Make one much larger than the other.

2. Cut pieces of string and use them to attach an action figure to one parachute. The strings should be attached with tape at the edges of the parachute and then attached to the action figure.

3. Make a mark high on the wall. You will drop the action figure with the parachute from that height every time.

4. Drop the action figure wearing the first parachute. **Record** the drop time in your *Science Notebook,* in a chart similar to the one below. Repeat the experiment three times. **Record** your data.

5. **Predict** how drops of the second parachute will compare with the first one. Repeat step 4, now with the action figure wearing the second parachute.

	Height of Drop	Drop Time
Small parachute		
Large parachute		

F44

Analyze and Conclude

1. What effect did the size of the parachute have? Suggest a **hypothesis** to explain any differences you observed in the rates of fall.

2. Parachutes come in many different sizes, for use with people, packages, machinery, and vehicles. How should parachute designs change for different uses?

3. Sky divers wear loose-fitting, baggy clothes. What, do you think, would be the benefit of wearing clothes like this?

INVESTIGATE FURTHER!

EXPERIMENT

What might happen if you parachute on a windy day? Repeat the activity, but add a wind factor by turning on a fan. Try tilting the fan at different angles. Does the direction of the wind have an effect? Do your observations support your explanation of how a parachute works?

Feather Falling on the Moon

As you know, there is a legend that Galileo dropped two cannonballs from the top of the Leaning Tower of Pisa. Although Galileo may never have done *this* experiment, he did experiment with the rates of fall for various objects.

As you read earlier, Galileo concluded that all objects fall at the same rate, regardless of their weight. What do you think might have happened if Galileo had experimented with a cannonball and a golf ball? What about a golf ball and a baseball? What about a hammer and a feather? In each case, do you think he would have gotten the same result?

Air Resistance

If all objects fall at the same rate, Galileo could have dropped any two objects, including a hammer and a feather, and both would have reached the ground at the same time. But perhaps Galileo suspected that a hammer and a feather dropped from a tower would not hit the ground at the same time. In fact, they wouldn't. Why not?

The additional factor in this experiment is air resistance. Air resistance is the force exerted by air against objects that are moving through the air. If you drop a metal ball from a tower, air resistance does not slow the ball very much. But if you drop a feather, air slows the feather so much that it can stay afloat quite easily. So Galileo's theory actually was that all objects fall with the same acceleration in a vacuum. In a vacuum there is no air, so there is no air resistance.

Scientists have used vacuum chambers to test Galileo's theory many times since his death in 1642. Each time, scientists

◀ July 30, 1971—Galileo is proven right as Astronaut Scott drops a hammer and a feather on the moon. They hit at the same time.

▲ No photographs exist of an actual landing on the Moon. In this picture drawn by NASA artists, what is being used to lower the Lunar Module to the Moon?

have shown that he was correct about the rate at which objects fall in a vacuum.

But the most dramatic test of Galileo's theory occurred on July 30, 1971, during the voyage of Apollo 15 to the Moon. During that voyage, astronaut David Randolph Scott dropped both a hammer and a feather at the same time while standing on the Moon's surface. Millions of television viewers saw Galileo's theory confirmed. The two objects struck the Moon's surface at exactly the same time.

Worlds Without Air

The success of Scott's experiment was due to the absence of air on the Moon. With no air resistance to hold the feather afloat, it followed the same law of acceleration as the hammer did. The difference in their masses had no effect on the way the objects fell.

The lack of air helped astronauts prove Galileo's theory once they had landed on the Moon. The lack of air also created a major headache for the scientists on Earth responsible for designing a system for safe landing on the Moon. On Earth, parachutes were used to lower spacecraft to the surface. But parachutes certainly were not going to work on the Moon. Can you explain why not?

Without a parachute, the astronauts had to use a different method for landing on the Moon's surface. What do you think they did? ■

F47

Sky Divers
and Their Parachutes

When referring to U.S. Army Airborne troops, an unknown pilot once said, "I will never understand why anyone would want to jump out of a perfectly good airplane!" Yet every day, people strap parachutes on and jump out of airplanes as part of their jobs and for fun.

Imagine standing at the open door of an airplane and then jumping out into the empty sky. Now imagine free-falling toward Earth, reaching a speed of about 192 km/h (about 120 mph). This is what sky divers do just for fun!

Patterns in the Sky

Frequently, sky divers jump individually, but sometimes they jump in large groups to create formations as they fall to Earth. As the divers leave the airplane, they don't open their parachutes.

These sky divers had less than 45 seconds to get into formation, separate, and pull their ripcords. ▼

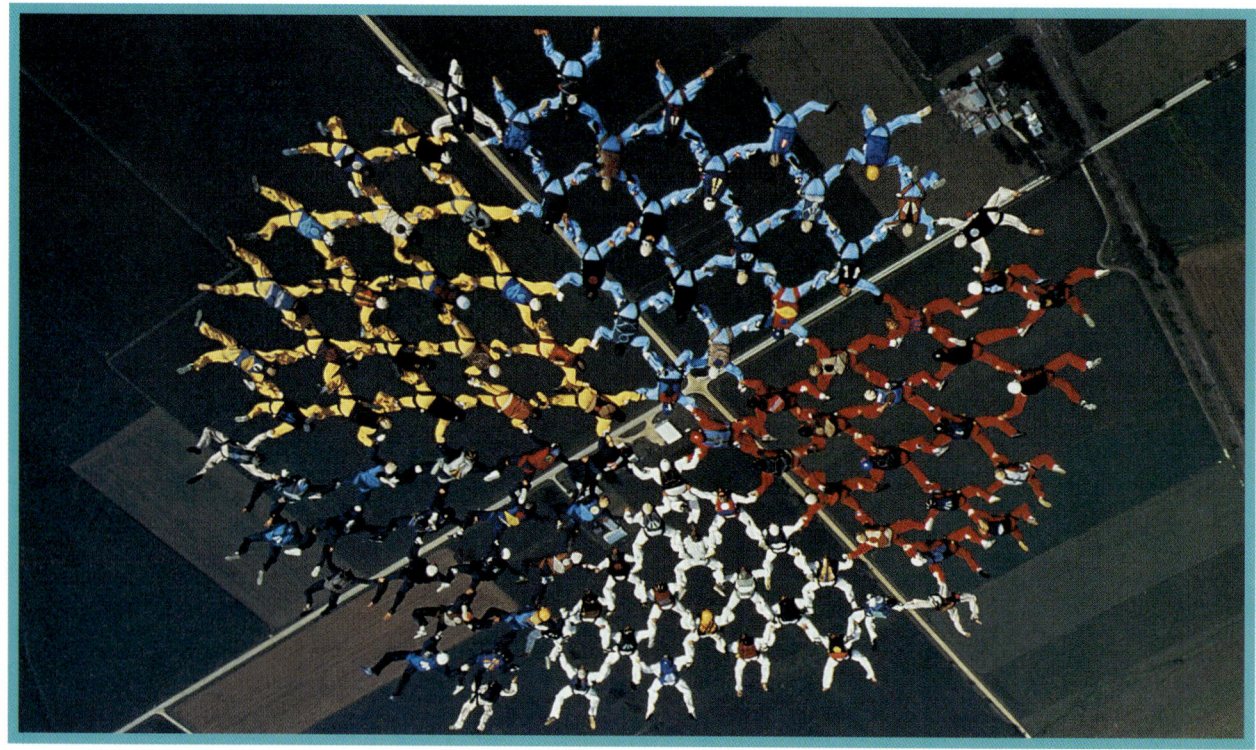

▲ A parachute without control slits will rock back and forth to allow some trapped air to escape. The result will be a very airsick parachutist.

▲ A parachute with control slits is more stable. It can also be steered so that the parachutist has more control over where he or she lands.

Instead, they free-fall. They can change their speed and direction by spreading their arms and legs to increase air resistance. As the divers fall, they reach out and grip each other's arms and legs to form the design chosen.

As sky divers create their formation, they often fall 2.4 km (about 1.5 mi) in 45 seconds. When they are no less than 670 m (about 2,200 ft) above the ground, they release their grips on one another and pull ripcords that open their parachutes. Some divers wear devices that pull their ripcords automatically when they are a certain distance above the ground. The large inside surface of a parachute offers a great deal of air resistance and slows the diver's fall to 32 km/h (about 20 mph) or less.

A parachute is actually easier to control when it has holes in it. If the parachute has no holes, the air trapped in it tries to escape through the sides. This causes the parachute to tip first one way and then another.

A small hole in the top of a parachute allows some air to escape and stops the parachute from tipping from side to side. Two slits in the sides of the parachute let more air escape. Sky divers can open and close the slits by pulling cords. This enables them to change speed and steer to a safe landing place where they land about as hard as if they had jumped off a platform 2.6 m (9 ft) above the ground.

Sky diving is much safer now than it used to be because of this ability to steer the parachute and the automatic opening feature. In 1991, around 125,000 sky divers made 2.25 million jumps. About 100,000 of these jumpers were sky diving for the first time. Some parachute

◀ Parachutes are nothing new. In the early 16th century, Leonardo da Vinci envisioned a primitive type of parachute.

centers now offer six hours of classroom training and a jump from an airplane on the same day.

Parachutes in History

Parachutes have a long history. When the great inventor Leonardo da Vinci died in 1519, he left behind the first drawings of a parachute. In 1797, Andre-Jacques Garnerin of France was the first person to use a parachute more or less successfully. Jumping from a hot-air balloon, he used a parachute that had no control slits. He was tossed around so much that he ended up airsick.

In 1917 during World War I, parachutes were used by pilots to bail out of planes that had been shot down. Parachutes were also used by soldiers to drop into enemy territory. Soldiers who did this were called paratroopers. Paratroopers attach the ripcord from the parachute to the inside of the plane. As they jump, the ripcords are pulled, and the parachutes open immediately.

Paratroopers usually need larger parachutes than do sky divers because paratroopers often carry heavy equipment and need more air resistance to slow their fall. Even bigger chutes or clusters of chutes are used for dropping cargo. For sky divers, though, one small parachute is big enough for an exciting afternoon of free-falling. ■

INVESTIGATION 3

1. Could you sky-dive on the Moon? Why or why not?

2. Sky divers sometimes do things to make themselves fall faster. What, do you think, can sky divers do to make themselves fall faster?

REFLECT & EVALUATE

WORD POWER

force
gravity
mass
weight

On Your Own
Review the terms in the list. Then use as many terms as you can to write a brief summary of the chapter.

With a Partner
Write each term in the list to make a word-search puzzle. See if your partner can find the hidden terms and tell you what each one means.

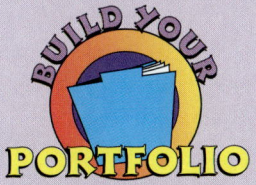

Make a poster that will help others understand the difference between mass and weight.

Analyze Information

Study the chart below. Then answer the following questions.

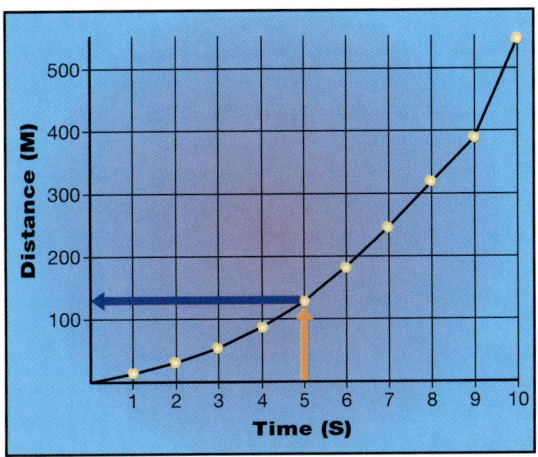

1. If an object has fallen 20 m, how long has it been falling?

2. If an object started falling 100 m off the ground and has been falling for 2 seconds, how far off the ground is it?

Assess Performance

Design, build, and test a container and parachute system that will land an egg, unbroken, after being dropped from the top of a three-story building. Make sure your teacher or a parent helps you with the test.

Problem Solving

1. Explain how the mass of an object doesn't change although its weight can change.

2. If all objects fall at the same rate, why would a car need a larger parachute than a human if both were dropped from a plane at the same time?

CHAPTER 3

MAKING AND MEASURING MOTION

Look around you on a busy street and you'll see all sorts of motion. Cars are speeding up and slowing down. People stop at curbs and then walk briskly across the street. Papers on the ground suddenly fly into the air in the breeze. What does all this changing motion have in common?

Thrills by Design

A person coming down a water slide is having fun with motion. If you've ever enjoyed the experience, you'll want to know about Andreas Tanzer. He designs water slides for amusement parks worldwide. What a great job!

Andreas says that the challenging part is making a safe ride that provides plenty of excitement as well. He has to decide how high and how long the water slide will be. Then he has to determine how people will react to the loops, turns, and curves in the design.

What do you think the slide designer must know about motion to make the slide safe as well as fun?

# Coming Up

How Are Objects at Rest and Objects in Motion Alike?
.... **F54**

How Do Forces Affect Motion?
.... **F62**

How Does Friction Affect the Motion of Objects?
.... **F70**

◀ Andreas Tanzer works with a computer-aided design for a water slide.

F53

How Are Objects at Rest and Objects in Motion Alike?

A magician approaches a table set with fine china and crystal glassware. She quickly grabs the tablecloth and pulls it from the table, leaving the dishes and glasses upright and undisturbed. How did she do it? To answer you'll need to know how objects at rest behave.

Activity
Rider Moves

MATERIALS
- 2 toy pickup trucks
- small block of wood
- *Science Notebook*

What do you feel when the car in which you are riding changes its motion suddenly?

Procedure

1. Place two toy pickup trucks, one in front of the other, on a flat hard floor. Place a wood block as a "rider" in the center of the first truck's bed. In your *Science Notebook*, **draw** a picture showing the positions of the trucks and the block.

2. Predict what will happen if you hit the first truck sharply from behind. Use the second truck to **test your prediction**. On your picture, show where the first truck was hit and what happened to it and the block.

Step 2

F54

Step 4

3. Repeat the activity twice to be sure of your results.

4. Repeat the activity, but this time hit the first truck from the front. **Record** your observations.

Analyze and Conclude

1. **Describe** what happened to the block when the truck was hit from the rear.

2. **Describe** what happened to the block when the truck was hit from the front.

3. **Explain** what happened to the block when the truck was moved suddenly.

INVESTIGATE FURTHER!

EXPERIMENT

Repeat the activity, using "passengers" of different shapes and materials. Does the shape of the passenger have any effect on the outcome? Does the material from which it's made have any effect? Report your results.

F55

Activity
Crash-test Dummies

When you ride in a car, you wear a seat belt to protect yourself from injury. How can you protect a crash-test dummy when a truck stops suddenly?

MATERIALS
- toy pickup truck
- small block of wood
- variety of materials
- ramp
- *Science Notebook*

Procedure

1. Select a block of wood that will fit in the back of a toy truck. This is now your crash-test dummy.

2. Carefully place the crash-test dummy in the back of the truck. Study its position and decide what safety equipment is needed.

3. Protect your crash-test dummy with whatever safety equipment you think is necessary.

4. As shown below set a ramp on a tilt so that the lowest part ends at a wall.

F56

5. Place your truck and crash-test dummy at the top of the ramp and release them.

6. Observe what happens to your crash-test dummy as a result of the collision. **Record** your observations in your *Science Notebook*. If the dummy flips out of the truck, tips over, or slides around in any way, you must consider the accident to be serious.

7. After the first test, **evaluate** your safety equipment and make revisions if necessary.

8. Repeat the activity, using any improved safety equipment. **Record** your observations and results.

9. Raise the ramp to make it steeper, and repeat the test. **Record** your observations.

Step 5

Analyze and Conclude

1. Make a list of all the safety devices you tried. **Describe** how well each device worked.

2. Add to your list the successful safety devices your classmates used.

3. From your observations, recommend new safety devices for real cars.

4. Why do you think the crash-test dummies tend to move around when the truck crashes into the wall?

5. What function do safety devices such as seat belts serve in car accidents?

INVESTIGATE FURTHER!

RESEARCH

Assume that your truck and dummy must ride on a track that turns upside down like a loop ride in an amusement park. Obtain some books on thrill-ride design and contact an amusement park to find out what kinds of safety precautions are built into the designs of such rides. Describe the safety precautions that amusement parks use on loop rides.

Sir Isaac Newton's First Law

Isaac Newton, born in England in 1642, spent most of his time working on his inventions. These included kites, a sundial, and a water clock. He graduated from Cambridge University in 1665, but made no particular impression on his teachers. He did not seem destined for fame.

Newton's Thoughts About Motion

Then Newton's life suddenly changed. A terrible epidemic known as the plague swept through Cambridge in 1665. To avoid the disease, Newton moved from Cambridge to his mother's farm near London. During the next 18 months, he made some of the most important discoveries in the history of mathematics and science.

Among Newton's discoveries were his hypotheses about the nature of motion. Until this time, scientists thought that a constant force was needed to keep an object in motion. It seemed obvious that if a force stopped acting on an object, the object slowed down and eventually stopped.

Newton thought differently. A story is often told that while sitting under a tree,

▲ Between 1665 and 1667, Isaac Newton revolutionized science with discoveries regarding gravity, motion, light, and mathematics.

he was struck on the head by a falling apple. While we don't know that this actually happened, we do know that late in his life Newton himself told the story to a friend. He explained that he wondered what had caused the apple's motion. Before long, Newton was looking beyond the problem of a single apple dropping from a tree. He wondered what caused the movement of Earth, the Moon, and the stars through the sky.

The Concept of Inertia

Over time, Newton worked out a number of hypotheses explaining the nature of motion. The basis of all these hypotheses is now known as Newton's **First Law of Motion**. According to this law, objects at rest tend to remain at rest. Objects in motion tend to stay in motion, traveling at a constant speed and in the same direction. The tendency of an object to remain at rest or in motion is called **inertia**.

We expect a rock to remain sitting at the top of a hill. A ball rolling across a table top will continue rolling; no force is needed to keep it in motion.

What we *do* have to explain are changes in these conditions. For example, suppose that the rock starts rolling down the hill. The problem is to explain why the rock changed its state. What made the rock start rolling down the hill?

Or suppose that a rolling ball speeds up, slows down, or changes direction. You'll discover Newton's explanation for those changes in the ball's condition in the next investigation.

Examples of Inertia

You can find many examples of inertia in everyday life. Think about the activity on page F56. What happened to the crash-test dummy when the truck suddenly stopped? Suppose you are standing in the aisle of a bus that is traveling at a constant speed of 40 km/h (25 mph). What would happen if the driver suddenly slammed on the brakes? Chances are you'd fall forward as the bus came to a

▲ Unless acted upon by some force, this rock will forever balance on top of the other rock.

stop. This would happen because your body has inertia while the bus is traveling forward. Your body is moving in the same direction and at the same speed as the bus. When the driver hits the brakes, the bus comes to a stop, but inertia keeps your body moving forward.

A similar explanation applies to sudden starts by the bus. You sit quietly in your seat while the bus waits for the last passenger to board. The driver suddenly steps on the accelerator. The bus lurches forward. What happens to you? How does inertia explain what happens? ■

Seat Belts and Airbags

 An automobile can provide a frightening lesson in inertia. A person riding in a car traveling at 88 km/h (55 mph) is also traveling at 88 km/h. If that person is unrestrained and the car is suddenly stopped by a wall or telephone pole, the person will continue to move forward at 88 km/h until stopped by the steering wheel, dashboard, or windshield.

Automobile Safety Systems

Automotive engineers have long been aware of the hazards associated with traveling in a car. Over time, they have developed a number of different systems to overcome inertia and prevent or reduce crash-related injuries.

Newer vehicles are equipped with head restraints. In a rear-end collision, a passenger's head is thrown back and hits the head restraint. This support prevents serious injury by stopping the backward motion of the head. Look at the photos of other automobile safety systems.

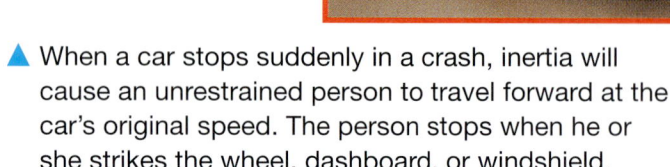

▲ When a car stops suddenly in a crash, inertia will cause an unrestrained person to travel forward at the car's original speed. The person stops when he or she strikes the wheel, dashboard, or windshield.

One of the great safety inventions of recent decades is the air bag. Stored in the dashboard or steering wheel of a car, the bag prevents the driver from being thrown into the steering column or dashboard. ▶

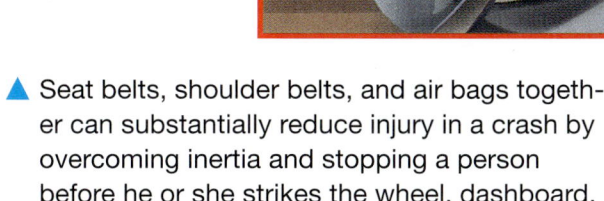

▲ Seat belts, shoulder belts, and air bags together can substantially reduce injury in a crash by overcoming inertia and stopping a person before he or she strikes the wheel, dashboard, or windshield.

INVESTIGATION 1

1. Compare two cars in terms of inertia. One is sitting in the driveway; the other is rolling along a level street.

2. As you come around a corner, you run into a table and a crystal vase tips toward you. You reach out in desperation and catch it before it hits the table. What made the vase tip? Why did it tip toward you and not away from you?

F61

INVESTIGATION 2

How Do Forces Affect Motion?

Two bike riders meet on James Street. One is coasting along and brakes to slow down. The other is pedaling hard to speed up. What forces are causing both of these changes in motion?

Activity

Starting and Stopping

What happens to the motion of a ball when you push it gently? What happens when you push it harder?

MATERIALS
- ball
- sheet of butcher paper
- ruler
- crayon
- *Science Notebook*

Procedure

1. Place a sheet of butcher paper on the floor. **Draw** a dot in the center of the paper.

2. Place a ball on top of the dot.

3. Use a ruler to **draw** a line extending away from the dot.

4. Hold a crayon over the line and behind the ball, aiming at the center of the ball. **Predict** the direction in which the ball will move if you gently push it with the crayon.

Step 3

Step 4

5. Push the ball. **Observe** the ball's path. Then **draw** the ball's path on the butcher paper.

6. Repeat steps 4 and 5, but this time hit the ball with more force. **Draw** the path of the ball on the paper.

7. Place the ball on the dot again. **Draw** another line on the paper, extending from the ball in a different direction.

8. Put the crayon over this line and gently strike the ball. **Draw** the ball's path on the paper.

Analyze and Conclude

1. When you hit the ball with the crayon, you are applying a force to the ball. **Suggest a hypothesis** that describes the relationship between the strength of the force applied and the resulting behavior of the ball.

2. The lines you drew on the butcher paper in steps 5, 6, and 8 show the direction in which the force acts. In a sentence, **suggest a hypothesis** that describes the relationship between the direction of each force and the resulting behavior of the ball.

INVESTIGATE FURTHER!

EXPERIMENT

In soccer most players can kick the ball in a straight line on the ground, and they can make the ball rise into the air. Skillful players can put sidespin on the ball to make it curve right or left. Really skillful players also can put backspin on a ball to make it stop dead or roll backward when it lands. Experiment to find out what you have to do to a soccer ball to make it curve or spin backward. Report your results to the class.

Activity
The Problem With Big Trucks

How is the motion of objects that have different masses affected by equal forces?

MATERIALS
- 2 toy trucks, one with a heavy load
- small wooden board
- metric ruler
- long wooden board
- books
- block of wood
- *Science Notebook*

Procedure

1. Place two toy trucks on a level floor.
2. Place a small wooden board behind both trucks.
3. **Predict** how the trucks will move if you apply equal force to each. Use the board to give both trucks a sudden, sharp push. Do not follow through.
4. **Measure the distance** that each truck moved, and **record** the data in your *Science Notebook*. Repeat the experiment twice. **Calculate** the average distance moved by each truck.
5. Build a ramp by propping up one end of a long wooden board on a stack of books.
6. Place the lighter truck at the top of the ramp. Place a block of wood at the bottom.
7. Release the truck so that it hits the block of wood squarely. **Measure** how far the truck travels after hitting the block. **Record** your measurement.
8. Repeat steps 6 and 7, using the heavier truck.

Step 1

Step 2

Step 6

Analyze and Conclude

1. Based on your observations, how does an equal force applied to two objects of different mass affect the acceleration of each?
2. What forces were acting to stop the trucks as they came down the ramp?
3. In which case was a greater force required to stop the truck? How do you know?

Sir Isaac Newton's
Second Law

When Isaac Newton left Cambridge, he was just looking for a way to avoid the plague. But during the next 18 months, Newton made observations that enabled him to explain the relationship between light and color and to invent a form of mathematics called calculus. He also explained how God holds the universe together by gravitation and laws of motion.

Although Newton completed his early investigations of gravity and motion in 1666, his theory of gravitation and laws of motion were not published until 1687. Newton's First Law of Motion states that all bodies have inertia. They tend to stay at rest or to travel at a constant speed in a constant direction.

Newton's **Second Law of Motion** picks up where the first law leaves off. An object that is at rest or in motion will not change its condition unless something causes the change. What might make an object move, speed up, slow down, stop, or change direction?

Force, Mass, and Acceleration

Newton hypothesized that the answer to the question asked above is a force. Remember that a **force** in science is a push or a pull. Newton's Second Law states that an object begins to move, speeds up, slows down, comes to a stop, or changes direction only when some force acts on that object.

For example, a rock on top of a hill might begin rolling down the hill if someone exerted a force on it. Once started down the hill, the rock would continue to gain speed because of the force of gravity

A push and a pull are both forces and both can result in a change in motion. ▼

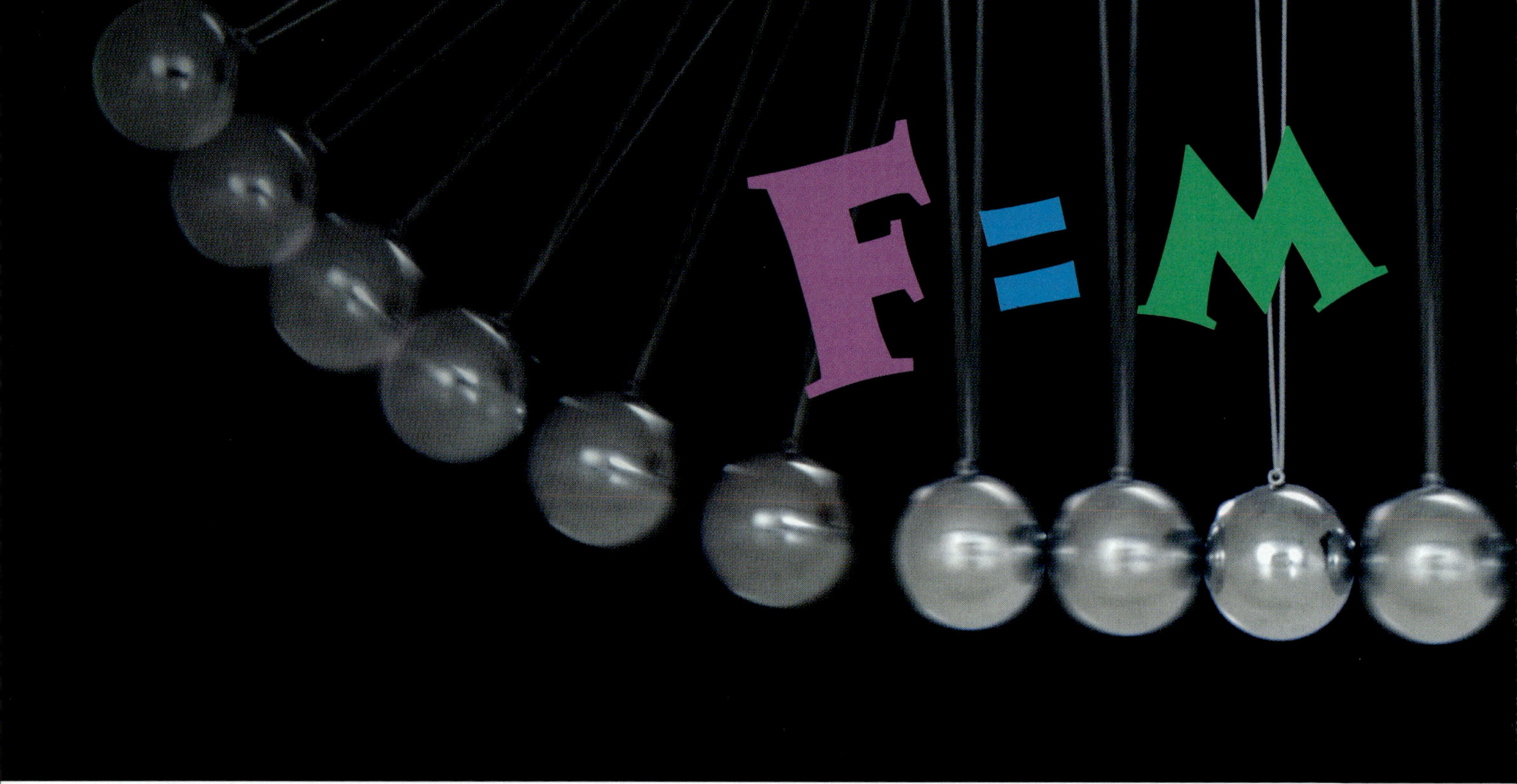

acting on it. The rock would continue moving down the hill until some new force acted on it to change its direction, slow it down, or stop it.

Consider a ball rolling across a billiard table. The ball might speed up, slow down, or change direction. Why? The Second Law says that changes such as these occur because a force has acted on the ball. What might provide the necessary force on a billiard ball?

Perhaps the billiard ball is hit by another ball from behind, in front, or from the side. If the contact with the other ball is from behind, a pushing force changes the speed of the first ball. If the contact is from the side or front, a pushing force changes not only the speed of the ball but also the direction in which the ball is moving.

Calculating Force

Newton discovered a mathematical formula that shows how force causes a change in the speed or direction of an object. That formula is

$$\text{Force} = \text{mass} \times \text{acceleration}$$
$$(F = m \times a)$$

The units used in this formula are newtons (N) for force, kilograms (kg) for mass, and meters per second per second (m/s^2) for acceleration. A **newton** is

The rocks in this picture moved down the hill because a force acted on them. ▼

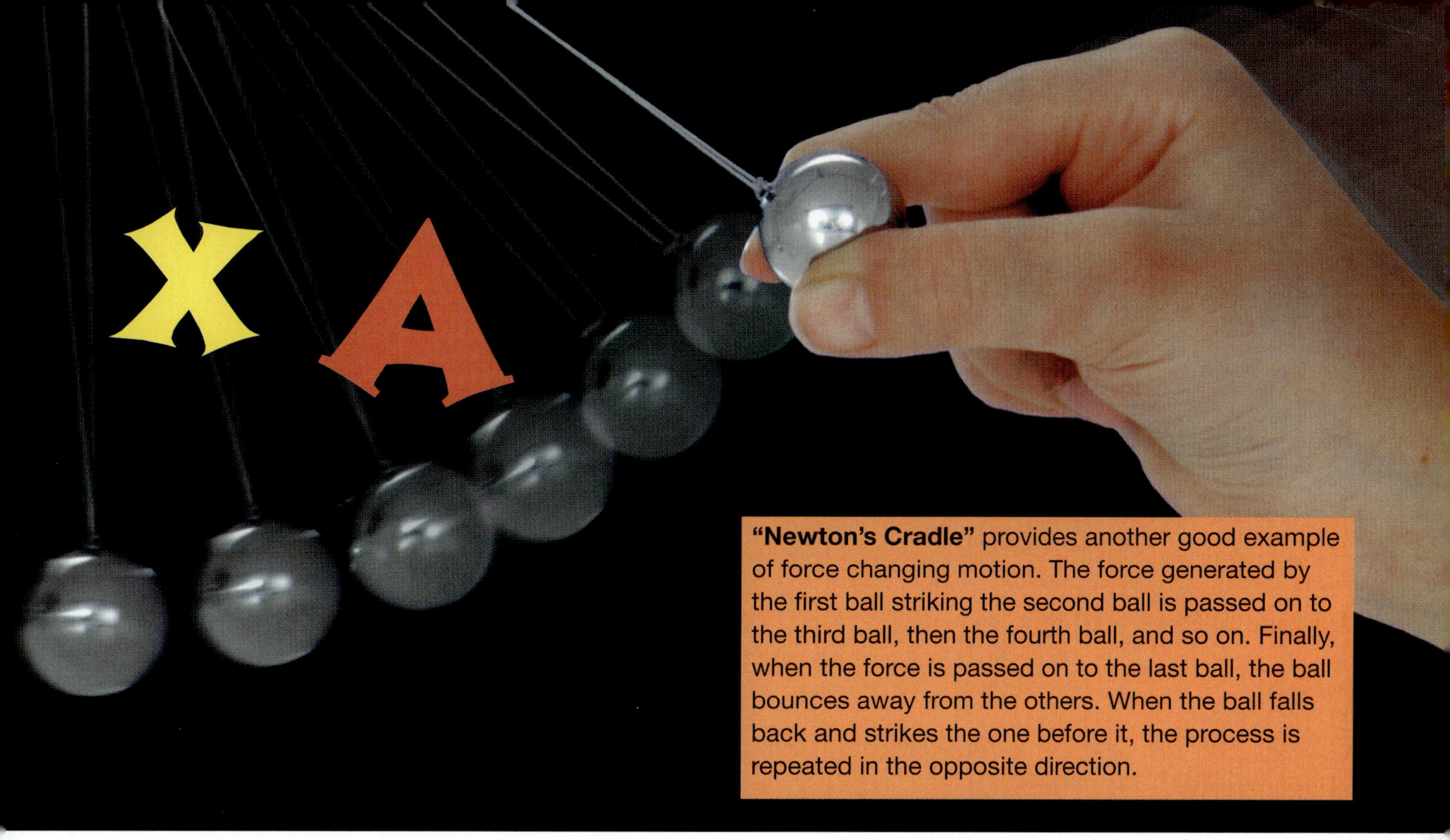

"Newton's Cradle" provides another good example of force changing motion. The force generated by the first ball striking the second ball is passed on to the third ball, then the fourth ball, and so on. Finally, when the force is passed on to the last ball, the ball bounces away from the others. When the ball falls back and strikes the one before it, the process is repeated in the opposite direction.

defined as the force needed to accelerate a 1-kg object by 1 meter per second every second.

$$(N = kg \times m/s^2)$$

The formula for force tells us many things about the way in which a force acts on an object. For example, suppose an object with a mass of 2 kg accelerates at 5 m/s². What force is required to achieve that acceleration? To answer that question, first write the formula for Newton's Second Law.

$$F = m \times a$$

Then substitute the values you know for this question.

$$m = 2 \text{ kg}; a = 5 \text{ m/s}^2$$

An Acceleration Problem ▶ Look at the engines in these two cars. The smaller car requires a smaller engine because it has a smaller mass. The larger car requires a larger engine because it has a larger mass. Which car probably requires the greater force to accelerate it to a speed of 88 km/h (55 mph) in 10 s?

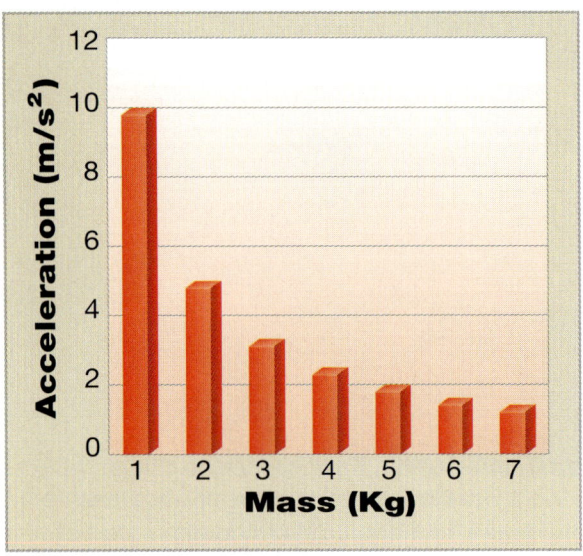

▲ Figure 1: Force = 10 N

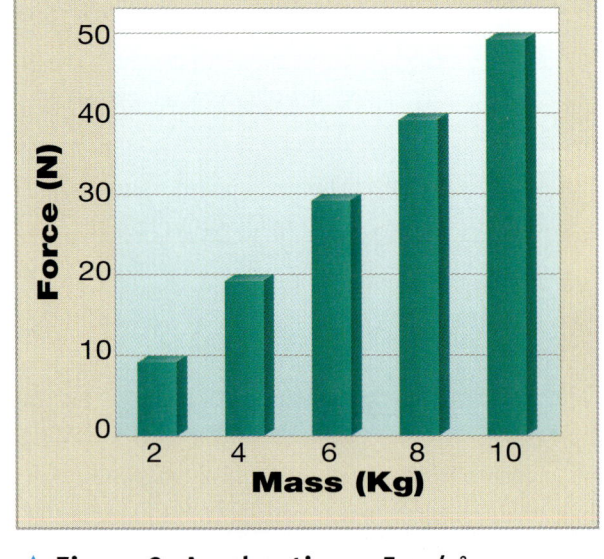

▲ Figure 2: Acceleration = 5 m/s²

Finally, use the formula to find the unknown quantity—force.

$$F = m \times a$$
$$F = 2 \text{ kg} \times 5 \text{ m/s}^2$$
$$F = 10 \text{ kg} \times \text{m/s}^2$$
$$F = 10 \text{ N}$$

It would require a force of 10 N to make a 2-kg object accelerate at the rate of 5 m/s every second, or 5 m/s².

What happens if the same force acts on a heavier body, one of 5 kg, for example? To find the answer to this question, use the bar graph in Figure 1. Notice that the x-axis of the graph shows seven different masses that are acted on by a force of 10 N. The y-axis shows the resulting acceleration.

When you solved this problem, you discovered an important general rule. A constant force, such as 10 N, causes greater acceleration in a lighter body than it does in a heavier body.

Other Applications of the Second Law

Suppose you wanted to give a heavier body the same acceleration as a lighter body. You can use $F = m \times a$ to find out how to do that, too. Look at the bar graph in Figure 2. Notice that the force required for an acceleration of 5 m/s² increases as mass increases. For example, a 4-kg mass requires a force of 20 N to accelerate to 5 m/s². A 2-kg mass only requires a force of 10 N to achieve the same acceleration.

Perhaps you'd like to know what happens to the acceleration of a 10-kg object if you change the force applied to it. Look at the bar graph in Figure 3. If you increase the force on a 10-kg mass, how is acceleration affected?

Finding the Mass of an Object

How can you find the mass of an object? Easy, you say—just put it on a balance and read the value. Scientists know another way to answer this question. They find the object's mass from the Second Law: $F = m \times a$.

Suppose you hit an object of unknown mass with a force of 15 N. Suppose that the object then moves with an acceleration of 5 m/s². Look at the bar graph in Figure 2. Can you use any of the information in this graph to solve the problem?

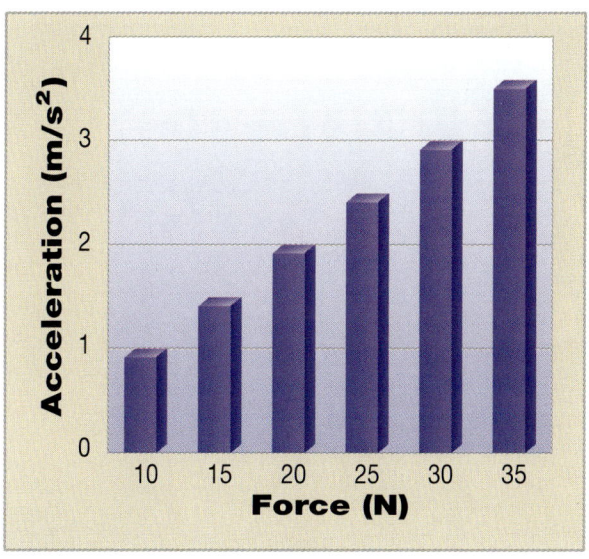

▲ Figure 3: Mass = 10 kg

▲ How are force, mass, and acceleration related in a BMX race?

You probably can. You can also try to rearrange the Second Law's formula to solve for mass. If you determined that the mass of the object is 3 kg, you're right on the mark! Congratulations!

In fact, the Second Law gives us a new way of thinking about mass. Mass is a measure of a body's inertia. If a large force is required to overcome the inertia of a body and get that body moving, the body has a lot of mass. If only a little force is needed to move a body, the body has a small amount of mass. Now you can find an exact number for the mass of a body, using Newton's Second Law of Motion. ■

INVESTIGATE FURTHER!

RESEARCH

Call a local car and truck dealership. Ask for information about their lightest car and their heaviest truck. Ask about differences in the engine and brake systems of the vehicles. Report the information to your class.

INVESTIGATION 2

1. What can you infer about the force necessary to throw a ball with an acceleration of 5 m/s^2 compared with the force required to throw it at 10 m/s^2?

2. A wagon has a mass of 20 kg. One child has a mass of 30 kg while another has a mass of 40 kg. A third child pushes the wagon. What force is needed to accelerate each child plus the wagon to 5 m/s^2?

How Does Friction Affect the Motion of Objects?

Investigation 3

A race car traveling at 240 km/h (149 mph) suddenly runs out of fuel. In less than 1 km, the car coasts to a stop. What slowed the car to 0 km/h so quickly? In this investigation you'll find out about the force that did it.

Activity

Friction Floors

According to the principle of inertia, a rolling car should roll forever. But it doesn't. Why not?

MATERIALS
- toy car that rolls well
- ramp that is at least 5 toy-car lengths long
- pieces of sandpaper, aluminum foil, wax paper, and a towel, each at least as long as 5 toy cars
- metric tape measure
- *Science Notebook*

Procedure

1. In your *Science Notebook*, **make a chart** in which you will list the different materials and how far the car traveled on each.

2. Tilt the ramp upward 5 to 8 cm, as shown in the photograph. Place a piece of sandpaper at the bottom of the ramp.

Step 2

F70

3. Release the car from the top of the ramp and watch it roll off the ramp and onto the sandpaper.

4. Measure how far the car traveled on the sandpaper. **Record** this information in the chart. Repeat the activity twice and **record** the distances.

5. Repeat steps 2, 3, and 4, using aluminum foil, wax paper, and towel. **Record** in the chart the distance the car travels over each material.

Step 5

Analyze and Conclude

1. Rank the four materials in order, from the one on which the car rolled farthest to the one on which the car rolled the shortest distance.

2. Each material is applying a force to the car to slow it down. Which material applied the most force? What evidence do you have to support your answer?

3. Compare the materials. What characteristics make some materials better than others at making the car stop?

INVESTIGATE FURTHER!

EXPERIMENT

When water freezes on a road, the road becomes slick. Freeze some water in a large flat pan, then experiment with different materials to make the ice less slippery. Which materials were most effective?

F71

Activity
Wheel Power

How do wheels help vehicles stay in motion?

MATERIALS
- toy truck that rolls well
- ramp at least as long as 10 toy cars
- box about the same size as the car
- *Science Notebook*

Procedure

1. Tilt a ramp as shown in the photo.

2. Place a toy truck on the ramp. Release it and **observe** what happens.

3. Place the box on the ramp. Release it and **observe** what happens.

4. **Record** your observations.

Analyze and Conclude

1. When two objects rub as they pass each other, friction is generated. Where does friction occur as the truck moves down the ramp? Where does friction occur when the box is on the ramp?

2. **Explain** what you observed in this activity in terms of friction. What are some ways of reducing friction between objects?

Step 3

INVESTIGATE FURTHER!

RESEARCH

Wheels are designed to minimize friction between objects. Look around for other objects and substances that reduce friction, such as ball bearings. Write a report about things that reduce the friction between moving objects.

Friction

▲ Spinning rapidly, the wheels of a drag racer rub against the surface of the track. Because the tires get hot and sticky, they grip the track better and the car can accelerate faster.

The driver pushes down on the accelerator, and the engine roars. The signal light turns green, and the driver releases the clutch. The car's wheels spin and scream. As smoke pours from the rapidly spinning tires, the car leaps forward. Less than four seconds later, the car reaches the end of the quarter-mile track, the driver hits the brakes, and a parachute pops out in back to stop the car.

Drag racing is an exciting sport. Car drivers compete with each other to see who can travel a quarter-mile course in the shortest time. Drivers usually smear a sticky material on the wheels of their cars at the beginning of the race. The sticky material increases the friction between tire and pavement. It helps cars grip the road and get off to a faster start.

What Is Friction?

Friction is a force that occurs between surfaces that are in contact with each other. Friction resists the motion of one surface over another. When a race car is at rest on the pavement, it has no motion. There is no friction between the car's tires and the pavement. But when the driver steps on the accelerator, the car's tires begin to rotate. Friction begins to develop between the tires and the pavement.

The amount of friction between two bodies depends on many factors but especially on the properties of each surface. Rough surfaces generally result in more friction than do smooth surfaces. Imagine sliding an ice cube across the frozen surface of a lake. Ice is usually very smooth, so there is little friction between the ice cube and the ice on the lake. The ice cube will slide a long way before coming to rest. What would happen if you slid the ice cube across rough pavement?

Friction also varies with the kind of motion taking place. Objects that roll over a surface produce less friction than objects that slide. Ball bearings are small metal balls inserted between two surfaces that rub against each other. There is

▲ **Bearings are used inside skateboard wheels to reduce the friction caused by pieces turning against one another.**

much less friction with the ball bearings rolling between the surfaces than with the two surfaces rubbing directly against each other.

Lubricants are liquids or fine powders used to reduce the friction between two surfaces. In many types of machinery,

SCIENCE AND FAITH

Friction is God's natural device to prevent objects from continuous motion. Friction can be good as in cases when you need to stop a bicycle or car. Friction can be damaging as when an engine self-destructs for lack of friction-reducing oil. As with all of God's creation, friction can be either a friend or an enemy depending on how it is used.

We sometimes use the word friction to describe tense or hostile relationships between people. Friction between two friends can end a friendship as quickly as too much friction can end an engine. But sometimes friction between friends is good. It's good when it drives friends to seek forgiveness and understanding. Forgiveness is like a lubricant that smooths out rough relationships.

Jesus died on the cross to earn forgiveness for us. Sometimes the friction between God and us returns, but repentance and forgiveness eliminates that friction. When God sets His forgiveness in motion, it never stops rolling!

metal surfaces rub against each other. A lot of friction results. The friction produces heat, which can damage the machinery. A few drops of oil can reduce this friction. If the friction is reduced, there is less damage to the machinery.

Friction in Sports

In many winter sports, participants want to reduce friction as much as possible. Downhill skiers often put wax on their skis. The wax reduces the friction between the skis and the snow, and the skier's speed increases.

Friction slows speed, but it can also be helpful. Walking is possible, for example, because friction prevents your feet from simply sliding back over the ground. In some sports, players want to increase friction. Someone who runs the 100-m dash wants the maximum possible amount of friction between his or her feet and the running track. What would happen if that friction suddenly disappeared? Why would friction be good for a basketball player or football player?

Shoes and Tires

In the last 50 years, a giant industry has developed that makes the right kind of shoe for each type of sport. In many cases, the right kind of shoe means a

▲ The shoes worn by a sprinter contain sharp spikes that penetrate the running surface. The spikes create greater friction between the runner and the track surface.

shoe that gives an athlete just the right amount of friction to do well in his or her particular sport.

Athletic shoes may have studs, cleats, or spikes on their soles to prevent the shoes from sliding over the ground. The bottom of a golfer's shoes, for example, are covered with metal spikes. The spikes dig into the ground and increase friction

---

UNIT PROJECT LINK

Choose two different motion rides to design. The rides should start, stop, and carry at least one marble. One of the rides should turn in circles. The other should use a swing. Give each ride a name. Then experiment with your rides to determine how fast each goes and the safety features each needs. Display this information beside each ride.

Various types of athletic shoes are designed to provide the proper amount of friction for an athlete to have a peak performance. ▼

to prevent the golfer from slipping as the club is swung.

Athletic footwear manufacturers produce several major kinds of shoes: those for running, walking, and training; for tennis and other court sports; for soccer, rugby, and other field sports; for track and field; and for specialty sports such as aerobics. In each case, the shoe's sole is designed to provide the right amount of friction between the shoe and the surface on which it is intended to be worn.

Interesting comparisons can be made between shoes, designed for human feet, and tires, designed for motor vehicles. When a wheel and tire roll, the tire surface does not slide over the pavement. In fact, some friction between tires and road is necessary to get a car moving in the first place and to bring it to a stop. Different kinds of tires have been invented to provide more or less friction, depending on the driving circumstances.

Snow tires, for example, are heavier and often wider than normal tires. These features increase the friction between a tire and the road. How are tires used by drag racers designed to increase friction? What can happen when there's not enough friction between the tires of a car and the road? ■

Tires are designed to provide friction under different circumstances. ▼

INVESTIGATION 3

1. How does friction help the movement of a car? How does friction hinder the movement of the car?

2. During the winter, highway department road crews often spread sand or cinders on ice. Why do they do this?

F76

REFLECT & EVALUATE

WORD POWER

First Law of Motion
force
friction
inertia
newton
Second Law of Motion

 On Your Own Review the terms in the list. Then use as many terms as you can in a paragraph about the laws of motion.

With a Partner Write each term in the list on one side of an index card and the definition on the other side. Use the cards to quiz your partner.

Design a banner for your classroom wall with everyday examples of Newton's First Law and Second Law on it. The laws should also be clearly stated on the banner.

Analyze Information

Study the bar graph below. Suppose equal forces had been applied to two objects. What can be inferred about their masses? Now suppose the objects are of equal mass. What can be inferred about the forces causing the accelerations?

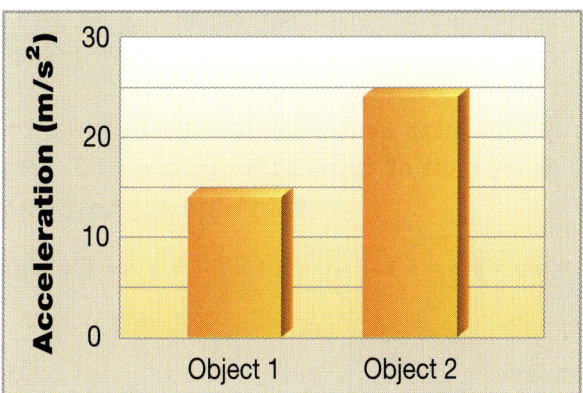

Assess Performance

Compare rolling friction and sliding friction. Hypothesize which friction is greater; then design an experiment to test your hypothesis. What materials would you need to conduct the experiment? Record and analyze your data and state whether you accept or reject your hypothesis.

Problem Solving

1. You have just watched another magician pull a tablecloth from under dishes. Explain this trick in terms of the principle of inertia.

2. Two books fall off a shelf. Both hit the floor at the same time. Your teacher tells you that both books had to fall with an acceleration of 9.8 m/s^2. If one book has a mass of 1.8 kg and the other has a mass of 3 kg, what is the force of gravity on each book?

CHAPTER 4
FORCES IN PAIRS

Some objects at rest require little force to move them. Other objects need a great deal of force to be influenced. What do you know about the forces that objects exert on each other?

The Physics Does the Work

How do you demolish a nine-story building in ten seconds? You "let physics do the work," says Anna Chong, president of Engineered Demolition of Minneapolis. The laws of physics cause the building to implode and fall down in a rubble.

In 1994 Anna Chong's company was responsible for imploding the Sears complex in Philadelphia, Pennsylvania. The enormous structure consisted of a nine-story merchandise building and a fourteen-story clock tower. Using 5,400 kg (12,000 lb) of dynamite, the blasters caused the building to implode instead of explode. The result was a towering heap of steel and concrete that took two months to cart away. How do you think engineers of the demolition company got the building to crumble in this way?

Coming Up

WHAT PROPERTY DO ALL MOVING OBJECTS SHARE?
............F80

HOW DO ACTIONS CAUSE REACTIONS?
............F88

HOW ARE ACTION-REACTION FORCES USED?
............F96

◀ Anna Chong placing dynamite in the Philadelphia Sears complex

F79

INVESTIGATION 1

WHAT PROPERTY DO ALL MOVING OBJECTS SHARE?

Traveling at 156.8 km/h (98 mph), a baseball streaks toward the player at bat. The batter swings hard and sends the ball sailing toward the stands 121 m (400 ft) away. What has happened to change the ball's speed and direction? In this investigation you'll find out what is shared by the bat and ball.

Activity
Marble Collisions

At one time or another, you've probably run smack into a person who was standing still. What happened? Use marbles to find out!

MATERIALS
- 2 small marbles
- 2 large marbles
- *Science Notebook*

SAFETY
Always direct the marbles away from yourself and others.

Procedure

1. Predict what will happen in each of the collisions listed in the tables below. Then create the collisions on a smooth, flat surface, and **describe** them in your *Science Notebook*.

Large Moving Marble Colliding With
a small stationary marble
a small moving marble
a large moving marble
the first marble in a row of two small stationary marbles

Small Moving Marble Colliding With
a small stationary marble
a small moving marble
a large moving marble
a small stationary marble that is directly in front of, and touching, a large stationary marble

2. Create each collision two more times to be certain of the results.

Analyze and Conclude

All moving objects have momentum. **Momentum** is a property related to the motion of an object. In a collision between a moving object and an object at rest, the moving object transfers some of its momentum to the object that is at rest.

1. Describe what happens to the momentum of the small marble when it hits another small marble at rest.

2. Describe what happens to the momentum of the large marble when it hits a small marble at rest.

3. Describe what happens to the momentum of the large marble when it hits two small marbles at rest.

4. What evidence did you find that momentum can be transferred during collisions?

INVESTIGATE FURTHER!

EXPERIMENT

Design an experiment to study momentum, using a beach ball and a basketball. Under exactly the same conditions, which ball has the greater momentum? What two things does momentum depend on?

Step 1

Activity
Football Momentum

Different-sized marbles can be compared to different-sized football players. How is momentum important in a football game?

MATERIALS
- 1 big marble
- 2 small marbles
- metric ruler
- *Science Notebook*

SAFETY
Always direct the marbles away from yourself and others.

Procedure

1. Pretend two marbles are football players. Let a big marble be a large lineman. Let a small marble be a smaller player. Let the large lineman tackle the smaller player by rolling the two marbles into each other at the same speed. **Record** in your *Science Notebook* what happens after the collision.

Step 1

2. Pretend that the big marble is a linebacker running into the backfield. This time the smaller player, who is carrying the ball, is running more than twice as fast as the larger player. To simulate this, make the small marble travel about twice as fast as the big marble. Have the marbles collide directly. **Record** what happens after the collision.

Step 2

Step 3

3. Assume that the small marble is the quarterback standing still, trying to find a receiver. A large lineman (the large marble) runs into the quarterback. With the small marble at rest, roll the large marble into it. **Record** what happens.

Analyze and Conclude

1. Look at your marble simulations of football tackles. Why are the football players on the scrimmage line usually very large and massive?

2. Why is it important for the smaller runners to run very fast before colliding with a larger player?

3. Suppose two football players of the same mass traveled toward each other at the same speed. **Predict** what would happen after the collision. Using the marbles and a metric ruler, **simulate** the collision and **record** the results.

4. What two factors determine an object's momentum?

UNIT PROJECT LINK

Bumper cars is a very popular amusement park attraction. Imagine two bumper cars racing toward one another and colliding. Describe what you think would happen after the collision. Sometimes a driver hits a bumper car that is touching another bumper car. Using three marbles of the same size, create a model of this crash. Watch what happens to the marbles. Describe what happens to each "car." Test as many different types of collisions as you can think of. Describe the result of each collision on a card next to a drawing of it.

Playing Pool

"Rack 'em up!" Anyone who has ever played pool has probably heard these words at the beginning of a game. To begin a game of pool, players rack, or arrange, 15 colored balls into the shape of a triangle at one end of the pool table.

Then one player stands at the opposite end of the table and uses a cue stick to strike the white cue ball. The cue ball travels across the table and "breaks" the triangle of colored balls. Often, one or more of the colored balls roll into pockets at the sides of the table. The game continues as the two players take turns hitting the cue ball at the colored balls. The game ends when all the balls except the cue ball have been hit into pockets.

A good pool player seems to understand how momentum works. When the cue ball is struck with the end of the cue stick, momentum is transferred from the cue stick to the cue ball. When the cue ball hits a single colored ball squarely, the cue ball stops rolling because all its momentum has been transferred. What happens to the colored ball?

Pool players often send a colored ball into a pocket by hitting it at an angle instead of hitting it squarely. When the cue ball strikes a colored ball on an angle, some of the momentum is maintained by the cue ball and some is transferred to the colored ball. The place where the cue ball hits the colored ball determines the direction in which the colored ball will roll. The path of the cue ball also changes because of impact. The game of pool is not as scientific as this description makes it sound. However, understanding the principle of momentum might just help you play the game better.

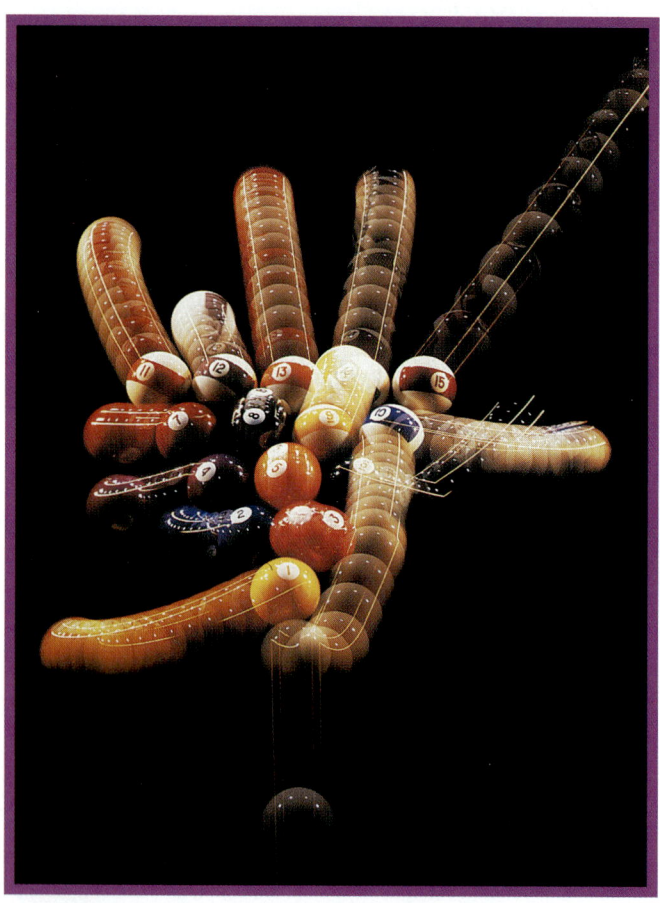

▲ In pool, momentum is transferred from the cue stick to the cue ball and from the cue ball to the balls it strikes.

Momentum Sharing

▲ Would you like to catch this baseball with your bare hand?

A baseball and a tennis ball have each been thrown to you at fairly high speeds. You must decide which one to catch barehanded. Which one will you choose?

Now the baseball has been lobbed underhand to you, and the tennis ball has been served to you by a professional tennis player. Which will you choose to catch barehanded this time?

Were your answers to the two questions the same or different? Why? What was the difference between the baseball and the tennis ball in the two situations?

How would you feel about catching this tennis ball? ▶

Momentum

The ability of a moving object to make something happen depends on how much mass it contains and how fast it's moving. In the original question, suppose both balls were thrown at a speed of 1 m/s (about 1 yd/s). Which ball do you think would sting more if you caught it with a bare hand?

Now compare what happens when the tennis ball moves toward you at 45 m/s (49 yd/s) and the baseball is thrown at 1 m/s (about 1 yd/s). Which ball do you think would sting more?

The concept that scientists use to express the combined effect of an object's mass and velocity is **momentum.**

The momentum of a body can be found by multiplying its mass by its velocity. In mathematical terms, that would be expressed as

$$p = m \times v$$

Note that the symbol p is often used to represent momentum.

In the formula shown above, mass (m) should be expressed in kilograms (kg), and velocity (v) in meters per second (m/s). Then, the unit of measure for momentum (p) is kilograms multiplied by meters per second.

You can use this formula to calculate the momentum of any object. For example, suppose that the baseball mentioned has a mass of 0.149 kg. What will be its momentum when traveling at a velocity of 6 m/s? To answer that question, write the formula for momentum.

$$p = m \times v$$

Then substitute the values for the mass (m) of the baseball and its velocity (v).

$$p = .149 \text{ kg} \times 6 \text{ m/s}$$
$$p = .894 \text{ kg} \times \text{m/s}.$$

What would be the momentum of the same baseball traveling at 8 m/s?

Conservation of Momentum

Some of the most interesting examples of momentum come from the world of sports. Think about the situation in which a pitcher throws a ball to a batter, who then hits a home run. When the ball was thrown, it had a momentum determined by its mass and velocity. It also had momentum after being hit, determined by its mass and its new velocity. In addition, the bat had momentum determined by its mass and the speed with which the batter swung.

Scientists can analyze such situations by using the **Law of Conservation of Momentum**. This law states that momentum can be transferred but can't be lost. When two or more objects collide, the total momentum at the end of the collision is the same as the total momentum at the beginning. When a bat hits a ball, the sum of the momentum of the bat and of the ball as it rebounds from the bat is equal to the sum of the momentum of the bat as it was swung and of the ball as it approached the bat. Can you apply this law to the activities on pages F80 and F82?

◀ Whenever objects collide, the resulting momentum of the objects is equal to the total momentum of the objects before the collision.

The momentum of a rocket in one direction is equal to the momentum of the burning gases in the opposite direction. ▶

The Rocket's Red Glare

Another example of the Law of Conservation of Momentum is found in a rocket launch. Imagine a rocket whose mass is 100,000 kg (220,000 lb) sitting on a launch pad. What is the rocket's momentum? Since the engines aren't firing, its momentum is zero.

But what happens once the engines fire? If you've ever seen a rocket launch, you know that the situation changes quickly once the fuel ignites. As burning gases move downward, the rocket moves upward.

Consider launching a model rocket with a mass of 1 kg (2.2 lb). Assume 0.1 kg (0.22 lb) of fuel is burned quickly, and the gases leave the rocket with a speed of 300 m/s (about 330 yd/s). How fast does the rocket go upward?

Remember that the total momentum before launch was zero. The Law of Conservation of Momentum tells us that the total momentum after launch also is zero because the rocket goes in one direction and the burning gases go in another direction. Mathematically, different directions are represented by opposite signs: a plus sign for the rocket momentum and a minus sign for the momentum of the burning gases.

rocket momentum − gas momentum = 0
(0.9 kg × v) − (0.1 kg × 300 m/s) = 0

Note that the rocket's mass includes the mass of its unburned fuel. Since the rocket has burned 0.1 kg of fuel, its mass has fallen to 0.9 kg. What is the value of v?

If you calculated that v = 33.3 m/s, you were correct. Remember that this is the value for the first moments of a liftoff. The rocket will gain velocity as more fuel is burned. ■

INVESTIGATION 1

1. A cue ball rolls quickly toward the racked pool balls. Colliding with the first ball in the triangle, the cue ball comes to a complete stop. The racked pool balls, however, scatter in all directions. Explain what has happened in terms of conservation of momentum.

2. Explain how conservation of momentum is involved in table tennis.

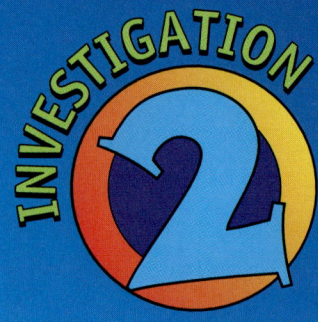

INVESTIGATION 2

How Do Actions Cause Reactions?

A child is roller-skating. Without thinking, he pushes on a wall, rolls backward, loses his balance, and falls into a puddle. You'll be able to explain what happened when you explore the relationship between action forces and reaction forces.

Activity

Bouncing Balls

When you drop a ball, it strikes Earth. What causes the ball to bounce back?

MATERIALS
- basketball or other large ball that bounces
- Science Notebook

Procedure

1. Drop a large ball on a flat floor. **Observe** the ball's speed. **Record** in your *Science Notebook* the point at which the ball is traveling the fastest and the point at which it is traveling the slowest.

2. Drop the ball again. This time, **observe** its direction. At what point does the ball's motion change direction?

3. **Predict** what will happen if you bounce the ball harder against the floor.

4. **Test** your prediction and **observe** the ball's motion. **Record** the results.

Analyze and Conclude

1. What exerted a force, or pushed back, on the ball when it hit the floor, causing the ball to change speed and direction?

2. How did bouncing the ball harder affect the force that changes the ball's speed and direction?

3. Identify two forces that act when the ball hits the floor.

Step 1

INVESTIGATE FURTHER!

EXPERIMENT

Drop a ball a short distance from the floor and watch it bounce. Then drop the same ball from a greater height and watch it bounce. What is the relationship between the force of the ball's hitting the floor and the floor's pushing against the ball? What is the relationship between the speed of the ball as it hits the floor and the speed of the ball as it bounces upward?

F89

Activity
Double-Ball Bounce

How can you use action and reaction forces to make a clay ball bounce?

MATERIALS
- modeling clay
- basketball
- metric tape measure
- Science Notebook

SAFETY
Don't throw the basketball or clay at anyone.

Procedure

1. Form some clay into a ball and drop it onto a hard floor. **Observe** the clay. What happened to it after it hit the floor? How did the clay change when it hit the floor? **Record** your observations in your *Science Notebook*.

2. Place the clay ball on top of the basketball.

3. Carefully drop the basketball so that the clay ball remains on top of the basketball.

4. **Make a drawing** of the basketball. **Draw** the location of the clay ball at the point when the basketball hits the ground.

5. **Draw** the path of the clay ball after the basketball has hit the floor and rebounded.

6. **Observe** how high the basketball bounces.

7. **Predict** how high the basketball will bounce without the clay ball on top of it. **Test your prediction** and **record** how high the basketball bounces.

Step 1

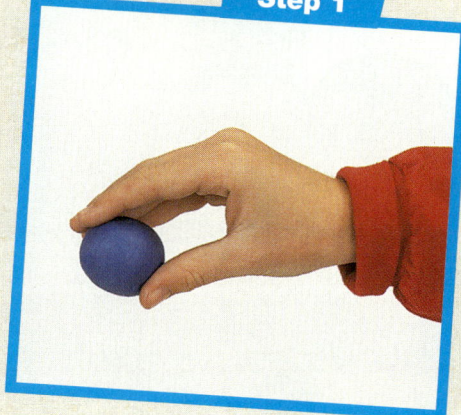

Step 2

Analyze and Conclude

1. What happened to the clay ball when it hit the floor? Why did this happen?

2. What happened to the clay ball when it was sitting on top of the dropped basketball? Why did this happen?

3. **Identify** the forces involved in this activity. What is the clay ball pushing against? What is the basketball pushing against?

4. **Compare** the height of the basketball's bounce with and without the clay sitting on the ball. How did the bounces differ? Why do you think they differed?

Actions Cause Reactions

The basketball is passed to you, and you drive down the court. The score is tied. There's only one defender between you and the basket. You hear the fans cheering and chanting. They're counting down the clock! "Ten, nine, eight, seven . . . !" This is your moment. You break left. The guard is right in your face. You break right. "Six, five, four. . . ." She's still in your face. Cutting left again, you catch her off balance, but she recovers and is coming back at you. "Three, two . . . ." At the top of the key, she's right on you! With one second to go, you push off the floor and rise high in the air with your head, arms, and hands well above the defender. With a flick of your wrists, you launch the ball toward the basket. The fans chant, "One!" The buzzer sounds, and silence falls throughout the arena as the ball arcs toward the basket.

What happened? How did you get into the air above the defender? What forces were involved in your last-second heroics?

Newton's Third Law of Motion

Had Sir Isaac Newton been watching you, he would have been happy to explain that you had just provided a wonderful demonstration of his Third Law of Motion. Once he stopped chanting with the crowd, he might have said, "Ah, my young friend, don't you know that for every action force there is an equal and opposite reaction force?" In this case, the action force was your feet pushing against the floor.

When you shoot a basketball the ball pushes on you just as hard as you push on it. ▶

The reaction force was the floor pushing against your feet. Because you exerted a force, the floor pushed back against you. This caused you to jump high above the defender trying to block you.

Newton's **Third Law of Motion** states that for every action force there is an equal and opposite reaction force. Two important things to remember about Newton's Third Law are: (1) forces always occur in pairs made up of an **action force** and a **reaction force**; (2) the action force and the reaction force always act on different bodies.

When you made your spectacular jump, you might have felt the action and reaction forces between your feet and the floor. But on a hard surface like a basketball court, it's difficult to see these forces work. If you jumped on a trampoline, though, it would be easy to observe the trampoline pushing back on you as you pushed on it.

Mass Matters

Now suppose that the defending player had jumped high enough to block your shot. Let's also suppose that she had pushed off the floor with a force exactly equal to the force you used to push off but that she had less mass than you. The Third Law explains that the reaction force of the floor would be equal to this player's action force. The reaction force, however, would be acting on a smaller mass. According to Newton's Second Law, this player would have a greater acceleration and would, therefore, go higher than you. If that had happened, she probably would have blocked your

SCIENCE AND FAITH

Newton's Third Law of Motion might remind us of an action and reaction that the Apostle Paul wrote about. He said, "But where sin increased, grace increased all the more, so that just as sin reigned in death, so also grace might reign through righteousness to bring eternal life through Jesus Christ our Lord" (Romans 5:20-21).

Another way of saying this is that when sin slams into us, forgiveness sends it flying away. But there's more. Unlike the objects Newton talked about in his Third Law, God's forgiveness applies far more force than any sin. It drives sin completely out of His sight. This is God's gift to us through His Son, Jesus Christ.

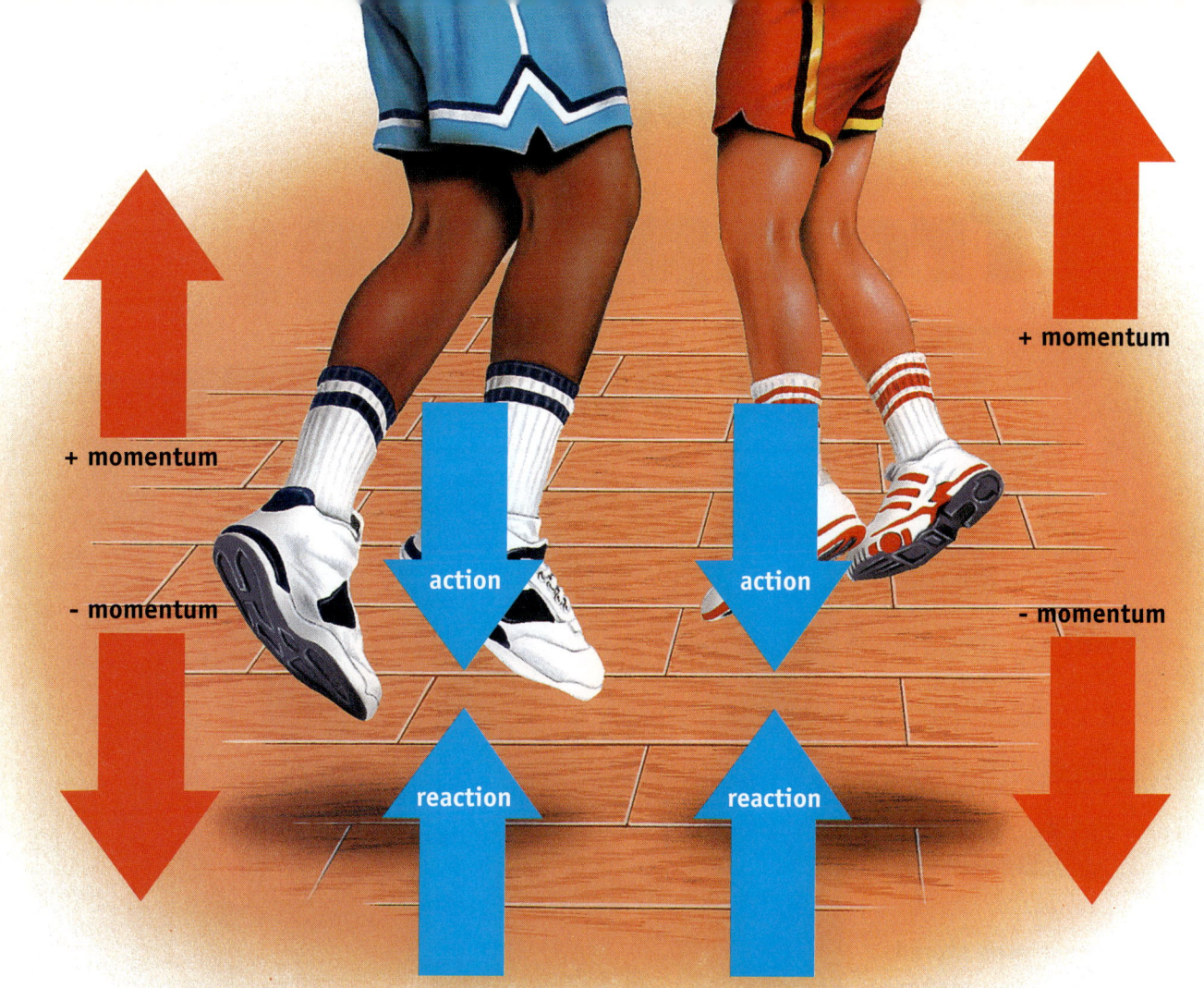

▲ If two people—one large and one small—both jump with the same force, which one is going to jump higher?

shot. But we know that wasn't the case, because the basketball is still arcing toward the basket as if in slow motion.

The Third Law and Earth's Surface

Think again about your leap. You already know that when your feet push downward against Earth, it pushes back. Your momentum is equal to your mass multiplied by your takeoff speed. Suppose you have a mass of 50 kg (110 lb) and jumped with a speed of 10 m/s (11 yd/s). Then your momentum would be

$$p = m \times v$$
$$p = 50 \text{ kg} \times 10 \text{ m/s}$$
$$p = 500 \text{ kg} \times \text{m/s}$$

What is Earth's reaction to your action? As you push against Earth, it pushes back, causing you to jump into the air. Since your momentum when you jumped is 500 kg × m/s, Earth's momentum must be −500 kg × m/s, the opposite of your momentum. Remember, momentum is conserved. How fast does Earth move backward in reaction to the action of your jump? You don't even have to calculate that number to know that Earth's backward velocity is very, very small. No one watching your jump shot will have any idea that Earth has moved at all! Actually, all the fans care about is whether or not the ball goes through the hoop!

So, what do you think? You took a shot at the last second. Are you a hero, or is the score still tied? ■

Trampoline Fun

▲ A gymnast uses stored energy to jump higher on a trampoline.

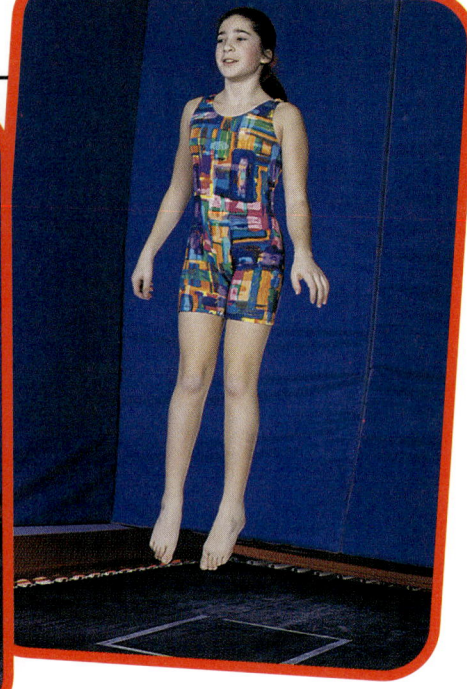

A gymnast bounces up and down on the trampoline. With each bounce the surface of the trampoline bends downward and then springs back. The gymnast rises high into the air and executes a beautiful midair somersault with a twist before landing again on the trampoline. Quickly her body again springs high into the air, and she completes another difficult maneuver.

Gymnasts practice for years and years to develop the body control necessary for a near-perfect gymnastics routine. A trampoline helps a gymnast sail much higher than he or she could if jumping from the ground. What is happening here? Does Newton's Third Law still apply?

The Third Law of Motion is still at work here. As you push down on the surface of a trampoline, the springs around the edges stretch and store energy. As the springs contract, the surface of the trampoline moves upward and the energy is returned to you. The trampoline pushes on you for a longer time than the ground would have, transferring a greater amount of energy to you.

As you bounce higher and fall from a higher point, you hit the trampoline with more force, storing more energy in the springs. The reaction force also increases and pushes against you even longer, sending you still higher into the air. Experts warn, though, that inexperienced bouncers should avoid high bounces.

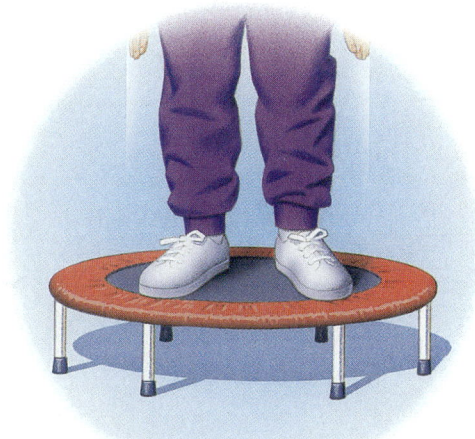

1. When you bounce on a trampoline, you begin by pushing against the trampoline's surface, which bends downward under you.

2. Eventually you and the trampoline's surface come to a stop and begin moving upward. Now the force that the trampoline exerts on you causes you to speed up.

3. Of course, you are exerting an equal and opposite force on the trampoline. Finally you leave the trampoline's surface and sail back into the air.

INVESTIGATE FURTHER!

EXPERIMENT

Turn a basketball into a rocket launcher. Design tiny rockets of paper and clay. Can you use the basketball to make your rockets sail across the room?

INVESTIGATION 2

1. Imagine a girl on a pair of in-line skates. She faces a brick wall and pushes forcefully on the wall. Explain what happens in terms of actions and reactions.

2. When a rocket lifts off a launch pad, where is the action force and where is the reaction force? Think! When the rocket is 2.2 km off the launch pad, where are the action and reaction forces?

F95

How Are Action-Reaction Forces Used?

Roaring to life, the rocket engines create an action force that causes hot gases to stream from the rocket. The restraining bolts explode free, and the reaction force thrusts the shuttle off the launch pad. In this investigation you'll examine some other ways that action-reaction forces make things move.

Activity

Action-Reaction Wheels

Have you ever noticed in which direction a car's wheels turn when the car moves? What gives a car its forward motion?

MATERIALS
- toy car with a pull-back friction engine
- *Science Notebook*

Procedure

1. With one hand, push a toy car backward on a table to wind up its engine.

2. Hold the car up and watch its wheels spin.

Step 2

F96

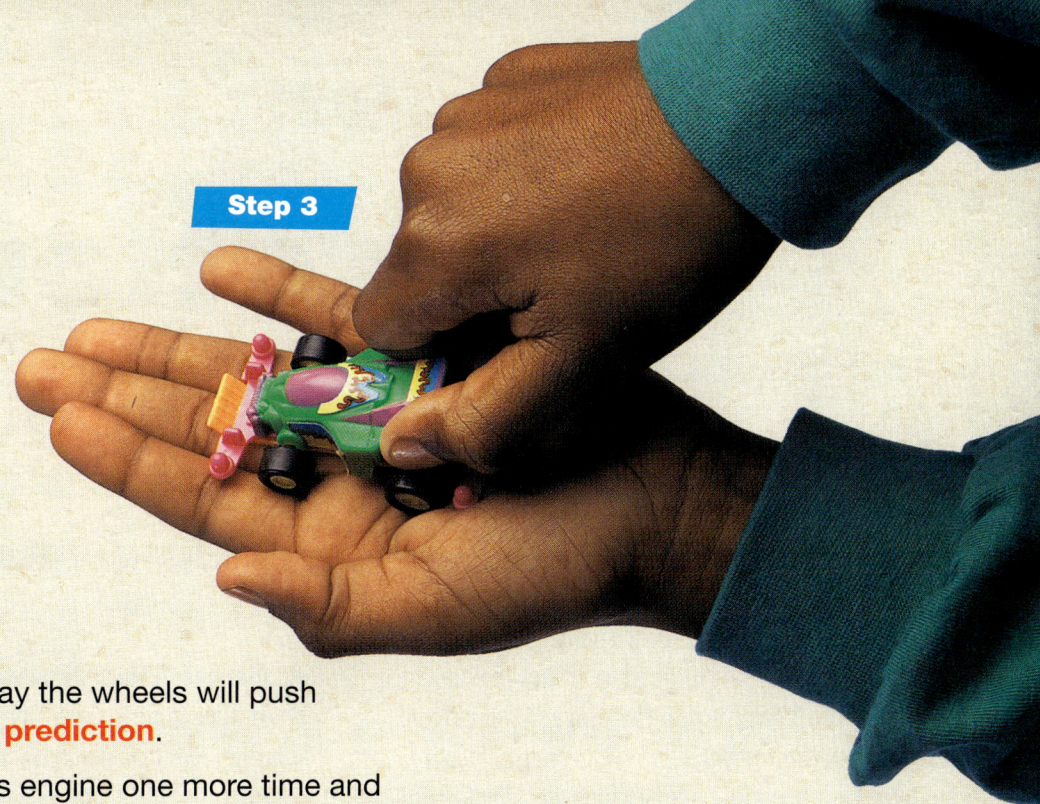

Step 3

3. Predict which way the wheels will push your hand. **Test your prediction**.

4. Wind up the car's engine one more time and release the car on the table.

5. In your *Science Notebook*, **make a drawing** of the car resting on the table. With one arrow, show the direction that the car traveled. With another arrow, show which way the wheels push on the ground.

Analyze and Conclude

1. Analyze your drawing. What gives the car its push to move forward? Remember that the car moves in the direction in which the force pushes it.

2. Identify two forces that act between the car and the surface.

INVESTIGATE FURTHER!

RESEARCH

What would happen if you changed the surface under the car? Try running the car on a soft pillow. Compare this to how the car runs on carpet or tile. Explain why you think the surface underneath is important.

Civilization and the Wheel

The name of the man or woman who invented the wheel will never be known. Perhaps the inventor was a warrior devising a chariot. The inventor might have been a hunter, tired of carrying the bodies of large animals. Or perhaps the inventor was a mourner, who sought a smoother ride for a loved one on the way to the grave. What *is* known is that the wheel was probably invented about 5,500 years ago.

In fact, the earliest picture we have of a wheel was drawn by a Sumerian accountant. It shows four rough-shaped wheels mounted on a funeral wagon pulled by oxen. The Sumerians lived in a part of the world known as the Fertile Crescent, between the Tigris and Euphrates rivers, in the country we know today as Iraq.

A Good Idea Spreads Quickly

If the ancient Sumerians invented the wheel, other people quickly adopted it. About 4,000 years ago, tribes from the steppes near the Black Sea appeared in the Tigris-Euphrates Valley. They brought with them strange animals called horses that were used to pull carts rolling on wheels. But these wheels were made with wooden rims and sturdy spokes fastened to a central hub. Soon the wheel with spokes found its way to Babylon, Greece, China, and Egypt, where it first appeared about 3,750 years ago. The ancient Celts of Western Europe also had the wheel by about this time.

▲ The earliest wheels were probably solid wooden wheels like the ones on this ancient toy.

As time went on, wheels became lighter and more efficient for speed. ▼

A Little Bit of Effort Does a Lot of Work

The wheel made life better and easier. It enabled people to accomplish more work with less effort. Before the wheel, some people used sledges, or dry-land sleds, to drag whatever they could not carry. Other people used travoises—two long poles tied together so that loads could be slung between the poles.

But the wheel greatly reduced friction and saved energy over the sledge and

▲ Before the introduction of the wheel, transporting large objects meant pushing or pulling them on sledges or travoises.

travois. Thus, the wheel offered a way to carry greater weight over a longer distance, at greater speeds, and with far less effort. A person on foot might be limited to traveling only about 56–64 km (35–40 mi) a day, carrying no more than 40 kg (88 lb). The wheel, however, enabled farmers, merchants, armies, and even whole towns to carry vast loads of food, trading goods, and other supplies over much longer distances. In time the wheel linked together settlements and speeded up the spread of civilization.

A Good Idea Gets Better

Make no mistake about it, a wheel is a machine that works on the principle of Newton's Third Law of Motion. A wheel pushes on the ground; the ground pushes on the wheel. The result is motion. Along with the lever, inclined plane, and wedge, the wheel is one of the four simple machines on which modern civilization has been built. And through the ages, the wheel has been improved many times.

At first wheels were mounted on axles, or rigid poles, which in turn were connected to the undersides of carts. The wheels and axles turned together as a unit. In time, the axles became fixed in position, and the wheels revolved around them.

The ancient Celts developed a crude forerunner of the roller bearing. They simply hollowed out separate channels inside the wheel's hub and lined each channel with hard wooden sticks. When the hub was mounted on the axle, the wheel and the sticks all turned together. As a result, the wheel turned more easily

It's very likely that rollers—a type of wheel—were used to move the Easter Island statues. ▼

and with less friction and wear on all its critical parts. The Celts were also the first to mount the front wheels on a movable platform so that a wagon could be turned and steered by its driver.

▲ The wheel became important to recreation, transportation, and work, as can be seen in this antique farming tractor.

The Pace of the Wheel Is the Pace of the Civilization

From the day the wheel was introduced, civilization has owed a tremendous debt to its inventor. The wheel has been used in hundreds of thousands of inventions that have improved civilization. Social scientists sometimes say that the pace of the wheel *is* the pace of the civilization. This means that the faster we travel on wheels, the faster we go in other ways, too.

This certainly seems true in this country. People moved westward in covered wagons. They built many of our cities around railroad stations, and then tied the cities together with a vast network of highways when the automobile appeared. We have even put wheels on our airplanes and moved our moon rockets and space shuttles into launching position on gigantic wheeled contraptions.

Can you imagine a world without wheels? From doorknobs to watches; from bicycles and baby buggies to trains, planes, and automobiles; from simple conveyor belts to the treads on gigantic military machines—almost every modern device with parts that move uses wheels in one way or another.

Beyond that, practically everything you eat, wear, play with, or live in was either produced, transported, or prepared for you by someone or something using wheels. It's probably fair to say that civilization could not exist without the wheel. Certainly the kind of society we're accustomed to would not be possible.

Even a shuttle depends on wheels to get it to the launch pad. ▶

Faster Fins

What do you use to move through the water when you swim? If you're like most people, you cup your hands and push them backward against the water. You probably also kick your feet to help you move through the water. As you push your hands backward against the water and kick your feet against the water, these action forces are responded to with the reaction force of the water pushing against you. The result is forward motion.

If you have ever watched championship swimmers in a race, you have probably noticed that their movements are very similar to the movements you use. The only difference is that their movements are more efficient than yours. But even the best swimmers only reach speeds of about 8 km/h (5 mph) for fairly short periods of time.

Most swimmers have one thing in common: They usually splash a lot of water around, especially with their feet. But do fish splash a lot of water? Except when they jump, fish very seldom splash any water.

Did you ever wonder how a fish swims? Some people think the fins on each side of the fish's body push it through the water. However, the fish uses its fins mostly for balance and turning. It swims by moving its tail and the middle section of its body back and forth.

The fish's body and tail push against the water, first on one side and then on the other. This motion is an action force against the water. The water in turn produces a reaction force that pushes the fish forward. In this way a sailfish can reach speeds of 108.8 km/h (68 mph).

Some marine mammals, such as seals, swim like fish. They move their rear

Humans just aren't built for speed in the water. ▼

Humans can become more efficient swimmers by using flippers, but they still can't match the efficiency and speed of even the slowest fish and mammals in the oceans. ▶

flippers back and forth in a powerful action force against the water. Other mammals, such as whales, porpoises, and dolphins, swim by moving their tails up and down.

Having watched fish and marine mammals swim, humans invented something to make swimming more efficient. Swim fins, which mimic the tail actions of fish and marine mammals, are worn by snorkelers and scuba divers to push against the water. The reaction force—the water pushing against the swim fins—pushes the diver through the water.

Long stiff fins push harder against the water than do short flexible fins. Long fins bend slightly as divers move their legs up and down in the water. However, a stiff fin will straighten itself out. The movement gives the diver a little extra push forward.

Snorkelers and scuba divers also can use their fins to help them tread water. They simply stand in the water and "walk" in place. The action force of their fins pushes down on the water. The reaction force is the water pushing the snorkelers and divers up.

With swim fins, humans become much more efficient swimmers. However, their efficiency does not come close to that of a trout, let alone a sailfish! ■

INVESTIGATION 3

1. Draw a car and its wheels. Diagram the action force and the reaction force needed for the car to go forward. Diagram the action force and the reaction force needed for the car to go backward.

2. You use action-reaction forces all the time. Explain how action-reaction forces affect you when you walk, climb stairs, roll over, or do a push-up.

REFLECT & EVALUATE

WORD POWER

action force
Law of Conservation of Momentum
momentum
reaction force
Third Law of Motion

 On Your Own
Review the terms in the list. Then use as many terms as you can in a paragraph about Newton's Third Law of Motion.

 With a Partner
Make up a quiz, using all the terms in the list. Challenge your partner to complete the quiz.

Develop a time line representing the history of the wheel. Illustrate your time line with drawings depicting its evolution.

Analyze Information

Study the table below. Using $p = m \times v$, fill in the missing data. What relationship do you notice between momentum and velocity? What relationship do you notice between momentum and mass?

Object	Momentum (kg × m/s)	Mass (kg)	Velocity (m/s)
1	50	5	10
2		5	20
3		10	10
4		25	10

Assess Performance

Design an experiment that compares the momentums of a small object with a mass of 1 kg (2.2 lb) and a larger object with a mass of 2 kg (4.4 lb) while traveling at the same speed. Hypothesize which object has the greater momentum. Design an experiment to test your hypothesis. What materials do you need to conduct the experiment? Record and analyze your data and state whether your hypothesis was correct.

Problem Solving

1. A truck is traveling north at 29 m/s on a narrow highway. It has a mass of 2,250 kg. A small car is traveling south on the same highway at 29 m/s. It has a mass of 900 kg. Which vehicle has greater momentum? What would happen if the vehicles hit head-on? Which vehicle would you rather be riding in? Why?

2. Explain how an accelerating bicycle illustrates Newton's Second and Third Laws of Motion.

F103

CHAPTER 5
REAL-WORLD FORCES

God created useful forces to work in the world. Planes, rockets, and space shuttles may seem to move in different ways, but the laws of motion apply to all of them.

Space Pioneer

When Mae Jemison was in grade school, she read books about astronomy and enjoyed science fiction. She never imagined that she would one day be an astronaut. But in September of 1992 she made history as a crew member on the eight-day mission of the *Endeavor* space shuttle.

As a medical doctor on the *Endeavor*, Mae Jemison gathered information on various medical aspects of space travel, such as motion sickness. She did biological experiments to see how tadpoles develop in space. As a crew member, she helped keep the space shuttle up and running.

The Mae C. Jemison Public School in Detroit has been named after her. She often visits schools, sharing her story and inspiring students with the same love of science that has made her own life so exciting.

Coming Up

INVESTIGATION 1

HOW DO HEAVY THINGS FLY?
.... F106

INVESTIGATION 2

HOW DO ROCKETS USE ACTION-REACTION FORCES?
.... F114

INVESTIGATION 3

HOW DO THINGS FLOAT?
.... F120

◄ Mae Jemison suited for her voyage into space

INVESTIGATION 1

How Do Heavy Things Fly?

Engines screaming, the powerful aircraft thunders toward the end of the runway. Nearly out of room, the pilot pulls back on the stick and the jet streaks into the sky. What forces are at work to get something so heavy to ever take off?

Activity
Making a Paper Glider

Under what conditions can the air support a paper glider—or a real glider?

MATERIALS
- sheet of notebook paper
- paper clips
- *Science Notebook*

SAFETY
Don't throw your plane at anyone.

Procedure

1. Using the following diagram, make a paper airplane.

Step 4

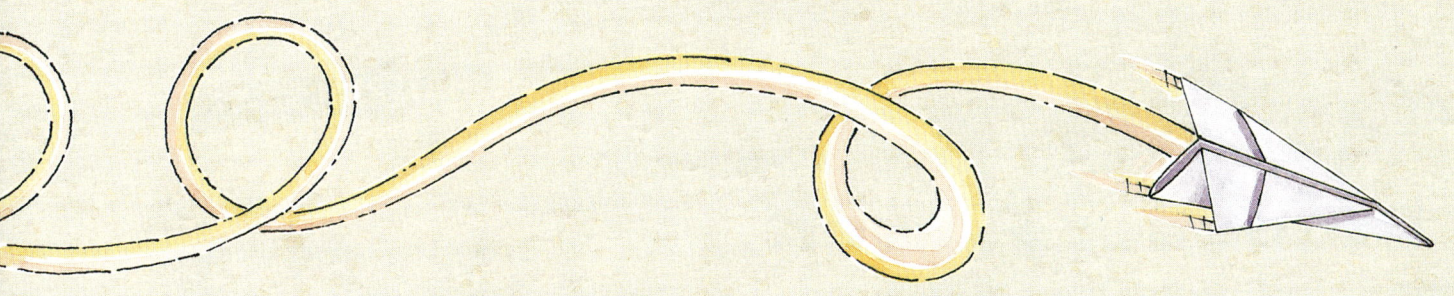

2. **Predict** how your airplane will fly. **Record** your prediction in your *Science Notebook*.

3. In your *Science Notebook*, **create a chart** like the one below. **Record** all your results in this chart.

Description of Flight Test	Result of Test
Forward glide test	
Spiral glide test	
Backward glide test	
Dropping test	

4. Practice tossing the airplane to make it glide forward.

5. Try creasing the wings until the plane turns in a spiral when you throw it.

6. Try throwing the plane backward. Does it fly as well backward as it does forward?

7. Drop the airplane without throwing it forward. Does it still float in the air?

Analyze and Conclude

1. Why do you think an airplane has to move forward through the air to fly?

2. Why is the shape of the airplane important? **Describe** the best shape for an airplane to have.

3. What must you do if you want a plane to spiral?

4. What do you think would make the plane turn to the left or right?

5. What conclusions can you draw about the forces that keep a glider in the air? Write your conclusions in your *Science Notebook*.

INVESTIGATE FURTHER!

EXPERIMENT

Create your own airplane. Make one that glides farther than the one you used in this activity. Use a full piece of paper in your design. Then have an air show with your classmates.

Activity
Propeller Power!

Helicopters don't have wings—they have large fast-spinning propellers. Try experimenting with some paper spinners to see what makes them stay in the air longer.

MATERIALS
- square sheets of paper
- *Science Notebook*

Procedure

1. Follow the diagrams below to make two paper spinners, one with wide wings and one with narrow wings.

2. Predict what will happen when you drop the spinners from the same height. **Record** your prediction in your *Science Notebook*.

3. Drop both spinners from the same height. **Record** what happens as they fall to the ground.

4. Repeat steps 2 and 3.

5. Make another narrow spinner and tape a penny to the bottom.

6. Drop the two narrow spinners—one with the penny and one without the penny—from the same height. **Record** what you observe.

Step 5

Analyze and Conclude

1. Do the spinners always turn in the same direction? Look at the wings and **infer** what causes the spinners to turn the way they do.

2. What effect does the wider wing have?

3. What effect does the extra weight have?

Designing Fliers

The Wright brothers flew their first plane at Kitty Hawk, North Carolina. Models tested in a wind tunnel helped them discover that twisted propellers work better than flat ones. On December 17, 1903, their plane, the *Flier*, made four flights. The longest flight lasted less than one minute.

1908
The Wright brothers build a plane capable of extended periods of flight. They demonstrate figure-eight flights.

1900
The Wright brothers obtained the most scientific knowledge available on aeronautics and flight. They build several successful gliders, improving on Lilienthal's designs.

1903
The Wright brothers announce that their new airplane had flown for 59 seconds. Many newspapers ignore the achievement. Some papers joke about it because everyone "knows" that flight is impossible.

1896
Orville and Wilbur Wright become interested in flying when they read about the death of Otto Lilienthal, a German engineer who built and flew the world's first successful gliders.

F109

Flying Forces

Greek mythology tells of an Athenian craftsman named Daedalus who went to the island of Crete. While in Crete, he and his son Icarus were imprisoned by the king. To escape, Daedalus built two sets of wings from wax, feathers, and string. He and Icarus flew from the prison out over the sea. But when Icarus flew too close to the Sun, the wax in his wings melted, and he fell to his death in the sea. Although saddened by the loss of his son, Daedalus flew on and eventually returned to Greece.

From the earliest times of recorded history, humans have dreamed of flying. With envy and wonder, people have

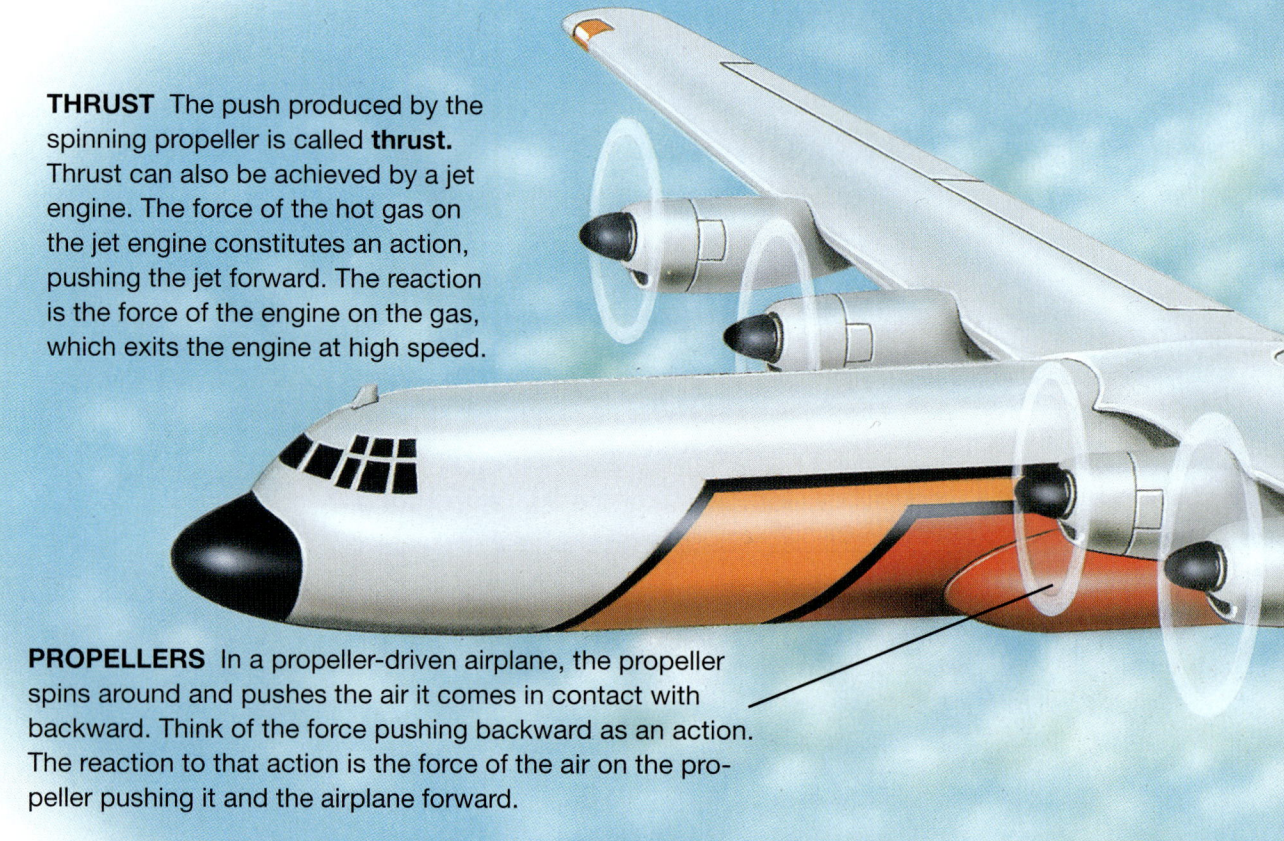

THRUST The push produced by the spinning propeller is called **thrust**. Thrust can also be achieved by a jet engine. The force of the hot gas on the jet engine constitutes an action, pushing the jet forward. The reaction is the force of the engine on the gas, which exits the engine at high speed.

PROPELLERS In a propeller-driven airplane, the propeller spins around and pushes the air it comes in contact with backward. Think of the force pushing backward as an action. The reaction to that action is the force of the air on the propeller pushing it and the airplane forward.

looked to the skies and have searched for ways to join the birds. Early attempts at flying were not much more successful than Icarus' effort and some proved just as deadly.

It wasn't until the Wright brothers mastered the forces required for flight that sustained-power flight became possible. However, the Wright brothers' first flight lasted just 12 seconds and covered a distance of only 37 m (120 ft)—a distance shorter than the wingspan of some modern aircraft!

Thrust and Lift

The whole idea of an airplane's design is to get a heavy piece of machinery off the ground and moving through the air. The first step in that process is to move the airplane forward on the ground. The airplane's engines do that job.

The wings of an airplane are curved on the top and flat on the bottom. Air passing over the top of a wing moves faster than air moving over the bottom of a wing. As a result of the higher speed on the top of the wing, air pressure is less in that area. Stronger air pressure on the bottom of the wing pushes the wing—and the rest of the airplane—upward.

You can easily observe this effect with a simple experiment. Hold a sheet of paper with both hands along one edge. Then blow over the top of the paper. In this experiment the paper is the wing of

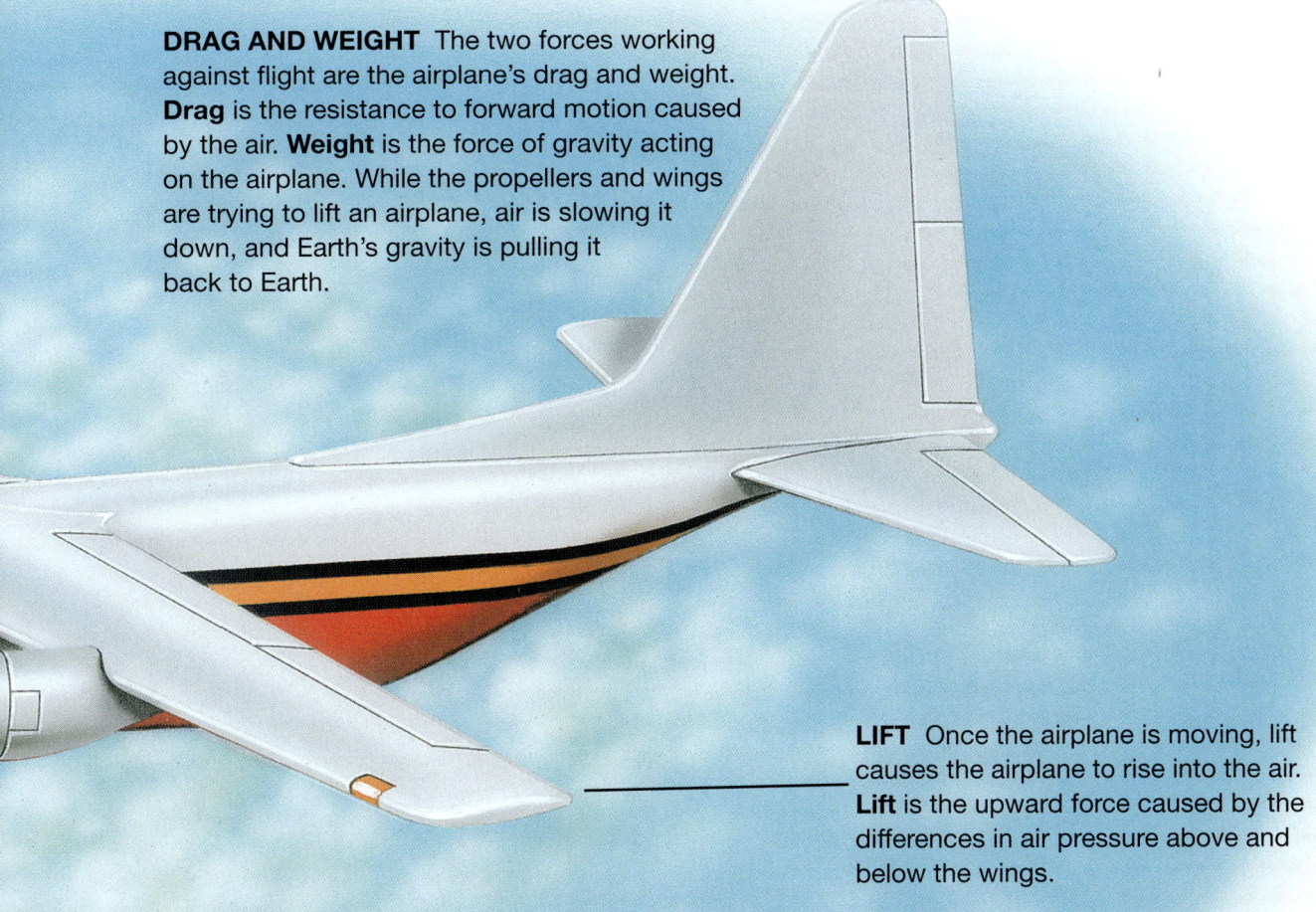

DRAG AND WEIGHT The two forces working against flight are the airplane's drag and weight. **Drag** is the resistance to forward motion caused by the air. **Weight** is the force of gravity acting on the airplane. While the propellers and wings are trying to lift an airplane, air is slowing it down, and Earth's gravity is pulling it back to Earth.

LIFT Once the airplane is moving, lift causes the airplane to rise into the air. **Lift** is the upward force caused by the differences in air pressure above and below the wings.

an airplane and your breath is the wind blowing over it.

How can thrust and lift of airplanes be improved? Larger, more efficient engines are one way to increase thrust. Changing the shape, number, and location of the wings increases lift. In fact, one interesting design for an airplane, called the flying wing, is in its shape—a large wing. The larger the wing, the greater the lift. So why not make the wing the size of the airplane itself? Some military planes have been designed in this way. While these planes do have a great deal of lift, they are very awkward to fly.

Drag

Since drag (the resistance between the plane and air) is a force that operates in the opposite direction of thrust, it would not seem to be desirable. However, it is very important. For a plane to slow down and come to a stop, it must have some way to increase drag. Most airplanes have flaps along the back edge of the wings. When the flaps are lowered, they increase both lift and drag, allowing the aircraft to fly and land at slower speeds. Wheel brakes, lift spoilers, and reverse thrust add drag to stop the plane on the ground.

Airplane Design and Testing

Modern airplanes are complicated machines. Engineers must test their designs long before the planes are ever built. One way to test new designs is to write computer programs that contain all

SCIENCE AND FAITH

"But those who hope in the Lord will renew their strength. They will soar on wings like eagles, they will run and not grow weary, they will walk and not be faint" (Isaiah 40:31).

God's people of the Old Testament knew about eagles. They watched them soar and dive and race toward the clouds. Like people of most civilizations, God's people probably wished they could fly like eagles. Isaiah, preaching God's Word, told people that faith in God was like having the strength of an eagle. God enables His people to fly in freedom and have the power to do great things in His name.

▲ A computer program determines the flight capabilities of the design and enables the engineer to make adjustments before actual construction of a new aircraft begins.

the design features. The computer can then predict what will happen when the plane attempts to take off, fly, and land.

Another step in airplane design is the wind tunnel. Research involving wind tunnels was pioneered by the Russian physicist Konstantin Tsiolkovsky before the turn of the twentieth century. A wind tunnel consists of a small chamber in which air is moved rapidly from one end to the other to simulate air rushing over an airplane's body. A small model of the airplane to be tested is placed inside the wind tunnel. Then the plane's behavior in a stream of air can be studied. Smoke is often introduced into the airstream to make it easier to see how the air flows over the model. Information collected in the wind tunnel is analyzed by engineers and used to make design changes that will improve the flight characteristics of the airplane. ■

INVESTIGATION 1

1. Make a drawing that shows and describes the forces acting on an airplane in flight.

2. Explain why the wings of a space shuttle are absolutely useless for most of its mission.

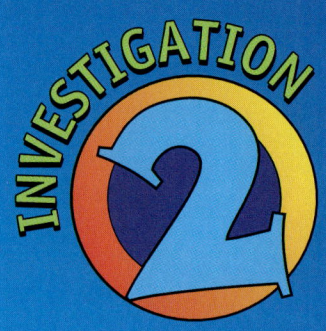

INVESTIGATION 2

How Do Rockets Use Action-Reaction Forces?

In space, there is no air, water, or ground to push against. How does a shuttle orbiter use its rockets to change direction in order to return to Earth? In this investigation you'll find out how rocket gases are involved in action-reaction forces.

Activity

Balloon Rocket Race

MATERIALS
- goggles
- long balloons
- string
- plastic straw
- tape
- metric tape
- *Science Notebook*

An inflated balloon can be a model for a rocket. Experiment with its action-reaction forces.

Procedure

1. Run a string through a straw and then stretch it across the classroom.

2. Tie the string to something at each end of the classroom. Clothing hooks and doorknobs work well.

3. Inflate your balloon and hold the end closed with your fingers. Do not inflate the balloon to its full size.

4. With the help of a group member, tape the balloon to the straw so that the straw runs along the length of the balloon.

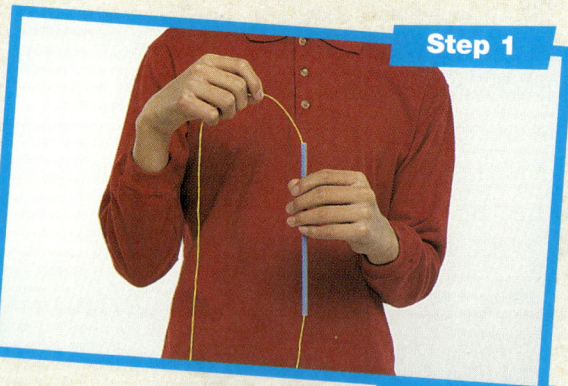
Step 1

Step 3

5. Move the straw and balloon on the string to one end of the room.

6. Predict what will happen if you release the end of the balloon. **Test your prediction** and **observe** what happens.

Step 5

7. Record how far the balloon traveled on the string.

8. Inflate the balloon again; this time, make it as big as you can.

9. Repeat the activity and **record** the distance the balloon traveled.

Analyze and Conclude

1. In your *Science Notebook*, **draw a picture** of the inflated balloon on the string. Draw arrows on your picture showing how the air in the balloon is pushing on the inflated balloon. Draw other arrows to show how the balloon is pushing back on the air inside.

2. Have an arrow show the direction in which the air moved as it escaped from the balloon. Draw another arrow to show the direction in which the balloon moved.

3. How did you increase the action force?

4. What happened to the reaction force when you increased the action force? What evidence can you cite?

INVESTIGATE FURTHER!

EXPERIMENT

Have a balloon race. Stretch several strings across the classroom. Be sure that each is level and stretched equally tight. Experiment with balloons of all sizes. Race several balloons at the same time. Draw the shape of each balloon and record the distance that it traveled.

Activity
Straw Rockets

Here's how the result of action-reaction forces can be directed to control movement.

MATERIALS
- goggles
- flexible plastic straw
- rubber band
- small balloon
- thin string
- tape
- *Science Notebook*

SAFETY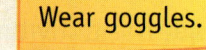
Wear goggles.

Procedure

1. Insert about 5 cm of a straw into a balloon, leaving the flexible bend outside the balloon. Use a rubber band to hold the straw tightly in place.

2. Inflate the balloon by blowing through the straw. Hold your finger over the end of the straw to prevent the air from escaping.

3. As shown at right, bend the flexible end of the straw so that it is pointing at a right angle to the rest of the straw.

4. Use tape to attach string to the balloon. Have a group member hold the string so that the straw is at right angles to the string, as shown.

Step 3

5. Predict what will happen if you release the air from the balloon. **Record** your prediction in your *Science Notebook*.

6. While a group member holds the string at arm's length, release the air inside the balloon. **Record** what happens.

Step 4

Analyze and Conclude

1. In your *Science Notebook*, draw the balloon and straw as if you were looking down on them.

2. With an arrow, show the direction that the air moves as it escapes from the balloon. With another arrow, show the way the balloon moves.

3. Draw arrows to indicate the action force and the reaction force that cause the motions of the balloon and straw. Label the arrows.

4. Explain how Newton's Third Law applies to this activity.

INVESTIGATE FURTHER!

EXPERIMENT

For this experiment, you need an empty milk carton, string, water, and a bucket. Punch a hole in the lower-right corner of each side of the milk carton. Also punch a hole through the center of the top of the carton. Thread the string through the hole in the top of the carton, and hang the carton over the bucket. While two group members cover the holes in the sides, fill the carton with water. Uncover the holes and watch what happens to the carton.

F117

Rocket Launch

The rockets developed by Goddard (*left*) and Tsiolkovsky (*center*) led directly to the powerful Saturn 5 (*right*).

At about the same time that the Wright brothers were experimenting with powered flight, Russian physicist Konstantin Tsiolkovsky and American physicist Robert Goddard were experimenting with rocket-powered flight. Each knew that a rocket would operate on Newton's Third Law of Motion, which states that any action force is accompanied by an equal reaction force in the opposite direction. Working independently of one another, Tsiolkovsky and Goddard both developed the foundation for space exploration.

The early rockets of Tsiolkovsky and Goddard seem simple compared to today's rockets. But their experiments led to the mighty Saturn 5 that would, in 1969, rocket Michael Collins, "Buzz" Aldrin, and Neil Armstrong on the Apollo 11 mission to the Moon.

Space-Shuttle Engines

In the more than 25 years since Apollo 11, no rocket produced has been as powerful as the Saturn 5. However, the rockets that lift the space shuttle are the most efficient ever produced.

The shuttle's solid-rocket boosters each contain 500,000 kg (1.1 million lbs) of aluminum metal, aluminum perchlorate, and a plasticlike material that holds these together. When the boosters ignite, the aluminum and aluminum perchlorate react to produce very hot gases that are pushed out of the engine nozzles.

The main engines of the shuttle operate on a mixture of liquid hydrogen and liquid oxygen. The liquid fuels are stored in a huge external fuel tank, which holds

550,000 L (143,000 gal.) of hydrogen and 1.5 million L (390,000 gal.) of oxygen. When ignited, the two liquid elements react to form steam. The steam exits the main engines at a temperature of about 2,000°C (3,600°F), providing a powerful thrust.

Shuttle Action and Reaction

As the space shuttle sits on its launch pad, its speed is zero. So its momentum is also zero. At the moment the engines ignite, all that changes. The effect of the shuttle engines firing is a stream of hot gases escaping from the engine nozzles at very high speeds. At that time the space shuttle begins ascending.

When the shuttle's engines fire, the hot gases push against the walls of the engine chamber. This action force pushes the chamber and the whole shuttle upward. At the same time, the walls of the chamber push back on the hot gases. This reaction force pushes the hot gases out of the bottom of the shuttle at high speed. The result is that the shuttle lifts off the pad and heads for orbit.

Since the shuttle has such a large mass, its velocity is small at first. As the engines continue to fire, the speed of the shuttle increases. By the time the main engines cut off, the shuttle has a velocity of about 27,000 km/h (16,200 mph).

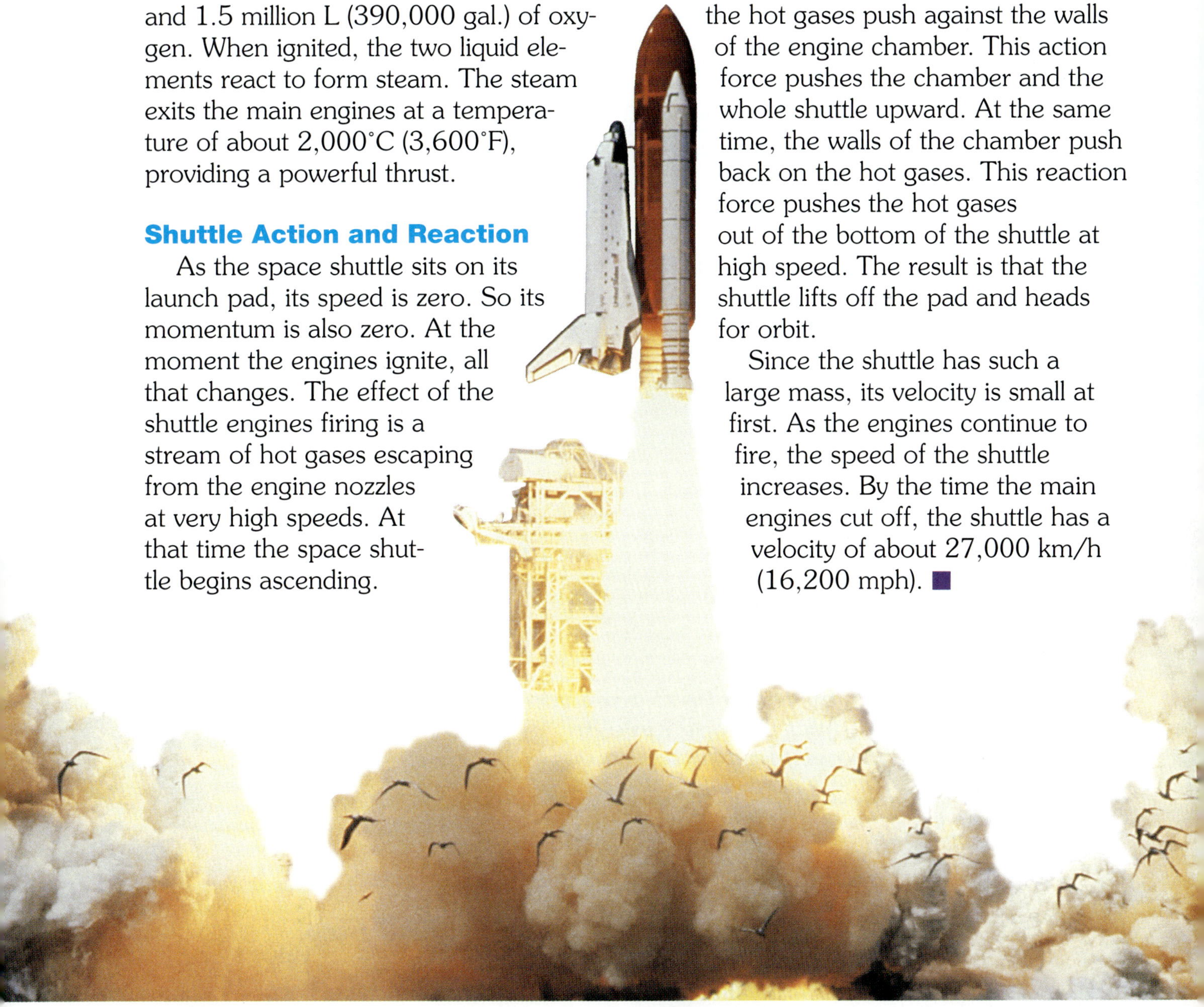

INVESTIGATION 2

1. How are action-reaction forces involved in launching a rocket?

2. How is blowing up a balloon and releasing it similar to launching a rocket in terms of action-reaction forces?

INVESTIGATION 3

How Do Things Float?

April 15, 1912—Hours ago, the luxury liner *Titanic* floated high in the water. Now she has sunk beneath the waves, down to the bottom of the Atlantic Ocean. What force keeps a ship afloat? What changes occurred to make this ship sink?

Activity

Clay Boats

What happens when you try to float a piece of clay on water? Does the object's shape have any effect on its ability to float? Experiment to find out.

MATERIALS
- goggles
- piece of clay
- large plastic container
- water
- marbles
- *Science Notebook*

SAFETY
Make sure you clean up any spills as soon as they occur to avoid slipping on wet floors.

Procedure

1. Roll the clay into a ball. Place it into a container filled with water. What happens?

2. Form the clay into a boat shape. Put your boat into the water to see if it floats.

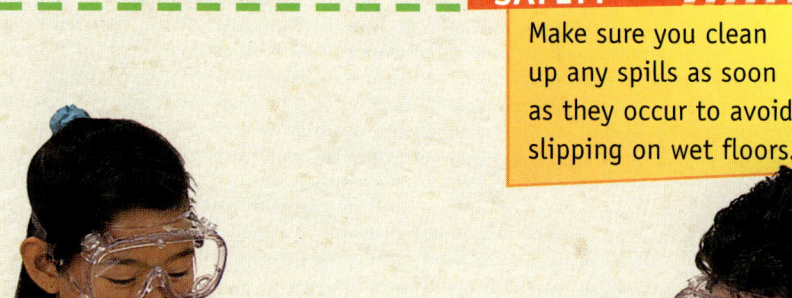

Step 2

3. **Draw a picture** of your boat in your *Science Notebook*.

4. **Predict** what would happen if you add marbles to your boat.

5. **Test your prediction** by adding marbles to your boat one by one. Continue adding marbles until your boat sinks.

6. **Record** the number of marbles your boat held before it sank.

7. Redesign your boat to hold more marbles before sinking, and repeat the experiment.

Analyze and Conclude

1. Describe how you increased the carrying capacity of your boat in step 7 without using more clay.

2. How did the shape of the boat affect its ability to float?

3. A boat floating in water is moving neither up nor down. Based on Newton's first two laws, what can you **infer** about the forces acting on the boat?

4. A boat floating in water is exerting a downward force on the water. Based on Newton's Third Law, what is causing the boat to float?

UNIT PROJECT LINK

Make a water ride for your park. You will need a pan of water to create the splash pool at the end of the ride. After you complete your design, make a three-dimensional model of the boat and the ride and place it in your park. On your model, show how many passengers will fit in each boat. Place a card next to the ride describing how fast the boat moves and what factors affect the size of the splash the boat makes.

Activity
Floating Egg

Do objects float better in fresh water or salt water? You'll find out in this activity.

MATERIALS
- goggles
- raw egg
- table salt
- large plastic container
- large spoon
- *Science Notebook*

SAFETY
Clean up spills immediately. If you must clean up a broken egg, wash your hands thoroughly.

Procedure

1. Half-fill a container with water.

2. Predict what will happen if you place an egg in the water. Using the spoon, carefully lower the egg into the container. In your *Science Notebook*, **record** what happens.

3. Predict what will happen if you add salt to the water. Gradually add salt to the water and **record** what happens.

Analyze and Conclude

1. In your *Science Notebook*, describe what happened to the egg during this experiment.

2. What else changed during the experiment?

3. How can you explain what you observed?

INVESTIGATE FURTHER!

RESEARCH
Go to the beach or talk to someone who has been to one. Ask what it is like to swim in salt water. Is it easier or harder than swimming in fresh water?

Step 2

F122

Forces in Fluids

▲ Thousands of tons of steel, aluminum, wood, cargo, and people float easily because the density of the ship is less than the density of the water.

What do you think would happen if you threw a piece of aluminum foil into a pan of water? Since aluminum is more dense than water—that is, it has more mass for a given volume than does water—you might expect to see the aluminum sink in the water. But will it?

What is at work here is a battle of forces: gravity in one corner and buoyancy in the other. Gravity is the force that tends to pull objects toward Earth's center. **Buoyancy** is the tendency of liquids like water to keep objects afloat. So what do you think? Who will win this battle of two great forces: gravity or buoyancy?

Archimedes' Principle

The answer to that question actually was discovered more than 2,200 years ago by Archimedes, a Greek mathematician and engineer. He had made the discovery while trying to solve another problem. According to the now-famous story, Archimedes was employed by Hiero, king of Syracuse, the largest Greek city in Sicily. The king suspected that his new crown was not made of pure gold, so he asked Archimedes to figure out if the goldsmith had cheated him.

While trying to find a way to solve the problem, Archimedes discovered that

F123

▲ As you can see in these pictures, one ship is riding higher in the water than the other ship. What's the difference?

when an object is placed in water, an amount of water equal to the object's volume will be displaced, or pushed out of the way. If the object's mass is equal to that of the water it displaces, the object floats.

What did Archimedes do with his discovery? He compared the amount of water displaced by the crown with the amount of water displaced by an equal amount of pure gold. When the crown displaced more water than the pure gold, Archimedes knew the crown was not pure gold and that the goldsmith had cheated the king.

Now consider a block of clay 10 cm × 10 cm × 10 cm. Assume that a block of clay that size has a mass of about 2,500 g. If you put the piece of clay into a container of water, the clay will displace a block of water 10 cm × 10 cm × 10 cm. A block of water that size has a mass of 1,000 g. In this example, the clay will sink because it has a greater mass than the water it displaces.

Think about the activity for a moment. What would happen if you were to make a boat from the block of clay? The boat might have walls only 1 cm thick all around. And, of course, it would have a much larger volume than the block of clay. Inside the walls of clay is air. Air has a very low mass, about 0.0013 g/mL. That is, a milliliter of air has a mass of only 0.0013 g.

The total mass of the boat made with clay walls plus the trapped air would be only slightly more than 2,500 g. But because of the boat's large volume, it eventually displaces a mass of water equal to its own mass. At this point the clay boat will float. *The secret in building a boat that will float, then, is to include as much air in it as possible.*

People are sometimes surprised that large ocean liners can be made of metals that would normally sink in water. Ocean liners also contain large heavy engines, pumps, cargo, furniture, and, of course, people. Yet ocean liners float because they have so much air trapped inside them. With a lot of air inside it, even a boat made from heavy metal can be made to float.

Factors Affecting Buoyancy

Any object that has a density of less than 1 g/mL will float in water. Wood with a density of 0.7 g/mL is an example. A milliliter of this wood has a mass of 0.7 g. In comparison, 1 mL of water has a mass of 1 g. According to Archimedes' Principle, the wood floats because it displaces a volume of water equal to its mass.

Can you make a block of iron float? You can if you choose the right liquid. For example, what happens if you put a block of iron in a bowl of liquid mercury? The density of the iron is 7.9 g/mL and the density of mercury is 13.5 g/mL.

Since iron has a lower density, it floats in mercury. What is the mass of 1 mL of iron? What is the mass of 1 mL of mercury displaced by 1 mL of iron that is floating?

You have already learned that shape affects the ability of an object to float. As you change an object's shape so that it includes more and more air, you are decreasing the object's density. An ocean liner has a density of less than 1 g/mL—hard to believe! Which boat would float better, one that is 10 m long, 2 m wide and 2 m deep, or one that is 10 m long, 3 m wide and 1.5 m deep? Why did adding marbles to the clay boat in the activity on pages F120 and F121 finally cause the boat to sink?

Underwater Diving

Humans have long been fascinated by the underwater world. However, two fac-

A penny sinks in water, but it doesn't sink in all liquids. ▼

When placed in mercury, a penny floats because it is less dense than mercury. ▼

▲ Scuba divers attach weights to their bodies to stay below the water.

tors have limited our abilities to explore that world. First, breathing underwater requires special equipment. People cannot hold their breath long enough to do much exploring underwater. A breakthrough in solving this problem was made by Jacques-Yves Cousteau and Emile Gagnan in 1943. They developed the Aqua-lung, one of the first underwater breathing devices that allowed the user to remain underwater for an extended time. Their invention is a type of self-contained underwater breathing apparatus, or scuba. Scuba equipment consists of a tank of compressed air for the diver to breathe and a system for regulating the intake of the air. Cousteau and Gagnan found designing the system difficult because the amount of air a diver needs changes as the depth of the water increases. Therefore, the regulating system has to continually adjust the amount of air released to the diver.

The second problem in exploring the underwater world is the density of the human body itself, which is just less than the density of water. When a person jumps into the water, the tendency is for the person to float. One way of overcoming the body's natural buoyancy is to add weights to the a person's waist, ankles, or wrists. By adjusting the number of weights attached, the diver can go as deep into the water as he or she wants to. ■

INVESTIGATION 3

1. How are action-reaction forces involved when you are floating in a pool?

2. A submarine is said to not only float in the water but also to "fly" through the water. Explain how a submarine "flies" in terms of action-reaction forces.

F126

REFLECT & EVALUATE

WORD POWER

buoyancy
drag
lift
thrust

On Your Own
Review the terms in the list. Then use each term in a different sentence that tells the meaning of the term.

With a Partner
Write a clue for each term in the list. Then challenge a partner to write the correct term for each clue.

Write a paragraph describing what might have been talked about in a meeting between Orville and Wilbur Wright and astronauts Michael Collins, Edwin E. "Buzz" Aldrin, and Neil Armstrong.

Analyze Information

Study the drawing. Then use the drawing to explain, in your own words, how a propeller-driven airplane works. Label the parts of the drawing and include the terms *thrust, drag,* and *lift* in your labels.

Assess Performance

Design and carry out an experiment to compare the buoyancy of diet cola and regular cola of the same brand. Before conducting the experiment, hypothesize which cola is more buoyant. Then compare the results of your experiment with those of your classmates. What do the results tell you about the relationship between density and buoyancy?

Problem Solving

1. How do the forces of lift and gravity on an airplane compare when the airplane is increasing in altitude?

2. You want to compare the densities of several different liquids: water, mercury, corn oil, rubbing alcohol, and syrup. How can you determine the liquids' densities, using only a tall glass cylinder

3. A stone and a cork are both placed in a container of water and they both displace the same amount of water, yet the stone sinks and the cork floats. Why?

INVESTIGATE FURTHER!

Throughout this unit you've investigated questions related to forces and motion. How will you use what you've learned and share that information with others? Here are some ideas.

Hold a Big Event to Share Your Unit Project

Now that you have created your model amusement park, prepare to display the results of your group's project. Create posters explaining each ride in your amusement park and include information about how each ride demonstrates each of Newton's Laws of Motion. Invite other classes, your parents, and your friends to visit your classroom for a demonstration of your amusement park. Compete with the other groups to see who has can create the highest roller coaster hill; the biggest water slide splash; or the fastest, wildest ride in general.

Experiment

Extend one of the activities in this unit by changing a material or method. You might redesign the garbage-bag parachute by adding holes or slits, or making it from cloth or paper. Then compare your results to the original parachute. You could also plan an experiment that tests different materials or designs for paper airplanes. After you have completed your plan discuss it with your teacher. If your teacher approves the plan, conduct your experiment and report on your results to the class. Then stage a competition to see which plane will fly the furthest, do the most loops, or fly the highest.

Research

What's your favorite set of wheels? a bicycle? in-line skates? a skateboard? how about really hot race car? Find out more about the wheels on your favorite vehicle. Research what these wheels are made of, how large they are, and what special features are in their design. Create a video presentation that demonstates how you make use of the wheels and also explains how the wheels make use of Newton's third law of motion. Then show your video to the class.

Science Handbook

Think Like a Scientist H2

    Does the Temperature of a Liquid Affect
    How Much Solute it Can Hold? H4

Safety H8

Science Tools H10

    Using a Microscope H10

    Using a Calculator H11

    Using a Balance H12

    Using a Spring Scale H13

    Using a Thermometer H14

    Measuring Volume H15

Measurements H16

Glossary H18

Index H38

THINK LIKE A SCIENTIST

"You don't have to be a professional scientist to act and think like one. Thinking like a scientist mostly means using common sense. It also means learning how to test your ideas in a careful way."

"In other words, *you* can think like a scientist."

Make a Hypothesis

Plan and Do a Test

Make Observations

To think like a scientist, you should learn as much as you can by observing things around you. Everything you hear and see is a clue about how the natural world works.

Ask a Question

Look for patterns. You'll get ideas and ask questions like these:

- Do all birds eat the same seeds?
- How does the time that the Sun sets change from day to day?

Make a Guess Called a Hypothesis

If you have an idea about why or how something happens, make an educated guess, or *hypothesis*, that you can test. For example, let's suppose that your hypothesis about the sunset time is that it changes by one minute each day.

Plan and Do a Test

Plan how to test your hypothesis. Your plan would need to consider some of these problems:

- How will you measure the time that the Sun sets?
- Will you measure the time every day?
- For how many days or weeks do you need to measure?

Record and Analyze What Happens

When you test your idea, you need to observe carefully and write down, or record, everything that happens. When you finish collecting data, you may need to do some calculations with it. For example, you might want to calculate how much the sunset time changes in a week or a month.

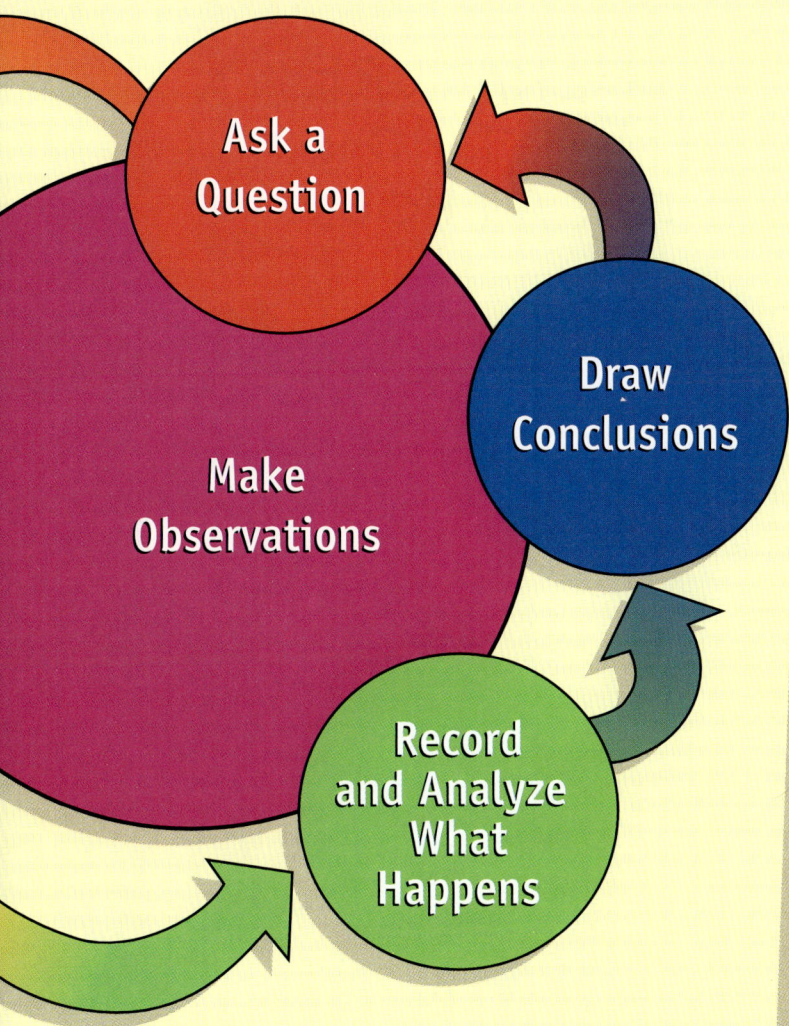

PRACTICE SCIENTIFIC REASONING SKILLS

To think like a scientist, you need to practice certain ways of thinking.

Always check for yourself.
Always ask, "How do I really know it's true?" Be willing to find out for yourself.

Be honest and careful about what you observe.
It's easy to only look for the results you expect. It's harder to see the unexpected. But unexpected results lead scientists to ask more questions. They also provide information on how things work.

Don't be afraid to be wrong.
Based on their observations, scientists make many hypotheses. Not all of these hypotheses turn out to be correct. But scientists can learn from wrong "guesses," because even wrong guesses result in information that leads to knowledge.

Keep an open mind about possible explanations.
Make sure to think about all the reasons why something might have happened. Consider all the explanations that you can think of.

Draw Conclusions

Whatever happens in a test, think about all the reasons for your results. For example, you might wonder what causes the time of sunset to change. You might also ask when the earliest and latest sunsets occur during the year. Sometimes this thinking leads to a new hypothesis.

If the time of the sunset changes by one minute each day, think about what else the data shows you. Can you predict the time that the Sun will set one month from now?

Think Like a Scientist

DOES THE TEMPERATURE OF A LIQUID AFFECT HOW MUCH SOLUTE IT CAN HOLD?

Here's an example of an everyday problem and how thinking like a scientist can help you explore it.

"I can't believe it."

"It's true."

"It's impossible! Ten?"

"That's right."

"A cup of herbal tea can't hold ten teaspoons of sugar."

"My mother's does," replied Mark. "She likes it sweet."

"I'll bet most of the sugar just sinks to the bottom of the cup," Nita asserted. "Doesn't it?"

"No, it doesn't," Mark said. "Would I lie to you?"

"Listen," Nita said, "Ms. Cobb's been teaching us about solutions. I'll bet if I asked her she'd say it's impossible."

Make Observations → Ask a Question

Nita explained the issue to Ms. Cobb and the other students. She asked Ms. Cobb to give her opinion, but she wouldn't. She simply asked the class what they thought. Some students thought it was possible, others thought it was impossible. Ms. Cobb suggested that the class figure out a way to find the answer.

Ms. Cobb invited the students to come up with questions that expressed the problem they want to solve. Two of the questions were:

H4

How much sugar can a cup of herbal tea hold?

Can hot water dissolve more sugar than cold water can?

Nita and Mark thought the second question was more interesting because it applied to more things—like coffee and lemonade. They were not sure what the answer to this question would be. But it was the kind of question that would tell them more about the nature of solutions.

> **Scientific investigations usually begin with something that you have noticed or read about. As you think about what you already know, you'll discover some ideas that you're not sure about. This will help you to ask the question that you really want to answer.**

Make a Hypothesis

Mark and Nita talked the problem over. Mark told Nita that his mother drank her herbal tea very hot; she always waited until the water was boiling violently before pouring it into her cup. "Maybe," Nita said, "if the water wasn't so hot, it would hold less sugar." Mark agreed that this was possible. But he wasn't sure.

Mark and Nita had a hunch that the hotter water is, the more solute, such as sugar, the water will hold. They came up with a hypothesis, a statement of what they thought was true. Their hypothesis was "The hotter the water, the more sugar it will dissolve."

Nita and Mark got a few heat-proof glass beakers, a cup measure, and thermometers. Ms. Cobb got 1-teaspoon measuring spoons and a bowl of sugar from the school cafeteria. She also borrowed several hotplates. Ms. Cobb reviewed the test procedure that Mark and Nita had planned.

> **When you use what you have observed to suggest a possible answer to your question, you are making a *hypothesis*. Be sure that your hypothesis is an idea that you can test somehow. If you can't think of an experiment or a model to test your hypothesis, try changing it. Sometimes it's better to make a simpler, clearer hypothesis that answers only part of your question.**

Think Like a Scientist

Make Observations → Plan and Do a Test

Mark and Nita knew they'd have to keep track of the different water temperatures in each beaker. They knew they'd have to put the same amount of water in each beaker. They would also have to keep track of how many teaspoons of sugar went into each beaker.

Nita knew that water boiled at 100 degrees Celsius (°C). So the beaker with the hottest water should be at this temperature. Another beaker could have water at 70°C; a third might have water at 40°C.

Mark suggested that they have a fourth beaker containing a cup of cold water at about 5°C—water whose temperature was close to freezing. This beaker would serve as their control. The control in this experiment would allow Mark and Nita to test the effect of heat on water's ability to dissolve sugar.

Ms. Cobb set up four water baths at the temperatures they agreed upon. Each was kept at a constant temperature. Each water bath had a thermometer in it.

One way to try out your hypothesis is to use a test called an experiment. When you plan an experiment, be sure that it helps you to answer your question. Even when you plan, things can happen that make the experiment confusing or make it not work properly. If this happens, you can change the plan for the experiment, and try again.

Make Observations → Record and Analyze What Happened

Mark and Nita asked two classmates to help them put teaspoons of sugar into the beakers. After each teaspoon of sugar went in, the solution was stirred with a glass stirring rod until the sugar dissolved. Each

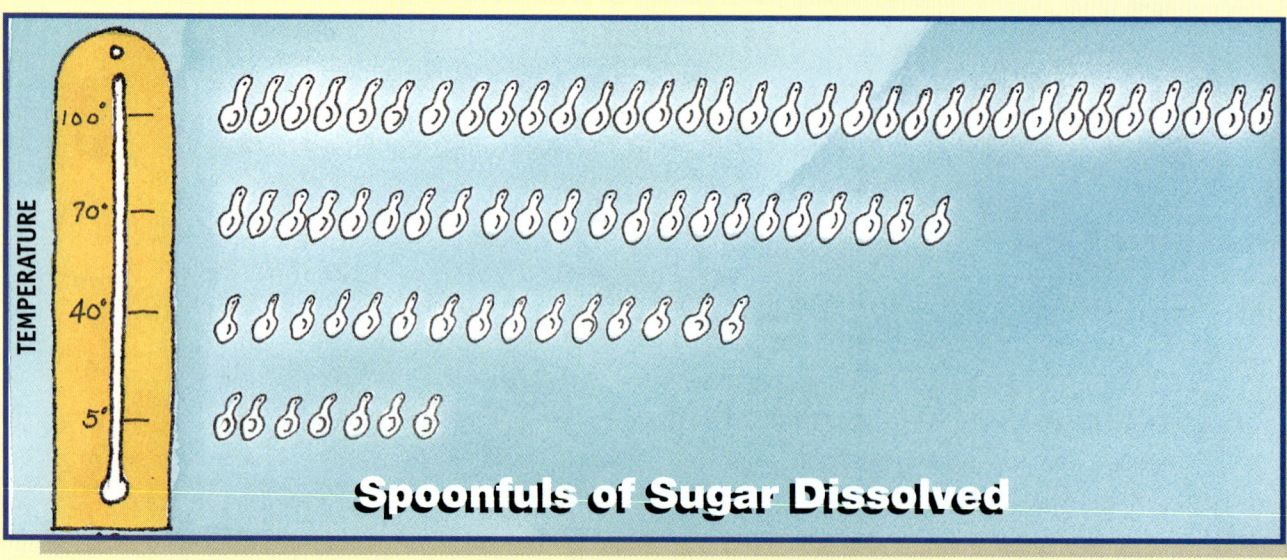

Spoonfuls of Sugar Dissolved

student kept track of the number of teaspoons of sugar that dissolved in it.

At the end of the experiment, each student looked at what he or she had written down. This information was organized in a graph like the one on page H6.

Mark and Nita studied the graph of the data they got during their experiment. They noticed that there was a definite relationship between water temperature and how much sugar could be dissolved in it.

Nita was surprised to see that Mark's mother's tea could really hold a lot more than 10 teaspoons of sugar. She and Mark agreed that people could drink their tea really sweet, unless, that is, they made it with cooler water.

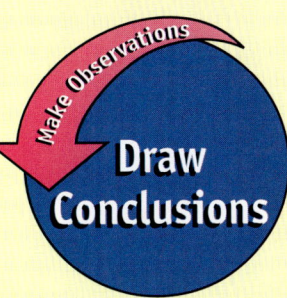

Mark and Nita decided that their test results supported their hypothesis. But they had noticed something odd that had happened in the beaker containing the hottest water. At some point after the water had cooled, a small amount of sugar added to the solution caused many sugar crystals to form.

They told Ms. Cobb about this strange result. Ms. Cobb congratulated them for having created a "supersaturated" solution. She suggested that Mark and Nita might want to plan another experiment to find out more about such solutions.

When you do an experiment, you need to write down, or record, your observations. Some of your observations might be a numbers – things that you counted or measured. Your recorded observations are called data. When you record your data, you need to organize it in a way that helps you to understand it. Graphs and tables are helpful ways to organize data. Then think about the information you have collected. Analyze what it tells you.

After you have analyzed your data, you should use what you have learned to draw a conclusion. A conclusion is a statement that sums up what you learned. The conclusion should be about the question you asked. Think about whether the information you have gathered supports your hypothesis or not. If it does, figure out how to check out your idea more thoroughly. Also think about new questions you can ask.

H7

SAFETY

The best way to be safe in the classroom is to use common sense. Prepare yourself for each activity before you start it. Get help from your teacher when there is a problem. Most important of all, pay attention. Here are some other ways that you can stay safe.

Stay Safe From Stains
- Wear protective clothing or an old shirt when you work with messy materials.
- If anything spills, wipe it up or ask your teacher to help you clean it up.

Stay Safe From Flames
- Keep your clothes away from open flames. If you have long or baggy sleeves, roll them up.
- Don't let your hair get close to a flame. If you have long hair, tie it back.

Stay Safe During Cleanup
- Wash up after you finish working.
- Dispose of things in the way that your teachers tells you to.

Stay Safe From Injuries
- Protect your eyes by wearing safety goggles when you are told that you need them.
- Keep your hands dry around electricity. Water is a good conductor of electricity, so you can get a shock more easily if your hands are wet.
- Be careful with sharp objects. If you have to press on them, keep the sharp side away from you.
- Cover any cuts you have that are exposed. If you spill something on a cut, be sure to wash it off immediately.
- Don't eat or drink anything unless your teacher tells you that it's okay.

MOST IMPORTANTLY
If you ever hurt yourself or one of your group members gets hurt, tell your teacher right away.

Science Tools

Using a Microscope

A microscope makes it possible to see very small things by magnifying them. Some microscopes have a set of lenses to magnify objects different amounts.

Examine Some Salt Grains

Handle a microscope carefully; it can break easily. Carry it firmly with both hands and avoid touching the lenses.

1. Turn the mirror toward a source of light. **NEVER** use the Sun as a light source.

2. Place a few grains of salt on the slide. Put the slide on the stage of the microscope.

3. While looking through the eyepiece, turn the adjustment knob on the back of the microscope to bring the salt grains into focus.

4. Raise the eyepiece tube to increase the magnification; lower it to decrease magnification.

Using a Calculator

After you've made measurements, a calculator can help you analyze your data. Some calculators have a memory key that allows you to save the result of one calculation while you do another.

Find an Average

The table shows the amount of rain that was collected using a rain gauge in each month of one year. You can use a calculator to help you find the average monthly rainfall.

1. Add the numbers. When you add a series of numbers, you don't need to press the equal sign until the last number is entered. Just press the plus sign after you enter each number (except the last one).

2. If you make a mistake while you are entering numbers, try to erase your mistake by pushing the clear entry (CE) key or the clear (C) key. Then you can continue entering the rest of the numbers you are adding. If you can't fix your mistake, you can push the (C) key once or twice until the screen shows 0. Then start over.

3. Your total should be 1,131. You can use the total to find the average. Just divide by the number of months in the year.

These keys run the calculator's memory functions.

This key erases the last entry.

Rainfall

Month	Rain (mm)
Jan.	214
Feb.	138
Mar.	98
Apr.	157
May	84
June	41
July	5
Aug.	23
Sept.	48
Oct.	75
Nov.	140
Dec.	108

SCIENCE TOOLS

Using a Balance

A balance is used to measure mass. Mass is the amount of matter in an object. Place the object to be massed in the left pan. Place standard masses in the right pan.

Measure the Mass of an Orange

1. Check that the empty pans are balanced, or level with each other. The pointer at the base should be on the middle mark. If it needs to be adjusted, move the slider on the back of the balance a little to the left or right.

2. Place an orange on the left pan. Notice that the pointer moves and that the pans are no longer level with each other. Then add standard masses, one at a time, to the right pan. When the pointer is at the middle mark again, the pans are balanced. Each pan holds the same amount of mass.

3. Each standard mass is marked to show the number of grams it contains. Add the number of grams marked on the masses in the pan. The total is the mass in grams of the orange.

Using a Spring Scale

A spring scale is used to measure force. You can use a spring scale to find the weight of an object in newtons. You can also use the scale to measure other forces.

Measure the Weight of an Object

1. Place the object in a net bag, and hang it from the hook on the bottom of the spring scale. Or, if possible, hang the object directly from the hook.

2. Slowly lift the scale by the top hook. Be sure the object to be weighed continues to hang from the bottom hook.

3. Wait until the pointer on the face of the spring scale has stopped moving. Read the number next to the pointer to determine the weight of the object in newtons.

Measure Friction

1. Hook the object to the bottom of the spring scale. Use a rubber band to connect the spring scale and object if needed.

2. Gently pull the top hook of the scale parallel to the floor. When the object starts to move, read the number of newtons next to the pointer on the scale. This number is the force of friction between the floor and the object as you drag the object.

SCIENCE TOOLS

Using a Thermometer

A thermometer is used to measure temperature. When the liquid in the tube of a thermometer gets warmer, it expands and moves farther up the tube. Different units can be used to measure temperature, but scientists usually use the Celsius scale.

Measure the Temperature of a Cold Liquid

1. Half-fill a cup with chilled liquid.

2. Hold the thermometer so that the bulb is in the center of the liquid.

3. Wait until you see the liquid in the tube stop moving. Read the scale line that is closest to the top of the liquid in the tube.

Measuring Volume

A graduated cylinder, a measuring cup, and a beaker are used to measure volume. Volume is the amount of space something takes up. Most of the containers that scientists use to measure volume have a scale marked in milliliters (mL).

Measure the Volume of Juice

1. Pour the juice into a measuring container.

2. Move your head so that your eyes are level with the top of the juice. Read the scale line that is closest to the surface of the juice. If the surface of the juice is curved up on the sides, look at the lowest point of the curve.

3. You can estimate the value between two lines on the scale to obtain a more accurate measurement.

▲ The bottom of the curve is at 50 mL.

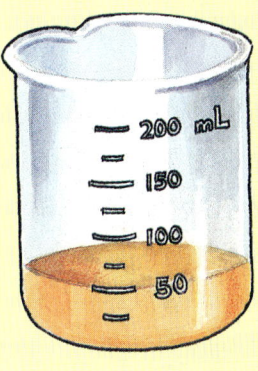

This beaker has marks for each 25 mL. ▼

This graduated cylinder has marks for every 1 mL. ▶

This measuring cup has marks for each 25 mL. ▼

Each container above has 50 mL of juice.

MEASUR

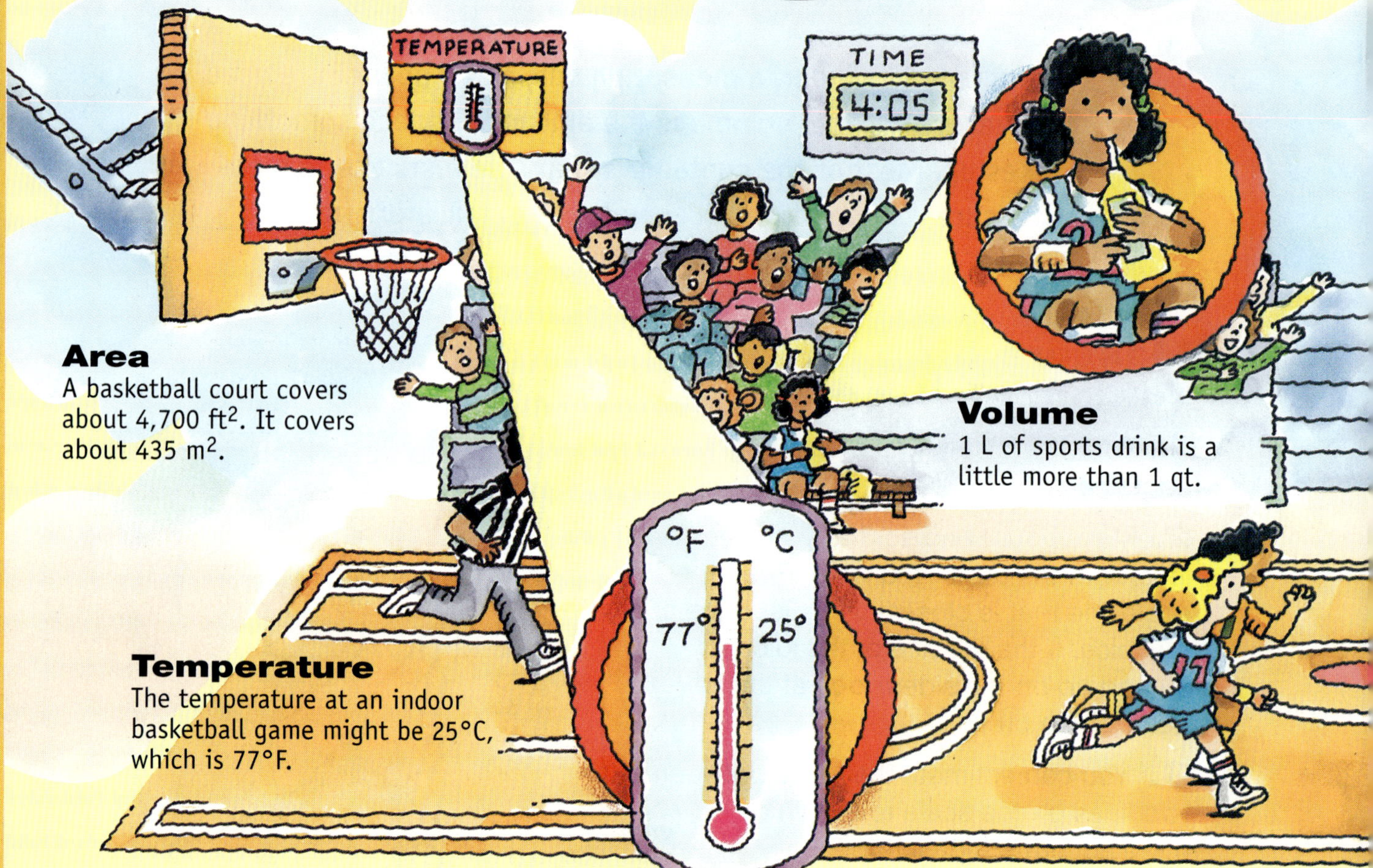

Area
A basketball court covers about 4,700 ft². It covers about 435 m².

Volume
1 L of sports drink is a little more than 1 qt.

Temperature
The temperature at an indoor basketball game might be 25°C, which is 77°F.

SI Measures

Temperature
Ice melts at 0 degrees Celsius (°C)
Water freezes at 0°C
Water boils at 100°C

Length and Distance
1,000 meters (m) = 1 kilometer (km)
100 centimeters (cm) = 1 m
10 millimeters (mm) = 1 cm

Force
1 newton (N) =
1 kilogram x meter/second/second
(kg x m/s²)

Volume
1 cubic meter (m³) = 1 m x 1 m x 1 m
1 cubic centimeter (cm³) =
1 cm x 1 cm x 1 cm
1 liter (L) = 1,000 milliliters (mL)
1 cm³ = 1 mL

Area
1 square kilometer (km²) = 1 km x 1 km
1 hectare = 10,000 m²

Mass
1,000 grams (g) = 1 kilogram (kg)
1,000 milligrams (mg) = 1 g

EMENTS

Mass and Weight
A basketball has a mass of about 650 g. It weighs about $1\frac{1}{2}$ lb.

Length/Distance
A basketball rim is about 10 ft high, or a little more than 3 m from the floor.

Rates (SI and English)

km/h = kilometers per hour
m/s = meters per second
mph = miles per hour

English Measures

Volume of Fluids
8 fluid ounces (fl oz) = 1 cup (c)
2 c = 1 pint (pt)
2 pt = 1 quart (qt)
4 qt = 1 gallon (gal)

Temperature
Ice melts at 32 degrees Fahrenheit (°F)
Water freezes at 32°F
Water boils at 212°F

Length and Distance
12 inches (in.) = 1 foot (ft)
3 ft = 1 yard (yd)
5,280 ft = 1 mile (mi)

Weight
16 ounces (oz) = 1 pound (lb)   2,000 pounds = 1 ton (T)

GLOSSARY

Pronunciation Key

Symbol	Key Words
a	cat
ā	ape
ä	cot, car
e	ten, berry
ē	me
i	fit, here
ī	ice, fire
ō	go
ô	fall, for
oi	oil
o͞o	look, pull
o͞o	tool, rule
ou	out, crowd
u	up
ʉ	fur, shirt
ə	a in ago e in agent i in pencil o in atom u in circus
b	bed
d	dog
f	fall

Symbol	Key Words
g	get
h	help
j	jump
k	kiss, call
l	leg
m	meat
n	nose
p	put
r	red
s	see
t	top
v	vat
w	wish
y	yard
z	zebra
ch	chin, arch
ŋ	ring, drink
sh	she, push
th	thin, truth
th	then, father
zh	measure

A heavy stress mark ′ is placed after a syllable that gets a heavy, or primary, stress, as in **picture** (pik′chər).

H18

abyssal plain (ə bis′əl plān) The broad, flat ocean bottom. (E34) The *abyssal plain* covers nearly half of Earth's surface.

acceleration (ak sel er ā′shən) The rate at which velocity changes over time. (F21) The spacecraft's *acceleration* increased as it soared into the air.

acid (as′id) A compound that turns blue litmus paper to red and forms a salt when it reacts with a base. (C81) *Acids* have a sour taste.

action force The initial force exerted in a force-pair. (F92) When you push against something, you are applying an *action force.*

aftershock A less powerful shock following the principal shock of an earthquake. (B58) Many *aftershocks* shook the ground in the days after the major earthquake.

algae (al′jē) Any of various plantlike protists. (A35) Diatoms and seaweed are kinds of *algae.*

allergy (al′ər jē) An oversensitivity to a specific substance that is harmless to most people, such as pollen, dust, animal hair, or a particular food. (G42) An *allergy* may cause such symptoms as sneezing, itching, or a rash.

alloy (al′oi) A solution of two or more metals. (C59) Bronze is an *alloy* of copper and tin.

antibiotic (an tī bī ät′ik) A substance, produced by microbes or fungi, that can destroy bacteria or stop their growth. Also, a synthetic substance with these properties. (A59) Doctors prescribe *antibiotics* to treat various bacteria-caused diseases.

antibody (an′ti bäd ē) A protein produced in the blood that destroys or weakens bacteria and other pathogens. (A59, G35) *Antibodies* are produced in response to infection.

aquaculture (ak′wə kul chər) The raising of water plants and animals for human use or consumption. (E80) Raising catfish on a catfish "farm" is a form of *aquaculture.*

asexual reproduction Reproduction involving a cell or cells from one parent and, resulting in offspring exactly like the parent. (D10) The division of an amoeba into two cells is an example of *asexual reproduction.*

asthenosphere (as then′ə sfir) The layer of Earth below the lithosphere; the upper part of the mantle. (B39) The *asthenosphere* contains hot, partially melted rock with plasticlike properties.

astronomical unit A unit of measurement equal to the distance from Earth to the Sun. (F9) Pluto is 39.3 *astronomical units* (A.U.) from the Sun.

atom The smallest particle of an element that has the chemical properties of that element. (C35) An *atom* of sodium differs from an *atom* of chlorine.

H19

atomic number (ə täm′ik num′bər) The number of protons in the nucleus of an atom of an element. (C73) The *atomic number* of oxygen is 8.

bacteria (bak tir′ē ə) Monerans that feed on dead organic matter or on living things. (A51, G33) Diseases such as pneumonia and tuberculosis are caused by *bacteria*.

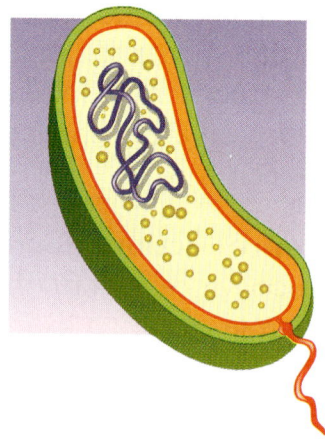

base A compound that turns red litmus paper blue and that forms a salt when it reacts with an acid. (C81) *Bases* have a slippery feel.

behavioral risk factor (bē hāv′yər əl risk fak′tər) A health risk factor that results from a person's choices about his or her lifestyle. (G53) Using drugs or alcohol is a *behavioral risk factor*.

benthos (ben′thäs) All the plants and animals that live on the ocean bottom. (E25) *Benthos* include oysters, crabs, and coral.

blue-green bacteria (blo͞o grēn bak tir′ē ə) Monerans that contain chlorophyll. (A51) Like plants, *blue-green bacteria* carry out photosynthesis and make their own food.

budding A form of asexual reproduction in which a new individual develops from a bump, or bud, on the body of the parent. (D13) Some one-celled organisms, such as yeast, reproduce by *budding*.

buoyancy (boi′ən sē) The tendency of liquids, like water, to keep objects afloat. (F123) Objects float better in salt water than in fresh water because salt water has greater *buoyancy*.

caldera (kal der′ə) A large circular depression, or basin, at the top of a volcano. (B104) The eruption formed a *caldera* that later became a lake.

cast fossil (kast fäs′əl) A fossil formed when minerals from rock move into and harden within the space left by a decaying organism. (D57) *Cast fossils* of shells can provide information about the animals from which the fossils formed.

cell The basic unit that makes up all living things. (A9) The human body is made up of trillions of *cells*.

cell differentiation (sel dif ər en shē-ā′shən) The development of cells into different and specialized cell types. (A25) Through *cell differentiation*, plant and animal cells develop into tissues.

cell membrane (sel mem′brān) The structure that surrounds and encloses a cell and controls the movement of substances into and out of the cell. (A10) The *cell membrane* shrank when the cell was placed in salt water.

cell respiration (sel res pə rā′shən) The process in cells in which oxygen is used to release stored energy by breaking down sugar molecules. (A19) The process of *cell respiration* provides energy for a cell's activities.

cell theory A theory that states that cells are the basic units of structure and function of all living things. (A10) The *cell theory* states that new cells are produced from existing cells.

cell wall The rigid structure surrounding the cells of plants, monerans, and some protists. (A10) The *cell wall* gives a cell its rigid shape.

chemical bond A force, or link, that holds atoms together in a molecule or in a crystal. (C73) In a water molecule, atoms of hydrogen and oxygen are held together by *chemical bonds*.

chemical change A change in matter that results in new substances with new properties. (C69) A *chemical change* occurs when wood burns and forms gases and ash.

chemical formula A group of symbols and numbers that shows what elements make up a compound. (C40) The *chemical formula* for carbon dioxide is CO_2.

chemical properties Characteristics of matter that describe how it changes when it reacts with other matter. (C34) The ability to burn is a *chemical property* of paper.

chemical symbol One or two letters used to stand for the name of an element. (C36) Ca is the *chemical symbol* for calcium.

chloroplast (klôr′ə plast) A tiny green organelle that contains chlorophyll and is found in plant cells and some protist cells. (A10) The chlorophyll inside a *chloroplast* enables a plant cell to capture solar energy.

cholesterol (kə les′tər ôl) A fatty substance, found in foods, that can lead to clogged blood vessels. (G60) A diet that is too high in *cholesterol* can increase the risk of heart disease.

chromosome (krō′mə sōm) A threadlike structure in the nucleus of a cell; it carries the genes that determine the traits an offspring inherits from its parent or parents. (A10, D22, G12) Most cells in the human body contain 23 pairs of *chromosomes*.

cilia (sil′ē ə) Small, hairlike structures lining the membranes of the respiratory system. (G33) *Cilia* help to filter the air that enters the body.

cinder-cone volcano (sin′dər kōn val kā′nō) A kind of volcano, usually small and steep-sloped, that is formed from layers of cinders, which are sticky bits of volcanic material. (B88) *Cinder-cone volcanoes* result from explosive eruptions.

communicable disease (kə myōō′ni-kə bəl di zēz) A disease that can be passed from one individual to another. (A58) Bacteria, which are easily passed from organism to organism, are the cause of many *communicable diseases*.

competition The struggle among organisms for available resources. (D77) *Competition* among members of a species is a factor in evolution.

composite-cone volcano (kəm päz′it kōn val cā′nō) A kind of volcano formed when explosive eruptions of sticky lava alternate with quieter eruptions of volcanic rock bits. (B89) Mount Vesuvius is a *composite-cone volcano* in southern Italy.

compound (käm′pound) A substance made up of two or more elements that are chemically combined. (C34) Water is a *compound* made up of hydrogen and oxygen.

condensation (kän dən sā′shən) The change of state from a gas to a liquid. (C28) The *condensation* of water vapor can form droplets of water on the outside of a cold glass.

continental edge (kän tə nent″l ej) The point at which the continental shelf, which surrounds each continent, begins to angle sharply downward. (E33) Beyond the *continental edge* the ocean increases rapidly in depth.

continental rise The lower portion of the continental slope, extending to the ocean floor. (E33) The *continental rise* usually starts angling down to the ocean floor about a mile beneath the ocean.

continental shelf The sloping shelf of land, consisting of the edges of the continents under the ocean. (E32) The *continental shelf* can extend hundreds of miles out into the ocean.

continental slope The steep clifflike drop from the continental edge to the ocean floor. (E33) The *continental slope* connects the continental shelf with the ocean bottom.

convection (kən vek′shən) The process by which heat energy is transferred through liquids or gases by the movement of particles. (B39) The pie in the oven was heated by *convection*.

convection current The path along which energy is transferred during convection. (B39) Scientists think that *convection currents* in the mantle cause Earth's tectonic plates to move.

convergent boundary (kən vur′jənt boun′də rē) A place where the plates that make up Earth's crust and upper mantle move together. (B40) Layers of rock may bend or break at a *convergent boundary*.

Coriolis effect (kôr ē ō′lis e fekt′) The tendency of a body or fluid moving across Earth's surface to have a curving motion due to Earth's rotation. (E56) The *Coriolis effect* causes air and water currents to move to the right in the Northern Hemisphere and to the left in the Southern Hemisphere.

crest The top of a wave. (E65) The *crest* of the wave seemed to tower over the surfer.

crust The thin outer layer of Earth. (B20) Earth's *crust* varies from 5 km to 48 km in thickness.

current Great rivers of water moving through the ocean. (E55) The *current* pulled the boat away from shore.

cytoplasm (sīt′ō plaz əm) The watery gel inside a cell. (A11) Various organelles are found inside the *cytoplasm* of a cell.

deceleration (dē sel ər ā′shən) A decrease in speed over time. (F23) Air resistance can cause the *deceleration* of objects.

density The amount of mass in a given volume of matter. (C13) Lead has a greater *density* than aluminum.

desalination (dē sal ə nā′shən) A process for obtaining fresh water from salt water by removing the salt. (E80) A few countries operate *desalination* plants, which obtain fresh water from ocean water.

diatom (dī′ə täm) A microscopic, one-celled alga with a glasslike cell wall. (A35) A single liter of sea water may contain millions of *diatoms*.

dietary fat A nutrient in food that provides energy. (G60) A small amount of *dietary fat* is part of a healthful diet.

diffusion (di fyoo′zhən) The tendency of substances to move from an area of greater concentration to an area of lesser concentration. (A16) Substances can pass in and out of cells by *diffusion*.

divergent boundary (di vur′jənt boun′də rē) A place where the plates that make up Earth's crust and upper mantle move away from one another. (B40) Most *divergent boundaries* are found on the floor of the ocean.

dome mountain A mountain formed when magma lifts Earth's surface, creating a broad dome, or bulge. (B47) Pikes Peak in Colorado is a *dome mountain*.

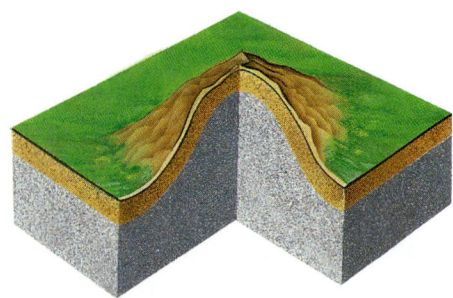

domesticated (dō mes'ti kāt əd) Tamed and/or bred to serve people's purposes. (D70) People breed *domesticated* animals such as horses for transportation and other uses.

dominant gene (däm'ə nənt jēn) A gene that has control over how a trait is expressed. (G14) A *dominant gene* will be expressed when paired with a recessive gene.

dominant trait (däm'ə nənt trāt) A trait that if inherited, will be expressed. (D45) Gregor Mendel found that tallness was a *dominant trait* in pea plants.

drag A force that resists forward motion through a fluid; it operates in the direction opposite to thrust. (F111) The air causes *drag* on an airplane.

earthquake A shaking or movement of Earth's surface, caused by the release of stored energy along a fault. (B58) Many *earthquakes* occur near the boundaries between tectonic plates.

egg A female sex cell. (G9) In sexual reproduction an *egg* is fertilized by a sperm.

electron (ē lek'trän) A negatively charged particle in an atom. (C71) The number of *electrons* in an atom usually equals the number of protons.

element (el'ə mənt) A substance that cannot be broken down into any other substance by ordinary chemical means. (C34) Oxygen, hydrogen, copper, iron, and carbon are *elements*.

embryo (em'brē ō) An early stage in the development of an organism. (G10) A fertilized egg develops into an *embryo*.

endangered species A species of animal or plant whose number has become so small that the species is in danger of becoming extinct. (D25) The rhinoceros has become an *endangered species* because poachers slaughter the animals for their horns.

endocrine gland (en'dō krin gland) A gland that produces hormones and releases them directly into the bloodstream. (G22) The thyroid and the pituitary are *endocrine glands*.

environmental risk factor A health risk factor that results from a person's environment. (G53) Breathing smoke from other people's cigarettes is an *environmental risk factor*.

epicenter (ep'i sent ər) The point on Earth's surface directly above an earthquake's point of origin. (B65) The *epicenter* of the earthquake was 2 km north of the city.

era (er'ə) One of the major divisions of geologic time. (D59) Many kinds of mammals developed during the Cenozoic *Era*.

ethanol (eth'ə nôl) A kind of alcohol used to make medicines, food products, and various other items. (A42) *Ethanol* is a flammable liquid.

evaporation (ē vap ə rā'shən) The change of state from a liquid to a gas. (C27) Heat from the Sun caused the *evaporation* of the water.

evolution (ev ə lōō'shən) The idea that all living things are descended from earlier forms of life, with new species developing over time. (D58) According to the theory of *evolution*, the plants and animals alive today descended from organisms that lived millions of years ago.

extinct (ek stiŋkt') With reference to species, no longer in existence. (D25) Dinosaurs are *extinct*.

extinction (ek stiŋk'shən) The disappearance of species from Earth. (D62) Scientists do not agree about what caused the *extinction* of the dinosaurs.

F

fault A break in rock along which rock slabs have moved. (B65) The shifting of Earth's tectonic plates can produce a *fault*, along which earthquakes may occur.

fault-block mountain A mountain formed when masses of rock move up or down along a fault. (B47) Mountains in the Great Rift Valley of Africa are *fault-block mountains*.

fermentation (fur mən tā'shən) A chemical change in which an organism breaks down sugar to produce carbon dioxide and alcohol or lactic acid. (A19, A42) The chemist used yeast to cause *fermentation* in the sugary liquid.

fertilization (fur tə li zā'shən) The process by which a sperm and an egg unite to form a cell that will develop into a new individual. (D24, G9) In humans, *fertilization* produces a cell containing 46 chromosomes, half from the female and half from the male.

H25

fetus (fēt′əs) A stage in the development of an organism that follows the embryo stage. (G10) After about eight weeks, a human embryo is called a *fetus*.

first law of motion The concept that objects at rest tend to remain at rest and objects in motion tend to remain in motion, traveling at a constant speed and in the same direction. (F59) According to the *first law of motion*, a stationary object will stay in place unless some force makes it move.

fission (fish′ən) A method of asexual reproduction in which a parent cell divides to form two new cells. (A51, D10) Many one-celled organisms, such as amoebas, reproduce by *fission*.

focus (fō′kəs) The point, or place, at which an earthquake begins. (B65) The *focus* of the earthquake was about 20 km beneath Earth's surface.

folded mountain A mountain formed when two tectonic plates collide. (B45) The Alps and the Himalayas are *folded mountains*.

food pyramid A model showing the relative amounts of different kinds of food a person should eat each day for a healthful diet. (G59) Grains, including breads, cereals, rice, and pasta, make up the base of the *food pyramid*.

force A push or a pull. (F33, F65) The *force* of friction caused the rolling wagon to slow and then stop.

fossil (fäs′əl) The remains or traces of a living thing, usually preserved in rock. (D56) *Fossils* are usually found in sedimentary rock.

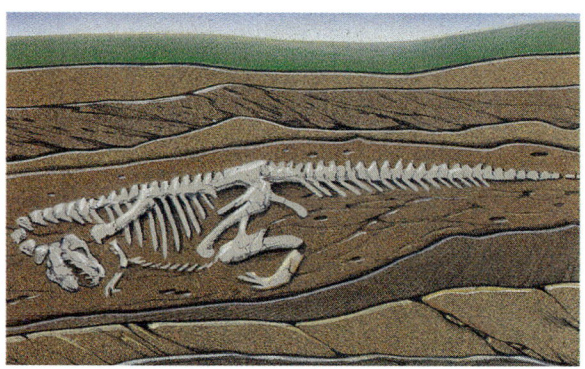

freezing The change of state from a liquid to a solid. (C28) The *freezing* of water occurs at 0°C.

friction (frik′shən) The rubbing of one thing against another. The force of friction resists motion between two surfaces that are in contact with each other. (F73) *Friction* keeps a car's tires from slipping off the road.

fungus (fuŋ′gəs) Any of a large group of organisms that feed on dead organisms or that are parasitic. (A43, G40) A mushroom is a *fungus*.

gene (jēn) One of the units that make up a chromosome; genes determine the traits an offspring inherits from its parent or parents. (D35, G13) Half of your *genes* come from your mother, and half come from your father.

gene splicing (jēn splīs′iŋ) A process by which genes are manipulated to alter the function or nature of an organism, usually by being transferred from one organism to another. (D48) Through *gene splicing*, scientists have transferred a gene for making insulin from one organism to another.

genetic engineering (jə net′ik en jə nir′iŋ) The process by which genes are manipulated to bring about biological change in species. (D47) Using *genetic engineering* techniques, scientists have successfully combined DNA from different organisms.

gravity (grav′i tē) The force that pulls objects toward Earth; also, the attractive force exerted by a body or object on other bodies or objects. (F33) *Gravity* causes a ball to fall to the ground after it is thrown into the air.

health risk factor An action or condition that increases the probability of getting a disease or becoming injured. (G52) Smoking cigarettes and living in an area with severe water pollution are two *health risk factors*.

heat Energy that flows from warmer to cooler regions of matter. (C26) *Heat* can cause matter to change from one state to another.

hereditary risk factor A health risk factor that is passed on through genes from parent to child. (G52) A family history of heart disease is a *hereditary risk factor*.

hormone (hôr′mōn) A chemical substance that acts as a messenger, causing a change in organs and tissues in the body. (G23) Growth *hormones* are released by the pituitary gland.

hot spot A place deep within Earth's mantle that is extremely hot and contains a chamber of magma. (B102) Magma rising from a *hot spot* can break through Earth's crust to form a volcano.

immune system (im myōōn′ sis′təm) The body's system that defends the body against pathogens. (A59, G33) The *immune system* produces antibodies to fight disease.

immunity (im myōōn′i tē) The body's resistance to a disease or infection. (G35) Polio vaccine gives people *immunity* to the disease.

incomplete dominance (in kəm plēt′ däm′ə nəns) The expression of both genes (traits) in a pair, producing a blended effect. (D46) A plant with pink flowers, produced by crossing a plant having red flowers with a plant having white flowers, is an example of *incomplete dominance*.

indicator (in'di kāt ər) A substance that changes color when mixed with an acid or a base. (C81) Paper treated with an *indicator* is used to test whether a compound is an acid or a base.

inertia (in ur'shə) The tendency of matter to remain at rest if at rest, or if in motion, to remain in motion in the same direction. (F59) *Inertia* results in passengers in a car moving forward when the driver applies the brakes.

inflammation (in flə mā'shən) A defense response by a part of the body, resulting from infection, injury, or irritation and marked by such symptoms as redness, pain, and swelling. (G33) The boy developed an *inflammation* where he had scraped his knee.

inherited trait (in her'it əd trāt) A trait that is passed on from parents to offspring by means of genes. (D34) Eye color is an *inherited trait*.

ion (ī'ən) An electrically charged atom. Ions form when atoms lose or gain electrons. (C73) A negative *ion* is formed when an atom gains electrons.

island arc A chain of volcanoes formed from magma that rises as a result of an oceanic plate sinking into the mantle. (B96) The Philippine Islands are part of an *island arc*.

kinetic energy (ki net'ik en'ər jē) Energy of motion. (C25) A ball rolling down a hill has *kinetic energy*.

lava (lä'və) Magma that flows out onto Earth's surface from a volcano. (B86) Flaming *lava* poured down the sides of the volcanic mountain.

law of conservation of mass The principle that states that matter can neither be created nor destroyed by a chemical or physical change. (C75) According to the *law of conservation of mass*, burning a log will not destroy any of the log's original mass.

law of conservation of momentum The principle that states that momentum can be transferred but cannot be lost. (F86) The *law of conservation of momentum* explains why the momentum resulting from the collision of two objects equals the total momentum of the objects before they collided.

learned trait (lurnd trāt) A trait that is acquired through learning or experience. (D36) The ability to speak Spanish is a *learned trait*.

lift The upward force, resulting from differences in air pressure above and below an airplane's wings, that causes the airplane to rise. (F111) Increasing the size of an airplane's wings increases *lift*.

lithosphere (lith′ō sfir) The solid, rocky layer of Earth, including the crust and top part of the mantle. (B38) The *lithosphere* is about 100 km thick.

magma (mag′mə) The hot, molten rock deep inside Earth. (B86) The *magma* rose through the volcano.

magnetic field (mag net′ik fēld) The space around a magnet within which the force of the magnet is exerted. (B28) The magnet attracted all the iron filings within its *magnetic field*.

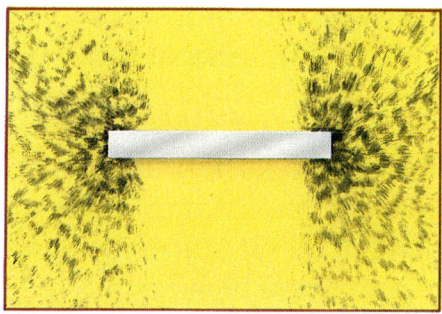

magnetic reversal (mag net′ik ri vur′səl) The switching or changing of Earth's magnetic poles such that the north magnetic pole becomes located at the south magnetic pole's position and vice versa. (B28) Scientists have found evidence of *magnetic reversals* in layers of rock along the ocean floor.

magnitude (mag′nə tōōd) The force or strength of an earthquake. (B59) *Magnitude* is a measure of the amount of energy released by an earthquake.

mantle The middle layer of Earth. (B19) The *mantle* is the thick layer of rock between the crust and the core.

mass The amount of matter in an object. (C10, F33) A large rock has more *mass* than a pebble.

matter Anything that has mass and takes up space. (C10) Rocks, water, and air are three kinds of *matter*.

meiosis (mī ō′sis) The process of cell division by which the number of chromosomes in sex cells is reduced to half the number in body cells. (D22) Because of *meiosis*, a sex cell in a human has only 23 chromosomes instead of 46.

melting The change of state from a solid to a liquid. (C27) The *melting* of the icicles began after sunrise.

menstrual cycle (men'strəl sī'kəl) A cycle of approximately 28 days during which an egg is released by the ovary and, if not fertilized, leaves the body with other tissue and blood. (G24) The *menstrual cycle* begins when a girl reaches puberty.

metric system A system of measurement based on a few defined units (such as the meter) and in which larger and smaller units are related by powers of 10. (F11) In the *metric system*, a centimeter is 10 times longer than a millimeter.

microorganism (mī krō ôr'gən iz-əm) An organism too small to be seen except with the aid of a microscope. (G40) Bacteria are *microorganisms*.

mid-ocean ridge A chain of mountains under the ocean. (B22, E34) The *mid-ocean ridge* extends almost 60,000 km.

mitochondria (mīt ō kän'drē ə) Cell organelles in which energy is released from food. (A11) The more *mitochondria* a cell has, the more energy it can release from food.

mitosis (mī tō'sis) The process in which one cell divides to form two identical new cells. (A23) The new cells formed by *mitosis* have the same number of chromosomes as the parent cell.

mixture A combination of two or more substances that can be separated by physical means. (C34) This jar contains a *mixture* of colored beads.

model Something used or made to represent an object or an idea. (C71) The plastic *model* showed the structure of the heart.

mold fossil (mōld fäs'əl) A fossil consisting of a hollowed space in the shape of an organism or one of its parts. (D56) Sediments collecting around a dead organism may lead to the formation of a *mold fossil* of the organism.

molecule (mäl'i kyo͞ol) A particle made up of a group of atoms that are chemically bonded. (C39) A *molecule* of water contains three atoms.

momentum (mō men'təm) A property of a moving object, calculated by multiplying the object's mass by its velocity. (F85) The train gathered *momentum* as its speed increased.

moneran (män'ər an) Any of mostly one-celled organisms in which the cell does not have a nucleus. (A50) Bacteria are *monerans*.

mucus (myo͞o'kəs) A thick, sticky fluid that lines the membranes of the respiratory system. (G33) *Mucus* helps trap particles that you breathe in.

multicellular (mul ti sel'yo͞o lər) Made up of more than one cell. (A33) Some protists are *multicellular*.

mutation (myo͞o tā′shən) A change in a gene that can result in a new characteristic, or trait. (D76) Certain *mutations* have helped species survive in their environment.

natural selection (nach′ər əl sə-lek′shən) The process by which those living things that have characteristics adapting them to their environment tend to live longest and produce the most offspring, passing on these favorable characteristics to their offspring. (D75) *Natural selection* helps explain why certain characteristics become common while others die out.

neap tide (nēp tīd) The tide occurring at the first and third quarters of the Moon, when the difference in level between high and low tide is smallest. (E71) *Neap tides* occur at two times during a month.

nekton (nek′tän) All the free-swimming animals that live in the ocean. (E25) *Nekton* include such animals as fish, octopuses, and whales.

neutralization (no͞o trəl ī zā′shən) The reaction between an acid and a base. (C83) *Neutralization* produces water and a salt.

neutron (no͞o′trän) A particle in the nucleus of an atom that has no electric charge. (C71) The mass of a *neutron* is about equal to that of a proton.

newton (no͞o′tən) A unit used to measure force. (F66) A *newton* is the force needed to accelerate a one-kilogram object by one meter per second every second.

nuclear fission (no͞o′klē ər fish′ən) The splitting of the nucleus of an atom, releasing great amounts of energy. (C77) Bombarding a nucleus with a neutron can cause *nuclear fission*.

nuclear membrane The structure that surrounds and encloses the nucleus and controls what substances move into and out of the nucleus. (A11) The *nuclear membrane* appears to be solid, but it actually has tiny holes through which materials can pass.

nucleus (no͞o′klē əs) 1. The dense, central part of an atom. (C71) The *nucleus* contains nearly all of an atom's mass. 2. The control center of a cell. (A11) The *nucleus* contains the cell's genetic information.

obese (ō bēs′) More than 20 percent over normal body weight. (G60) *Obese* people have more health problems than people of normal weight.

organ A part of a multicellular organism made up of a group of tissues that work together to perform a certain function. (A26) The heart and the lungs are *organs* of the human body.

H31

organ system A group of organs that work together to perform one or more functions. (A26) The stomach and the intestines are part of the *organ system* that digests food.

osmosis (äs mō′sis) The diffusion of water through a membrane. (A16) *Osmosis* maintains the balance of water inside and outside a cell.

paleontologist) (pā lē ən täl′ə jist) A scientist who studies fossils. (D58) A team of *paleontologists* discovered the remains of a dinosaur.

Pangaea (pan jē′ə) A supercontinent that existed about 200 million years ago. (B9) *Pangaea* broke apart into several continents.

pathogen (path′ə jən) A microorganism that can cause a disease. (G40) A virus is a *pathogen*.

period 1. A division of geologic time that is a subdivision of an era. (D59) The Jurassic *Period* is part of the Mesozoic Era. 2. The interval of time between two successive wave crests. (E65) The *period* for the ocean waves was about ten seconds.

petrification (pe tri fi kā′shən) The changing of the hard parts of a dead organism to stone. (D57) Fossils of trees have been preserved by *petrification*.

photosynthesis (fōt ō sin′thə sis) The process by which green plants and other producers use light energy to make food. (A18, E24) In *photosynthesis*, plant cells use light energy to make glucose from carbon dioxide and water.

physical change A change in size, shape, or state of matter, with no new kind of matter being formed. (C68) The freezing of water into ice cubes is an example of a *physical change*.

physical properties (fiz′i kəl präp′ər tēz) Characteristics of matter that can be measured or detected by the senses. (C34) Color is a *physical property* of minerals.

phytoplankton (fīt ō plaŋk′tən) Any of the usually microscopic plantlike protists that live near the surface of the ocean. (E10) *Phytoplankton* drift with the ocean currents.

plankton (plaŋk′tən) Organisms, generally microscopic in size, that float or drift in the ocean. (A35, E11) *Plankton* is a source of food for fish.

plate One of the slabs that make up Earth's crust and upper mantle; also called *tectonic plate*. (B19) Some of Earth's *plates* carry continents.

plate boundary A place where the plates that make up Earth's crust and upper mantle either move together or apart or else move past one another. (B20, B40) Earthquakes occur along *plate boundaries*.

pollution The contamination of the environment with waste materials or other unwanted substances. (E91) Dangerous chemicals dumped into the ocean are one source of *pollution*.

polymer (päl′ə mər) A compound consisting of large molecules formed from many smaller, linked molecules. (C92) Proteins are *polymers*.

protist (prōt′ist) Any of a large group of mostly single-celled, microscopic organisms. (A33) Amoebas and algae are *protists*.

proton (prō′tän) A positively charged particle found in the nucleus of an atom. (C71) The atomic number of an atom equals the number of *protons* in the atom's nucleus.

protozoan (prō tō zō′ən) Protists that have animal-like traits. (A34, G40) A paramecium is a *protozoan*.

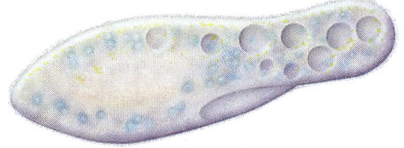

puberty (pyo͞o′bər tē) The state of physical development when a person becomes capable of producing offspring. (G22) Girls generally reach *puberty* earlier than boys.

radioactive element (rā dē ō ak′tiv el′ə mənt) An element made up of atoms whose nuclei break down, or decay, into nuclei of other atoms. (C76) As the nucleus of a *radioactive element* decays, energy is released.

reaction force The force exerted in response to an action force. (F92) A *reaction force* is equal in strength to an action force but opposite in direction.

recessive gene (ri ses′iv jēn) A gene that is able to control how a trait is expressed only when paired with another recessive gene. (G14) A *recessive gene* will not be expressed when paired with a dominant gene.

recessive trait (ri ses′iv trāt) A trait that will be hidden if paired with a dominant trait. (D45) In his experiments with pea plants, Gregor Mendel learned that shortness was a *recessive trait*.

reproduction The process by which organisms produce more of their own kind. (D10) *Reproduction* ensures the survival of the species.

Richter scale (rik′tər skāl) A scale of numbers by which the magnitude of earthquakes is measured. (B59) Each increase of 1.0 on the *Richter scale* represents an increase of 30 times in the energy released by an earthquake.

H33

rifting (rift′iŋ) The process by which magma rises to fill the gap between two plates that are moving apart. (B108) *Rifting* in eastern Africa may split the continent into two parts.

salinity (sə lin′ə tē) The total amount of dissolved salts in ocean water. (E9) The *salinity* of the ocean varies in different parts of the world.

salt A compound that can be formed when an acid reacts with a base. (C83) When vinegar and baking soda interact, they produce a *salt*.

saprophyte (sap′rə fīt) An organism that lives on dead or decaying matter. (A44) Molds are *saprophytes*.

sea-floor spreading The process by which new ocean floor is continually being formed as magma rises to the surface and hardens into rock. (B30) *Sea-floor spreading* occurs as magma fills the space between separating plates.

seamount (sē′mount) An underwater mountain that formed from a volcano. (E34) Thousands of *seamounts* rise from the floor of the Pacific.

second law of motion The concept that an object's acceleration is related to the strength of the force acting on it and on the object's mass. (F65) A gust of wind blowing an open umbrella out of your hands illustrates the *second law of motion*.

seismograph (sīz′mə graf) An instrument that records the intensity, duration, and nature of earthquake waves. (B74) Scientists use information from *seismographs* to determine the location of earthquakes.

seismometer (sīz mäm′ə tər) An instrument that detects and records Earth's movements. (B98) Data from the *seismometer* suggested that a volcanic eruption might soon occur.

selective breeding Breeding of living things to produce offspring with certain desired characteristics. (D70) People have used *selective breeding* to produce domesticated animals.

sex cell A female or male reproductive cell; an egg cell or sperm cell. (D22) Reproduction can occur when *sex cells* unite.

sexual reproduction Reproduction that involves the joining of a male sex cell and a female sex cell. (D22, G9) Most animals and plants produce offspring through *sexual reproduction*.

shield volcano A kind of volcano that is large and gently sloped and that is formed when lava flows quietly from a crack in the Earth's crust. (B89) Mauna Loa, a *shield volcano* in Hawaii, is the largest volcano on Earth.

solute (säl′yo͞ot) The material present in the smaller amount in a solution; the substance dissolved in a solution. (C57) If you dissolve sugar in water, sugar is the *solute*.

solution A mixture in which the different particles are spread evenly throughout the mixture. (C57) Dissolving salt in water makes a *solution*.

solvent (säl′vənt) The material present in the greater amount in a solution; the substance in a solution, usually a liquid, that dissolves another substance. (C57) If you mix sugar and water, water is the *solvent*.

speed The distance traveled in a certain amount of time; rate of movement. (F16) The truck was moving at a *speed* of 40 mph.

sperm (spurm) A male sex cell. (G9) A *sperm* combines with an egg during fertilization.

spore A reproductive cell that can develop into a new organism. (A43) Ferns and mushrooms produce *spores*.

spring tide A tide occurring at or just after the new moon and full moon; usually the highest tide of the month. (E71) At the time of a *spring tide*, both the Sun and the Moon are in line with Earth.

state of matter Any of the three forms that matter may take: solid, liquid, or gas. (C20) Water's *state of matter* depends on its temperature.

substance Matter of a particular kind, or chemical makeup. (C34) Elements and compounds are *substances*.

symbiosis (sim bī ō′sis) A relationship between two organisms in which at least one organism benefits. (A61) Some fungi and algae grow together in *symbiosis*.

tectonic plate *See* plate.

temperature A measure of the average kinetic energy of the particles in matter. (C26) Water *temperature* rises as the motion of water molecules increases.

theory of continental drift A theory that states that the continents formed a single land mass at one time in the past and have drifted over time to their present positions. (B10) The idea of *continental drift* was first suggested by Alfred Wegener.

theory of plate tectonics The theory that Earth's lithosphere is broken into enormous slabs, or plates, that are in motion. (B19, B41) Scientists use the *theory of plate tectonics* to explain how Earth's continents drift.

third law of motion The concept that for every action force there is an equal and opposite reaction force. (F92) When you watch someone's feet bouncing off a trampoline, you see the *third law of motion* at work.

thrust (thrust) The push or driving force that causes an airplane, rocket, or other object to move forward. (F110) *Thrust* can be produced by a spinning propeller or by a jet engine.

tide The daily rise and fall of the surface of the ocean or other large body of water, caused by the gravitational attraction of the Moon and the Sun. (E70) As the *tide* came in, we moved our blanket back from the water's edge.

tissue A group of similar, specialized cells working together to carry out the same function. (A25) Muscle *tissue* contains cells that contract.

toxin (täks'in) A poison produced by an organism. (A58) *Toxins* produced by bacteria can cause serious illness.

trade wind A prevailing wind that blows from east to west on either side of the equator. (E56) South of the equator, the *trade wind* comes from the southeast.

transform-fault boundary (trans-fôrm fôlt boun'də rē) A place where the plates that make up Earth's crust and upper mantle move past one another. (B41) Movement occurring at a *transform-fault boundary* may cause cracks to form in Earth's rocks.

tsunami (tsōō nä'mē) A large and powerful ocean wave usually caused by an underwater earthquake. (B76) A *tsunami* can cause great destruction if it strikes a land area.

turbidity current (tʉr bid'i tē kʉr'ənt) A current of water carrying large amounts of sediment. (E38, E61) *Turbidity currents* may cause sediment to build up in some places.

upper mantle (up'ər man'təl) The outermost part of the mantle. (B20) Earth's plates consist of a thin layer of crust lying over the *upper mantle*.

upwelling The rising of deep water to the surface that occurs when winds move surface water. (E60) *Upwelling* brings pieces of shells and dead organisms up from the ocean floor.

vaccine (vak sēn′) A preparation of dead or weakened bacteria or viruses that produces immunity to a disease. (A59, G35) The *vaccine* for smallpox has eliminated that disease.

vacuole (vak′yōō ōl) A structure in the cytoplasm in which food and other substances are stored. (A11) A *vacuole* in a plant cell is often quite large.

vegetative propagation (vej ə tāt′iv präp ə gā′shən) A form of asexual reproduction in which a new plant develops from a part of a parent plant. (D15) Using a cutting taken from a houseplant to grow a new plant is a method of *vegetative propagation*.

velocity (və läs′ə tē) The rate of motion in a particular direction. (F21) The *velocity* was northwest at 880 km/h.

virus (vī′rəs) A tiny disease-causing life form consisting of genetic material wrapped inside a capsule of protein. (A52, G40) *Viruses* cause such diseases as AIDS, chickenpox, and rabies.

volcano An opening in Earth's crust through which hot gases, rock fragments, and molten rock erupt. (B48, B86) Lava flowed out of the *volcano*.

volume (väl′yōōm) The amount of space that matter takes up. (C11) A large fuel tank holds a greater *volume* of gasoline than a small tank.

wave The up-and-down movement of the surface of water, caused by the wind. (E65) Ocean *waves* crashed against the shoreline.

wavelength The distance between the crests of two successive waves. (E65) At the height of the storm, the waves had a *wavelength* of 10 m.

weight A measure of the force of gravity on an object. (F33) The *weight* of this package is five pounds.

westerly (wes′tər lē) A prevailing wind that blows from west to east. (E56) Ships that sailed from North America to Europe were aided by the power of the *westerlies*.

zooplankton (zō ō plaŋk′tən) Any of the tiny animal-like organisms that live near the surface of the ocean. (E11) Zooplankton float in the sea.

zygote (zī′gōt) A fertilized egg cell. (D24, G10) A *zygote* develops into an embryo by means of cell division.

Note: Recognizing that many schools teach health as a separate subject, Science DiscoveryWorks Concordia Edition does not include Unit G, a health unit.

INDEX

A
Abyssal plain, E34
Accelerate, F19
Acceleration, F21–F23, F66–F69
  graphing, F40–F41
  units of, F22
Acid rain, C84–C85
Acid(s), C78–C84*
Actions and reactions, F88–F89*, F90*, F91–F95, F96–F97*, F101–F102, F114–F115*, F116–F117
Adaptation to environment, D24
Adolescence, G21, G24
Adulthood, F21
  celebrating, G25–G26
Africa, B10–B11, B13–B15, B108–B110
African Plate, B21
Agar, A54
AIDS, A46, A47, A53, A55, A59, A60
Air, E92
Air pollution, C85
Air resistance, F46–F47
Air bags, F60–F61
Algae, A34–A35, D6*, E86
  pigment of, A34–A35
Alginic acid, A34, E81
Allergies, G42–G43
Alloy, C59
Amalgams, C60
Amber, D58
Ammonia, E86
Amniocentesis, G16–G17
Amoeba, A22, A31, A36–A37, D10, D12
  amoebic dysentery, A38
  food-gathering of, A36
  movement of, A36

Amphibians, B13
Antarctica, B13, B15, B34–B35, E60
Antarctic Bottom Water, E59
Antibodies, A59, G35–G36
Antibiotics, A55, A59
Aquaculture, E80, E83
Archaeologists, B92
Archaeopteryx, B12–B13
Archimedes' principle, F123–F125
Asexual reproduction, D9*, D10, D15, D17
Asia, B13
Asteroids, D62–D63
Asthenosphere, B39, B102
Astronauts, F118, F127
Astronomical unit (AU), F9
Atlantic Ocean, B13, E38, E55, E57, E59
Atom(s), A13, C35, C71–C74, C76
  and chemical bonding, C74
  models of, C72
  nuclei of, C71, C76
  structure of, C71
Atomic number, C73
Australia, B11, B13, B15

B
Bacteria, A46–A62
  and animals, A61
  blue-green, A50, A51
  classification of, A48, A49, A50–A51
  and diseases, A54–A55, A56, A58–A59
  helpful, A60, A62
  and plants, A61
  reproduction of, A51
  shapes of, A49–A51
Base(s), C78–C79*, C80*, C81–C82

baking soda, C82
  neutralization of, C83
  sodium hydroxide (lye), C82
Bathyscaphs, E48
Bathyspheres, E48
Benthos, E26–E27
Bicycle(s), F4, F14
Birds, B13, B15, E92, E94
Bison, D25
Blood, A24
  artificial, A24–A25
  transfusion, A24
Blood types, G13–G14
Body defenses, G31*, G32–G35. See also Immune system.
Bohr models, C72
Bohr, Niels, C72
Boiling, C28
Bones, D64–D65*, D66–D67
Boric acid, C82
Brake system, automobile, F24–F25
Braking distance, F25–F26
Bromine, E80
Bronze, C57, C59
Bryophyllum (air plant), D14
Budding, D8–D9*, D13–D14
Buoyancy, F123–F125

C
Caldera, B104
Carbon, C40–C41, C91–C92, E86
Carbon dioxide, A18–A19, C69, E92
Cell(s), A6–A25, D8–D9*, D11, D18–D19*, D20–D21*, D22–D24, D34–D35, D39*, D40–D41*, D45, D47, G8*, G9, G23
  animal, A8*, A9–A10, A12,

*Activity

A18–A19
blood, D22, D24
bone, D22, D24
differentiation of, A25–A26
division of, A20–A21*, A23, A25
egg, D18–D19*, D20–D21*, D22, D24, D34–D35, D39*, D40–D41*, D44, G8*, G9
membranes of, A6–A7*, A8*, A10–A11, A14–A15*, A16, A22, D11
nuclei of, A7*, A9–A10, D22
plant, A6–A7*, A8*, A9–A11, A12, A18–A19
reproductive, D18–D19*, D21*, D22–D24
skin, D22, D24
sperm, D18–D19*, D20–D21*, D22, D24, D34–D35, D39*, D40–D41*, D44, G8*, G9, G23
transport in, A16
walls of, A2, A6
wastes, A18, A22, A25
Centimeter, F11. See also Metric units.
Changes, C68–C69
  chemical, C69–C71
  physical, C68
Chemical(s), C20–C21, C34, C36, C40, C46*, C64–C65*, C66*, C67*, C69–C71, C74, C86–C87*, C88–C89*, C90*, D10, D19*, D22, E80–E81, E93
  analysis of, C93
  bonding of, C74, C91
  changes in, C64–C65*, C66*, C67*, C69–C71
  coding of cells by, D10, D19*, D22
  equations for, C70

forces, C20–C21
formulas for, C40, C70
mixtures of, C46*, C47*, C54*, C55*, C58, C64–C65*, C66*, C67*, C90*
properties of, C34, C86–C87*, C88–C89*
reactions, C70
symbols for, C36
synthesis of, C93–C94
Chemical reactions, C70, C93–C94
Chemistry, C93
Chemists, C93
Childhood, G20
Chlorella, A35
Chlorine, C40, C73
Chlorophyll, A18, A34–A35, A37
Chloroplast, A6, A9, A18, A32. See also Cells.
Cholesterol, C41, G60
Chromosomes, A10, A23, D18–D19*, D20–D21*, D22–D24, D35, D44, D47, D76, G12–G14
Cilia, A36–A37, G33
Climate, B9, B11
  zones, B11
Coal, B10–B11
Cohesion, C58
Cold, A59
Collisions, F80–F81*, F82–F83*, F84–F85
Comets, E37
Compass, B28–B29
Compounds, C34, C39–C41, C49, C78–C79*, C80*, C81–C83, C91, C94
Condensation, C28
Conifers, B13
Conservation of mass, law of, C75
Conservation of momentum, law of, F86–F87

Continent, B6–B7*, B8, B11–B12, B14–B15, B19
Continental drift, B6*, B8–B12
Continental rise, E34
Continental shelf, B8, B10, E32–E33
Continental slope, E33
Convection, B39–B40
Convection current, B39–B40
Copper, E81
Coriolis effect, E56
Crystals, C27
Curie, Marie, C75
Currents, E52–E53*, E54*, E55–E61
Cuttings, plant, D15
Cyclometer, F14
Cytoplasm, A6*, A9–A11, A36. See also Cell(s).

D

Dalton, John, C43
Darwin, Charles, D68–D71, D74–D79
Deceleration, F23
Density, C13–C15, E54*, E58–E59, F120–F121*, F123–F126
  calculating, C13
  and flotation, C15, F120–F121*, F124–F125
  identifying materials by, C14
  and purity, C15
  and temperature, C14–C15
Diamonds, B10
Diatoms, A34–A35
Diffusion, A14–A15*, A16–A17
Digestive system, A26
Dinosaurs, B13–B14, D61–D63, D67, D75, E39
Diseases, A53, A54–A55
  communicable, A58–A59
  infectious, A38
DNA, D34–D35, D76, G12
Dolphins, E74, E92, E94
Domestic animals, D70

*Activity

H39

Down syndrome, G16
Drag, F112. *See also* Forces.

E

Earth, B4, B11, B13–B15,
    B16–B17*, B18*, B19,
    B28–B29, B32, B38–B40,
    B43, B99, E55, E70–E71.
    See also Tectonic plate(s);
    World.
  core of, B19–B28
  crust of, B16–B17*,
    B19–B20, B38
  features map, B43
  geographic poles of, B11,
    B28
  magnetic field of, B28–B30
  magnetic poles of, B28
  mantle of, B38–B40
  and ozone layer, B99
  and position relative to Sun
    and Moon, E71
  rotation of, E55, E70
  surface of, B4, B11–B12
Earthquake(s), B9, B16–B17*,
    B18*, B20, B31,
    B56–B61, B62–B63*,
    B65–B67, B68–B69*,
    B70–B71*, B72–B73*,
    B74, B76–B77, B79–B81,
    B92, B97–B98
  aftershocks, B58
  Anchorage, Alaska (1964),
    B63, B77, B81
  architecture and, B72–B73*,
    B79–B80
  epicenters of, B63,
    B70–B71
  focus of, B65
  highways and, B80
  locations, B56–B57, B61,
    B63, B65–B66, B77–B78,
    B81
  Loma Prieta (1989), B61
  measuring magnitude of,
    B59
  on ocean floor, B76–B77

  predicting, B60–B61
  San Francisco (1906),
    B56–B57, B65–B66
  as volcano warnings, B92,
    B97–B98
  waves from, B66–B67,
    B70–B71*, B79
Echo, E40–E41*
Ecosystems, E92
Einstein, Albert, C75
Electricity, B32, C85
  generation of, C85
Electrons, C71, C73–C74
  sharing of, C74
Elements, C34–C38, C42,
    C76
  radioactive, C76
El Niño, E57, E61
Elodea, A6–A7*, A9, A18
Embryo, G10
Endangered species, D25
Endocrine gland, G22–G23
Energy, B31–B32, B36–B37*,
    C25–C26, E74, E78*,
    E80, E84, E87
  and chemical bonding, C74
  electrical, B32, E87
  from food, A16–A17, A19
  geothermal, B31–B32
  hydroelectric, B32
  kinetic, C26
  light, from Sun, A18–A19
  and matter, C22–C23, C24*
  nuclear, B32
  solar, B32
  tidal, E87
Environment(s), D24,
    D32–D33*, D34,
    D36–D37
  conditions in, D32–D33*
Equator, B11
Erosion, B91
Ethanol, A42
Euglena, A37
Eurasian Plate, B21, B31
Europe, B11, B13

Evaporation, C27–C28, E9
Evidence, B8–B11
Evolution, D58, D69, D76
Extinction, D25, D62

F

Fat, dietary, G60
Fathom, F9
Fault(s), B57–B60, B64–B65
  San Andreas, B58–B60
  types of, B64
Fermentation, A19, A42
Ferns, B13
Ferret, black-footed, D26
Fertilization, D22, D24, D28,
    D35, G9, G13
Fertilizers, E81, E93
Fetus, G10–G11
Fever, G47
Fish, B15, E23, E79–E81,
    E82, E92, E93–E94
Fishing, commercial, E79
Fission, A37, A77, D10,
    D12–D13
  nuclear, A77
  reproductive, A37, D10,
    D12–D13
Flagellum, A37
Flight, F106–F107*, F108*,
    F109–F110
Flowers, D46
Food, A16–A18, A22, E74,
    E79–E81
Food chain, A35, E26,
    E60–E61
Food pyramid, G59
Force, F18–F19, F33,
    F65–F69, F78,
    F110–F112, F123–F126
  drag, F112
  in fluid, F123–F126
  lift, F111
  in motion, F18–F19
  thrust, F110–F112
  weight, F112
Fossil fuels, C85
Fossils, B8–B11, D52–D53*,

D54–D55*, D56–D63
Freezing, C28
Friction, F73–F77
Fructose, C91
Fungi, A28, A40–A41*,
   A42–A44, D8*, G40–G41
   reproduction of, A43

G

Galápagos Islands, D69, D78
Galilei, Galileo, F38, F46–F47
Gamma rays, C77
Gases, C20, C25, C27
Generators, E87
Genes, D34–D37, D38–D39*,
   D46–D47, D76, G13–G15
   combinations of, D44, D46
   defects in, D48
   dominant, D40*, D45, D46
   recessive, D40*, D46, G15
   splicing of, D48
Genetic disorders, G15
Geneticists, D28
Genetics, D46
Geography, B13–B15
Geologic eras, D59–D63
Geologic periods, B10, D60–D61
Geologic time scale, D59–D61
Geothermal energy, B31–B32
Glaciers, C4, E37, E80
Glaciologists, C4
Glands, G22
   endocrine, G22–G23
   pituitary, G23
Global warming, B99
Glossopteris, B11
Gold, C60, E38
Graduate (cylinder), C11–C12
Grafting, D17
Gravity, B4, E68–E69*,
   E70–E71, F28, F30–F31*,
   F33–F34, F36, F38,
   F42–F43*, F44–F45*
Greenhouse effect, B99
Gulf Stream, E55, E57

H

Habitats, natural, D25
Hawaiian Islands,
   B100–B101*,
   B102–B105, E35
   formation of, B102–B105
Heart, A26
Heat, B32, B36–B37*, C26
Height, F14
Herculaneum, B92
Hereditary traits. See Trait(s).
Heredity, D28, D45
HIV (AIDS virus), A46, A47, A55, A60
Hormones, G23
Hot spots, B100, B102
Human Genome Project, G17
Humans, D4, D12, D22, E92
Hydras, D8*, D13–D14
Hydrogen, C37, C39, E86
Hypothesis, A45, B8

I

Ice, E37, E80
Icebergs, E37, E80
Icecaps, E80
Immune system, A59, A60, A62
Immunity, G35
Incomplete dominance, D46
Indian Ocean, B13, E38
Indicators, C81
Inertia, F59–F61, F69, F70*
Infancy, G20
Infectious diseases, A38
Inflammation, G33
Inherited traits. See Traits.
Insects, B14–B15
Insulin, D48
Interests, G19*, G20
Interferons, G45–G46
Interleukin, G46
Ionic compounds, C73
Ions, C73
Iridium, E39
Iron, B28–B29, E81
Island arcs, B96. See also Volcanoes.
Islands, B90–B91, B96–B99, B100–B101*, B102–B105, E34–E35
   Hawaiian, B100–B101*, B102–B105
   Philippines, B96–B99
   seamounts, B103
   Surtsey, B90–B91
   volcanic, B90–B91

J

Jurassic period, D61

K

Karat, C60
Kelp, A34, E86
Kilogram, F11. See also Metric units.
Kilometer, F11. See also Metric units.
Kilowatt, E84
Krill, E26

L

Lactic acid, A19
Land bridge, B8
Land mass, B8–B9, B11, B13
Lava, B86, B88–B89, B104
Lift, F111
Liquids, C20, C25, C27, C33*, C67*
   converted from solids, C33*
   converting to solids, C67*
Liter, F11. See also Metric units.
Lithosphere, B39
Litmus paper, C80*, C81
Liver, A26
Lubricants, F74
Lymphocytes, G35

M

Macrophages, G33–G35, G45
Magma, B22*, B29, B31–B32, B48, B86, B97
Magnet, B28
Magnetic field, B28–B29

*Activity

Magnetic poles, B28
Magnetic reversal, B28
Magnetism, B28
Magnetometer, B29
Mammals, B12, B15
Manganese, E38
Mantle of Earth, B19–B20, B29
  upper, B20
Mariana Trench, E18–E21, E28–E29
Marsupials, D61
Mass, C6*, C10, D72–D73*, F32–F34, F66–F69
  measuring, C10
Matter, C4–C24*
  energy and, C22–C23*, C24*
  gases as, C20, C25, C27
  liquids as, C20, C25, C27
  movement within, C19–C20
  solids as, C20, C25, C27
  structure of, C16–C17*, C18*, C19, C22–C23*
  temperature and, C22–C23*, C24*, C25–C26
Measurement, units of, F8–F11
  conversion charts for, F11, F27
Mediterranean Sea, E58–E59
Meiosis, D18*, D22–D24, D35
Melting, C27
Mendel, Gregor, D44
Mendeleev, Dmitri, C37, C43
Meniscus, C11
Menstrual cycle, G24
Mercuric oxide, C39
Mercury, C39
Mesosaurus, B11
Metal, properties of, C32*
Meteors, E37, E39
Methane, C91, E86
Metric units, C11, F10–F11
Microorganisms, A30*–A32*, A33–A41, D48, E92, G30*, G40. *See also*
  Protists; Protozoans.
  growing, A37, A40–A41*
  movement of, A30, A36
Microscope(s), A6–A7*, A8*, A12–A13, D6*, D8*
  electron, A12
  lens of, A12
Mid-Atlantic Ridge, B31
Mid-Ocean Ridge, E34, E38
Minerals, E74, E92
Mitochondria, A9–A10, A19. *See also* Cell(s).
Mitosis, A23, D35, G10. *See also* Cell(s).
Mixtures, C34, C44*, C47*, C48, C54*, C55*, C58
Model, C71
Molecules, C74
Momentum, F81*, F82–F83*, F84–F87, F103
  definition of, F85–F86
Monerans. *See* Bacteria.
Moon, E68–E69*, E70–E72
Mosquitoes, A38–A39
  Anopheles, A38
  breeding, A38
Motion, F52, F54–F55*, F56–F57*, F58–F59, F62–F63*, F64*, F65–F68, F70–F72*
  Newton's first law of, F58–F59, F65
  Newton's second law of, F65–F68
  Newton's third law of, F91–F94, F99, F118
Mountain(s), B4, B10, B23*, B27, B31, B43, B45–B50. *See also* Volcanoes.
  adaptation to life in, B49–B50
  dome, B46–B47
  fault-block, B46–B47
  folded, B45
  formation of, B45
  underwater, B4, B23*, B27, B31, E33–E34
Mucus, G33
Mud, E81
Mudflow, B92
Mushrooms, A28, A40
Mutation, D76

N

Natural gas, B27, E81, E84, E86
Natural selection, D74–D79
Neap tides, E71
Nekton, E25, E27
Nepal, B49–B50
Neutralization, C83
Neutron, C71
Newton (N), F34, F66
Newton, Sir Isaac, F38, F58–F59, F65–F66
Nickel, B28
Nitric acid, C84
North America, B10, B13–B15
North American Plate, B21, B31, B44, B59
North Atlantic Deep Water, E59
Nuclear fission, C77
Nuclear membrane, A10. *See also* Cell(s).
Nuclear radiation, C76
Nuclear reactor, C77
Nucleus, A7*, A9–A10. *See also* Cell(s).

O

Obesity, G60
Ocean(s), B4, B8, B20, B26, E4–E93
  Atlantic, B13
  basin of, E32
  currents in, E52–E53*, E54*, E55–E61
  density of, E20–E21
  depth of, B26–B27
  exploration of, E44–E46
  floor of, B4, B22*, B23*,

H42

*Activity

B24–B25*, B26, B29, E30*, E32, E33–E34, E40–E41*, E47
  gases in, E10
  housing in, E48
  Indian, B13
  life in, E24–E27, E81
  mid-ocean ridge, B22*, B29
  minerals in, E38–E39
  mountains in, E34
  Pacific, E28–E29, E34, E57
  particles in, E6–E7*
  pollution in, E11, E74, E88*, E91–E94
  pressure in, E18–E21
  resources from, E78*, E81, E88*
  salinity of, E8–E10, E21, E58–E59
  sea-floor spreading in, B22*, B29
  sediments in, E11, E31*, E36–E39, E61, E81, E86
  temperature of, E18–E21
  tides, E68–E69*, E70–E72
  waves, E62–E63*, E64*, E65–E67, E84–E85
Ocean Thermal Energy Conversion (OTEC), E86
Offspring, D10, D20*, D24, D34–D35, D40*, D44–D45
  variation in, D24
Oil, B27, E81, E84, E86, E94
Oil spill(s), A62, E88–E89*, E90*, E94
Organs, A26
  heart, A26
  liver, A26
  sexual, G23
Organ systems (in animals and plants), A26
Organelles, A10. *See also* Cell(s).
Organic chemistry, C91
Ovaries, G9, G23

Oxygen, A16, A18–A19, A24, C39–C40
Ozone layer, B99

P
Pacific Plate, B21, B59, B76, B87
Paleontologists, D58
Pangaea, B9, B11–B12, B44
Parachutes, F44*, F48–F50
Paramecium(s), A36, D6–D7*, D10
  movement of, A36
Parasites, A36, A38, A44
Parent cell, D9*, D10–D11, D13, D22
Parent plant, D15
Pasteur, Louis, A52, A54
Pasteurization, A54
Pathogens, G40–G41, G44–G48
Penicillin, A55
Penicillium, A44
Periodic table, C37–C38
Pesticides, E93
Philippine Islands, B96–B99
Photosynthesis, A18–A19, E24
pH scale, C83
Physical change, C68
Physical properties, C34
Phytoplankton, E11, E24–E26, E92
Pituitary gland, G23
Plankton, A35–A36, E10–E11, E24–E25, E27
Plant(s), B8, B11, B13, D14–D15, D32–D33*, D36–D37, D44–D45
  flowering, B14
  parts of, D16
  seed, B15
  self-pollination of, D45
  tubers of, D17
Plate boundaries, B20, B40–B41
Plate tectonics, theory of, B19,

B30, B41. *See also* Tectonic plate(s).
Polar zone, B11
Pollen, D28
Pollution, B99, E11, E74, E88*, E91–E94
Polymers, C92
Pompeii, B92
Population, E80
Prenatal care, G16–G17
Producers, A18
Propagation, vegetative, D15–D16
Properties, C34
  chemical, C34
  physical, C34
Protist(s), A28, A30*–A32*, A33–A39, A40–A41*, D6–D7*, D10
  algae, A34–A35
  animal-like, A31*
  multicellular, A33
  plantlike, A32*
  reproduction of, A37
Proton, C71, C73
Protozoan(s), A36–A38, G40–G41
  diseases caused by, A38, G41
  movement of, A36–A37
  parasitic, A36, A38
  Plasmodium, A38–A39
Pseudopods, A36
Puberty, G22–G24

R
Radiation, C77
Radioactivity, C76–C77
Rain forests, C62
  plants and animals in, C62
Reaction time, F25–F26
Reproduction, D4, D6*, D8*, D9*, D10, D12–D13, D15, D17, D18*, D22, D25, G9
  asexual, D6*, D8*, D9*, D10, D13, D15, D17

*Activity

H43

sexual, D10, D18*, D22, D24, G9
Reptiles, B11
Respiration, A19
Rhizoids, A43
Rhizopus, A43
Richter scale, B56, B59
Rifting, B107
Ring of Fire, B87, B95–B96
Risk factors, G52–G60
    behavioral, G53, G56–G57*, G58*, G59–G60
    environmental, G53–G55
    health, G52
    hereditary, G52
Rivers, E91, E93
Rock, D56, E81, E86
Rockets, F112
Rust, C69

S

Salinity, E9
Salt, C83, E8–E10, E80
San Andreas Fault, B41, B58–B60
Sandstone, B10
Saprophytes, A44
Sargasso Sea, E53
Sargassum, A35
Scuba, E17, F126
Sea, E76*, E91. *See also* Ocean(s).
Sea floor. *See* Ocean(s), floor of.
Sea rockets, B90
Seafood, E79
Seamounts, E33–E34
Seat belts, F60–F61
Seaweed, A34–A35, E81, E86
Secchi disk, E12–E13*
Sediments, E31*, E36–E37, E61, E81, E86
Selective breeding, D70–D71
Self-pollination, D45
Seismograph, B68–B69*, B74–B75
Seismologists, B60, E50

Seismometer, B98
Sewage, A62
Sexual characteristics, secondary, G23–G24
Sexual reproduction, D10, D18*, D22, D24, G9
Sharks, E15, E35
Sierra Nevada range, B43
Sloths, D50
Sodium, C40, C73
Sodium chloride, C40, C73
Soil, B27
Solids, C20, C25, C27, C33*
    converted from liquids, C67*
    converting to liquids, C33*
Solute, C57
Solutions, C52–C53*, C57–C60
Solvent, C57
Sonar, B24–B25*, B26–B27, E42*, E43, E74, E79
Sound, B26–B27
South America, B10–B11, B13–B15
Space shuttle, F118–F119
Species, D10, D25
    endangered, D25
    survival of, D25
Speed, F12–F13, F15–F19, F20*
    averaging, F16
    calculating, F12–F13
    definition of, F16
    measuring, F12–F13
    of pendulum, F20*
    predicting, F12–F13
    racing, F15
    recording, F12–F13
    and stress, F17
Spirogyra, A32, A35
Spores, A43
Spring tides, E71
Stages of growth, G18*, G19*, G20–G21
Sterilization, A54
Stolons, A43

Subduction zones, B87
Submersibles, E28–E29, E48
Substance, C34
Sugar, A18–A19
Sulfur dioxide, B98–B99
Sulfuric acid, B99, C40, C82, C84
Sun, E70–E72, E84
Sunlight, E92
Supercontinent, B7*. *See also* Pangaea.
Surface tension, C58
Surtsey, B90–B91
Symbiosis, A61

T

Talus blocks, B104
Tectonic plate(s), B18*, B19–B21, B31, B36–B37*, B38–B41, B42–B43*, B44*, B54–B55*, B86–B87, B102, B107–B110
    boundaries of, B20, B40–B41
    collision of, B42–B43*, B44*, B45, B49
    and earthquakes, B57, B66
    Eurasian, B31
    map of, B20–B21, B43
    movement of, B40–B41
    North American, B21, B31, B44, B59
    Pacific, B21, B59, B76, B87
    rifting of, B107–B110
    theory of plate tectonics, B19, B30, B41
    volcanoes and, B86–B87, B96–B97
Temperate zone, B11
Temperature, C26
Thrust, F110
Tides, E68–E69*, E70–E72
    neap, E71
    spring, E71
Tiltmeter, B98
Tissues, A25–A26

*Activity

muscle tissue, A25–A26
nerve tissue, A26
Toxins, A58
Trade winds, E56
Trait(s), D28, D30–D31*,
    D32–D33*, D34, D36,
    D44, D46, G6–G7*,
    G12–G13, G15
  dominant, G6–G7*, G13
  eye color, D37, D46
  gene-controlled, D37
  height, D35, D37, D45
  learned, D36
  recessive, G6–G7*, G13,
    G15
  skin color, D46
Trees, fossils of, B11
Trenches, B4, B25*
Tropical zone, B11
Tsunamis, B63, B76–B77,
    E50, E67
  locations of, B77–B78
  predicting, B78
Tubers, D17
Turbidity current, E38, E61
Turbines, E87

U
Ultrasound technology,
    G16–G17
Upwelling, E60

V
Vaccination, G36
Vaccine(s), A59, A60
Vacuoles, A7*. See also Cell(s).
Vegetative propagation,
    D15–D16
Velocity, F21
Vertebrates, D60, D66–D67
Viruses, A47, A52, A53, A60
  and disease, A53, A56,
    A58–A59
Vitamin C, C91
Volcanoes, B4, B16*, B18*,
    B20, B31–B32, B48, B82,
    B84–B85*, B86–B93,
    B94–B95*, B96–B99,
    B100–B101*,
    B102–B106, B109–B110,
    E35, E37
  debris from, B87–B89, B92,
    B97
  eruptions of, B4, B16*,
    B31–B32, B82,
    B84–B85*, B87,
    B90–B93, B94–B95*
  formation of, B102
  island arc, B96
  predicting eruptions of, B82,
    B97–B98
  robots exploring, B106
  types of, B88–B89
Volcanologists, B92
Volume, C8*, C11–C12
  measuring, C11–C12
Volvox, A35

W
Wastes, E91–E93
Water, A18, A28, A30, A32,
    A33, B4, B8, B13, B32,
    C22–C23*, C24*,
    C25–C28, C30,
    C56–C57, C69, C74,
    E12–E13*, E14–E15*,
    E16*, E19, E22–E23*,
    E74, E77*, E80, E91–E92,
    F120–F121*, F122*,
    F123–F126
  density of, E14–E15*,
    F123–F126
  desalination of, C30, E77*,
    E80
  flotation in, F120–F121*,
    F124–F125
  fresh, C30, E74, E80, F122*
  ground, B32
  microorganisms in, A28,
    A30, A32, A33–A37
  particles in, E12–E13*, E19
  plants in, E22–E23*
  salt, C30, C56–C57, E80,
    F122*
Wave(s), E62–E63*, E64*,
    E65–E67
  measuring, E65
  movement of, E65–E66
Weather, B10
Wegener, Alfred, B8–B11,
    B19
Weight, C10, F33–F35, F112
  units of measurement, F34
Westerlies, E56
Whales, E92, E94
Wheels, F96–F100
Wind, E52–E53*, E55–E56,
    E60, E66, E84
Wind tunnel, F113
World, B6*, B9. *See also*
    Earth.

Y
Yard (Old English), F9
Yeasts, A42–A43, D8*, D13
Yogurt, A57, A61

Z
Zambia, G25
Zinc, E81
Zoo(s) D25–D26
Zooplankton, E11, E24–E26,
    E92
Zygote, D20–D21*, D22, D24,
    D34, D39*, D41*, D46,
    G9–G10, G12–G13

Note: Recognizing that many schools teach health as a separate subject, Science Discovery Works Concordia Edition does not include Unit G, a health unit.

*Activity

CREDITS

Cover: *Underwater:* J & L Weber/Peter Arnold, Inc.
Lava: © Shipp/Science Photo Library/Photo Researchers, Inc.

ILLUSTRATORS

UNIT 6A Opener: Lane Yerkes. **Chapter A1:** Keith Kasnot: 22, 23; Briar Lee Mitchell: 26; Michael Kress-Russick: 17, 26; Teri McDermott: 10, 11; Walter Stuart: 25; Ray Vella: 18, 19. **Chapter A2:** David Flaherty: 43, 44; Virge Kask: 33; Kirk Moldoff: 37; Yvonne Walston: 39; Lane Yerkes: 28, 29. **Chapter A3:** Barbara Cousins: 50, 51, 53; Eldon Doty: 55; Ken Tiessen: 61, 62.

UNIT 6B Chapter B1: Skip Baker: 22; Dolores Bego: 7, 30; Warren Budd: 19, 20, 31; Eldon Doty: 8, 9; Eureka Cartography: 17, 18, 20, 21; Geo Systems: 12, 13, 14, 15; Dale Glasgow & Assoc.: 10; Brad Gaber: 29; Greg Harris: 26, 27; Bill Morris: 28; Claudia Karabaic Sargent: 11; Ray Smith: 12, 13, 14, 15. **Chapter B2:** Julie Carpenter: 40, 41; Brad Gaber: 38, 39, 40, 41; Eureka Cartography: 41, 43, 51; Ben Perini 49; Bob Swanson: 45, 47, 48; Randy Verougstraete: 49. **Chapter B3:** Dolores Bego: 77; Bob Brugger: 64; Julie Carpenter: 76, 77, 78; Eldon Doty: 56, 57; Eureka Cartography: 55, 59; Patrick Gnan: 79, 80; Greg Harris: 76, 77, 102; Robert Roper: 64, 65, 67, 81; Robert Schuster: 60; Joe Spencer: 75. **Chapter B4:** Stephen Baur: 107; Dolores Bego: 87; Eldon Doty: 93; Eureka Cartography: 90, 101, 102, 110; Dale Glasgow & Assoc.: 105; Greg Harris: 102, 103, 111; Susan Johnson Carlson: 110; Laszlo Kubini: 92, 96; Bob Swanson: 86, 96, 97; John Youssi: 88, 89, 108, 109.

UNIT 6C Chapter C1: Terry Boles: 15; Patrick Gnan: 11; Mark McIntosh: 29; Andy Meyer: 10, 11, 12; Robert Pasternack: 26, 27; Scott Ross: 12, 19, 20, 21. **Chapter C2:** Bob Brugger: 51; Bill Fox: 34; Adam Mathews: 58; Bob Radigan: 57; Nadine Sokol: 39, 40, 41; Paul Woods: 36, 37, 61. **Chapter C3:** Eldon Doty: 75; Patrick Gnan: 69, 90; George Hardebeck: 76; Steven Mach: 82, 83; Ken Rosenborg: 76, 77; Robert Schuster: 92, 94; Nadine Sokol: 70, 72, 73, 74.

UNIT 6D Chapter D1: Karl Edwards: 10, 11, 12; J.A.K. Graphics: 19, 21, 23; Nina Laden: 10, 11; Kirk Moldoff: 24; Wendy Smith-Griswold: 15, 16, 17. **Chapter D2:** Barbara Cousins: 38, 40, 45; Terry Kovalcik: 37; Sudi McCollum: 33; Teri McDermott: 34, 35, 36, 37, 47; Marjorie Muns: 44, 45; Linda Nye: 42. **Chapter D3:** Drew Brook Cormack: 68, 69; Mona Conner: 74, 75, 76; Richard Courtney: 62; Andy Lendway: 59, 79; Christine Schaar: 66, 67; Raymond Smith: 59, 60, 61; David Uhl: 56, 57; Rosemary Volpe: 70.

UNIT 6E Chapter E1: Terry Boles: 17; Adam Mathews: 17; Bob Radigan: 8, 9, 10, 11; Jim Salvati: 24, 25; Robert Schuster: 11. **Chapter E2:** Barbara Hoopes Ambler: 43; Adam Mathews: 38; Joe McDermott: 32, 33, 49; Steven Nau: 36, 37, 38, 39; Jon Prud' Homme: 36; Bob Radigan: 44, 45; Jeff Seaver: 39. **Chapter E3:** Greg Harris: 65, 73; Jeffery Hitch: 56, 59; Catherine Leary: 65, 66; Adam Mathews: 58, 59, 60, 61; Steven Nau: 62, 63; Jon Prud' Homme: 70, 71; Peter Spacek: 55, 56, 57; Bob Radigan: 92, 93; Gary Torrisi: 84, 85. **Chapter E4:** Eldon Doty: 82, 83; Bob Radigan: E92, E93; Michael Sloan: 80; Dean St. Clair: 91, 92, 93, 94, 95; Gary Torrisi: 84, 85, 86.

UNIT 6F Opener: Ron Fleming **Chapter F1:** Terry Boles: 8, 9, 10; Art Cumings: 24; David Klug: 26; A. J. Miller: 14; Jeffrey Oh: 16, 17; Linda Richards: 25. **Chapter F2:** Terry Boles: 32, 33, 35; Eldon Doty: 38; Don Dixon: 47; Larry Jost: 48, 49; Rebecca Merrilees: 43; Lois Leonard Stock: 46, 47. **Chapter F3:** Terry Boles: 65; Ron Fleming: 52, 53; Dale Glasgow & Assoc.: 68, 69, 77; Jeffery Lynch: 60, 61; Linda Richards: 73, 74, 75, 76; Scott Ross: 58, 59; Michael Sloan: 55, 56, 57. **Chapter F4:** Larry Jost: 95; Bob Novak: 93; Sergio Roffo: 84; Ron Young: 82, 83. **Chapter F5:** Terry Boles: 106, 107, 117; Julie Carpenter: 109; Bob Novak 110, 111, 124; Pete Spacek: 123, 124, 125, 126.

UNIT 6G Opener: Iskra Johnson. **Chapter G1:** Anatoly Chernistov: 22, 23; Iskra Johnson: 4, 5; Claude Martinot: 12, 13, 14, 15; Briar Lee Mitchell: 7; Mary Ellen Niates: 9, 10, 11, 17; Julie Peterson: 25, 26; Stephen Schudlich: 9, 10, 11, 16; Matt Straub: 20, 21; Kate Sweeney: 13, 14, 27. **Chapter G2:** Barbara Cousins: 40, 41; David Flaherty: 32; Marcia Hartsock: 46; Jackie Heda: 32, 33, 34, 35, 47; Briar Lee Mitchell: 42, 43; Leonid Mysakov: 36. **Chapter G3:** Mark Bender: 51, 52, 53; Glasgow & Assoc.: 57; Steven Stankiewicz: 54, 55; Rod Thomas: 59, 60, 61, 62, 63; Beth Anne Willert: 61.

Glossary: Warren Budd and Assoc., Barbara Cousins, Brad Gaber, Patrick Gnan, Verlin Miller, Bob Swanson, David Uhl, John Youssi.

Handbook: Kathleen Dunne, Laurie Hamilton, Catherine Leary, Andy Meyer

Unit A Opener 1–3: © M.I. Walker/Science Source/Photo Researchers. 2: *l.* Grant Heilman Photography. **Chapter 1** 4–5: *bkgd.* David M. Phillips/Visuals Unlimited; *inset* Richard Hutchings for SBG. 6: Ken Karp for SBG. 7: *t.* Ken Karp for SBG; *b.l.* Ken Karp for SBG; *b.r.* © Nursidsany et Perennou/Photo Researchers, Inc. 8: Ken Karp for SBG. 10: © Biophoto Associates/Science Source/Photo Researchers, Inc. 12: *t.* The Science Museum, London/Science & Society Picture Library; *b.* The Science Museum/Science & Society Picture Library. 13: *b.* © Photo Researchers, Inc. 14–16: Ken Karp for SBG. 18: Ruth Dixon/Stock Boston. 19: PhotoEdit. 20: Ken Karp for SBG. 21: Carolina

H46

Biological/Phototake. 22: *l.* © M. Abbey/Photo Researchers, Inc.; *m.* © M. Abbey/Photo Researchers, Inc.; *r.* © M. Abbey/Photo Researchers, Inc. 23: *l.* © M. Abbey/Photo Researchers, Inc.; *r.* © M. Abbey/Photo Researchers, Inc. 24: Merritt A. Vincent/Photo Edit. 25: David Dennis/Tom Stack & Associates. 26: *t.m.* John Cunningham/Visuals Unlimited; *b.* Cabisco/Visuals Unlimited. **Chapter 2** 28: S. Rannels/Grant Heilman Photography. 30: *t.* Carolina Biological Supply Co.; *b.l.* © Photo Researchers, Inc.; *b.r.* © M.I. Walker/Photo Researchers, Inc. 31: *b.* Carolina Biological Supply/Custom Medical Stock. 32: *b.* Bruce Iverson. 33: *t.* J. Robert Waaland/Biological Photo Service; *b.* Alfred Owczarzak/Biological Photo Service. 34: *t.l.* © Photo Researchers, Inc.; *t.r.* Custom Medical Stock; *b.* Manfred Kage/Peter Arnold. 35: *t.l.* © Nuridsany et Pereennou/Photo Researchers, Inc.; *t.m.l.* © Walker/Photo Researchers, Inc.; *t.m.r.* Roger Klocek/Visuals Unlimited; *t.r.* © Photo Researchers, Inc.; *m.* Manfred Kage/Peter Arnold; *b.* Carolina Biological/Phototake. 36: © M.I. Walker/Photo Researchers, Inc. 38: E. R. Degginger/Color-Pics, Inc. 41: *r.* © Photo Researchers, Inc. 43: *b.* Carolina Biological Supply Co. 44: *t.* © Sidney Moulds/Photo Researchers, Inc.; *b.l.* E. R. Degginger/Color-Pics, Inc.; *b.r.* Sherman Thomson/Visuals Unlimited. **Chapter 3** 46: *bkgd.* Institut Pasteur/CNRI/Phototake. 47: *inset* Ian Howarth. 51: E. R. Degginger/Color-Pics, Inc.; 52: J.L. Carson/Custom Medical Stock. 53: © Biophoto Association/Photo Researchers, Inc.; 54–55: The Bettmann Archive. AP/Wide World Photos; *m.r.* Sipa Press; *b.l.* The Bettmann Archive; *b.m.* The Schomberg Collection/The New York Public Library; *b.r.* Sipa Press. 59: J. L. Carson/Custom Medical Stock. 60: Kevin Walsh/UCSD. 61: © Photo Researchers, Inc. 62: *l.* © Will & Deni McIntyre/Photo Researchers, Inc; 2: © Stephen J. Kraseman/Photo Researchers, Inc.

Unit B Opener: Liaison International. 2: Peter French. **Chapter 1** 4: *inset* © Tom Van Sant/Geosphere Project, Santa Monica/Photo Researchers, Inc. 4–5: *bkgd.* Richard Johnston/FPG International: 9: Courtesy, Dover Publications. 31: Bob Krist. **Chapter 2** 34: *r. inset* Lamont-Doherty Earth Observatory. 34.35: *bkgd.* Don Blankenship-UTIG; *l.inset* Jean Miele; *m. inset* Lawrence A. Lanver. 39: Phil Degginger/Color-Pics, Inc. 40: Bob Krist. 41: © David Parker/Science Photo Library/Photo Researchers, Inc. . 45: *r.* Superstock. 47: *t.* Dr. E. R. Degginger/Color-Pics, Inc.; *b* Rich Buzzelli/Tom Stack & Associates. 48: © Emil Muench/Photo Researchers, Inc.; *m.* Ralph Perry/Tony Stone Images; *b.* Larry Nielsen/Peter Arnold. 50: *l.* Superstock; *r.* AP/Wide World Photos. **Chapter 3** 52–53: *bkgd.* Les Stone/Sygma; *inset* Gaylon Wampler/Sygma. 56: *t.* The Bettmann Archive; *b.* The Granger Collection. 58: © Will and Deni McIntyre/Photo Researchers, Inc. 61: © David Parker/Science Photo Library/Photo Researchers, Inc. 62: AP/Wide World Photos. 67: Shahn Kermani/Liaison International. 72–73: Grant Huntington for SBG. 74: Michael Holford. 78: Ken Biggs/Tony Stone Images. 79: James Stanfield/ © National Geographic Society. 80: Mark Downey/Liaison International. **Chapter 4** 82–83: *bkgd.* Dean Conger/© National Geographic Society. 86: © 1991 *Discover* Magazine. 87: *l.* Mikhail Zhilin/Bruce Coleman; *r.* Franco Salmoiraghi. 88: Robert Frerck/Odyssey Productions. 89: *t.* Tony Stone Images; *b.* Phil Degginger/Color-Pics, Inc. 90: *l.* Stella Snead/Bruce Coleman; *r.* K. Eriksson/Liaison International. 92: *l.* Scala/Art Resource; *r.* Alinari/Art Resource. 97: © Robert M. Carey/NOAA/Science Photo Library/Photo Researchers, Inc. 98: *t.* AP/Wide World Photos; *b.* AP/Wide World Photos. 99: Peter French. 103: Werner Forman Archive/British Museum/Art Resource. 104: *t.* Dr. Alexander Malahoff/HURL; *b.* James Cachero/Sygma. 106: NASA. 109: Rick Carson/Liaison International.

Unit C Opener: 1–3: ©William McCoy/Rainbow. 2: David Young–Wolff/PhotoEdit. **Chapter 1** 4: *bkgd.* Tom Bean/The Stock Market; *inset* David S. Hik/Nunatak International. 6–24: Richard Hutchings for SBG. 25: © Francois Gohier/Photo Researchers, Inc. 28: *l.* © Scott Camazine/Photo Researchers, Inc. **Chapter 2** 30: *bkgd.* Tom Stack & Associates; *inset* ESA/TSADO/Tom Stack & Associates. 32–35: Grant Huntington for SBG. 39–40: *l.* Yoav Levy/Phototake. 42: *l.* © George Holton/National Archaeological Museum/Photo Researchers, Inc.; *r.* Culver Pictures. 43: *t.b.* Culver Pictures 44–49: Grant Huntington for SBG. 50: *l.* Robert Yager/Tony Stone Images; *r.* Bill Ross/Tony Stone Images. 51: Steve Weinrebe/Stock Boston. 52–55: Grant Huntington for SBG. 56: NASA/Tom Stack & Associates. 57: *l.r.* Grant Huntington for SBG. 58: David Young–Wolff/PhotoEdit. 59: *t.* Ken Lax for SBG; *b.l., b.m., b.r.* Boltin Picture Library. **Chapter 3** 62: *bkgd.* Michael Fogden/DRK Photo; *inset* Steve Winter/Black Star. 65–68: *t.* Ken Karp for SBG. 69: *t.* D. Cavagnaro/DRK Photo; *m.* John Gerlach/DRK Photo. 74–75: The Bettman Archive. 78–82: Ken Karp for SBG. 84: Tom Stack & Associates. 85: © Jim Corwin/Photo Researchers, Inc. 86–92: Ken Karp for SBG. 93: Pat Lanza Field/Bruce Coleman. 95: E. R. Degginger/Color-Pics, Inc.; *r.* Phil Degginger/Color-Pics, Inc.

Unit D Opener: 1–3: Custom Medical Stock. 2: Hinterleitner/Gamma Liaison. **Chapter 1** 4: *bkgd.* Corey Meitchik/Custom Medical Stock ; *inset* Grace Moore/Morristown Memorial Hospital. 6: Grant Huntington for SBG. 7: © M. Abbey/Photo Researchers, Inc.; 8: Grant Huntington for SBG. 9: © Biophoto Associates/Photo Researchers, Inc. 11: Dwight R. Kuhn. 13: © Biophoto Associates/Photo Researchers, Inc.; *m.t. m. b* © M. I. Walker/Photo Researchers, Inc. 14: William E. Ferguson. 15: *bkgd.* Lefever/Grushow/Grant Heilman Photography; *inset* Lefever/Grushow/Grant Heilman Photography. 16: *t.* Dwight R. Kuhn; *m.l.* Runk/Schoenberger/Grant Heilman Photography; *m.r.,b.* Grant Heilman Photography. 17: *l.* Larry Lefever/Grant Heilman Photography; *m.* Dwight R. Kuhn; *r.* The Granger Collection. 18–20: Grant Huntington for SBG. 22: © David M. Phillips/Photo Researchers, Inc. 25: *t.* E. R. Degginger/Color-Pics, Inc.; *b.* The Granger Collection. 26: *t.* Ron Garrison/Zoological Society of San Diego; *b.* Steve Kaufman/DRK Photo. 27: © M. Abbey/Photo Researchers, Inc. **Chapter 2** 28: *bkgd.* Dr. Jack Hearn/U.S. Department of Agricultural Research; *inset* Dr. Jack Hearn/U.S. Department of Agricultural Research. 30–35: Grant Huntington for SBG. 36: *l.* Focus on Sports; *m.* Michael Ponzini/Focus on Sports; *r.* Sports Chrome. 39–41: Grant Huntington for SBG. 44: Bill Horseman Photography/Stock Boston. 45: Austrian Institute. 46: Courtesy, Marcus Rhoades. 48: *l.* David M. Dennis/Tom Stack & Associates; *r.* Bob Daemmrich. **Chapter 3** 50: *bkgd.* Larry Dale Gordon/The Image Bank; *inset* Robert Maier/Animals Animals. 52: Ken Lax for SBG. 53: *t.* Ken Lax for SBG; *m.* Breck Kent/Earth Scenes; *b.l.* © James Amos/Photo Researchers, Inc.; *b.r.* Breck Kent/Earth Scenes. 54–55: Ken Lax for SBG. 57: *l.* © Eric Hosking/Photo Researchers, Inc.; *r.* Wendell Metzen/Bruce Coleman.

58: Hinterleitner/Liaison International; *m.t., m.b., r.* Kenneth Garrett/© National Geographic Society. 63: *t.* NASA; *b.* Peter Ward. 68: © Darwin Museum. 71: Robert Frerck/Odyssey Productions; 72–73: Ken Lax for SBG. 77: Wardene Weissler/Bruce Coleman. 78: J. & C. Kroeger/Animals Animals.

Unit E Opener: 1–3: Mike Severns/Tom Stack & Associates. 2: *b.* © Carl Purcell/Photo Researchers, Inc. **Chapter 1** 4: *bkgd.* Susan Van Etten/Photo Edit; *inset* New Jersey Newsphotos. 8: *l.* © Francois Gohier/Photo Researchers, Inc.; *r.* William Johnson/Stock Boston. 9: *t.* Owen Franken/Stock Boston; *b.* © Carl Purcell/Photo Researchers, Inc. 10: *t.* © Gregory Ochocki/Photo Researchers, Inc.; *b.* Ralph Oberlander/Stock Boston. 17: Michael Grecco/Stock Boston. 18–19: Thomas J. Abercrombie/© National Geographic Society. 20: *t.* Paul Steel/The Stock Market; *b.* Jack Stein Grove/PhotoEdit. 24: *t.* © Eric Grave/Science Source/Photo Researchers, Inc.; *b.* © D. P. Wilson/Science Source/Photo Researchers, Inc. 25: *t.* © Charles V. Angelo/Photo Researchers, Inc.; *b.* Larry Tackett/Tom Stack & Associates. 26: *t.* Frank Oberlander/Stock Boston; *b.* Denise Tackett/Tom Stack & Associates. **Chapter 2** 28: *bkgd.* Greg Vaughn/Tom Stack & Associates; *inset* Courtesy, Scientific Search Project. 34: Fred Bavendam/Peter Arnold. 35: Jeff Greenberg/The Picture Cube. 37: *t.* Superstock; *b.* M. Timothy O'Keefe/Bruce Coleman. 45: *t.* The Bettmann Archive; *b.* Woods Hole Oceanographic Institution. 46–47: *t.* Michael Holford. 48: Wildlife Conservation Society. **Chapter 3** 50: *bkgd.* AP/Wide World Photos; *inset* Ann Summa. 52–54: Ken Karp for SBG. 55: NASA. 57: *l.* © 1996 Adam Woolfitt/Woodfin Camp and Associates; *r.* © 1996 Momatiuk/Eastcott/Woodfin Camp and Associates. 58: Superstock. 59: John Beatty/Oxford Scientific/Earth Scenes. 60: *t.* © Francois Gohier/Photo Researchers, Inc.; *b.* E.R. Degginger/Color-Pics, Inc. 61: George Goodwin/Color-Pics, Inc. 62–63: Ken Karp for SBG. 67–71: The Bettman Archive. 72: *l.* ©Leroux-Explorer/Photo Researchers, Inc.; *r.* ©Leroux-Explorer/Photo Researchers, Inc. **Chapter 4** 74: *bkgd.* Jack Stein Grove/PhotoEdit; *inset* Flip Nicklin/Minden Pictures. 76–77: Ken Karp for SBG. 79: *t.* Richard Hutchings for SBG; *b.l.* Thomas D. Mangelsen/Peter Arnold; *b.r.* Larry Brock/Tom Stack & Associates. 80: *l.* Greg Vaughn/Tom Stack & Associates; *r.* © Porterfield-Chickering/Photo Researchers, Inc. 81: *t.r.* Runk/Schoenberger/Grant Heilman Photography; *b.l.* Runk/Schoenberger/Grant Heilman Photography. 83: J & L Weber/Peter Arnold. 84: Greg Ryan & Sally Beyer/Positive Reflections. 87: *l.* Nancy Dudley/Stock Boston; *r.* Nancy Dudley/Stock Boston. 88–90: Ken Karp for SBG. 91: *t.* Stacy Pick/Stock Boston; *b.* Robert Winslow/Tom Stack & Associates. 93: *t.* NASA; *b.* The Heirs of W. Eugene Smith/Black Star. 94: *l., r.* Exxon Co., U.S.A. 95: John Paul/FSP/Liaison International.

Unit F Opener: 1–3: Chris Hamilton/The Stock Market. 2: Courtesy, Wet 'n Wild. **Chapter 1** 4: *bkgd.* Steven Pumphey/© National Geographic Society. 11: Imagery/Picture Perfect USA. 15: Courtesy, Edwards Air Force Base. 21: Courtesy, Wet'n Wild. 22: © NASA/Mark Marten/Science Source/Photo Researchers, Inc. 23: Co Rentmeester/The Image Bank. **Chapter 2** 28: *bkgd.* John Turner/Tony Stone Images; l. *inset* Carolyn Russo/Smithsonian Institution; r. *inset* Budd Davison/Courtesy, Smithsonian Institution. 39: *l.* Al Tielemans/Duomo; *r.* David Madison/Duomo. 41: Courtesy, Estes Industries. 45: E. Bordis/Leo de Wys. 46: NASA. 48: Tom Sanders/The Stock Market. 50: The Bettman Archive. **Chapter 3** 52: Richard T. Nowitz/© National Geographic Society. 58: SuperStock. 59: Jeff Foott/Bruce Coleman. 61: Romilly Lockyer/The Image Bank. 63: *b.* © H. Zwarc/Petit Format/Photo Researchers, Inc. 66: Leverett Bradley/Tony Stone Images. 69: Steven Pumphey/© National Geographic Society. 73: Richard T. Bryant/The Stock Source. 75: Focus on Sports. **Chapter 4** 78: *bkgd.* Nina Bermann/Sipa Press; *inset* Engineered Demolition. 84: Henry Groskinsky/Peter Arnold. 85: *t.* © Jerry Wachter/Photo Researchers, Inc.; *b.* Mitchell Layton/Duomo. 86: Rick Rickman/Duomo. 87: NASA/Starlight. 89: *l.* Grant Huntington for SBG; *r.* Globus Studios. 90: *t.,b.* Grant Huntington for SBG. 91: Focus on Sports. 98: Erich Lessing/Art Resource; 99: *t.* Kingston Collection/Profiles West; *b.* © George Holton/Photo Researchers, Inc. 100: *t.* Kim Taylor/Bruce Coleman; *b.* Bruce Coleman. 101: David Madison. 102: Stephen Frink/Southern Stock Photos. **Chapter 5** 104: NASA. 109: North Wind Picture Archives. 113: Bruno de Hogues/Tony Stone Images. 118: *l.* The Bettman Archive; *m.* The Granger Collection; *r.* NASA. 119: Roger Ressmeyer/Starlight. 120–121: Grant Huntington for SBG. 123: Paul Kenward/Tony Stone Images. 125: Richard Megna/Fundamental Photographs. 126: Adam Zetter/Leo de Wys.

Unit G Opener: 1–3: Bob Daemmrich/The Image Works. 2: *l.* © Biophoto/Science Source/Photo Researchers, Inc. **Chapter 1** 4: *bkgd.* Movie Stills Archive; *inset* John Schultz. **Chapter 2** 28: *bkgd.* © NIBSC/Photo Researchers, Inc.; *l. inset* © CNRI/Photo Researchers, Inc.; *r. inset* Center for Disease Control. 30–31: Ken Lax for SBG. 34: Lennart Nilsson; 35: David Young-Wolff/PhotoEdit. 36: © Jean-Loup Charnet/Science Photo Library/Photo Researchers, Inc. 37: *t.* The Bettmann Archive; *b.* © S. Nagendra/Photo Researchers, Inc. 38–39: Ken Lax for SBG. 40: *l.* © East Malling Research Station/Science Photo Library/Science Source/Photo Researchers, Inc.; *m.* © CNRI/Science Photo Library/Photo Researchers, Inc.; *r.* © Dr. Chris Bjornberg/Photo Researchers, Inc. 42: *t.* © John Kaprielian/Photo Researchers, Inc.; *b.* © Biophoto/Photo Researchers, Inc. 44: *l.r.* © National Cancer Institute/Photo Researchers, Inc.; *m.* © Science Source/Photo Researchers, Inc.; *r.* © CDC/Photo Researchers, Inc. 45: *l., r.* © Philippe Plailly/Science Photo Library/Photo Researchers, Inc.; © Hank Morgan/Science Source/Photo Researchers, Inc. **Chapter 3** 48: *bkgd.* Tom Tracy/The `Stock Market; *insets* Courtesy, Eastern Intermediate School. 51: *l.* Richard Hutchings; *m.* David Young-Wolff/PhotoEdit; *r.* Michael Newman/PhotoEdit. 52: Robert Brenner/PhotoEdit. 53: *t.* © David Grossman/Photo Researchers, Inc.; 56–58: Richard Hutchings for SBG. 62: Bob Daemmrich.